The Voice
of
Reflection:
A Writer's Reader

The Voice
of
Reflection:
A Writer's Reader

Janet Marting

The University of Akron

HarperCollinsCollegePublishers

Senior Acquistion Editor: *Patricia A. Rossi*
Developmental Editor: *Maris L. L'Heureux*
Project Coordination: *York Production Services*
Cover Design: *York Production Services*
Cover Painting: *Will Barnet,* Child Reading-Pink, *1966. Cincinnati Art
        Museum, Cincinnati OH. © 1994 Will Barnet/Licensed by
        VAGA, New York, NY.*
Electronic Production Manager: *Christine Pearson*
Composition: *R. R. Donnelley*
Printer and Binder: *R. R. Donnelley*
Cover Printer: *Coral Graphics Services Inc.*

The Voice of Reflection: A Writer's Reader

Library of Congress Cataloging-in-Publication Data

The Voice of reflection: a writer's reader / [compiled by] Janet Marting.
    p.   cm.
  Includes bibliographical references (p.).
  ISBN 0-673-46934-4
  ISBN (teacher edition) 0-673-99046-X
  1. College readers.   2. English language—Rhetoric.   I. Marting, Janet
PE1417.V65 1995
808'.042—dc20   94-1385
                                                         CIP

9   8   7   6   5   4   3   2   1

For Catherine

Contents

Chapter 3: *Learning from the Past*

Chapter 4: *On Friendship*

Chapter 5: *Self-Portaits*

Chapter 6: *Country and City Life*

Chapter 7: *Living in America*

Chapter 8: *The Circle Unbroken*

Preface

The Voice of Reflection compiles fifty-eight autobiographical, expressive essays that are models of reflective, introspective nonfiction. Part of the appeal of the personal, expressive essay is that it invites students to write about what they know the best: their experiences and observations. From descriptions of people and places they know well to narratives about significant events in their lives, from essays that probe how an event brought about a new understanding of people, places, or events to writing that explains or analyzes something of importance, the personal, expressive essay is appropriate for first-year composition courses as well as intermediate- and advanced-level writing courses.

Because students possess the raw material that autobiographical writing requires, they are more apt to be motivated to write and compose more freely than if they were stumped by or simply uninterested in the subject matter. Moreover, because they have a stake in the content of their papers, they are more prone to work on and re-work their writing, thus gaining first-hand experience with the power of the writing process — something with which experienced writers are familiar.

In recent years, much attention has been given to the essay. Indeed, the host of titles used to describe the essay is telling: expressive, personal, familiar, reflective, open, and introspective — to name but a few. Such an array of terms suggests a profession intent on better understanding and defining the form. Scholarly books and articles have sought to redefine and offer ways to best teach the essay; papers and even entire sessions at national conferences such as the Conference on College Composition and Communication and the Modern Language Association have been devoted to it.

There appears to be a resurgence of essays as a literary genre in journals and magazines alike: and with increasing regularity, the term "literary nonfiction" is commonplace, with graduate schools offering courses and degrees in the writing of nonfiction (as opposed to "creative" or "scholarly" writing). It seems clear that the essay, in the tradition set forth by Michel de Montaigne in the sixteenth century, is being resurrected as a viable, exciting genre worthy of attention in all levels of composition courses.

The combination of these two factors — the increased interest in the essay as a genre and the utilitarian nature of the essay — was the impetus for my assembling a collection of well-crafted, accessible, and compelling essays. It is my hope that *The Voice of Reflection* will provide stimulating models to interest, challenge, and motivate students in their own writing.

The Voice of Reflection begins with five essays that focus on the autobiographical impulse and detail what the writers derive from the act of writing. Their descriptions of themselves as writers help to shatter the mystique often associated with writing, and their discussions of their writing backgrounds aids in putting into context not only the product but the process of writing.

Chapter 2, "Family Matters," consists of essays that examine family relationships. The precept of this theme is that there is little in life that so affects us as family. The authors represented in this chapter write thoughtfully, objectively, often lovingly about family members who have had an impact on their lives.

The next chapter, "Learning from the Past," focuses on the formal and informal educations that are a part of all people's lives. As the chapter title's *double entendre* suggests, we take with us lessons from the past and have the opportunity to learn from those lessons. The selections in this chapter exemplify such learning.

Chapter 4, "On Friendship," as the title reflects, looks at yet another part of life: the role of friendships. The essays not only describe the authors' friendships but examine their nature and importance.

Chapter 5, "Self-Portraits," features writers reflecting on who and what they are as people. The essays are thoughtful and courageous self-examinations of topics ranging from bulimia to alcoholism to the impact that small stature and male role models have on the writers. The selections in this chapter show writers putting a mirror in front of themselves, and speak openly and sometimes even critically about what they see.

In Chapter 6, "Country and City Life," the authors describe their experiences living in rural and urban settings. The essays explore the ways in which environment helps to shape us into who we are as people. Thus, we become privy to how people interact with their settings, often becoming a part of them.

Chapter 7, "Living in America," features the experiences of minorities — be they minorities because of ethnicity, race or sexual orientation — as the writers describe how they have dealt with living in a country where they do not fit into the confines of the dominant cultural norm.

The final chapter, "The Circle Unbroken," presents essays that deal with illness and death. Instead of mourning the losses in their lives, the authors pay homage to and celebrate the power of the human spirit and the ways in which they have benefited from what might otherwise be considered tragedy.

Distinguishing themselves by their reflective, introspective explorations, the essays are outstanding examples of personal, expressive writing on topics that are central to people's lives. As Willa Cather once stated, there are but a handful of themes that "go on repeating themselves as fiercely as if they had never happened at all." The selections in *The Voice of Reflection* commemorate what I believe Cather had in mind.

Apparatus

Each chapter begins with a series of epigraphs related to the theme of the chapter. Meant to whet readers' interest in the theme, the epigraphs attempt to capture the essence of the topic. Chapter introductions discuss the overall theme of the chapter and offer brief summaries of each of the essays. Before the essays, headnotes provide pertinent biographical information on the authors in an effort to provide a context for what students are about to read. The introductions also offer brief summaries of the essays with prereading suggestions.

Following each essay are Discussion Questions designed to elicit students' own understandings of what they read, and to call their attention to specific writing techniques and matters of style the authors used in their essays. Instead of asking objective reading-quiz-type questions, the Discussion Questions are meant to foster student reflection on and discussion of what they have just read.

Writing Topics appear at the end of each chapter of the book. Drawn from the essays' ideas and the authors' writing techniques, they offer a wide selection of engaging possibilities for students to explore in their own writing.

Acknowledgments

While compiling the essays in this book resulted in much difficult decision making, I would be remiss in not confessing that this project was a labor of love. Not only did it provide me with an excuse to immerse myself in my favorite kind of reading, it offered me the opportunity to discuss my passion with friends and colleagues. For their support, encouragement, and helpful suggestions, I thank Virginia P. Clark, Thomas Dukes, Pat C. Hoy II, Carole Keller, Laura B. Monroe, Bill Murphy, Bob Pope, Diana C. Reep, Sheryl Stevenson, and Debra Thompson. I also thank my students at The University of Akron for being so receptive to my ideas concerning the reading and writing of personal essays.

My reviewers offered me sound helpful suggestions, and I thank them for their insightful and supportive comments: Chris Anderson, Oregon State University, Dana Beckelman, University of Wisconsin, Mary Jane Dickerson, University of Vermont; Susan Peck McDonald, University of California, San

Diego; Carol S. Olsen, Valparaiso University, and Jane Bowman Smith, Winthrop University.

Again, I have been fortunate to work with editors at HarperCollins who are models of excellence in their profession: Patricia A. Rossi, sponsoring editor, for her continuing interest in my ideas and for her tireless good cheer; and Marisa L. L'Heureux, developmental editor, for believing in this project from the very start and for her reassurance, perspicacity, and delightful humor.

Finally, thanks to Bill and Chelsea whose unswerving belief in my work has made all the difference.

Janet Marting

Preface for Students

The essays that constitute *The Voice of Reflection* are autobiographical, expressive explorations of topics central to people's lives. Because of their personal involvement with the topics, the authors have created the most powerful, provocative, and dynamic kind of writing that you can read — and write yourself. That may sound like an exaggeration, but I think the reasons for my interest in and excitement about this kind of writing are understandable: most people are naturally curious and want to know about other people's experiences, observations, and beliefs. It is a way for people to connect with others, establish a common bond, and maybe even figure out their own lives in the process. By reading other people's essays and writing our own, we have the opportunity to reaffirm our humanity. That is the type of essay you will read in this book and be encouraged to write.

The essays in this collection distinguish themselves in several ways. Unlike writing that narrates a story or describes a person, place, or thing, these essays go a few crucial steps further: they explore, examine, and think about and through their topics. Because of the authors' careful scrutiny and daring, you will see writers discovering things they weren't previously aware of: you will witness writing as discovery. Such are the fruits of mindful exploration. There's no way that reading — or writing — can be boring and humdrum when a new perspective or understanding is reached.

Another way in which the personal, expressive essay differs from other kinds of writing is that the writers reflect on the topics in their essays. As reader, you are privy to hearing the authors muse over, reflect upon, and interpret their experiences and their world. Hence, the title of this book: *The Voice of Reflection*. One of the results of such mindful reflection is that the writers are able to make sense of their experiences, make meaning from what might previously have been unknown, acknowledged, or unclear. Because of such introspection, you will have a chance to know the authors in ways no other genre affords.

Not only is the personal, expressive essay something you can enjoy reading, it is something you can take pleasure in writing. Again I say this for a number of reasons. First, such writing centers around someone you know more about than anyone else — you. When you write about what you know, care about, are interested in and committed to, you have a stake in your writing and are likely to put the time and effort into creating the most important essays you have ever written: essays that mean something to you. You will have the opportunity to make important connections between your writing and your life. By reflecting on the topics of your writing — your experiences and observations — you will be able to understand them in new ways, discover meanings that were once unclear or unknown. In essence, you will put yourself in a position to reap the benefits described in the preceding three paragraphs.

Reading good essays is one of the strongest motivations to writing them. As Susan Sontag states in the introduction to *The Best American Essays* (1992), "One becomes a writer not so much because one has something to say as because one has experienced ecstacy as a reader." I hope the essays in this collection will provide you with that ecstacy, so much so you will want to experience another pleasure: that of producing pieces of writing that matter — to you and to those who read them.

Janet Marting

Chapter 1

The Autobiographical Impulse

We humanize what is going on in the world and in ourselves by speaking of
it, and in the course of speaking of it we learn to be human.

—Hannah Arendt

To be ourselves we must have ourselves—possess, if need be repossess, our
life-stories. We must 'recollect' ourselves, re-collect the inner drama, the narrative, of ourselves. A man needs such a narrative, a continuous inner narrative, to maintain his identity, his self.

—Oliver Saks

It seems to me that writing is a marvelous way to make sense of one's life,
both for the writer and for the reader.

—John Cheever

An experience isn't finished until it's written.

—Anne Morrow Lindbergh

We write to heighten our own awareness of life. . . . We write to be able to
transcend our life, to reach beyond it . . . to teach ourselves to speak with
others.

—Anaïs Nin

Ever since you first started speaking, you have produced autobiographical accounts of your life. Telling your parents what you did while at play, keeping diaries or journals of your activities and thoughts, writing descriptions of significant events in your life for class assignments, producing essays about your accomplishments for job or school letters of application—all of these required you to draw on your personal experiences.

Autobiography is at the heart of whatever you write because, whether you are consciously aware of it or not, your writing is filtered through a lifetime of your own experiences and impressions. To better understand this idea, try to recall the last time you vacationed at a special place or attended a memorable concert. Although hundreds, if not thousands, of other people also visited that place or listened to that concert, your own experiences and impressions are what matter. Only *you* can convey what an activity meant to you. And part of your appreciation of an event is based on what preceded it: what you brought to the experience from your own past.

It is also important to understand that autobiography can be more than the mere written record of your life. Much more. The writing of autobiography offers you the opportunity to pause and reflect on your life, to observe from a distance (whether of time or of space) not only the people who populate and events that occupy your life, but how you have been shaped by them.

The writing of autobiography also offers you a means by which to discover what was not consciously known, a way to make sense of what was previously unclear. The epigraphs that begin this chapter offer additional thoughts on the heightened understanding that reflecting on your life can produce. Powerful attributes for a powerful genre, to be sure.

The authors in Chapter 1 of *The Voice of Reflection* examine not only the autobiographical impulse—what propels them to write—but all that autobiography has to offer. The first two essays, by George Orwell and Joan Didion, both entitled "Why I Write," answer the question posed in the title. Then Pat C. Hoy II adds another voice to the conversation when he discusses what he finds of value in writing. Next, James Baldwin describes his origins and the difficulties of being an African-American writer. Finally, Patricia Hampl offers her ideas about the role of memory in writing.

As you read these essays, you will hear the authors' thoughts on the benefits they derive from writing. You will also notice interplay among the five selections. On what points do you think the five writers would agree and disagree? Just as importantly, when you consider the writing you have done in the past, do you find any connections between it and what these authors have to say? Join the conversation as these writers reflect on their past writing experiences and what they find of value in their work.

Why I Write

George Orwell

George Orwell, the pen name for Eric Arthur Blair, was born in Bengal, India, in 1903. As a child, his family returned to England where he was educated at Eton. A member of the Indian Imperial Police in Burma, India, Orwell resigned from police work to become a writer. He is the author of such novels as Burmese Days *(1934),* A Clergyman's Daughter *(1935),* Keep the Apidistra Flying *(1936), and* Coming Up for Air *(1939).* Down and Out in Paris and London *(1933) is the title of his autobiography, and* The Road to Wigan Pier *(1937) and* Homage to Catalonia *(1938) are books of social criticism and autobiography. Orwell is best known for* Animal Farm *(1945) and* 1984 *(1949), satirical novels depicting the dangers of totalitarianism. In fact, Orwell was a staunch critic of totalitarianism and an advocate for the oppressed. In "Why I Write," Orwell recounts his memories as a writer, all of which led him "to make political writing into an art."*

1   From a very early age, perhaps the age of five or six, I knew that when I grew up I should be a writer. Between the ages of about seventeen and twenty-four I tried to abandon this idea, but I did so with the consciousness that I was outraging my true nature and that sooner or later I should have to settle down and write books.

2   I was the middle child of three, but there was a gap of five years on either side, and I barely saw my father before I was eight. For this and other reasons I was somewhat lonely, and I soon developed disagreeable mannerisms which made me unpopular throughout my schooldays. I had the lonely child's habit of making up stories and holding conversations with imaginary persons, and I think from the very start my literary ambitions were mixed up with the feeling of being isolated and undervalued. I knew that I had a facility with words and a power of facing unpleasant facts, and I felt that this created a sort of private world in which I could get my own back for my failure in everyday life. Nevertheless the volume of serious— *i.e.,* seriously intended—writing which I produced all through my childhood and boyhood would not amount to half a dozen pages. I wrote my first poem at the age of four or five, my mother taking it down to dictation. I cannot remember anything about it except that it was about a tiger and the tiger had "chair-like teeth"—a good enough phrase, but I fancy the poem was a plagiarism of Blake's "Tiger, Tiger." At eleven, when the war of 1914–18 broke out, I wrote a patriotic poem which was printed in the local newspaper, as was another, two years later, on the death of Kitchener. From time to time, when I was a bit older, I wrote bad and usually unfinished "nature poems" in the Georgian style. I also, about

twice, attempted a short story which was a ghastly failure. That was the total of the would-be serious work that I actually set down on paper during all those years.

3   However, throughout this time I did in a sense engage in literary activities. To begin with there was the made-to-order stuff which I produced quickly, easily and without much pleasure to myself. Apart from school work I wrote *vers d'occasion*, semi-comic poems which I could turn out at what now seems to me astonishing speed—at fourteen I wrote a whole rhyming play, in imitation of Aristophanes, in about a week—and helped to edit school magazines, both printed and in manuscript. These magazines were the most pitiful burlesque stuff that you could imagine, and I took far less trouble with them than I now would with the cheapest journalism. But side by side with all this, for fifteen years or more, I was carrying out a literary exercise of a quite different kind: this was the making up of a continuous "story" about myself, a sort of diary existing only in the mind. I believe this is a common habit of children and adolescents. As a very small child I used to imagine that I was, say, Robin Hood, and picture myself as the hero of thrilling adventures, but quite soon my "story" ceased to be narcissistic in a crude way and became more and more a mere description of what I was doing and the things I saw. For minutes at a time this kind of thing would be running through my head: "He pushed the door open and entered the room. A yellow beam of sunlight, filtering through the muslin curtains, slanted on to the table, where a matchbox, half open, lay beside the inkpot. With his right hand in his pocket he moved across to the window. Down in the street a tortoisehell cat was chasing a dead leaf," etc., etc. This habit continued till I was about twenty-five, right through my non-literary years. Although I had to search, and did search, for the right words, I seemed to be making this descriptive effort almost against my will, under a kind of compulsion from outside. The "story" must, I suppose, have reflected the styles of the various writers I admired at different ages, but so far as I remember it always had the same meticulous descriptive quality.

4   When I was about sixteen I suddenly discovered the joy of mere words, *i.e.* the sounds and associations of words. The lines from *Paradise Lost*—

> *So hee with difficulty and labour hard*
> *Moved on: with difficulty and labour hee,*

which do not now seem to me so very wonderful, sent shivers down my backbone; and the spelling "hee" for "he" was an added pleasure. As for the need to describe things, I knew all about it already. So it is clear what kind of books I wanted to write, in so far as I could be said to want to write books at that time. I wanted to write enormous naturalistic novels with unhappy endings, full of detailed descriptions and arresting similes, and also full of purple passages in which words were used partly for the sake of their sound. And in fact my first completed novel, *Burmese Days*, which I wrote when I was thirty but projected much earlier, is rather that kind of book.

I give all this background information because I do not think one can assess a writer's motives without knowing something of his early development. His subject matter will be determined by the age he lives in—at least this is true in tumultuous, revolutionary ages like our own—but before he ever begins to write he will have acquired an emotional attitude from which he will never completely escape. It is his job, no doubt, to discipline his temperament and avoid getting stuck at some immature stage, or in some perverse mood: but if he escapes from his early influences altogether, he will have killed his impulse to write. Putting aside the need to earn a living, I think there are four great motives for writing, at any rate for writing prose. They exist in different degrees in every writer, and in any one writer the proportions will vary from time to time, according to the atmosphere in which he is living. They are:

(1) Sheer egoism. Desire to seem clever, to be talked about, to be remembered after death, to get your own back on grownups who snubbed you in childhood, etc., etc. It is humbug to pretend that this is not a motive, and a strong one. Writers share this characteristic with scientists, artists, politicians, lawyers, soldiers, successful businessmen—in short, with the whole top crust of humanity. The great mass of human beings are not acutely selfish. After the age of about thirty they abandon individual ambition—in many cases, indeed, they almost abandon the sense of being individuals at all—and live chiefly for others, or are simply smothered under drudgery. But there is also the minority of gifted, wilful people who are determined to live their own lives to the end, and writers belong in this class. Serious writers, I should say, are on the whole more vain and self-centred than journalists, though less interested in money.

(2) Esthetic enthusiasm. Perception of beauty in the external world, or, on the other hand, in words and their right arrangement. Pleasure in the impact of one sound on another, in the firmness of good prose or the rhythm of a good story. Desire to share an experience which one feels is valuable and ought not to be missed. The esthetic motive is very feeble in a lot of writers, but even a pamphleteer or a writer of textbooks will have pet words and phrases which appeal to him for non-utilitarian reasons; or he may feel strongly about typography, width of margins, etc. Above the level of a railway guide, no book is quite free from esthetic considerations.

(3) Historical impulse. Desire to see things as they are, to find out true facts and store them up for the use of posterity.

(4) Political purpose—using the word "political" in the widest possible sense. Desire to push the world in a certain direction, to alter other people's idea of the kind of society that they should strive after. Once again, no book is genuinely free from political bias. The opinion that art should have nothing to do with politics is itself a political attitude.

It can be seen how these various impulses must war against one another, and how they must fluctuate from person to person and from time to time. By nature—taking your "nature" to be the state you have attained when you are first adult—I am a person in whom the first three motives would outweigh the fourth. In a peaceful age I might have written ornate or merely descriptive books, and might have remained almost unaware of my political loyalties. As it is I have been forced into becoming a sort of pamphleteer. First I spent five years in an unsuitable profession (the Indian Imperial Police, in Burma), and then I underwent poverty and the sense of failure. This increased my natural hatred of authority and made me for the first time fully aware of the existence of the working classes, and the job in Burma had given me some understanding of the nature of imperialism: but these experiences were not enough to give me an accurate political orientation. Then came Hitler, the Spanish civil war, etc. By the end of 1935 I had still failed to reach a firm decision. I remember a little poem that I wrote at that date, expressing my dilemma:

A happy vicar I might have been
Two hundred years ago,
To preach upon eternal doom
And watch my walnuts grow;

But born, alas, in an evil time,
I missed that pleasant haven,
For the hair has grown on my upper lip
And the clergy are all clean-shaven.

And later still the times were good,
We were so easy to please,
We rocked our troubled thoughts to sleep
On the bosoms of the trees.

All ignorant we dared to own
The joys we now dissemble;
The greenfinch on the apple bough
Could make my enemies tremble.
But girls' bellies and apricots,
Roach in a shaded stream,
Horses, ducks in flight at dawn,
All these are a dream.

It is forbidden to dream again;
We maim our joys or hide them;

Horses are made of chromium steel
And little fat men shall ride them.

I am the worm who never turned,
The eunuch without a harem;
Between the priest and the commissar
I walk like Eugene Aram;

And the commissar is telling my fortune
While the radio plays,
But the priest has promised an Austin Seven,
For Duggie always pays.

I dreamed I dwelt in marble halls,
And woke to find it true;
I wasn't born for an age like this;
Was Smith? Was Jones? Were you?

11

The Spanish war and other events in 1936–7 turned the scale and thereafter I knew where I stood. Every line of serious work that I have written since 1936 has been written, directly or indirectly, *against* totalitarianism and *for* democratic socialism, as I understand it. It seems to me nonsense, in a period like our own, to think that one can avoid writing of such subjects. Everyone writes of them in one guise or another. It is simply a question of which side one takes and what approach one follows. And the more one is conscious of one's political bias, the more chance one has of acting politically without sacrificing one's esthetic and intellectual integrity.

12 What I have most wanted to do throughout the past ten years is to make political writing into an art. My starting point is always a feeling of partisanship, a sense of injustice. When I sit down to write a book, I do not say to myself, "I am going to produce a work of art." I write it because there is some lie that I want to expose, some fact to which I want to draw attention, and my initial concern is to get a hearing. But I could not do the work of writing a book, or even a long magazine article, if it were not also an esthetic experience. Anyone who cares to examine my work will see that even when it is downright propaganda it contains much that a full-time politician would consider irrelevant. I am not able, and I do not want, completely to abandon the world-view that I acquired in childhood. So long as I remain alive and well I shall continue to feel strongly about prose style, to love the surface of the earth, and to take a pleasure in solid objects and scraps of useless information. It is no use trying to suppress that side of myself. The job is to reconcile my ingrained likes and dislikes

with the essentially public, non-individual activities that this age forces on all of us.

13   It is not easy. It raises problems of construction and of language, and it raises in a new way the problem of truthfulness. Let me give just one example of the cruder kind of difficulty that arises. My book about the Spanish civil war, *Homage to Catalonia,* is, of course, a frankly political book, but in the main it is written with a certain detachment and regard for form. I did try very hard in it to tell the whole truth without violating my literary instincts. But among other things it contains a long chapter, full of newspaper quotations and the like, defending the Trotskyists who were accused of plotting with Franco. Clearly such a chapter, which after a year or two would lose its interest for any ordinary reader, must ruin the book. A critic whom I respect read me a lecture about it. "Why did you put in all that stuff?" he said. "You've turned what might have been a good book into journalism." What he said was true, but I could not have done otherwise. I happened to know, what very few people in England had been allowed to know, that innocent men were being falsely accused. If I had not been angry about that I should never have written the book.

14   In one form or another this problem comes up again. The problem of language is subtler and would take too long to discuss. I will only say that of late years I have tried to write less picturesquely and more exactly. In any case I find that by the time you have perfected any style of writing, you have always outgrown it. *Animal Farm* was the first book in which I tried, with full consciousness of what I was doing, to fuse political purpose and artistic purpose into one whole. I have not written a novel for seven years, but I hope to write another fairly soon. It is bound to be a failure, every book is a failure, but I do know with some clarity what kind of book I want to write.

15   Looking back through the last page or two, I see that I have made it appear as though my motives in writing were wholly public-spirited. I don't want to leave that as the final impression. All writers are vain, selfish and lazy, and at the very bottom of their motives there lies a mystery. Writing a book is a horrible, exhausting struggle, like a long bout of some painful illness. One would never undertake such a thing if one were not driven on by some demon whom one can neither resist nor understand. For all one knows that demon is simply the same instinct that makes a baby squall for attention. And yet it is also true that one can write nothing readable unless one constantly struggles to efface one's own personality. Good prose is like a window pane. I cannot say with certainty which of my motives are the strongest, but I know which of them deserve to be followed. And looking back through my work, I see that it is invariably where I lacked a *political* purpose that I wrote lifeless books and was betrayed into purple passages, sentences without meaning, decorative adjectives and humbug generally.

Discussion Questions

1. Based on your own experiences, can you identify with Orwell's "motives for writing"? Why or why not? What other motives can you add?

2. The beginning of "Why I Write" recaps Orwell's interests and experiences in writing at an early age. What early writing experiences do you remember that can help others to better understand you as an adult writer?

3. Orwell lists his "four great motives for writing" and then states that "these various impulses must war against one other." Do you see this as posing problems for a writer? Why or why not?

4. In paragraph 12, Orwell states his desire "to make political writing into an art." To what extent do you think the two interests are compatible?

5. Explain what you understand Orwell to mean when he writes, at the end of his essay, "good prose is like a window pane."

Why I Write
Joan Didion

Born in Sacramento, California, in 1934, Joan Didion graduated from the University of California at Berkeley. She began her writing career in 1956 at Vogue *magazine. A prolific writer, Didion is the author of five novels,* River Run *(1963),* Play It as It Lays *(1970),* A Book of Common Prayer *(1977), and* Democracy *(1984), and* Run River *(1994). Her three collections of essays,* Slouching toward Bethlehem *(1968),* The White Album *(1979), and* Sentimental Journeys *(1993) examine the deterioration of the American spirit since the 1960s.* Salvador *(1983) and* Miami *(1987) are journalistic accounts of two places that recently have experienced social upheaval.* After Henry *(1992) reports on current events, from the 1988 Presidential campaign to the case of the New York investment banker who was raped and beaten nearly to death as she jogged in Central Park. In the following selection, Didion examines the "three short unambiguous words" of the title, "Why I Write." As you read, pay particular attention to the reasons she offers. How are they similar to or different from Orwell's—and your own?*

1   Of course I stole the title for this talk, from George Orwell. One reason I stole it was that I like the sound of the words: Why I Write. There

you have three short unambiguous words that share a sound, and the sound they share is this:

/

/

/

2   In many ways writing is the act of saying *I,* of imposing oneself upon other people, of saying *listen to me, see it my way, change your mind.* It's an aggressive, even a hostile act. You can disguise its aggressiveness all you want with veils of subordinate clauses and qualifiers and tentative subjunctives, with ellipses and evasions—with the whole manner of intimating rather than claiming, of alluding rather than stating—but there's no getting around the fact that setting words on paper is the tactic of a secret bully, an invasion, an imposition of the writer's sensibility on the reader's most private space.

3   I stole the title not only because the words sounded right but because they seemed to sum up, in a no-nonsense way, all I have to tell you. Like many writers I have only this one "subject," this one "area": the act of writing. I can bring you no reports from any other front. I may have other interests: I am "interested," for example, in marine biology, but I don't flatter myself that you would come out to hear me talk about it. I am not a scholar. I am not in the least an intellectual, which is not to say that when I hear the word "intellectual" I reach for my gun, but only to say that I do not think in abstracts. During the years when I was an undergraduate at Berkeley I tried, with a kind of hopeless late-adolescent energy, to buy some temporary visa into the world of ideas, to forge for myself a mind that could deal with the abstract.

4   In short I tried to think. I failed. My attention veered inexorably back to the specific, to the tangible, to what was generally considered, by everyone I knew then and for that matter have known since, the peripheral. I would try to contemplate the Hegelian dialectic and would find myself concentrating instead on a flowering pear tree outside my window and the particular way the petals fell on my floor. I would try to read linguistic theory and would find myself wondering instead if the lights were on in the bevatron up the hill. When I say that I was wondering if the lights were on in the bevatron you might immediately suspect, if you deal in ideas at all, that I was registering the bevatron as a political symbol, thinking in shorthand about the military-industrial complex and its role in the university community, but you would be wrong. I was only wondering if the lights were on in the bevatron, and how they looked. A physical fact.

5   I had trouble graduating from Berkeley, not because of this inability to deal with ideas—I was majoring in English, and I could locate the house-and-garden imagery in *The Portrait of a Lady* as well as the next person, "imagery" being by definition the kind of specific that got my attention—but simply because I had neglected to take a course in Milton. For reasons which now sound baroque I needed a degree by the end of that summer, and the English department finally agreed, if I would come

down from Sacramento every Friday and talk about the cosmology of *Paradise Lost,* to certify me proficient in Milton. I did this. Some Fridays I took the Greyhound bus, other Fridays I caught the Southern Pacific's City of San Francisco on the last leg of its transcontinental trip. I can no longer tell you whether Milton put the sun or the earth at the center of his universe in *Paradise Lost,* the central question of at least one century and a topic about which I wrote 10,000 words that summer, but I can still recall the exact rancidity of the butter in the City of San Francisco's dining car, and the way the tinted windows on the Greyhound bus cast the oil refineries around Carquinez Straits into a grayed and obscurely sinister light. In short my attention was always on the periphery, on what I could see and taste and touch, on the butter, and the Greyhound bus. During those years I was traveling on what I knew to be a very shaky passport, forged papers: I knew that I was no legitimate resident in any world of ideas. I knew I couldn't think. All I knew then was what I couldn't do. All I knew then was what I wasn't, and it took me some years to discover what I was.

6   Which was a writer.

7   By which I mean not a "good" writer or a "bad" writer but simply a writer, a person whose most absorbed and passionate hours are spent arranging words on pieces of paper. Had my credentials been in order I would never have become a writer. Had I been blessed with even limited access to my own mind there would have been no reason to write. I write entirely to find out what I'm thinking, what I'm looking at, what I see and what it means. What I want and what I fear. Why did the oil refineries around Carquinez Straits seem sinister to me in the summer of 1956? Why have the night lights in the bevatron burned in my mind for twenty years? *What is going on in these pictures in my mind?*

8   When I talk about pictures in my mind I am talking, quite specifically, about images that shimmer around the edges. There used to be an illustration in every elementary psychology book showing a cat drawn by a patient in varying stages of schizophrenia. This cat had a shimmer around it. You could see the molecular structure breaking down at the very edges of the cat: the cat became the background and the background the cat, everything interacting, exchanging ions. People on hallucinogens describe the same perception of objects. I'm not a schizophrenic, nor do I take hallucinogens, but certain images do shimmer for me. Look hard enough, and you can't miss the shimmer. It's there. You can't think too much about these pictures that shimmer. You just lie low and let them develop. You stay quiet. You don't talk to many people and you keep your nervous system from shorting out and you try to locate the cat in the shimmer, the grammar in the picture.

9   Just as I meant "shimmer" literally I mean "grammar" literally. Grammar is a piano I play by ear, since I seem to have been out of school the year the rules were mentioned. All I know about grammar is its infinite power. To shift the structure of a sentence alters the meaning of that sentence, as definitely and inflexibly as the position of a camera alters the meaning of the object photographed. Many people know about camera

angles now, but not so many know about sentences. The arrangement of the words matters, and the arrangement you want can be found in the picture in your mind. The picture dictates the arrangement. The picture dictates whether this will be a sentence with or without clauses, a sentence that ends hard or a dying-fall sentence, long or short, active or passive. The picture tells you how to arrange the words and the arrangement of the words tells you, or tells me, what's going on in the picture. *Nota bene.*

10   It tells you.

11   You don't tell it.

12   Let me show you what I mean by pictures in the mind. I began *Play It as It Lays* just as I have begun each of my novels, with no notion of "character" or "plot" or even "incident." I had only two pictures in my mind, more about which later, and a technical intention, which was to write a novel so elliptical and fast that it would be over before you noticed it, a novel so fast that it would scarcely exist on the page at all. About the pictures, the first was of white space. Empty space. This was clearly the picture that dictated the narrative intention of the book—a book in which anything that happened would happen off the page, a "white" book to which the reader would have to bring his or her own bad dreams—and yet this picture told me no "story," suggested no situation. The second picture did. This second picture was of something actually witnessed. A young woman with long hair and a short white halter dress walks through the casino at the Riviera in Las Vegas at one in the morning. She crosses the casino alone and picks up a house telephone. I watch her because I have heard her paged, and recognize her name: she is a minor actress I see around Los Angeles from time to time, in places like Jax and once in a gynecologist's office in the Beverly Hills Clinic, but have never met. I know nothing about her. Who is paging her? Why is she here to be paged? How exactly did she come to this? It was precisely this moment in Las Vegas that made *Play It as It Lays* begin to tell itself to me, but the moment appears in the novel only obliquely, in a chapter which begins:

> "Maria made a list of things she would never do. She would never: walk through the Sands or Caesar's alone after midnight. She would never: ball at a party, do S-M unless she wanted to, borrow furs from Abe Lipsey, deal. She would never: carry a Yorkshire in Beverly Hills."

13   That is the beginning of the chapter and that is also the end of the chapter, which may suggest what I meant by "white space."

14   I recall having a number of pictures in my mind when I began the novel I just finished, *A Book of Common Prayer.* As a matter of fact one of these pictures was of that bevatron I mentioned, although I would be hard put to tell you a story in which nuclear energy figures. Another was a newspaper photograph of a hijacked 707 burning on the desert in the Middle East. Another was the night view from a room in which I once

spent a week with paratyphoid, a hotel room on the Colombian coast. My husband and I seemed to be on the Colombian coast representing the United States of America at a film festival (I recall invoking the name "Jack Valenti" a lot, as if its reiteration could make me well), and it was a bad place to have fever, not only because my indisposition offended our hosts but because every night in this hotel the generator failed. The lights went out. The elevator stopped. My husband would go to the event of the evening and make excuses for me and I would stay alone in this hotel room, in the dark. I remember standing at the window trying to call Bogotá (the telephone seemed to work on the same principle as the generator) and watching the night wind come up and wondering what I was doing eleven degrees off the equator with a fever of 103. The view from that window definitely figures in *A Book of Common Prayer,* as does the burning 707, and yet none of these pictures told me the story I needed.

15   The picture that did, the picture that shimmered and made these other images coalesce, was the Panama airport at 6 A.M. I was in this airport only once, on a plane to Bogotá that stopped for an hour to refuel, but the way it looked that morning remained superimposed on everything I saw until the day I finished *A Book of Common Prayer.* I lived in that airport for several years. I can still feel the hot air when I step off the plane, can see the heat already rising off the tarmac at 6 A.M. I can feel my skirt damp and wrinkled on my legs. I can feel the asphalt stick to my sandals. I remember the big tail of a Pan American plane floating motionless down at the end of the tarmac. I remember the sound of a slot machine in the waiting room. I could tell you that I remember a particular woman in the airport, an American woman, *a norteamericana,* a thin *norteamericana* about forty who wore a big square emerald in lieu of a wedding ring, but there was no such woman there.

16   I put this woman in the airport later. I made this woman up, just as I later made up a country to put the airport in, and a family to run the country. This woman in the airport is neither catching a plane nor meeting one. She is ordering tea in the airport coffee shop. In fact she is not simply "ordering" tea but insisting that the water be boiled, in front of her, for twenty minutes. Why is this woman in this airport? Why is she going nowhere, where has she been? Where did she get that big emerald? What derangement, or disassociation, makes her believe that her will to see the water boiled can possibly prevail?

17   "She had been going to one airport or another for four months, one could see it, looking at the visas on her passport. All those airports where Charlotte Douglas's passport had been stamped would have looked alike. Sometimes the sign on the tower would say "Bienvenidos" and sometimes the sign on the tower would say "Bienvenue," some places were wet and hot and others dry and hot, but at each of these airports the pastel concrete walls would rust and stain and the swamp off the runway would be littered with the fuselages of cannibalized Fairchild F-227's and the water would need boiling.

18   "I knew why Charlotte went to the airport even if Victor did not.

19   "I knew about airports."

20   These lines appear about halfway through *A Book of Common Prayer*, but I wrote them during the second week I worked on the book, long before I had any idea where Charlotte Douglas had been or why she went to airports. Until I wrote these lines I had no character called "Victor" in mind: the necessity for mentioning a name, and the name "Victor," occurred to me as I wrote the sentence. *I knew why Charlotte went to the airport* sounded incomplete. *I knew why Charlotte went to the airport even if Victor did not* carried a little more narrative drive. Most important of all, until I wrote these lines I did not know who "I" was, who was telling the story. I had intended until then that the "I" be no more than the voice of the author, a nineteenth-century omniscient narrator. But there it was:

21   "I knew why Charlotte went to the airport even if Victor did not.

22   "I knew about airports."

23   This "I" was the voice of no author in my house. This "I" was someone who not only knew why Charlotte went to the airport but also knew someone called "Victor." Who was Victor? Who was this narrator? Why was this narrator telling me this story? Let me tell you one thing about why writers write: had I known the answer to any of these questions I would never have needed to write a novel.

Discussion Questions

---

1. Didion begins her essay by admitting that she "stole the title" of her piece from George Orwell. What would you choose as a title for an essay that discusses *your* feelings about writing? Why?

2. In paragraph 2, Didion claims that writing is saying to others, *"listen to me, see it my way, change your mind. . . .* setting words on paper is the tactic of a secret bully, an invasion, an imposition of the writer's sensibility on the reader's most private space." Do you see your own writing the way Didion sees her own? Why or why not?

3. Didion talks about writing in terms of "pictures in . . . [her] mind." How effective do you find that image? Can you come up with your own metaphor for the way you envision writing?

4. Explain what you understand Didion to mean in paragraph 9 when she states that "grammar is a piano I play by ear."

5. What similarities and differences do you find in Didion's and Orwell's accounts of why they write?

Immortality
Pat C. Hoy II

*P*at C. Hoy II was born in Hamburg, Arkansas, in 1938. Educated at the University of Pennsylvania, Hoy has taught at the
United States Military Academy at West Point and has served as a senior preceptor in the Expository Writing Program of Harvard University. Currently, Hoy is the Director of Writing at New York
University. *His essays have appeared in such publications as* Agni, Sewanee Review, Virginia Quarterly Review, *the* Georgia Review, *and*
Home Ground: Southern Autobiography. *The following essay appears in* Instinct for Survival *(1992), a volume of his collected essays.
Notice the way Hoy uses memories and stories from his past as ways to
frame his discussion of the importance he finds in writing. Also, pay
attention to the way he uses Joan Didion's ideas as a springboard for
examining his own reasons for writing.*

> As for writing, I want to express beauty too . . . showing all the traces of the
> mind's passage through the world; & achieve in the end, some kind of whole
> made of shivering fragments; to me this seems the natural process; the flight
> of the mind.
>
> —VIRGINIA WOOLF

> the lies of poets are lies in the service of truth
>
> —JOHN OF SALISBURY

1   I sit in my office curtained behind the morning sun and tell myself that
nothing is ever finished. For the moment, that seems to be the story of my
life. And when I say those words to myself, say them over and over as I try
to arrange the countless messages and all the tasks large and small that are
laid out before me for the day's work, I wonder what that simple story
might mean if I just relax and let my mind wander over it, making of the
story what it will.

2   Nothing is ever finished. Nothing.

3   When Joan Didion reminds us that we tell ourselves stories in order to
live, she has in mind a saving act of desperation. For her, storytelling ar-
rests the "shifting phantasmagoria" of life, puts a stop to the movement.
Didion is on to something, of course, but I think she's a little shy of the
truth. We tell ourselves stories not so much to order the chaotic but to
reach an understanding, perhaps indirectly, of the lives we are living. Our
stories do freeze the frames of our experience, but those stories also carry
meaning as old as life itself. Embedded in each is a nugget of truth. The
truth varies, of course, according to the way we tell the stories. But with-

out them, we are lost, alone, cut adrift. Stories provide context and continuity. Without them we begin to think there's nothing left to say, nothing left to write. With them we keep our lives at the center of our imaginations—just where they belong.

4   My mother spent much of her life—about forty of her ninety years— running a bus station in a small south Arkansas town. She went to the station day in and day out during all those years, meeting the buses, serving the customers, entertaining friends and their children, providing a home away from home in the most unlikely place—"A place," she'd say, "where folks could sit down and take the load off their feet." She's been dead six years, and I still can't get her out of my head. Her life sits at the center of my imagination, a monument against the ravages of time. She's not at all a lifeless thing.

5   Today, her words about endurance come back again. "Honey," she'd say, "what can't be cured must be endured." The simplest of stories. A cliché, perhaps, out of any mouth but hers. She lost two husbands, one to cancer, the other to a wandering spirit, a son to war. She lived alone almost twenty-five years, finally gave up the bus station at eighty-five, in the aftermath of a tornado that left her hunkered under an old oak desk, rain pouring through the roof destroying her most prized possessions—the pictures and letters and cards from family and friends. But even in the nursing home, later, she managed somehow to gather about her the fragments, the bits and pieces from here and there that pleased her—a favorite chair from my brother, pictures, lots of pictures, on the tables, in the drawers, on the walls, cards from grandchildren, a telephone right by her head, and always a small box of stationery on the bedside table. She wrote as best she could against the palsied movement of her hand, telling her stories until almost the day she died, writing out the wisdom of her life. Even at the very end, her mind was razor sharp, memory serving her, steadying her spirit. She had a hold on things. The stories she had in her head did it for her, I suspect. Simple stories.

6   What can't be cured must be endured.

7   My father, I had thought in my younger days, couldn't be endured. He left us high and dry when I was five, and I had reason over time to resent him. There were embarrassing moments through my school days when he wouldn't come back for the big events, and there were other times when he would come bleary-eyed and a bit tipsy, glowing with false pride. I felt distanced from him then, out of touch, almost as if I didn't know him. But finally, his not being there made little difference. He hadn't been around for the daily rituals, hadn't had time for commitment. He had consumed his life living it, and nothing from the living spilled over for the rest of us.

8   Over the years, trying to face my own self, I have come to love and respect my father's wandering spirit. I know now how compelling the heart can be, and I imagine he had no choice but to follow his wherever it took

him. But the loving spirit that led him on and gave him satisfaction also did him in. He lived a less cerebral life than I do, a life closer to the bone. He knew little, if anything, about restraint. I'm a luckier man. I sit and write and sustain myself with stories, chasing always my dad and the others I have loved. He had no knack for storytelling; never knew much about the mana of the mind. I have no idea what he thought, ever . . . and know only a little, even today, about what he did. I suspect though that memory served him ill, that he never knew the storyteller's peace, that he simply couldn't reconcile his heart to the daily grind, couldn't fit the pieces of his life together and settle his restlessness.

9   In the thick of middle age, I long to sit uninterrupted for lazy stretches of time or to lollygag outdoors, meandering away from people and organizations and schedules. I have to contend with a touch of my father's restlessness, but I'm more interested in solitude now than adventure. I yearn to do my wandering over a patch of ground that might bless me occasionally with surprise. I have a younger friend who has moved to the country with acres and acres of land, and she has begun to move over that bounded space, exploring its contours, observing its wildlife, learning the promise and the confinement afforded by fences and good neighbors. Today she called to tell me that she and her husband may have to give it up. The farm is one of twenty-five targeted sites for the dumping of toxic wastes. A lawyer by profession, she understands the processes that can claim her space; she knows about the laws of dominion. But the slightest prospect of personal, legal entanglements rustles her spirit, and her mind moves quickly to devise schemes of surrender that will keep her life free of legal brambles, even if it means giving up the land without a fight. She doesn't want to have to walk around the law when she roams over the fields.

10   Solitude is hard to come by these days, and I, like my friend, yearn for it. I need more time for the stories. Behind the urge to put all the pieces of my life together there seems to be a gathering instinct at work, something driving me back into memory and out into the world, something compelling me to bring the pieces together. It's as if I'm finally beginning to understand that going down far enough into my own soul is the same as going out into the world. I can do both simultaneously, and when I do, I begin to unearth nuggets of truth. Finding those surprises seems to be my primary business as I search for a clearer picture, hoping to find there in the images of my life the earth's treasure.

11   This searching may very well be a matriarchal thing. It's certainly not the kind of searching my dad did. Nor is it the kind of searching I did as a young Army officer. Eleven or so years after graduating from West Point, after my first stint with troops in Virginia and Korea after a year and a half of graduate school at the University of Pennsylvania, after three years of teaching writing and literature at West Point, after all that, I chose these representative words for the plaque the English department gave me as I left West Point to rejoin the Regular Army: "The ULTIMATE most holy form of theory is action. . . . It is not God who will save us—it is we who

will save God, by battling, by creating, and by transmuting matter into spirit." I look at those words now and think of the naive and necessary heroism that lay behind my efforts. I had loved the brashness and the struggle to excel, knowing that I had to act, had to learn to stand on my own. But there came a time when action seemed less important than contemplation. When I discovered that the Army was claiming my heart and my mind and that I was losing my place beside my children, I had to face a hard and necessary fact: I would not be able to stay on that imaginary train that could take me one day to the Chief of Staff's office in Washington. I wasn't cut out for it.

12   What I was cut out for was teaching. During those early years in the Army, whether leading troops or working with cadets at West Point, I had been a teacher. My greatest satisfaction had not come from commanding but from developing young men who were learning to live together in a community, many for the first time. Everywhere I went, I was teaching, teaching how to prepare the Nike Hercules missile for firing, how to fire and maintain a howitzer, how to compute the firing data that would put artillery rounds on the target, how to assemble nuclear weapons, how to select and occupy field positions in a combat zone, how to keep men alive and effective in the middle of a rice paddy in Vietnam, how to coordinate and manage the activities of a battalion of artillery. Every one of those tasks required teamwork and cooperation and intensive training, and in each of those places where I worked, I was the trainer, the teacher. When the time came for graduate school and an assignment back to the West Point faculty, I chose to study literature rather than mathematics or thermodynamics, subjects the career counselor in Washington urged me to consider because they had more utility. My imagination led me to the stories. I was interested in literature as a way into life.

13   What I found at the University of Pennsylvania surprised me. I was not prepared for the literary historians on Penn's faculty, some of whom, even in the late sixties, were just getting to the New Critics. Only two of my teachers put the primary texts, the stories themselves, at the center of their classes. Both encouraged us to set the critics aside and read with lively imaginations. They encouraged us to reach out and connect, to imagine that there were new answers to life's old problems. They seemed to know that the stories we were reading stretched back in time and forward, and that if we read them with care and diligence, they might reveal a pearl of great value.

14   It was in Herbert Howarth's class that I first read *The Man Who Died,* that little novella D.H. Lawrence wrote at the end of his life on earth. Lawrence's consuming rage for understanding still fascinates me. He wanted to possess the knowledge of what it meant to be man and woman living together—in bed and in culture. Marriage was always out there in front of him, tormenting, leading, beckoning him toward understanding, and he never tired of the search that compelled him to fit the pieces together. In *The Man Who Died,* he tells us about the life of Christ following

the resurrection, insisting that the resurrection story has no meaning unless Christ comes back flesh and blood, back into life a man, freed of his own consuming urge to save God by battling, by creating, by transmuting flesh into spirit. Lawrence insists on bringing Christ back resurrected, erect and upright, a living man.

15   The resurrection itself required a woman; it always does. Coming back from the dead is serious business, too serious, I suspect, to leave to the men . . . even in Lawrence's imagination. As the foundation for his story, Lawrence turned to the Egyptian myth of Isis and Osiris. There he found the image of a woman who could take the broken body of Christ and resurrect it; she could bring him back to life. Isis twice had her husband taken away, each time by a jealous brother, Seth. When Isis found Osiris's body the first time and returned it to Egypt, Seth cut it into fourteen pieces and scattered them throughout Egypt. Again Isis lovingly and dutifully went after Osiris, this time seeking to gather all the pieces and reassemble her husband's body. She found all of him except the genitals and therefore had to make an image of the phallus, fashioning it out of wax and spices. Having put the severed parts of Osiris's body together again, she resuscitated him long enough to conceive Horus who would revenge their suffering.

16   What interests me, and what interested Lawrence, about this story is not Osiris's heroic kingship but Isis's loving devotion, her configuring imagination, and her defiance in the face of established order. In the end, she had the gods granting her favors. Like Lawrence, I am intrigued by her persistence, by her relentless effort to search for and find, to collect and reassemble, the lost or scattered parts of her husband's body. Were I to be blessed by a goddess in my life, I would wish her to be Isis. In her search, I find the story of my life, the meaning at the very heart of things. I find there the key to my life as teacher and writer.

17   Writing has always been for me an act of collecting and reconfiguring, imagining and reconceiving, a reaching out into life and libraries to find meaning. I have, like searching Isis, been trying to find the pieces that would make life whole—a task that's never finished. The search itself carries over to my classroom, where day after day and year after year I try to set in motion searches like that of the mythic woman who's always hovering in the back of my mind. I want my students to be grasped by a single necessity that will set their minds in motion and engender the gathering instinct. I want them to know that the search has no value unless they aim to unearth the mythic nuggets, the stories and the ideas that give us bearing, connecting us with our past and leading us into the future.

18   Each year as a prelude to more formal, academic writing, I try to put students in an exploratory frame of mind, setting them free to follow what my friend Sam Pickering calls the "vagaries of their own willful curiosities." I send them back into memory, asking only that they retrieve a fragment from their past. What I want them to find, of course, is not some lifeless thing, but a story stolen out of time, a story that reverberates and plays on their imaginations. I want the students to be able to pluck that

initial fragment out of memory so that they can set it beside other fragments and begin to make sense of things . . . if only temporarily.

19   It's not just a simple matter of telling a story. The stories constitute
the foundation, but their inherent truths are not always self-evident. Only
the writer can bring them together, arranging and shaping them to re
veal the missing part, the *idea* itself. That idea must be configured, must
be imagined. The stories generate it, but the writer, having gathered the
stories together, must decide, finally, what they mean. Meaning, however
elusive and changing, is the hidden nugget, that treasure the imagination
seeks. Behind that never-ending search is the urge to understand, the human need to make things whole, to create something lasting.

20   About a year ago, when I was writing an essay about soldiering, I
asked my students how young men and women at Harvard might be
heroic, suggesting to them at the outset that my own notions about heroism had changed over time, that acts of physical grandeur now seem far
less important to me than acts of mind. I wanted them to think a little bit
about the never-ending struggle for self-definition. I was hoping too that I
would be able to get them to think about how some of our heroic urges
carry over into the latter stages of life, depriving us of solace. I wanted
them to think about what a hero is supposed to do when the spaces on the
map have been charted, when there is no longer a home to protect, a family to nurture, a beast to slay, a war to win. How do men and women sustain themselves when the tasks have been completed or when there is no
cultural need for the old heroics? I gave the briefest sketch of what I had in
mind, and discovered very quickly that my own middle-aged dis-ease
didn't interest them.

21   My students had notions of heroism that differed markedly from
mine, differed even from those I had when I was their age. Many spoke of
their struggle to develop a voice that could meet the voice behind the
lectern in their classroom. They spoke of the enormous difficulty of facing
day after day the respected voices of authority all over the university. They
talked too of the importance of thinking hard enough, struggling actually,
to utter a response, to say something finally that would make them feel
satisfied with themselves. One young woman, having listened long enough
to the men in the room, spoke of the difficulty at Harvard of being smart
and being pretty. She said that in the minds of the men, it was impossible
to be both. You couldn't be both and be a Harvard woman. To try was to
be heroic. A pall fell over the room as she adjusted herself in the chair,
tucked her legs up into the seat beneath her skirt, and faced them.

22   Following close order on the heels of that discussion, Elizabeth began
a new essay. Intrigued by Ingres's *La Grande Odalisque,* she saw in the
painting a woman whose "fluid" body is "anatomically impossible: the
back and arm are far too long and her legs cross over each other in what
would be a highly uncomfortable position for anyone with solid bones."
She saw this woman as an "enigma," just as she saw something "fraudulent" about Rita Hayworth's *Gilda* who "was a whore and a virtuous

woman . . . two women inhabiting a beautiful shell whose two sides were irreconcilable." Elizabeth thought of these two women in terms of an ideal woman of her own, one she occasionally drew in the margins of her notebook. She brought all these women together in her essay, placing them alongside scenes from her life that accentuated her own struggle to control her weight, to make her body thin by following a "regimen" that alternated days of eating "enormous amounts" with days of fasting.

23 In junior high school, Elizabeth turned to "self-induced vomiting" to maintain her own façade. In my class, she turned to Yeats to clarify her idea about beauty:

There is a line in Yeats' "Adam's Curse" that cries bitterness—

To be born woman is to know—
Although they do not talk of it at school—
That we must labor to be beautiful

I have only just discovered that I have been misquoting these lines for years. In my mind the last line, though essentially the same, has always had a slightly different nuance. . . . We must suffer to be beautiful.

Therein lies the story of Elizabeth's heroism: We must suffer to be beautiful. Turning to Yeats, she turns away from the autobiographical details of her life to the idea itself. Her story gives us insight, reminds us about the perils of beauty, and asks us indirectly to think about how we create those perils. The essay itself is deeply rooted in the particularity of Elizabeth's own experiences—her stories as well as her treasures from the art museum—but she tells her tale in such a way that it links us all together. Leaving her essay, we know that Elizabeth will have to endure forever in a culture where beauty inflicts intense pain. The rest of us, because of her tale, will probably never see beauty again in the same light.

24 Virginia Woolf once reminded us that emotion is also form. She had in mind something other than the architectonic scaffolding Percy Lubbock thought of as structure. Woolf saw through that surface order to something much deeper, something emotional, something deeply felt, that sets in motion the play of our mind on paper. That movement of mind, that grounded search, leads to the mythic nuggets—the larger, more comprehensive treasure we fashion out of the waxy substance of our imaginations, those ideas that give meaning to our struggles.

25 At the very beginning of *The Unbearable Lightness of Being,* Milan Kundera expresses concern that each generation seems destined to relive the same old stories. He wonders quite simply what the myth of the eternal return might "signify." According to Kundera's reckoning, "We must

live our lives without knowing in advance the answer to life's most troubling questions. And what can life be worth," he asks, "if the first rehearsal
for life is life itself?" Yet in the end, Kundera seems to take comfort in the
happiness his characters find against the sad fact of recurrence. The lives
that Thomas, Sabina, and Tereza live are no more perfect than the lives
any of us live, and yet, in Kundera's mind, there is happiness.

26   "The sadness was the form," he says, "the happiness content."

27   Kundera, like Didion, I think, is a little shy of the truth. We do indeed
tell ourselves stories in order to live; the stories themselves order our lives
and record our occasional happiness. So be it. But we also tell ourselves
stories to satisfy a restless and insatiable urge to understand why we are living. Stories give us bearing, stabilize us . . . momentarily. They also record
our legacy; they are the human trace we spread across the world, recording
our movement from generation to generation. If we lay those generational
stories side by side, we find the history of our progress and our failure.

28   Kundera's modern mind, looking at the story of the eternal return
asks, in a thoroughly modern way, what the myth can *signify* . . . as if he's
afraid of the old-fashioned word meaning, as if he can't risk an intellectual
foray into *meaning* itself. Yet there's something old-fashioned and traditional in his question, no matter how he chooses to frame it. Kundera is
not, after all, "nothing but a devouring flame of thought" like Matthew
Arnold's Empedocles, who was compelled in the face of the modern
dilemma to *take* his life as a retreat from "despondency and gloom." For
Kundera, there is at least the content that is happiness.

29   But there is more. There is possibility and promise in those stories we
tell ourselves. If the stories never change, if we are destined to repeat them
over and over, generation after generation, it is because we fail to read them
as if our very lives depend on them. If we see in them a pattern that compels us to live as our forebears have always lived, they bequeath a burden
that is unbearably heavy. But if, occasionally, we can look beneath the surface into the form that is emotion, we might just catch a glimpse of the very
impulses that set our lives in motion. We may discover that there are indeed
new possibilities, new ways to live out the impulses. We may find that the
old heroics no longer seem worthy of our imaginations . . . or our lives.

30   As I continue to gather the fragments of my own life, I like to think
that the stories I tell myself have something to do with other lives, that my
story could be everyone's. I know of course that the larger story I'm trying
to tell will not be finished. Nothing ever is. As I give in to my own needs,
wandering and looking for solitude so that I can find time to let my gathering instinct reveal new secrets to me, as I sit and wait and try to open
myself to the wisdom of the stories themselves, I am sustained by a rhythm
of involvement that binds me to those I love and chase in my imagination,
whether they be the living or the dead. And like my mom, I continue to
write. The smaller stories steady me against the ravages of time; they teach
me about endurance and quell my wandering spirit, reminding me to sit
still, telling me that this is the only life I'll ever live. From them, on the

best of occasions, I relax into life's complexities, and I garner, if only for a moment, the storyteller's peace, the revelation that even the fragments of my own life can shiver into wholeness.

Discussion Questions

1. Hoy begins his essay and weaves it with personal narrative. How effective do you find this technique? Explain your response.

2. In paragraph 3, Hoy introduces the way in which he disagrees with Joan Didion. With whom do you agree: Hoy or Didion? Why?

3. Explain your understanding of Hoy's title "Immortality" and the epigraph by John of Salisbury, "the lies of poets are lies in the service of truth."

4. Do you agree with Hoy when in paragraph 27 he states that we "tell ourselves stories in order to live; the stories themselves order our lives and record our occasional happiness. . . . we also tell ourselves stories to satisfy a restless and unsatiable urge to understand why we are living. Stories give us bearing, stabilize us . . . momentarily"? Why or why not? Why do *you* tell stories?

5. In the last paragraph, Hoy states, "I like to think that the stories I tell myself have something to do with other lives, that my story could be everyone's." To what extent has "Immortality" accomplished those goals? Can you remember writing something that fits Hoy's description?

Autobiographical Notes
James Baldwin

James Baldwin was born in the Harlem ghetto of New York City in 1924. In 1948 he moved to Paris where he began his writing career. Baldwin was a prolific writer: his novels include Go Tell It on the Mountain *(1953),* Giovanni's Room *(1956),* Another Country *(1962), and* If Beale Street Could Talk *(1974); he also wrote plays, including* The Amen Corner *(1955) and* Blues for Mister Charlie *(1964); his essay collections include* Notes of a Native Son *(1955)—in which the following essay appears,* Nobody Knows My Name *(1961),* The Fire Next Time *(1963),* No Name in the Street *(1972), and* The Price of the Ticket *(1985). Baldwin was most noted for writing about issues of race, sexual identity, and social injustice in America. He died in 1987.*

1   I was born in Harlem thirty-one years ago. I began plotting novels at about the time I learned to read. The story of my childhood is the usual bleak fantasy, and we can dismiss it with the restrained observation that I certainly would not consider living it again. In those days my mother was given to the exasperating and mysterious habit of having babies. As they were born, I took them over with one hand and held a book with the other. The children probably suffered, though they have since been kind enough to deny it, and in this way I read *Uncle Tom's Cabin* and *A Tale of Two Cities* over and over and over again; in this way, in fact, I read just about everything I could get my hands on—except the Bible, probably because it was the only book I was encouraged to read. I must also confess that I wrote—a great deal—and my first professional triumph, in any case, the first effort of mine to be seen in print, occurred at the age of twelve or thereabouts, when a short story I had written about the Spanish revolution won some sort of prize in an extremely short-lived church newspaper. I remember the story was censored by the lady editor, though I don't remember why, and I was outraged.

2   Also wrote plays, and songs, for one of which I received a letter of congratulations from Mayor La Guardia, and poetry, about which the less said, the better. My mother was delighted by all these goings-on, but my father wasn't; he wanted me to be a preacher. When I was fourteen I became a preacher, and when I was seventeen I stopped. Very shortly thereafter I left home. For God knows how long I struggled with the world of commerce and industry—I guess they would say they struggled with *me*—and when I was about twenty-one I had enough done of a novel to get a Saxton Fellowship. When I was twenty-two the fellowship was over, the novel turned out to be unsalable, and I started waiting on tables in a Village restaurant and writing book reviews—mostly, as it turned out, about the Negro problem, concerning which the color of my skin made me automatically an expert. Did another book, in company with photographer Theodore Pelatowski, about the store-front churches in Harlem. This book met exactly the same fate as my first—fellowship, but no sale. (It was a Rosenwald Fellowship.) By the time I was twenty-four I had decided to stop reviewing books about the Negro problem—which, by this time, was only slightly less horrible in print than it was in life—and I packed my bags and went to France, where I finished, God knows how, *Go Tell It on the Mountain.*

3   Any writer, I suppose, feels that the world into which he was born is nothing less than a conspiracy against the cultivation of his talent—which attitude certainly has a great deal to support it. On the other hand, it is only because the world looks on his talent with such a frightening indifference that the artist is compelled to make his talent important. So that any writer, looking back over even so short a span of time as I am here forced to assess, finds that the things which hurt him and the things which helped him cannot be divorced from each other; he could be helped in a certain way only because he was hurt in a certain way; and his help is simply to be

enabled to move from one conundrum to the next—one is tempted to say that he moves from one disaster to the next. When one begins looking for influences one finds them by the score. I haven't thought much about my own, not enough anyway; I hazard that the King James Bible, the rhetoric of the store-front church, something ironic and violent and perpetually understated in Negro speech—and something of Dickens' love for bravura—have something to do with me today; but I wouldn't stake my life on it. Likewise, innumerable people have helped me in many ways; but finally, I suppose, the most difficult (and most rewarding) thing in my life has been the fact that I was born a Negro and was forced, therefore, to effect some kind of truce with this reality. (Truce, by the way, is the best one can hope for.)

4   One of the difficulties about being a Negro writer (and this is not special pleading, since I don't mean to suggest that he has it worse than anybody else) is that the Negro problem is written about so widely. The bookshelves groan under the weight of information, and everyone therefore considers himself informed. And this information, furthermore, operates usually (generally, popularly) to reinforce traditional attitudes. Of traditional attitudes there are only two—For or Against—and I, personally, find it difficult to say which attitude has caused me the most pain. I am speaking as a writer; from a social point of view I am perfectly aware that the change from ill-will to good-will, however motivated, however imperfect, however expressed, is better than no change at all.

5   But it is part of the business of the writer—as I see it—to examine attitudes, to go beneath the surface, to tap the source. From this point of view the Negro problem is nearly inaccessible. It is not only written about so widely; it is written about so badly. It is quite possible to say that the price a Negro pays for becoming articulate is to find himself, at length, with nothing to be articulate about. ("You taught me language," says Caliban to Prospero, "and my profit on't is I know how to curse.") Consider: the tremendous social activity that this problem generates imposes on whites and Negroes alike the necessity of looking forward, of working to bring about a better day. This is fine, it keeps the waters troubled; it is all, indeed, that has made possible the Negro's progress. Nevertheless, social affairs are not generally speaking the writer's prime concern, whether they ought to be or not; it is absolutely necessary that he establish between himself and these affairs a distance which will allow, at least, for clarity, so that before he can look forward in any meaningful sense, he must first be allowed to take a long look back. In the context of the Negro problem neither whites nor blacks, for excellent reasons of their own, have the faintest desire to look back; but I think that the past is all that makes the present coherent, and further, that the past will remain horrible for exactly as long as we refuse to assess it honestly.

6   I know, in any case, that the most crucial time in my own development came when I was forced to recognize that I was a kind of bastard of the West; when I followed the line of my past I did not find myself in

Europe but in Africa. And this meant that in some subtle way, in a really profound way, I brought to Shakespeare, Bach, Rembrandt, to the stones of Paris, to the cathedral at Chartres, and to the Empire State Building, a special attitude. These were not really my creations, they did not contain my history; I might search in them in vain forever for any reflection of myself. I was an interloper; this was not my heritage. At the same time I had no other heritage which I could possibly hope to use—I had certainly been unfitted for the jungle or the tribe. I would have to appropriate these white centuries, I would have to make them mine—I would have to accept my special attitude, my special place in this scheme—otherwise I would have no place in *any* scheme. What was the most difficult was the fact that I was forced to admit something I had always hidden from myself, which the American Negro has had to hide from himself as the price of his public progress; that I hated and feared white people. This did not mean that I loved black people; on the contrary, I despised them, possibly because they failed to produce Rembrandt. In effect, I hated and feared the world. And this meant, not only that I thus gave the world an altogether murderous power over me, but also that in such a self-destroying limbo I could never hope to write.

7   One writes out of one thing only—one's own experience. Everything depends on how relentlessly one forces from this experience the last drop, sweet or bitter, it can possibly give. This is the only real concern of the artist, to recreate out of the disorder of life that order which is art. The difficulty then, for me, of being a Negro writer was the fact that I was, in effect, prohibited from examining my own experience too closely by the tremendous demands and the very real dangers of my social situation.

8   I don't think the dilemma outlined above is uncommon. I do think, since writers work in the disastrously explicit medium of language, that it goes a little way towards explaining why, out of the enormous resources of Negro speech and life, and despite the example of Negro music, prose written by Negroes has been generally speaking so pallid and so harsh. I have not written about being a Negro at such length because I expect that to be my only subject, but only because it was the gate I had to unlock before I could hope to write about anything else. I don't think that the Negro problem in America can be even discussed coherently without bearing in mind its context; its context being the history, traditions, customs, the moral assumptions and preoccupations of the country; in short, the general social fabric. Appearances to the contrary, no one in America escapes its effects and everyone in America bears some responsibility for it. I believe this the more firmly because it is the overwhelming tendency to speak of this problem as though it were a thing apart. But in the work of Faulkner, in the general attitude and certain specific passages in Robert Penn Warren, and, most significantly, in the advent of Ralph Ellison, one sees the beginnings—at least—of a more genuinely penetrating search. Mr. Ellison, by the way, is the first Negro novelist I have ever read to utilize in language, and brilliantly, some of the ambiguity and irony of Negro life.

9   About my interests: I don't know if I have any, unless the morbid desire to own a sixteen-millimeter camera and make experimental movies can be so classified. Otherwise, I love to eat and drink—it's my melancholy conviction that I've scarcely ever had enough to eat (this is because it's *impossible* to eat enough if you're worried about the next meal)—and I love to argue with people who do not disagree with me too profoundly, and I love to laugh. I do *not* like bohemia, or bohemians, I do not like people whose principal aim is pleasure, and I do not like people who are *earnest* about anything. I don't like people who like me because I'm a Negro; neither do I like people who find in the same accident grounds for contempt. I love America more than any other country in the world, and exactly for this reason, I insist on the right to criticize her perpetually. I think all theories are suspect, that the finest principles may have to be modified, or may even be pulverized by the demands of life, and that one must find, therefore, one's own moral center and move through the world hoping that this center will guide one aright. I consider that I have many responsibilities, but none greater than this: to last, as Hemingway says, and get my work done.

10   I want to be an honest man and a good writer.

Discussion Questions

1. In paragraph 3, Baldwin states that "the things which hurt him and the things which helped him cannot be divorced from each other." From your own experience, do you find that statement believable? Why or why not?

2. Baldwin begins paragraph 4 with "One of the difficulties of being a Negro writer. . . ." Use your own experiences to fill in and complete the following sentence: "One of the difficulties of being a __ writer is __."

3. In paragraph 5, Baldwin states that "it is part of the business of the writer . . . to examine attitudes, to go beneath the surface, to tap the source." From your own experiences as a writer and reader, what do you see as the "business" of the writer?

4. Baldwin devotes the next to last paragraph to listing his interests. What do you think is the purpose of this paragraph? If you were to list your own interests, what would they be and what relationship would they have to the topics about which you write?

5. On what points do you think Baldwin, Hoy, Didion, and Orwell would agree? How does this information help you as a writer? Explain your answer.

Memory and Imagination

Patricia Hampl

*Born in 1946 in St. Paul, Minnesota, Patricia Hampl was edu-
cated at the University of Minnesota and the University of Iowa.
She has received awards and fellowships from the Guggenheim Foundation, the MacArthur Foundation, and the National Endowment
for the Arts. She is the author of two volumes of poetry,* Woman Before
an Aquarium *(1978) and* Resort and Other Poems *(1983),*
Spillville, *a prose poem (1987), and two memoirs,* A Romantic Education *(1981) and* Virgin Time: In Search of the Contemplative
Life *(1992). Hampl's work has also appeared in the* Paris Review, The
New Yorker, The New York Times Book Review, *and the* American
Poetry Review. *She resides in St. Paul and is a professor of English at
the University of Minnesota. In the following essay, Hampl recalls her
first piano lesson as a way to discuss the role of memory in her own
writing.*

1   When I was seven, my father, who played the violin on Sundays with a
nicely tortured flair which we considered artistic, led me by the hand down
a long, unlit corridor in St. Luke's School basement, a sort of tunnel that
ended in a room full of pianos. There many little girls and a single sad boy
were playing truly tortured scales and arpeggios in a mash of troubled
sound. My father gave me over to Sister Olive Marie, who did look remarkably like an olive.

2   Her oily face gleamed as if it had just been rolled out of a can and laid
on the white plate of her broad, spotless wimple. She was a small, plump
woman; her body and the small window of her face seemed to interpret
the entire alphabet of olive: her face was a sallow green olive placed upon
the jumbo ripe olive of her black habit. I trusted her instantly and smiled,
glad to have my hand placed in the hand of a woman who made sense,
who provided the satisfaction of being what she was: an Olive who looked
like an olive.

3   My father left me to discover the piano with Sister Olive Marie so that
one day I would join him in mutually tortured piano-violin duets for the
edification of my mother and brother who sat at the table meditatively
spooning in the last of their pineapple sherbet until their part was called
for: they put down their spoons and clapped while we bowed, while the
sweet ice in their bowls melted, while the music melted, and we all melted
a little into each other for a moment.

4   But first Sister Olive must do her work. I was shown middle C, which
Sister seemed to think terribly important. I stared at middle C and then
glanced away for a second. When my eye returned, middle C was gone, its
slim finger lost in the complicated grasp of the keyboard. Sister Olive
struck it again, finding it with laughable ease. She emphasized the impor-

tance of middle C, its central position, a sort of North Star of sound. I remember thinking, "Middle C is the belly button of the piano," an insight whose originality and accuracy stunned me with pride. For the first time in my life I was astonished by metaphor. I hesitated to tell the kindly Olive for some reason; apparently I understood a true metaphor is a risky business, revealing of the self. In fact, I have never, until this moment of writing it down, told my first metaphor to anyone.

5   Sunlight flooded the room; the pianos, all black, gleamed. Sister Olive, dressed in the colors of the keyboard, gleamed; middle C shimmered with meaning and I resolved never—never—to forget its location: it was the center of the world.

6   Then Sister Olive, who had had to show me middle C twice but who seemed to have drawn no bad conclusions about me anyway, got up and went to the windows on the opposite wall. She pulled the shades down, one after the other. The sun was too bright, she said. She sneezed as she stood at the windows with the sun shedding its glare over her. She sneezed and sneezed, crazy little convulsive sneezes, one after another, as helpless as if she had the hiccups.

7   "The sun makes me sneeze," she said when the fit was over and she was back at the piano. This was odd, too odd to grasp in the mind. I associated sneezing with colds, and colds with rain, fog, snow and bad weather. The sun, however, had caused Sister Olive to sneeze in this wild way, Sister Olive who gleamed benignly and who was so certain of the location of the center of the world. The universe wobbled a bit and became unreliable. Things were not, after all, necessarily what they seemed Appearance deceived: here was the sun acting totally out of character, hurling this woman into sneezes, a woman so mild that she was named, so it seemed, for a bland object on a relish tray.

8   I was given a red book, the first Thompson book, and told to play the first piece over and over at one of the black pianos where the other children were crashing away. This, I was told, was called practicing. It sounded alluringly adult, practicing. The piece itself consisted mainly of middle C, and I excelled, thrilled by my savvy at being able to locate that central note amidst the cunning camouflage of all the other white keys before me. Thrilled too by the shiny red book that gleamed, as the pianos did, as Sister Olive did, as my eager eyes probably did. I sat at the formidable machine of the piano and got to know middle C intimately, preparing to be as tortured as I could manage one day soon with my father's violin at my side.

9   But at the moment Mary Katherine Reilly was at my side, playing something at least two or three lessons more sophisticated than my piece. I believe she even struck a chord. I glanced at her from the peasantry of single notes, shy, ready to pay homage. She turned toward me, stopped playing, and sized me up.

10   Sized me up and found a person ready to be dominated. Without introduction she said, "My grandfather invented the collapsible opera hat."

11   I nodded, I acquiesced, I was hers. With that little stroke it was de-

cided between us—that she should be the leader, and I the sidekick. My job was admiration. Even when she added, "But he didn't make a penny from it. He didn't have a patent"—even then, I knew and she knew that this was not an admission of powerlessness, but the easy candor of a master, of one who can afford a weakness or two.

12   With the clairvoyance of all fated relationships based on dominance and submission, it was decided in advance: that when the time came for us to play duets, I should always play second piano, that I should spend my allowance to buy her the Twinkies she craved but was not allowed to have, that finally, I should let her copy from my test paper, and when confronted by our teacher, confess with convincing hysteria that it was I, I who had cheated, who had reached above myself to steal what clearly belonged to the rightful heir of the inventor of the collapsible opera hat. . . .

13   There must be a reason I remember that little story about my first piano lesson. In fact, it isn't a story, just a moment, the beginning of what could perhaps become a story. For the memoirist, more than for the fiction writer, the story seems already *there,* already accomplished and fully achieved in history ("in reality," as we naively say). For the memoirist, the writing of the story is a matter of transcription.

14   That, anyway, is the myth. But no memoirist writes for long without experiencing an unsettling disbelief about the reliability of memory, a hunch that memory is not, after all, *just* memory. I don't know why I remembered this fragment about my first piano lesson. I don't, for instance, have a single recollection of my first arithmetic lesson, the first time I studied Latin, the first time my grandmother tried to teach me to knit. Yet these things occurred too, and must have their stories.

15   It is the piano lesson that has trudged forward, clearing the haze of forgetfulness, showing itself bright with detail more than thirty years after the event. I did not choose to remember the piano lesson. It was simply there, like a book that has always been on the shelf, whether I ever read it or not, the binding and title showing as I skim across the contents of my life. On the day I wrote this fragment I happened to take that memory, not some other, from the shelf and paged through it. I found more detail, more event, perhaps a little more entertainment than I had expected, but the memory itself was there from the start. Waiting for me.

16   Or was it? When I reread what I had written just after I finished it, I realized that I had told a number of lies. I *think* it was my father who took me the first time for my piano lesson—but maybe he only took me to meet my teacher and there was no actual lesson that day. And did I even know then that he played the violin—didn't he take up his violin again much later, as a result of my piano playing, and not the reverse? And is it even remotely accurate to describe as "tortured" the musicianship of a man who began everyday by belting out "Oh What a Beautiful Morning" as he shaved?

17   More: Sister Olive Marie did sneeze in the sun, but was her name Olive? As for her skin tone—I would have sworn it was olive-like; I would

have been willing to spend the better part of an afternoon trying to write the exact description of imported Italian or Greek olive her face suggested: I wanted to get it right. But now, were I to write that passage over, it is her intense black eyebrows I would see, for suddenly they seem the central fact of that face, some indicative mark of her serious and patient nature. But the truth is, I don't remember the woman at all. She's a sneeze in the sun and a finger touching middle C. That, at least, is steady and clear.

18   Worse: I didn't have the Thompson book as my piano text. I'm sure of that because I remember envying children who did have this wonderful book with its pictures of children and animals printed on the pages of music.

19   As for Mary Katherine Reilly. She didn't even go to grade school with me (and her name isn't Mary Katherine Reilly—but I made that change on purpose). I met her in Girl Scouts and only went to school with her later, in high school. Our relationship was not really one of leader and follower; I played first piano most of the time in duets. She certainly never copied anything from a test paper of mine: she was a better student, and cheating just wasn't a possibility with her. Though her grandfather (or someone in her family) did invent the collapsible opera hat and I remember that she was proud of that fact, she didn't tell me this news as a deft move in a childish power play.

20   So, what was I doing in this brief memoir? Is it simply an example of the curious relation a fiction writer has to the material of her own life? Maybe. That may have some value in itself. But to tell the truth (if anyone still believes me capable of telling the truth), I wasn't writing fiction. I was writing memoir—or was trying to. My desire was to be accurate. I wished to embody the myth of memoir: to write as an act of dutiful transcription.

21   Yet clearly the work of writing narrative caused me to do something very different from transcription. I am forced to admit that memoir is not a matter of transcription, that memory itself is not a warehouse of finished stories, not a static gallery of framed pictures. I must admit that I invented. But why?

22   • Two whys: why did I invent, and then, if a memoirist must inevitably invent rather than transcribe, why do I—why should anybody—write memoir at all?

23   I must respond to these impertinent questions because they, like the bumper sticker I saw the other day commanding all who read it to QUESTION AUTHORITY, challenge my authority as a memoirist and as a witness.

24   It still comes as a shock to realize that I don't write about what I know: I write in order to find out what I know. Is it possible to convey to a reader the enormous degree of blankness, confusion, hunch and uncertainty lurking in the act of writing? When I am the reader, not the writer, I too fall into the lovely illusion that the words before me (in a story by Mavis Gallant, an essay by Carol Bly, a memoir by M. F. K. Fisher), which *read* so inevitably, must also have been *written* exactly as they appear, rhythm and cadence, language and syntax, the powerful waves of the sentences laying themselves on the smooth beach of the page one after another faultlessly.

25   But here I sit before a yellow legal pad, and the long page of the preceding two paragraphs is a jumble of crossed-out lines, false starts, confused order. A mess. The mess of my mind trying to find out what it wants to say. This is a writer's frantic, grabby mind, not the poised mind of a reader ready to be edified or entertained.

26   I sometimes think of the reader as a cat, endlessly fastidious, capable, by turns, of mordant indifference and riveted attention, luxurious, recumbent, and ever poised. Whereas the writer is absolutely a dog, panting and moping, too eager for an affectionate scratch behind the ears, lunging frantically after any old stick thrown in the distance.

27   The blankness of a new page never fails to intrigue and terrify me. Sometimes, in fact, I think my habit of writing on long yellow sheets comes from an atavistic fear of the writer's stereotypic "blank white page." At least when I begin writing, my page isn't utterly blank; at least it has a wash of color on it, even if the absence of words must finally be faced on a yellow sheet as truly as on a blank white one. Well, we all have our ways of whistling in the dark.

28   If I approach writing from memory with the assumption that I know what I wish to say, I assume that intentionality is running the show. Things are not that simple. Or perhaps writing is even more profoundly simple, more telegraphic and immediate in its choices than the grating wheels and chugging engine of logic and rational intention. The heart, the guardian of intuition with its secret, often fearful intentions, is the boss. Its commands are what a writer obeys—often without knowing it. Or, I do.

29   That's why I'm a strong adherent of the first draft. And why it's worth pausing for a moment to consider what a first draft really is. By my lights, the piano lesson memoir is a first draft. That doesn't mean it exists here exactly as I first wrote it. I like to think I've cleaned it up from the first time I put it down on paper. I've cut some adjectives here, toned down the hyperbole there, smoothed a transition, cut a repetition—that sort of housekeeperly tidying-up. But the piece remains a first draft because I haven't yet gotten to know it, haven't given it a chance to tell me anything. For me, writing a first draft is a little like meeting someone for the first time. I come away with a wary acquaintanceship, but the real friendship (if any) and genuine intimacy—that's all down the road. Intimacy with a piece of writing, as with a person, comes from paying attention to the revelations it is capable of giving, not by imposing my own preconceived notions, no matter how well-intentioned they might be.

30   I try to let pretty much anything happen in a first draft. A careful first draft is a failed first draft. That may be why there are so many inaccuracies in the piano lesson memoir: I didn't censor, I didn't judge. I kept moving. But I would not publish this piece as a memoir on its own in its present state. It isn't the "lies" in the piece that give me pause, though a reader has a right to expect a memoir to be as accurate as the writer's memory can make it. No, it isn't the lies themselves that makes the piano lesson memoir a first draft and therefore "unpublishable."

31   The real trouble: the piece hasn't yet found its subject; it isn't yet about what it wants to be about. Note: what *it* wants, not what I want. The difference has to do with the relation a memoirist—any writer, in fact—has to unconscious or half-known intentions and impulses in composition.

32   Now that I have the fragment down on paper, I can read this little piece as a mystery which drops clues to the riddle of my feelings, like a culprit who wishes to be apprehended. My narrative self (the culprit who has invented) wishes to be discovered by my reflective self, the self who wants to understand and make sense of a half-remembered story about a nun sneezing in the sun. . . .

33

       We only store in memory images of value. The value may be lost over the passage of time (I was baffled about why I remembered that sneezing nun, for example), but that's the implacable judgment of feeling: *this*, we say somewhere deep within us, is something I'm hanging on to. And of course, often we cleave to things because they possess heavy negative charges. Pain likes to be vivid.

34   Over time, the value (the feeling) and the stored memory (the image) may become estranged. Memoir seeks a permanent home for feeling and image, a habitation where they can live together in harmony. Naturally, I've had a lot of experiences since I packed away that one from the basement of St. Luke's School; that piano lesson has been effaced by waves of feeling for other moments and episodes. I persist in believing the event has value—after all, I remember it—but in writing the memoir I did not simply relive the experience. Rather, I explored the mysterious relationship between all the images I could round up and the even more impacted feelings that caused me to store the images safely away in memory. Stalking the relationship, seeking the congruence between stored image and hidden emotion—that's the real job of memoir.

35   By writing about that first piano lesson, I've come to know things I could not know otherwise. But I only know these things as a result of reading this first draft. While I was writing, I was following the images, letting the details fill the room of the page and use the furniture as they wished. I was their dutiful servant—or thought I was. In fact, I was the faithful retainer of my hidden feelings which were giving the commands.

36   I really did feel, for instance, that Mary Katherine Reilly was far superior to me. She was smarter, funnier, more wonderful in every way—that's how I saw it. Our friendship (or she herself) did not require that I become her vassal, yet perhaps in my heart that was something I wanted; I wanted a way to express my feeling of admiration. I suppose I waited until this memoir to begin to find the way.

37   Just as, in the memoir, I finally possess that red Thompson book with the barking dogs and bleating lambs and winsome children. I couldn't (and still can't) remember what my own music book was, so I grabbed the name and image of the one book I could remember. It was

only in reviewing the piece after writing it that I saw my inaccuracy. In pondering this "lie," I came to see what I was up to: I was getting what I wanted. At last.

38   The truth of many circumstances and episodes in the past emerges for the memoirist through details (the red music book, the fascination with a nun's name and gleaming face), but these details are not merely information, not flat facts. Such details are not allowed to lounge. They must work. Their work is the creation of symbol. But it's more accurate to call it the *recognition* of symbol. For meaning is not "attached" to the detail by the memoirist: meaning is revealed. That's why a first draft is important. Just as the first meeting (good or bad) with someone who later becomes the beloved is important and is often reviewed for signals, meanings, omens, and indications.

39   Now I can look at that music book and see it not only as "a detail," but for what it is, how it *acts*. See it as the small red door leading straight into the dark room of my childhood longing and disappointment. That red book *becomes* the palpable evidence of that longing. In other words, it becomes symbol. There is no symbol, no life-of-the-spirit in the general or the abstract. Yet a writer wishes—indeed all of us wish—to speak about profound matters that are, like it or not, general and abstract. We wish to talk to each other about life and death, about love, despair, loss, and innocence. We sense that in order to live together we must learn to speak of peace, of history, of meaning and values. Those are a few.

40   We seek a means of exchange, a language which will renew these ancient concerns and make them wholly and pulsingly ours. Instinctively, we go to our store of private images and associations for our authority to speak of these weighty issues. We find, in our details and broken and obscured images, the language of symbol. Here memory impulsively reaches out its arms and embraces imagination. That is the resort to invention. It isn't a lie, but an act of necessity, as the innate urge to locate personal truth always is.

41   All right. Invention is inevitable. But why write memoir? Why not call it fiction and be done with all the hashing about, wondering where memory stops and imagination begins? And if memoir seeks to talk about "the big issues," about history and peace, death and love—why not leave these reflections to those with expert and scholarly knowledge? Why let the common or garden variety memoirist into the club? I'm thinking again of that bumper sticker: why Question Authority?

42   My answer, of course, is a memoirist's answer. Memoir must be written because each of us must have a created version of the past. Created: that is, real, tangible, made of the stuff of a life lived in place and in history. And the down side of any created thing as well: we must live with a version that attaches us to our limitations, to the inevitable subjectivity of our points of view. We must acquiesce to our experience and our gift to

transform experience into meaning and value. You tell me your story, I'll tell you my story.

43   If we refuse to do the work of creating this personal version of the past, someone else will do it for us. That is a scary political fact. "The struggle of man against power," a character in Milan Kundera's novel *The Book of Laughter and Forgetting* says, "is the struggle of memory against forgetting." He refers to willful political forgetting, the habit of nations and those in power (Question Authority!) to deny the truth of memory in order to disarm moral and ethical power. It's an efficient way of controlling masses of people. It doesn't even require much bloodshed, as long as people are entirely willing to give over their personal memories. Whole histories can be rewritten. As Czeslaw Milosz said in his 1980 Nobel Prize lecture, the number of books published that seek to deny the existence of the Nazi death camps now exceeds one hundred.

44   What is remembered is what *becomes* reality. If we "forget" Auschwitz, if we "forget" My Lai, what then do we remember? And what is the purpose of our remembering? If we think of memory naively, as a simple story, logged like a documentary in the archive of the mind, we miss its beauty but also its function. The beauty of memory rests in its talent for rendering detail, for paying homage to the senses, its capacity to love the particles of life, the richness and idiosyncrasy of our existence. The function of memory, on the other hand, is intensely personal and surprisingly political.

45   Our capacity to move forward as developing beings rests on a healthy relation with the past. Psychotherapy, that widespread method of mental health, relies heavily on memory and on the ability to retrieve and organize images and events from the personal past. We carry our wounds and perhaps even worse, our capacity to wound, forward with us. If we learn not only to tell our stories but to listen to what our stories tell us—to write the first draft and then return for the second draft—we are doing the work of memoir.

46   Memoir is the intersection of narration and reflection, of story-telling and essay-writing. It can present its story *and* reflect and consider the meaning of the story. It is a peculiarly open form, inviting broken and incomplete images, half-recollected fragments, all the mass (and mess) of detail. It offers to shape this confusion—and in shaping, of course it necessarily creates a work of art, not a legal document. But then, even legal documents are only valiant attempts to consign the truth, the whole truth and nothing but the truth to paper. Even they remain versions.

47   Locating touchstones—the red music book, the olive Olive, my father's violin playing—is deeply satisfying. Who knows why? Perhaps we all sense that we can't grasp the whole truth and nothing but the truth of our experience. Just can't be done. What can be achieved, however, is a version of its swirling, changing wholeness. A memoirist must acquiesce to selectivity, like any artist. The version we dare to write is the only truth, the only relationship we can have with the past. Refuse to write your life and you have no life. At least, that is the stern view of the memoirist.

48   Personal history, logged in memory, is a sort of slide projector flashing images on the wall of the mind. And there's precious little order to the slides in the rotating carousel. Beyond that confusion, who knows who is running the projector? A memorist steps into this darkened room of flashing, unorganized images and stands blinking for a while. Maybe for a long while. But eventually, as with any attempt to tell a story, it is necessary to put something first, then something else. And so on, to the end. That's a first draft. Not necessarily the truth, not even *a* truth sometimes, but the first attempt to create a shape.

49   The first thing I usually notice at this stage of composition is the appalling inaccuracy of the piece. Witness my first piano lesson draft. Invention is screamingly evident in what I intended to be transcription. But here's the further truth: I feel no shame. In fact, it's only now that my interest in the piece truly quickens. For I can see what isn't there, what is shyly hugging the walls, hoping not to be seen. I see the filmy shape of the next draft. I see a more acute version of the episode or—this is more likely—as entirely new piece rising from the ashes of the first attempt.

50   The next draft of the piece would have to be a true re-vision, a new seeing of the materials of the first draft. Nothing merely cosmetic will do—no rouge buffing up the opening sentence, no glossy adjective to lift a sagging line, nothing to attempt covering a patch of gray writing. None of that. I can't say for sure, but my hunch is the revision would lead me to more writing about my father (why was I so impressed by that ancestral inventor of the collapsible opera hat? Did I feel I had nothing as remarkable in my own background? Did this make me feel inadequate?). I begin to think perhaps Sister Olive is less central to this business than she is in this draft. She is meant to be a moment, not a character.

51   And so I might proceed, if I were to undertake a new draft of the memoir. I begin to feel a relationship developing between a former self and me.

52   And, even more compelling, a relationship between an old world and me.

Discussion Questions

1. Hampl confesses in paragraph 16 that when she rereads what she has just written, she realizes she has "told a number of lies." Do you think that reaction is typical of most writers? What do *you* see when you reread what you have just written? Explain your answer.

2. In paragraph 26, Hampl likens a reader to a cat and a writer to a dog. How effective do you find her associations? Can you offer

analogies of your own that more clearly represent how you envision a reader and a writer?

3. In paragraph 29, Hampl discusses her reasons for being such a "strong adherent of the first draft." Do you agree with her? If so, why? If not, discuss what would you consider yourself an advocate for in the writing process.

4. Why does Hampl believe it is important for people to write their memoirs? Do you agree with her reasons? Can you add some of your own?

5. Hampl's essay advances the idea that writing creates self-understanding. Can you recall a time when something you wrote provided you with self-understanding? Explain your answer.

Chapter 1 Writing Topics

1. Write a profile of yourself as a writer. Be sure to reflect on the situations that created your self-image.

2. Many writers have a favorite place to write (e.g., a carrel in the library, a comfortable chair in their bedroom, etc.). They also have favorite writing utensils (e.g., yellow, lined, legal-sized pads of paper, felt tip pens, a laptop or notebook computer, etc.). Describe the place and writing materials that provide a writing environment for you to do your best work.

3. Write an essay in which you detail the way you went about writing something important to you. You might want to contrast it with the way you went about writing something in which you had no interest or stake.

4. What does revision mean to you? Describe the way you go about revising a piece of writing so others can understand not only something about you but about the revision process.

5. Chronicle your own life as a writer in an essay in which you examine why you write—or don't write—and the people who have had a positive and/or negative influence on you as a writer.

6. George Orwell knew at a very early age that he wanted to be a writer when he grew up. When you were a child, what did *you* want to be when you grew up? Examine how that choice has changed (or remained the same) over the years.

7. Recall something a parent, grandparent, sibling, or friend has said to you that has had a powerful influence in the way you have lived your life. Write an essay that shows the way those words influenced you.

8. Think about a piece of literature, a film, a song, or an art work that has meant a great deal to you. Explore the ways in which you have been enlightened by that particular work of art.

9. In "Why I Write," Joan Didion speaks of images that "shimmer around the edges." Choose an image that has haunted you and write an essay in which you show its significance in your life.

Chapter 2

Family Matters

Relationships and communion are the most significant clues surrounding the mystery of our human nature. They tell us the most about who we are.

—Susan Cahill

The family, not the individual, is the real molecule of society, the key link in the social chain of being.

—Robert Nisbet

No man is an island, entire of itself; every man is a piece of the continent, a part of the main; if a clod be washed away by the sea, Europe is the less, as well as if a promontory were, as well as if a manor of thy friends or of thine own were; any man's death diminishes me, because I am involved in mankind; and therefore never send to know for whom the bells toll: It tolls for thee.

—John Donne

We are creatures of outside influences—we originate nothing within. Whenever we take a new line of belief or action, the impulse is always suggested from the outside.

—Mark Twain

It is in the thrill of the pull between someone else's authority and our own, between submission and independence that we must discover how to define ourselves.

—Nancy Sommers

Families come in all shapes and sizes. Whether the family is nuclear, extended, blended, or adopted, one thing is certain: the first and most influential relationships we have are with our families. After all, they are our first contact with the world. From the time we are born and through childhood and adolescence, we learn values, morals, and ethics from family members simply by living with them. There is virtually no chance of *not* being affected positively and/or negatively by our families.

The family we enter, whether by birth, adoption, or choice, can leave an indelible mark on who we become as adults. Whether we choose to emulate family members or follow different paths, our familial relationships are revealing because they speak to the kind of people we become. To explore our relationships with our families is to explore ourselves. The readings in this chapter do just that.

Chapter 2 begins with four essays that present the perspective of children as they remember their parents. Annie Dillard recounts her mother in a series of stories and anecdotes. In the next essay, Janice E. Fein recalls a wish, common in childhood, to have a family resembling her friend's—a wish that she, as an adult, realized was mistaken. Next, Sherwood Anderson recalls when he learned how very special it was to be his father's son. In "Missing: A Man with a Briefcase," Susan Allen Toth reminisces about the few but powerful memories she has of her father.

From *The Broken Cord,* Michael Dorris speaks from the perspective of a father who weighs his conflicting emotions of wanting to care for his adult son against his knowledge that it is time for his son to care for himself. "On Going Home," by Joan Didion, is a fascinating exploration of the adage, "You can't go home again." Finally, N. Scott Momaday details the return to his grandmother's funeral and to his ancestral roots.

In this chapter, you will notice that the readings are more than just narratives about family members or incidents. Besides hearing people and events described, you will have a chance to hear the authors reaching new understandings of their families. Listen to the writers as they reflect on their relationships. Imagine what musings you might have about you own ancestry or offspring.

An American Childhood
Annie Dillard

Born in 1945, Annie Dillard received B.A. and M.A. degrees from Hollins College. A poet, essayist, critic, and American naturalist, Dillard is the author of Tickets for a Prayer Wheel *(1974);* Pilgrim at Tinker Creek *(1974), for which she won the Pulitzer Prize;* Holy the Firm *(1977);* Living By Fiction *(1982);* Teaching a Stone to Talk *(1982);* Encounters with Chinese Writers *(1984); and* An American Childhood *(1987). She is also the author of a novel,* The Living *(1992). Delighting in the wonders of nature, Dillard has distinguished herself as a keen observer of natural life. The following essay from her autobiography,* An American Childhood, *vividly describes Dillard's mother, largely by anecdotes and stories.*

1   One Sunday afternoon Mother wandered through our kitchen, where Father was making a sandwich and listening to the ball game. The Pirates were playing the New York Giants at Forbes Field. In those days, the Giants had a utility infielder named Wayne Terwilliger. Just as Mother passed through, the radio announcer cried—with undue drama—"Terwilliger bunts one!"

2   "Terwilliger bunts one?" Mother cried back, stopped short. She turned. "Is that English?"

3   "The player's name is Terwilliger," Father said. "He bunted."

4   "That's marvelous," Mother said. "'Terwilliger bunts one.' No wonder you listen to baseball. 'Terwilliger bunts one.'"

5   For the next seven or eight years, Mother made this surprising string of syllables her own. Testing a microphone, she repeated, "Terwilliger bunts one"; testing a pen or a typewriter, she wrote it. If, as happened surprisingly often in the course of various improvised gags, she pretended to whisper something else in my ear, she actually whispered, "Terwilliger bunts one." Whenever someone used a French phrase, or a Latin one, she answered solemnly, "Terwilliger bunts one." If Mother had had, like Andrew Carnegie, the opportunity to cook up a motto for a coat of arms, hers would have read simply and tellingly, "Terwilliger bunts one."(Carnegie's was "Death to Privilege.")

6   She served us with other words and phrases. On a Florida trip, she repeated tremulously, "That . . . is a royal poinciana." I don't remember the tree; I remember the thrill in her voice. She pronounced it carefully, and spelled it. She also liked to say "portulaca."

7   The drama of the words "Tamiami Trail" stirred her, we learned on the same Florida trip. People built Tampa on one coast, and they built Miami on another. Then—the height of visionary ambition and folly—they piled a slow, tremendous road through the terrible Everglades to

connect them. To build the road, men stood sunk in muck to their armpits. They fought off cottonmouth moccasins and six-foot alligators. They slept in boats, wet. They blasted muck with dynamite, cut jungle with machetes; they laid logs, dragged drilling machines, hauled dredges, heaped limestone. The road took fourteen years to build up by the shovelful, a Panama Canal in reverse, and cost hundreds of lives from tropical, mosquito-carried diseases. Then, capping it all, some genius thought of the word Tamiami: they called the road from Tampa to Miami, this very road under our spinning wheels, the Tamiami Trail. Some called it Alligator Alley. Anyone could drive over this road without a thought.

8   Hearing this, moved, I thought all the suffering of road building was worth it (it wasn't my suffering), now that we had this new thing to hang these new words on—Alligator Alley for those who liked things cute, and, for connoisseurs like Mother, for lovers of the human drama in all its boldness and terror, the Tamiami Trail.

9   Back home, Mother cut clips from reels of talk, as it were, and played them back at leisure. She noticed that many Pittsburghers confuse "leave" and "let." One kind relative brightened our morning by mentioning why she'd brought her son to visit: "He wanted to come with me, so I left him." Mother filled in Amy and me on locutions we missed. "I can't do it on Friday," her pretty sister told a crowded dinner party, "because Friday's the day I lay in the stores."

10   (All unconsciously, though, we ourselves used some pure Pittsburghisms. We said "tele pole," pronounced "telly pole," for that splintery sidewalk post I loved to climb. We said "slippy"—the sidewalks are "slippy." We said, "That's all the farther I could go." And we said, as Pittsburghers do say, "This glass needs washed," or "The dog needs walked"—a usage our father eschewed; he knew it was not standard English, nor even comprehensible English, but he never let on.)

11   "Spell 'poinsettia,'" Mother would throw out at me, smiling with pleasure. "Spell 'sherbet.'" The idea was not to make us whizzes, but, quite the contrary, to remind us—and I, especially, needed reminding—that we didn't know it all just yet.

12   "There's a deer standing in the front hall," she told me one quiet evening in the country.

13   "Really?"

14   "No. I just wanted to tell you something once without your saying, 'I know.'"

15   Supermarkets in the middle 1950s began luring, or bothering, customers by giving out Top Value Stamps or Green Stamps. When, shopping with Mother, we got to the head of the checkout line, the checker, always a young man, asked, "Save stamps?"

16   "No," Mother replied genially, week after week, "I build model airplanes." I believe she originated this line. It took me years to determine where the joke lay.

17   Anyone who met her verbal challenges she adored. She had surgery on one of her eyes. On the operating table, just before she conked out, she appealed feelingly to the surgeon, saying, as she had been planning to say for weeks, "Will I be able to play the piano?" "Not on me," the surgeon said. "You won't pull that old one on me."

18   It was, indeed, an old one. The surgeon was supposed to answer, "Yes, my dear, brave woman, you will be able to play the piano after this operation," to which Mother intended to reply, "Oh, good, I've always wanted to play the piano." This pat scenario bored her; she loved having it interrupted. It must have galled her that usually her acquaintances were so predictably unalert; it must have galled her that, for the length of her life, she could surprise everyone so continually, so easily, when she had been the same all along. At any rate, she loved anyone who, as she put it, saw it coming, and called her on it.

19   She regarded the instructions on bureaucratic forms as straight lines. "Do you advocate the overthrow of the United States government by force or violence?" After some thought she wrote, "Force." She regarded children, even babies, as straight men. When Molly learned to crawl, Mother delighted in buying her gowns with drawstrings at the bottom, like Swee'pea's, because, as she explained energetically, you could easily step on the drawstring without the baby's noticing, so that she crawled and crawled and crawled and never got anywhere except into a small ball at the gown's top.

20   When we children were young, she mothered us tenderly and dependably; as we got older, she resumed her career of anarchism. She collared us into her gags. If she answered the phone on a wrong number, she told the caller, "Just a minute," and dragged the receiver to Amy or me, saying, "Here, take this, your name is Cecile," or, worse, just, "It's for you." You had to think on your feet. But did you want to perform well as Cecile, or did you want to take pity on the wretched caller?

21   During a family trip to the Highland Park Zoo, Mother and I were alone for a minute. She approached a young couple holding hands on a bench by the seals, and addressed the young man in dripping tones: "Where have you been? Still got those baby-blue eyes; always did slay me. And this"—a swift nod at the dumbstruck young woman, who had removed her hand from the man's—"must be the one you were telling me about. She's not so bad, really, as you used to make out. But listen, you know how I miss you, you know where to reach me, same old place. And there's Ann over there—see how she's grown? See the blue eyes?"

22   And off she sashayed, taking me firmly by the hand, and leading us around briskly past the monkey house and away. She cocked an ear back, and both of us heard the desperate man begin, in a high-pitched wail, "I swear, I never saw her before in my life. . . ."

23   On a long, sloping beach by the ocean, she lay stretched out sunning

with Father and friends, until the conversation gradually grew tedious, when without forethought she gave a little push with her heel and rolled away. People were stunned. She rolled deadpan and apparently effortlessly, arms and legs extended and tidy, down the beach to the distant water's edge, where she lay at ease just as she had been, but half in the surf, and well out of earshot.

24   She dearly loved to fluster people by throwing out a game's rules at whim—when she was getting bored, losing in a dull sort of way, and when everybody else was taking it too seriously. If you turned your back, she moved the checkers around on the board. When you got them all straightened out, she denied she'd touched them; the next time you turned your back, she lined them up on the rug or hid them under your chair. In a betting rummy game called Michigan, she routinely played out of turn, or called out a card she didn't hold, or counted backward, simply to amuse herself by causing an uproar and watching the rest of us do double takes and have fits. (Much later, when serious suitors came to call, Mother subjected them to this fast card game as a trial by ordeal; she used it as an intelligence test and a measure of spirit. If the poor man could stay a round without breaking down or running out, he got to marry one of us, if he still wanted to.)

25   She excelled at bridge, playing fast and boldly, but when the stakes were low and the hands dull, she bid slams for the devilment of it, or raised her opponents' suit to bug them, or showed her hand, or tossed her cards in a handful behind her back in a characteristic swift motion accompanied by a vibrantly innocent look. It drove our stolid father crazy. The hand was over before it began, and the guests were appalled. How do you score it, who deals now, what do you do with a crazy person who is having so much fun? Or they were down seven, and the guests were appalled. "Pam!" "Dammit, Pam!" He groaned. What ails such people? What on earth possesses them? He rubbed his face.

26   She was an unstoppable force; she never let go. When we moved across town, she persuaded the U.S. Post Office to let her keep her old address—forever—because she'd had stationery printed. I don't know how she did it. Every new post office worker, over decades, needed to learn that although the Doaks' mail is addressed to here, it is delivered to there.

27   Mother's energy and intelligence suited her for a greater role in a larger arena—mayor of New York, say—than the one she had. She followed American politics closely; she had been known to vote for Democrats. She saw how things should be run, but she had nothing to run but our household. Even there, small minds bugged her; she was smarter than the people who designed the things she had to use all day for the length of her life.

28   "Look," she said. "Whoever designed this corkscrew never used one. Why would anyone sell it without trying it out?" So she invented a better one. She showed me a drawing of it. The spirit of American enterprise never faded in Mother. If capitalizing and tooling up had been as interesting as theorizing and thinking up, she would have fired up a new factory

every week, and chaired several hundred corporations.

29   "It grieves me," she would say, "it grieves my heart," that the company that made one superior product packaged it poorly, or took the wrong tack in its advertising. She knew, as she held the thing mournfully in her two hands, that she'd never find another. She was right. We children wholly sympathized, and so did Father; what could she do, what could anyone do, about it? She was Samson in chains. She paced.

30   She didn't like the taste of stamps so she didn't lick stamps; she licked the corner of the envelope instead. She glued sandpaper to the sides of kitchen drawers, and under kitchen cabinets, so she always had a handy place to strike a match. She designed, and hounded workmen to build against all norms, doubly wide kitchen counters and elevated bathroom sinks. To splint a finger, she stuck it in a light-weight cigar tube. Conversely, to protect a pack of cigarettes, she carried it in a Band-Aid box. She drew plans for an over-the-finger toothbrush for babies, an oven rack that slid up and down, and—the family favorite—Lendalarm. Lendalarm was a beeper you attached to books (or tools) you loaned friends. After ten days, the beeper sounded. Only the rightful owner could silence it.

31   She repeatedly reminded us of P. T. Barnum's dictum: You could sell anything to anybody if you marketed it right. The adman who thought of making Americans believe they needed underarm deodorant was a visionary. So, too, was the hero who made a success of a new product, Ivory soap. The executives were horrified, Mother told me, that a cake of this stuff floated. Soap wasn't supposed to float. Anyone would be able to tell it was mostly whipped-up air. Then some inspired adman made a leap: Advertise that it floats. Flaunt it. The rest is history.

32   She respected the rare few who broke through to new ways. "Look," she'd say, "here's an intelligent apron." She called upon us to admire intelligent control knobs and intelligent pan handles, intelligent andirons and picture frames and knife sharpeners. She questioned everything, every pair of scissors, every knitting needle, gardening glove, tape dispenser. Hers was a restless mental vigor that just about ignited the dumb household objects with its force.

33

Torpid conformity was a kind of sin; it was stupidity itself, the mighty stream against which Mother would never cease to struggle. If you held no minority opinions, or if you failed to risk total ostracism for them daily, the world would be a better place without you.

34   Always I heard Mother's emotional voice asking Amy and me the same few questions: Is that your own idea? Or somebody else's? "*Giant* is a good movie," I pronounced to the family at dinner. "Oh, really?" Mother warmed to these occasions. She all but rolled up her sleeves. She knew I hadn't seen it. "Is that your considered opinion?"

35   She herself held many unpopular, even fantastic, positions. She was scathingly sarcastic about the McCarthy hearings while they took place,

right on our living-room television; she frantically opposed Father's wait-and-see calm. "We don't know enough about it," he said. "I do," she said. "I know all I need to know."

36   She asserted, against all opposition, that people who lived in trailer parks were not bad but simply poor, and had as much right to settle on beautiful land, such as rural Ligonier, Pennsylvania, as did the oldest of families in the finest of hidden houses. Therefore, the people who owned trailer parks, and sought zoning changes to permit trailer parks, needed our help. Her profound belief that the country-club pool sweeper was a person, and that the department-store saleslady, the bus driver, telephone operator, and housepainter were people, and even in groups the steelworkers who carried pickets and the Christmas shoppers who clogged intersections were people—this was a conviction common enough in democratic Pittsburgh, but not altogether common among our friends' parents, or even, perhaps, among our parents' friends.

37   Opposition emboldened Mother, and she would take on anybody on any issue—the chairman of the board, at a cocktail party, on the current strike; she would fly at him in a flurry of passion, as a songbird selflessly attacks a big hawk.

38   "Eisenhower's going to win," I announced after school. She lowered her magazine and looked me in the eyes: "How do you know?" I was doomed. It was fatal to say, "Everyone says so." We all knew well what happened. "Do you consult this Everyone before you make your decisions? What if Everyone decided to round up all the Jews?" Mother knew there was no danger of cowing me. She simply tried to keep us all awake. And in fact it was always clear to Amy and me, and to Molly when she grew old enough to listen, that if our classmates came to cruelty, just as much as if the neighborhood or the nation came to madness, we were expected to take, and would be each separately capable of taking, a stand.

Discussion Questions

1. How would you describe Dillard's mother from the many anecdotes provided in this essay?

2. Which anecdote do you think best captures Dillard's mother? Why?

3. What do you gather Dillard's attitude was toward her mother? Cite specific passages to support your answer.

4. What specifically do you think Dillard learned from her mother? Explain your response.

5. Do you find the last sentence of Dillard's essay believable? Why or why not?

A New Perspective

Janice E. Fein

*J**anice E. Fein was born in 1948 and delayed her college education
until her two children were in school. A psychology major, Fein
graduated** magna cum laude *from the University of Akron in 1992.
Currently, she works as a social services case worker for abused and neglected children. She wrote the following essay for a freshman composition class. The assignment was to choose a haunting image from childhood and write an essay in which the image is thoroughly explored. "A
New Perspective" was published in* Fresh Inc., *a collection of the best
essays written in freshman composition courses at Akron. As you read
it, pay attention to the essay's details and to the childhood anger Fein
experienced.*

1   Our lives are shaped by the seemingly insignificant events of our youth.
My childhood has become a series of mental snips of celluloid edited from
the long playing film entitled "Cheated in Life."

2   My mother is walking me to kindergarten. I'm sure it must be kindergarten. In future years it would become vitally important for me to remember just exactly when it was. If it were first or second grade we would
have been walking in the opposite direction but I can clearly see each familiar house as we pass by: Leedom's, Neiman's, Salem's, yes, it was definitely kindergarten. The film clip does not take us to our final destination,
nor does it begin at home. It's a simple walk down a simple block in time.
I can still feel my left fingers cradled in the smooth grip of her hand, one
not much bigger than that of my own. I actually feel the warmth of the rising sun on my face as I look up at her each time she speaks. Aha! It was
kindergarten! The sun always rose from behind that row of houses. If we
had been walking anywhere else, the sun would have been in her face, not
mine. She never walked me to elementary school. She only walked me to
kindergarten, and very possibly, only that one time. Was it the first day of
school? Or Parent's Day? It was unimportant. What became important, in
later years, was my ability to woefully lament, "I only remember my
mother walking one time in my life. She walked me to kindergarten."

3   Thereafter, all recollections of her were in her hospital bed, a massive
ugly thing that took up a good portion of my parents' room. The debilitating effects of rheumatoid arthritis confined her to that bed. There were,
however, what she referred to as "good days," days in which she was able
to drag herself from her bed and onto a small kitchen chair with curved
metal legs. She would then muster enough energy to force her hips in an
awkward motion. Each painful hip movement would inch the chair labori-
ously forward, commanding it to perform the tasks that her frozen
arthritic joints could not accomplish. My friends never came to my room
to play. To do so they would have to pass by my parents' room. I remem-

ber that bed and that chair as embarrassing eyesores and how, once again, I had felt cheated.

4   Connie had the best playroom in the neighborhood. She was my very best friend and every day after school I would race home to change clothes and, in a heartbeat, I was at her door. Half of her basement was converted into a wonderful playhouse with panelling, carpets, and lace curtains to match. I was sure that every toy ever created was in that room. Despite the lure of all those treasures, what I remember most were the marvelous sounds and smells that drifted down to us from the kitchen above. Pots and pans clanging, water rushing through the pipes, and best of all, Connie's mother humming softly as she worked. One particular evening, the aroma was so compelling that I had to ask. Connie wrinkled her nose in disgust and said, "Lasagna . . . again!" I pretended to have to use the bathroom so that I could pass through the kitchen and briefly glimpse what a lasagna looked like.

5   The oven timer was the saddest sound. When I heard it I knew what was coming next. "Connie, come wash up for supper," and I would have to leave. At a snail's pace, I would wander back to my own kitchen door. No wonderful aromas ever greeted me there. Sometimes there would be cold macaroni and cheese left over by one of my brothers or sisters. Most often I would prepare something on my own. Frozen hamburger patties, fish sticks, maybe I'll just have a can of soup. It never really mattered. It would never be lasagna. One evening, as I wander into my mother's room, bologna sandwich in hand, she shakes her head and says, "Is that the best you can find out there?" "I'm not very hungry," I lie. Only now can I see that the look in her eyes matched the despair in my heart, and yet, I felt cheated.

6   As childhood progressed, certain actions became innate. Handouts at school calling for volunteer room mothers and field trip chaperones were surreptitiously discarded along the nine-block journey home. I'll never forget those nine long blocks. In January and February they might just as well have been ninety! My classmates are piling into their mothers' warm waiting station wagons. I hunch my shoulders to my ears and silently watch as they disappear into the swirling gusts of snow. No steaming mug of hot cocoa is awaiting my arrival, just those sad eyes. Cheated.

7   I've rolled the film a thousand times. The scenes have never changed, only my perspective. It took the birth of my first child to truly see the whole picture. I've often tried to imagine what it would be like to see my son in pain and not be able to brush away a tear, mend a knee or simply hold him in my arms. I've seen the look in his eyes when he hit his first home run. I've "hugged him warm" on snowy days and "tickled him happy" when life was cruel. I've knelt with him to say his prayers and thanked God for my ability to do so. I may never understand why some of us are cheated in life. I only know, from this perspective, that I am not the one who was.

Discussion Questions

1. Why do you think it is important for Fein to identify exactly when the first experience she describes in paragraph 2 took place? In your own life, do you find it necessary to identify the exact time an experience happened? Why or why not?

2. What specifically in Fein's essay makes her childhood experiences believable?

3. Instead of relying solely on the sense of sight to describe moments from her childhood, Fein uses all five senses. Identify examples of each of the senses. Which strike you as the most powerful? Why?

4. What effect is created by the repetition of the word "cheated" throughout the essay? Why isn't the repetition tedious and unnecessary?

5. In what ways do you think the birth of Fein's first child justified her "new perspective"?

Discovery of a Father

Sherwood Anderson

Born in Camden, Ohio, in 1876, Sherwood Anderson dropped out of school to work a series of odd jobs. He did not seriously begin writing until he was thirty-six years old. After extensive traveling around the world to pursue his literary interests, Anderson finally settled in West Virginia, where he edited two local newspapers. Anderson is the author of over a dozen books, including Windy McPherson's Son *(1916),* Marching Men *(1917),* Winesburg, Ohio *(1919),* Horses and Men *(1923),* Tar: A Midwest Childhood *(1926), and* Dark Laughter *(1927). Anderson died in 1941. The following essay, originally appearing in Anderson's* Memoirs, *examines "one of the strangest relationships in the world": the one between father and son. In it, Anderson chronicles his growing understanding of how very special it was to be his father's son.*

1   One of the strangest relationships in the world is that between father and son. I know it now from having sons of my own.

2   A boy wants something very special from his father. You hear it said that fathers want their sons to be what they feel they cannot themselves be, but I tell you it also works the other way. I know that as a small boy I wanted my father to be a certain thing he was not. I wanted him to be a proud, silent, dignified father. When I was with other boys and he passed along the street, I wanted to feel a glow of pride: "There he is. That is my father."

3   But he wasn't such a one. He couldn't be. It seemed to me then that he was always showing off. Let's say someone in our town had got up a show. They were always doing it. The druggist would be in it, the shoe-store clerk, the horse doctor, and a lot of women and girls. My father would manage to get the chief comedy part. It was, let's say, a Civil War play and he was a comic Irish soldier. He had to do the most absurd things. They thought he was funny, but I didn't.

4   I thought he was terrible. I didn't see how Mother could stand it. She even laughed with the others. Maybe I would have laughed if it hadn't been my father.

5   Or there was a parade, the Fourth of July or Decoration Day. He'd be in that, too, right at the front of it, as Grand Marshal or something, on a white horse hired from a livery stable.

6   He couldn't ride for shucks. He fell off the horse and everyone hooted with laughter, but he didn't care. He even seemed to like it. I remember once when he had done something ridiculous, and right out on Main Street, too. I was with some other boys and they were laughing and shouting at him and he was shouting back and having as good a time as they were. I ran down an alley back of some stores and there in the Presbyterian Church sheds I had a good long cry.

7   Or I would be in bed at night and Father would come home a little lit up and bring some men with him. He was a man who was never alone. Before he went broke, running a harness shop, there were always a lot of men loafing in the shop. He went broke, of course, because he gave too much credit. He couldn't refuse it and I thought he was a fool. I had got to hating him.

8   There'd be men I didn't think would want to be fooling around with him. There might even be the superintendent of our schools and a quiet man who ran the hardware store. Once, I remember, there was a white-haired man who was a cashier of the bank. It was a wonder to me they'd want to be seen with such a windbag. That's what I thought he was. I know now what it was that attracted them. It was because life in our town, as in all small towns, was at times pretty dull and he livened it up. He made them laugh. He could tell stories. He'd even get them to singing.

9   If they didn't come to our house they'd go off, say at night, to where there was a grassy place by a creek. They'd cook food there and drink beer and sit about listening to his stories.

10   He was always telling stories about himself. He'd say this or that wonderful thing happened to him. It might be something that made him look like a fool. He didn't care.

11   If an Irishman came to our house, right away father would say he was Irish. He'd tell what county in Ireland he was born in. He'd tell things that happened there when he was a boy. He'd make it seem so real that, if I hadn't known he was born in southern Ohio, I'd have believed him myself.

12   If it was a Scotchman, the same thing happened. He'd get a burr into

his speech. Or he was a German or a Swede. He'd be anything the other man was. I think they all knew he was lying, but they seemed to like him just the same. As a boy that was what I couldn't understand.

13 And there was Mother. How could she stand it? I wanted to ask but never did. She was not the kind you asked such questions.

14 I'd be upstairs in my bed, in my room above the porch, and Father would be telling some of his tales. A lot of Father's stories were about the Civil War. To hear him tell it he'd been in about every battle. He'd known Grant, Sherman, Sheridan and I don't know how many others. He'd been particularly intimate with General Grant so that when Grant went East, to take charge of all the armies, he took Father along.

15 "I was an orderly at headquarters and Sam Grant said to me, 'Irve,' he said, 'I'm going to take you along with me.'"

16 It seems he and Grant used to slip off sometimes and have a quiet drink together. That's what my father said. He'd tell about the day Lee surrendered and how, when the great moment came, they couldn't find Grant.

17 "You know," my father said, "about General Grant's book, his memoirs. You've read of how he said he had a headache and how, when he got word that Lee was ready to call it quits, he was suddenly and miraculously cured.

18 "Huh," said Father. "He was in the woods with me.

19 "I was there with my back against a tree. I was pretty well corned. I had got hold of a bottle of pretty good stuff.

20 "They were looking for Grant. He had got off his horse and come into the woods. He found me. He was covered with mud.

21 "I had the bottle in my hand. What'd I care? The war was over. I knew we had them licked."

22 My father said that he was the one who told Grant about Lee. An orderly riding by had told him, because the orderly knew how thick he was with Grant. Grant was embarrassed.

23 "But, Irve, look at me. I'm all covered with mud," he said to Father.

24 And then, my father said, he and Grant decided to have a drink together. They took a couple of shots and then, because he didn't want Grant to show up potted before the immaculate Lee, he smashed the bottle against the tree.

25 "Sam Grant's dead now and I wouldn't want it to get out on him," my father said.

26 That's just one of the kind of things he'd tell. Of course, the men knew he was lying, but they seemed to like it just the same.

27 When we got broke, down and out, do you think he ever brought anything home? Not he. If there wasn't anything to eat in the house, he'd go off visiting around at farm houses. They all wanted him. Sometimes he'd stay away for weeks, Mother working to keep us fed, and then home he'd come bringing, let's say, a ham. He'd got it from some farmer friend. He'd slap in on the table in the kitchen. "You bet I'm going to see that my kids have something to eat," he'd say, and Mother would just stand

smiling at him. She'd never say a word about all the weeks and months he'd been away, not leaving us a cent for food. Once I heard her speaking to a woman in our street. Maybe the woman had dared to sympathize with her. "Oh," she said, "it's all right. He isn't ever dull like most of the men in this street. Life is never dull when my man is about."

28   But often I was filled with bitterness, and sometimes I wished he wasn't my father. I'd even invent another man as my father. To protect my mother I'd make up stories of a secret marriage that for some strange reason never got known. As though some man, say the president of a railroad company or maybe a Congressman, had married my mother, thinking his wife was dead and then it turned out she wasn't.

29   So they had to hush it up but I got born just the same. I wasn't really the son of my father. Somewhere in the world there was a very dignified, quite wonderful man who was really my father. I even made myself half believe these fancies.

30   And then there came a certain night. Mother was away from home. Maybe there was church that night. Father came in. He'd been off somewhere for two or three weeks. He found me alone in the house, reading by the kitchen table.

31   It had been raining and he was very wet. He sat and looked at me for a long time, not saying a word. I was startled, for there was on his face the saddest look I had ever seen. He sat for a time, his clothes dripping. Then he got up.

32   "Come on with me," he said.

33   I got up and went with him out of the house. I was filled with wonder but I wasn't afraid. We went along a dirt road that led down into a valley, about a mile out of town, where there was a pond. We walked in silence. The man who was always talking had stopped his talking.

34   I didn't know what was up and had the queer feeling that I was with a stranger. I don't know whether my father intended it so. I don't think he did.

35   The pond was quite large. It was still raining hard and there were flashes of lightning followed by thunder. We were on a grassy bank at the pond's edge when my father spoke, and in the darkness and rain his voice sounded strange.

36   "Take off your clothes," he said. Still filled with wonder, I began to undress. There was a flash of lightning and I saw that he was already naked.

37   Naked, we went into the pond. Taking my hand, he pulled me in. It may be that I was too frightened, too full of a feeling of strangeness, to speak. Before that night my father had never seemed to pay any attention to me.

38   "And what is he up to now?" I kept asking myself. I did not swim very well, but he put my hand on his shoulder and struck out into the darkness.

39   He was a man with big shoulders, a powerful swimmer. In the darkness I could feel the movements of his muscles. We swam to the far edge of the pond and then back to where we had left our clothes. The rain con-

tinued and the wind blew. Sometimes my father swam on his back, and when he did he took my hand in his large powerful one and moved it over so that it rested always on his shoulder. Sometimes there would be a flash of lightning, and I could see his face quite clearly.

40   It was as it was earlier, in the kitchen, a face filled with sadness. There would be the momentary glimpse of his face, and then again the darkness, the wind and the rain. In me there was a feeling I had never known before.

41   It was a feeling of closeness. It was something strange. It was as though there were only we two in the world. It was as though I had been jerked suddenly out of myself, out of my world of the schoolboy out of a world in which I was ashamed of my father.

42   He had become blood of my blood; he the strong swimmer and I the boy clinging to him in the darkness. We swam in silence, and in silence we dressed in our wet clothes and went home.

43   There was a lamp lighted in the kitchen, and when we came in, the water dripping from us, there was my mother. She smiled at us. I remember that she called us "boys." "What have you boys been up to?" she asked, but my father did not answer. As he had begun the evening's experience with me in silence, so he ended it. He turned and looked at me. Then he went, I thought, with a new and strange dignity, out of the room.

44   I climbed the stairs to my room, undressed in darkness and got into bed. I couldn't sleep and did not want to sleep. For the first time I knew that I was the son of my father. He was a storyteller as I was to be. It may be that I even laughed a little softly there in the darkness. If I did, I laughed knowing that I would never again be wanting another father.

Discussion Questions

1.   To what extent are Anderson's initial feelings about his father fairly typical of a young boy's? To what extent are Anderson's descriptions of his father believable?

2.   What accounts for Anderson's changing his opinion of his father? Do you find his turnaround plausible? Why or why not?

3.   Anderson's new understanding of his father begins as they remove their clothes to swim in the pond. What symbolism do you find in this scene?

4.   Throughout the essay, Anderson seems to criticize his father's stories, yet at the end he admits to becoming a storyteller himself. How is this change of heart justified? Is it convincing?

5.   Who is this essay really about: Anderson's father, Anderson himself, or father-son relationships? Explain your answer.

Missing: A Man with a Briefcase
Susan Allen Toth

Born in Ames, Iowa, in 1940, Susan Allen Toth was educated at Smith College, the University of California at Berkeley, and the University of Minnesota. She has taught English at Macalester College since 1969 and is the author of Blooming: A Small-Town Childhood *(1978),* Ivy Days: Making My Way Out East *(1984),* How to Prepare for Your High School Reunion and Other Midlife Musings *(1988), and* My Love Affair with England: A Traveler's Memoir *(1992). The following essay appears in* Family Portraits: Remembrances by Twenty Distinguished Writers *(1989), edited by Carolyn Anthony. In it, Toth uses a family photograph to evoke memories of her father.*

1   Almost all our family pictures show just the three of us, my mother, my older sister Karen, and me. At first a young wife in a floral dress and with neat braids, Mother stands self-consciously before the camera. In her middle years, dressed in trim suits, she changes to an upswept pompadour. Over the years, as she relaxes, so does her hairdo, gradually turning into a graying brisk bob. Karen and I appear in rompers, then starched pinafores, eventually wedding dresses, and finally jeans and baggy sweaters.

2   Someone is obviously missing from this sequence of snapshots. For years I thought we three were an ordinary family. But now, studying the empty space, I know better. I see the ghost who haunts it. For although he is invisible to the lens of the camera, my father is standing beside us in every picture. Only he does not age. Tall, lean, almost handsome except for a Roman nose, he is always thirty-nine.

3   Here on my desk is his worn black briefcase, hauled out from under a dusty pile of high school annuals and college notebooks. The thick leather is glazed with cracks, and the clasps are coated with rust. When I asked my mother a few years ago if I could take this briefcase from her old trunk, I thought perhaps I would revive it and give it new life. Could I use it to carry books to my office? Even though it was heavy, could I perhaps stuff it with unfinished manuscripts and lug it on plane trips? My father might like that, I thought. His name is still there: EDWARD D. ALLEN, printed in gold leaf under the lock. Whenever I see his name in print, I have a faint sense of shock. After forty-two years, no one speaks or writes it anymore.

4   Of course, I didn't ever use his briefcase. It was too shabby and unwieldy. I kept it lying on my desk for many months, thinking each day I'd take it with me, before I finally let loose the string of that romantic but useless idea. Feeling a little guilty, I tucked the briefcase in my storage closet. Someday I suppose my daughter will have to toss it out.

5   I don't have much from which to reconstruct my father. Although I have an often alarming recall of many details of my life, my years with him

are surprisingly blank, like an old-fashioned photograph album with only an occasional snapshot stuck there, a scene I seem to have mentally snapped and firmly glued down with corner mounts.

6   For a long time I didn't think losing my father had affected me very much. He died at thirty-nine, when I had just turned seven, and my mother, a strong, determined, and resourceful woman, took over the support and raising of Karen and me. Although my mother and I were very close when I was growing up, we didn't talk much about my father. We never set off our feelings like Roman candles—our heritage was Scandinavian and English, a blend that stands up better to cold weather than to dazzling heat—and we had to get on with our lives. My mother watched well over my sister and me, providing whatever she thought we needed—music lessons, bicycles, trips—and if someone had asked me, at eight or twelve or eighteen, what I had missed by not having a father, I don't think I could have told them.

7   Of course, I did notice his absence on Father's Day. I could ignore the official June day by walking quickly past the dimestore greeting-card aisle. But other kinds of Father's Days appeared at awkward times and places. Invite your father for Dad's Day at Camp! Take him to the Father-Daughter Dinner! Let him buy your corsage for the Dads-and-Daughters Dance! Living in a small town, I didn't have any friends who lacked a visible father, and I dreaded the events when I was supposed to produce one. Zac Dunlap, the kindhearted family man next door, was always glad to take me, but, uncertain what to say or do, I was on my company behavior—not, I realized, the way most kids acted with their fathers.

8   I was almost forty before I began to understand that, although my father had vanished so early, his influence had not. At thirty-nine, the age when he died, I found myself wracked by a strange and pervasive anxiety. Living beyond that milestone seemed odd, almost unthinkable, and perhaps impossible. As I struggled to understand my turbulent feelings, I gradually realized that, although I could not conjure up his face with a photograph, my father must have helped shape how I thought, how I felt, and who I was. For the first time, I asked myself what Edward D. Allen had really been like, and how we were related.

9   The clearest connection I could trace to my father was fear. A courageous man, he would hate knowing that. My mother has told me how bravely he endured his long illness, which began almost as soon as I was born. He had a brain tumor, but for many years no one recognized what it was. His symptoms resembled stroke or epilepsy. Sometimes, in the midst of a sentence, he would stop, blank-eyed; moments later he would resume, not realizing what had happened. Worse, he was struck by seizures. The word our family used was "spells." Once, in a mental snapshot so short it is a moment's click, my mother, father, sister, and I are sitting together in the dining nook of our small kitchen. It has a red-brick linoleum floor. "Hazel," my father says quietly to my mother, "I think I'm going to have a spell." He gets up from the table. Everything in my mind goes black for

a moment, as it must have for him, and then I see him lying on the red linoleum, my mother bending over him. I do not know what happened next.

10   I do not remember any other "spells," though of course he had many of them. He also had terrible headaches; when I first was struck by a migraine, I thought I too had a brain tumor. But he continued his teaching, writing, and other professorial responsibilities. He was a proud man, my mother says, and he bore the agonizing knowledge that at any time, during a lecture or a meeting, he might lose control of himself. In another snapshot, my mother and I are walking down the steep polished-granite stairs inside the Agricultural Economics building at Iowa State College. My father's office is somewhere high above us. She is holding my hand tightly. "Watch your step," she says, and I hear a warning tone in her voice. I try to place my feet on the funny raspy-feeling strips that roughen the stair edges. Has she told me my father once fell here? Is that what I believe has caused his "spells"? In my memory, the stairs are cold and ominous.

11   Almost every day my father must have carried his heavy black briefcase up and down those stairs. He never gave up, my mother says. He did not like to talk about what was happening to him. I think I can see him, leaving home for his office, a tall lean man in a long overcoat, his hand firmly on the handle of the briefcase bulging with papers. It looked very important, an emblem of the College that he served so loyally. "He was a brilliant economist," my mother told me, "and he had a wonderful future ahead of him." When people spoke of my father in later years, they often echoed her. Among the remarkable group of young economists who worked at Iowa State in the early 1940s, most went on to make national and international reputations. Through the years I heard their names as a litany of achievement: Kenneth Boulding, Bill Nichols, Oswald Brownlee, Rainer Schickele. My father, I knew, should have been one of them.

12   So, not intending to, he left me his burden of unfulfilled promise. Without having to be asked, I picked it up. Like mountain climbers who gradually adjust to a rarefied atmosphere, children soon find the air of high expectations completely natural. From kindergarten, when I was embarrassed to bring home a report card because it had one minus among my pluses—under "Deportment," Miss Sawyer had written with unblinking severity: "Susan picks her nose"—I knew I needed to be a very good student. I was someone who ought to excel, someone with that exciting but demanding word "potential." Sometimes I was afraid that I would fail, that I too would not be able to redeem my promise.

13   But that fear came later. Another had hovered over my life from its beginning. I do not know how aware I was of my father's illness, of my mother's worry, of doctors, diagnoses, and medicines. Although I knew he had "spells," I did not know he was dying. Perhaps he didn't know himself. The summer before he died, a specialist at the University of Wisconsin, where my mother and father had gone for help, found a tiny

pinpoint of a tumor in his brain. "Come back in six months, at Christmas," the doctor told him. But my mother says my father was so busy, so involved in his forthcoming book, so concentrated on his work at the College, that he didn't go back at Christmas. One bright July morning the following summer, they were having breakfast. My father suddenly threw up, a violent projectile vomiting, and when they called our family doctor, she advised them to go to Madison immediately.

14   If I was sitting in the kitchen that awful morning, I have locked the memory away in a dark closet without a key. I know I was sent to stay across the street with friends, while my sister Karen went to other neighbors. My father was ill, I was told, and he had gone to Madison—a city so remote in my imagination it might have been Oz—in order to get better. I don't believe I was very worried. The Zickefooses were a jolly family, and I was great friends with their daughter Kay, who was my age. On those hot July days, I'm sure we cut out paper dolls, hid under the lilacs, and ran through the sprinkler, just as we usually did.

15   One afternoon soon after my parents had left, Mrs. Zickefoose told me I had to pay a visit across the alley to the E. S. Allens—the *other* Edward Allens, not related, though I regarded them as an older aunt and uncle. Going to see E. S. and Aunt Minne was always a slightly exotic occasion; they were Quakers and pacifists, and Aunt Minne, who was German, still had an accent. Their house was filled with antique furniture and German knickknacks. Somehow it always felt dark and hushed, as if the curtains were drawn, and Aunt Minne's kitchen had a lingering aroma of unfamiliar pungent spices. The atmosphere was not frightening, just different, a little like church. But today, the way Mrs. Zickefoose spoke, I somehow didn't want to go the Allens'.

16   Behind the E. S. Allens' house was a large garden, partly vegetables, but with lots of flowers. We had had a Victory garden once, and I can picture my father, in another mental snapshot, digging a pitchfork in the damp black dirt of early spring. I see the colorful Burpee's seed packets on stakes, marking each row, and the white string stretching over the deep furrows. I must have telescoped the time to midsummer, for I also see next to our garage another garden, a blur of rosy-red and white hollyhocks, sweet-smelling peonies, and orange nasturtiums. We had a small orchard too, in that narrow but deep city lot, and I remember my father once lifted me up into the white-flowering branches of the cherry tree. I sat there, perched above the whole world, while he worked among the lettuce and sweet corn below.

17   Walking to the Allens' house that afternoon, not wanting to hurry, not wanting to get there at all, I crunched the black cinders of the alley under my shoes. Despite the heat, I wasn't barefoot because I knew the cinders would hurt too much. Slowly I passed through their backyard garden, past what seemed like fields of daisies, petunias, and zinnias. I remember how brightly the sun shone.

18   My sister was there in the darkened living room, waiting for me. We sat next to Aunt Minne on the stiff-backed sofa. I do not remember how

she led us toward what she had to say. It didn't take long. When she came to the end, I heard her words very clearly: "Your father was so sick they had to go to Madison. He had an operation in the hospital there, and during the night, he died."

19   I didn't completely understand what she had told us, but I knew she had pronounced something that had the sound of doom. I began to cry. Karen was tight-faced and silent; later, walking back through the blooming flowers of the back garden, I accused her of not caring enough. Even then I knew I was being mean, but with a shamed self-awareness, I realized I had cried partly because I knew I was expected to.

20   I never forgot Aunt Minne's last sentence: "And during the night he died." Far away and in a setting I couldn't imagine, my father had gone to sleep and never woke up. During the night, he had simply disappeared. Where had he gone? I'm sure I brushed aside as unreal any talk of heaven and angels. After the funeral, which my sister and I didn't attend—the grown-ups thought we were too young—we were taken to the cemetery. I remember the mound of fresh earth, heaped with flowers. My mother says I asked if Daddy was really down there, under the ground. This time I am sure my sister and I both wept.

21   "And during the night he died." It was such a matter-of-fact statement. How could Aunt Minne have said it better? Yet it haunts me still. I have never liked staying alone at night. Before my daughter was born, if my husband was going to be out of town, I occasionally drove across town to a friend's house to sleep. Even now, if I am by myself, I leave a few lights on, double-lock the doors, and keep the telephone nearby. I sometimes am reluctant to fall asleep. Lost in the night, my father closed his eyes and never opened them again.

22   So I grew up knowing how fragile and vulnerable were the people I loved. While I was not a brooding or depressed child—in fact, like my father, I usually showed a very cheerful face—I was a worrier. I still am. Not long ago, as my husband, James, and I were walking up the steps of the National Gallery in Washington, he suddenly stopped and gripped the railing. I paused too and looked at him anxiously. I am always edgy when we are traveling. He seemed far away from me, standing so silently on the steps, utterly preoccupied. "What is it?" I asked, reaching for his arm, wondering how I could get an ambulance and wishing I'd taken that Red Cross course in cardiopulmonary resuscitation. Hearing the urgency in my voice, James looked at me in surprise. "Nothing," he said, "except I was trying to remember where I left the car keys."

23   So I have to try to curb my catastrophic imagination. If I can stand far enough back from my frightening pictures, I can even sometimes see how funny-awful they are. Once a therapist asked me to go to a swimming pool and just float. "I want you to experience fully the feeling of being supported, of being held up without your having to make any effort," she explained. I dutifully went to the pool and floated, though I didn't much like it. I wanted to do laps; like my father, I'm used to keeping busy. Later

I had to give the therapist a report. "And what did you think about?" she asked. I was embarrassed, but I had to answer truthfully. "Sharks," I said. "I thought about sharks."

24   I can see the fear my father left with me from another perspective, of course. Writers often turn things around and look at them from strange angles. Mine is one of gratitude, for I believe that when I became painfully aware of the possibility of sudden loss, I focused acutely and passionately on the world around me. I wanted to hold it close and never let it go. When my first two books of memoirs were published, readers assumed I had kept a journal. How else could I have remembered so much detail? Until they began asking me, I had not thought my memory was at all unusual. No, I hadn't kept a journal. I just kept those living pictures stored in my mind, piled in overfull bags spilling their contents onto the floor, until, by writing, I cleaned at least a corner of my attic and set it in order.

25   Fear was certainly not all my father gave me, however, and when I try to bring him back, I can focus on other pictures. On Sunday nights, my father liked to listen to the Jack Benny show. He stretched out on the sofa near the radio in the living room, and I climbed up to his lap and snuggled next to him. As he laughed, his stomach shook, and I rocked with the gentle waves of his laughter. Lying there on the sofa, I was sheltered and safe. Afterward, Mother often served us a special Sunday supper of soft-boiled eggs, Velveeta cheese, and milk toast. Though I didn't understand most of the jokes, I loved the Jack Benny show.

26   In the years since his death, several people have told me how much my father loved to laugh. "That's where you get your verve," my mother says to me wistfully. Old friends reminisce vaguely about how they enjoyed him, though few can think of any particular incidents I can grasp and make my own. Humor vanishes even more quickly than loosed balloons.

27   Though he could be lighthearted, my father believed in discipline. Once, going downstairs from my bedroom, I paused and looked over the banister into the kitchen. Mother was cooking oatmeal. Whatever I said— I didn't like oatmeal—brought my father swiftly out of the bathroom. "Don't let me ever hear you speak to your mother like that again," he said sternly. Another day, when I used some bad language—or was I "backtalking" again?—he took me into the bathroom and washed my mouth out with soap. I can still taste it, acrid and unpleasant. Just last week, when I hadn't thoroughly rinsed out a drinking glass, I spat out the soapy water with an instinctive revulsion and thought of my father.

28   I think of my father at other odd times. Although I haven't played tennis for years, he used to float into my mind during a game or even backboard practice. My mother told me when I was quite young how he had enjoyed tennis. His old racket stayed on a shelf in our house for many years. One of my mother's pictures shows him smiling, racket in hand, tennis sweater flung casually over his shoulders. Like everything else my father did, he was very good at tennis. Thinking perhaps I'd inherited some genetic skills, I signed up for a tennis class in college, but I barely passed. I

imagined my father dashing and lunging over the court; I puffed and lumbered.

29   My father had been light on his feet, a wonderful dancer. I never learned any steps beyond a basic fox-trot, and I stumbled over my partner's shoes. My parents loved to dance. When they went out as a young married couple with another pair of married friends, Mother remembers, still with some irritation, she'd get stuck with Dan, the other husband, who couldn't dance at all, because Dan's wife, Helen, insisted on waltzing around the floor with Edward. I know how Dan must have felt.

30   I followed him a little better in music. My father loved to sing too, and one of our most precious possessions was a 78 record, made by someone at the College, of a barbershop quartet that included my father. Over and over my sister and I would play "Ol' Man River," because for a few bars my father sang alone: "Hearts get weary and sick of tryin'." We held our breath and listened as hard as we could. That was our father's voice, rich and resonant, and, above all, alive.

31   I couldn't sing more than a few notes above middle C, but I did take piano lessons. My father's sister, Aunt Mary, had been a magnificent pianist, my mother said. Music ran in the family. She and my father liked concerts, and they had a small but prized collection of symphony records. On the piano was a thick volume of Gilbert and Sullivan songs, which my father had especially liked. Gathering all these clues, I made an effort to include music in my own life. When, at twenty, I sat alone in a cheap seat at the Sadler's Wells Theatre in London and entered eagerly into the D'Oyly Carte's production of *The Mikado,* I kept a paperback copy of the lyrics in my lap. I didn't want to miss a word.

32   A tennis racket, a book of Gilbert and Sullivan, a vision of my father whirling Helen Prince around the dance floor—these bits and scraps are not much from which to piece a coherent pattern. My father flashes in and out of my mind, yet each flash is illuminating. That is why I am frustrated that I cannot see him as a whole. I was an English major; I know what a well-rounded literary character should be like. I wish I could make my father into one. As a graduate student, I had some skill as a researcher, and I worked with primary source materials. So I have read the few letters my mother treasures, scrutinized the yellowed pages of the college newspaper he edited, and tried to read his posthumously published textbook. Our family was very proud of that book. I used to roll its title on my tongue, because it sounded so impressive: Allen and Brownlee, *The Economics of Public Finance.* I wasn't surprised that I couldn't understand it.

33   But my father has remained elusive, or, rather, frozen. He is captured only in those poses I have examined, again and again, in my mother's actual photograph album or in the one I have assembled in my mind. Sometimes I can enter my mother's black-and-white snapshots and briefly meet my father there. Daddy, his arm tucked in Mother's, poses on our front doorsteps, with my sister and me standing in front of them in our Sunday best. As I look at the picture, I can feel the touch of the soft velvet

collar on my coat and the crispness of the plaid ribbon bows on my pig-tails. Daddy stands knee-deep in the chilly water during our summer vaca-tion at Lake Carlos. Afterward, I think I can see him stroking away from me, laughing and splashing, a strong swimmer moving easily through the water.

34   Why is it so difficult to bring my father back? I feel I ought to be able to do it, but I can't. I am left with random pieces, flashes, snapshots. Those people who still remember him tend to repeat the same phrases, over and over: "He was a wonderful man." "He had such a terrific sense of humor!" "What a tragedy he died so young." "He did so love you girls!" More, I think, I need more.

35   During the search I conducted in my early forties, my mother con-tributed an unexpected gift. When I was a toddler and Karen perhaps three, a neighbor who had acquired a movie camera—a rarity in those days—had shot a few minutes' footage of our family. Mother had it copied for Karen and me, and I promptly had my film transferred onto videotape. When I put it into our VCR, I thought that now, finally, I would see my father as he really was.

36   But I didn't. Although I was fascinated by the silent images, I didn't feel part of them. My father swung me up to his shoulders, where I grinned and clutched his hair. Karen grabbed one of my toys, and my mother bent over her, gently but reprovingly. My parents looked young and happy, and my sister and I were cute and wriggly. But I couldn't re-member being there. I was less connected to that film than to the old fa-miliar snapshots, Mother's and mine.

37   "Can you think of anything *bad* about my father?" I once asked my Uncle Don, his only brother. He and my aunt looked puzzled. There was an awkward pause. "It's just that he doesn't quite seem *real*," I tried to ex-plain, but my words hung like discordant notes over the luncheon table, jarring them into silence. I knew then that I was asking questions no one could answer anymore.

38   My father's idealized portrait has hung, lit with a loving glow, in his family's and friends' memories for forty-two years: a tall, almost hand-some, eager man, who knew how to laugh, who sang and danced and played tennis, who worked hard and brilliantly at his career. I grew up with this portrait, and I am glad I have it. But I long for a few flaws to make it come alive. I sometimes wonder if that is why I remember so vividly the taste of soap in my mouth.

39   Today, or tomorrow, I will pack away the old black briefcase. I am not sure when, if ever, I will look at it again. I won't need it. I have many dif-ferent bags and satchels to carry my books and papers. My current favorite is a plastic "shopper" in a William Morris design that I found in a National Trust shop in England. I liked it so much I got an apron to match. The tote bag doesn't look very professional, but it is lightweight, waterproof, and very capacious. On top of a stack of papers, I can still jam a pair of shoes and a bag lunch. Besides, I like the twining leaves and flowers. If I

had died when my daughter was only seven, could she reconstruct my personality from this flimsy satchel?

40   Though the black briefcase has not told me everything I want to know, it is not completely silent. A briefcase is the mark of a college professor; I became one. It once held my father's books and papers; my life sinks its deepest roots into all the books I have (at least partly) read and all the pieces of paper on which I have written. The man who carried that briefcase was someone I could talk to.

41   I could ask him about his work, his writing, and his teaching, and he could ask about mine. We could talk about families, my mother and sister, his granddaughters, my husband; about gardening; about summers at the lake. Maybe he would tell me stories about growing up as the youngest child of a Congregational minister in a small Iowa town, or his college years at Grinnell, or how he met and married my mother. He could explain how he managed to live with fear; what he felt when he left Karen and me to take the train to Madison, what he wished he could have said to us then. He could tell me about tennis, and music, and the economics of public finance. I'm sure we would laugh together, and we would talk, I think, for a very long time.

Discussion Questions

---

1.   Toth uses her father's briefcase as a recurrent image and emblem of her father. Have you ever associated specific items with the people who used them? Discuss how important you think such icons are in remembering people.

2.   Toth informs her readers in paragraph 5 that she "[doesn't] have much from which to reconstruct [her] father." Given her shortage of memories, how effective do you think Toth *is* in portraying him? Explain your response.

3.   In paragraph 12, Toth discusses the "burden of unfulfilled promise" her father left her. To what extent do you think Toth's fear of failure is realistic? Explain your answer.

4.   Why do you think it took Toth until she was almost forty years old to recognize the influence her father had on her? To what extent do you think this is characteristic of most people?

5.   Toth discusses the fear her father left with her. After having read her essay, what else do you see her father leaving her? Cite specific passages in the essay to support your response.

Adam
Michael Dorris

Born in 1945, Michael Dorris earned his doctorate in anthropology from Yale University. He has taught anthropology and Native American Studies at many schools, including Franconia College and Dartmouth College. A member of the Modoc tribe, Dorris is the au-thor of Native Americans: Five Hundred Years After *(1975); two novels,* A Yellow Raft in Blue Water *(1987) and* The Crown of Columbus *(1991), co-written with his wife, Louise Erdrich; a novel for adolescent readers,* Morning Girl *(1992); a collection of essays en-titled* Paper Trail *(1994); a collection of short stories,* Working Men *(1993); and* The Broken Cord *(1989), an account of Adam, Dor-ris's adopted child. Adam was the victim of fetal alcohol syndrome, the result of his mother drinking during her pregnancy. In the book, Dor-ris relates the story of his discovery of the origins of Adam's condition and discusses the problem of alcoholism on Indian reservations.* The Broken Cord *won the National Book Critics Circle Award and was made into a television movie in 1992. The following excerpt from the book takes place when Adam ventures out on his own as a young man. Dorris shows himself caught between wanting to continue caring for his son and letting him manage by himself. Two years after Dorris' book was published, Adam was killed in an automobile accident.*

1   It was a good while before I visited Adam at his place of employment, and when I saw him, I knew why. I walked into the almost empty restau-rant of the bowling alley—The Red Rooster—and caught a glimpse of my son through the open door that led into the kitchen. It was only the most fleeting look, snatched as he passed from view in the space of a few strides, but it was enough. He was a collection of repeated admonitions left unchecked, an impression he confirmed as, a few minutes later, he sat across from me in a booth.

2   I had determined in advance to under no circumstances be disapprov-ing, so it was only to myself that I said: "Adam, where are your glasses? You can't see without them." I did not mention the fact that he had not shaved or washed his face in some time. I did not criticize his choice of clothing: a torn T-shirt in frigid November, a shabby pair of sweat pants, worn obviously without underwear, the ravaged running shoes I had begged him to discard weeks before. The nails on his fingers were long and jagged, his teeth not clean, his hair unbrushed. There was a spot of fresh blood on his lower lip, the result of his tendency for chapped skin in winter dryness. All through public school, from October through March, I would apply balm to his lips as my last act before he left the house. Today I controlled my urge to remind him.

3   Rather, I asked about his recent injury, a burn he had sustained on his forearm when he had stumbled into a hot stove. No one, least of all Adam, seemed sure how this accident had happened, but it was probable that on one of the many days he had neglected to take his midday medicine—or skipped lunch—he had suffered a minor seizure. That one was not a major attack, but those had occurred as well. In just a few months on the job, Adam had been sent in an ambulance to the emergency room at Mary Hitchcock Hospital on three separate occasions after collapsing. He had banged his head on the floor, bruised his leg, bloodied his nose, and each time it was later discovered that the convulsions had been released because the medication level in his bloodstream was too low.

4   When responsible for his own care, Adam sometimes became confused about his dosage, "remembering" he had taken his Dilantin or Tegretol but warping the time frame. After seventeen years of instruction he still mixed up breakfast and lunch, lunch and dinner, the hours intervening from one meal to the other evaporating in his memory. Or, conversely, the minutes seemed to him to multiply between the event of swallowing a pill and the event of sitting at the table; at those times he overdosed and became drowsy, lethargic. Every now and then, I was convinced, his failure to take his medicine was, to the extent Adam was capable of it, intentional—a nonact rising out of anger at his need, at routine, at infirmity. He got mad at the pills and spurned them, only to pay dearly later for his defiance.

5   Now he held up his arm for me to examine. A long red scar shaped like the blade of a sword extended from his wrist to his elbow. The doctor on the case had complained to me that Adam had not kept the bandages clean, had removed them often to examine the wound, and that as a consequence the healing process had been neither quick nor ideal. There would be more of a lasting disfigurement than there had to be.

6   But I didn't bring this up. "It looks much better," I said.

7   Adam, like me, is astigmatic—that is, without his glasses he has a "lazy eye." While one eye focuses, the other drifts. He seemed to be looking over my shoulder, even as he opened the clear plastic bag that held the food he had brought from his boarding home.

8   "What happened to your lunch box?" I asked, referring to the expensive contraption Louise had purchased for him when he started the job.

9   "The handle is loose," he said. "So to make sure, I don't use it." He unpacked three sandwiches, three hard-boiled eggs, and a banana and methodically began to eat. The blood on his lip was wiped with every bite, then reappeared as he worked his jaws. I wanted to reach across the table with my napkin and blot it. I wanted to run next door to the drugstore and buy Vaseline. I wanted to do a lot of things, but Adam would immediately discontinue doing them when I was gone.

10   Instead, I thought of all the school lunches I had fixed, early in the morning. There was a period of perhaps a year during which Adam consumed the entire contents of his lunch box on the school bus, minutes after he had eaten breakfast. At lunchtime he would have nothing to eat.

Then there was another phase during which he didn't eat at all. One day I was looking for something in his closet and discovered a cache of decayed, moldy sandwiches, cookies, and fruit stuffed into a corner.

11   Today Adam's meal consisted of dry pieces of white bread framing thin slices of baloney. No mayonnaise or mustard. "I think they'd taste better if you jazzed them up a little bit," I offered. He labored to crack an egg, bending low over the table in his myopia and tapping the shell until a series of fissures appeared, then he peeled it, dropping each fragment, one at a time, into the plastic bag. When the surface of the egg was clear, he took a bite, and I couldn't stop myself. "Try just a bit of salt," I suggested. "It will bring out the flavor." He obliged me, prompting yet another memory as he virtually pressed the salt shaker against the egg skin. Years of instruction echoed in my brain: "Hold the ketchup away from the hot dog when you pour it, Adam." "Don't touch the potatoes with the pepper shaker, Adam." "Hold the milk carton above the glass, Adam."

12   He tried the salted egg and pronounced it an improvement, but as he progressed through the other two eggs, he forgot the salt. So did I. By all evidence Adam didn't take much notice of what he ate. Feeding, for him, seemed to be an act independent of sensation, of preference or enjoyment. He put what was before him into his mouth, chewed and swallowed it, and continued the exercise until there was nothing left. No matter what was served, one dish seemed indistinguishable from another to him. This impression had alternately irritated and depressed me; a well-prepared meal was one of life's small pleasures to which Adam was oblivious. It was a gift that a thoughtful host might serve a guest; but no matter what was offered, Adam reciprocated—unless he was prodded each time to do so—with not the slightest appreciation.

13   The conversation between my nearly twenty-one-year-old son and me consisted as usual of me asking questions and him answering.

14   "How's work going?"

15   "Good."

16   "Have you seen any movies?"

17   "I haven't gotten around to it yet."

18   I gestured to the wooden lanes visible through the interior windows. "Have you been bowling since you've worked here?"

19   "Not yet."

20   "What's your favorite program on TV these days?"

21   "I guess 'Mama's Family'"

22   "What did you have for dinner last night?"

23   "A TV dinner."

24   "What kind?"

25   He paused in thought, searched his memory. "I can't say. Probably it was macaroni or turkey."

26   All this time he worked his way through the food he had brought like a beaver devouring a tree trunk.

27   "Don't you want something to drink?" I asked. "Some milk or a Coke?"

28   "No," he said. "I generally don't drink anything."

29   "You know, you've got a cracked lip. It's bleeding. Did you run out of the stuff you need this time of year?"

30   Adam touched his finger to the wound, then held it before him and examined the blood. "No," he said and turned his attention back to the egg.

31   "What's work been like today?"

32   This was a question he was equipped to handle, and he started with the beginning of the morning when he boarded the bus. He got off the bus at the bus stop. He came into the Red Rooster through the front door. He hung his jacket on the hook. He swept the floor with the broom. He stacked dishes from the dishwasher. He got his jacket and zipped it up. He went outside. He picked trash off the parking lot. A milk carton. A piece of newspaper. Two pop cans. Something else he couldn't remember. He came back inside. He took off his jacket and hung it on the hook.

33   I listened as Adam recounted, like a videocassette playback, the blow by blow of his day. The hours existed for him as a series of unrelated acts, connected neither by analysis nor by critical perspective, uncolored by like or dislike, undistinguished by incident. As I nodded, inviting him to continue, I yearned to put words in his mouth, to break through the barrier of his plodding progress, to find in him some spark of sarcasm or wit. "So Adam," I wanted to say. "Who are you going to vote for in the presidential election? What do you think of the new Soviet foreign policy? I just read this great mystery novel—you've got to try it."

34   This was my problem, not his. Where was the fine line between acceptance of a condition I could never change and despair or, worse, indifference? When did I stop wanting, demanding, feeling that Adam had been cheated? When did I let go, quell my passion to power his life, direct his interests, think his thoughts? I was not proud of my complaints; they had long since ceased to do Adam much good and, in fact, interfered with the rhythm of the father-son relationship that he would probably prefer. I tried to imagine this lunch through his perspective, and everything was perfectly satisfactory, better even than satisfactory: Dad had said he would come, and Dad came. No problem. No anxiety that the instructions had been remembered wrong. Adam had not forgotten his lunch. He had brought his medicine and taken it. He had not been criticized. He was on a turf with which he was familiar, at ease. He had not made a mistake. There were no questions he had to struggle to answer. There was no disruption of familiar pattern, and the rest of the day would proceed on schedule, no surprises.

35   I had no doubt that Adam was glad to see me, that my presence alone was for him a good thing. On an emotional level, he required no more of me than my tacit approval. He liked having the category "Dad" in his life—characters on TV had dads, and so did he. He liked having a person with whom he shared enough history to make some small talk. I confirmed his world, and that's all he wanted. The desire for more came only from me.

❦

36   Adam's birthdays are, I think, the hardest anniversaries, even though as an adoptive father I was not present to hear Adam's first cry, to feel the aspirated warmth of his body meeting air for the first time. I was not present to count his fingers, to exclaim at the surprise of gender, to be comforted by the hope at the heart of his new existence.

37   From what I've learned, from the sum of gathered profiles divided by the tragedy of each case, the delivery of my premature son was unlikely to have been a joyous occasion. Most fetal alcohol babies emerged not in a tide, the facsimile of saline, primordial, life-granting sea, but instead enter this world tainted with stale wine. Their amniotic fluid literally reeks of Thunderbird or Ripple, and the whole operating theater stinks like the scene of a three-day party. Delivery room staff who have been witness time and again tell of undernourished babies thrown into delirium tremens when the cord that brought sustenance and poison is severed. Nurses close their eyes at the memory. An infant with the shakes, as cold turkey as a raving derelict deprived of the next fix, is hard to forget.

38   Compared to the ideal, Adam started far in the hole, differently from the child who began a march through the years without the scars of fetters on his ankles, with eyes and ears that worked, with nothing to carry except what he or she collected along the path.

39   Adam's birthdays are reminders for me. For each celebration commemorating that he was born, there is the pang, the rage, that he was not born whole. I grieve for what he might have, what he should have been. I magnify and sustain those looks of understanding or compassion or curiosity that fleet across his face, fast as a breeze, unexpected as the voice of God—the time he said to me in the car, the words arising from no context I could see, "Kansas is between Oklahoma and Texas." But when I turned in amazement, agreeing loudly, still ready after all these years to discover a buried talent or passion for geography, for anything, that possible person had disappeared.

40   "What made you say that?" I asked.

41   "Say what?" he answered. "I didn't say anything."

42   The sixteenth birthday, the eighteenth. The milestones. The driver's license, voting, the adult boundary-marker birthdays. The days I envisioned while watching the mails for the response to my first adoption application, the days that set forth like distant skyscrapers as I projected ahead through my years of fatherhood. I had given little specific consideration to what might come between, but of those outstanding days I had been sure. They were the pillars I followed, the oases of certainty. Alone in the cabin in Alaska or in the basement apartment near Franconia while I waited for the definition of the rest of my life to commence, I planned the elaborate cake decorations for those big birthdays, the significant presents I would save to buy. Odd as it may seem, the anticipation of the acts of letting Adam go began before I even knew his name. I looked forward to the proud days on which the world would recognize my son as progres-

sively more his own man. Those were among the strongest hooks that bonded me to him in my imagination.

43 As each of these anniversaries finally came and went, nothing like I expected them to be, I doubly mourned. First, selfishly, for me, and second for Adam, because he didn't know what he was missing, what he had already missed, what he would miss. I wanted to burst through those birthdays like a speeding train blasts a weak gate, to get past them and back into the anonymous years for which I had made no models, where there were no obvious measurements, no cakes with candles that would never be lit.

44 It was a coincidence that Adam turned twenty-one as this book neared completion, but it seemed appropriate. On the morning of his birthday, I rose early and baked him a lemon cake, his favorite, and left the layers to cool while I drove to Hanover to pick him up. His gifts were wrapped and on the kitchen table—an electric shaver, clothes, a Garfield calendar. For his special dinner he had requested tacos, and as always I had reserved a magic candle—the kind that keeps reigniting no matter how often it is blown out—for the center of his cake.

45 I was greeted at Adam's house by the news that he had just had a seizure, a small one this time, but it had left him groggy. I helped him on with his coat, bent to tie his shoelace, all the while talking about the fun we would have during the day. He looked out the window. Only the week before he had been laid off from his dishwashing job. December had been a bad month for seizures, some due to his body's adjustment to a change in dosage and some occurring because Adam had skipped taking medicine altogether. The bowling alley's insurance carrier was concerned and that, combined with an after-Christmas slump in business, decided the issue. Now he was back at Hartford for a few weeks while Ken Kramberg and his associates sought a new work placement. I thought perhaps Adam was depressed about this turn of events, so I tried to cheer him up as we drove south on the familiar road to Cornish.

46 "So, Adam," I said, making conversation, summoning the conventional words, "do you feel any older? What's good about being twenty-one?"

47 He turned to me and grinned. There *was* something good.

48 "Well," he answered, "now the guys at work say I'm old enough to drink."

49 His unexpected words kicked me in the stomach. They crowded every thought from my brain.

50 "Adam, you can't," I protested. "I've told you about your birthmother, about your other father. Do you remember what happened to them?" I knew he did. I had told him the story several times, and we had gone over it together as he read, or I read to him, parts of this book.

51 Adam thought for a moment. "They were sick?" he offered finally. "That's why I have seizures?"

52 "No, they weren't sick. They died, Adam. They died from drinking. If

you drank, it could happen to you." My memory played back all the statistics about sons of alcoholic fathers and their particular susceptibility to substance abuse. "It would not mix well with your medicine."

53   Adam sniffed, turned away, but not before I recognized the amused disbelief in his expression. He did not take death seriously, never had. It was an abstract concept out of his reach and therefore of no interest to him. Death was less real than Santa Claus—after all, Adam had in his album a photograph of himself seated on Santa Claus's lap. Death was no threat, no good reason to refuse his first drink.

54   My son will forever travel through a moonless night with only the roar of wind for company. Don't talk to him of mountains, of tropical beaches. Don't ask him to swoon at sunrises or marvel at the filter of light through leaves. He's never had time for such things, and he does not believe in them. He may pass by them close enough to touch on either side, but his hands are stretched forward, grasping for balance instead of pleasure. He doesn't wonder where he came from, where he's going. He doesn't ask who he is, or why. Questions are a luxury, the province of those at a distance from the periodic shock of rain. Gravity presses Adam so hard against reality that he doesn't feel the points at which he touches it. A drowning man is not separated from the lust for air by a bridge of thought—he is one with it—and my son, conceived and grown in an ethanol bath, lives each day in the act of drowning. For him there is no shore.

Discussion Questions

1. Dorris provides many examples of his frustration with Adam's behavior. What sustains you and keeps your interest as you read them?

2. Dorris states that Adam's birthdays are the hardest anniversaries because they remind him that Adam was not "born whole." Do you find this reaction justifiable or selfish? Why?

3. Dorris admits that "This [wanting a more "normal" father-son relationship] was my problem, not his [Adam's]." Given this admission, do you find yourself more sympathetic to Adam or to Dorris? Explain your response.

4. What do you think was Dorris's purpose in writing about his son: to gain your sympathy? to complain about his plight as a father? to instruct you about the dangers of women drinking while pregnant? Explain your answer.

5. How would you describe Dorris's last paragraph? In what ways is it a fitting conclusion to the essay?

On Going Home
Joan Didion

*B*orn in Sacramento, California, in 1934, Joan Didion graduated from the University of California at Berkeley. She began
her writing career in 1956 at Vogue magazine. A prolific writer,
Didion is the author of five novels, River Run (1963), Play It as It
Lays (1970), A Book of Common Prayer (1977), and Democracy
(1984), and Run River (1994). Her three collections of essays,
Slouching toward Bethlehem (1968), The White Album (1979),
and Sentimental Journeys (1993) examine the deterioration of the
American spirit since the 1960s. Salvador (1983) and Miami
(1987) are journalistic accounts of two places that recently have experienced social upheaval. After Henry (1992) reports on current
events, from the 1988 Presidential campaign to the case of the New
York investment banker who was raped and beaten nearly to death
as she jogged in Central Park. "On Going Home," the following selection, is representative of Didion's sharp, analytical, and caring
eye. The essay presents Didion's observations and thoughts as she returns to her childhood home to celebrate her daughter's birthday.

1   I am home for my daughter's first birthday. By "home" I do not mean
the house in Los Angeles where my husband and I and the baby live, but
the place where my family is, in the Central Valley of California. It is a vital
although troublesome distinction. My husband likes my family but is uneasy in their house, because once there I fall into their ways, which are difficult, oblique, deliberately inarticulate, not my husband's ways. We live in
dusty houses ("D-U-S-T," he once wrote with his finger on surfaces all
over the house, but no one noticed it) filled with mementos quite without
value to him (what could the Canton dessert plates mean to him? how
could he have known about the assay scales, why should he care if he did
know?), and we appear to talk exclusively about people we know who have
been committed to mental hospitals, about people we know who have
been booked on drunk-driving charges, and about property, particularly
about property, land, price per acre and C-2 zoning and assessments and
freeway access. My brother does not understand my husband's inability to
perceive the advantage in the rather common real-estate transaction known
as "sale-leaseback," and my husband in turn does not understand why so
many of the people he hears about in my father's house have recently been
committed to mental hospitals or booked on drunk-driving charges. Nor
does he understand that when we talk about sale-leasebacks and right-of-
way condemnations we are talking in code about the things we like best,
the yellow fields and the cottonwoods and the rivers rising and falling and
the mountain roads closing when the heavy snow comes in. We miss each

other's points, have another drink and regard the fire. My brother refers to my husband, in his presence, as "Joan's husband." Marriage is the classic betrayal.

2   Or perhaps it is not any more. Sometimes I think that those of us who are now in our thirties were born into the last generation to carry the burden of "home," to find in family life the source of all tension and drama. I had by all objective accounts a "normal" and a "happy" family situation, and yet I was almost thirty years old before I could talk to my family on the telephone without crying after I had hung up. We did not fight. Nothing was wrong. And yet some nameless anxiety colored the emotional charges between me and the place that I came from. The question of whether or not you could go home again was a very real part of the sentimental and largely literary baggage with which we left home in the fifties; I suspect that it is irrelevant to the children born of the fragmentation after World War II. A few weeks ago in a San Francisco bar I saw a pretty young girl on crystal take off her clothes and dance for the cash prize in an "amateur-topless" contest. There was no particular sense of moment about this, none of the effect of romantic degradation, of "dark journey," for which my generation strived so assiduously. What sense could that girl possibly make of, say, *Long Day's Journey into Night*? Who is beside the point?

3   That I am trapped in this particular irrelevancy is never more apparent to me than when I am home. Paralyzed by the neurotic lassitude engendered by meeting one's past at every turn, around every corner, inside every cupboard, I go aimlessly from room to room. I decide to meet it head-on and clean out a drawer, and I spread the contents on the bed. A bathing suit I wore the summer I was seventeen. A letter of rejection from *The Nation*, an aerial photograph of the site for a shopping center my father did not build in 1954. Three teacups hand-painted with cabbage roses and signed "E.M.," my grandmother's initials. There is no final solution for letters of rejection from *The Nation* and teacups hand-painted in 1900. Nor is there any answer to snapshots of one's grandfather as a young man on skis, surveying around Donner Pass in the year 1910. I smooth out the snapshot and look into his face, and do and do not see my own. I close the drawer, and have another cup of coffee with my mother. We get along very well, veterans of a guerrilla war we never understood.

4   Days pass. I see no one. I come to dread my husband's evening call, not only because he is full of news of what by now seems to me our remote life in Los Angeles, people he has seen, letters which require attention, but because he asks what I have been doing, suggests uneasily that I get out, drive to San Francisco or Berkeley. Instead I drive across the river to a family graveyard. It has been vandalized since my last visit and the monuments are broken, overturned in the dry grass. Because I once saw a rattlesnake in the grass I stay in the car and listen to a country-and-Western station. Later I drive with my father to a ranch he has in the foothills. The man who runs his cattle on it asks us to the roundup, a week

from Sunday, and although I know that I will be in Los Angeles I say, in the oblique way my family talks, that I will come. Once home I mention the broken monuments in the graveyard. My mother shrugs.

5   I go to visit my great-aunts. A few of them think now that I am my cousin, or their daughter who died young. We recall an anecdote about a relative last seen in 1948, and they ask if I still like living in New York City. I have lived in Los Angeles for three years, but I say that I do. The baby is offered a horehound drop, and I am slipped a dollar bill "to buy a treat." Questions trail off, answers are abandoned, the baby plays with the dust motes in a shaft of afternoon sun.

6   It is time for the baby's birthday party: a white cake, strawberry-marshmallow ice cream, a bottle of champagne saved from another party. In the evening, after she has gone to sleep, I kneel beside the crib and touch her face, where it is pressed against the slats, with mine. She is an open and trusting child, unprepared for and unaccustomed to the ambushes of family life, and perhaps it is just as well that I can offer her little of that life. I would like to give her more. I would like to promise her that she will grow up with a sense of her cousins and of rivers and of her great-grandmother's teacups, would like to pledge her a picnic on a river with fried chicken and her hair uncombed, would like to give her *home* for her birthday, but we live differently now and I can promise her nothing like that. I give her a xylophone and a sundress from Madeira, and promise to tell her a funny story.

Discussion Questions

1. Didion begins her essay by referring to her daughter's birthday. Can you recall a family ritual that spurred your thinking about family in a way you never did before?

2. In the first paragraph, Didion states that the difference between what she considers "the house" and "home" is a "vital although troublesome distinction." Consider your own past and discuss a word that might cause similar confusion if you didn't explain it.

3. In what ways might Didion be considered a victim of her past? In what ways is she a participant in the victimization?

4. What do you make of Didion's statement that she was almost thirty before she was able to speak to her family on the telephone without crying after she hung up?

5. With whom are you most sympathetic in this essay: Didion, Didion's brother, her husband? Why?

A Kiowa Grandmother

N. Scott Momaday

*N. Scott Momaday, a Native American of Kiowa and Cherokee
descent, was born in 1934 in New Mexico. A poet, novelist, and
essayist, Momaday is also an artist and a Kiowa tribal dancer and
member of the Gourd Dance Society of the Kiowa tribe. He is the author of* House Made of Dawn *(1968), which won the Pulitzer Prize,*
The Way to Rainy Mountain *(1969), in which the following essay appears,* The Gourd Dancer *(1976),* The Names: A Memoir *(1976),
and* In the Presence of the Sun: Stories and Poems, *1961–1991
(1992). Momaday grew up on a reservation in New Mexico and has
taught at the University of California at Berkeley. He is currently Regents Professor of English at the University of Arizona. In the following piece, Momaday describes scenes from his childhood and the ways
in which his grandmother influenced his life.*

1   A single knoll rises out of the plain in Oklahoma, north and west of
the Wichita Range. For my people, the Kiowas, it is an old landmark, and
they gave it the name Rainy Mountain. The hardest weather in the world
is there. Winter brings blizzards, hot tornadic winds arise in the spring,
and in summer the prairie is an anvil's edge. The grass turns brittle and
brown, and it cracks beneath your feet. There are green belts along the
rivers and creeks, linear groves of hickory and pecan, willow and witch
hazel. At a distance in July or August the steaming foliage seems almost to
writhe in fire. Great green and yellow grasshoppers are everywhere in the
tall grass, popping up like corn to sting the flesh, and tortoises crawl about
on the red earth, going nowhere in the plenty of time. Loneliness is an aspect of the land. All things in the plain are isolate; there is no confusion of
objects in the eye, but *one* hill or *one* tree or *one* man. To look upon that
landscape in the early morning, with the sun at your back, is to lose the
sense of proportion. Your imagination comes to life, and this, you think, is
where Creation was begun.

2   I returned to Rainy Mountain in July. My grandmother had died in
the spring, and I wanted to be at her grave. She had lived to be very old
and at last infirm. Her only living daughter was with her when she died,
and I was told that in death her face was that of a child.

3   I like to think of her as a child. When she was born, the Kiowas were
living the last great moment of their history. For more than a hundred
years they had controlled the open range from the Smoky Hill River to the
Red, from the headwaters of the Canadian to the fork of the Arkansas and
Cimarron. In alliance with the Comanches, they had ruled the whole of
the southern Plains. War was their sacred business, and they were among
the finest horsemen the world has ever known. But warfare for the Kiowas
was preeminently a matter of disposition rather than of survival, and they

never understood the grim, unrelenting advance of the U.S. Cavalry. When at last, divided and ill-provisioned, they were driven onto the Staked Plains in the cold rains of autumn, they fell into panic. In Palo Duro Canyon they abandoned their crucial stores to pillage and had nothing then but their lives. In order to save themselves, they surrendered to the soldiers at Fort Sill and were imprisoned in the old stone corral that now stands as a military museum. My grandmother was spared the humiliation of those high gray walls by eight or ten years, but she must have known from birth the affliction of defeat, the dark brooding of old warriors.

4 Her name was Aho, and she belonged to the last culture to evolve in North America. Her forebears came down from the high country in western Montana nearly three centuries ago. They were a mountain people, a mysterious tribe of hunters whose language has never been positively classified in any major group. In the late seventeenth century they began a long migration to the south and east. It was a journey toward the dawn, and it led to a golden age. Along the way the Kiowas were befriended by the Crows, who gave them the culture and religion of the Plains. They acquired horses, and their ancient nomadic spirit was suddenly free of the ground. They acquired Tai-me, the sacred Sun Dance doll, from that moment the object and symbol of their worship, and so shared in the divinity of the sun. Not least, they acquired the sense of destiny, therefore courage and pride. When they entered upon the southern Plains they had been transformed. No longer were they slaves to the simple necessity of survival; they were a lordly and dangerous society of fighters and thieves, hunters and priests of the sun. According to their origin myth, they entered the world through a hollow log. From one point of view, their migration was the fruit of an old prophecy, for indeed they emerged from a sunless world.

5 Although my grandmother lived out her long life in the shadow of Rainy Mountain, the immense landscape of the continental interior lay like memory in her blood. She could tell of the Crows, whom she had never seen, and of the Black Hills, where she had never been. I wanted to see in reality what she had seen more perfectly in the mind's eye, and traveled fifteen hundred miles to begin my pilgrimage.

6 Yellowstone, it seemed to me, was the top of the world, a region of deep lakes and dark timber, canyons and waterfalls. But, beautiful as it is, one might have the sense of confinement there. The skyline in all directions is close at hand, the high wall of the woods and deep cleavages of shade. There is a perfect freedom in the mountains, but it belongs to the eagle and the elk, the badger and the bear. The Kiowas reckoned their stature by the distance they could see, and they were bent and blind in the wilderness.

7 Descending eastward, the highland meadows are a stairway to the plain. In July the inland slope of the Rockies is luxuriant with flax and buckwheat, stonecrop and larkspur. The earth unfolds and the limit of the land recedes. Clusters of trees, and animals grazing far in the distance, cause the vision to reach away and wonder to build upon the mind. The

sun follows a longer course in the day, and the sky is immense beyond all comparison. The great billowing clouds that sail upon it are shadows that move upon the grain like water, dividing light. Farther down, in the land of the Crows and Blackfeet, the plain is yellow. Sweet clover takes hold of the hills and bends upon itself to cover and seal the soil. There the Kiowas paused on their way; they had come to the place where they must change their lives. The sun is at home on the plains. Precisely there does it have the certain character of a god. When the Kiowas came to the land of the Crows, they could see the dark lees of the hills at dawn across the Bighorn River, the profusion of light on the grain shelves, the oldest deity ranging after the solstices. Not yet would they veer southward to the caldron of the land that lay below; they must wean their blood from the northern winter and hold the mountains a while longer in their view. They bore Tai-me in procession to the east.

8   A dark mist lay over the Black Hills, and the land was like iron. At the top of a ridge I caught sight of Devil's Tower upthrust against the gray sky as if in the birth of time the core of the earth had broken through its crust and the motion of the world was begun. There are things in nature that engender an awful quiet in the heart of man; Devil's Tower is one of them. Two centuries ago, because they could not do otherwise, the Kiowas made a legend at the base of the rock. My grandmother said:

> *Eight children were there at play, seven sisters and their brother. Suddenly the boy was struck dumb; he trembled and began to run upon his hands and feet. His fingers became claws, and his body was covered with fur. Directly there was a bear where the boy had been. The sisters were terrified; they ran, and the bear after them. They came to the stump of a great tree, and the tree spoke to them. It bade them climb upon it, and as they did so it began to rise into the air. The bear came to kill them, but they were just beyond its reach. It reared against the tree and scored the bark all around with its claws. The seven sisters were borne into the sky, and they became the stars of the Big Dipper.*

From that moment, and so long as the legend lives, the Kiowas have kinsmen in the night sky. Whatever they were in the mountains, they could be no more. However tenuous their well-being, however much they had suffered and would suffer again, they had found a way out of the wilderness.

9   My grandmother had a reverence for the sun, a holy regard that now is all but gone out of mankind. There was a wariness in her, and an ancient awe. She was a Christian in her later years, but she had come a long way about, and she never forgot her birthright. As a child she had been to the Sun Dances; she had taken part in those annual rites, and by then she had learned the restoration of her people in the presence of Tai-me. She was about seven when the last Kiowa Sun Dance was held in 1887 on the Washita River above Rainy Mountain Creek. The buffalo were gone. In order to consummate the ancient sacrifice—to impale the head of a buffalo

bull upon the medicine tree—a delegation of old men journeyed into Texas, there to beg and barter for an animal from the Goodnight herd. She was ten when the Kiowas came together for the last time as a living Sun Dance culture. They could find no buffalo; they had to hang an old hide from the sacred tree. Before the dance could begin, a company of soldiers rode out from Fort Sill under orders to disperse the tribe. Forbidden without cause the essential act of their faith, having seen the wild herds slaughtered and left to rot upon the ground, the Kiowas backed away forever from the medicine tree. That was July 20, 1890, at the great bend of the Washita. My grandmother was there. Without bitterness, and for as long as she lived, she bore a vision of deicide.

10   Now that I can have her only in memory, I see my grandmother in the several postures that were peculiar to her: standing at the wood stove on a winter morning and turning meat in a great iron skillet; sitting at the south window, bent above her beadwork, and afterwards, when her vision failed, looking down for a long time into the fold of her hands; going out upon a cane, very slowly as she did when the weight of age came upon her; praying. I remember her most often at prayer. She made long, rambling prayers out of suffering and hope, having seen many things. I was never sure that I had the right to hear, so exclusive were they of all mere custom and company. The last time I saw her she prayed standing by the side of her bed at night, naked to the waist, the light of a kerosene lamp moving upon her dark skin. Her long, black hair, always drawn and braided in the day, lay upon her shoulders and against her breasts like a shawl. I do not speak Kiowa, and I never understood her prayers, but there was something inherently sad in the sound, some merest hesitation upon the syllables of sorrow. She began in a high and descending pitch, exhausting her breath to silence; then again and again—and always the same intensity of effort, of something that is, and is not, like urgency in the human voice. Transported so in the dancing light among the shadows of her room, she seemed beyond the reach of time. But that was illusion; I think I knew then that I should not see her again.

11   Houses are like sentinels in the plain, old keepers of the weather watch. There, in a very little while, wood takes on the appearance of great age. All colors wear soon away in the wind and rain, and then the wood is burned gray and the grain appears and the nails turn red with rust. The windowpanes are black and opaque; you imagine there is nothing within, and indeed there are many ghosts, bones given up to the land. They stand here and there against the sky, and you approach them for a longer time than you expect. They belong in the distance; it is their domain.

12   Once there was a lot of sound in my grandmother's house, a lot of coming and going, feasting and talk. The summers there were full of excitement and reunion. The Kiowas are a summer people; they abide the cold and keep to themselves, but when the season turns and the land becomes warm and vital they cannot hold still; an old love of going returns upon them. The aged visitors who came to my grandmother's house when I was a child were made of lean and leather, and they bore themselves up-

right. They wore great black hats and bright ample shirts that shook in the wind. They rubbed fat upon their hair and wound their braids with strips of colored cloth. Some of them painted their faces and carried the scars of old and cherished enmities. They were an old council of warlords, come to remind and be reminded of who they were. Their wives and daughters served them well. The women might indulge themselves; gossip was at once the mark and compensation of their servitude. They made loud and elaborate talk among themselves, full of jest and gesture, fright and false alarm. They went abroad in fringed and flowered shawls, bright beadwork and German silver. They were at home in the kitchen, and they prepared meals that were banquets.

13   There were frequent prayer meetings, and great nocturnal feasts. When I was a child I played with my cousins outside, where the lamplight fell upon the ground and the singing of the old people rose up around us and carried away into the darkness. There were a lot of good things to eat, a lot of laughter and surprise. And afterwards, when the quiet returned, I lay down with my grandmother and could hear the frogs away by the river and feel the motion of the air.

14   Now there is a funeral silence in the rooms, the endless wake of some final word. The walls have closed in upon my grandmother's house. When I returned to it in mourning, I saw for the first time in my life how small it was. It was late at night, and there was a white moon, nearly full. I sat for a long time on the stone steps by the kitchen door. From there I could see out across the land; I could see the long row of trees by the creek, the low light upon the rolling plains, and the stars of the Big Dipper. Once I looked at the moon and caught sight of a strange thing. A cricket had perched upon the handrail, only a few inches away from me. My line of vision was such that the creature filled the moon like a fossil. It had gone there, I thought, to live and die, for there, of all places, was its small definition made whole and eternal. A warm wind rose up and purled like the longing within me.

15   The next morning I awoke at dawn and went out on the dirt road to Rainy Mountain. It was already hot, and the grasshoppers began to fill the air. Still, it was early in the morning, and the birds sang out of the shadows. The long yellow grass on the mountain shone in the bright light, and a scissortail hied above the land. There, where it ought to be, at the end of a long and legendary way, was my grandmother's grave. Here and there on the dark stones were ancestral names. Looking back once, I saw the mountain and came away.

Discussion Questions

1. Instead of beginning with a description of his grandmother or himself, Momaday starts with a description of the land. Discuss how this picture helps prepare you to meet Momaday and his grandmother.

2. Why do you think Momaday states in paragraph 3 that he likes to think of his grandmother "as a child"? How does this help Momaday—and you—to understand her?

3. In what ways does Momaday make his grandmother sound mythical and legendary? Why is this an important part of his description of her?

4. Although this essay focuses on Momaday's grandmother, to what extent is it about Momaday himself? Explain your answer.

5. What do you think Momaday gained from his trip to Rainy Mountain? Cite specific passages that influence your response.

Chapter 2 Writing Topics

1. Was there ever a time in your life when you felt a special closeness with a parent or sibling? Explore the situation(s) that precipitated that feeling.

2. Write an essay in which you describe your father's or mother's physical appearance and actions. Pay particular attention to the details that make him or her come alive on the page.

3. Children are frequently envious of something their classmates or friends have that they don't, much as Janice E. Fein examined in her essay. Recall a time when you were jealous of a peer. Describe the situation and how it rectified itself.

4. Recall a time when your mature, adult understanding allowed you to reevaluate and put into better perspective a childhood impression. Write an essay that shows the marked contrast.

5. Children sometimes wish they weren't related to their father, mother, or siblings. Write an essay in which you describe a time when you felt that way.

6. Susan Allen Toth recalls the briefcase her father always used. Is there an item you associate with an important person in your life? In an essay, examine the reasons for that item so strongly representing that person.

7. Michael Dorris vacillates between wanting to treat his son, Adam, as a child and treat him as an adult. Can you recall a situation in which your parents (or you as a parent) had a similar dilemma? Show the confusion this tension created.

8. Was there ever a time when you wanted a kind of relationship with someone different from the one he or she was willing or able to offer? Write an essay in which you recreate that situation and your reflections on it, then and now.

9. Was there ever a time when you were jealous of one of your parents? What was the basis of that reaction, and what came of it?

10. When you were growing up, what behavior—good or bad—did your father or mother display with which you will always associate him or her? Write an essay in which you show the ways you were affected by that behavior.

11. Joan Didion states that her husband does not understand when her family talks "in code." What characteristics of your own family would come across as strange or difficult for others to understand because of their choice of words? What "codes" make your family distinctive?

12. In what ways does a particular place remind you of a special person? Examine, as N. Scott Momaday did in his essay, the connection between person and place.

Chapter 3

Learning from the Past

The past is a foreign country: they do things differently there.

—L. P. Hartley

But there is more to the present than a series of snapshots. We are not merely sensitized film; we have feelings, a memory for information and an eidetic memory for the imagery of our own pasts.

—Annie Dillard

Nothing can be brought to an end in the unconscious; nothing is past or forgotten.

—Sigmund Freud

All serious daring starts from within.

—Eudora Welty

We write to taste life twice, in the moment, and in retrospection.

—Anaïs Nin

As we grow, we build a storehouse of memories, some of which include the people, places, and events that have helped to shape us into the people we now are. One of the abundant sources of those memories involves our education, whether it takes place in school (formal education) or in less formal settings (informal education). Those memories are often rich, vivid, and important because of the impact—good or bad—that they had on us. Recalling our school days or particular things we learned from others is a common occurence: I daresay you have described to friends the exceptional teachers who had a positive impact on your life or the teachers who, for whatever reason, turned you off to a particular subject. Likewise, you can recall situations—again positive or negative—in which you learned something from a person or an event that has had a lasting effect on you.

The selections in this chapter center around learning. Instead of simply narrating an experience or describing a person, however, the authors reflect on the people and events about which they are writing. You will be privy to the mindful, sensitive, courageous, and honest insights these authors reached. In the process, you also will be able to better understand the writers, human nature, and perhaps even yourselves vicariously.

Chapter 3 begins with two writers' reflections on experiences that taught them about the nature of education: Frank Conroy looks back to a time when playing jazz with other musicians and speaking to his girlfriend's father and Supreme Court Justice William O. Douglas promoted "understanding [that] came with a kind of click, a resolving kind of click." Then Frederick Buechner provides glimpses of his student days as a backdrop for his understanding of the search for and the discovery of self.

In "Listening" from *One Writer's Beginning,* Eudora Welty recalls the powerful role that reading played in her education. The next two selections grapple with the recognition and acknowledgment of adulthood: Joyce Maynard comes to terms with her life when she compares herself to her five-year-old friend. Cruising the countryside with his friends provides the occasion for Paul Milo Miller to reflect on finishing one stage of his formal education and his fear of committing himself to the responsibilities that accompany adulthood. Next, Andre Dubus recounts his love of baseball in childhood and the education that accompanied his involvement with that sport.

The theme of satisfying the expectations of society and of others while remaining true to oneself is examined in the next pair of essays: first, Lorene Cary explores her need to make a statement to the world while still living in a restricted school setting; next, in "The Achievement of Desire," Richard Rodriguez ponders the difficulty of straddling two worlds: being successful in academic achievements while being sensitive to his less-educated parents' feelings and remaining in tune with his Mexican-American heritage.

As you read the essays in this chapter, you will learn not only about the writers' pasts but about their *understanding* of those pasts. You will read more than "stories"; you will hear the authors' thoughts about those stories. You surely will be able to recall some of your own experiences that are conducive to such scrutiny; no doubt learning from the past is a theme you can examine in your own writing.

Think about It

Frank Conroy

*F rank Conroy was born in New York City in 1936. After having at-
tended schools in New York and Florida, he graduated from
Haverford College in 1958. A fiction writer, Conroy is the author of
Stop-Time (1967), his memoir of growing up. In the following essay,
which originally appeared in* Harper's *magazine in 1988, Conroy recalls selling hot dogs, working as a jazz musician, and meeting his girlfriend's father and Supreme Court Justice William O. Douglas as experiences which taught him that we must "continually remake democracy
and the law" and that "education doesn't end until life ends."*

1   When I was sixteen I worked selling hot dogs at a stand in the
Fourteenth Street subway station in New York City, one level above the
trains and one below the street, where the crowds continually flowed back
and forth. I worked with three Puerto Rican men who could not speak
English. I had no Spanish, and although we understood each other well with
regard to the tasks at hand, sensing and adjusting to each other's body movements in the extremely confined space in which we operated, I felt isolated
with no one to talk to. On my break I came out from behind the counter and
passed the time with two old black men who ran a shoeshine stand in a dark
corner of the corridor. It was a poor location, half hidden by columns, and
they didn't have much business. I would sit with my back against the wall
while they stood or moved around their ancient elevated stand, talking to
each other or to me, but always staring into the distance as they did so.

2   As the weeks went by I realized that they never looked at anything in
their immediate vicinity—not at me or their stand or anybody who might
come within ten or fifteen feet. They did not look at approaching customers once they were inside the perimeter. Save for the instant it took to
discern the color of the shoes, they did not even look at what they were
doing while they worked, but rubbed in polish, brushed, and buffed by
feel while looking over their shoulders, into the distance, as if awaiting the
arrival of an important person. Of course there wasn't all that much distance in the underground station, but their behavior was so focused and
consistent they seemed somehow to transcend the physical. A powerful
mood was created, and I came almost to believe that these men could see
through walls, through girders, and around corners to whatever hyper-
space it was where whoever it was they were waiting and watching for
would finally emerge. Their scattered talk was hip, elliptical, and hinted at
mysteries beyond my white boy's ken, but it was the staring off, the long,
steady staring off, that had me hypnotized. I left for a better job, with
handshakes from both of them, without understanding what I had seen.

3   Perhaps ten years later, after playing jazz with black musicians in vari-

ous Harlem clubs, hanging out uptown with a few young artists and intellectuals, I began to learn from them something of the extraordinarily varied and complex riffs and rituals embraced by different people to help themselves get through life in the ghetto. Fantasy of all kinds—from playful to dangerous—was in the very air of Harlem. It was the spice of uptown life.

4   Only then did I understand the two shoeshine men. They were trapped in a demeaning situation in a dark corner in an underground corridor in a filthy subway system. Their continuous staring off was a kind of statement, a kind of dance. Our bodies are here, went the statement, but our souls are receiving nourishment from distant sources only we can see. They were powerful magic dancers, sorcerers almost, and thirty-five years later I can still feel the pressure of their spell.

5   The light bulb may appear over your head, is what I'm saying, but it may be a while before it actually goes on. Early in my attempts to learn jazz piano, I used to listen to recordings of a fine player named Red Garland, whose music I admired. I couldn't quite figure out what he was doing with his left hand, however; the chords eluded me. I went uptown to an obscure club where he was playing with his trio, caught him on his break, and simply asked him. "Sixths," he said cheerfully. And then he went away.

6   I didn't know what to make of it. The basic jazz chord is the seventh, which comes in various configurations, but it is what it is. I was a self-taught pianist, pretty shaky on theory and harmony, and when he said sixths I kept trying to fit the information into what I already knew, and it didn't fit. But it stuck in my mind—a tantalizing mystery.

7   A couple of years later, when I began playing with a bass player, I discovered more or less by accident that if the bass played the root and I played a sixth based on the fifth note of the scale, a very interesting chord involving both instruments emerged. Ordinarily, I suppose I would have skipped over the matter and not paid much attention, but I remembered Garland's remark and so I stopped and spent a week or two working out the voicings, and greatly strengthened my foundations as a player. I had remembered what I hadn't understood, you might say, until my life caught up with the information and the light bulb went on.

8   I remember another, more complicated example from my sophomore year at the small liberal-arts college outside Philadelphia. I seemed never to be able to get up in time for breakfast in the dining hall. I would get coffee and a doughnut in the Coop instead—a basement area with about a dozen small tables where students could get something to eat at odd hours. Several mornings in a row I noticed a strange man sitting by himself with a cup of coffee. He was in his sixties, perhaps, and sat straight in his chair with very little extraneous movement. I guessed he was some sort of distinguished visitor to the college who had decided to put in some time at a student hangout. But no one ever sat with him. One morning I approached his table and asked if I could join him.

9   "Certainly," he said. "Please do." He had perhaps the clearest eyes I

had ever seen, like blue ice, and to be held in their steady gaze was not, at first, an entirely comfortable experience. His eyes gave nothing away about himself while at the same time creating in me the eerie impression that he was looking directly into my soul. He asked a few quick questions, as if to put me at my ease, and we fell into conversation. He was William O. Douglas from the Supreme Court, and when he saw how startled I was he said, "Call me Bill. Now tell me what you're studying and why you get up so late in the morning." Thus began a series of talks that stretched over many weeks. The fact that I was an ignorant sophomore with literary pretensions who knew nothing about the law didn't seem to bother him. We talked about everything from Shakespeare to the possibility of life on other planets. One day I mentioned that I was going to have dinner with Judge Learned Hand. I explained that Hand was my girlfriend's grandfather. Douglas nodded, but I could tell he was surprised at the coincidence of my knowing the chief judge of the most important court in the country save the Supreme Court itself. After fifty years on the bench Judge Hand had become a famous man, both in and out of legal circles—a living legend, to his own dismay. "Tell him hello and give him my best regards," Douglas said.

10   Learned Hand, in his eighties, was a short, barrel-chested man with a large, square head, huge, thick, bristling eyebrows, and soft brown eyes. He radiated energy and would sometimes bark out remarks or questions in the living room as if he were in court. His humor was sharp, but often leavened with a touch of self-mockery. When something caught his funny bone he would burst out with explosive laughter—the laughter of a man who enjoyed laughing. He had a large repertoire of dramatic expressions involving the use of his eyebrows—very useful, he told me conspiratorially, when looking down on things from behind the bench. (The court stenographer could not record the movement of his eyebrows.) When I told him I'd been talking to William O. Douglas, they first shot up in exaggerated surprise, and then lowered and moved forward in a glower.

11   "*Justice* William O. Douglas, young man," he admonished. "Justice Douglas, if you please." About the Supreme Court in general, Hand insisted on a tone of profound respect. Little did I know that in private correspondence he had referred to the Court as "The Blessed Saints, Cherubim and Seraphim," "The Jolly Boys," "The Nine Tin Jesuses," "The Nine Blameless Ethiopians," and my particular favorite, "The Nine Blessed Chalices of the Sacred Effluvium."

12   Hand was badly stooped and had a lot of pain in his lower back. Martinis helped, but his strict Yankee wife approved of only one before dinner. It was my job to make the second and somehow slip it to him. If the pain was particularly acute he would get out of his chair and lie flat on the rug, still talking, and finish his point without missing a beat. He flattered me by asking for my impression of Justice Douglas, instructed me to convey his warmest regards, and then began talking about the Dennis case, which he described as a particularly tricky and difficult case involving the prosecution of eleven leaders of the Communist party. He had just

started in on the First Amendment and free speech when we were called in to dinner.

13   William O. Douglas loved the outdoors with a passion, and we fell into the habit of having coffee in the Coop and then strolling under the trees down toward the duck pond. About the Dennis case, he said something to this effect: "Eleven Communists arrested by the government. Up to no good, said the government; dangerous people, violent overthrow, etc. First Amendment, said the defense, freedom of speech, etc." Douglas stopped walking. "Clear and present danger."

14   "What?" I asked. He often talked in a telegraphic manner, and one was expected to keep up with him. It was sometimes like listening to a man thinking out loud.

15   "Clear and present danger," he said. "That was the issue. Did they constitute a clear and present danger? I don't think so. I think everybody took the language pretty far in Dennis." He began walking, striding along quickly. Again, one was expected to keep up with him. "The FBI was all over them. Phones tapped, constant surveillance. How could it be clear and present danger with the FBI watching every move they made? That's a ginkgo," he said suddenly, pointing at a tree. "A beauty. You don't see those every day. Ask Hand about clear and present danger."

16   I was in fact reluctant to do so. Douglas's argument seemed to me to be crushing—the last word, really—and I didn't want to embarrass Judge Hand. But back in the living room, on the second martini, the old man asked about Douglas. I sort of scratched my nose and recapitulated the conversation by the ginkgo tree.

17   "What?" Hand shouted. "Speak up, sir, for heaven's sake."

18   "He said the FBI was watching them all the time so there couldn't be a clear and present danger," I blurted out, blushing as I said it.

19   A terrible silence filled the room. Hand's eyebrows writhed on his face like two huge caterpillars. He leaned forward in the wing chair, his face settling, finally, into a grim expression. "I am astonished," he said softly, his eyes holding mine, "at Justice Douglas's newfound faith in the Federal Bureau of Investigation." His big, granite head moved even closer to mine, until I could smell the martini. "I had understood him to consider it a politically corrupt, incompetent organization, directed by a power-crazed lunatic." I realized I had been holding my breath throughout all of this, and as I relaxed, I saw the faintest trace of a smile cross Hand's face. Things are sometimes more complicated than they first appear, his smile seemed to say. The old man leaned back. "The proximity of the danger is something to think about. Ask him about that. See what he says."

20   I chewed the matter over as I returned to campus. Hand had pointed out some of Douglas's language about the FBI from other sources that seemed to bear out his point. I thought about the words "clear and present danger," and the fact that if you looked at them closely they might not be as simple as they had first appeared. What degree of danger? Did the word "present" allude to the proximity of the danger, or just the fact that the

danger was there at all—that it wasn't an anticipated danger? Were there other hidden factors these great men were weighing of which I was unaware?

21   But Douglas was gone, back to Washington. (The writer in me is tempted to create a scene here—to invent one for dramatic purposes—but of course I can't do that.) My brief time as a messenger boy was over, and I felt a certain frustration, as if, with a few more exchanges, the matter of *Dennis* v. *United States* might have been resolved to my satisfaction. They'd left me high and dry. But, of course, it is precisely because the matter did not resolve that has caused me to think about it, off and on, all these years. "The Constitution," Hand used to say to me flatly, "is a piece of paper. The Bill of Rights is a piece of paper." It was many years before I understood what he meant. Documents alone do not keep democracy alive, nor maintain the state of law. There is no particular safety in them. Living men and women, generation after generation, must continually remake democracy and the law, and that involves an ongoing state of tension between the past and the present which will never completely resolve.

22   Education doesn't end until life ends, because you never know when you're going to understand something you hadn't understood before. For me, the magic dance of the shoeshine men was the kind of experience in which understanding came with a kind of click, a resolving kind of click. The same with the experience at the piano. What happened with Justice Douglas and Judge Hand was different, and makes the point that understanding does not always mean resolution. Indeed, in our intellectual lives, our creative lives, it is perhaps those problems that will never resolve that rightly claim the lion's share of our energies. The physical body exists in a constant state of tension as it maintains homeostasis, and so too does the active mind embrace the tension of never being certain, never being absolutely sure, never being done, as it engages the world. That is our special fate, our inexpressibly valuable condition.

Discussion Questions

1. Throughout Conroy's essay, he says that he "didn't understand" information that "didn't fit," that was a "tantalizing mystery." Given his confusion, is Conroy successful in sustaining your interest in the essay? Why or why not?

2. In your own education, have you ever had the "resolving kind of click" that Conroy describes in paragraph 22? Explain the circumstances of that experience.

3. In the last paragraph, Conroy discusses what he has learned about education. Do you find this ending convincing or does it smack too much of "the moral of the story"? Explain your answer.

4. Whom do you think Conroy envisioned as his audience? What leads you to your answer?

5. Given that his essay is about education, what did *you* learn from Conroy's essay?

Once upon a Time
Frederick Buechner

Frederick Buechner, born in 1925, earned his A.B. degree from Princeton University in 1948 and his B.D. degree from the Union Theological Seminary in 1958. An ordained minister of the United Presbyterian Church, Buechner has also taught writing at New York University and Harvard University. He is the author of some thirteen books of fiction and twelve books of nonfiction. Some of those publications include A Long Day's Dying *(1950),* The Final Beast *(1965),* The Hungering Dark *(1968),* The Magnificent Defeat *(1969),* The Alphabet of Grace *(1970),* The Entrance of Porlock *(1970),* Lion's Country *(1971),* Wishful Thinking *(1973),* The Faces of Jesus *(1974),* Godric *(1980),* The Sacred Journey *(1982), from which the following essay is excerpted,* Now and Then *(1983), and* The Son of Laughter *(1993). Buechner has been nominated for a Pulitzer Prize, is the recipient of the O. Henry Memorial Award, and has been honored by the American Academy and Institute of Arts and Letters. In the following piece, Buechner explores his search "for a self to be, for other selves to love, and for work to do," three searches that many people would consider universal.*

1 Lawrenceville was the name of the school in New Jersey that I went to that fall before Pearl Harbor, and pimply, nonathletic, my mother's son, I sat under the maples by the tennis courts with my tears staining the paper and wrote what I hoped were cheerful letters home. I pictured the terrace under the sleeping porch where I had loved to lie reading in a ragged canvas hammock, pictured Grandpa Kuhn sitting in the living room with his straw hat on listening to the war news on the radio, pictured my brother and a cousin trying to make a mud dam across the muddy little Pacolet river. But my homesickness was not just a longing for home, I think. It was a fear that home would somehow get lost before I ever got a chance to see it again, or that I would somehow get lost myself, and as things turned out, my fears proved well grounded on both points. That fall my mother was married to a widower she had known in Bermuda so that home was no

longer North Carolina but New England, and before the end of that first year away at school, I was no longer the boy who had sat under the maples in tears.

2   It is hard to evoke the year 1940 for people who were not alive then—the great excitement of it, the extraordinary sense of aliveness. It was the war that did it, of course. I doubt if there has ever been a war that seemed so much a struggle between the forces of light and the forces of darkness be-cause, although Hitler, Mussolini, Tojo, have come to seem since no worse than crazy uncles at a wake—criminals and lunatics, to be sure, but part of the human family at least, part of the same history that produces us all—at the time they seemed the very incarnation and caricature of evil. In America, on the other hand, we had for a leader that same president whom I had seen in the Mayflower, held upright under the arms by his two sons, but a pillar of strength and stability now who had been president for so long that he seemed to embody the very continuity of civilization that the war imperiled. For people born since, it must be hard to imagine a time when this country seemed so much on the side of the angels or a cause so just. Even as a child I had sensed the purposelessness and disillusion of the Depression years—I remember the anti-Roosevelt jokes, the anti-W.P.A. jokes, the roads into Washington when we lived there jammed by the jalopies of the gaunt, un-shaven Hunger Marchers, remembered my own father's years of rootless wandering—and all of this was suddenly gone now with rich and poor alike caught up in a sense of common purpose and destiny. Ingenuous, sentimen-tal, propagandizing as they were, you could not watch the great war movies like *Mrs. Miniver* and *In Which We Serve* unmoved, and when the theater lights came on at the end and "The Star Spangled Banner" was piped out over the loudspeaker system, you stood to it stirred in ways that in this post-Hiroshima, post-Dallas, post-Vietnam, post-Watergate age is perhaps no longer possible and may never be possible again. The war tapped reserves of strength and emotion that for years had gone forgotten or unrecognized, and this was true not only for the nation as a whole, but for the little nation of the school where I went and in some measure for me as a part of it.

3   The art class that I was assigned to was taught by a man who was an ex-cellent draughtsman. He painted marvelous still lifes of almost photo-graphic clarity—translucent glass vases of roses, bowls of sunlit fruit—and in order to teach us to do the same, he set us to making charcoal sketches of spheres, cubes, pyramids with the object of showing us how by getting the perspective right and the proper play of light and shade we could create the illusion of depth. All of this was fine for people who wanted to do still lifes, I thought, but it was not fine for me. It was not still life that interested me but alive life. Most particularly it was the endless and subtly changing variations of the human face—the moist glitter of eyes, the shadow of lips, the way the hair grew—and it was not long before I decided that if I could not paint what I wanted, then I did not want to be a painter at all.

4   At the same time I happened to have for an English teacher an en-tirely different sort of man. He had nothing of the draughtsman about

him, no inclination to drill us in anything, but instead a tremendous, Irishman's zest for the blarney and wizardry of words. I had always been a reader and loved words for the tales they can tell and the knowledge they can impart and the worlds they can conjure up like the Scarecrow's Oz and Claudius' Rome; but this teacher, Mr. Martin, was the first to give me a feeling for what words are, and can do, in themselves. Through him I started to sense that words not only convey something, but *are* something; that words have color, depth, texture of their own, and the power to evoke vastly more than they mean; that words can be used not merely to make things clear, make things vivid, make things interesting and whatever else, but to make things happen inside the one who reads them or hears them. When Gerard Manley Hopkins writes a poem about a blacksmith and addresses him as one who "didst fettle for the great gray drayhorse his bright and battering sandal," he is not merely bringing the blacksmith to life, but in a way is bringing us to life as well. Through the sound, rhythm, passion of his words, he is bringing to life in us, as might otherwise never have been brought to life at all, a sense of the uniqueness and mystery and holiness not just of the blacksmith and his great gray drayhorse, but of reality itself, including the reality of ourselves. Mr. Martin had us read wonderful things—it was he who gave me my love for *The Tempest,* for instance—but it was a course less in literature than in language and the great power that language has to move and in some measure even to transform the human heart.

5   He had us do a good deal of writing, of course, and one day I got a paper back from him with what in an English class was the unheard-of grade of 100. It was an extremely overripe character sketch of an eighteenth century French courtier, like the ones I had seen in the *Marie Antoinette* movie, pulling on a pair of jeweled gloves as he stands on a balcony watching the sun go down, but it was as full of as many rich and marvelous words as I could dig up, and when he gave me 100 on it, I think it is not too much to say that, from that moment on, I knew that what I wanted to be more than anything else was a writer.

6   What I wanted to write especially was poetry, and I have wondered since why. The answer, I suspect, is that after all those childhood years of wandering around the surface of the east coast, after all the different places I had lived and schools I had been to, after all the tales Naya had told me of still other places, other people, I had had enough of breadth for a while, enough of surface, enough even of faces. What I was suddenly most drawn to now was the dimension of what lay beneath the surface and behind the face. What was going on inside myself, behind my own face, was the subject I started trying to turn to in my half-baked way, and I suppose it was no coincidence that, for the first time in my life, I began to be able to tell a few friends the true story of how my father had died, which was the innermost secret I had.

7   Chief among these friends was my friend Jimmy Merrill, who had a "cube" across the corridor from mine—cubes being the cheerless little

three-sided cells where they housed the younger boys in those days with only a curtain at the open side for privacy. Like me, he was either no good at sports and consequently disliked them, or possibly the other way around. Like me—though through divorce rather than death—he had lost his father. Like me, he was a kind of oddball—plump and not very tall then with braces on his teeth and glasses that kept slipping down the short bridge of his nose and a rather sarcastic, sophisticated way of speaking that tended to put people off—and for that reason, as well as for the reason that he was a good deal brighter than most of us, including me, boys tended to make his life miserable. But it was Jimmy who became my first great friend, and it was through coming to know him that I discovered that perhaps I was not, as I had always suspected, alone in the universe and the only one of my kind. He was another who saw the world enough as I saw it to make me believe that maybe it was the way the world actually was—who cried at the same kinds of things that made me cry, and laughed at the same kind of foolery, and was helpless, hapless, ludicrous in many of the ways I felt I was. The Jigger Shop was the place that the whole school flocked to for candy and food and college banners and athletic equipment and Heaven only knows what-all else, and I remember being there one crowded Saturday afternoon when, in an excess of high spirits, another boy I knew dashed a dollop of tomato ketchup in my face from the bottle he was anointing his hamburger with, whereupon Jimmy handed me a great spoonful of butterscotch sauce from the sundae he had just ordered, and I smeared it lavishly down first one of my assailant's red cheeks and then the other with spectacular effect. Singly we could neither of us ever have pulled it off. Together we were a match for the world.

8   And together, too, we wrote poetry. We were endlessly impressed by each other's work, but we were also the keenest rivals, and in poem after poem competed for prizes and grades and the marvel of our teachers. As I look back over the ones that I wrote, I cringe with embarrassment at their terrible staginess and bathos, but I can remember still the enormous excitement of writing them, of waking up in the morning and looking at the poem of the evening before with the richest possible sense of having written something that seemed to me beautiful, lasting, and true. What I cannot remember is what it was that led me in so many of them to make references to Jesus. I had forgotten that I had until I looked back at them recently. It is true that I joined a confirmation class at school, of which I remember absolutely nothing except the dark, thin-boned profile of the young Episcopal priest who taught it and the fact that I was eventually confirmed in the school chapel, by the florid, medieval-looking Bishop of New Jersey. But I have the feeling that I gave no more serious thought to what I was doing than when I had arranged for my own christening a year or so earlier. If I had to guess at my motive for putting Jesus in so many of my poems, I would guess that it was for effect as much as anything, to give them some sort of aura or authority that I was afraid they lacked, to suggest that I was a much more substantial and fancier poet than I secretly be-

lieved myself to be. Maybe, too, I remembered the Da Vinci study for *The Last Supper* and hoped that the mention of his name might touch people as much as the sight of that sad, tired face had touched me. I do not know. But for whatever the reason or lack of one, I find to my surprise that Jesus appears again and again in those early, embarrassing poems as he has appeared in many another embarrassing poem both before and since. I cannot explain why he is there any more than I can explain why he is anywhere. And perhaps the explanation is not important. He was there, of all places, even there, and that is important enough.

9   We search, on our journeys, for a self to be, for other selves to love, and for work to do, and by the June I graduated from Lawrenceville, just a month short of seventeen, I had come farther along the way to discovering at least something of each than I believe I supposed at the time.

10   It is all but impossible, I think, to remember, in any very inward sense, any of the selves that we have been along the way, to recapture, from the vantage of thirty, forty, fifty, what it felt like to be sixteen. But I can remember at least the sense of having become, or started to become, a self with boundaries somewhat wider than and different from those set me by my family. I no more knew who I was then than in most ways I know who I am now, but I knew that I could survive more or less on my own in more or less the real world. I knew, as I had not before, the sound of my own voice both literally and figuratively—knew something of what was different about my way of speaking from anybody else's way and knew something of the power of words spoken from the truth of my own heart or from as close to that truth as I was able to come then. In Tyron, with the onset of adolescence and knocked silly by all the dreams, hungers, fears that I figured I was going to have to live with for the rest of my days, I remember my scalp going cold at the thought that nothing was real, least of all me. There were nightmarish times when even those closest to me seemed strangers as I seemed a stranger to myself, and I was sure that I must be losing my mind. But by sixteen I had found others, both like me and unlike me, and if they could be my friends, I decided, then I must be real enough and sane enough at least to get by.

11   And I loved them, these others, those friends and teachers. I would never have used the word *love,* saving that for what I had felt for the girl with the mouth that turned up at the corners, and for Naya, my mother and brother, but love of a kind it nonetheless was. Even the ones I did not all that much like I think I knew I would miss when the time came. I sensed in them, as in myself, an inner battle against loneliness and the great dark, and to know that they were also battling was to be no longer alone in the same way within myself. I loved them for that. I wished them well. And then there was Jimmy, my first fast friend; and Huyler, who of all of them heard out most healingly the secret of my father; and Bill, skinny and full of life and the brightest of us all, who would have added God only knows what richness to the great ragbag of things if the war had

not ended him before he more than got started. I could not imagine who I would have been without them, nor can I imagine it to this day because they are in so many ways a part of me still.

12   And if part of my search, those Lawrenceville years, was the search also for a father, I found fathers galore—Mr. Martin, who may have just changed the whole course of my life with that one preposterous grade; and Mr. Thurber, who gave hour after hour to going over with me in great detail those ghastly, promising poems; and Mr. Bowman, my Greek teacher, who was mad as a hatter and recommended that I read Norman Douglas' *South Wind* because he said it would corrupt me; and Mr. Heely, the headmaster, who on the day before school was to start once said to his faculty, "Gentlemen, never forget that when you enter your classrooms tomorrow, you will frequently find yourselves in the presence of your intellectual superiors." On All Saints' Day, it is not just the saints of the church that we should remember in our prayers, but all the foolish ones and wise ones, the shy ones and overbearing ones, the broken ones and whole ones, the despots and tosspots and crackpots of our lives who, one way or another, have been our particular fathers and mothers and saints, and whom we loved without knowing we loved them and by whom we were helped to whatever little we may have, or ever hope to have, of some kind of seedy sainthood of our own.

13   And I found work to do. By the time I was sixteen, I knew as surely as I knew anything that the work I wanted to spend my life doing was the work of words. I did not yet know what I wanted to say with them. I did not yet know in what form I wanted to say it or to what purpose. But if a vocation is as much the work that chooses you as the work you choose, then I knew from that time on that my vocation was, for better or worse, to involve that searching for, and treasuring, and telling of secrets which is what the real business of words is all about.

14   Something like all of this was what I had at least started to find by the spring of 1943 with the world at war and in a way more alive to the issues of light and dark than it has ever been since. What I had not found, I could not name and, for the most part, knew of only through my sense of its precious and puzzling and haunting absence. And maybe we can never name it by its final, true, and holy name, and maybe it is largely through its absence that, this side of Paradise, we will ever know it.

Discussion Questions

1. What do you think Buechner's purpose was in writing this essay: to describe how he chose a profession, to tell of his love of friends and family, to ponder the nature of experience? Explain your answer.

2. To what extent do you agree with Buechner in paragraph 10 when he writes that "It is all but impossible, I think, to remember, in any very inward sense, any of the selves that we have been along the way, to recapture, from the vantage of thirty, forty, fifty, what it felt like to be sixteen." Is his statement more a condemnation of the power of memory or an observation about the power of understanding? Explain your response.

3. Do you agree with Buechner when he claims that the reason for his putting Jesus in his poems is unimportant? Why or why not?

4. Explain your understanding of what Buechner is getting at in the last two sentences of his essay.

5. What points of agreement do you find between Frank Conroy's and Buechner's views of education and of life? Cite specific statements in each essay that lead you to your response.

Listening

Eudora Welty

Eudora Welty was born in Mississippi in 1909 and received her education at the University of Wisconsin and the Columbia Business School. She began her career as a journalist and copywriter, and during the Depression she worked for the Works Progress Administration as a writer and photographer. She later wrote stories and novels about the people she met in Mississippi. The recipient of a Pulitzer Prize, a PEN/Malamud Award, and the National Endowment for the Humanities' Frankel Prize, Welty's novels include The Robber Bridegroom *(1962),* Delta Wedding *(1946), and* The Optimist's Daughter *(1969). Her stories appear in* Thirteen Stories *(1970) and* The Collected Stories of Eudora Welty *(1980). Originally a series of lectures presented at Harvard University in 1983,* One Writer's Beginnings *(1984) is about the people and events that have influenced her life as a writer. The following excerpt from that book describes Welty's early love of reading.*

1   In our house on North Congress Street in Jackson, Mississippi, where I was born, the oldest of three children, in 1909, we grew up to the striking of clocks. There was a mission-style oak grandfather clock standing in the hall, which sent its gong-like strokes through the livingroom, diningroom, kitchen, and pantry, and up the sounding board of the stairwell. Through the night, it could find its way into our ears; sometimes, even on the sleeping porch, midnight could wake us up. My parents' bedroom had a smaller striking clock that answered it. Though the kitchen clock did nothing but show the time, the diningroom clock was a cuckoo clock with weights on long chains, on one of which my baby brother, after climbing

on a chair to the top of the china closet, once succeeded in suspending the cat for a moment. I don't know whether or not my father's Ohio family, in having been Swiss back in the 1700s before the first three Welty brothers came to America, had anything to do with this; but we all of us have been time-minded all our lives. This was good at least for a future fiction writer, being able to learn so penetratingly, and almost first of all, about chronology. It was one of a good many things I learned almost without knowing it; it would be there when I needed it.

2   My father loved all instruments that would instruct and fascinate. His place to keep things was the drawer in the "library table" where lying on top of his folded maps was a telescope with brass extensions, to find the moon and the Big Dipper after supper in our front yard, and to keep appointments with eclipses. There was a folding Kodak that was brought out for Christmas, birthdays, and trips. In the back of the drawer you could find a magnifying glass, a kaleidoscope, and a gyroscope kept in a black buckram box, which he would set dancing for us on a string pulled tight. He had also supplied himself with an assortment of puzzles composed of metal rings and intersecting links and keys chained together, impossible for the rest of us, however patiently shown, to take apart; he had an almost childlike love of the ingenious.

3   In time, a barometer was added to our diningroom wall; but we didn't really need it. My father had the country boy's accurate knowledge of the weather and its skies. He went out and stood on our front steps first thing in the morning and took a look at it and a sniff. He was a pretty good weather prophet.

4   "Well, I'm *not*," my mother would say with enormous self-satisfaction.

5   He told us children what to do if we were lost in a strange country. "Look for where the sky is brightest along the horizon," he said. "That reflects the nearest river. Strike out for a river and you will find habitation." Eventualities were much on his mind. In his care for us children he cautioned us to take measures against such things as being struck by lightning. He drew us all away from the windows during the severe electrical storms that are common where we live. My mother stood apart, scoffing at caution as a character failing. "Why, I always loved a storm! High winds never bothered me in West Virginia! Just listen at that! I wasn't a bit afraid of a little lightning and thunder! I'd go out on the mountain and spread my arms wide and *run* in a good big storm!"

6   So I developed a strong meteorological sensibility. In years ahead when I wrote stories, atmosphere took its influential role from the start. Commotion in the weather and the inner feelings aroused by such a hovering disturbance emerged connected in dramatic form. (I tried a tornado first, in a story called "The Winds.")

7   From our earliest Christmas times, Santa Claus brought us toys that instruct boys and girls (separately) how to build things—stone blocks cut to the castle-building style, Tinker Toys, and Erector sets. Daddy made for us himself elaborate kites that needed to be taken miles out of town to a

pasture long enough (and my father was not afraid of horses and cows watching) for him to run with and get up on a long cord to which my mother held the spindle, and then we children were given it to hold, tugging like something alive at our hands. They were beautiful, sound, shapely box kites, smelling delicately of office glue for their entire short lives. And of course, as soon as the boys attained anywhere near the right age, there was an electric train, the engine with its pea-sized working headlight, its line of cars, tracks equipped with switches, semaphores, its station, its bridges, and its tunnel, which blocked off all other traffic in the upstairs hall. Even from downstairs, and through the cries of excited children, the elegant rush and click of the train could be heard through the ceiling, running around and around its figure eight.

8   All of this, but especially the train, represents my father's fondest beliefs—in progress, in the future. With these gifts, he was preparing his children.

9   And so was my mother with her different gifts.

10   I learned from the age of two or three that any room in our house, at any time of day, was there to read in, or to be read to. My mother read to me. She'd read to me in the big bedroom in the mornings, when we were in her rocker together, which ticked in rhythm as we rocked, as though we had a cricket accompanying the story. She'd read to me in the diningroom on winter afternoons in front of the coal fire, with our cuckoo clock ending the story with "Cuckoo," and at night when I'd got in my own bed. I must have given her no peace. Sometimes she read to me in the kitchen while she sat churning, and the churning sobbed along with *any* story. It was my ambition to have her read to me while *I* churned; once she granted my wish, but she read off my story before I brought her butter. She was an expressive reader. When she was reading "Puss in Boots," for instance, it was impossible not to know that she distrusted *all* cats.

11   It had been startling and disappointing to me to find out that story books had been written by *people,* that books were not natural wonders, coming up of themselves like grass. Yet regardless of where they came from, I cannot remember a time when I was not in love with them—with the books themselves, cover and binding and the paper they were printed on, with their smell and their weight and with their possession in my arms, captured and carried off to myself. Still illiterate, I was ready for them, committed to all the reading I could give them.

12   Neither of my parents had come from homes that could afford to buy many books, but though it must have been something of a strain on his salary, as the youngest officer in a young insurance company, my father was all the while carefully selecting and ordering away for what he and Mother thought we children should grow up with. They bought first for the future.

13   Besides the bookcase in the livingroom, which was always called "the library," there were the encyclopedia tables and dictionary stand under windows in our diningroom. Here to help us grow up arguing around the diningroom table were the Unabridged Webster, the Columbia Encyclopedia,

Compton's Pictured Encyclopedia, the Lincoln Library of Information, and later the Book of Knowledge. And the year we moved into our new house, there was room to celebrate it with the new 1925 edition of the Britannica, which my father, his face always deliberately turned toward the future, was of course disposed to think better than any previous edition.

14   In "the library," inside the mission-style bookcase with its three diamond-latticed glass doors, with my father's Morris chair and the glass-shaded lamp on its table beside it, were books I could soon begin on—and I did, reading them all alike and as they came, straight down their rows, top shelf to bottom. There was the set of Stoddard's Lectures, in all its late nineteenth-century vocabulary and vignettes of peasant life and quaint beliefs and customs, with matching halftone illustrations: Vesuvius erupting, Venice by moonlight, gypsies glimpsed by their campfires. I didn't know then the clue they were to my father's longing to see the rest of the world. I read straight through his other love-from-afar: the Victrola Book of the Opera, with opera after opera in synopsis, with portraits in costume of Melba, Caruso, Galli-Curci, and Geraldine Farrar, some of whose voices we could listen to on our Red Seal records.

15   My mother read secondarily for information; she sank as a hedonist into novels. She read Dickens in the spirit in which she would have eloped with him. The novels of her girlhood that had stayed on in her imagination, besides those of Dickens and Scott and Robert Louis Stevenson, were *Jane Eyre, Trilby, The Woman in White, Green Mansions, King Solomon's Mines*. Marie Corelli's name would crop up but I understood she had gone out of favor with my mother, who had only kept *Ardath* out of loyalty. In time she absorbed herself in Galsworthy, Edith Wharton, above all in Thomas Mann of the *Joseph* volumes.

16   *St. Elmo* was not in our house; I saw it often in other houses. This wildly popular Southern novel is where all the Edna Earles in our population started coming from. They're all named for the heroine, who succeeded in bringing a dissolute, sinning roué and atheist of a lover (St. Elmo) to his knees. My mother was able to forgo it. But she remembered the classic advice given to rose growers on how to water their bushes long enough: "Take a chair and *St. Elmo*."

17   To both my parents I owe my early acquaintance with a beloved Mark Twain. There was a full set of Mark Twain and a short set of Ring Lardner in our bookcase, and those were the volumes that in time united us all, parents and children.

18   Reading everything that stood before me was how I came upon a worn old book without a back that had belonged to my father as a child. It was called *Sanford and Merton*. Is there anyone left who recognizes it, I wonder? It is the famous moral tale written by Thomas Day in the 1780s, but of him no mention is made on the title page of *this* book; here it is *Sanford and Merton in Words of One Syllable* by Mary Godolphin. Here are the rich boy and the poor boy and Mr. Barlow, their teacher and interlocutor, in long discourses alternating with dramatic scenes—danger and

rescue allotted to the rich and the poor respectively. It may have only words of one syllable, but one of them is "quoth." It ends with not one but two morals, both engraved on rings: "Do what you ought, come what may," and "If we would be great, we must first learn to be good."

19   This book was lacking its front cover, the back held on by strips of pasted paper, now turned golden, in several layers, and the pages stained, flecked, and tattered around the edges; its garish illustrations had come unattached but were preserved, laid in. I had the feeling even in my heedless childhood that this was the only book my father as a little boy had had of his own. He had held onto it, and might have gone to sleep on its coverless face: he had lost his mother when he was seven. My father had never made any mention to his own children of the book, but he had brought it along with him from Ohio to our house and shelved it in our bookcase.

20   My mother had brought from West Virginia that set of Dickens; those books looked sad, too—they had been through fire and water before I was born, she told me, and there they were, lined up—as I later realized, waiting for *me*.

21   I was presented, from as early as I can remember, with books of my own, which appeared on my birthday and Christmas morning. Indeed, my parents could not give me books enough. They must have sacrificed to give me on my sixth or seventh birthday—it was after I became a reader for myself—the ten-volume set of Our Wonder World. These were beautifully made, heavy books I would lie down with on the floor in front of the diningroom hearth, and more often than the rest volume 5, *Every Child's Story Book*, was under my eyes. There were the fairy tales—Grimm, Andersen, the English, the French, "Ali Baba and the Forty Thieves"; and there was Aesop and Reynard the Fox; there were the myths and legends, Robin Hood, King Arthur, and St. George and the Dragon, even the history of Joan of Arc; a whack of *Pilgrim's Progress* and a long piece of *Gulliver*. They all carried their classic illustrations. I located myself in these pages and could go straight to the stories and pictures I loved; very often "The Yellow Dwarf" was first choice, with Walter Crane's Yellow Dwarf in full color making his terrifying appearance flanked by turkeys. Now that volume is as worn and backless and hanging apart as my father's poor *Sanford and Merton*. The precious page with Edward Lear's "Jumblies" on it has been in danger of slipping out for all these years. One measure of my love for Our Wonder World was that for a long time I wondered if I would go through fire and water for it as my mother had done for Charles Dickens; and the only comfort was to think I could ask my mother to do it for me.

22   I believe I'm the only child I know of who grew up with this treasure in the house. I used to ask others, "Did you have Our Wonder World?" I'd have to tell them The Book of Knowledge could not hold a candle to it.

23   I live in gratitude to my parents for initiating me—and as early as I begged for it, without keeping me waiting—into knowledge of the word, into reading and spelling, by way of the alphabet. They taught it to me at home in time for me to begin to read before starting to school. I believe

the alphabet is no longer considered an essential piece of equipment for traveling through life. In my day it was the keystone to knowledge. You learned the alphabet as you learned to count to ten, as you learned "Now I lay me" and the Lord's Prayer and your father's and mother's name and address and telephone number, all in case you were lost.

24   My love for the alphabet, which endures, grew out of reciting it but, before that, out of seeing the letters on the page. In my own story books, before I could read them for myself, I fell in love with various winding, enchanted-looking initials drawn by Walter Crane at the heads of fairy tales. In "Once upon a time," an "O" had a rabbit running it as a treadmill, his feet upon flowers. When the day came, years later, for me to see the Book of Kells, all the wizardry of letter, initial, and word swept over me a thousand times over, and the illumination, the gold, seemed a part of the word's beauty and holiness that had been there from the start.

25   Learning stamps you with its moments. Childhood's learning is made up of moments. It isn't steady. It's a pulse.

26   In a children's art class, we sat in a ring on kindergarten chairs and drew three daffodils that had just been picked out of the yard; and while I was drawing, my sharpened yellow pencil and the cup of the yellow daffodil gave off whiffs just alike. That the pencil doing the drawing should give off the same smell as the flower it drew seemed part of the art lesson—as shouldn't it be? Children, like animals, use all their senses to discover the world. Then artists come along and discover it the same way, all over again. Here and there, it's the same world. Or now and then we'll hear from an artist who's never lost it.

27   In my sensory education I include my physical awareness of the *word*. Of a certain word, that is; the connection it has with what it stands for. At around age six, perhaps, I was standing by myself in our front yard waiting for supper, just at that hour in a late summer day when the sun is already below the horizon and the risen full moon in the visible sky stops being chalky and begins to take on light. There comes the moment, and I saw it then, when the moon goes from flat to round. For the first time it met my eyes as a globe. The word "moon" came into my mouth as though fed to me out of a silver spoon. Held in my mouth the moon became a word. It had the roundness of a Concord grape Grandpa took off his vine and gave me to suck out of its skin and swallow whole, in Ohio.

28   This love did not prevent me from living for years in foolish error about the moon. The new moon just appearing in the west was the rising moon to me. The new should be rising. And in early childhood the sun and moon, those opposite reigning powers, I just as easily assumed rose in east and west respectively in their opposite sides of the sky, and like partners in a reel they advanced, sun from the east, moon from the west, crossed over (when I wasn't looking) and went down on the other side. My father couldn't have known I believed that when, bending behind

me and guiding my shoulder, he positioned me at our telescope in the front yard and, with careful adjustment of the focus, brought the moon close to me.

29   The night sky over my childhood Jackson was velvety black. I could see the full constellations in it and call their names; when I could read, I knew their myths. Though I was always waked for eclipses, and indeed carried to the window as an infant in arms and shown Halley's Comet in my sleep, and though I'd been taught at our diningroom table about the solar system and knew the earth revolved around the sun, and our moon around us, I never found out the moon didn't come up in the west until I was a writer and Herschel Brickell, the literary critic, told me after I misplaced it in a story. He said valuable words to me about my new profession: "Always be sure you get your moon in the right part of the sky."

30   My mother always sang to her children. Her voice came out just a little bit in the minor key. "Wee Willie Winkie's" song was wonderfully sad when she sang the lullabies.

31   "Oh, but now there's a record. She could have her own record to listen to," my father would have said. For there came a Victrola record of "Bobby Shafftoe" and "Rock-a-Bye Baby", all of Mother's lullabies, which could be played to take her place. Soon I was able to play her my own lullabies all day long.

32   Our Victrola stood in the diningroom. I was allowed to climb onto the seat of a diningroom chair to wind it, start the record turning, and set the needle playing. In a second I'd jumped to the floor, to spin or march around the table as the music called for—now there were all the other records I could play too. I skinned back onto the chair just in time to lift the needle at the end, stop the record and turn it over, then change the needle. That brass receptacle with a hole in the lid gave off a metallic smell like human sweat, from all the hot needles that were fed it. Winding up, dancing, being cocked to start and stop the record, was of course all in one the act of *listening*—to "Overture to *Daughter of the Regiment*," "Selections from *The Fortune Teller*," "Kiss Me Again," "Gypsy Dance from *Carmen*," "Stars and Stripes Forever," "When the Midnight Choo-Choo Leaves for Alabam," or whatever came next. Movement must be at the very heart of listening.

33   Ever since I was first read to, then started reading to myself, there has never been a line read that I didn't *hear*. As my eyes followed the sentence, a voice was saying it silently to me. It isn't my mother's voice, or the voice of any person I can identify, certainly not my own. It is human, but inward, and it is inwardly that I listen to it. It is to me the voice of the story or the poem itself. The cadence, whatever it is that asks you to believe, the feeling that resides in the printed word, reaches me through the reader-voice. I have supposed, but never found out, that this is the case with all readers—to read as listeners—and with all writers, to write as listeners. It may be part of the desire to write. The sound of what falls on the page be-

gins the process of testing it for truth, for me. Whether I am right to trust so far I don't know. By now I don't know whether I could do either one, reading or writing, without the other.

34   My own words, when I am at work on a story, I hear too as they go, in the same voice that I hear when I read in books. When I write and the sound of it comes back to my ears, then I act to make my changes. I have always trusted this voice.

Discussion Questions

1. Welty describes a world in which reading was a central part. To what extent do you think Welty's experiences are typical of young children? How do your own experiences compare with Welty's?

2. Welty writes in paragraph 8 of her father "preparing his children." In your own past, how did your parents prepare you for the future?

3. What do you see as the connection between the strong influence of reading and Welty becoming a writer? That is, why is reading an integral part of writing? How does reading influence your own writing?

4. What do you think Welty means by the term "sensory education" in paragraph 27?

5. In paragraph 33, Welty states, "Ever since I was first read to, then started reading to myself, there has never been a line read that I didn't *hear*." What do *you* see as the connection between the written word and sound? When you read, do you "hear" the words? Why is this important?

Looking Back
Joyce Maynard

*J*oyce Maynard *was born in 1953 and grew up in New Hampshire. Educated at Yale University, Maynard distinguished herself by publishing her first book,* Looking Backward: A Chronicle of Growing Old in the Sixties *(1973) when she was a nineteen-year-old sophomore in college. Since then Maynard has been a syndicated columnist and a reporter for* The New York Times. *Her essays have appeared in such magazines as* Mademoiselle, *and she has published two novels,* Baby Love *(1981) and* To Die For *(1992). Her columns have also been reprinted in a collection entitled* Domestic Affairs *(1988). Currently, Maynard writes and publishes the newsletter* Domestic Affairs *from her home in Keene, New Hampshire. In the following essay taken from* Looking Backward, *Maynard reflects on growing up by comparing herself to Hanna, her five-year-old friend.*

1   To my friend Hanna, at five, I am a grown-up. I do not feel like one—at nineteen, I'm at the midway point between the kindergartner and her mother, and I belong to neither generation—but I can vote, and drink in New York, and marry without parental consent in Mississippi, and get a life sentence, not reform school, if I shoot someone premeditatedly. Walking with Hanna in New York and keeping to the inside, as the guidebooks tell me, so that doorway muggers lunging out will get not her but me, I'm suddenly aware that, of the two of us, I am the adult, the one whose life means less, because I've lived more of it already; I've moved from my position as protected child to child protector; I am the holder of a smaller hand where, just ten years ago, *my* hand was held through streets whose danger lay not in the alleys but in the roads themselves, the speeding cars, roaring motorcycles. I have left childhood, and though I longed to leave it, when being young meant finishing your milk and missing "Twilight Zone" on TV because it came on too late, now that it's gone I'm uneasy. Not fear of death yet (I'm still young enough to feel immortal) or worry over wrinkles and gray hair, but a sense that the fun is over before it began, that I'm old before my time—why isn't someone holding *my* hand still, protecting *me* from the dangers of the city, guiding me home?

2   I remember kneeling on the seat of a subway car, never bothering to count the stops or peer through all those shopping bags and knees to read the signs, because *she* would know when to get off, she'd take my hand; I remember looking out the window to see the sparks fly, underpants exposed to all the rush-hour travelers and never worrying that they could see, while all around me, mothers had to cross their legs or keep their knees together. And later, driving home, leaning against my mother's shoulder while her back tensed on the seat and her eyes stared out at the yellow lines, it was so nice to know I was responsible for nothing more than brushing my teeth when we got home, and not even that, if we got home late enough.

3   Hanna doesn't look where we're going, never bothers to make sure she can find her way home again, because she knows I will take care of those things, and though I feel I am too young to be so old in anybody's eyes, it's just a feeling, not a fact. When it rains, she gets the plastic rain hat, and when the ball of ice cream on her cone falls off, I give her mine. But if Hanna uses my ice cream and my hat, my knowledge of the subways and my hand, well, I use Hanna too: she's my excuse to ride the Ferris wheel, to shop for dolls. And when the circus comes to town—Ringling Brothers, no less—and I take her, everything evens up. Walking to Madison Square Garden, stepping over sidewalk lines and dodging muggers, she is my escort more than I am hers.

4   I think of one time in particular.

5   There we sat, in our too-well-cushioned seats, Hanna in her navy blue knee socks and flower barrettes, I beside her, holding the overpriced miniature flashlight she had shamed me into buying (because everyone else in our row had one), earnestly obeying the ringmaster's instructions to wave it when the lights went out—frantically, a beacon in the night—because Hanna's hands were too full of other circus-going apparatus: a celluloid doll whose arm already hung loose, the Cracker Jack she wanted for the prize inside, the Jujubes that she swallowed dutifully like pills. We all seemed a little sad, Hanna and me and all the other flashlight wavers who surrounded us, like people I'd see in a movie and feel sorry for—the grown-ups, the ticket buyers, because the admission fee hadn't really bought us into youngness again, even the little kids, because most of them had barely had it to begin with. We grew up old, Hanna even more than I. We are cynics who see the trap door in the magic show, the pillow stuffing in Salvation Army Santa Clauses, the camera tricks in TV commercials ("That isn't really a genie's hand coming out of the washing machine," Hanna tells me, "it's just an actor with gloves on."). So at the circus, there was a certain lack of wonder in the crowd, a calm, shrugging atmosphere of "So what else is new?" She leaned back on her padded seat, my four-year-old, watching me twirl her flashlight for her ("Keep up with those flashlights, kids," the ringmaster had said), chewing her hot dog, anticipating pratfalls, toughly, smartly, sadly, wisely, agedly unenthralled, more wrapped up in the cotton candy than in the Greatest Show on Earth. Above us, a man danced on a tightrope while, below, poodles stood on their heads and elephants balanced, two-legged, over the spangled bodies of trusting circus girls, and horses leapt through flaming hoops and jugglers handled more balls than I could count and never dropped one.

6   Perhaps it was that we had too much to look at and so weren't awed by any one thing. But even more, it was that we had seen greater spectacles, unmoved, that our whole world was a visual glut, a ten-ring circus even Ringling Brothers couldn't compete with. A man stuck his head into a tiger's mouth and I pointed it out, with more amazement than I really felt, to my cool, unfazed friend, and when she failed to look (I, irritated now—"these seats cost money. . . ") turned her head for her, forced her to take the sight in. The tiger could have bitten the tamer's head off, I think, swallowed him whole and turned into a monkey and she wouldn't have blinked. We watched what must have been two dozen clowns pile out of a Volkswagen without Hanna's knowing what the point of all that was. It isn't just the knowledge that they emerge from a trap door in the sawdust that keeps Hanna from looking up, either. Even if she didn't know the trick involved, she wouldn't care.

7   I don't think I'm reading too much into it when I say that, at five, she has already developed a sense of the absurd—the kind of unblinking world-weariness that usually comes only to disillusioned middle-aged men and eighty-year-old rocking-chair sitters. I sometimes forget that Hanna is

just five, not eighty; that she believes she will grow up to be a ballerina and tells me that someday she'll marry a prince; that she is afraid of the dark, she isn't big enough for a two-wheeler; her face clouds over in the sad parts of a Shirley Temple movie and lights up at the orange roof of a Howard Johnson's. Maybe I'm projecting on Hanna the feelings I have about my own childhood and growing up when I say that she seems, sometimes, to be so jaded. I think not, though. I watch her watching the monkeys dance and, sensing my eyes on her, and for my benefit, not from real mirth, she laughs a TV-actress laugh. She throws her head back (a shampoo ad) and smiles a toothpaste commercial smile so that baby teeth show—sex appeal?—and says, for my benefit, "This is lots of fun, isn't it?" the way people who aren't enjoying themselves much, but feel they should be, try to convince themselves they are.

8   What all this has to do with growing up old—Hanna and me, five and nineteen, watching the circus—is that Hanna has already begun her aging and I, once having aged, am trying to return. We're different generations, of course, but—though Hanna doesn't know what Vietnam is, or marijuana— we've both been touched by the sixties or, at least, its aftermath. I've grown up old, and I mention Hanna because she seems to have been born that way, almost, as if each generation tarnishes the innocence of the next. In 1957 I was four going on twenty, sometimes; Hanna at the circus borders on middle age . . . I feel the circle—childhood and senility—closing in.

9   A word like *disillusioned* doesn't apply to a five-year-old's generation or—though they call my generation "disillusioned" all the time—to mine. I grew up without many illusions to begin with, in a time when fairy tales were thought to be unhealthy (one teacher told my mother that), when fantasy existed mostly in the form of Mr. Clean and Speedy Alka-Seltzer. We were sensible, realistic, literal-minded, unromantic, socially conscious and politically minded, whether we read the papers (whether we could even read, in fact) or not. The Kennedys were our fairy-tale heroes, integration and outer space and The Bomb the dramas of our first school years. It was not a time when we could separate our own lives from the outside world. The idea then was *not* to protect the children—"expose" them, that was the term, and surely there's some sense, at least, in that— but it was carried too far with us. We were dragged through the mud of Relevance and Grim Reality, and now we have a certain tough, I've-been-there attitude. Not that we really know it all, but we often think we do. Few things shock or surprise us, little jolts our stubborn sureness that our way is right or rattles our early formed and often ill-founded, opinionated conclusions. We imagine hypocrisy in a politician's speeches. We play at vulnerability—honesty, openness, the sensitivity-group concept of *trust,* but what we're truly closer to is venerability. I think of the sixteen-year-old McGovern worker who tells me she was an idealistic socialist when she was young, and of the whole new breed, just surfacing, of drug users who have come full circle and, at twenty, given up dope (before some of us have begun, even).

10   All of which adds to this aged, weary quality I'm talking about. Oh yes, I know we are the Pepsi Generation. I know what they all say about our "youthful exuberance"—our music, our clothes, our freedom and energy and go-power. And it's true that, physically, we're strong and energetic, and that we dance and surf and ride around on motorbikes and stay up all night while the parents shake their heads and say "Oh, to be young again . . . " What sticks in my head, though, is another image. I hear low, barely audible speech, words breathed out as if by some supreme and nearly superhuman effort, I see limp gestures and sedentary figures. Kids sitting listening to music, sitting rapping, just sitting. Or sleeping—that, most of all. Staying up late, but sleeping in later. We're tired, often more from boredom than exertion, old without being wise, worldly not from seeing the world but from watching it on television.

11   Every generation thinks it's special—my grandparents because they remember horses and buggies, my parents because of the Depression. The over-thirties are special because they knew the Red Scare and Korea, bobby socks and beatniks. My older sister is special because she belonged to the first generation of teen-agers (before that, people in their teens were *adolescents*), when being a teen-ager was still fun. And I am caught in the middle. Mine is the generation of unfulfilled expectations. "When you're older," my mother promised, "you can wear lipstick." But when the time came, of course, lipstick wasn't being worn. "When we're big, we'll dance like that," my friends and I whispered, watching Chubby Checker twist on "American Bandstand." But we inherited no dance steps; ours was a limp, formless shrug to watered-down music that rarely made the feet tap. "Just wait till we can vote," I said, bursting with ten-year-old fervor, ready to fast, freeze, march and die for peace and freedom as Joan Baez, barefoot, sang, "We Shall Overcome." Well, now we can vote, and we're old enough to attend rallies and knock on doors and wave placards, and suddenly it doesn't seem to matter any more. My generation is special because of what we missed rather than what we got, because in a certain sense we are the first and the last. The first to take technology for granted. (What was a space shot to us, except an hour cut from social studies to gather before a TV in the gym as Cape Canaveral counted down?) The first to grow up with TV. My sister was eight when we got our set, so to her it seemed magic and always somewhat foreign. She had known books already and would never really replace them. But for me, the TV set was like the kitchen sink and the telephone, a fact of life.

12   We inherited a previous generation's hand-me-downs and took in the seams, turned up the hems, to make our new fashions. We took drugs from the college kids and made them a high school commonplace. We got the Beatles, but not those lovable look-alikes in matching suits with barber cuts and songs that made you want to cry. They came to us like a bad joke—aged, bearded, discordant. And we inherited the Vietnam war just

after the crest of the wave—too late to burn draft cards and too early not to be drafted. The boys of 1953—my year—will be the last to go.

13   So where are we now? Generalizing is dangerous. Call us the apathetic generation and we will become that. Say times are changing, nobody cares about prom queens and getting into the college of his choice any more—say that (because it sounds good, it indicates a trend, gives a symmetry to history) and you make a movement and a unit out of a generation unified only in its common fragmentation. We tend to stay in packs, of course—at rock concerts and protest marches, but not so much because we are a real group as because we are, for all our talk of "individuality" and "doing one's thing," conformists who break traditions, as a rule, only in the traditional ways.

14   Still, we haven't all emerged the same because our lives were lived in high school corridors and drive-in hamburger joints as well as in the pages of *Time* and *Life* and the images on the TV screen. National and personal memory blur so that, for me, November 22, 1963, was a birthday party that had to be called off and Armstrong's moon walk was my first full can of beer. But memory—shared or unique—is, I think, a clue to why we are where we are now. Like over-anxious patients in analysis, we treasure the traumas of our childhood. Ours was more traumatic than most. The Kennedy assassination has become our myth: talk to us for an evening or two—about movies or summer jobs or the weather—and the subject will come up ("where were *you* when you heard . . . "), as if having lived through Jackie and the red roses, John-John's salute and Oswald's on-camera murder justifies our disenchantment. If you want to know who we are now—if you wonder whether ten years from now we will end up just like all those other generations that thought they were special—with 2.2 kids and a house in Connecticut—if that's what you're wondering, look to the past because, whether we should blame it or not, we do.

15   Durham, New Hampshire, where I come from, is a small town. There are no stop lights or neon signs on Main Street. We used to have an ice-cube machine but the zoning board and the town grandfathers sent it away to someplace less concerned with Old New England charm—some place where cold drinks are more important than tourists in search of atmosphere. The ugliest part of town is a row of gas stations that cluster at the foot of Church Hill and the Historical Society's rummage sale museum. Supershellwegivestampsmobiloilyoumayhavealreadywon . . . their banners blow in our unpolluted winds like a Flag Day line-up at the UN. Dropouts from Oyster River High man the pumps and the greasers who are still in school, the shop boys, screech into the stations at lunchtime to study their engines and puff on cigarettes and—if there's been an accident lately—to take a look at the wrecks parked out back. When the rivers melt for swimming, sixth-grade boys bike to the stations—no hands—to pump up their tires and collect old inner tubes. Eighth graders come in casual, blushing troups to check out the dispensers in the Shell station's men's room. Nobody stays at the gas stations for long. They rip out to the high-

way or down a dirt road that leads to the rapids or back to town where even the grocery store is wreathed in ivy.

16   Proud of our quaintness, we are self-conscious, as only a small New Hampshire town that is also a university town just on the edge of sophistication can be. The slow, stark New England accents are cultivated with the corn. We meet in the grocery store and shake our heads over changes—the tearing down of Mrs. Smart's house to make way for a parking lot; the telephone company's announcement that dialing four digits was no longer enough, we'd need all seven; the new diving board at the town pool. . . . Durham is growing. Strange babies eat sand in the wading water and the mothers gathered to watch them no longer know each others' names. The old guard—and I am one—feel almost resentful. What can they know, those army-base imports, those Boston commuters with the Illinois license plates, those new faculty members and supermarket owners who weren't around the year it snowed so hard we missed four days of school and had to make it up on Saturdays. . . .

17   Yet all the while I was growing up in this town, I itched to leave. In September I'd visit the city for school clothes and wish I lived there always. In Boston, where I could go shopping every day and never worry about shoveling snow or pulling weeds. I tried hard for sophistication— with my Boston dresses and my New York magazines and my Manchester high-heeled boots. Now that I've left I've discovered my loyalties—I play the small-town girl and pine for a Thornton Wilder dream that never really existed, a sense of belonging, the feeling that I'm part of a community.

18   In truth, what I have always been is an outsider. Midnight on New Year's Eve I would be reading record jackets or discussing the pros and cons of pass-fail grading with an earnest, glasses-polishing scholar who spoke of "us" and "we" as if I were just like him, or cleaning up the floor and the clothes of some ninth-grade boy who hadn't learned yet that you don't gulp down scotch the way you gulp down Kool-Aid. Many paper cups of Bourbon past the point where others began to stumble and slur and put their arms around each other in moments of sudden kinship, I remained clear-headed, unable to acquire that lovely warm fog that would let me suspend judgment, sign "Love always" in yearbooks (thinking that I meant it), put down my pencil and just have a good time. But liquor seems almost to sharpen my quills, to set me farther apart.

19   Sometimes I pretend, but I can always hear, off in the distance, the clicking of a typewriter. I see myself in the third person, a character in a book, an actor in a movie. I don't say this proudly but as a confession that, even as a friend told me another friend had died the night before I felt not only shock and grief but someday-I'll-write-about-this. And here I am now, doing it.

20   It must seem, to people who don't know me and even more, perhaps, to the ones who do, as if I'm a cold-blooded traitor, informing on a world that trusted me enough to let me in. So let me say first off that, whatever I say about the Girl Scouts and the cheerleaders and the soccer players and

the high school drama club, the person I'm informing on most of all is myself. I'm not writing nostalgically, so the memories may not come out the way some people would like to remember them. (Listen to a twelve-year-old, sometime, reminiscing about the good old days when she was eight. Unable to feel wholeness and happiness in the present, we fabricate happy memories.) I don't look back in anger, either; maybe it's Freudian psychology that has made us so suspicious of our pasts. Whatever the reason, there's an awful lot of bitterness around, too many excuses made, too much stuffed in closets and blamed on things beyond control—parents and wars and teachers and traumas that became real only after the event, when we learned what traumas were.

21   As for looking back, I do it reluctantly. Sentimentality or bitterness— it breeds one or the other almost inevitably. But the fact is that there's no understanding the future without the present, and no understanding where we are now without a glance, at least, to where we have been.

Discussion Questions

1. Maynard begins her essay by stating that at nineteen she does not feel grown-up. Do you find the reasons Maynard offers for that reaction convincing? How commonplace do you think that feeling is among people in their late teens? Can you add some of your own?

2. How do you account for Maynard stating in paragraph 8 that "Hanna has already begun her aging and I, once having aged, am trying to return"? Do you agree with her assessment of the situation? Have you ever felt similarly?

3. In paragraph 11 Maynard states, "Every generation thinks it's special." Do you think *your* generation is special? Why or why not?

4. Maynard writes in paragraph 13 that people her age "tend to stay in packs . . . not so much because we are a real group as because we are, for all our talk of 'individuality' and 'doing one's own thing,' conformists who break traditions, as a rule, only in the traditional ways." Can you find examples of this behavior among your own peers? Or is this a behavior peculiar to Maynard's generation?

5. Do you view the ending of Maynard's essay as optimistic or pessimistic? Explain your answer.

Chasing the Night
Paul Milo Miller

P aul Milo Miller was born in Vermont in 1967 and moved to Ohio when he was eleven years old. After graduating from high school, he took a year off to "try to make some sense and find some direction in life." When he graduated from college in 1991, he had no immediate plans but thought he would attend graduate school sometime in the future. Miller wrote the following essay in a freshman composition class at the University of Akron. "Chasing the Night" takes place during an evening's outing in which Miller and his friends go "cruising." More importantly, Miller reflects on a situation in which many students his age find themselves: graduating from high school and considering what they want to do with their lives. Before you read his essay, think back to the times when your life was in transition. What were your thoughts and feelings? How did the situation resolve itself? As you read Miller's essay, notice the careful attention he pays to reflection and introspection.

1   We were out on the dark back roads, penetrating the quiet summer night with a nearly unholy roar as Bob pushed his GTO up towards the 100 mph mark, sometimes slowing down to a more manageable 65 or 70 for a particularly threatening turn. I was sunk low in the back seat, the wind from the open windows nearly pinning me back. I considered suggesting we slow it down a bit, but thought better of it. It would have been a futile effort and merely opened the door for derision. Anyway, I figured at this speed if we hit anything we'd practically disintegrate on impact; if we slowed down it would just be a more painful and lingering death.

2   I realized that Bowden was turned around in the front passenger seat, yelling something at me. The wind-tunnel effect of the back seat was too great to make out much of anything. I forced myself forward and yelled, "What?!"

3   "You want to get something to eat?" Bowden hollered. Bowden had a first name but we never used it. Before I even answered Bob had pulled the car onto the shoulder and was ripping the beast around. In a shower of gravel we were off back towards town, the car screeching like a banshee in the hot darkness.

4   I sipped a beer that I had been holding between my legs. Bob didn't drink—that's why he always ended up driving. My mind wandered as it always did when I found myself on one of these late night rides across the Ohio countryside. You couldn't very well talk with all the wind, so the three of us would just sit back and take in the night, content with our own thoughts. I always thought of the same thing.

5   I knew this stage of my life would be coming to an end soon. I'd be

back at college. All this pointless roaming through the boondocks would be replaced by a sense of direction. These late night toasts to freedom would disappear in a sobering sense of responsibility. The commitment to nothing and no one I felt roaring through the open farm country would become victim to the constricted, limited charm of settling down. I could feel it all stirring within me already: That desire to make good for my parents, that sense of starting to lay roots, thinking about a career, a purpose—not so much a purpose, I reminded myself, as a function—for my life.

6   I thought about my girlfriend. I knew she had already been thinking about marriage. It scared me because I could picture it. For the first time I felt the middle class world that I had grown up in, and which had been so good to me, start to drag me in. Maybe it scared me because part of me knew that I would end up there—there on Main Street U.S.A. with a wife, two kids, and a dog. I would be sucked into that existence, forgetting the dreams that I had once entertained on summer nights just like this one, blasting through the night like werewolves on acid.

7   I think that's why my girlfriend hated it so much when I went out with these guys. She wasn't worried about me seeing other girls—she could've competed with that if she had wanted to. But she knew she couldn't compete with the exhilaration, the freedom I felt hurtling through the dark with no destination, no purpose other than the experience itself. She knew that was when I got closest to discovering myself, closest to saying, "Screw the real world, the world of rules, expectations, and commitments." Closest to forgetting that world I realized was really the adult world.

8   I just didn't want to grow up. Really, I thought, none of us did. It was the Peter Pan syndrome; we'd rather be out howling at the moon and occasionally running down stray cats or a sluggish ground hog in the GTO than worrying about supporting a family and getting a job. There was something about the hours we'd spend in that car driving recklessly around that somehow seemed to put things in a perspective that we could all deal with. Maybe it was the recklessness, the wildness of youth, knowing that we could all buy it on a tricky curve and that the instrument of our epiphany could just as easily be our coffin. A fuel-injected thanatopsis that somehow affirmed living was enough; that the trappings of growing up we had been enticed with for so long in our journey to adulthood and "our place in society" really didn't count for much after the dust had cleared and all we'd have left would be a tombstone.

9   Maybe in rocketing out into the countryside we were trying to get away from what everybody was telling us: what we should do, who we should be, and how we would be happy if we played by the rules. In a sense, it was the dying gasp of final rebellion before we closed the chapter on our youth and moved into a new stage, a stage that would not be so free and blissfully ignorant of the views of others. When we were young (and especially when we were out driving) we could, in a sense, create our own reality, ignoring what "everybody else," what society, had to say; but in this new stage we would

have to begin listening more to what those other people were saying just to survive. Of course we would have to, we couldn't help but grow up. Time was a trap that Bob's gas guzzling dinosaur of a car could never outrun.

10 We pulled into the Big Boy parking lot; the breakfast bar was waiting for us, open all night. "Hey Mil, what you thinking?"

11 "Nothing," I said, but went on anyway. "Do you think if we started robbing 7–11's and gas stations we could make it to Mexico before the cops'd catch up to us?"

12 We all laughed. After eating, we headed back towards the outskirts of town, chasing the night and hoping to stay oblivious to the fact that our young dreams of freedom were on a collision course with reality. Sooner or later it would happen, we'd crash and burn in that American dream and find ourselves thrown clear of the wreckage into homes with white-picket fences and jobs that would get us up at six. But for now we'd just hear that engine rev and try to achieve escape velocity from what was pulling us all in.

Discussion Questions

1. How accurately do you think Miller portrays young men; that is, are his reactions representative or atypical of the thinking of people his own age? Explain your response.

2. To what extent does Miller's essay apply only to young men, or do you think the same can be said of young women's thoughts and feelings as well?

3. In paragraph 7, Miller muses on his girlfriend's reactions to his behavior. Do you agree with his thinking? Why or why not?

4. Explain your understanding of the following lines that appear in paragraph 8: "A fuel-injected thanatopsis that somehow affirmed living was enough; that the trappings of growing up we had been enticed with for so long in our journey to adulthood and 'our place in society' really didn't count for much after the dust had cleared and all we'd have left would be a tombstone."

5. Given what you know of Miller in his essay, what do you suppose will happen to him in say, one year, five years, twenty years? Explain your reasons for thinking the way you do.

Under the Lights
Andre Dubus

*A*ndre Dubus was born in 1936; he earned his B.A. degree from McNeese State University and his M.F.A. degree from the University of Iowa. His short stories have appeared in such publications as Sewanee Review, New Yorker, and Ploughshares. Dubus's short-

story collections include Separate Flight *(1975),* Adultery and Other Choices *(1977),* Finding a Girl in America *(1980),* The Times Are Never So Bad *(1983),* We Don't Live Here Anymore *(1984),* Land Where My Fathers Died *(1984), and* The Last Worthless Evening *(1986). Appearing in his collection of essays,* Broken Vessels *(1991), "Under the Lights" recalls Dubus's boyhood love of baseball.*

1   The first professional baseball players I watched and loved were in the Class C Evangeline League, which came to our town in the form of the Lafayette Brahman Bulls. The club's owner raised these hump-backed animals. The league comprised teams from other small towns in Louisiana, and Baton Rouge, the capital. The Baton Rouge team was called the Red Sticks. This was in 1948, and I was eleven years old. At the Lafayette municipal golf course, my father sometimes played golf with Harry Strohm, the player-manager of the Bulls. Strohm was a shortstop. He seemed very old to me and, for a ballplayer, he was: a wiry deeply tanned greying man with lovely blue eyes that were gentle and merry, as his lined face was.

2   Mrs. Strohm worked in the team's business office; she was a golfer too, and her face was tan and lined and she had warm grey-blue eyes with crinkles at their corners. In the Bulls' second season, she hired me and my cousin Jimmy Burke and our friend Carroll Ritchie as ball boys. The club could not afford to lose baseballs, and the business manager took them from fans who caught fouls in the seats. No one on the club could afford much; the players got around six hundred dollars for a season, and when one of them hit a home run the fans passed a hat for him. During batting practice we boys stood on the outside of the fence and returned balls hit over it, or fouled behind the stands. At game time a black boy we never met appeared and worked on the right field fence; one of us perched on the left, another of us stood in the parking lot behind the grandstands, and the third had the night off and a free seat in the park. Our pay was a dollar a night. It remains the best job I ever had, but I would have to be twelve and thirteen and fourteen to continue loving it.

3   One late afternoon I sat in the stands with the players who were relaxing in their street clothes before pre-game practice. A young outfielder was joking with his teammates, showing them a condom from his wallet. The condom in his hand chilled me with disgust at the filth of screwing, or doing it, which was a shameful act performed by dogs, bad girls, and thrice by my parents to make my sisters and me; and chilled me too with the awful solemnity of mortal sin: that season, the outfielder was dating a young Catholic woman, who later would go to Lourdes for an incurable illness; she lived in my neighborhood. Now, recalling what a foolish boy the outfielder was, I do not believe the woman graced him with her loins any more than baseball did, but that afternoon I was only confused and frightened, a boy who had opened the wrong door, the wrong drawer.

4   Then I looked at Harry Strohm. He was watching the outfielder, and his eyes were measuring and cold. Then with my own eyes I saw the outfielder's career as a ballplayer. He did not have one. That was in Harry's

eyes, and his judgment had nothing, of course, to do with the condom: it was the outfielder's cheerful haplessness, sitting in the sun, with no manhood in him, none of the drive and concentration and absolute seriousness a ballplayer must have. This was not a professional relaxing before losing himself in the long hard moment-by-moment work of playing baseball. This was a youth with little talent, enough to hit over .300 in Class C, and catch fly balls that most men could not, and throw them back to the infield or to home plate. But his talent was not what Harry was staring at. It was his lack of regret, his lack of retrospection, this young outfielder drifting in and, very soon, out of the profession that still held Harry, still demanded of him, still excited him. Harry was probably forty, maybe more, and his brain helped his legs cover the ground of a shortstop. He knew where to play the hitters.

5   My mother and father and I went to most home games, and some nights in the off-season we ate dinner at Poorboy's Restaurant with Harry and his wife. One of those nights, while everyone but my mother and me was smoking Lucky Strikes after dinner, my father said to Harry: My son says he wants to be a ballplayer. Harry turned his bright eyes on me, and looked through my eyes and into the secret self, or selves, I believed I hid from everyone, especially my parents and, most of all, my father: those demons of failure that were my solitary torment. I will never forget those moments in the restaurant when I felt Harry's eyes, looking as they had when he stared at the young outfielder who, bawdy and jocular, had not seen them, had not felt them.

6   I was a child, with a child's solipsistic reaction to the world. Earlier that season, on a morning before a night game, the Bulls hosted a baseball clinic for young boys. My friends and I went to it, driven by one of our mothers. That was before seatbelts and other sanity, when you put as many children into a car as it could hold, then locked the doors to keep them closed against the pressure of bodies. By then I had taught myself to field ground and fly balls, and to bat. Among my classmates at school, I was a sissy, because I was a poor athlete. Decades later I realized I was a poor athlete at school because I was shy, and every public act—like standing at the plate, waiting to swing at a softball—became disproportionate. Proportion is all; and, in sports at school, I lost it by surrendering to the awful significance of my self-consciousness. Shyness has a strange element of narcissism, a belief that how we look, how we perform, is truly important to other people.

7   In the fall of 1947 I vowed—I used that word—to redeem myself in softball season in the spring. I used the word *redeem* too. We had moved to a new neighborhood that year, and we had an odd house, two-storied and brick, built alone by its owner, our landlord. It had the only basement in Lafayette, with a steep driveway just wide enough for a car and a few spare inches on either side of it, just enough to make a driver hold his breath, glancing at the concrete walls rising beside the climbing or descending car. The back wall of the living room, and my sisters' shared bedroom above it, had no windows. So I practiced there, throwing a baseball

against my sisters' wall for flies, and against the living room wall for grounders. In that neighborhood I had new friends and, since they did not know me as a sissy, I did not become one. In autumn and winter we played tackle football, wearing helmets and shoulder pads; when we weren't doing that, I was practicing baseball. Every night, before kneeling to say the rosary then going to bed, I practiced batting. I had learned the stance and stride and swing from reading John R. Tunis's baseball novels, and from *Babe Ruth Comics,* which I subscribed to and which, in every issue, had a page of instructions in one of the elements of baseball. I opened my bedroom door so the latch faced me, as a pitcher would. The latch became the ball and I stood close enough to hit it, my feet comfortably spread, my elbows away from my chest, my wrists cocked, and the bat held high. Then one hundred times I stepped toward the latch, the fastball, the curve, and kept my eyes on it and swung the bat, stopping it just short of contact.

8   In the spring of 1948, in the first softball game during the afternoon hour of physical education in the dusty schoolyard, the two captains chose teams and, as always, they chose other boys until only two of us remained. I batted last, and first came to the plate with two or three runners on base, and while my teammates urged me to try for a walk, and the players on the field called Easy out, Easy out, I watched the softball coming in waist-high, and stepped and swung, and hit it over the right fielder's head for a double. My next time at bat I tripled to center. From then on I brought my glove to school, hanging from a handlebar.

9   That summer the Bulls came to town, and we boys in the neighborhood played baseball every morning, on a lot owned by the father of one of our friends. Mr. Gossen mowed the field, built a backstop, and erected foul poles down the left and right field foul lines. Beyond them and the rest of the outfield was tall grass. We wore baseball shoes and caps, chewed bubble gum and spat, and at the wooden home plate we knocked dirt from our spikes. We did not have catcher's equipment, only a mask and a mitt, so our pitchers did not throw hard. We did not want them to anyway. But sometimes we played a team from another neighborhood and our catcher used their shin guards and chest protector, and we hit fast balls and roundhouse curves. I don't know about my other friends, but if Little League ball had existed then I would not have played: not with adult coaches and watching parents taking from me my excitement, my happiness while playing or practicing, and returning me to the tense muscles and cool stomach and clumsy hands and feet of self-consciousness. I am grateful that I was given those lovely summer days until we boys grew older and, since none of us was a varsity athlete, we turned to driving lessons and romance.

10   There were three or four of those baseball seasons. In that first one, in 1948, we went one morning to the Bulls' clinic. The ball field was a crowd of boys, young ones like us, eleven or twelve, and teenagers too. The day began with short drills and instruction and demonstrations; I don't remember how it ended. I only remember the first drill: a column of us in

the infield, and one of the Bulls tossing a ground ball to the first boy, then the next boy, and so on: a fast, smooth exercise. But waiting in line, among all those strangers, not only boys but men too, professional ballplayers, I lost my months of backyard practice, my redemption on the softball field at school and the praise from my classmates that followed it, lost the mornings with my friends on our field. When my turn came I trotted toward the softly bouncing ball, crouched, took my eyes off the ball and saw only the blankness of my secret self, and the ball went between and through my legs. The player tossed me another one, which I fielded while my rump puckered as in anticipation of a spanking, a first day at school. Harry Strohm was watching.

11   So later that summer, amid the aroma of coffee and tobacco smoke at the table at Poorboy's, when he gazed at me with those eyes like embedded gems, brilliant and ancient, I saw in them myself that morning, bound by the strings of my fear, as the ball bounced over my stiffly waiting gloved hand. Harry Strohm said nothing at the table; or, if he did, I heard it as nothing. Perhaps he said quietly: That's good.

12   I was wrong, and I did not know I was wrong until this very moment, as I write this. When Harry looked at me across the table, he was not looking at my body and into my soul and deciding I would never be a ballplayer, he was not focusing on my trifling error on that long day of the clinic. He was looking at my young hope and seeing his own that had propelled him into and kept him in this vocation, this game he had played nearly all his life. His skin was deeply, smoothly brown; the wrinkles in his face delineated his skin's toughness. He wore a short-sleeved shirt and slacks. I cannot imagine him in a suit and tie, save in his casket; cannot imagine him in any clothing but a baseball uniform, or something familiar, something placed in a locker before a game, withdrawn from it after the game and the shower, some assembly of cotton whose only function was to cover his nakedness until the next game, the next season. He had once played Triple A ball.

13   So had Norm Litzinger, our left fielder. A shoulder injury was the catalyst for his descent from the top of the wall surrounding the garden where the very few played major league baseball. I do not remember the effect of the injury on his performance in the Evangeline League. Perhaps there was none, as he threw on smaller fields, to hold or put out slower runners, and as he swung at pitches that most major leaguers could hit at will. He was brown, and broad of shoulder and chest, handsome and spirited, and humorous. He was fast too, and graceful, and sometimes, after making a shoestring catch, he somersaulted to his feet, holding the ball high in his glove. Once, as he was sprinting home from third, the catcher blocked the plate. Litzinger ducked his head and ran into the catcher, who dropped the ball as the two men fell; then Litzinger rose from the tumble and dust, grinning, holding his shoulders sloped and his arms bent and hanging like an ape's, and walked like one into applause and the dugout.

14   He was in his thirties. At the end of every season he went home, to

whatever place in the North. For us, everything but Arkansas above us was the North; everything but California, which was isolate and odd. One season he dated a beautiful woman who sat with another beautiful woman in a box seat behind home plate. I was thirteen or fourteen. Litzinger's lady had black hair and dark skin, her lips and fingernails were bright red, her cheeks rouged. Her friend was blonde, with very red lips and nails. They both smoked Chesterfields, and as I watched them drawing on their cigarettes, marking them with lipstick, and blowing plumes of smoke into the humid and floodlit night air, and daintily removing bits of tobacco from their tongues, I felt the magical and frightening mystery of their flesh. The brunette married Norman Litzinger; and one night, before the game, the blonde married Billy Joe Barrett with a ceremony at home plate.

15   One season I read a book by Joe DiMaggio. I believe it was a book of instruction, for boys. I only remember one line from that book, and I paraphrase it: If you stay in Class D or C ball for more than one season, unless you have been injured, you should get out of professional baseball. Perhaps DiMaggio wrote the word *quit*. I can't. I've spent too much of my life in angry dread of that word.

16   How could I forget DiMaggio's sentence? I loved young ballplayers who, with the Bulls, were trying to rise through the minor leagues, to the garden of the elect. I loved young ballplayers who, like the outfielder with the condom, were in their second or third seasons in Class C ball. And I loved old ballplayers, like Harry Strohm; and Bill Thomas, a fifty-year-old pitcher with great control, and an assortment of soft breaking balls, who one night pitched a no-hitter; and once, when because of rain-outs and doubleheaders, the Bulls had no one to pitch the second game of a double header, he pitched and won both of them. And I loved players who were neither old nor young, for baseball: men like Tom Spears, a pitcher in his mid-twenties, who had played in leagues higher than Class C, then pitched a few seasons for us on his way out of professional baseball. He was a gentle and witty man, and one morning, because we asked him to, he came to one of our games, to watch us play.

17   Late one afternoon Mrs. Strohm gave both my cousin Jimmy and me the night off, and we asked the visiting manager if we could be his batboys. Tom Spears pitched for the Bulls that night. This was a time in baseball when, if a man was pitching a no-hitter, no one spoke about it. Radio announcers hinted, in their various ways. Fans in seats looked at each other, winked, raised an eyebrow, nodded. We were afraid of jinxing it; and that belief made being a fan something deeper than watching a game. An uninformed spectator, a drunk, even a thirteen-year-old boy could, by simply saying the words *no-hitter*, destroy it. So you were connected with everyone watching the game, and everyone listening to it too, for a man alone with his radio in his living room, a man who lacked belief, could say those two sacred words and break the spell.

18   But Jimmy and I did not know until the night Spears pitched a no-hitter, while we were batboys for the New Iberia Pelicans, that the opposing

team transcended their desire to win, and each player his desire to perform, to hit, and instead obeyed the rules of the ritual. We were having fun, and we were also trying to do perfect work as batboys; we did not know Spears was pitching a no-hitter. We sat in the dugout while the Pelicans were in the field, sat with pitchers and the manager and reserve ballplayers. When the Pelicans were at bat we stayed close to the on-deck circle, watched hitter after hitter returning to the dugout without a hit. And no one said a word. Then the last batter struck out on a fastball, a lovely glint of white, and the crowd was standing and cheering and passing the hat, and the Bulls in the field and from the dugout were running to the mound, to Spears. Then the Pelicans were saying the two words, surrounding them with the obscenities I first heard and learned from ballplayers, and they went quickly to their bus—there were no visiting locker rooms in the league—and left their bats. Jimmy and I thrust them into the canvas bat bag and ran, both of us holding the bag, to the parking lot, to the bus. The driver, a player, had already started it; the team was aboard. Your bats, we called; Your bats. From the bus we heard the two words, the obscenities; a player reached down through the door and hoisted in the bag of Louisville Sluggers.

19   How could I forget DiMaggio's sentence? Our first baseman, in the Bulls' first season, was a young hard-hitting lefthander whose last name was Glenn. We were in the Detroit Tiger system, and after Glenn's season with us, he went up to Flint, Michigan, to a Class A league. I subscribed to *The Sporting News* and read the weekly statistics and box scores, and I followed Glenn's performance, and I shared his hope, and waited for the season when he would stand finally in the garden. At Flint he batted in the middle of the order, as he had for us, and he did well; but he did not hit .300, or thirty home runs. In the next season I looked every week at the names in *The Sporting News,* searched for Glenn in double A and triple A, and did not find him there, or in Class A or B, and I never saw his name again. It was as though he had come into my life, then left me and died, but I did not have the words then for what I felt in my heart. I could only say to my friends: I can't find Glenn's name anymore.

20   I believed Billy Joe Barrett's name would be part of baseball for years. I believed he would go from us to Flint, then to double and finally triple A, and would have a career there, at the top of the garden wall. And, with the hope that is the essence of belief, I told myself that he would play in the major leagues; that one season, or over several of them, he would discover and claim that instant of timing, or that sharper concentration, or whatever it was that he so slightly lacked, and that flawed his harmony at the plate. In the field he was what we called then a Fancy Dan. He was right-handed and tall, fast and graceful and lithe. He leaped high and caught line drives as smoothly as an acrobat, as though the hard-hit ball and his catching it were a performance he and the batter had practiced for years. On very close plays at first, stretching for a throw from an infielder,

he did a split, the bottom of one leg and the top of the other pressed against the earth; then quickly and smoothly, without using his hands, he stood. He stole a lot of bases. He often ended his slide by rising to his feet, on the bag. He batted left-handed and was a line drive hitter, and a good one; but not a great one.

21   I have never seen a first baseman whose grace thrilled me as Barrett's did; and one night in Lafayette he hit a baseball in a way I have never seen again. He batted lead-off or second and every season hit a few home runs, but they were not what we or other teams and fans or Barrett himself considered either a hope or a threat when he was at the plate. But that night he hit a fast ball coming just above his knees. It started as a line drive over the second baseman, who leaped for it, his gloved hand reaching up then arcing down without the ball that had cleared by inches, maybe twelve of them, the glove's leather fingers. Then in short right field the ball's trajectory sharply rose, as though deflected higher and faster by angled air, and the right fielder stopped his motion toward it and simply stood and watched while the ball rose higher and higher and was still rising and tiny as it went over the lights in right field. Billy Joe Barrett's career ended in Lafayette.

22   How could I forget DiMaggio's sentence? Before I got out of high school, the Bulls' park was vacant, its playing field growing weeds. The Strohms had moved on, looking for another ball club; and Norm Litzinger and Billy Joe Barrett and their wives had gone to whatever places they found, after Lafayette, and after baseball. I was driving my family's old Chevrolet and smoking Lucky Strikes and falling in love with girls whose red lips marked their cigarettes and who, with painted fingernails, removed bits of tobacco from their tongues; and, with that immortal vision of mortality that youth holds in its heart, I waited for manhood.

23   DiMaggio was wrong. I know that now, over forty years after I read his sentence. Or, because I was a boy whose hope was to be a different boy with a new body growing tall and fast and graceful and strong, a boy who one morning would wake, by some miracle of desire, in motion on the path to the garden, I gave to DiMaggio too much credence; and his sentence lost, for me, all proportion, and insidiously became a heresy. Which I am renouncing now, as I see Billy Joe Barrett on the night when his whole body and his whole mind and his whole heart were for one moment in absolute harmony with a speeding baseball and he hit it harder and farther than he could at any other instant in his life. We never saw the ball start its descent, its downward arc to earth. For me, it never has. It is rising white over the lights high above the right field fence, a bright and vanishing sphere of human possibility soaring into the darkness beyond our vision.

Discussion Questions

1. Dubus describes in paragraph 6 the importance of proportion. Can you remember times as a child feeling self-conscious? Is this feeling peculiar to children? Explain your response.

2. Explain the importance of Dubus "redeeming" himself in softball.

3. What do you see as the significance of Dubus stating in paragraph 12, "I did not know I was wrong until this very moment, as I write this"? What is Dubus implying about the act of writing?

4. Can you remember reading something that greatly affected you, much as Dubus was affected by Joe DiMaggio's book? Describe that event in your life.

5. Explain what you understand Dubus to mean in the last sentence of his essay. How is it a fitting conclusion to his essay?

Turning It Out

Lorene Cary

Born in 1956, Lorene Cary is a 1974 graduate of St. Paul's School. She received her B.A. and M.A. degrees from the University of Pennsylvania in 1978. After earning another M.A. degree from the University of Sussex in England in 1979, Cary worked as a writer for Time *magazine and as an associate editor at* TV Guide. *An African-American writer, Cary has published short fiction and is the author of* Black Ice *(1991), a reminiscence of her days at the formerly all-white, all-male St. Paul's School, an elite New Hampshire prep school. In the following excerpt from that book, Cary, an exceptionally strong student, recalls moving from Yeadon, her previous high school in West Philadelphia, to St. Paul's, known for being the "bootcamp" for future American leaders. Jimmy, another new African-American student at St. Paul's, becomes her friend and confidante, as they pursue succeeding without selling out.*

1   I was not afraid to go to St. Paul's School, although it was becoming clear to me from the solicitous white faces that people thought I was—or ought to be. I had no idea that wealth and privilege could confer real advantages beyond the obvious ones sprawled before us. Instead, I believed that rich white people were like poodles: overbred, inbred, degenerate. All the coddling and permissiveness would have a bad effect, I figured, now that they were up against those of us who'd lived a real life in the real world.

2   I knew that from a black perspective Yeadon had been plenty cushy, but after all, I had been a transplant. West Philly had spawned me, and I was loyal to it. Jimmy felt just as unafraid, just as certain as Darwin that we would overcome. Jimmy had grown up in the projects, the son of a steadfast father and a mother who was a doer, a mover who led tenant-action and community groups. Together, his parents had raised a boy who had a job to do.

3   "Listen to me, darling," he said. "We are going to turn this motherfucker out!"

4   And why not? I, too, had been raised for it. My mother and her mother, who had worked in a factory, and her mother, who had cleaned apartments in Manhattan, had been studying these people all their lives in preparation for this moment. And I had studied them. I had studied my mother as she turned out elementary schools and department stores.

5   I always saw it coming. Some white department-store manager would look at my mother and see no more than a modestly dressed young black woman making a tiresome complaint. He'd use that tone of voice they used when they had *important* work elsewhere. Uh-oh. Then he'd dismiss her with his eyes. I'd feel her body stiffen next to me, and I'd know that he'd set her off.

6   "Excuse me," she'd say. "I don't think you understand what I'm trying to say to you . . . "

7   And then it began in earnest, the turning out. She never moved back. It didn't matter how many people were in line. It didn't matter how many telephones were ringing. She never moved back, only forward, her body leaning over counters and desk tops, her fingers wrapped around the offending item or document, her face getting closer and closer. Sometimes she'd talk through her teeth, her lips moving double time to bite out the consonants. Then she'd get personal. "How dare you," would figure in. "How dare you sit there and tell me . . . " Finally, when she'd made the offense clear, clearer even than the original billing error or the shoddy seam, she'd screw up her eyes: "Do you hear me? Do you hear what I'm saying to you?"

8   They'd eventually, inevitably, take back the faulty item or credit her charge or offer her some higher-priced substitute ("like they should've done in the first place," she'd say, and say to them). They would do it because she had made up her mind that they would. Turning out, I learned, was not a matter of style; cold indignation worked as well as hot fury. Turning out had to do with will. I came to regard my mother's will as a force of nature, an example of and a metaphor for black power and black duty. *My* duty was to compete in St. Paul's classrooms. I had no option but to succeed and no doubt that I could will my success.

9   Jimmy understood. He knew the desperate mandate, the uncompromising demands, and the wild, perfect, greedy hope of it. If we could succeed here—earn high marks, respect, awards; learn these people, study

them, be in their world but not of it—we would fulfill the prayers of our ancestors. Jimmy knew as I did that we could give no rational answer to white schoolmates and parents who asked how we had managed to get to St. Paul's School. How we got there, how we found our way to their secret hideout, was not the point. The point was that we had been bred for it just as surely as they. The point was that we were there to turn it out . . .

10   Early in my first term at St. Paul's I began to dream old dreams. They were childhood dreams that I had thought I'd done with, like bed-wetting. In one dream, I was encircled by bears, friendly, round-faced teddies as big as I. The bears were animated, sepia-colored versions of pen-and-ink drawings in one of my books. In the dream I was a child again, joyfully naked. The bears held paws and danced around me in a circle. We sang together. They protected and adored me. Then—as I knew would happen, the foreknowledge lending betrayal to their song—they began to leer and sneer. Their eyes shone with malice. They closed in about me. I was naked, and their teeth gleamed sharp and white against the sepia.

11   I ran from them, ducking under their interlocked paws, pricking my skin on hairs as sharp as the pen that had drawn them. I ran and ran and ran to the edge of a precipice and awakened just as they were about to catch me.

12   The first time I dreamt this dream at St. Paul's, I expected to wake up on Addison Street in West Philadelphia. But there were no city noises to comfort me, and no headlights sweeping like searchlights across the blinds.

13   I dreamt that I was watching my own funeral. I was a small, grayish corpse in a short coffin. From the back of the church I could see the tips of my feet and my folded hands above the polished mahogany. I observed the mourning with self-absorbed satisfaction.

14   In another dream, I was walking on the sidewalk on Addison Street toward my friend Siboney to ask if she wanted to play. Under my feet the sidewalk shimmered with broken glass. Then the shimmering became movement. The cement squares began to shift. They had been shifting, in fact, from the beginning of time. The solidity had been an illusion. So, too, had been the unbroken surface. Holes yawned between the squares, small ones, then bigger and bigger. They emitted radiant heat and the sounds of souls in despair. An anthropomorphic sea of magma howled and gurgled fire. I had to walk. I had to walk the walk, but at every step, the holes swirled around. If I made one wrong step, I would tumble into hell.

15   I did not talk about my nightmare vision in religion class, but I thought about it. I did not speak to the girls in my room about the bears, but I thought of them, too, while I laughed and listened for betrayal. The bears warned me to beware of slipping into friendship.

16   Girls came and went in my room. I liked it that way. I wanted the company—and the prosperous appearance of company. They taught me about tollhouse cookies; Switzerland; the names of automobiles, shampoos, rock groups, Connecticut cities; casual shoes and outdoor-equip-

ment catalogues. I learned that other girls, too, tired during sports, that their calf muscles, like mine, screamed out pain when they walked down the stairs. I learned about brands of tampons. I learned that these girls thought their hair dirty when they did not wash it daily.

17   "I hear what you're saying, but I just don't see it. I'm looking at your hair, but I don't see grease."

18   "Oh, my God, it's, like, hanging down in clumps!" One girl pulled a few strands from her scalp to display the offending sheen. "Look."

19   I learned that their romanticized lusts sounded like mine felt, as did their ambivalent homesickness, and their guarded, girlish competitiveness.

20   As they came to sit and stay, however, differences emerged between us. Taken together, these girls seemed more certain than I that they deserved our good fortune. They were sorry for people who were poorer than they, but they did not feel guilty to think of the resources we were sucking up—forests, meadows and ponds, the erudition of well-educated teachers, water for roaring showers, heat that blew out of opened windows everywhere, food not eaten but mixed together for disgusting fun after lunch. They took it as their due. It was boot-camp preparation for America's leaders, which we were told we would one day be. They gave no indication that they worried that others, smarter or more worthy, might, at that very moment, be giving up hope of getting what we had.

21   I did not, however, tell the girls what I was thinking. We did not talk about how differently we saw the world. Indeed my black and their white heritage was not a starting point for our relationship, but rather was the outer boundary. I could not cross it, because there sprang up a hard wall of denial impervious to my inexperienced and insecure assault. "Well, as far as I'm concerned," one girl after another would say, "it doesn't matter to me if somebody's white or black or green or purple. I mean people are just people."

22   The motion, having been made, would invariably be seconded.

23   "Really. I mean, it's the person that counts."

24   Having castigated whites' widespread inability to see individuals for the skin in which they were wrapped, I could hardly argue with "it's the person that counts." I didn't know why they always chose green and purple to dramatize their indifference, but my ethnicity seemed diminished when the talk turned to Muppets. It was like they were taking something from me.

25   "I'm not purple." What else could you say?

26   "The truth is," somebody said, "I . . . this is *so* silly . . . I'm really embarrassed, but, it's like, there *are* some things you, God, you just feel ashamed to admit that you think about this stuff, but I always kind of wondered if, like, black guys and white guys were, like, different . . . "

27   They shrieked with laughter. Sitting on the afghan my mother had crocheted for me in the school colors of red and white, their rusty-dusty feet all over my good afghan, they laughed and had themselves a ball.

28   "Now, see, that's why people don't want to say anything," one girl said. "Look, you're getting all mad."

29   "I'm not mad."

30   "You look it."

31   "I'm not mad. I don't even know about any differences between white guys and black guys," I said deliberately avoiding the word boys. (Black manhood seemed at stake. Everything seemed at stake.) Then I added as archly as possible: "I don't mess around with white boys."

32   The party broke up soon after. I sat still, the better to control my righteous anger. It always came down to this, I thought, the old song of the South. I wanted something more meaningful. I wanted it to mean something that I had come four hundred miles from home, and sat day after day with them in Chapel, in class. I wanted it to mean something that after Martin Luther King's and Malcolm X's assassinations, we kids sweated together in sports, ate together at Seated Meal, studied and talked together at night. It couldn't be just that I was to become like them or hang onto what I'd been. It couldn't be that lonely and pointless.

33   I looked across the quad to Jimmy's window, and waved. He was not in his room, but the mere sight of his lighted window brought me back to my purpose. It was not to run my ass ragged trying to wrench some honesty out of this most disingenuous of God's people. I had come to St. Paul's to turn it, out. How had I lost sight of the simple fact?

Discussion Questions

1. Explain what you understand "turning out" to mean, given Cary's example of her mother in the department store.

2. In what way do Cary's dreams symbolize her presence and experience at St. Paul's? Do you see her sentiments shared by your own peers?

3. When Cary's schoolmates claim that "people are just people" and that "it's the person that counts," to what extent are they being unrealistic and discounting the experiences of minorities, such as Cary's?

4. Explain how important you think Cary's inclusion of her friend Jimmy's background is in this essay. How different would her story have been had she not included Jimmy in it?

5. How successful do you think Cary was in "turning it out" at St. Paul's? What in her essay leads you to your answer?

The Achievement of Desire

Richard Rodriguez

The son of working-class Mexican immigrant parents, Richard Rodriguez was born in San Francisco in 1944. Spanish was his first language, and he barely spoke English when he started school at the age of five. He holds a B.A. degree from Stanford University, an M.A. degree from Columbia University, and a Ph.D. in English from the University of California at Berkeley. Since 1981 he has been a full-time writer. Rodriguez is the author of Hunger of Memory: The Education of Richard Rodriguez *(1982), a series of autobiographical essays in which the following essay appears, and* Days of Obligation: An Argument with My Mexican Father *(1992). Rodriguez writes with care and thoughtfulness about the tug he feels between assimilating into the American culture and pleasing his parents. Notice the way Rodriguez uses parentheses to make his readers privy to what he was really thinking.*

1   I stand in the ghetto classroom—"the guest speaker"—attempting to lecture on the mystery of the sounds of our words to rows of diffident students. "Don't you hear it? Listen! The music of our words. *'Sumer is i-cumen in. . . .'* And songs on the car radio. We need Aretha Franklin's voice to fill plain words with music—her life." In the face of their empty stares, I try to create an enthusiasm. But the girls in the back row turn to watch some boy passing outside. There are flutters of smiles, waves. And someone's mouth elongates heavy, silent words through the barrier of glass. Silent words—the lips straining to shape each voiceless syllable: *"Meet meee late errr."* By the door, the instructor smiles at me, apparently hoping that I will be able to spark some enthusiasm in the class. But only one student seems to be listening. A girl, maybe fourteen. In this gray room her eyes shine with ambition. She keeps nodding and nodding at all that I say; she even takes notes. And each time I ask a question, she jerks up and down in her desk like a marionette, while her hand waves over the bowed heads of her classmates. It is myself (as a boy) I see as she faces me now (a man in my thirties).

2   The boy who first entered a classroom barely able to speak English, twenty years later concluded his studies in the stately quiet of the reading room in the British Museum. Thus with one sentence I can summarize my academic career. It will be harder to summarize what sort of life connects the boy to the man.

3   With every award, each graduation from one level of education to the next, people I'd meet would congratulate me. Their refrain always the same: "Your parents must be very proud." Sometimes then they'd ask me how I managed it—my "success." (How?) After a while, I had several

quick answers to give in reply. I'd admit, for one thing, that I went to an excellent grammar school. (My earliest teachers, the nuns, made my success their ambition.) And my brother and both my sisters were very good students. (They often brought home the shiny school trophies I came to want.) And my mother and father always encouraged me. (At every graduation they were behind the stunning flash of the camera when I turned to look at the crowd.)

4   As important as these factors were, however, they account inadequately for my academic advance. Nor do they suggest what an odd success I managed. For although I was a very good student, I was also a very bad student. I was a "scholarship boy," a certain kind of scholarship boy. Always successful, I was always unconfident. Exhilarated by my progress. Sad. I became the prized student—anxious and eager to learn. Too eager, too anxious—an imitative and unoriginal pupil. My brother and two sisters enjoyed the advantages I did, and they grew to be as successful as I, but none of them ever seemed so anxious about their schooling. A second-grade student, I was the one who came home and corrected the "simple" grammatical mistakes of our parents. ("Two negatives make a positive.") Proudly I announced—to my family's startled silence—that a teacher had said I was losing all trace of a Spanish accent. I was oddly annoyed when I was unable to get parental help with a homework assignment. The night my father tried to help me with an arithmetic exercise, he kept reading the instructions, each time more deliberately, until I pried the textbook out of his hands, saying, "I'll try to figure it out some more by myself."

5   When I reached the third grade, I outgrew such behavior. I became more tactful, careful to keep separate the two very different worlds of my day. But then, with ever-increasing intensity, I devoted myself to my studies. I became bookish, puzzling to all my family. Ambition set me apart. When my brother saw me struggling home with stacks of library books, he would laugh, shouting: "Hey, Four Eyes!" My father opened a closet one day and was startled to find me inside, reading a novel. My mother would find me reading when I was supposed to be asleep or helping around the house or playing outside. In a voice angry or worried or just curious, she'd ask: "What do you see in your books?" It became the family's joke. When I was called and wouldn't reply, someone would say I must be hiding under my bed with a book.

6   (How did I manage my success?)

7   What I am about to say to you has taken me more than twenty years to admit: *A primary reason for my success in the classroom was that I couldn't forget that schooling was changing me and separating me from the life I enjoyed before becoming a student.* That simple realization! For years I never spoke to anyone about it. Never mentioned a thing to my family or my teachers or classmates. From a very early age, I understood enough, just enough about my classroom experiences to keep what I knew repressed, hidden beneath layers of embarrassment. Not until my last months as a graduate student, nearly thirty years old, was it possible for me to think much about the rea-

sons for my academic success. Only then. At the end of my schooling, I needed to determine how far I had moved from my past. The adult finally confronted, and now must publicly say, what the child shuddered from knowing and could never admit to himself or to those many faces that smiled at his every success. ("Your parents must be very proud. . . .")

I

8   At the end, in the British Museum (too distracted to finish my dissertation) for weeks I read, speed-read, books by modern educational theorists, only to find infrequent and slight mention of students like me. (Much more is written about the more typical case, the lower-class student who barely is helped by his schooling.) Then one day, leafing through Richard Hoggart's *The Uses of Literacy,* I found, in his description of the scholarship boy, myself. For the first time I realized that there were other students like me, and so I was able to frame the meaning of my academic success, its consequent price—the loss.

9   Hoggart's description is distinguished, at least initially, by deep understanding. What he grasps very well is that the scholarship boy must move between environments, his home and the classroom, which are at cultural extremes, opposed. With his family, the boy has the intense pleasure of intimacy, the family's consolation in feeling public alienation. Lavish emotions texture home life. *Then,* at school, the instruction bids him to trust lonely reason primarily. Immediate needs set the pace of his parents' lives. From his mother and father the boy learns to trust spontaneity and nonrational ways of knowing. *Then,* at school, there is mental calm. Teachers emphasize the value of a reflectiveness that opens a space between thinking and immediate action.

10   Years of schooling must pass before the boy will be able to sketch the cultural differences in his day as abstractly as this. But he senses those differences early. Perhaps as early as the night he brings home an assignment from school and finds the house too noisy for study.

> He has to be more and more alone, if he is going to "get on."
> He will have, probably unconsciously, to oppose the ethos of the hearth, the intense gregariousness of the working-class family group. Since everything centres upon the living-room, there is unlikely to be a room of his own; the bedrooms are cold and inhospitable, and to warm them or the front room, if there is one, would not only be expensive, but would require an imaginative leap—out of the tradition—which most families are not capable of making. There is a corner of the living-room table. On the other side Mother is ironing, the wireless is on, someone is singing a snatch of song or Father says intermittently whatever

comes into his head. The boy has to cut himself off mentally, so as to do his homework, as well as he can.[1]

The next day, the lesson is as apparent at school. There are even rows of desks. Discussion is ordered. The boy must rehearse his thoughts and raise his hand before speaking out in a loud voice to an audience of classmates. And there is time enough, and silence, to think about ideas (big ideas) never considered at home by his parents.

11   Not for the working-class child alone is adjustment to the classroom difficult. Good schooling requires that any student alter early childhood habits. But the working-class child is usually least prepared for the change. And, unlike many middle-class children, he goes home and sees in his parents a way of life not only different but starkly opposed to that of the classroom. (He enters the house and hears his parents talking in ways his teachers discourage.)

12   Without extraordinary determination and the great assistance of others—at home and at school—there is little chance for success. Typically most working-class children are barely changed by the classroom. The exception succeeds. The relative few become scholarship students. Of these, Richard Hoggart estimates, most manage a fairly graceful transition. Somehow they learn to live in the two very different worlds of their day. There are some others, however, those Hoggart pejoratively terms "scholarship boys," for whom success comes with special anxiety. Scholarship boy: good student, troubled son. The child is "moderately endowed," intellectually mediocre, Hoggart supposes—though it may be more pertinent to note the special qualities of temperament in the child. High-strung child. Brooding. Sensitive. Haunted by the knowledge that one *chooses* to become a student. (Education is not an inevitable or natural step in growing up.) Here is a child who cannot forget that his academic success distances him from a life he loved, even from his own memory of himself.

13   Initially, he wavers, balances allegiance. ("The boy is himself [until he reaches, say, the upper forms] very much of *both* the worlds of home and school. He is enormously obedient to the dictates of the world of school, but emotionally still strongly wants to continue as part of the family circle.") Gradually, necessarily, the balance is lost. The boy needs to spend more and more time studying, each night enclosing himself in the silence permitted and required by intense concentration. He takes his first step toward academic success, away from his family.

14   From the very first days, through the years following, it will be with his parents—the figures of lost authority, the persons toward whom he feels deepest love—that the change will be most powerfully measured. A separation will unravel between them. Advancing in his studies, the boy notices that his mother and father have not changed as much as he.

1. All quotations in this chapter are from Richard Hoggart, *The Uses of Literacy* (London: Chatto and Windus, 1957), chapter 10. [author's note]

Rather, when he sees them, they often remind him of the person he once was and the life he earlier shared with them. He realizes what some Romantics also know when they praise the working class for the capacity for human closeness, qualities of passion and spontaneity, that the rest of us experience in like measure only in the earliest part of our youth. For the Romantic, this doesn't make working-class life childish. Working-class life challenges precisely because it is an *adult* way of life.

15   The scholarship boy reaches a different conclusion. He cannot afford to admire his parents. (How could he and still pursue such a contrary life?) He permits himself embarrassment at their lack of education. And to evade nostalgia for the life he has lost, he concentrates on the benefits education will bestow upon him. He becomes especially ambitious. Without the support of old certainties and consolations, almost mechanically, he assumes the procedures and doctrines of the classroom. The kind of allegiance the young student might have given his mother and father only days earlier, he transfers to the teacher, the new figure of authority. "[The scholarship boy] tends to make a father-figure of his form-master," Hoggart observes.

16   But Hoggart's calm prose only makes me recall the urgency with which I came to idolize my grammar school teachers. I began by imitating their accents, using their diction, trusting their every direction. The very first facts they dispensed, I grasped with awe. Any book they told me to read, I read—then waited for them to tell me which books I enjoyed. Their every casual opinion I came to adopt and to trumpet when I returned home. I stayed after school "to help"—to get my teacher's undivided attention. It was the nun's encouragement that mattered most to me. (She understood exactly what—my parents never seemed to appraise so well—all my achievements entailed.) Memory gently caressed each word of praise bestowed in the classroom so that compliments teachers paid me years ago come quickly to mind even today.

17   The enthusiasm I felt in second-grade classes I flaunted before both my parents. The docile, obedient student came home a shrill and precocious son who insisted on correcting and teaching his parents with the remark: "My teacher told us. . . ."

18   I intended to hurt my mother and father. I was still angry at them for having encouraged me toward classroom English. But gradually this anger was exhausted, replaced by guilt as school grew more and more attractive to me. I grew increasingly successful, a talkative student. My hand was raised in the classroom; I yearned to answer any question. At home, life was less noisy than it had been. (I spoke to classmates and teachers more often each day than to family members.) Quiet at home, I sat with my papers for hours each night. I never forgot that schooling had irretrievably changed my family's life. That knowledge, however, did not weaken ambition. Instead, it strengthened resolve. Those times I remembered the loss of my past with regret, I quickly reminded myself of all the things my teachers could give me. (They could make me an educated man.) I tightened my grip on pencil and books. I evaded nostalgia.

Tried hard to forget. But one does not forget by trying to forget. One only remembers. I remembered too well that education had changed my family's life. I would not have become a scholarship boy had I not so often remembered.

19   Once she was sure that her children knew English, my mother would tell us, "You should keep up your Spanish." Voices playfully groaned in response. *"¡Pochos!"* my mother would tease. I listened silently.

20   After a while, I grew more calm at home. I developed tact. A fourth-grade student, I was no longer the show-off in front of my parents. I became a conventionally dutiful son, politely affectionate, cheerful enough, even—for reasons beyond choosing—my father's favorite. And much about my family life was easy then, comfortable, happy in the rhythm of our living together: hearing my father getting ready for work; eating the breakfast my mother had made me; looking up from a novel to hear my brother or one of my sisters playing with friends in the backyard; in winter, coming upon the house all lighted up after dark.

21   But withheld from my mother and father was any mention of what most mattered to me: the extraordinary experience of first-learning. Late afternoon: In the midst of preparing dinner, my mother would come up behind me while I was trying to read. Her head just over mine, her breath warmly scented with food. "What are you reading?" Or, "Tell me all about your new courses." I would barely respond, "Just the usual things, nothing special." (A half smile, then silence. Her head moving back in the silence. Silence! Instead of the flood of intimate sounds that had once flowed smoothly between us, there was this silence.) After dinner, I would rush to a bedroom with papers and books. As often as possible, I resisted parental pleas to "save lights" by coming to the kitchen to work. I kept so much, so often, to myself. Sad. Enthusiastic. Troubled by the excitement of coming upon new ideas. Eager. Fascinated by the promising texture of a brand-new book. I hoarded the pleasures of learning. Alone for hours. Enthralled. Nervous. I rarely looked away from my books—or back on my memories. Nights when relatives visited and the front rooms were warmed by Spanish sounds, I slipped quietly out of the house.

22   It mattered that education was changing me. It never ceased to matter. My brother and sisters would giggle at our mother's mispronounced words. They'd correct her gently. My mother laughed girlishly one night, trying not to pronounce *sheep* as *ship*. From a distance I listened sullenly. From that distance, pretending not to notice on another occasion, I saw my father looking at the title pages of my library books. That was the scene on my mind when I walked home with a fourth-grade companion and heard him say that his parents read to him every night. (A strange-sounding book—*Winnie the Pooh.*) Immediately, I wanted to know, "What is it like?" My companion, however, thought I wanted to know about the plot of the book. Another day, my mother surprised me by asking for a "nice" book to read. "Something not too hard you think I might like." Carefully I chose one, Willa Cather's *My Ántonia*. But when, several weeks later, I

happened to see it next to her bed unread except for the first few pages, I was furious and suddenly wanted to cry. I grabbed up the book and took it back to my room and placed it in its place, alphabetically on my shelf.

23   "Your parents must be very proud of you." People began to say that to me about the time I was in sixth grade. To answer affirmatively, I'd smile. Shyly I'd smile, never betraying my sense of the irony: I was not proud of my mother and father. I was embarrassed by their lack of education. It was not that I ever thought they were stupid, though stupidly I took for granted their enormous native intelligence. Simply, what mattered to me was that they were not like my teachers.

24   But, "Why didn't you tell us about the award?" my mother demanded, her frown weakened by pride. At the grammar school ceremony several weeks after, her eyes were brighter than the trophy I'd won. Pushing back the hair from my forehead, she whispered that I had "shown" the *gringos*. A few minutes later, I heard my father speak to my teacher and felt ashamed of his labored, accented words. Then guilty for the shame. I felt such contrary feelings. (There is no simple road-map through the heart of the scholarship boy.) My teacher was so soft-spoken and her words were edged sharp and clean. I admired her until it seemed to me that she spoke too carefully. Sensing that she was condescending to them, I became nervous. Resentful. Protective. I tried to move my parents away. "You both must be very proud of Richard," the nun said. They responded quickly. (They were proud.) "We are proud of all our children." Then this afterthought: "They sure didn't get their brains from us." They all laughed. I smiled.

25   Tightening the irony into a knot was the knowledge that my parents were always behind me. They made success possible. They evened the path. They sent their children to parochial schools because the nuns "teach better." They paid a tuition they couldn't afford. They spoke English to us.

26   For their children my parents wanted chances they never had—an easier way. It saddened my mother to learn that some relatives forced their children to start working right after high school. To *her* children she would say, "Get all the education you can." In schooling she recognized the key to job advancement. And with the remark she remembered her past.

27   As a girl new to America my mother had been awarded a high school diploma by teachers too careless or busy to notice that she hardly spoke English. On her own, she determined to learn how to type. That skill got her jobs typing envelopes in letter shops, and it encouraged in her an optimism about the possibility of advancement. (Each morning when her sisters put on uniforms, she chose a bright-colored dress.) The years of young womanhood passed, and her typing speed increased. She also became an excellent speller of words she mispronounced. "And I've never been to college," she'd say, smiling, when her children asked her to spell words they were too lazy to look up in a dictionary.

28   Typing, however, was dead-end work. Finally frustrating. When her youngest child started high school, my mother got a full-time office job once again. (Her paycheck combined with my father's to make us—in fact—what we had already become in our imagination of ourselves—middle class.) She worked then for the (California) state government in numbered civil service positions secured by examinations. The old ambition of her youth was rekindled. During the lunch hour, she consulted bulletin boards for announcements of openings. One day she saw mention of something called an "anti-poverty agency." A typing job. A glamorous job, part of the governor's staff. "A knowledge of Spanish required." Without hesitation she applied and became nervous only when the job was suddenly hers.

29   "Everyone comes to work all dressed up," she reported at night. And didn't need to say more than that her co-workers wouldn't let her answer the phones. She was only a typist, after all, albeit a very fast typist. And an excellent speller. One morning there was a letter to be sent to a Washington cabinet officer. On the dictating tape, a voice referred to urban guerrillas. My mother typed (the wrong word, correctly): "gorillas." The mistake horrified the anti-poverty bureaucrats who shortly after arranged to have her returned to her previous position. She would go no further. So she willed her ambition to her children. "Get all the education you can; with an education you can do anything." (With a good education *she* could have done anything.)

30   When I was in high school, I admitted to my mother that I planned to become a teacher someday. That seemed to please her. But I never tried to explain that it was not the occupation of teaching I yearned for as much as it was something more elusive: I wanted to *be* like my teachers, to possess their knowledge, to assume their authority, their confidence, even to assume a teacher's persona.

31   In contrast to my mother, my father never verbally encouraged his children's academic success. Nor did he often praise us. My mother had to remind him to "say something" to one of his children who scored some academic success. But whereas my mother saw in education the opportunity for job advancement, my father recognized that education provided an even more startling possibility: It could enable a person to escape from a life of mere labor.

32   In Mexico, orphaned when he was eight, my father left school to work as an "apprentice" for an uncle. Twelve years later, he left Mexico in frustration and arrived in America. He had great expectations then of becoming an engineer. ("Work for my hands and my head.") He knew a Catholic priest who promised to get him money enough to study full time for a high school diploma. But the promises came to nothing. Instead there was a dark succession of warehouse, cannery, and factory jobs. After work he went to night school along with my mother. A year, two passed. Nothing much changed, except that fatigue worked its way into the bone;

then everything changed. He didn't talk anymore of becoming an engineer. He stayed outside on the steps of the school while my mother went inside to learn typing and shorthand.

33   By the time I was born, my father worked at "clean" jobs. For a time he was a janitor at a fancy department store. ("Easy work; the machines do it all.") Later he became a dental technician. ("Simple.") But by then he was pessimistic about the ultimate meaning of work and the possibility of ever escaping its claims. In some of my earliest memories of him, my father already seems aged by fatigue. (He has never really grown old like my mother.) From boyhood to manhood, I have remembered him in a single image: seated, asleep on the sofa, his head thrown back in a hideous corpselike grin, the evening newspaper spread out before him. "But look at all you've accomplished," his best friend said to him once. My father said nothing. Only smiled.

34   It was my father who laughed when I claimed to be tired by reading and writing. It was he who teased me for having soft hands. (He seemed to sense that some great achievement of leisure was implied by my papers and books.) It was my father who became angry while watching on television some woman at the Miss America contest tell the announcer that she was going to college. ("Majoring in fine arts.") "College!" he snarled. He despised the trivialization of higher education, the inflated grades and cheapened diplomas, the half education that so often passed as mass education in my generation.

35   It was my father again who wondered why I didn't display my awards on the wall of my bedroom. He said he liked to go to doctors' offices and see their certificates and degrees on the wall. ("Nice.") My citations from school got left in closets at home. The gleaming figure astride one of my trophies was broken, wingless, after hitting the ground. My medals were placed in a jar of loose change. And when I lost my high school diploma, my father found it as it was about to be thrown out with the trash. Without telling me, he put it away with his own things for safekeeping.

36   These memories slammed together at the instant of hearing that refrain familiar to all scholarship students: "Your parents must be very proud. . . ." Yes, my parents were proud. I knew it. But my parents regarded my progress with more than mere pride. They endured my early precocious behavior—but with what private anger and humiliation? As their children got older and would come home to challenge ideas both of them held, they argued before submitting to the force of logic or superior factual evidence with the disclaimer, "It's what we were taught in our time to believe." These discussions ended abruptly, though my mother remembered them on other occasions when she complained that our "big ideas" were going to our heads. More acute was her complaint that the family wasn't close anymore, like some others she knew. Why weren't we close, "more in the Mexican style"? Everyone is so private, she added. And she

mimicked the yes and no answers she got in reply to her questions. Why didn't we talk more? (My father never asked.) I never said.

37   I was the first in my family who asked to leave home when it came time to go to college. I had been admitted to Stanford, one hundred miles away. My departure would only make physically apparent the separation that had occurred long before. But it was going too far. In the months preceding my leaving, I heard the question my mother never asked except indirectly. In the hot kitchen, tired at the end of her workday, she demanded to know, "Why aren't the colleges here in Sacramento good enough for you? They are for your brother and sister." In the middle of a car ride, not turning to face me, she wondered, "Why do you need to go so far away?" Late at night, ironing, she said with disgust, "Why do you have to put us through this big expense? You know your scholarship will never cover it all." But when September came there was a rush to get everything ready. In a bedroom that last night I packed the big brown valise, and my mother sat nearby sewing initials onto the clothes I would take. And she said no more about my leaving.

38   Months later, two weeks of Christmas vacation: The first hours home were the hardest. ("What's new?") My parents and I sat in the kitchen for a conversation. (But, lacking the same words to develop our sentences and to shape our interests, what was there to say? What could I tell them of the term paper I had just finished on the "universality of Shakespeare's appeal"?) I mentioned only small, obvious things: my dormitory life; weekend trips I had taken; random events. They responded with news of their own. (One was almost grateful for a family crisis about which there was much to discuss.) We tried to make our conversation seem like more than an interview.

II

39   From an early age I knew that my mother and father could read and write both Spanish and English. I had observed my father making his way through what, I now suppose, must have been income tax forms. On other occasions I waited apprehensively while my mother read onion-paper letters airmailed from Mexico with news of a relative's illness or death. For both my parents, however, reading was something done out of necessity and as quickly as possible. Never did I see either of them read an entire book. Nor did I see them read for pleasure. Their reading consisted of work manuals, prayer books, newspaper, recipes.

40   Richard Hoggart imagines how, at home,

. . . [The scholarship boy] sees strewn around, and reads regularly himself, magazines which are never mentioned at school, which seem not to belong to the world to which the school introduces him; at school he hears about and reads books never mentioned at home. When he brings those books into the house they do not take their place with other books which the family are reading, for often there are none or almost none; his books look, rather, like strange tools.

In our house each school year would begin with my mother's careful instruction: "Don't write in your books so we can sell them at the end of the year." The remark was echoed in public by my teachers, but only in part: "Boys and girls, don't write in your books. You must learn to treat them with great care and respect."

41   OPEN THE DOORS OF YOUR MIND WITH BOOKS, read the red and white poster over the nun's desk in early September. It soon was apparent to me that reading was the classroom's central activity. Each course had its own book. And the information gathered from a book was unquestioned. READ TO LEARN, the sign on the wall advised in December. I privately wondered: What was the connection between reading and learning? Did one learn something only by reading it? Was an idea only an idea if it could be written down? In June, CONSIDER BOOKS YOUR BEST FRIENDS. Friends? Reading was, at best, only a chore. I needed to look up whole paragraphs of words in a dictionary. Lines of type were dizzying, the eye having to move slowly across the page, then down, and across. . . . The sentences of the first books I read were coolly impersonal. Toned hard. What most bothered me, however, was the isolation reading required. To console myself for the loneliness I'd feel when I read, I tried reading in a very soft voice. Until: "Who is doing all that talking to his neighbor?" Shortly after, remedial reading classes were arranged for me with a very old nun.

42   At the end of each school day, for nearly six months, I would meet with her in the tiny room that served as the school's library but was actually only a storeroom for used textbooks and a vast collection of *National Geographics.* Everything about our sessions pleased me: the smallness of the room; the noise of the janitor's broom hitting the edge of the long hallway outside the door; the green of the sun, lighting the wall; and the old woman's face blurred white with a beard. Most of the time we took turns. I began with my elementary text. Sentences of astonishing simplicity seemed to me lifeless and drab: "The boys ran from the rain . . . She wanted to sing . . . The kite rose in the blue." Then the old nun would read from her favorite books, usually biographies of early American presidents. Playfully she ran through complex sentences, calling the words alive with her voice, making it seem that the author somehow was speaking directly to me. I smiled just to listen to her. I sat there and sensed for the very first time some possibility of fellowship between a reader and a writer, a communication, never *intimate* like that I heard spoken words at home convey, but one nonetheless *personal.*

43   One day the nun concluded a session by asking me why I was so reluctant to read by myself. I tried to explain; said something about the way written words made me feel all alone—almost, I wanted to add but didn't, as when I spoke to myself in a room just emptied of furniture. She studied my face as I spoke; she seemed to be watching more than listening. In an uneventful voice she replied that I had nothing to fear. Didn't I realize that reading would open up whole new worlds? A book could open doors for me. It could introduce me to people and show me places I never imagined existed. She gestured toward the bookshelves. (Bare-breasted African women danced, and the shiny hubcaps of automobiles on the back covers of the *Geographic* gleamed in my mind.) I listened with respect. But her words were not very influential. I was thinking then of another consequence of literacy, one I was too shy to admit but nonetheless trusted. Books were going to make me "educated." *That* confidence enabled me, several months later, to overcome my fear of the silence.

44   In fourth grade I embarked upon a grandiose reading program. "Give me the names of important books," I would say to startled teachers. They soon found out that I had in mind "adult books." I ignored their suggestion of anything I suspected was written for children. (Not until I was in college, as a result, did I read *Huckleberry Finn* or *Alice's Adventures in Wonderland*.) Instead, I read *The Scarlet Letter* and Franklin's *Autobiography*. And whatever I read I read for extra credit. Each time I finished a book, I reported the achievement to a teacher and basked in the praise my effort earned. Despite my best efforts, however, there seemed to be more and more books I needed to read. At the library I would literally tremble as I came upon whole shelves of books I hadn't read. So I read and I read and I read: *Great Expectations;* all the short stories of Kipling; *The Babe Ruth Story;* the entire first volume of the *Encyclopaedia Britannica* (A-ANSTEY); the *Iliad; Moby Dick; Gone with the Wind; The Good Earth; Ramona; Forever Amber; The Lives of the Saints; Crime and Punishment; The Pearl*. . . . Librarians who initially frowned when I checked out the maximum ten books at a time started saving books they thought I might like. Teachers would say to the rest of the class, "I only wish the rest of you took reading as seriously as Richard obviously does."

45   But at home I would hear my mother wondering, "What do you see in your books?" (Was reading a hobby like her knitting? Was so much reading even healthy for a boy? Was it the sign of "brains"? Or was it just a convenient excuse for not helping about the house on Saturday mornings?) Always, "What do you see . . . ?"

46   What *did* I see in my books? I had the idea that they were crucial for my academic success, though I couldn't have said exactly how or why. In the sixth grade I simply concluded that what gave a book its value was some major idea or theme it contained. If that core essence could be mined and memorized, I would become learned like my teachers. I decided to record in a notebook the themes of the books that I read. After reading *Robinson*

Crusoe, I wrote that its theme was "the value of learning to live by oneself." When I completed *Wuthering Heights,* I noted the danger of "letting emotions get out of control." Rereading these brief moralistic appraisals usually left me disheartened. I couldn't believe that they were really the source of reading's value. But for many more years, they constituted the only means I had of describing to myself the educational value of books.

47   In spite of my earnestness, I found reading a pleasurable activity. I came to enjoy the lonely good company of books. Early on weekday mornings, I'd read in my bed. I'd feel a mysterious comfort then, reading in the dawn quiet—the blue-gray silence interrupted by the occasional churning of the refrigerator motor a few rooms away or the more distant sounds of a city bus beginning its run. On weekends I'd go to the public library to read, surrounded by old men and women. Or, if the weather was fine, I would take my books to the park and read in the shade of a tree. A warm summer evening was my favorite reading time. Neighbors would leave for vacation and I would water their lawns. I would sit through the twilight on the front porches or in backyards, reading to the cool, whirling sounds of the sprinklers.

48   I also had favorite writers. But often those writers I enjoyed most I was least able to value. When I read William Saroyan's *The Human Comedy,* I was immediately pleased by the narrator's warmth and the charm of his story. But as quickly I became suspicious. A book so enjoyable to read couldn't be very "important." Another summer I determined to read all the novels of Dickens. Reading his fat novels, I loved the feeling I got—after the first hundred pages—of being at home in a fictional world where I knew the names of the characters and cared about what was going to happen to them. And it bothered me that I was forced away at the conclusion, when the fiction closed tight, like a fortune-teller's fist—the futures of all the major characters neatly resolved. I never knew how to take such feelings seriously, however. Nor did I suspect that these experiences could be part of a novel's meaning. Still, there were pleasures to sustain me after I'd finish my books. Carrying a volume back to the library, I would be pleased by its weight. I'd run my fingers along the edge of the pages and marvel at the breadth of my achievement. Around my room, growing stacks of paperback books reenforced my assurance.

49   I entered high school having read hundreds of books. My habit of reading made me a confident speaker and writer of English. Reading also enabled me to sense something of the shape, the major concerns, of Western thought. (I was able to say something about Dante and Descartes and Engels and James Baldwin in my high school term papers.) In these various ways, books brought me academic success as I hoped that they would. But I was not a good reader. Merely bookish, I lacked a point of view when I read. Rather, I read in order to acquire a point of view. I vacuumed books for epigrams, scraps of information, ideas, themes—anything to fill the hollow within me and make me feel educated. When one

of my teachers suggested to his drowsy tenth-grade English class that a person could not have a "complicated idea" until he had read at least two thousand books, I heard the remark without detecting either its irony or its very complicated truth. I merely determined to compile a list of all the books I had ever read. Harsh with myself, I included only once a title I might have read several times. (How, after all, could one read a book more than once?) And I included only those books over a hundred pages in length. (Could anything shorter be a book?)

50   There was yet another high school list I compiled. One day I came across a newspaper article about the retirement of an English professor at a nearby state college. The article was accompanied by a list of the "hundred most important books of Western Civilization." "More than anything else in my life," the professor told the reporter with finality, "these books have made me all that I am." That was the kind of remark I couldn't ignore. I clipped out the list and kept it for the several months it took me to read all of the titles. Most books, of course, I barely understood. While reading Plato's *Republic*, for instance, I needed to keep looking at the book jacket comments to remind myself what the text was about. Nevertheless, with the special patience and superstition of a scholarship boy, I looked at every word of the text. And by the time I reached the last word, relieved, I convinced myself that I had read *The Republic*. In a ceremony of great pride, I solemnly crossed Plato off my list.

III

51   The scholarship boy pleases most when he is young—the working-class child struggling for academic success. To his teachers, he offers great satisfaction; his success is their proudest achievement. Many other persons offer to help him. A businessman learns the boy's story and promises to underwrite part of the cost of his college education. A woman leaves him her entire library of several hundred books when she moves. His progress is featured in a newspaper article. Many people seem happy for him. They marvel. "How did you manage so fast?" From all sides, there is lavish praise and encouragement.

52   In his grammar school classroom, however, the boy already makes students around him uneasy. They scorn his desire to succeed. They scorn him for constantly wanting the teacher's attention and praise. "Kiss Ass," they call him when his hand swings up in response to every question he hears. Later, when he makes it to college, no one will mock him aloud. But he detects annoyance on the faces of some students and even some teachers who watch him. It puzzles him often. In college, then in graduate school, he behaves much as he always has. If anything is different about him it is that he dares to anticipate the successful conclusion of his studies. At last he feels that he belongs in the classroom, and this is exactly the source of the dissatisfaction he causes. To many persons around him, he

appears too much the academic. There may be some things about him that recall his beginnings—his shabby clothes; his persistent poverty; or his dark skin (in those cases when it symbolizes his parents' disadvantaged condition)—but they only make clear how far he has moved from his past. He has used education to remake himself.

53 It bothers his fellow academics to face this. They will not say why exactly. (They sneer.) But their expectations become obvious when they are disappointed. They expect—they want—a student less changed by his schooling. If the scholarship boy, from a past so distant from the classroom, could remain in some basic way unchanged, he would be able to prove that it is possible for anyone to become educated without basically changing from the person one was.

54 Here is no fabulous hero, no idealized scholar-worker. The scholarship boy does not straddle, cannot reconcile, the two great opposing cultures of his life. His success is unromantic and plain. He sits in the classroom and offers those sitting beside him no calming reassurance about their own lives. He sits in the seminar room—a man with brown skin, the son of working-class Mexican immigrant parents. (Addressing the professor at the head of the table, his voice catches with nervousness.) There is no trace of his parents' accent in his speech. Instead he approximates the accents of teachers and classmates. Coming from *him* those sounds seem suddenly odd. Odd too is the effect produced when *he* uses academic jargon—bubbles at the tip of his tongue: "*Topos* . . . negative capability . . . vegetation imagery in Shakespearean comedy." He lifts an opinion from Coleridge, takes something else from Frye or Empson or Leavis. He even repeats exactly his professor's earlier comment. All his ideas are clearly borrowed. He seems to have no thought of his own. He chatters while his listeners smile—their look one of disdain.

55 When he is older and thus when so little of the person he was survives, the scholarship boy makes only too apparent his profound lack of *self*-confidence. This is the conventional assessment that even Richard Hoggart repeats:

> [The scholarship boy] tends to over-stress the importance of examinations, of the piling-up of knowledge and of received opinions. He discovers a technique of apparent learning, of the acquiring of facts rather than of the handling and use of facts. He learns how to receive a purely literate education, one using only a small part of the personality and challenging only a limited area of his being. He begins to see life as a ladder, as a permanent examination with some praise and some further exhortation at each stage. He becomes an expert imbiber and doler-out; his competence will vary, but will rarely be accompanied by genuine enthusiasms. He rarely feels the reality of knowledge, of other men's thoughts and imaginings, on his own pulses. . . . He has something of the blinkered pony about him. . . .

But this is criticism more accurate than fair. The scholarship boy is a very bad student. He is the great mimic; a collector of thoughts, not a thinker; the very last person in class who ever feels obliged to have an opinion of his own. In large part, however, the reason he is such a bad student is because he realizes more often and more acutely than most other students—than Hoggart himself—that education requires radical self-reformation. As a very young boy, regarding his parents, as he struggles with an early homework assignment, he knows this too well. That is why he lacks self-assurance. He does not forget that the classroom is responsible for remaking him. He relies on his teacher, depends on all that he hears in the classroom and reads in his books. He becomes in every obvious way the worst student, a dummy mouthing the opinions of others. But he would not be so bad—nor would he become so successful, a *scholarship* boy—if he did not accurately perceive that the best synonym for primary "education" is "imitation."

56   Those who would take seriously the boy's success—and his failure—would be forced to realize how great is the change any academic undergoes, how far one must move from one's past. It is easiest to ignore such considerations. So little is said about the scholarship boy in pages and pages of educational literature. Nothing is said of the silence that comes to separate the boy from his parents. Instead, one hears proposals for increasing the self-esteem of students and encouraging early intellectual independence. Paragraphs glitter with a constellation of terms like *creativity* and *originality*. (Ignored altogether is the function of imitation in a student's life.) Radical educationalists meanwhile complain that ghetto schools "oppress" students by trying to mold them, stifling native characteristics. The truer critique would be just the reverse: not that schools change ghetto students too much, but that while they might promote the occasional scholarship student, they change most students barely at all.

57   From the story of the scholarship boy there is no specific pedagogy to glean. There is, however, a much larger lesson. His story makes clear that education is a long, unglamorous, even demeaning process—*a nurturing never natural to the person one was before one entered a classroom.* At once different from most other students, the scholarship boy is also the archetypal "good student." He exaggerates the difficulty of being a student, but his exaggeration reveals a general predicament. Others are changed by their schooling as much as he. They too must re-form themselves. They must develop the skill of memory long before they become truly critical thinkers. And when they read Plato for the first several times, it will be with awe more than deep comprehension.

58   The impact of schooling on the scholarship boy is only more apparent to the boy himself and to others. Finally, although he may be laughable—a blinkered pony—the boy will not let his critics forget their own change. He ends up too much like them. When he speaks, they hear themselves echoed. In his pedantry, they trace their own. His ambitions are theirs. If his failure were singular, they might readily pity him. But he is more troubling than that. They would not scorn him if this were not so.

IV

59 Like me, Hoggart's imagined scholarship boy spends most of his years in the classroom afraid to long for his past. Only at the very end of his schooling does the boy-man become nostalgic. In this sudden change of heart, Richard Hoggart notes:

> He longs for the membership he lost, "he pines for some Nameless Eden where he never was." The nostalgia is the stronger and the more ambiguous because he is really "in quest of his own absconded self yet scared to find it." He both wants to go back and yet thinks he has gone beyond his class, feels himself weighted with knowledge of his own and their situation, which hereafter forbids him the simpler pleasures of his father and mother. . . .

According to Hoggart, the scholarship boy grows nostalgic because he remains the uncertain scholar, bright enough to have moved from his past, yet unable to feel easy, a part of a community of academics.

60 This analysis, however, only partially suggests what happened to me in my last year as a graduate student. When I traveled to London to write a dissertation on English Renaissance literature, I was finally confident of membership in a "community of scholars." But the pleasure that confidence gave me faded rapidly. After only two or three months in the reading room of the British Museum, it became clear that I had joined a lonely community. Around me each day were dour faces eclipsed by large piles of books. There were the regulars, like the old couple who arrived every morning, each holding a loop of the shopping bag which contained all their notes. And there was the historian who chattered madly to herself. ("Oh dear! Oh! Now, what's this? What? Oh, my!") There were also the faces of young men and women worn by long study. And everywhere eyes turned away the moment our glance accidentally met. Some persons I sat beside day after day, yet we passed silently at the end of the day, strangers. Still, we were united by a common respect for the written word and for scholarship. We did form a union, though one in which we remained distant from one another.

61 More profound and unsettling was the bond I recognized with those writers whose books I consulted. Whenever I opened a text that hadn't been used for years, I realized that my special interests and skills united me to a mere handful of academics. We formed an exclusive—eccentric!—society, separated from others who would never care or be able to share our concerns. (The pages I turned were stiff like layers of dead skin.) I began to wonder: Who, beside my dissertation director and a few faculty members, would ever read what I wrote? And: Was my dissertation much more than an act of social withdrawal? These questions went unanswered in the silence of the Museum reading room. They remained to trouble me after

I'd leave the library each afternoon and feel myself shy—unsteady, speaking simple sentences at the grocer's or the butcher's on my way back to my bed-sitter.

62   Meanwhile my file cards accumulated. A professional, I knew exactly how to search a book for pertinent information. I could quickly assess and summarize the usability of the many books I consulted. But whenever I started to write, I knew too much (and not enough) to be able to write anything but sentences that were overly cautious, timid, strained brittle under the heavy weight of footnotes and qualifications. I seemed unable to dare a passionate statement. I felt drawn by professionalism to the edge of sterility, capable of no more than pedantic, lifeless, unassailable prose.

63   *Then* nostalgia began.

64   After years spent unwilling to admit its attractions, I gestured nostalgically toward the past. I yearned for that time when I had not been so alone. I became impatient with books. I wanted experience more immediate. I feared the library's silence. I silently scorned the gray, timid faces around me. I grew to hate the growing pages of my dissertation on genre and Renaissance literature. (In my mind I heard relatives laughing as they tried to make sense of its title.) I wanted something—I couldn't say exactly what. I told myself that I wanted a more passionate life. And a life less thoughtful. And above all, I wanted to be less alone. One day I heard some Spanish academics whispering back and forth to each other and their sounds seemed ghostly voices recalling my life. Yearning became preoccupation then. Boyhood memories beckoned, flooded my mind. (Laughing intimate voices. Bounding up the front steps of the porch. A sudden embrace inside the door.)

65   For weeks after, I turned to books by educational experts. I needed to learn how far I had moved from my past—to determine how fast I would be able to recover something of it once again. But I found little. Only a chapter in a book by Richard Hoggart. . . . I left the reading room and the circle of faces.

66   I came home. After the year in England, I spent three summer months living with my mother and father, relieved by how easy it was to be home. It no longer seemed very important to me that we had little to say. I felt easy sitting and eating and walking with them. I watched them, nevertheless, looking for evidence of those elastic, sturdy strands that bind generations in a web of inheritance. I thought as I watched my mother one night: Of course a friend had been right when she told me that I gestured and laughed just like my mother. Another time I saw for myself: My father's eyes were much like my own, constantly watchful.

67   But after the early relief, this return, came suspicion, nagging until I realized that I had not neatly sidestepped the impact of schooling. My desire to do so was precisely the measure of how much I remained an academic. *Negatively* (for that is how this idea first occurred to me): My need to think so much and so abstractly about my parents and our relationship was

in itself an indication of my long education. My father and mother did not pass their time thinking about the cultural meanings of their experience. It was I who described their daily lives with airy ideas. And yet, *positively:* The ability to consider experience so abstractly allowed me to shape into desire what would otherwise have remained indefinite, meaningless longing in the British Museum. If, because of my schooling, I had grown culturally separated from my parents, my education finally had given me ways of speaking and caring about that fact.

68 My best teachers in college and graduate school, years before, had tried to prepare me for this conclusion, I think, when they discussed texts of aristocratic pastoral literature. Faithfully, I wrote down all that they said. I memorized it: "The praise of the unlettered by the highly educated is one of the primary themes of 'elitist' literature." But, "the importance of the praise given the unsolitary, richly passionate and spontaneous life is that it simultaneously reflects the value of a reflective life." I heard it all. But there was no way for any of it to mean very much to me. I was a scholarship boy at the time, busily laddering my way up the rungs of education. To pass an examination, I copied down exactly what my teachers told me. It would require many more years of schooling (an inevitable miseducation) in which I came to trust the silence of reading and the habit of abstracting from immediate experience—moving away from a life of closeness and immediacy I remembered with my parents, growing older—before I turned unafraid to desire the past, and thereby achieved what had eluded me for so long—the end of education.

Discussion Questions

1. Rodriguez writes of his education separating himself culturally from his parents. Do you think education is the culprit or is it an excuse? If you know of other people whose education—or lack of it—alienated them from their families, how similar are their experiences to Rodriguez's?

2. In paragraph 7, Rodriguez confesses that "what [he is] about to say . . . has taken . . . more than twenty years to admit." Why do you think it has taken so long? Is his explanation believable?

3. Rodriguez uses parentheses to signal to the reader his own unspoken thoughts. How effective do you find this technique? Explain your answer.

4. Paragraphs 51 through 58 are devoted to the scholarship student who uses education to "remake" himself. Do you agree with Rodriguez's assessment of such students? Why or why not?

5. Explain what you see as the significance of the title of Rodriguez's essay.

Chapter 3 Writing Topics

1. As children, we often dream of being old enough to do something we are not yet allowed to do (e.g., drive a car, date, vacation without parents). Describe a time when, as an adult, you fulfilled a childhood fantasy. Did the reality live up to the dream?

2. Write an essay in which you recall several experiences you had while working or important discussions with others in which you learned a valuable lesson.

3. Many people might not fully appreciate the excitement of living during a certain time. Choose a specific event when you felt truly excited about living, "the extraordinary sense of alivement" as Frederick Buechner calls it, and describe what was happening in the world and in you at that time.

4. Some of our journeys in life involve searches for our own identities as individuals, for other people to love, or even for suitable occupations. Select one such journey and describe it so others can understand what you went through and who you became.

5. Have you ever experienced being disappointed by what was supposed to have been a happy and momentous occasion (e.g., an important date, a big party, a high school graduation)? Write an essay in which you sharply contrast your expectations with what actually transpired.

6. Recall a time when your perspective was different from that of someone younger than yourself, thus making you feel "older and wiser." What precipitated this feeling? How did it feel being "grown up"?

7. Each generation seems to be characterized by a certain term (e.g., the "me" generation). In an essay, examine the ways in which you are (or are not) representative of your generation. Cite specific examples that lead you to your answer and be sure to choose a term that aptly describes your generation.

8. Examine a turning point in your life, a time when one stage of life was coming to an end and another starting. What was happening in your life at that time? What emotions did you experience? What were your thoughts?

9. Was there ever a time in your life when you didn't want to "grow up," when being where and who you were at that time felt too comfortable to relinquish? Describe such a time.

10. Recall a time in your life when you would go to any lengths to "fit in." What did you do? Were you successful? Were you pleased with the outcome or did you regret your actions?

11. Can you remember a time when you surprised even yourself at how well you performed a task? Describe it so that others can experience the surprise along with you.

12. How has your race, ethnic background, or gender put upon you strong pressures to act in a certain way, either in keeping with or breaking from others' expectations? Did you regret the way you acted, or did you feel comfortable with it? Describe the situation.

13. Analyze the ways in which your education has separated you from or drawn you closer to your family and friends.

14. Has there ever been a time when you felt your parents or friends were unable to understand something important about you because they were not "in tune" with your life? Describe such a time, its outcome, and your reactions to what unfolded.

Chapter 4

On Friendship

Fate makes relatives, but choice makes friends.

—Delile

Whatever people I take into my life I take in because they challenge me and I challenge them at the deepest level.

—May Sarton

Two friends, two bodies with one soul inspired.

—Homer

Friendship of a kind that cannot easily be reversed tomorrow must have its roots in common interests and shared beliefs, and even between nations, in some personal feeling.

—Barbara Tuchman

Without a horse and a dog and a friend, man would expire.

—Rudyard Kipling

Just as family relationships and educational experiences provide rich material worthy of further inquiry, so does friendship. From the time we are children to the time we die, we rely on friends as playmates, confidantes, and supporters in ways in which we can rely on no other people. Rarely is there a time in our lives when we don't count on friends and take pride in being called a friend.

If you were to look around, you would find ample evidence of the way friends are portrayed in our society. Turn on the television, for example, and see a demonstration of male bonding in the Levi's Dockers commercials. Switch the channel and hear the reminiscences of two old roommates spurred on by their drinking General Foods International coffee. Or close to any holiday, watch Merlin Olson urge us to send flowers to our loved ones who live far away.

Nowhere is the importance of friendship more evident than in the arts. Friendship has long been a theme in literature, visual arts, and music lyrics. Recent films, too, have focused on the value of friendship: *Butch Cassidy and the Sundance Kid, The Big Chill, The Breakfast Club, Best Friends, Thelma and Louise, Beaches, Stella, Fried Green Tomatoes, Steel Magnolias,* and *A League of Their Own,* to name a few. Friendship has been portrayed as more than a means of giving and receiving, helping others in times of crisis and having the favor returned. Justifiably, people view it as an essential part of their lives.

Consider the following questions: What do you look for in a friend? What does it mean to have a friend and to be a friend? How do your friends influence and help shape you into the person you are? How have your friendships changed as you matured? And why are friendships such an integral part of your life? These are but a handful of questions that the essays in Chapter 4 address.

The first pair of essays deal with gender-related issues: Barbara Ehrenreich starts off by pondering the importance of "best" friendship, specifically the reasons why it is applauded in men and belittled in women. Then Steve Tesich focuses on the differences he finds in his friendships with men as opposed to those with women. In "Fish Gotta Swim," Susan Allen Toth recounts her first real date and the boyfriends who followed. Next, Jennifer Crichton describes why forming friendships during the first semester in college is so difficult yet so essential.

The last four essays center around the authors' special friendships. May Sarton details her friendship with her hired hand, Perley Cole. Zora Neale Hurston describes the friendships she had with two influential women in her life. Then Bill Murphy reflects on the ways in which his brother is also his friend. In the final selection, Gary Soto looks forward to a visit with some good friends.

The essays in this chapter no doubt will motivate you to think about your own friends, the importance you attach to friendship, your definition of a real friend, and the ways in which you have been a friend to others. Pay attention to the way all of the writers go about describing their friends, reflecting on the topic of friendship, and showing how they have been changed or shaped by their friendships. What can you learn from their experiences? Just as importantly, what can you contribute from yours?

In Praise of "Best" Friends

Barbara Ehrenreich

*B*orn in 1941 in Montana, Barbara Ehrenreich holds a B.A. degree *from Reed College and a Ph.D. degree from Rockefeller University. While a fellow at the Institute for Policy Studies in Washington, D.C., she edited* Seven Days *magazine. A contributing editor of* Ms. *magazine since 1981, Ehrenreich also writes for* Time *magazine. Ehrenreich has taught at the State University of New York at Old Westbury. Her essays have appeared in such magazines as* Mother Jones, Nation, *and the* New York Times Magazine. *She is the author of* Fear of Falling: The Inner Life of the Middle Class *(1989),* The Worst Years of Our Lives: Irreverent Notes from a Decade of Greed *(1990) and* Kipper's Game *(1994). The following essay, which first appeared in* Ms. *magazine, makes a strong case for the importance—indeed the necessity—of people having "best" friends.*

1   All the politicians, these days, are "profamily," but I've never heard of one who was "profriendship." This is too bad and possibly short-sighted. After all, most of us would never survive our families if we didn't have our friends.

2   I'm especially concerned about the fine old institution of "best friends." I realized that it was on shaky ground a few months ago, when the occasion arose to introduce my own best friend (we'll call her Joan) at a somewhat intimidating gathering. I got as far as saying, "I am very proud to introduce my best friend, Joan . . . " when suddenly I wasn't proud at all. I was blushing. "Best friend," I realized as soon as I heard the words out loud, sounds like something left over from sixth-grade cliques: the kind of thing where if Sandy saw you talking to Stephanie at recess, she might tell you after school that she wasn't going to be your best friend anymore, and so forth. Why couldn't I have just said "my good friend Joan" or something *grown-up* like that?

3   But Joan is not just any friend, or even a "good friend"; she is my best friend. We have celebrated each other's triumphs together, nursed each other through savage breakups with the various men in our lives, discussed the Great Issues of Our Time, and cackled insanely over things that were, objectively speaking, not even funny. We have quarreled and made up; we've lived in the same house and we've lived thousands of miles apart. We've learned to say hard things, like "You really upset me when . . . " and even "I love you." Yet, for all this, our relationship has no earthly weight or status. I can't even say the name for it without sounding profoundly silly.

4   Why is best friendship, particularly between women, so undervalued and unrecognized? Partly, no doubt, because women themselves have always been so undervalued and unrecognized. In the Western tradition, male best friendships are the stuff of history and high drama. Reread

Homer, for example, and you'll realize that Troy did not fall because Paris, that spoiled Trojan prince, loved Helen, but because Achilles so loved Patroclus. It was Patroclus's death, at the hands of the Trojans, that made Achilles snap out of his sulk long enough to slay the Trojans' greatest warrior and guarantee victory to the Greeks. Did Helen have a best friend, or any friend at all? We'll never know, because the only best friendships that have survived in history and legend are man-on-man: Alexander and Hephaestion, Orestes and Pylades, Heracles and Iolas.

5   Christianity did not improve the status of female friendship. "Every woman ought to be filled with shame at the thought that she is a woman," declaimed one of the early church fathers, Clement of Alexandria, and when two women got together, the shame presumably doubled. Male friendship was still supposed to be a breeding ground for all kinds of upstanding traits—honor, altruism, courage, faith, loyalty. Consider Arthur's friendship with Lancelot, which easily survived the latter's dalliance with Queen Guinevere. But when two women got together, the best you could hope for, apparently, was bitchiness, and the worst was witchcraft.

6   Yet, without the slightest encouragement from history, women have persisted in finding best friends. According to recent feminist scholarship, the nineteenth century seems to have been a heyday of female best friendship. In fact, feminism might never have gotten off the ground at all if it hadn't been for the enduring bond between Elizabeth Cady Stanton, the theoretician of the movement, and Susan B. Anthony, the movement's first great pragmatist.

7   And they are only the most famous best friends. According to Lillian Faderman's book *Surpassing the Love of Men,* there were thousands of anonymous female couples who wrote passionate letters to each other, exchanged promises and tokens of love, and suffered through the separations occasioned by marriage and migration. Feminist scholars have debated whether these great best friendships were actually lesbian, sexual relationships—a question that I find both deeply fascinating (if these were lesbian relationships, were the women involved conscious of what a bold and subversive step they had taken?) and somewhat beside the point. What matters is that these women honored their friendships, and sought ways to give them the kind of coherence and meaning that the larger society reserved only for marriage."

8   In the twentieth century, female best friendship was largely eclipsed by the new ideal of the "companionate marriage." At least in the middle-class culture that celebrated "togetherness," your *husband* was now supposed to be your best friend, as well, of course, as being your lover, provider, co-parent, housemate, and principal heir. My own theory (profamily politicians please take note) is that these expectations have done more damage to the institution of marriage than no-fault divorce and the sexual revolution combined. No man can be all things to even one woman. And the foolish idea that one could has left untold thousands of women not only divorced, but what is in the long run far worse—friendless.

9   Yet even feminism, when it came back to life in the early seventies, did not rehabilitate the institution of female best friendship. Lesbian relationships took priority, for the good and obvious reason that they had been not only neglected, but driven underground. But in our zeal to bring lesbian relationships safely out of the closet, we sometimes ended up shoving best friendships further out of sight. "Best friends?" a politically ever-so-correct friend once snapped at me, in reference to Joan, "why aren't you lovers?" In the same vein, the radical feminist theoretician Shulamith Firestone wrote that after the gender revolution, there would be no asexual friendships. The coming feminist Utopia, I realized sadly, was going to be a pretty lonely place for some of us.

10   Then, almost before we could get out of our jeans and into our corporate clone clothes, female friendship came back into fashion—but in the vastly attenuated form of "networking." Suddenly we were supposed to have dozens of women friends, hundreds if time and the phone bill allow, but each with a defined function: mentors, contacts, connections, allies, even pretty ones who might be able to introduce us, now and then, to their leftover boyfriends. The voluminous literature on corporate success for women is full of advice on friends: whom to avoid ("turkeys" and whiners), whom to cultivate (winners and potential clients), and how to tell when a friend is moving from the latter category into the former. This is an advance, because it means we are finally realizing that women are important enough to be valued friends and that friendship among women is valuable enough to write and talk about. But in the pushy new dress-for-success world, there's less room than ever for best friendships that last through thick and thin, through skidding as well as climbing.

11   Hence my campaign to save the institution of female best friendship. I am not asking you to vote for anyone, to pray to anyone, or even to send me money. I'm just suggesting that we all begin to give a little more space, and a little more respect, to the best friendships in our lives. To this end, I propose three rules:

12   1. Best friendships should be given social visibility. If you are inviting Pat over for dinner, you would naturally think of inviting her husband, Ed. Why not Pat's best friend, Jill? Well, you may be thinking, how childish! They don't have to go everywhere together. Of course they don't, but neither do Pat and Ed. In many settings, including your next dinner party or potluck, Pat and Jill may be the combination that makes the most sense and has the most fun.

13   2. Best friends take time and nurturance, even when that means taking time and nurturance away from other major relationships. Everyone knows that marriages require "work." (A ghastly concept, that. "Working on a marriage" has always sounded to me like something on the order of lawn maintenance.) Friendships require effort, too, and best friendships require our very best efforts. It should be possible to say to husband Ed or whomever, "I'm sorry I can't spend the evening with you because I need

to put in some quality time with Jill." He will only be offended if he is a slave to heterosexual couple-ism—in which case you shouldn't have married him in the first place.

14   3. Best friendship is more important than any work-related benefit that may accrue from it, and should be treated accordingly. Maybe your best friend will help you get that promotion, transfer, or new contract. That's all well and good, but the real question is: Will that promotion, transfer, or whatever help your best friendship? If it's a transfer to San Diego, and your best friend's in Cincinnati, it may not be worth it. For example, as a writer who has collaborated with many friends, including "Joan," I am often accosted by strangers exclaiming, "It's just amazing that you got through that book [article, or other project] together and you're still friends!" The truth is, in nine cases out of ten, that the friendship was always far more important than the book. If a project isn't going to strengthen my friendship—and might even threaten it—I'd rather not start.

15   When I was thinking through this column—out loud of course, with a very good friend on the phone—she sniffed, "So what exactly do you want—formal, legalized friendships, with best-friend licenses and showers and property settlements in case you get in a fight over the sweaters you've been borrowing from each other for the past ten years?" No, of course not, because the beauty of best friendship, as opposed to, say, marriage, is that it's a totally grass-roots, creative effort that requires no help at all from the powers-that-be. Besides, it would be too complicated. In contrast to marriage—and even to sixth-grade cliques—there's no rule that says you can have only one "best" friend.

Discussion Questions

1. Ehrenreich's essay applauds the institution of "best friends." What in your own experience makes you agree or disagree with her?

2. In paragraph 4, Ehrenreich claims that best friendship between women is "undervalued and unrecognized," whereas best friendship between men has been "the stuff of history and high drama." Can you generate some of your own examples to support or refute her contention?

3. Ehrenreich, in paragraph 8, presents the notion that one's spouse (or significant other) should be one's best friend. Drawing on your own experience and observations, discuss your reasons for agreeing or disagreeing with her.

4. In paragraph 10, Ehrenreich lists some of the "defined functions" of friends. How many of your own friends would qualify for that list? Can you add some additional categories of your own?

5. What is your reaction to Ehrenreich's three rules in paragraphs 12 through 14? Which seems most plausible? Which the least? Why?

Focusing on Friends
Steve Tesich

Steve Tesich was born in 1942 in Yugoslavia. At the age of fourteen, he emigrated to the United States and earned an undergraduate degree from Indiana University and an M.A. degree in Russian literature from Columbia University. A novelist and playwright, Tesich wrote the screenplay for the movie Breaking Away *(1979), for which he received an Academy Award. His other screenplays include* Four Friends *(1981) and* The World According to Garp *(1982). Tesich is also the author of* Touching Bottom *(1980) and* Square One *(1990). The following essay originally appeared in 1983 in the* New York Times Magazine*'s section "About Men." In it, Tesich ruminates on the differences he finds between his relationships with women and those with men.*

1   When I think of people who were my good friends, I see them all, as I do everything else from my life, in cinematic terms. The camera work is entirely different for men and women.

2   I remember all the women in almost extreme close-ups. The settings are different—apartments, restaurants—but they're all interiors, as if I had never spent a single minute with a single woman outside. They're looking right at me, these women in these extreme close-ups; the lighting is exquisite, worthy of a Fellini or Fosse film, and their lips are moving. They're telling me something important or reacting to something even more important that I've told them. It's the kind of movie where you tell people to keep quiet when they chew their popcorn too loudly.

3   The boys and men who were my friends are in an entirely different movie. No close-ups here. No exquisite lighting. The camera work is rather shaky but the background is moving. We're going somewhere, on foot, on bicycles, in cars. The ritual of motion, or action, makes up for the inconsequential nature of the dialogue. It's a much sloppier film, this film that is not really a film but a memory of real friends: Slobo, Louie, Sam. Male friends. I've loved all three of them. I assumed they knew this, but I never told them.

4   Quite the contrary is true in my female films. In close-up after close-up. I am telling every woman who I ever loved that I love her, and then lingering on yet another close-up of her face for a reaction. There is a perfectly appropriate musical score playing while I wait. And if I wait long enough, I get an answer. I am loved. I am not loved. Language clears up the suspense. The emotion is nailed down.

5   Therein lies the difference, I think, between my friendships with men and with women. I can tell women I love them. Not only can I tell them. I am compulsive about it. I can hardly wait to tell them. But I can't tell the men. I just can't. And they can't tell me. Emotions are never nailed down. They run wild, and I and my male friends chase after them, on foot, on bicycles, in cars, keeping the quarry in sight but never catching up.

6   My first friend was Slobo. I was still living in Yugoslavia at the time, and not far from my house there was an old German truck left abandoned after the war. It had no wheels. No windshield. No doors. But the steering wheel was intact. Slobo and I flew to America in that truck. It was our airplane. Even now, I remember the background moving as we took off down the street, across Europe, across the Atlantic. We were inseparable: The best of friends. Naturally, not one word concerning the nature of our feelings for one another was ever exchanged. It was all done in actions.

7   The inevitable would happen at least once a day. As we were flying over the Atlantic, there came, out of nowhere, that wonderful moment: engine failure! "We'll have to bail out," I shouted. "A-a-a-a-a!" Slobo made the sound of a failing engine. Then he would turn and look me in the eye: "I can't swim," he'd say. "Fear not." I put my hand on his shoulder. "I'll drag you to shore." And, with that, both of us would tumble out of the truck onto the dusty street. I swam through the dust. Slobo drowned in the dust, coughing, gagging. "Sharks!" he cried. But I always saved him. The next day the ritual would be repeated, only then it would be my turn to say "I can't swim," and Slobo would save me. We saved each other from certain death over a hundred times, until finally a day came when I really left for America with my mother and sister. Slobo and I stood at the train station. We were there to say goodbye, but, since we weren't that good at saying things and since he couldn't save me, he just cried until the train started to move.

8   The best friend I had in high school was Louie. It now seems to me that I was totally monogamous when it came to male friends. I would have several girl friends but only one real male friend. Louis was it at that time. We were both athletes, and one day we decided to "run till we drop." We just wanted to know what it was like. Skinny Louie set the pace as we ran around our high-school track. Lap after lap. Four laps to a mile. Mile after mile we ran. I had the reputation as being a big-time jock. Louie didn't. But this was Louie's day. There was a bounce in his step and, when he turned back to look at me, his eyes were gleaming with the thrill of it all. I

finally dropped. Louie still looked fresh; he seemed capable, on that day, of running forever. But we were the best of friends, and so he stopped. "That's it," he lied. "I couldn't go another step farther." It was an act of love. Naturally, I said nothing.

9   Louie got killed in Vietnam. Several weeks after his funeral, I went to his mother's house, and, because she was a woman, I tried to tell her how much I had loved her son. It was not a good scene. Although I was telling the truth, my words sounded like lies. It was all very painful and embarrassing. I kept thinking how sorry I was that I had never told Louie himself.

10   Sam is my best friend now, and has been for many years. A few years ago, we were swimming at a beach in East Hampton. The Atlantic! The very Atlantic I had flown over in my German truck with Slobo. We had swum out pretty far from the shore when both of us simultaneously thought we spotted a shark. Water is not only a good conductor of electricity but of panic as well. We began splashing like madmen toward shore. Suddenly, at the height of my panic, I realized how much I loved my friend, what an irreplaceable friend he was, and, although I was the faster swimmer, I fell back to protect him. Naturally, the shark in the end proved to be imaginary. But not my feelings for my friend. For several days after that I wanted to share my discovery with him, to tell him how much I loved him. Fortunately, I didn't.

11   I say fortunately because on reflection, there seems to be sufficient evidence to indicate that, if anybody was cheated and shortchanged by me, it was the women, the girls, the very recipients of my uncensored emotions. Yes. I could hardly wait to tell them I loved them. I did love them. But once I told them, something stopped. The emotion was nailed down, but, with it, the enthusiasm and the energy to prove it was nailed down, too. I can remember my voice saying to almost all of them, at one time or another: "I told you I love you. What else do you want?" I can now recoil at the impatient hostility of that voice but I can't deny it was mine.

12   The tyranny of self-censorship forced me, in my relations with male friends, to seek alternatives to language. And just because I could never be sure they understood exactly how I felt about them, I was forced to look for ways to prove it. That is, I now think, how it should be. It is time to make adjustments. It is time to pull back the camera, free the women I know, and myself, from those merciless close-ups and have the background move.

Discussion Questions

1. Based on your own experiences and observations, do you think Tesich echoes the sentiments of most men when he discusses the difference he perceives in friendships with men versus those with women? Do you think women have similar feelings about their friendships with men? Why or why not?

2. How effective do you think Tesich's choice is of framing his essay in cinematic terms? Explain your response.

3. Do you think it was wise for Tesich not to tell his friend he loved him. Why? What would you have done? Explain your answer.

4. Do you agree with Tesich's realization in paragraph 11 that he "cheated and shortchanged" the women in his life? Why or why not?

5. In the last paragraph, Tesich claims that "it is time to make adjustments." Do you believe Tesich will change? Why or why not? If he does, what specific adjustments do you think he will make in his behavior? Or do you think his statement is just an easy, obvious way to end his essay?

Fish Gotta Swim

Shirley Abbott

Born in Hot Springs, Arkansas, in 1934, Shirley Abbott earned her A.B. degree from Texas State College for Women and pursued graduate studies at the University of Grenoble and Columbia University. She has been the editor of Horizon *magazine and has been the recipient of a Fulbright scholarship. Her articles have appeared in a number of magazines including* Smithsonian, Harper's, American Heritage, *and* Southern Living. *Abbott is the author of* The Art of Food *(1977),* The National Museum of American History *(1981), and* Historic Charleston *(1985). Her two autobiographical memoirs are* Womenfolks: Growing Up Down South *(1983) and* The Bookmaker's Daughter *(1991), in which the following essay appears. Currently, Abbott lives in New York and works as a writer for a health newsletter. "Fish Gotta Swim" begins with recounting her preparations for her first real date in high school and proceeds with a discussion of her subsequent boyfriends.*

1   My high school adventures in love were limited by my parents' circumstances as well as by the odd ideas I had absorbed from excess reading. I was a mermaid in search of a marble prince. I had considered several candi-

dates, unsuccessfully, but when I was about sixteen, a boy called Tommy, tall and moderately handsome, seemed to qualify. Some two dozen boys in my class fell into the "cute" category, every one of them an athlete. (Never mind that our teams lost every game.) Girls were supposed to want these boys and scorn the tuba players in the band or kids who merely showed up for classes. The top two dozen girls already had them cornered, but not a girl in the whole high school refused to join the chase.

2   One of my classmates, a slow-witted, unkempt, obese girl named Myrtle, had been shunted along from grade to grade. But though she could not master arithmetic, Myrtle understood who the right boys were, and she used to stand grinning at their elbows and refuse to go away in the teeth of their insults. She tormented them with love notes, which they destroyed before her face. They called her a fat turd and other names, threatened to beat her up, stole her bookbag, pretended to befriend her and then wrote her lush love notes signed with somebody else's name. She would hang her head and blush violently, but she never fought back, and nothing permanently extinguished her hope. The guidance counselor, Miss Telliard, a high school version of Miss Love without the wooden paddles, spent a lot of time drying Myrtle's tears and pleading with her to leave the boys alone, offering them sympathy but requiring mercy and forbearance in return, recruiting the coaching staff to back her up. In her run-down saddle oxfords and greasy blue jacket, Myrtle chased the football team along the hallways and up the stairs, an unconscious parody of every girl in the school.

3   Tommy ranked perhaps twenty-second in the top two dozen, not swaggeringly good-looking or a first-string halfback, but so much the better, I thought. I was determined to make him mine. I was relentlessly at the top of my class, the girl who always raised her hand, who knew the answer that stumped everyone else, who made 100 percent on the test and ruined the curve—definitely not the statue in any boy's garden. But in my dreams I offered the sea witch my tongue, my feet, my pride, my grade-point average, anything. Bunking parties as a girlish pastime had given way to other games, including one called TWIRP week: The Woman Is Requested to Pay. That week, girls asked boys for dates, provided the transportation, bought the gas and hamburgers. I didn't understand that the game was fixed. The boys just arranged everything with the girls beforehand. Steadies went with steadies. This was anything but open season on men. Nevertheless, I accosted Tommy in the hall and asked if he'd go to the dance with me the next Saturday. He said yes, and I can now imagine what he endured in the locker room that week, having been trapped by the valedictorian, a tall person with legs like a wading bird's and a streak of vulnerability that you could see from across the street.

4   I cast bright smiles at him whenever I saw him in the hallway, and he ducked his head and smiled back. It didn't bother me that he never sought me out, or asked what the plans were, or came and leaned on my locker door, the way other football players did with their girls, so tall, so massive,

just sort of swinging on the door and—quick—pushing their heads inside for a kiss and a feel. Next week, I figured, after he'd spent an evening with me, he'd have overcome his natural shyness and his hesitation. Having sampled my company and my kisses, he'd be right there by my locker door, pushing my head inside for a fast but meaningful kiss, wanting me to wear his football jacket, offering me his class ring on a golden chain to wear around my neck, to bounce suggestively around my sweater front. Somehow, I knew, I was about to be forgiven for being too tall and too gangly and the only person out of two hundred in the junior class who genuinely liked Keats's odes. I would show him, and them, that it didn't matter. Meanwhile, I had an important occasion to prepare for, girlfriends to consult about which skirt, which sweater, were they wearing loafers and socks or flats and hose, would it be cold enough for a coat, did they think, or would my leather jacket do? I looked better in the jacket, less like somebody on the way to Sunday school. I arranged to spend the night with a girlfriend, who also had a date with a football player, her steady. We planned to pick the boys up in her car. She would drive. Tommy and I would be alone in the back seat. Friday afternoon, I managed to stop my man in the hallway long enough to tell him when to expect me. He was all grins and shyness, enough to melt my heart.

5   I spent the next afternoon at my girlfriend's house shampooing my hair, doing my nails. Not an inch of my body escaped my attention. I filed, brushed, polished, cleaned, clipped, plucked, curled, and groomed until I was perfect. I had bought a new lipstick, with a little mirror attached to the tube (two dollars extra). I took a bubble bath before I dressed. I put perfume on my pulse spots and promised myself to reapply it before leaving. I used every trick magazines could suggest, and a few left over from *Gone With the Wind,* such as pinching my cheeks to make them rosy. I considered eating a large dinner so I wouldn't appear hungry at the dance, but that seemed silly. I measured my waist. A fat twenty-three. How had Scarlett gotten it down to sixteen? I sucked my stomach in brutally, considered and rejected the idea of wearing a panty girdle.

6   Standing in the bathroom with the door locked, half an hour before time to leave, I inspected the effect of Kleenex in the bra cups, wondering whether it was worth the risk. No, big breasts weren't even what men wanted, just think of Lauren Bacall, only I really was awfully small compared with most football players' girls, not to mention Grace Kelly. The phone rang, and I somehow knew it tolled for me. I stopped fidgeting with the Kleenex and the mirror and stood there. After a long time, my girlfriend knocked.

7   "Hey, I've got some news. Tommy isn't coming. He says he can't talk to you, but he told me to tell you he just can't make it. He said to tell you he was sorry." She sounded calm and noncommittal. Happens every day, nothing to get excited about. I knew that being stood up was a social ca tastrophe in the same category as being abandoned at the altar or left pregnant. A girl that could have this done to her wasn't worth much. She

wasn't desirable enough, did not evoke enough masculine respect. Could not expect the rest of the male community to rally in her defense. Could not even expect her girlfriends to be indignant; only cool and slightly embarrassed. In each hand I held the folded Kleenex I had so recently removed from my brassiere. Each fingernail was perfectly manicured and polished bright pink. My tongue was as inoperative as if the sea witch had extracted it and fed it to the sharks.

8   "I can't call off my date," my friend continued through the door. "I know you wouldn't want me to. Mom and Dad are going to be here watching TV. They'd love to have you, they said. Honestly, I haven't got time to drive you home. I guess you could tag along to the dance with us, if you want to. Maybe that's what you should do. But I'm afraid Tommy might be there with somebody else."

9   I opened the bathroom door and saw the concern on her face. "No thanks, I guess I'll just stay here and watch TV." I wasn't angry with Tommy. I had reached womanhood: I internalized the event as neatly as Madame Bovary swallowed the poison. Forgiveness in my heart, I cast myself numbly into the sea foam. I should have known better, I should never have asked him. When at last I reached the privacy of my own bedroom, I believe I must have wept a good deal. I gave up eating. I spent long hours in silence, without moving. I refused to return to school for several days. This was my first sustained experience with humiliation and grief. I'd no idea how to escape from this dark cave, where my own foolishness had chained me to the wall (it never occurred to me that Tommy had been foolish or cruel).

10   My parents never asked me exactly what happened, though my mother seemed to know without being told, for she kept muttering, in my general direction, "Stupid, rude boys. You're better off not to worry about them." She had been the belle of the county, with suitors swarming around the door by the time she was sixteen. One wrote her sonnets and threatened suicide. She had had six or seven proposals by the time she found my father. People still teased her about her boyfriends, and she in turn teased me about all the fathers I might have had but didn't.

11   My father was angry, though I couldn't tell at what. He had been opposed to the TWIRP dance anyway, a stupid idea, just a chance for young girls to get their feelings hurt and expose themselves to ridicule. So I could hardly describe my emotional bruises to him now, and in any case, I had defied him. How could I expect him to comfort me? He had, after all, spoken his mind about headstrong girls and drugstore cowboys who had football jackets now but would end up pumping gas for a living and why didn't I just forget it and translate fifty lines of Virgil for extra credit the way my Latin teacher had suggested, instead of going off to some dance? I didn't need to worry about men at my tender age, he thundered. His ranting was a kind of ultra-high-frequency message that no woman could live the life of the body in tandem with the life of the mind. You must choose—be the servant of men or an independent creature. But I was the

person who had rewritten *Little Women* in order to marry Jo to Laurie. I still had no idea that Jo March, with her handsome suitor whom she oh-so-sensibly rejects and her eventual cozy marriage and gemütlich boys' school, was a fake. I was beginning to understand, however, why so few female names appeared on the spines of leather-bound volumes. How did you love men and have a brain at the same time? I had no answers, but my father's preaching suddenly alienated me and, more than anything else, gave me strength to show up for school once more.

12   Tommy and I never spoke to each other again or looked each other in the eye. I pretended he was in another dimension, and avoided the floor where his locker was. I had dreaded being the subject of gossip, but—final humiliation—no one except me seemed to care. I wondered at the gap between my stories and my life. I hardened into my role as class brain. I'd knock the curve so high those football players would all flunk.

13   In spite of my father—indeed, in spite of myself—I found other boys, with other lessons for me. One of them was also a football player, who seldom showed up for practice but somehow acquired the coveted jacket, probably by stealing it. Billy and I worked on the school yearbook together, which required frequent visits to the printing plant in a village nearby. He always drove his old Ford, which always broke down. I sat in the front seat while he tinkered with the carburetor, happy that although the car really wouldn't start, he wanted to kiss me. He was less reliable even than his Ford, and as marginal socially as I was. His grades were so hopeless that he didn't mind necking with the valedictorian. He didn't know what a valedictorian was. Grades, F's or A's, were without any significance to Billy. He never took me on a standard date, but he never demolished me either.

14   I didn't think of these encounters in the car as love, or of Billy as a lover. Lovers were tall and handsome, called for you at the door, gave you their class ring, sent you gardenias, gave your mother something to gossip with other mothers about. Other girls had lovers, steadies, and wore little pins on their sweaters. One night another girl's boyfriend, also called Tommy, cornered me in her kitchen and kissed me until my head swam with pleasure and desire and I had to hold on to him to stand up. "I wanted you to know what this was like," he explained, while I was still too dizzy to see. "I didn't know if anybody had ever kissed you." I was a charity case, but it was okay.

15   Love notes were part of adolescence then—secret, identical, spelled out in pencil on lined paper in the illiterate hand most high school boys wrote, having laid aside all that Miss Love and her colleagues had ever taught them. "You sure are one nice girl, and I hope we can see each other some time." "I sure do hope you like me as much as I like you. I'll never forget what happened Saturday night" "You sure are one sweet girl, and I like you." This Tommy began writing me such notes, and once showed up at my house, unannounced, driving a battered old car. His girlfriend either didn't know or didn't care, and whenever we managed to get in an hour's kissing, he made no promises and offered no trophies. Nevertheless, my wounds healed a little.

16   Another boy invited me to go driving, and without even asking if I'd first like a barbecue sandwich, he headed straight for the airport parking lot, deserted at night since the airport closed at 5 P.M. He was one of those unremarkable boys who just showed up at school. He wanted more than kisses—not everything, just more than I had done before. I was terrified of pregnancy and convinced that one time was all it took; indeed, I figured you could probably absorb those fearful little male cells through you fingers—a comic but sensible enough attitude for one not yearning to become a housewife at age seventeen. I was deeply ashamed, however, of my own cowardice. Having been raised on romantic fiction, I thought it was a disgrace to abstain from sex, like going to the end of the diving board and not jumping. Luckily for me, the young man was not a reader of novels. He wanted to go to some big college in the East and wasn't running any risks. He knew about rubbers but neither trusted them nor had the courage to buy any. That didn't mean you couldn't unbutton buttons and unzip zippers. Neither of us swore that we loved each other, but the little quick places responded urgently, and he seemed to like mine fine, in spite of my daunting grade-point average. For once I forgot about grades.

17   We spent many evenings that summer experimenting with self-control in the airport parking lot. It was good exercise. It made me happy, gave me courage. Emotionally and physically, there was parity to what we did. You could do these things with a boy and still be friends. No important vows or gametes were exchanged, and nobody had to commit suicide. I hadn't yet realized that sensuality between equals might be a better bargain than romance, yet for the first time, in the crowded theater of my mind, the marble prince and the mermaid got pushed temporarily offstage. Casanova, my old friend, had tried to tell me that love might be entirely dispensable but tenderness never could be. Poor old rake, poor panting Casanova, disillusioned in every encounter, restlessly seeking another. And a great deal easier to have in one's arms than Tristan and Romeo and the love-death. Still, in my youth and ignorance, I had no intention of renouncing romance.

Discussion Questions

1. From your own experience and observations, how typical do you think Abbott's experiences are with members of the opposite sex?

2. Is there anything in Abbott's essay—or in your own experiences or observations—that prepares you for Tommy standing Abbott up? Explain your answer.

3. How typical is Abbott's thinking after Tommy stood her up? her mother's? her father's? If she had stood Tommy up, do you think he would have felt similarly? Why or why not?

4. What do you think Abbott means by the "marble prince and the mermaid" she mentions in paragraphs 1 and 17?

5. Do you think the last sentence of Abbott's essay is a commonly held sentiment? Do you think it effectively concludes the essay? Explain your response.

College Friends

Jennifer Crichton

J ennifer Crichton was born in 1957 and attended Brown University from 1974 to 1977 and Barnard College from 1977 to 1979. She is the author of Delivery: A Nurse Midwife's Story *(1986), which combines her research of obstetrical practices with her creation of fictional characters. Crichton is a full-time writer, and the following essay was first published in* Ms. *magazine. In it, she discusses the importance of friendship, especially in the first semester of college when her loneliness was particularly strong. As you read this essay, see if you recognize yourself in it.*

1   As far as I'm concerned, the first semester away at college is possibly the single worst time to make friends. You'll make them, but you'll probably get it all wrong, through no fault of your own, for these are desperate hours.

2   Here's desperation: standing in a stadium-like cafeteria, I became convinced that a thousand students busy demolishing the contents of their trays were indifferent to me, and studying me with ill-disguised disdain at the same time. The ability to mentally grasp two opposing concepts is often thought of as the hallmark of genius. But I credit my mind's crazed elasticity to panic. Sitting alone at a table, I see the girl I'd met that morning in the showers. I was thrilled to see her. The need for a friend had become violent. Back at the dorm, I told her more about my family's peculiarities and my cataclysmic summer fling than I'd ever let slip before. All the right sympathetic looks crossed her face at all the right moments, whereupon I deduced that through the good graces of the housing department, I'd stumbled upon a soulmate. But what seemed like two minds mixing and matching on a cosmic plane was actually two lonely freshmen under the influence of unprecedented amounts of caffeine and emotional upheaval. This wasn't a meeting of souls. This was a talking jag of monumental proportions.

3   By February, my first friend and I passed each other in the hall with lame, bored smiles, and now I can't remember her name for the life of me. But that doesn't make me sad in the least.

4   Loneliness and the erosion of high school friendships through change and distance leave yawning gaps that beg to be filled. Yet, I never made a

real friend by directly applying for the position of confidante or soulmate. I made my best friendships by accident, with instant intimacy marking none of them—it wasn't mutual loneliness that drew us together.

5   I met my best friend Jean in a film class when she said Alfred Hitchcock was overrated. I disagreed and we argued out of the building and into a lifelong friendship where we argue still. We became friends without meaning to, and took our intimacy step by step. Deliberate choice, not desperate need, moved us closer. Our friendship is so much a part of us now that it seems unavoidable that we should have become friends. But there was nothing inevitable about it. It's easy to imagine Jean saying to me in that classroom, "Hitchcock's a hack, you're a fool, and that's all I have to say." But that was not all she had to say. Which is why we're friends today. We always have more to say.

6   Friendship's value wasn't always clear to me. In the back of my mind, I believed that platonic friendships were a way of marking time until I struck the pay dirt of serious romance. I'd managed to digest many romantic notions by my first year of college, and chief among them was the idea that I'd meet the perfect lover who would be everything to me and make me complete. I saw plunging into a relationship as an advanced form of friendship, friendship plus sex. Lacking sex, platonic friendships seemed like a lower standard of living. As long as my boyfriend offered me so much in one convenient package, women friends were superfluous. I thought I was the girl who had everything.

7   But what made that relationship more—the sex—made it a bad replacement for friendship. Sexual tension charged the lines of communication between us. White noise crackled on the wire as desire and jealousy, fear of loss, and the need to be loved conspired to cloud and distort expression. Influenced by these powerful forces, I didn't always tell the truth. And on the most practical level, when my boyfriend and I broke up, I had lost more than my lover, I lost my best friend.

8   "You can't keep doing this," Suzanne told me later that same year.

9   "What?"

10   "Start up our friendship every time your relationship falls apart."

11   "I don't do that," I said. It was exactly what I did.

12   "Yes, you do, and I'm sick of it. I'm not second best. I'm something entirely different."

13   Once you see that relationships and friendships are different beasts, you'll never think of the two things as interchangeable again, with friendships as the inferior version. . . .

14   Friendships made in college set a standard for intimacy other friendships are hard-pressed ever to approach. "I've become a narrow specialist in my friendships since graduation," says Pam. "With one friend I'll talk about work. With another, we're fitness fanatics together. But I don't really know much about them—how they live their lives, what they eat for breakfast, or if they eat breakfast at all, who their favorite uncle is, or when they got their contact lenses. I don't even know who they voted for for

President. There will be a close connection in spots, but in general I feel as if I'm dealing with fractions of people. With my college friends, I feel I know them *whole*."

15   In college, there's time to reach that degree of intimacy. One night, my best friend and I spent hours describing how our respective families celebrated Christmas. My family waited until everyone was awake and caffeinated before opening presents, hers charged out of bed to rip open the boxes before they could wipe the sleep out of their eyes. We were as self-righteous as religious fanatics, each convinced our own family was the only one that did Christmas right. Did we really spend an entire night on a subject like that? Did we really have that much time?

16   Operating on college time, my social life was unplanned and spontaneous. Keeping a light on in our rooms was a way of extending an invitation. We had time to hang out, to learn to tell the difference between ordinary crankiness and serious depressions in each other, and to follow the digressions that were at the heart of our friendships. But after college, we had to change, and in scheduling our free-form friendships we felt, at first, self-conscious and artificial.

17   When I had my first full-time job, I called my best friend to make a dinner date a week in advance. She was still in graduate school, and thought my planning was dire evidence that I'd tumbled into the pit of adult convention. "Why don't you have your girl call my girl and we'll set something up?" she asked. Heavy sarcasm. While the terms of the friendship have shifted from digressive, spontaneous socializing to a directed, scheduled style, and we all feel a certain sense of loss, the value of friendship has, if anything, increased.

18   If my college journals were ever published in the newspaper, the headline would most likely read, "FFM WRITER PENS GOO," but I did find something genuinely moving while reading through my hyper-perceptions the other day. Freshman year I'd written: "I am interested in everything. Nothing bores me. I hope I don't die before I can read everything, visit every place, and feel all there is to feel."

19   The sentiment would be a lot more poignant if I'd actually gone ahead and died young, but I find it moving anyway because it exemplifies what's good about being young: that you exist as the wide-eyed adventurer, fueled by the belief that you might amount to something and anything, and that your possibilities are endless. When I feel this way now, I'm usually half-dreaming in bed on a breezy Saturday morning. Or I'm with a college friend—someone with whom I'd pictured the future, back when the future was a dizzying haze viewed with the mind's eye from the vantage point of a smoky dorm room. Together we carved out life with words and hopes. When I'm with her now, I remember that feeling and experience it all over again, because there's still a lot of hazy future to imagine and life to carve. With my friend, I can look to my future and through my past and remember who I am.

Discussion Questions

1. From your own experiences, what makes you agree or disagree with Crichton when she states in the opening paragraph that "the first semester away at college is possibly the single worst time to make friends"?

2. Explain what you see as the difference between relationships and friendships that Crichton presents in paragraph 13. To what extent do you agree with her assessment?

3. Do you think that college friendships are substantively different from those made before or after college? Why or why not?

4. Explain what you think is meant in paragraph 14 when Pam claims that "with my college friends, I feel I know them *whole*." From your own experiences, has that been the case? Why or why not?

5. In the last paragraph, Crichton seems to find her identity when recalling her days in college. Do you think her perception is realistic, or is it tainted by sentimentality? Explain your answer.

Perley Cole

May Sarton

*B*orn near Ghent, Belgium, in 1912, May Sarton has had a prolific *career as a writer. The author of over ten volumes of poetry, over fifteen novels, and seven books of nonfiction, Sarton's most famous collections of poetry include* A Grain of Mustard Seed *(1971),* A Durable Fire *(1972), and* Halfway to Silence *(1980). Among her most acclaimed novels are* Faithful Are the Wounds *(1955),* Mrs. Stevens Hears the Mermaids Singing *(1965),* Kinds of Love *(1970), and* As We Now Are *(1973). Sarton's memoirs and journals include* I Knew a Phoenix *(1959),* Journal of a Solitude *(1973),* A World of Light *(1976),* The House by the Sea *(1977),* Recovering: A Journal *(1980),* At Seventy: A Journal *(1984), and* Plant Dreaming Deep *(1968), in which the following essay appears. Perley Cole is the work-man Sarton hired to help her with her home in Nelson, New Hampshire. More than a hired hand, he became Sarton's trusted friend.*

1   Out of the magic that is Nelson, the person I needed was on the way, as the Quigleys had been on the way that first autumn although we did not meet for months. Perley Cole did not come into my life for three years.

2   At first—it seems incredible now—we were hardly aware of his pres-

ence in the village. We saw lights in the old house up the hill back of the brick schoolhouse, and figured the deer would no longer come down of an autumn night to pick windfalls from the orchard there. Someone had moved in, and that is usually good news. We didn't know who he was, nor why he had come. It takes time to penetrate the thickets of private life in Nelson, and I suppose it must have been several months before I ran into Perley Cole, at the dump, for at that time I was still hauling my own rubbish, unaware that it might be possible to get someone to do it for me. We introduced ourselves formally among the ash cans, and I remember admiring the neat way he had painted his old pick-up, black with a red lining. It looked shipshape in a way that few cars around here do, and he himself had an air about him—an old man, but an old man with a keen eye and a look of being able to command the situation whatever it might be.

3   Then one June day, the ancient bell on my front door tinkled rather more imperatively than usual, and there he was. He launched at once into a long speech which managed to seem laconic because of the manner in which it was delivered. It went something like this: "I know I'm an old man, an old fool some might say, but I've done some farming here and there in my time, and it might happen that you could need some help . . . Mind you, I ain't goin' to starve, one way or t'other, and I have plenty to do on my own place, but . . . "

4   I let him know that there were about a million things that needed doing, and pointed out a few of them.

5   "I'll be around one of these days," he said, and vanished.

6   It was my first experience of his abrupt departures. Every now and then Perley comes to a boil, and utters. When he has uttered, he vanishes into thin air. It can be disconcerting until you get used to it. He is shy and touchy, and I have come to believe that he vanishes because he is suddenly afraid that the answer he has elicited may not be the one he wants to hear.

7   I watched him walk away that day, his back slightly stooped, his stride the long slow stride of the farmer who can keep going from daylight to dark without tiring. And I thought over the face I had just seen for the second time, an American Gothic face, lean, sharply lined, with a high forehead and a long stubborn chin, a sharply defined nose, shy, piercing eyes. Why had he settled here among us? "I'm an old man," he had said, but there was a certain fierceness in the tone that clearly meant "an untamed old man."

8   During the interval between our meeting at the dump and his call, a good deal had happened on his place. It had been spruced up like nothing we had seen around here lately. Not only had the house itself been painted and the barn rebuilt and reroofed, but the meadow around it had been scythed down. Beds of flowers had made their appearance around the granite rocks. The apple trees had been pruned. The untamed old man was clearly a man of many skills, and he had standards we were not used to seeing. It is wonderful, in a village like this, to see a derelict place reclaimed. It somehow gives us all a lift as we struggle to keep the wilderness from taking over.

9 Had he been serious, I wondered? Had I put him off by saying the wrong thing? By being too eager, or not eager enough? For I sensed already that this was a man of prickly pride, sensitivity, touchiness, shyness.

10 Then early one morning, I was woken by a soft sound I could not place, a kind of whispering out in the field between house and barn. From my bed, I pulled the shade up and looked out on a clear bright summer morning, the dew shining on the grass, and there was Perley Cole scything down the jungle. It was the first time I had seen a man scything (even around here we are motorized these days). I watched the long steady sweeps, and how often he stopped and stood the scythe up to whet it— watched and hugely enjoyed the whole operation, repeated over and over, as if in slow motion, the continuous rhythm of it, and the man himself, as tall and angular as his tool. I saw, too, how he handled it with a wary, loving touch. And I saw, too, that this was no rough-and-ready job but a matter of skill and grace. When I went out, later on, he was on his knees trimming with a sickle, although the scythe itself had been used so delicately that only a perfectionist would have seen the need for additional work around the edges. The old barn stood up now as trim as could be.

11 "See that?" Perley said, lifting the scythe to show me. "Made in England. I wouldn't take a hundred dollars for it!"

12 The collar of his dark-gray shirt was turned in, and I could see a dew of sweat on his throat; his eyes looked dark blue in the morning light, and his cheeks were pink. There, triumphant, he was surely in the prime of life, and I would never have guessed that he was then over seventy. But he has learned to handle himself as skillfully as a fine tool.

13 We didn't talk much that day, nor for many days to come. But gradually he shaped and pruned and cleared the place for me. And as he worked I saw that I had lived here for three years in ignorance. Now the light was beginning to dawn. One of the first revelations was what a little pruning can do. Perley trimmed out three small trees around a rock that stands in the middle of my big meadow and suddenly the whole large scene had a focus. You could rest your eyes somewhere. Little by little he enlarged the "lawn" to include all the rough field between house and barn, and brought back the front green to something delightful to behold. He would have none of my power motor. "I wouldn't be seen dead with one of those G— d—noisy bastards," he informed me in that half-aggressive, half-apologetic tone of voice I have come to know so well. He assured me that he could do a better job with my hand machine. Could he? I wondered, for the area is large. After the first time around I was convinced, and I finally gave the power motor away. You don't offer Paderewski a player piano!

14 Little by little we began to tame each other, finding our way slowly into friendship, sealed with many a glass of sherry when Perley knocked off at noon. The sherry is downed in one gulp. Down it goes, and then, after a moment, up comes a story.

15 "Court's in session. Now you listen to me!"

16   I sit on the kitchen stool, drink my sherry slowly, and listen.

17   So it is that I have come to know a good deal about him, about him and his "bird," as he sometimes calls Angie, and about Parker, their son, who came back from World War II with a permanent cloak of silence around him, as shy as a deer. Parker and his mother are made of the same delicate stuff, but Perley arrived in this world weighing eleven pounds and screaming. He was the youngest of four brothers, and he was not the favorite; he ran away at twelve to work for a neighboring farmer. "I was not one to hang on my mother's tit!" he told me with savage pride. By the time he was eighteen he was a man and he knew whom he was going to marry. "But first the cage, then the bird," he told me, and he did not propose to Angie until he could offer her a house and ten acres of land, which he had bought for $620 from two old-lady schoolteachers who were retiring. He got it because they wanted him to have it. "And I didn't pay a cent down," he told me to prove how good his credit was in that neighborhood.

18   The young couple had barely settled in when a friend turned up from the county jail and said, "I need you, Perley."

19   Perley Cole was the youngest guard they had ever had, but he had eyes in the back of his head, and I can imagine that he was both fierce and just. He has told me that he could size up the troublemakers the day they arrived, and it was for that prescience, no doubt, that he was respected. At any rate condemned men asked that it be young Perley to lead them to the gallows. His myth-making nature thrived in the prison. I have come to understand that he lives in a heroic world of his own making, where everything is a little larger than life-size, where he expects the worst and is ready for it, ready with a quip or a blow, and ready with an ornery kind of patience as well. If he sees I am depressed about something, he doesn't console; he says, "Life is like a stone wall; let one stone start sliding and you're done for! Well, good-by—and good luck!" I find this view of life exhilarating.

20   I have never heard him say anything that did not come from deep inside his own experience, and when he tells me to be patient and not to be in such a hurry, I take it because I know that he has learned his own patience and his own rhythm through a long life. In the years I have known him, he has taught me a great deal. I have soaked him up like some healthy primal source, and he has nourished the poet as well as the gardener. He uses language like a poet himself, and savors his own pithy turns of phrase, so they come back like recurring themes in a fugue. One of my favorites is "He knows as much about farming as a goose knows about Jesus."

21   What he talks about is often himself, himself as a legendary figure who inhabits the center of the myth, for he likes to look back on his life and ruminate on it. After seven years as a prison guard, he went back to farming, first working for richer men and then on his own, but wherever he was, whether master or servant, he must always have been enclosed in the armor of an immensely self-reliant and essentially solitary man. For he has

chosen a kind of solitude even within his family. Joining a church would seem as ludicrous to him as joining any other sort of club. I haven't yet been able to persuade him to come to a Town Meeting. On Old Home Day in August, when the village gathers on the green for games, speeches, and a band concert, Perley Cole gets into his new blue pick-up and disappears. Last year he decided to revisit old haunts and pay a few calls on relatives in and near Cornish.

22   As usual after any expedition, he came round a few days later to tell me all about it in great detail. This time it was a saga of changing times. He told me how he sat in the Chevy and looked out on what remained of a rich farm where he had worked forty or more years ago, a farm of great silos and barns, of many acres of pasture and corn.

23   "It's a wilderness," he said. "It's all gone to pot, grown up into brush, barns fallen in or burned. I tell you if I had stayed there another five minutes, I'd have gone crazy!"

24   He stopped in Cornish to look up old acquaintances, talked to a man and named names.

25   "Brother," the man told him, "if you want to see any of them, you'll have to go to the cemetery!"

26   "You should never have left Nelson," I teased him. "Around here we're most of us alive."

27   That's how we talk, veering away from what is too painful to contemplate. But after he had left I thought over all he had said, and shivered as the shadow of death and decay passed over the house like a cloud. And then the sun came out as I felt in my bones the resilience of the old man, the way he himself has handled change, not by resisting it but by playing his own game within it.

28   In his late sixties, when he still had a herd of cows and it was becoming harder and harder to get help he could afford, he went through a period of black depression. "It got so as when I went into the barn and looked at all those cows, I sat down on a stool and wept!" The time had come to make a radical change, and unlike many a farmer who dies in harness, Perley had the wit to recognize that he had reached the limit. He and Angie said goodby to the cows and to Hillsboro and looked around for a little place where they could settle in, free of the anxieties and responsibilities of a working farm.

29   So it came about that they were brought to Nelson to look at the old place back of the schoolhouse. Angie, as he has often explained to me, has the last word about everything indoors but his word is law on anything outside the house. Nevertheless, I have noticed that she manages to sneak some flower seeds into the vegetable garden, and it was she, not he, who made the final decision on their house. Perley was not enthusiastic—I have never been able to find out why. At any rate they moved in. He was kept busy the first year sprucing up the old place. He spent the first winter on snowshoes tracking down hedgehogs (as the porcupine is called in New Hampshire). But by their second year, he no doubt began to feel pretty

restless, especially as he keeps his eyes open and he could see how much needed doing all over the village. And so one day he appeared on my doorstep.

30   He might have been an apparition from another age, an age when a workman still had the time and the patience and the wish to do a patient, perfect job, not for the money, not even for the praise he might get at the end of the day, but out of self-respect and out of the love of the work for its own sake. In this Perley is very much like a poet, and he stands before me as an exemplar. Thinking of the way he kneels down to clip a border after he has cut the grass, I sometimes have revised a page for the fifth time instead of letting it go after the fourth. In fact I find that when he is on the place I work better. There he is somewhere off in the woods cutting brush, and here I am at my desk pruning out a thicket of words. It gives me a little extra zip to know he is there. It's both companionable, in a curious solitary way, and inspiring.

31   I can't imagine how I should ever have managed without him. Until very recently no friend has turned up here whose joy it is to work out of doors with me. If in those first years I had looked ahead to all that was to be done, to all that needed doing, I should have despaired. But little by little, together, Perley and I have lifted the place out of its neglect and chaos into something like beauty and order. Sometimes he surprises me with a job of his own invention. Last year when I came back from a semester away as Poet in Residence at a Midwestern college, I found that the barn, which had become a general dump for anything and everything, had been completely organized and tidied up. Garden stakes were tied into bundles according to size. Flowerpots were arranged in one corner, according to shape. A huge mass of odd lumber and two-by-fours left by the builders had been cut to kindling size and neatly stacked. Every tool had been cleaned and put into the best possible shape. Well, it was a glorious homecoming!

32   In these last years Perley has been getting rid of bracken and brush to clear out the whole hillside below the garden, and so set off the stone wall and the big trees at its foot. He has pruned out around a single birch, the only one I can see from the house, so that elegant white figure stands out at the end of one meadow. He has penetrated a small, ragged wood behind the barn and cleared it so that six small ash trees in lines of three now "finish" that end of the barn when I sit on the back porch on a summer evening. One fall he pruned along the stone wall that divides my property from the church grounds, so that too has shape and form at last. Little by little what was a derelict farm is becoming a small estate. We have a continuous joke about this, for when I have been away and come back, it is not unusual for Perley to tell me that "a man" stopped in a car and offered $100,000 for it. The sum grows each year, and with reason. My answer is, "I'm not selling!"

33   "Not for a hundred thousand?" Perley asks, lifting his eyebrows.

34   "Not for a million."

35   Perley's domain is the woods and fields; mine is the garden proper.

For flowers are not his specialty and he knows next to nothing about them. Nevertheless it is he who comes to dig big holes for me when (and always unexpectedly) an order of bushes and plants arrives from a nursery-man. It is he who prunes the little fruit trees that I planted eight years ago and that have begun to bear at last. It is he who limes and rolls and cuts the lawns and trims the borders. It is he who goes out and cuts the spruce and hemlock to lay on the borders when I put them to bed in November. And when I am away, as I often have to be—when I go out on a teaching stint to help pay the bills, it is he who can be depended on to see that everything is well taken care of in my absence. Of all that Nelson has given me he is the pearl of great price.

36   But if Perley often resembles a guardian angel, the angel has two faces and one is less benign. He is a "good scrapper" he informs me, as if I didn't know! Every now and then he is seized on by a fury. I have thought about this a lot because I recognize the same symptoms in myself. Pressure of one kind or another builds up and finally blows itself off in anger. Once he walked off the place and did not come back for two days, leaving a job half finished. I called Angie, finally, to ask what the matter was.

37   "Oh, you know Perley," she said in her gentle voice. "I can't say, but he'll get over it."

38   "You tell him to come down here and have it out," I said.

39   Much to my surprise he did come down, prepared with a speech of considerable color and length which I suspect he had been rehearsing. He had come down to tell me to get a younger man, that he was through. It took some doing but I finally penetrated his meaning, which was that I had said at the end of the morning two days before, "You've been at it long enough, Perley." I am always slightly anxious for fear his passionate concern for the job will lead him to overdo. (The man is, after all, seventy-seven now.) Perley had taken my statement to mean that he had been *slow,* an old man not worth his pay! The court was in session and I listened. After I had listened, I persuaded him that if he went home and didn't come back the salt would lose its savor and nothing ever feel quite right again.

40   But if that storm blew over, there is always a new one in the air whenever Perley comes down with a bill. No one could possibly pay him enough for what he does, but for some reason he always behaves like a horse about to shy. There is a defiant look in his eye, as if he imagined the bill would be thrown in his face as exorbitant.

41   "Now if you don't want me around after this," he says, as if he had committed some crime, "there'll be no hard feelings. You'll always be welcome at our house."

42   By this time I'm as nervous as he is and prepared to pay out a fortune, considering what has been accomplished. He then hands me an itemized bill with every hour accounted for, and I am abashed to see how little it turns out to be after all. Why all this fuss?

43   Now and then the myth-making inner world swells up and floods all

sense of reality. It is as if an enraged bear were loose inside Perley, and I have learned that it is best at such times to keep away. But the violence he directs against others, a violence of speech rather than action as I have known him, he sometimes directs against himself. Once when he confessed to uprooting a rare plant by mistake, he said, "I should be shot right through the heart!"

44　　Perley's moods are rather like the New England weather, and, like the weather, he keeps me on my toes, for I never know what to expect. Sometimes he is in a mood to tease. When he learned that I had got a rifle to scare woodchucks off, he was delighted, and ever since has woven many a tall story around my imaginary exploits. "I hear so and so is in hospital, shot through the tail and groaning like a wounded bear," he will say, referring to an ornery local character with whom I have had words. "Looks like he won't live," Perley says, letting out a brief guffaw as he saunters off.

45　　Am I wrong in believing that he is happier now than he has ever been? that finding a village that needed a lot of trimming up was just what he hankered after when the cows had gone?—not to mention his being cock of the walk in a village of old ladies, all of whom need his help. He does exactly what he pleases and when he pleases, knocks off at noon and takes a long nap, and sometimes decides to take a holiday for a week or so. "I'm going into my tunnel," he says, and vanishes until whatever he does in the tunnel has been accomplished. Lately Angie has been ill for a long time, away in a hospital, and he has taken to reading intensively. "I read and I meditate," he told me the other day, and added, "Meditation is like religion."

46　　For a second I felt the phrase was out of character, but I have thought about it and I think that Perley, like all of us, is changing. In all those first years, he and I stood, as it were, outside time. Old? In a given day he did twice the work of most men of thirty. But in these last five years I have been learning that middle age is not youth. My work day is not as long as it used to be. And in these five years Perley has moved from what still felt like the prime of life when he was seventy to old age. I face the fact that he will not be with me forever. But when he tries to persuade me that he is through, we come to settle for "just one more year and then we'll see."

47　　And it will still take a while to get us tidied up here in the village. There is nothing that pleases Perley more than to survey a tangled jungle of rotten trees and brush and to carve it into shape. Contemplating what would look to most of us like an impossible task, he begins to hum with anticipation; his face, often harsh in repose, lights up with the joy of battle, with the artist's joy. Hours later he emerges, his straw hat pulled down over his eyes, his shirt collar tucked in, and swallows a glass of sherry as if it were water. Behind him beauty and order have been restored.

48　　When he and I are working side by side here, as we do, for a few hours anyway we are neither old nor young. We are outside time.

Discussion Questions

1. What do you think Sarton values the most in her friendship with Cole? Cite specific passages that influence your response. Do you also value such qualities in your friendships? Why?

2. Sarton uses dialogue to evoke the spirit of Perley Cole. Discuss how his speech aids you in envisioning and getting to know the man better.

3. Although Sarton never overtly states that she and Perley Cole are friends, how does she create that impression?

4. Perley Cole becomes Sarton's friend by being her co-worker. Do you think that employer and employee have an easier or a more difficult time becoming friends and maintaining friendships? Why?

5. What do you think Sarton means in the last paragraph when she describes working with Cole? Have you ever experienced similar feelings while working with a friend?

Two Women in Particular

Zora Neale Hurston

Zora Neale Hurston was born in 1909 and grew up in Eatonville, Florida, the first incorporated African-American community in the United States. The first African-American woman to be admitted to Barnard College, Hurston studied anthropology and later worked as a folklorist with the famed anthropologist, Franz Boaz. She is the author of Mules and Men *(1935), a study of voodoo among southern blacks; a novel entitled* Their Eyes Were Watching God *(1937); and an autobiography,* Dust Tracks on a Road *(1942), from which the following essay is taken. Hurston died in 1960. In "Two Women in Particular," Hurston pays tribute to two friends who had a powerful impact on her life.*

1   Two women, among the number whom I have known intimately force me to keep them well in mind. Both of them have rare talents, are drenched in human gravy, and both of them have meant a great deal to me in friendship and inward experience. One, Fannie Hurst, because she is so young for her years, and Ethel Waters because she is both so old and so young for hers.

2   Understand me, their ages have nothing to do with their birthdays. Ethel Waters is still a young woman. Fannie Hurst is far from old.

3   In my undergraduate days I was secretary to Fannie Hurst. From day

to day she amazed me with her moods. Immediately before and after a very serious moment you could just see her playing with her dolls. You never knew where her impishness would break out again.

4   One day, for instance, I caught her playing at keeping house with company coming to see her. She told me not to leave the office. If the doorbell rang, Clara, her cook, was to answer it. Then she went downstairs and told Clara that I was to answer the doorbell. Then she went on to another part of the house. Presently I heard the bell, and it just happened that I was on my way downstairs to get a drink of water. I wondered why Clara did not go to the door. What was my amazement to see Miss Hurst herself open the door and come in, greet herself graciously and invite herself to have some tea. Which she did. She went into that huge duplex studio and had toasted English muffins and played she had company with her for an hour or more. Then she came on back up to her office and went to work.

5   I knew that she was an only child. She did not even have cousins to play with. She was born to wealth. With the help of images, I could see that lonely child in a big house making up her own games. Being of artistic bent, I could see her making up characters to play with. Naturally she had to talk for her characters, or they would not say what she wanted them to. Most children play at that at times. I had done that extensively so I knew what she was doing when I saw her with the door half open, ringing her own doorbell and inviting herself to have some tea and muffins. When she was tired of her game, she just quit and was a grown woman again.

6   She likes for me to drive her, and we have made several tours. Her impishness broke out once on the road. She told me to have the car all serviced and ready for next morning. We were going up to Belgrade Lakes in Maine to pay Elizabeth Marbury a visit.

7   So soon next day we were on the road. She was Fannie Hurst, the famous author as far as Saratoga Springs. As we drove into the heart of town, she turned to me and said, "Zora, the water here at Saratoga is marvelous. Have you ever had any of it?"

8   "No, Miss Hurst, I never did."

9   "Then we must stop and let you have a drink. It would never do for you to miss having a drink of Saratoga water."

10   We parked near the famous United States Hotel and got out.

11   "It would be nice to stop over here for the night," she said. "I'll go see about the hotel. There is a fountain over there in the park. Be sure and get yourself a drink! You can take Lummox for a run while you get your water."

12   I took Lummox out of the car. To say I took Lummox for a run would be merely making a speech-figure. Lummox weighed about three pounds, and with his short legs, when he thought that he was running he was just jumping up and down in the same place. But anyway, I took him along to get the water. It was so-so as far as the taste went.

13   When I got back to the car, she was waiting for me. It was too early in the season for the hotel to be open. Too bad! She knew I would have en-

joyed it so much. Well, I really ought to have some pleasure. Had I ever seen Niagara Falls?

14   "No, Miss Hurst. I always wanted to see it, but I never had a chance."

15   "Zora! You mean to tell me that you have never seen Niagara Falls?"

16   "No." I felt right sheepish about it when she put it that way.

17   "Oh, you must see the Falls. Get in the car and let's go. You must see those Falls right now." The way she sounded, my whole life was bare up to then and wrecked for the future unless I saw Niagara Falls.

18   The next afternoon around five o'clock, we were at Niagara Falls. It had been a lovely trip across Northern New York State.

19   "Here we are, now, Zora. Hurry up and take a good look at the Falls. I brought you all the way over here so that you could see them."

20   She didn't need to urge me. I leaned on the rail and looked and looked. It was worth the trip, all right. It was just like watching the Atlantic Ocean jump off Pike's Peak.

21   In ten minutes or so, Miss Hurst touched me and I turned around.

22   "Zora, have you ever been across the International Bridge? I think you ought to see the Falls from the Canadian side. Come on, so you can see it from over there. It would be too bad for you to come all the way over here to see it and not see it from the Bridge."

23   So we drove across the Bridge. A Canadian Customs Official tackled us immediately. The car had to be registered. How long did we intend to stay?

24   "You'd better register it for two weeks," Miss Hurst answered and it was done. The sun was almost down.

25   "Look, Zora, Hamilton is only a short distance. I know you want to see it. Come on, let's drive on, and spend the night at Hamilton."

26   We drove on. I was surprised to see that everything in Canada looked so much like everything in the United States. It was deep twilight when we got into Hamilton.

27   "They tell me Kitchener is a most interesting little place, Zora. I know it would be fun to go on there and spend the night." So on to Kitchener we went.

28   Here was Fannie Hurst, a great artist and globe famous, behaving like a little girl, teasing her nurse to take her to the zoo, and having a fine time at it.

29   Well, we spent an exciting two weeks motoring over Ontario, seeing the countryside and eating at quaint but well-appointed inns. She was like a child at a circus. She was a run-away, with no responsibilities.

30   Fannie Hurst, the author, and the wife of Jacques Danielson, was not with us again until we hit Westchester on the way home. Then she replaced Mrs. Hurst's little Fannie and began to discuss her next book with me and got very serious in her manner.

31   While Fannie Hurst brings a very level head to her dressing, she exults in her new things like any debutante. She knows exactly what goes with her very white skin, black hair and sloe eyes, and she wears it. I doubt if any woman on earth has gotten better effects than she has with black,

white and red. Not only that, she knows how to parade it when she gets it on. She will never be jailed for uglying up a town. I am due to have this friendship with Ethel Waters, because I worked for it.

32   She came to me across the footlights. Not the artist alone, but the person, and I wanted to know her very much. I was too timid to go backstage and haunt her, so I wrote her letters and she just plain ignored me. But I kept right on. I sensed a great humanness and depth about her; I wanted to know someone like that.

33   Then Carl Van Vechten gave a dinner for me. A great many celebrities were there, including Sinclair Lewis, Dwight Fiske, Anna May Wong, Blanche Knopf, an Italian soprano, and my old friend, Jane Belo. Carl whispered to me that Ethel Waters was coming in later. He was fond of her himself and he knew I wanted to know her better, so he had persuaded her to come. Carl is given to doing nice things like that.

34   We got to talking, Ethel and I, and got on very well. Then I found that what I suspected was true. Ethel Waters is a very shy person. It had not been her intention to ignore me. She felt that I belonged to another world and had no need of her. She thought that I had been merely curious. She laughed at her error and said, "And here you were just like me all the time." She got warm and friendly, and we went on from there. When she was implored to sing, she asked me first what I wanted to hear. It was "Stormy Weather," of course, and she did it beautifully.

35   Then I did something for her. She told us that she was going to appear with Hall Johnson's Choir at Carnegie Hall, and planned to do some spirituals. Immediately, the Italian soprano and others present advised her not to do it. The argument was that Marian Anderson, Roland Hayes and Paul Robeson had sung them so successfully that her audience would make comparisons and Ethel would suffer by it. I saw the hurt in Ethel's face and jumped in. I objected that Ethel was not going to do any concertized versions of spirituals. She had never rubbed any hair off her head against any college walls and she was not going to sing that way. She was going to sing those spirituals just the way her humble mother had sung them to her.

36   She turned to me with a warm, grateful smile on her face, and said, "Thank you."

37   When she got ready to leave, she got her wraps and said, "Come on, Zora. Let's go on uptown." I went along with her, her husband, and faithful Lashley, a young woman spiritual singer from somewhere in Mississippi, whom Ethel has taken under her wing.

38   We kept up with each other after that, and I got to know her very well. We exchanged confidences that really mean something to both of us. I am her friend, and her tongue is in my mouth. I can speak her sentiments for her, though Ethel Waters can do very well indeed in speaking for herself. She has a homely philosophy that reaches all corners of Life, and she has words to fit when she speaks.

39   She is one of the strangest bundles of people that I have ever met. You can just see the different folks wrapped up in her if you associate with her

long. Just like watching an open fire—the color and shape of her personality is never the same twice. She has extraordinary talents which her lack of formal education prevents her from displaying. She never had a chance to go beyond the third grade in school. A terrible fear is in me that the world will never really know her. You have seen her and heard her on the stage, but so little of her capabilities are seen. Her struggle for adequate expression throws her into moods at times. She said to me Christmas Day of 1941, "You have the advantage of me, Zora. I can only show what is on the stage. You can write a different kind of book each time."

40   She is a Catholic, and deeply religious. She plays a good game of bridge, but no card-playing at her house on Sundays. No more than her mother would have had in her house. Nobody is going to dance and cut capers around her on the Sabbath, either. What she sings about and acts out on the stage, has nothing to do with her private life.

41   Her background is most humble. She does not mind saying that she was born in the slums of Philadelphia in an atmosphere that smacked of the rural South. She neither drinks nor smokes and is always chasing me into a far corner of the room when I light a cigarette. She thanks God that I don't drink.

42   Her religious bent shows in unexpected ways. For instance, we were discussing her work in "Cabin in the Sky." She said, "When we started to rehearse the spirituals, some of those no-manners people started to swinging 'em, and get smart. I told 'em they better not play with God's music like that. I told 'em if I caught any of 'em at it, I'd knock 'em clean over into the orchestra pit." Her eyes flashed fire as she told me about it. Then she calmed down and laughed. "Of course, you know, Zora, God didn't want me to knock 'em over. That was an idea of mine."

43   And this fact of her background has a great deal to do with her approach to people. She is shy and you must convince her that she is really wanted before she will open up her tender parts and show you. Even in her career, I am persuaded that Ethel Waters does not know that she has arrived. For that reason, she is grateful for any show of love or appreciation. People to whom she has given her love and trust have exploited it heartlessly, like hogs under an acorn tree—guzzling and grabbing with their ears hanging over their eyes, and never looking up to see the high tree that the acorns fell from.

44   She went on the stage at thirteen and says that she got eight dollars a week for her first salary. She was so frightened that she had to be pushed on to sing her song, and then another member of the cast had to come on with her until she could get started. Then too, they had to place a chair for her to lean on to overcome her nervousness.

45   At fifteen, she introduced the "St. Louis Blues" to the world. She saw a sheet of the music, had it played for her, then wrote to W. C. Handy for permission to use it. Handy answered on a postal card and told her to go as far as she liked, or words to that effect. If W. C. Handy had only known at that time the importance of his act!

46   She is gay and sombre by turns. I have listened to her telling a story and noticed her change of mood in mid-story. I have asked her to repeat something particularly pungent that she has said, and had her tell me, "I couldn't say it now. My thoughts are different. Sometime when I am thinking that same way, I'll tell it to you again."

47   The smiles and metaphors just drip off her lips. One day I sat in her living-room on Hobart Street in Los Angeles, deep in thought. I had really forgotten that others were present. She nudged Archie Savage and pointed at me. "Salvation looking at the temple forlorn," she commented and laughed. "What you doing, Zora? Pasturing in your mind?"

48   "It's nice to be talking things over with you, Zora," she told me another time. "Conversation is the ceremony of companionship."

49   Speaking of a man we both know, she said, "The bigger lie he tells, the more guts he tells it with."

50   "That man's jaws are loaded with big words, but he never says a thing," she said speaking of a mutual friend. "He got his words out of a book. I got mine out of life."

51   "She shot him lightly and he died politely," she commented after reading in the *Los Angeles Examiner* about a woman killing her lover.

52   Commenting on a man who had used coarse language, she said, "I'd rather him to talk differently, but you can't hold him responsible, Zora, they are all the words he's got."

53   Ethel Waters has known great success and terrible personal tragedy, so she knows that no one can have everything.

54   "Don't care how good the music is, Zora, you can't dance on every set."

55   I am grateful for the friendship of Fannie Hurst and Ethel Waters. But how does one speak of honest gratitude? Who can know the outer ranges of friendship? I am tempted to say that no one can live without it. It seems to me that trying to live without friends is like milking a bear to get cream for your morning coffee. It is a whole lot of trouble, and then not worth much after you get it.

Discussion Questions

1. How important do you think age is in Hurston's friendships? How important do you think it *should* be?

2. What do you see as the significance of Hurston having to work for her friendship with Ethel Waters? Do you think that friendships that have to be "worked for" are more valuable than those that don't? Explain your answer.

3. What do you think Hurston means in the last paragraph when she talks about the "outer ranges of friendship"?

4. To what extent is Hurston's essay proof that "trying to live without friends is like milking a bear to get cream for your morning coffee"? How effective is her analogy?

5. How effective do you think Hurston's essay is, given that it is based on only two examples? Explain your answer.

My Brother, My Friend
Bill Murphy

*B*orn *in 1955 in Massachusetts, Bill Murphy attended Boston University before earning his B.A. and M.A. degrees from the University of Arkon. A fiction and personal essay writer, his work has appeared in* Akros *and* Elysian Fields. *Murphy teaches composition at the University of Akron and is also a staff columnist for* The Medina County Gazette, *in which a version of this essay originally appeared. In the following essay, Murphy examines the dual relationship he has with his brother, that of sibling and friend.*

1   I'll always be a little brother. I guess I can stand it. I have only one brother in this world, my big brother, and though that will never change, I do wonder if I'll always be his friend.

2   I've been staying with my brother Tim during my vacation in the Florida Keys. His decision to move here some ten years ago has ensured that he has his share of winter visitors, whether he likes it or not, and he is under orders to never consider moving.

3   Of course, he's not on vacation while I'm down here, but with our mother living a couple of miles away, it's something of a family reunion, which in our family is something of a mixed blessing.

4   Tim, my only sibling, is eight years older than I, and I of course always looked up to him, yearned to spend time with him as I was growing up. I'm sure I was too little to be much fun most of the time, but he did let me hang around sometimes while his friends were around. I'm sure we weren't friends then—I must have been more of a curiosity, a conversation piece—but I learned a lot about the world and my brother just by listening and watching, until I was 10. Then he was off to college and I saw him only sporadically, summers and holidays and weekends after that, until we shared an apartment for a year when I was in my early 20s.

5   I was trying to be his friend then, as I moved in with him after his girlfriend of 10 years moved out after a relationship-ending dispute. I thought Tim and I would hang out and be pals, but he quickly found a woman to rebound with and they spent much more time together than we did. I've come to realize that friendship often takes a back seat to romance/sex, but

I didn't think of it as an aspect of friendship back then.

6   We've seen each other on and off since, but I've visited him during the holidays for four years in a row now. He's duty-bound as a participating family member to allow me into his climate, which in the winter is pretty spectacular, highs in the 80s and continually-cooling breezes, but it's the friend in him that invites me with enthusiasm and never deliberately makes me feel uncomfortable at being there.

7   I have felt uncomfortable being with him. When I think of Tim in the abstract, I feel warmly—he's my brother, he's a good guy, he's my friend—but after spending several weeks with him, I realize it's a lot more complicated than that.

8   For one thing, we're really very different from each other, not just in personality, but in outlook. Although we're both part of the baby-boomer generation, when he was in high school, the Beatles and Stones were popular, Vietnam was ravaging teenage men, and the Sixties spread its magic dust, but when I was in high school, Elton John ruled, Nam was no longer much of a worry and the Disco Seventies were underway.

9   Just eight years apart, but different worlds. Even in our family we lived in different worlds. Alcohol played a large and unfortunate part in our upbringing, and while that created its share of uncertainties for both of us, for his first eight years he had no one to share with and after that only a relatively inarticulate companion, while I always had a big brother to shield me and guide me. He had to construct a method of bravery to cope, and it was well in place by the time I was born. In several ways I grew up in a safer world than he did, and some of that I owe to him.

10   As the years have gone by, the essentials of our roles haven't changed. His job as big brother has been to explain the world, from politics to sports to music to our family, to me, and my job has been to listen to his disclosures, which have often amounted to monologues, and I have been happy to have his attention.

11   He's always decided what we'll do and where we'll go, and I've gone along, glad to be with his company and with his friends. His decision-making tendencies are, I think, a manifestation of his courage, an attempt to make order of a disordered world, and that's always been there for me. He's invited and brought me to hundreds of baseball and basketball games, concerts and clubs and restaurants, while I've only brought him to a handful. That's the way we've operated as big and little brother—I don't know if it's seemed odd or not, but it has seemed perfectly natural.

12   While it's a privilege to be Tim's little brother. I've come to understand that he needs me in my role—he needs to have someone to explain to, someone to show things to. Even though he's 45 years old now, the world is still a scary enough place, and I know having a little brother to talk to still helps him make sense of things.

13   Now it's perfectly possible for friends to have this sort of relationship—I'm sure I wouldn't be the first to suggest that friendship roles sometimes mimic family roles—but here's where our friendship might have gone

south. For a few years there, I was not comfortable in this role as listener and tried to reject it. I'd listen as long as I could to the monologues that I'd loved as a youth and then get fed up and stop. I'd reached the point where I too had something to say but didn't know how, didn't feel comfortable in saying it, and I'm not sure Tim had the slightest idea what my problem was.

14   Our friendship could have ended there, as friendships often do, in a swirl of hazy understanding and shifting personality patterns that might have led to a cloudburst of anger and an atmosphere of resentment, but because we were brothers, we couldn't drift too far apart.

15   And now, as I grow older and possibly wiser myself, I've managed to get beyond the resentment and frustration and can interject my thoughts and create what amounts to actual conversation, though it rarely is a smooth process. He talks and when I think of it I respond, sometimes to his surprise, and sometimes he is able to respond to my response. Sometimes I actually initiate discussion, but tentatively, unsure if it's my place to do so, and I'm still surprised when he takes me seriously enough to react, unaccustomed as he may be to the notion. We are nurturing a new friendship, and should the conditions remain stable for awhile, some healthy creature may grow from this.

16   I don't know if we'd be friends if we weren't brothers, but if we weren't brothers, I do know it wouldn't be this hard either. We wouldn't have years of subconscious role-playing to recognize and try and break out of. Then again, since friends can come and go, and as brothers we'll be struggling with this until one of us, at least, dies, we may have several opportunities to grow out of one friendship and into another.

17   Maybe as the years go by, I can somehow be the big brother he never had and help him relax that facade of bravery, but now that I understand, I really do think I can stand, in any case, to be his little brother, especially since it is as a little brother that I write this, explaining the world to my invisible brothers and sisters as my brother did for me.

18   Of course, it does help our friendship that my big brother lives in the Keys.

Discussion Questions

---

1. From your own experiences and observations, how important do you think age is in the relationships people have with their siblings? Explain your response.

2. Do you think that siblings have an easier time being friends with one another than with persons outside the family? Or is there something inherent in family relations that makes friendships with family members more difficult? Explain your response.

3. Explain the importance of role playing between siblings. Do you think this improves or harms the chance of siblings being friends? Why?

4. What do you think Murphy learned from having written this essay? Cite specific lines that influence your response. What did *you* learn?

5. In the next-to-last paragraph, Murphy states "Maybe as the years go by, I can somehow be the big brother he [Tim] never had and help him relax that facade of bravery....." What in Murphy's essay leads you to believe that this will or will not happen? Explain your answer.

Expecting Friends
Gary Soto

Gary Soto, a Mexican-American poet and fiction writer from California, was born in 1952. He earned his B.A. degree from California State University, Fresno, in 1974 and his M.F.A. degree from the University of California, Irvine, in 1976. Soto's publications include The Elements of San Joaquin *(1977), for which he recieved the United States Award of the International Poetry Forum,* The Tale of Sunlight *(1978),* Father Is a Pillow Tied to a Broom *(1980),* Where Sparrows Work Hard *(1981),* Black Hair *(1985),* Baseball in April and Other Stories *(1990),* A Summer Life *(1990), and* Home Course in Religion: New Poems *(1991). His books of essays are entitled* Living Up the Street: Narrative Recollections *(1985),* Lesser Evils: Ten Quartets *(1988), and* Small Faces *(1986), in which the following essay appears. In it, Soto focuses on friendships between men.*

1   My friends are coming—Jon the Estonian and Omar the Mexican—and what we want is to sit under the apricot tree in the backyard and talk about friends who couldn't come—Chris the one-book scholar and Leonard the two-beat drummer. We're going to talk poetry, ours mostly, and open beers one after another until we're a little drunk and a little wiser than the chairs we're sitting on. But we're going to take this slowly. We may, in fact, not sit under that tree but first take a drive to Tilden Park, where we'll hike as if there's a place to go and maybe sit waist-deep in wild grass, chewing long stalks that are springboards for the ants. Later we could go to the Country Club and slouch in leather chairs that overlook the green and its small rise of hills. Men in plaid kneeling over golf balls.

Clouds over the trees. Trees like pieces of the sea standing up. The day will be so open, so filled with blue air, that we won't believe it's all for us.

2   But who are these friends? Jon was a classmate in poetry, roommate in Laguna Beach, and the best man in my wedding, a guy who drank to all the causes of the heart. A friend writes of Jon and the day of the wedding:

> *The best man, lifting*
>
> *at least his fifth bottle of champagne,*
>
> *stands on a table in his white tuxedo;*
>
> *and turning slowly toward us, like Tommy Dorsey*
>
> *to the band, invites us to toast the moon,*
>
> *the clear Fresno moon, which he finds gone.*

And the moon did disappear, for my wife and I married on a night of an eclipse that comes every twenty years, a rare treat for the astronomer's wife. We didn't know. We planned the wedding from an old calendar, sent out homemade invitations, and stood in front of a churchroom of relatives who gave money, clock radios, vases, a quilt, and a new bed to wear down over the years. Here are sensible gifts, they were saying. Now make a home. Make a laughing baby in your arms.

3   And Omar? He was already a poet when I was a naive college student who carried books under both arms when we first met in a hallway at Fresno State in 1972. I put down my books and asked, "Are you really Omar?" He smiled, offered a clammy hand, and said, "Keep reading, young man," when I told him how much I admired his poetry. And I did. I read lines like "Someone is chasing me up my sleeve" and "If I remember the dying maybe I'll be all right."

4   Later in the year I saw him with friends in front of the student union. Omar looked tattered, like a sailor roughed up by the sea, for his face was stubbled, his eyes red and milky in the corners, and his hair stiff as a shirt collar. I joined him and his friends who were hunched in old trench coats, feet moving a little because it was a gray December. No one was talking or about to talk. They looked around like sparrows, heads turning nervously left and then right, and shivered the cold from their shoulders. I looked around too and shivered, shaking off the cold. Trying to be friendly, I asked Omar how he was doing. He turned to me with a crazed look and said, "Go ask the dead!" I was taken back, surprised by his tone and half-eclipsed eye. Then he relaxed and chuckled; his friends chuckled. I opened my mouth into a stiff smile, stood with them for a while longer, and finally said goodbye as I hurried away with my sophomore books under my arms.

5   Omar the Crazy Gypsy, Lord Byron in Mexican clothes, cheerleader of the acid set of the late 60s, is now a quiet poet in the rural town of Sanger where, on weekends with an uncle, he sells pants, shirts, cowboy hats, and whatever workers buy from the back of a station wagon or

sweaty tents at swap meets. He is a merchant, he says, and when I ask jokingly if he sells his poetry too, he says, "Yes, they cost too. Right here." He touches his heart, and I know what he means.

6   These friends are coming to visit. We may drive to Tilden Park; we may drive across the San Rafael Bridge and search the water for migrating whales through binoculars. We'll pass the C&H Sugar Refinery in Hercules, then San Quentin, and finally come to the moss-green hills of Sonoma. We'll drive talking and looking left, then right, between bites of apples and slapped-together sandwiches. We may stop to take pictures of cows; we may stop at a roadside bar with a name like The South Forty or The Trail's End and stand drinking frosty beers. After a beer or two we may become so at ease that we invite a cowpoke who, after two or three or four beers, may call us city queers and hit us on our silly grins.

7   If we were smart we'd only drink one beer and get out—or just stay home, my home in Berkeley, under that apricot tree in the feathery light of an early spring day. The world is in blossom: apple and apricot, the tulip and yellow daffodil that is broken by wind. The sky is like no other: blue over the garage and silver-blue where the sun is coming through behind a rack of clouds. The breeze is doing things in the trees; my neighbor's dog is wagging his tail against the fence.

8   This will be Saturday. I will get my winter wish: to sit with friends who mean much to me and talk about others who mean much to us. I've been waiting for this moment. I've been waiting months to open up to others, laugh, and flick beer tops at kidding friends who have drunk too much. We'll carry chairs from the kitchen and set them under the tree. My wife may join us; I'll slap my lap and she'll sit with a sparkling wine glass in her hand. And our daughter may come out with her flying dolphin, a stuffed animal that's taped together and just hanging on. This will be Saturday, the weather faintly remembered from another time. In the backyard we may talk, or not talk, but be understood all the same.

Discussion Questions

1. How helpful are Soto's descriptions of his friends in aiding you to understand something about the friendship he has with them? Explain your answer.

2. Much of the essay is spent on Soto anticipating what he and his friends could or might do when they visit. What reasons do you see behind such speculation? Have you ever engaged in such thinking before the arrival of some friends?

3. Throughout the essay, Soto includes pieces of information not necessarily pertinent to his discussion of friendship (e.g., in para-

graph 7, "my neighbor's dog is wagging his tail against the fence"). Why do you think Soto included such snippets?

4. Explain your understanding of the last sentence, "In the back-yard we may talk, or not talk, but be understood all the same." Can you recall some friendships in which you felt similarly?

5. How do you think Barbara Ehrenreich and Steve Tesich would respond to Soto's essay? That is, on what points do you think they would agree? Why

Chapter 4 Writing Topics

1. Write an essay in which you discuss whether men's relationships with other men (or women's relationships with women) are stronger than with those of the opposite sex. Be sure to provide specific examples in your essay and examine what you believe are the causes of your observations.

2. In your own life, how have your friendships changed over the years? To what extent do you think your experiences are characteristic of other people's?

3. Write an essay that explores this question: In what ways do people idealize relationships that are far from perfect? Why do people insist on seeing those relationships as something they are not? Use your own experiences and observations to support the ideas you raise in your essay.

4. If you have the clear, objective perspective that time and distance often provide, recall your first "romance" and describe it so others can see the emotions you experienced at that time.

5. From your own experience and observations, how do friends and/or family members influence romantic relationships? That is, what impact does peer or family pressure have on dating, the seriousness of relationships, the breakup of relationships, etc.?

6. In an essay, examine the ways the friendships you formed in college have differed from friendships you formed at other times in your life and in different circumstances. Which do you think will last longer? Why?

7. Do you think it is possible for your boyfriend or girlfriend to be your best friend as well? Why or why not? Explore the dynamics of being (or not being) both types of friends.

8. Has there ever been a time in your life when developing friendships proved unusually easy or difficult? Examine the time(s) when that was the case.

9. Write an essay about a friendship that you would call one of the most important in your life. Describe the person, your relationship with him or her, the experiences you shared, etc., in order to help explain the friendship. Why does this particular friendship qualify as one of the most significant in your life?

10. To what extent do you think friendship with others helps to shape your self-image or self-identity? Write an essay in which you investigate the connection.

11. Have you ever been friends with two people who were markedly different from each other, people who spanned the range of friendship? Describe those people, their effect on you, and what could be learned about the nature of friendship—and you—from such a situation.

12. Think about the friendships you have had and examine the importance age has had in those relationships. Are there special advantages to having friends who are the same age as you, or is a wide range of ages preferable? Be sure to draw on your own experiences and observations as examples of your beliefs.

13. How important do you think setting is in entertaining friends? Describe a time in which the place where you met contributed to the success of the gathering.

14. Write an essay in which you reflect on the reasons for people placing so much importance on friendship. Do you think the importance is justified, or are people making too much of friendship?

Chapter 5

Self-Portraits

The chief characteristic of the mind is to be constantly describing itself.

—Henry Focillon

The consciousness of self, this capacity to see one's self as though from the outside, is the distinctive characteristic of man.

—Rollo May

All of our lives we are accompanied vaguely by the selves we might be

—Lance Morrow

I find myself saying briefly and prosaically that it is much more important to be oneself than anything else.

—Virginia Woolf

But we can never be—in the deepest sense—anybody than we always were from the very beginning.

—Curtis Harnack

At some time in our lives, it seems that all of us are on a quest to know "who we are." As teenagers, we often struggle with questions concerning our identity and how we fit into the world. Later on, some people experience a midlife crisis in which they rethink not only what they have done with their lives, but who they are as individuals. A glance at the "self-help" shelf in any bookstore reveals a society seemingly obsessed with wanting to better understand themselves. Of course the task is more complicated than reading a book or opting for a new lifestyle. As we mature and change physically so too do our thoughts and beliefs change. With each new job, each new relationship, each new challenge, we are given the opportunity for growth. "What does not change/is the will to change" is the way the poet Charles Olson described this human phenomenon.

Examining who we are is indeed a challenging and informative enterprise. Describing ourselves requires not only observing from the outside but looking at the inside. To restrict ourselves to describing only from the outside would amount to placing a mirror in front of ourselves and reporting what we see. More interesting and informative is examining the inside, what we think and feel.

The essays in Chapter 5 of *The Voice of Reflection* offer eight such self-portraits. The issues the writers examine range from beauty to addiction, physical handicaps to gender roles. The first two essays concern physical beauty: Gloria Steinem, in an excerpt from *Revolution from Within,* examines the way she grew to accept her self-image. Then Elizabeth MacDonald provides a stunning description of her quest for an idealized self that resulted in her acquiring bulimia.

The next pair of essays deals with physical disability: Leonard Kriegel recounts how he had to learn to "fall into life," and Matthew Soyster describes his anger and frustration with multiple sclerosis. Both essays provide unusual and powerful examinations of what it means to be physically challenged in a world designed primarily for people without restrictions.

From his autobiography, *Self-Consciousness,* John Updike details his history with a skin disorder, psoriasis. In "Short Subject," Joseph Epstein offers his perspective on being short in a world of seemingly populated by tall people. In "Time in a Bottle," Linda Ellerbee recounts her battle with alcoholism and her route to recovery. Finally, Scott Russell Sanders reflects on all of the role models he had as a child and how they failed to help him understand what it is to be a man.

As you read these essays, you will see something much different from self-absorbed or egocentric descriptions of the authors. You will be invited to witness epiphany: how the writers' understandings have taken shape and the ways they have transformed "looking" into "vision." Perhaps the essays can spur *you* on to experiment with self-portraiture.

Bodies of Knowledge

Gloria Steinem

Gloria Steinem was born in Toledo, Ohio, in 1934. A graduate of Smith College, Steinem is the founding editor of New York *maga-zine and the cofounder of the Women's Action Alliance. She is most noted, however, for cofounding* Ms. *magazine in 1971 and for her ac-tive involvement in feminist issues and politics. Steinem is the author of* Outrageous Acts and Everyday Rebellions *(1983) and* Revolution from Within: A Book of Self-Esteem *(1992), from which the following essay is excerpted and* Moving Beyond Words *(1994). In this piece, Steinem reflects on how feminism "rescued" her from a poor self-image.*

1   It was only when I looked for the *why* of that big, plump, vulnerable girl in my own head—who had made me do everything from becoming stoop-shouldered in an effort to be shorter to hiding behind any available screen of hair and huge glasses—that she began to change at all, and she's not completely there yet. I had left her for too many years sealed up and alone, a chubby girl growing up in an isolated family whose food addic-tions and body image she absorbed.

2   I think of my father, who weighed over 300 pounds most of his life, got in the car even to mail a letter, and organized his days around food. He knew every restaurant with an unlimited buffet on his peripatetic sales route from the Midwest to the West Coast, and when we saw each other, our emotional connections always took place over double-thick malteds or apple pie à la mode. I loved him for his sense of adventure, for looking af-ter me when I was very little and my mother could not, and for so much more; yet I was often ashamed of his huge size, his inability to fit into movie seats, his suits and shirts that often bore clear traces of the last meal, and his habit of falling asleep in any company after the soporific of food. At the time and for years after his death, I thought I was separate from him—but of course, I was not. I am his daughter. Like a recovering alco-holic, I'm a foodaholic who can't keep food in the house. I'm still trying to stay healthy, one day at a time. As Gabriel García Márquez says through one of his characters in *Love in the Time of Cholera:* "I am not rich. I am a poor man with money, which is not the same thing." Well, I am not a thin woman, I'm a fat woman who's not fat at the moment.

3   I also think of my mother, whose problem was her sad heart and un-dervalued head, not the rest of her body, yet her soft maternal hips and breasts seemed connected in my child's mind to her fate of sadness. I real-ize that I've continued to worry about and feel protective of women who are big-breasted and vulnerable, at the same time that I've longed for a more slender, boyish body to distance me from my mother's fate. But when I did begin to lose some plumpness after childhood, it was because I shot up to my full height of five feet seven by the time I was ten or eleven,

which made me tower over my girlfriends and internalize a sense of being huge and galumphing. Still, this new height did reward me by enabling me to look older, and thus make money dancing at local clubs, a small-time version of the show-business career that seemed the only way out of our neighborhood. In retrospect, however, this was also a case of growing up too soon that probably added to my feelings of loss as my mother's care-taker. By fifteen, I was pretending to be eighteen in order to enter a local talent/beauty contest and feeling inordinately depressed when I failed to win a chance to compete in Florida for a title I recall as "Miss Capehart TV." When I belatedly began ballet lessons to add to the tap dancing I'd been learning, my ballet teacher also dimmed my dreams of dancing my way out of Toledo by saying I was too tall *en pointe* for most male partners. Since I never questioned the need to be shorter than dates and an eventual husband, a lifetime of creative slumping stretched before me.

4   Later, when college had got me out of Toledo, I gave up dancing— my only exercise. All other forms seemed beyond me. I thought tennis was for rich kids, field hockey was for prep-school girls, and besides, I'd never learned a sport. In high school, the only desirable sport for girls was being a drum majorette or cheerleader, both of which I envied but didn't at-tempt. Each time I tried one in college, the instructors—perhaps unaccus-tomed to having to start from scratch—suggested I try something else. Furthermore, I was downright shocked the first time I heard someone say "I'm going for a walk" when she didn't have to. In my neighborhood in those prefitness times, having a car signaled prosperity and walking meant poverty. College only confirmed my habit of living in my head: I just stud-ied, ate, and gained my part of what was known as "the freshman ton." If there had been a sport called sitting-and-reading, I would have been an all-time champion.

5   By the time I was out of college, back from a two-year fellowship in India, and trying to make a living as a freelance writer in New York, there were media images that gave me other ways to distance myself from my background and my family. I remember crying over Audrey Hepburn in *Breakfast at Tiffany's* because I identified with the poor and prematurely responsible childhood she had escaped by walking down a dirt road a little farther every day—until finally, she just kept going. I laced my dark hair with obvious blond streaks, just as she had done. The kerchiefs she wore turned out to be perfect for hiding my fat cheeks. I also copied her huge sunglasses in order to hide the fleshiness left over from a chubby child-hood that overhung my eyelids and displaced my contact lenses so often that I gave up wearing them. Short skirts like hers were also satisfyingly unladylike and showed the one part of me still fit from dancing: legs. I re-alized that, if I patched myself together with just the right combination of flaunting and hiding, I could be counted as pretty, even though I was far from that in my mind. A friend from that era described me as a mousy girl with harlequin glasses and a ponytail who had turned herself into a myste-rious Holly Golightly overnight.

6   Thus, I inched along that narrow you-can't-win continuum of female images, escaping from 1950s "collegiate" into 1960s "rebellious" without once thinking who *I* was.

7   Fortunately, feminist ideas began to explode at the end of the 1960s and helped us all to realize that we shared an overarching problem: being judged on how we looked instead of what was in our heads and hearts. Thanks to this unifying and liberating revelation, we began to rebel against the more obvious forms of imprisonment, like feeling we couldn't go to the grocery without lipstick, or giving more thought to what we wore than what we read. I abandoned clothes anxiety with relief and evolved a simple, comfortable, jeans-sweater-and-boots uniform that I wore for one entire decade. Somehow, it took me that long to burn the cheap dressing-up of Toledo plus the expensive dressing-down of the Ivy League out of my brain.

8   Only in the last decade have I been able to achieve what I really enjoy; what Marge Piercy described so well in her futurist novel, *Woman on the Edge of Time:* soft, comfortable, semiandrogynous clothes for everyday, and a pool of fanciful clothes shared with friends so we can all decorate ourselves for an occasional party or dancing at night. Perhaps the one attitude that has persisted from Toledo days is my fear of looking ladylike: then, because the wives of the factory owners looked that way (and unfortunately, I thought of them as the enemy); now, because those fussy clothes seem like a prison. I noticed several studies remarking on the frequency with which women's dreams involve feeling imprisoned by their clothes—and I believe it. I'd like to print cards for little girls in button-in-the-back frilly dresses (as well as for their grown-up sisters suffering in their own versions of those dresses): *Help! I am a prisoner in my clothes.*

9   But though I was rescued by feminism, it had one result for which I was ill prepared: finding myself referred to as "the pretty one"—jeans and all. Rationally, I knew it was a response of surprise, based on what the media thought feminists looked like (if a woman could get a man, why would she need equal pay?), and this was especially clear to me because I was judged much prettier *after* I was identified as a feminist than I ever had been *before.* Identifying women by appearance again, flattering some and insulting others, was a way of reducing feminism to form without content—and dividing us. Since I didn't feel prettier (or even pretty), I didn't trust the press's image of me, and I just kept hiding out in my uniform of jeans, hair, and sunglasses, hoping that other women wouldn't be alienated by what the media said.

10   Because the internal image was so much realer than reality, it never occurred to me to question the childhood roots of that self-image—to ask myself why I hid my face, stood round-shouldered, always felt enormous, and when someone complimented me, gave them reasons why they were wrong—instead of just saying thank you.

11   It was in that stage that I saw my real physical self on television. (This is a self-revelation now available to anyone with a video camera, and one that I highly recommend; somehow, it's much more powerful than look-

ing in a mirror, perhaps because our media craziness makes us think what we see on a screen is almost more real than reality.) Once I got past the shock of wondering who that was, I had to admit there was something called body image. Seeing myself looking so calm on the screen, and knowing that I had been petrified inside—paradoxically, it takes a little confidence to reveal one's *lack* of confidence—also gave me more sympathy for other people. I began to do less envying, judging, or worrying about women based on their appearance, since it now dawned on me that one can never know how others see themselves.

12   But once I realized that image was different from reality, I also began to wonder how my own mother had seen herself. One of my earliest memories was of brushing her hair or dabbing powder on her pale cheeks while she sat docile as a child, depending on me to "fix her up" for a rare outing. By the time I knew her, she was a woman who paid almost no attention to her physical self. Before those long years of depression, how had she seen herself when she was a young girl?

13   As we sat in her basement apartment in my sister's house—for my mother still could not live alone—she described how raw-boned and gawky she'd felt next to her littler, rounder, "prettier" sister, and how angry she had been at her mother for giving them both a message that women's bodies were shameful. She had eloped with my father because he made her laugh, but also because she was grateful to be chosen. It was the first time in our lives we'd ever talked about anything as basic as our feelings about our bodies, and my mother, then in her seventies, surprised me by saying she wanted to do something about what she called "my dewlaps," loose facial skin that was the result of a hard life that included several years in mental hospitals, and little self-care. For years, I'd noticed that she told new acquaintances she was much older than she really was, and I suddenly understood why: she'd been trying to match inner and outer reality. Now, there was a spark of hope that made her want to *be* that inner person. In spite of my skepticism (then a bias) about plastic surgery, I encouraged her and set about making the necessary arrangements; it was so clearly a sign of hope that she wanted it. But when we talked again, all her old anxieties and depression had returned. Nothing I said could convince her that her body was worth any attention at all. Our talk had come too late.

14   I look at the photograph she gave me that day, and when I see the tall, spare, "gawky" young woman that my mother was in her early twenties, I realize with irony that she was exactly the free, androgynous image I would later try to become. When I was in my mother's body, had I absorbed this authentic self emanating from her bones? Are there generations of daughters, each one rebelling against the false image forced on the generation before, never knowing that we would have loved and admired our mothers all the more if they had been able to blossom as their true selves?

15   Over the years since my mother's death, I've been trying to enjoy and appreciate my own authentic body, and to learn what it has to teach. "The

body never forgets" is the motto of therapists who help people use somatic memories as bridges to the past, and I've come to believe that the body image never forgets either. I know a woman who saw herself with such shameful and distorted breasts that she wanted to have breast surgery. She remembered only a week before her scheduled operation that her grandmother had made her wear painful bindings as a developing girl, and that she had assumed this was necessary to keep her safe from boys at school. Suddenly, she saw that surgery was not the healing she needed. But I wonder: How many people try to change the part of the body that is only trying to help them remember?

16   As for myself, I'm still learning. I only recently understood, for instance, why nausea has always felt like the end of the world to me; so much so that I once endangered my health by resisting the need to throw up with food poisoning. By focusing on one current feeling of nausea, I rediscovered the day that I realized I was solely responsible for my mother. My father, long separated from her, had driven me home from Girl Scout camp, and after he had dropped me off, I was alone with my very depressed mother. As I felt the fear of understanding there was no one to turn to, I also felt in my stomach the malted and hamburger my father had bought me. They seemed to remain in the pit of my stomach for days.

17   But once I had followed this thread to the past, its fearfulness began to dim. The amazing thing is this: The moment we find the true reason for some feeling that has an irrationally powerful hold over us, whether it has to do with body image or anything else, the spell is broken. It may take a long time, but the negative grooves it has left in our minds can be filled in with conscious and positive affirmations. With our ideas about our bodies, as with all things human, saying yes works better than saying no. So I've been trying to recall positive parts of my family legacy and then expand on them.

18   While working on this book, for instance, I've been thinking how grateful I am to my parents for respecting my body as a child and never making me think it deserved spanking, hitting, or abuse of any kind. This has helped me not only to be rebellious on my own behalf, but to believe in and to fight against abuse experienced by others—for I have no personal stake in denying its reality. I've also tried to focus on parts of my body that I like, and to imagine expanding that empowering feeling to the rest of me. I recently realized that the one part of my body of which I am unequivocally proud is the hands I inherited from my father. They are long, tapering, graceful hands, something about him of which I was never ashamed. Just imagining how this self-esteem might feel if expanded to my whole body gives me a glimpse of how energizing true body-pride could be. I think of all the women I know who take pleasure in their bodies but are made to feel guilty about it, as if they were giving in to a culture that has used women's bodies for fetishes and consumerism. I think of other women who give up body-pride and even jeopardize their health by ignoring their physical selves, retreating into their minds, and trying to defeat the culture by treating flesh and skin as unfortunate necessity. What won-

ders have they and all of us been missing? What might we become if we were body-proud from the beginning?

19 The whole answer remains for future generations to discover, but I've found my own small beginning. Sometimes when my hand rests on a surface, I see the middle finger tap involuntarily, exactly as my father's used to do. For that one second, I feel his visceral presence. I hope he knows that I'm no longer ashamed—of either of us.

Discussion Questions

1. In her essay, Steinem discusses the sources that affected her sense of self-image. Who and/or what has been instrumental in influencing your own self-image?

2. In paragraph 6, Steinem admits to "inch[ing] along that narrow you-can't-win continuum of female images . . . without once thinking who *I* was." Can you identify a moment in your own life when you felt pulled by outside forces and neglected to consider who you really were? Describe such a time and how you were affected by it.

3. Steinem in paragraph 11 recommends that people see themselves on video to see their "real physical sel[ves]." If you have already done this, describe what you saw. Was it what you expected to see? If you haven't seen yourself on video, what do you think you would see? Why?

4. Answer the question Steinem raises in the next-to-last paragraph: "What might we become if we were body-proud from the beginning?"

5. Steinem's essay addresses the inner versus the outer self. To what extent do you think many people find disparities between those two selves? To what extent do you see this issue as New Age, media hype? Explain your response.

Odalisque

Elizabeth MacDonald

E lizabeth MacDonald was born in 1971 and grew up in New York City. A Fine Arts major at Harvard University, MacDonald wrote "Odalisque" as a student in an Expository Writing class taught by Pat C. Hoy II. In her essay, MacDonald recounts her history of be-

ing obsessed with weight, and she analyzes the neoclassical artist Ingres'
painting of the Turkish harem slave's body that is "everything that I
wish I could permit mine to be." After you read this essay, reread Hoy's
"Immortality" that appears in Chapter 1. Hoy states that "Leaving
her essay, we know that Elizabeth will have to endure in a culture
where beauty inflicts intense pain. The rest of us, because of her tale,
will probably never see beauty again in the same light." What in Mac-
Donald's essay makes you agree or disagree with Hoy's observation?

1   I am in eighth grade—perhaps two weeks, or even a week before all
the trouble started—and walking one evening with a friend on the east
side of Manhattan. I catch sight of my reflection in a plate-glass window
and, in these formative years, observe what I am becoming. My hair is
short and less feminine at this time, my face rounder, my body plumper. I
was happy with what I saw.

2   I am in ninth grade and my waist is the thickness of a bottleneck. Lying
on my bed I hear my parents talking about me as they walk along the hall.

3   "This diet has gone on too long," my mother is saying, "she's gotten
very weak."

4   "She is very thin," says my father.

5   I am in tenth grade and fatter than I have ever been. In a book written
during the Twiggy-influenced sixties I read that every day that you fast you
lose two pounds of fat. This seems easier than recovering the discipline
that I had once in such abundance and have now lost. I begin a regimen in
which I eat enormous amounts for a few days and fast on the others. I
want very much to regain the beauty that was once mine, to re-discover
the indestructible, perfect creature of angles and spare planes that lies hidden under this amorphous mass of lumps. I want more than anything to be
thin again. This seems to be a way. For a desperate girl who has no assurance that she will ever be desirable, almost no price is too high.

6   I do not remember the first time that I made myself throw up. It may
have been in eleventh grade, but the circumstances have faded under the
shame and horror. As I understand it many people try self-induced vomiting. Few are successful on the first attempt and most give up. Some of us
persist: some of us even become quite talented.

7   In that talent I originally found salvation. Self-indulgence and beauty
seemed, for the first time, compatible. I could give myself everything I
wanted and retain the figure of the ascetic. I could have my cake, and I
could eat it too. Nothing, however, is that easy. Maintaining the façade
becomes indispensable. Every compliment is a knife in the gut and an impulse to retain what I have, though I pay, and pay dearly. There is a line in
Yeats' "Adam's Curse" that cries bitterness—

To be born woman is to know—

Although they do not talk of it at school—

That we must labor to be beautiful

I have only just discovered that I have been misquoting these lines for years. In my mind the last line, though essentially the same, has always had a slightly different nuance.

8   . . . We must suffer to be beautiful.

9   The most famous photograph of Rita Hayworth, as Gilda, immortalizes her as an extraordinary beauty. In black satin she stands, mysterious and gorgeous—a stunning beauty, with allure and come-hither confidence. Her skin glows alabaster against a black background and on her beautiful face, slightly turned to the side, is a look of encouragement and, conversely, knowing distance. She tilts her chin up in the arrogance of her beauty: she knows very well that she stops traffic and hearts. Her hair is long, her waist is small, and her strapless dress clings to her perfect figure. Her self-presentation is more than feminine; it is the essence of female. Rita Hayworth played a woman all men wanted and all women wanted to be. She sets the standard of what it is to be an ideal woman—a flesh Goddess.

10   I have heard that she could not reconcile her beauty and herself, that she felt herself to be an illusion created by lights and other people's vision of what she should be. You could never tell that from this photograph. This woman revels in nothing more than her sexuality and beauty. And for all that, all the power and joy in her physical presence that she presents to the world in this still, Rita Hayworth never believed in the image she presented. She felt that the façade was fraudulent and that she was two people inhabiting a beautiful shell whose two sides were irreconcilable. Her most famous quotation is a cry of pain. "Every man I ever knew went to bed with Gilda and woke up with me." They saw in her the realization of all their dreams and found that she was just a woman. Men looked in her for Gilda and a goddess. Inside she knew that she was as mortal as Mary Sixpack and she could not bear the split between her image and what she felt to be her real self. She suffered in her beauty.

11   In the margins of most of my notebooks is the sketch of a woman's head in a three-quarter view. Her hair is long and her cheekbones are far more pronounced than mine will ever be, no matter how thin I get. Her jaw is very defined. I gave her a name once, a name that has much to do with ethereality and fragility and a name as imaginary as is Gilda. I only christen the sketches that turn out well with that name. I only want to draw a Gilda, and I only want to be a Gilda, even knowing what Gilda did to Rita Hayworth.

12   I would never presume to compare my looks with those of Rita Hayworth, but I am a woman, and I know about laboring. I too have learned that there is a price to be paid for beauty. I live the same deception as she did. I am not what I seem, and the deception battles my soul.

13   "Yes, I am attracted," I overheard him say once, "but I don't think she's my type." He did not know me at that point. I was a shell and a body, long hair and green eyes and long legs and a small waist, nice curves for one so thin. I know that he wants the flesh envelope that I walk in. I and others have seen him looking at me, my hair, my face, my legs. He has twisted around in chairs to watch me as I go by, and I know that he is aware of me whenever I am around him. My physicality is a magnet. He wants and he wants, but he just wants a body. He does not want me. He himself is easy in his corporeality: he has the athlete's presence and the athlete's ability to live within his skin and take pleasure in the way his body works. I think I felt that if he—so easy in his skin—believed in my entirety then I too would believe. Only my body sold. Uninterested in the interior, he cannot divorce himself of his attraction for the façade, and I am caught. The façade always sells first, and therefore the façade must always be maintained, no matter what.

14   I met him for breakfast one morning this winter when the snow was falling softly. I walked alone in the quiet of early morning. I could feel the snow collecting on the gauze of my hair. Alone with him in a near-empty dining hall, I felt cold, and my food had no taste. I ate very little. After breakfast I disappeared.

15   Sometimes, when I have disappeared and I am unrecognizable, invisible, I run my hands over the planes of my face, telling myself that I am, I am, I am. I exist, I am alive, I tell myself, running my fingertips over the sockets of bone in which those green eyes lie, and I discover the line of my jaw beneath my skin. My eyelashes tickle my hands, and my hands worship my flesh and my bones. I am reassuring myself that somewhere under my rib cage my heart beats, that though invisible I am not gone.

16   I remember the first time I threw up blood.

17   The modern artist Giorgio di Chirico painted in a classical manner. His subjects seem to be informed by Italian Renaissance models but the classical vision has been tortured and twisted and made strange. His paintings recede into depth in skewed perspective, and nature has been warped into something that is both recognizable and alien. In his lonely, dark settings the shadows are like none ever seen in reality but are still frighteningly real. "There are more enigmas in the shadow of a man who walks in the sun," he said, "than in all the religions of past, present and future." In the medium he devoted his life to he could find no answers: mysteries were easier than a simple darkness, the shadow of a man in the sun. The lines of his paintings are invariably ruler straight, but there is no peace or ease to be found in his art. His paintings are disorienting: they are the representation of a human imbalance and uncertainty in the world.

18   I am uneasy in my shell.

19   The neoclassical artist Ingres painted figures of dubious anatomical construction but used the questions to glorify the beauty of the human shape rather than to disorient the viewer. It is the male body that is said to represent best the human form for its shape follows the lines of the core and is undisguised by curves and softness. Ingres painted women. In "The Turkish Bath" many women lie in splendor, impossibly twisted into sensuous shapes. He celebrates the disguising curves and softness, emphasizing them, asserting roundness as beautiful. In another celebration of Woman, "La Grande Odalisque," a beautiful woman reclines alone. I first saw this painting in grisaille, a technique that simulates statuary, molding the human shape in shades of grey.

20   The body of this Turkish harem slave is everything that I wish I could permit mine to be. It is voluptuous and smooth; it is classically feminine. In the line of breast and hip, of round arm and thigh, globes and arcs connect and flow, defining grace and beauty. Hers is a celebration of existence, of the flesh and the senses. Nude she reclines, luxuriating in herself as a living being and a body. Her setting reflects and enhances the luxury of her being: royal blue, oriental cushions, self-indulgence and self-love. She cares for her own pleasure. Her skin is pale, and the feminine aspects of her figure have been emphasized to the point of distortion. Her shoulders are narrow; her waist is small, and her lower back is far too long. The elongation highlights the flesh at the hip and leads into her legs. They appear shorter than they would were she thin. Her feet and hands are fragile, her visible eye luminous, and the bones of her face have a delicate beauty. She is direct and beautiful. She is sensuous and sensual. She is enigmatic and she is feminine. Her glance over her round shoulder beckons and arrogantly asserts her power. Nude, she revels in herself as a sexual being. She does not hide.

21   In my dreams, though, I take on the attributes not of the Odalisque, but of my impossibly idealized sketch. The world celebrates my fragility and stunning physical presence. I define gorgeous. The earth congratulates itself that I pass time on its surface. I am delicate and so breathtakingly beautiful that I put Gilda to shame.

22   Ingres chose not to make his Odalisque's body anatomically correct. By the standards of reality it is warped and strangely twisted, wrong like di Chirico's perspective. Her arm and her lower back are far too long, her leg twists around her other leg. Her body is more than imperfect, it is impossible, but in its impossibility the necessities of bone and blood have been sacrificed to the beauty of line and form. Where di Chirico skews perspective to disorient, Ingres twists a body and liberates it. Without the bones that constrain the normal human figure, she is freer in her flesh. She is more conscious of her own power and presence. She inhabits her body in joy, accepting it, loving her curves and sensuality, hedonism inherent in the hookah and crumpled sheets. She flows feminine.

23   In Ingres' world—though not in mine—she need not suffer to be easy in her skin.

Discussion Questions

1. What emotion(s) do you think MacDonald wanted to evoke in her readers: anger? pity? fear? sympathy? Explain your answer.

2. What effect is created by MacDonald never coming out and saying she has bulimia? Do you think this adds to the effect of the essay? Why or why not?

3. Why do you think MacDonald includes references to movie stars and modern artists in her essay? Could she have achieved the same effects had she not included them? Explain your response.

4. Throughout her essay, MacDonald uses one-sentence paragraphs. Discuss their level of effectiveness.

5. Do you agree with Pat Hoy when he claims that we "will probably never see beauty again in the same light" after we read MacDonald's essay? Why or why not?

Falling into Life

Leonard Kriegel

Born in 1933 in New York, Leonard Kriegel received his B.A. degree from Hunter College, his M.A. from Columbia University, and his Ph.D. from New York University. He has taught English at Long Island University and, since 1961, at City College of the City University of New York. Kriegel is the author of The Long Walk Home *(1964),* Edmund Wilson *(1971),* Working Through: A Teacher's Journey in the Urban University *(1972),* Notes for the Two Dollar Window *(1976),* Of Man and Manhood *(1979),* Quilting Time *(1982), and* Falling into Life *(1991). The following essay from that most recent book first appeared in* The American Scholar *and was selected for* Best American Essays 1989. *In it, Kriegel recalls episodes from his life as a victim of polio and how he literally—and perhaps figuratively—had to "just let go and fall."*

1   It is not the actual death a man is doomed to die but the deaths his imagination anticipates that claim attention as one grows older. We are constantly being reminded that the prospect of death forcefully concentrates the mind. While that may be so, it is not a prospect that does very much else for the imagination—other than to make one aware of its limitations and imbalances.

2   Over the past five years, as I have moved into the solidity of middle age, my own most formidable imaginative limitation has turned out to be

a surprising need for symmetry. I am possessed by a peculiar passion: I want to believe that my life has been balanced out. And because I once had to learn to fall in order to keep that life mine, I now seem to have convinced myself that I must also learn to fall into death.

3   Falling into life wasn't easy, and I suspect that is why I hunger for such awkward symmetry today. Having lost the use of my legs during the polio epidemic that swept across the eastern United States during the summer of 1944, I was soon immersed in a process of rehabilitation that was, at least when looked at in retrospect, as much spiritual as physical.

4   That was a full decade before the discovery of the Salk vaccine ended polio's reign as the disease most dreaded by America's parents and their children. Treatment of the disease had been standardized by 1944: following the initial onslaught of the virus, patients were kept in isolation for a period of ten days to two weeks. Following that, orthodox medical opinion was content to subject patients to as much heat as they could stand. Stiff paralyzed limbs were swathed in heated, coarse woolen towels known as "hot packs." (The towels were that same greenish brown as blankets issued to American GIs, and they reinforced a boy's sense of being at war.) As soon as the hot packs had baked enough pain and stiffness out of a patient's body so that he could be moved on and off a stretcher, the treatment was ended, and the patient faced a series of daily immersions in a heated pool.

5   I would ultimately spend two full years at the appropriately named New York State Reconstruction Home in West Haverstraw. But what I remember most vividly about the first three months of my stay there was being submerged in a hot pool six times a day, for periods of between fifteen and twenty minutes. I would lie on a stainless steel slab, my face alone out of water, while the wet heat rolled against my dead legs and the physical therapist was at my side working at a series of manipulations intended to bring my useless muscles back to health.

6   Each immersion was a baptism by fire in the water. While my mind pitched and reeled with memories of the "normal" boy I had been a few weeks earlier, I would close my eyes and focus not, as my therapist urged, on bringing dead legs back to life but on my strange fall from the childhood grace of the physical. Like all eleven-year-old boys, I had spent a good deal of time thinking about my body. Before the attack of the virus, however, I thought about it only in connection with my own lunge toward adolescence. Never before had my body seemed an object in itself. Now it was. And like the twenty-one other boys in the ward—all of us between the ages of nine and twelve—I sensed I would never move beyond the fall from grace, even as I played with memories of the way I once had been.

7   Each time I was removed from the hot water and placed on a stretcher by the side of the pool, there to await the next immersion, I was fed salt tablets. These were simply intended to make up for the sweat we lost, but salt tablets seemed to me the cruelest confirmation of my new status as spiritual debtor. Even today, more than four decades later, I still shiver at

the mere thought of those salt tablets. Sometimes the hospital orderly would literally have to pry my mouth open to force me to swallow them. I dreaded the nausea the taste of salt inspired in me. Each time I was resubmerged in the hot pool, I would grit my teeth—not from the flush of heat sweeping over my body but from the thought of what I would have to face when I would again be taken out of the water. To be an eater of salt was far more humiliating than to endure pain. Nor was I alone in feeling this way. After lights-out had quieted the ward, we boys would furtively whisper from cubicle to cubicle of how we dreaded being forced to swallow salt tablets. It was that, rather than the pain we endured, that anchored our sense of loss and dread.

8   Any recovery of muscle use in a polio patient usually took place within three months of the disease's onset. We all knew that. But as time passed, every boy in the ward learned to recite stories of those who, like Lazarus, had witnessed their own bodily resurrection. Having fallen from physical grace, we also chose to fall away from the reality in front of us. Our therapists were skilled and dedicated, but they weren't wonder-working saints. Paralyzed legs and arms rarely responded to their manipulations. We could not admit to ourselves, or to them, that we were permanently crippled. But each of us knew without knowing that his future was tied to the body that floated on the stainless steel slab.

9   We sweated out the hot pool and we choked on the salt tablets, and through it all we looked forward to the promise of rehabilitation. For, once the stiffness and pain had been baked and boiled out of us, we would no longer be eaters of salt. We would not be what we once had been, but at least we would be candidates for re-entry into the world, admittedly made over to face its demands encased in leather and steel.

10   I suppose we might have been told that our fall from grace was permanent. But I am still grateful that no one—neither doctors nor nurses nor therapists, not even that sadistic orderly, himself a former polio patient, who limped through our lives and through our pain like some vengeful presence—told me that my chances of regaining the use of my legs were nonexistent. Like every other boy in the ward, I organized my needs around whatever illusions were available. And the illusion I needed above any other was that one morning I would simply wake up and rediscover the "normal" boy of memory, once again playing baseball in French Charley's Field in Bronx Park rather than roaming the fields of his own imagination. At the age of eleven, I needed to weather reality, not face it. And to this very day, I silently thank those who were concerned enough about me, or indifferent enough to my fate, not to tell me what they knew.

11   Like most boys, sick or well, I was an adaptable creature—and rehabilitation demanded adaptability. The fall from bodily grace transformed each of us into acolytes of the possible, pragmatic Americans for whom survival was method and strategy. We would learn, during our days in the New York State Reconstruction Home, to confront the world that was.

We would learn to survive the way we were, with whatever the virus had left intact.

12   I had fallen away from the body's prowess, but I was being led toward a life measured by different standards. Even as I fantasized about the past, it disappeared. Rehabilitation, I was to learn, was ahistorical, a future devoid of any significant claim on the past. Rehabilitation was a thief's primer of compensation and deception: its purpose was to teach one how to steal a touch of the normal from an existence that would be striking in its abnormality.

13   When I think back to those two years in the ward, the boy who made his rehabilitation most memorable was Joey Tomashevski. Joey was the son of an upstate dairy farmer, a Polish immigrant who had come to America before the Depression and whose English was even poorer than the English of my own shtetl-bred father. The virus had left both of Joey's arms so lifeless and atrophied that I could circle where his bicep should have been with pinky and thumb and still stick the forefinger of my own hand through. And yet, Joey assumed that he would make do with whatever had been left him. He accepted without question the task of making his toes and feet over into fingers and hands. With lifeless arms encased in a canvas sling that looked like the breadbasket a European peasant might carry to market, Joey would sit up in bed and demonstrate how he could maneuver fork and spoon with his toes.

14   I would never have dreamed of placing such confidence in my fingers, let alone my toes. I found, as most of the other boys in the ward did, Joey's unabashed pride in the flexibility and control with which he could maneuver a forkful of mashed potatoes into his mouth a continuous indictment of my sense of the world's natural order. We boys with dead legs would gather round his bed in our wheelchairs and silently watch Joey display his dexterity with a vanity so open and naked that it seemed an invitation to being struck down yet again. But Joey's was a vanity already tested by experience. For he was more than willing to accept whatever challenges the virus threw his way. For the sake of demonstrating his skill to us, he kicked a basketball from the auditorium stage through the hoop attached to a balcony some fifty feet away. When one of our number derisively called him lucky, he proceeded to kick five of seven more balls through that same hoop.

15   I suspect that Joey's pride in his ability to compensate for what had been taken away from him irritated me, because I knew that, before I could pursue my own rehabilitation with such singular passion, I had to surrender myself to what was being demanded of me. And that meant I had to learn to fall. It meant that I had to learn, as Joey Tomashevski had already learned, how to transform absence into opportunity. Even though I still lacked Joey's instinctive willingness to live with the legacy of the virus, I found myself being overhauled, re-created in much the same way as a car engine is rebuilt. Nine months after I arrived in the ward, a few weeks before my twelfth birthday, I was fitted for double long-legged

braces bound together by a steel pelvic band circling my waist. Lifeless or not, my legs were precisely measured, the steel carefully molded to form, screws and locks and leather joined to one another for my customized benefit alone. It was technology that would hold me up—another offering on the altar of compensation. "You get what you give," said Jackie Lyons, my closest friend in the ward. For he, too, was now a novitiate of the possible. He, too, now had to learn how to choose the road back.

16   Falling into life was not a metaphor; it was real, a process learned only through doing, the way a baby learns to crawl, to stand, and then to walk. After the steel bands around calves and thighs and pelvis had been covered over by the rich-smelling leather, after the braces had been precisely fitted to allow my fear-ridden imagination the surety of their holding presence, I was pulled to my feet. For the first time in ten months, I stood. Two middle-aged craftsmen, the hospital bracemakers who worked in a machine shop deep in the basement, held me in place as my therapist wedged two wooden crutches beneath my shoulders.

17   They stepped back, first making certain that my grip on the crutches was firm. Filled with pride in their technological prowess, the three of them stood in front of me, admiring their skill. Had I been created in the laboratory of Mary Shelley's Dr. Frankenstein, I could not have felt myself any more the creature of scientific pride. I stood on the braces, crutches beneath my shoulders slanting outward like twin towers of Pisa. I flushed, swallowed hard, struggled to keep from crying, struggled not to be overwhelmed by my fear of falling.

18   My future had arrived. The leather had been fitted, the screws had been turned to the precise millimeter, the locks at the knees and the bushings at the ankles had been properly tested and retested. That very afternoon I was taken for the first time to a cavernous room filled with barbells and Indian clubs and crutches and walkers. I would spend an hour each day there for the next six months. In the rehab room, I would learn how to mount two large wooden steps made to the exact measure of a New York City bus's. I would swing on parallel bars from one side to the other, my arms learning how they would have to hurl me through the world. I balanced Indian clubs like a circus juggler because my therapist insisted it would help my coordination. And I was expected to learn to fall.

19   I was a dutiful patient. I did as I was told because I could see no advantage to doing anything else. I hungered for the approval of those in authority—doctors, nurses, therapists, the two bracemakers. Again and again, my therapist demonstrated how I was to throw my legs from the hip. Again and again, I did as I was told. Grabbing the banister with my left hand, I threw my leg from the hip while pushing off my right crutch. Like some baby elephant (despite the sweat lost in the heated pool, the months of inactivity in bed had fattened me up considerably), I dangled from side to side on the parallel bars. Grunting with effort, I did everything demanded of me. I did it with an unabashed eagerness to please

those who had power over my life. I wanted to put myself at risk. I wanted to do whatever was supposed to be "good" for me. I believed as absolutely as I have ever believed in anything that rehabilitation would finally placate the hunger of the virus.

20   But when my therapist commanded me to fall, I cringed. For the prospect of falling terrified me. Every afternoon, as I worked through my prescribed activities, I prayed that I would be able to fall when the session ended. Falling was the most essential "good" of all the "goods" held out for my consideration by my therapist. I believed that. I believed it so intensely that the belief itself was painful. Everything else asked of me was given—and given gladly. I mounted the bus stairs, pushed across the parallel bars until my arms ached with the effort, allowed the medicine ball to pummel me, flailed away at the empty air with my fists because my therapist wanted me to rid myself of the tension within. The slightest sign of approval from those in authority was enough to make me puff with pleasure. Other boys in the ward might not have taken rehabilitation seriously, but I was an eager servant cringing before the promise of approval.

21   Only I couldn't fall. As each session ended, I would be led to the mats that took up a full third of the huge room. "It's time," the therapist would say. Dutifully, I would follow her, step after step. Just as dutifully, I would stand on the edge of those two-inch-thick mats, staring down at them until I could feel my body quiver. "All you have to do is let go," my therapist assured me. "The other boys do it. Just let go and fall."

22   But the prospect of letting go was precisely what terrified me. That the other boys in the ward had no trouble in falling added to my shame and terror. I didn't need my therapist to tell me the two-inch-thick mats would keep me from hurting myself. I knew there was virtually no chance of injury when I fell, but that knowledge simply made me more ashamed of a cowardice that was as monumental as it was unexplainable. Had it been able to rid me of my sense of my own cowardice, I would happily have settled for bodily harm. But I was being asked to surrender myself to the emptiness of space, to let go and crash down to the mats below, to feel myself suspended in air when nothing stood between me and the vacuum of the world. *That* was the prospect that overwhelmed me. *That* was what left me sweating with rage and humiliation. The contempt I felt was for my own weakness.

23   I tried to justify what I sensed could never be justified. Why should I be expected to throw myself into emptiness? Was this sullen terror the price of compensation, the badge of normality? Maybe my refusal to fall embodied some deeper thrust than I could then understand. Maybe I had unconsciously seized upon some fundamental resistance to the forces that threatened to overwhelm me. What did matter that the ground was covered by the thick mats? The tremors I feared were in my heart and soul.

24   Shame plagued me—and shame is the older brother to disease. Flushing with shame, I would stare down at the mats. I could feel myself wanting to cry out. But I shriveled at the thought of calling more atten-

tion to my cowardice. I would finally hear myself whimper, "I'm sorry. But I can't. I can't let go."

25   Formless emptiness. A rush of air through which I would plummet toward obliteration. As my "normal" past grew more and more distant, I reached for it more and more desperately, recalling it like some movie whose plot has long since been forgotten but whose scenes continue to comfort through images disconnected from anything but themselves. I remembered that there had been a time when the prospect of falling evoked not terror but joy: football games on the rain-softened autumn turf of Mosholu Parkway, belly-flopping on an American Flyer down its snow-covered slopes in winter, rolling with a pack of friends down one of the steep hills in Bronx Park. Free falls from the past, testifying not to a loss of the self but to an absence of barriers.

26   My therapist pleaded, ridiculed, cajoled, threatened, bullied. I was sighed over and railed at. But I couldn't let go and fall. I couldn't sell my terror off so cheaply. Ashamed as I was, I wouldn't allow myself to be bullied out of terror.

27   A month passed—a month of struggle between me and my therapist. Daily excursions to the rehab room, daily practice runs through the future that was awaiting me. The daily humiliation of discovering that one's own fear had been transformed into a public issue, a subject of discussion among the other boys in the ward, seemed unending.

28   And then, terror simply evaporated. It was as if I had served enough time in that prison. I was ready to move on. One Tuesday afternoon, as my session ended, the therapist walked resignedly alongside me toward the mats. "All right, Leonard. It's time again. All you have to do is let go and fall." Again, I stood above the mats. Only this time, it was as if something beyond my control or understanding had decided to let my body's fall from grace take me down for good. I was not seized by the usual paroxysm of fear. I didn't feel myself break out in a terrified sweat. It was over.

29   I don't mean that I suddenly felt myself spring into courage. That wasn't what happened at all. The truth was I had simply been worn down into letting go, like a boxer in whose eyes one recognizes not the flicker of defeat—that issue never having been in doubt—but the acceptance of defeat. Letting go no longer held my imagination captive. I found myself quite suddenly faced with a necessary fall—a fall into life.

30   So it was that I stood above the mat and heard myself sigh and then felt myself let go, dropping through the quiet air, crutches slipping off to the sides. What I didn't feel this time was the threat of my body slipping into emptiness, so mummified by the terror before it that the touch of air pre-empted even death. I dropped. I did not crash. I dropped. I did not collapse. I dropped. I did not plummet. I felt myself enveloped by a curiously gentle moment in my life. In that sliver of time before I hit the mat, I was kissed by space.

31   My body absorbed the slight shock and I rolled onto my back, braced

legs swinging like unguided missiles into the free air, crutches dropping away to the sides. Even as I fell through the air, I could sense the shame and fear drain from my soul, and I knew that my sense of my own cowardice would soon follow. In falling, I had given myself a new start, a new life.

32   "That's it!" my therapist triumphantly shouted. "You let go! And there it is!"

33   *You let go! And there it is!* Yes, and you discover not terror but the only self you are going to be allowed to claim anyhow. You fall free, and then you learn that those padded mats hold not courage but the unclaimed self. And if it turned out to be not the most difficult of tasks, did that make my sense of jubilation any less?

34   From that moment, I gloried in my ability to fall. Falling became an end in itself. I lost sight of what my therapist had desperately been trying to demonstrate for me—that there was a purpose in learning how to fall. For she wanted to teach me through the fall what I would have to face in the future. She wanted to give me a wholeness I could not give myself. For she knew that mine would be a future so different from what confronts the "normal" that I had to learn to fall into life in order not to be overwhelmed.

35   From that day, she urged me to practice falling as if I were a religious disciple being urged by a master to practice spiritual discipline. Letting go meant allowing my body to float into space, to turn at the direction of the fall and follow the urgings of emptiness. For her, learning to fall was learning the most essential of American lessons: how to turn incapacity into capacity.

36   "You were afraid of hurting yourself," she explained to me. "But that's the beauty of it. When you let go, you can't hurt yourself."

37   An echo of the streets and playgrounds I called home until I met the virus. American slogans: go with the flow, roll with the punch, slide with the threat until it is no longer a threat. They were simply slogans, and they were all intended to create strength from weakness, a veritable world's fair of compensation.

38   I returned to the city a year later. By that time, I was a willing convert, one who now secretly enjoyed demonstrating his ability to fall. I enjoyed the surprise that would greet me as I got to my feet, unscathed and undamaged. However perverse it may seem, I felt a certain pleasure when, as I walked with a friend, I felt a crutch slip out of my grasp. Watching the thrust of concern darken his features, I felt myself in control of my own capacity. For falling had become the way my body sought out its proper home. It was an earthbound body, and mine would be an earthbound life. My quest would be for the solid ground beneath me. Falling with confidence, I fell away from terror and fear.

39   Of course, some falls took me unawares, and I found myself letting go too late or too early. Bruised in ego and sometimes in body, I would pull myself to my feet to consider what had gone wrong. Yet I was essentially untroubled. Such defeats were part of the game, even when they confined

me to bed for a day or two afterward. I was an accountant of pain, and sometimes heavier payment was demanded. In my mid-thirties, I walked my two-year-old son's babysitter home, tripped on the curbstone, and broke my wrist. At forty-eight, an awkward fall triggered by a carelessly unlocked brace sent me smashing against the bathtub and into surgery for a broken femur. It took four months for me to learn to walk on the crutches all over again. But I learned. I already knew how to fall.

40   I knew such accidents could be handled. After all, pain was not synonymous with mortality. In fact, pain was insurance against an excessive consciousness of mortality. Pain might validate the specific moment in time, but it didn't have very much to do with the future. I did not yet believe that falling into life had anything to do with falling into death. It was simply a way for me to exercise control over my own existence.

41   It seems to me today that, when I first let my body fall to those mats, I was somehow giving myself the endurance I would need to survive in this world. In a curious way, falling became a way of celebrating what I had lost. My legs were lifeless, useless, but their loss had created a dancing image in whose shadowy gyrations I recognized a strange but potentially interesting new self. I would survive. I knew that now. I could let go, I could fall, and, best of all, I could get up.

42   To create an independent self, a man had to rid himself of both the myths that nurtured him and the myths that held him back. Learning to fall had been the first lesson in how I yet might live successfully as a cripple. Even disease had its inviolate principles. I understood that the most dangerous threat to the sense of self I needed was an inflated belief in my own capacity. Falling rid a man of excess baggage; it taught him how each of us is dependent on balance.

43   But what really gave falling legitimacy was the knowledge that I could get to my feet again. That was what taught me the rules of survival. As long as I could pick myself up and stand on my own two feet, brace-bound and crutch-propped as I was, the fall testified to my ability to live in the here and now, to stake my claim as an American who had turned incapacity into capacity. For such a man, falling might well be considered the language of everyday achievement.

44   But the day came, as I knew it must come, when I could no longer pick myself up. It was then that my passion for symmetry in endings began. On that day, spurred on by another fall, I found myself spinning into the inevitable future.

45   The day was actually a rainy night in November of 1983. I had just finished teaching at the City College Center for Worker Education, an off-campus degree program for working adults, and had joined some friends for dinner. All of us, I remember, were in a jovial, celebratory mood, although I no longer remember what it was we were celebrating. Perhaps it was simply the satisfaction of being good friends and colleagues at dinner together.

46   We ate in a Spanish restaurant on Fourteenth Street in Manhattan. It was a dinner that took on, for me at least, the intensity of a time that would assume greater and greater significance as I grew older, one of those watershed moments writers are so fond of. In the dark, rain-swept New York night, change and possibility seemed to drift like a thick fog all around us.

47   Our mood was still convivial when we left the restaurant around eleven. The rain had slackened off to a soft drizzle and the street glistened beneath the play of light on the wet black creosote. At night, rain in the city has a way of transforming proportion into optimism. The five of us stood around on the slicked-down sidewalk, none of us willing to be the first to break the richness of the mood by leaving.

48   Suddenly, the crutch in my left hand began to slip out from under me, slowly, almost deliberately, as if the crutch had a mind of its own and had not yet made the commitment that would send me down. Apparently, I had hit a slick patch of city sidewalk, some nub of concrete worn smooth as medieval stone by thousands of shoppers and panhandlers and tourists and students who daily pounded the bargain hustlings of Fourteenth Street.

49   Instinctively, I at first tried to fight the fall, to seek for balance by pushing off from the crutch in my right hand. But as I recognized that the fall was inevitable, I simply went slack—and for the thousandth time my body sought vindication in its ability to let go and drop. These good friends had seen me fall before. They knew my childish vanities, understood that I still thought of falling as a way to demonstrate my control of the traps and uncertainties that lay in wait for us all.

50   Thirty-eight years earlier, I had discovered that I could fall into life simply by letting go. Now I made a different discovery—that I could no longer get to my feet by myself. I hit the wet ground and quickly turned over and pushed up, trying to use one of the crutches as a prop to boost myself to my feet, as I had been taught to do as a boy of twelve.

51   But try as hard as I could, I couldn't get to my feet. It wasn't that I lacked physical strength. I knew that my arms were as powerful as ever as I pushed down on the wet concrete. It had nothing to do with the fact that the street was wet, as my friends insisted later. No, it had to do with a subtle, if mysterious, change in my own sense of rhythm and balance. My body had decided—*and decided on its own, autonomously*—that the moment had come for me to face the question of endings. It was the body that chose its time of recognition.

52   It was, it seems to me now, a distinctively American moment. It left me pondering limitations and endings and summations. It left me with the curiously buoyant sense that mortality had quite suddenly made itself a felt presence rather than the rhetorical strategy used by the poets and novelists I taught to my students. This was what writers had in mind when they spoke of the truly common fate, this sense of ending coming to one unbidden. This had brought with it my impassioned quest for symmetry. As I

lay on the wet ground—no more than a minute or two—all I could think of was how much I wanted my life to balance out. It was as if I were staring into a future in which time itself had evaporated.

53   Here was a clear, simple perception, and there was nothing mystical about it. There are limitations we recognize and those that recognize us. My friends, who had nervously been standing around while I tried to get to my feet, finally asked if they could help me up. "You'll have to," I said. "I can't get up any other way."

54   Two of them pulled me to my feet while another jammed the crutches beneath my arms, as the therapist and the two bracemakers had done almost four decades earlier. When I was standing, they proceeded to joke about my sudden incapacity in that age-old way men of all ages have, as if words might codify loss and change and time's betrayal. I joined in the joking. But what I really wanted was to go home and contemplate this latest fall in the privacy of my apartment. The implications were clear: I would never again be an eater of salt, I would also never again get to my feet on my own. A part of my life had ended. But that didn't depress me. In fact, I felt almost as exhilarated as I had thirty-eight years earlier, when my body surrendered to the need to let go and I fell into life.

55   Almost four years have passed since I fell on the wet sidewalk of Fourteenth Street. I suppose it wasn't a particularly memorable fall. It wasn't even particularly significant to anyone who had not once fallen into life. But it was inevitable, the first time I had let go into a time when it would no longer even be necessary to let go.

56   It was a fall that left me with the knowledge that I could no longer pick myself up. That meant I now needed the help of others as I had not needed their help before. It was a fall that left me burning with this strange passion for symmetry, this desire to balance my existence out. When the day comes, I want to be able to fall into my death as nakedly as I once had to fall into my life.

57   Do not misunderstand me. I am not seeking a way out of mortality, for I believe in nothing more strongly than I believe in the permanency of endings. I am not looking for a way out of this life, a life I continue to find immensely enjoyable—even if I can no longer pull myself to my own two feet. Of course, a good deal in my life has changed. For one thing, I am increasingly impatient with those who claim to have no use for endings of any sort. I am also increasingly embarrassed by the thought of the harshly critical adolescent I was, self-righteously convinced that the only way for a man to go to his end was by kicking and screaming.

58   But these are, I suppose, the kinds of changes any man or woman of forty or fifty would feel. Middle-aged skepticism is as natural as adolescent acne. In my clearer, less passionate moments, I can even laugh at my need for symmetry in beginnings and endings as well as my desire to see my own eventual death as a line running parallel to my life. Even in mathematics, let alone life, symmetry is sometimes too neat, too closed off from

the way things actually work. After all, it took me a full month before I could bring myself to let go and fall into life.

59   I no longer talk about how one can seize a doctrine of compensation from disease. I don't talk about it, but it still haunts me. In my heart, I believe it offers a man the only philosophy by which he can actually live. It is the only philosophy that strips away both spiritual mumbo jumbo and the procrustean weight of existential anxiety. In the final analysis, a man really is what a man does.

60   Believing as I do, I wonder why I so often find myself trying to frame a perspective that will prove adequate to a proper sense of ending. Perhaps that is why I find myself sitting in a bar with a friend, trying to explain to him all that I have learned from falling. "There must be a time," I hear myself tell him, "when a man has the right to stop thinking about falling."

61   "Sure," my friend laughs. "Four seconds before he dies."

Discussion Questions

1. At any point in his essay, do you think Kriegel is asking for pity? If so, how does that influence your reaction to him and to the essay? If not, how does that affect your reading of the piece?

2. What do you make of Kriegel's inability or unwillingness to fall when his therapist commands him to, even when Kriegel calls himself a "dutiful patient"? Do you think he is typical of most people? Why or why not?

3. Although Kriegel states in paragraph 16 that falling is *not* a metaphor, do *you* think it is? If not, why not? If so, what it is a metaphor of?

4. Did you find Kriegel's justifications in paragraph 22 for being terrified to fall believable? Why or why not?

5. In paragraph 42 Kriegel states, "To create an independent self, a man had to rid himself of both the myths that nurtured him and the myths that held him back." Identify incidents in your own life that support this observation.

Living under Circe's Spell
Matthew Soyster

M atthew Soyster is a writer who lives in Northern California. The following essay appeared in the October 11, 1993, Newsweek *magazine's "My Turn" column. In it Soyster muses on the ways in which "each disabled person is crippled in his [her] own way." Soyster has multiple sclerosis, the chronic, degenerative disease of the central nervous system. Once a marathon runner, cyclist, and skier, Soyster reflects on how the passions that once "defined" him are gone and how, confined to a wheelchair, he must search for other passions.*

1   "Life is brief, time's a thief." This ribbon of pop lyricism keens from an an apartment-house radio into the hot afternoon air. Across the street I am sprawled in the gutter behind my minivan, bits of glass and scrap metal chewing at my knees and elbows, a cut on my hand beginning to well crimson.

2   There has been no assailant, no wound except to my psyche. I'm just a clumsy cripple whose legs buckled before he reached his wheelchair. A moment ago I yanked it from my tailgate, as I've done a thousand times. But when it spun off at a crazy angle I missed the seat and slumped to the ground.

3   Now the spasms start, shooting outward from the small of my back, forcing me prone, grinding my cheek into the asphalt. What will I look like to the first casual passerby before he catches sight of the telltale chair? A wine-soaked rummy? A hit-and-run victim? Maybe an amateur mechanic checking the rear suspension, wrong side up.

4   I'm too young and vital looking to be this helpless. I shrink from the inevitable clucking and concern. Then again, this isn't the best neighborhood. The first person to come along may simply kick me and take my wallet. No wonder I'm ambivalent about rescue, needing but not wanting to be discovered. With detachment I savor the hush of this deserted street, the symphony of birdsong in the treetops.

5   I am trying to remember Rilke's line about waiting without hope, because hope would be hope for the wrong thing. Instead, that idiot TV commercial for the medical alarm-pager keeps ringing through my brain: "Help me. I've fallen and I can't get up."

6   It was only a matter of time. I've known for months that my hair's-breadth maneuvering would eventually fail me. For years, in fact. When I first learned that I had multiple sclerosis I was a marathon runner and whitewater-rafting guide, a cyclist and skier, the quintessential California golden boy. Cardiovascular fitness had long since become our state religion. I lived for and through my legs.

7   But that's only the ad-slick surface of the California dream, the sunshine without the shadow. The town I live in is also the mecca of the disabled, the home of the Independent Living Movement, the place where broken people come to patch together their dignity and their dreams.

8   Yin and yang. In Berkeley, there are wheelchair users on every corner. Propped in sagging hospital-issue chairs. Space-age sports chairs. Motor-driven dreadnoughts. When I could still walk, I crossed the street to avoid them. What an odd tribe they seemed, with their spindly, agitated limbs, always hurtling down the avenue on some manic errand.

9   How could I imagine my own swift decline? A few months or years passed. Soon I was relying on a cane, then crutches, and finally—after many thigh-bruising falls and a numbness so intense it turned my legs to driftwood—a wheelchair. My response to these limitations was compensation and denial. I thought I could become a disabled Olympian: wheelchair racing, tennis, rugby. I thought I could go on as before.

10   Wrong again. To paraphrase Tolstoy, all able-bodied people are alike, but each disabled person is crippled in his own way. MS not only played havoc with my upper-body strength and agility; it clouded my mind and sapped my energy. I could totter a few steps supported at both wrists, but my days in the winter surf, high peaks and desert canyons were over.

11   So what is it like to spend your life forked at the waist, face-level with children? The syndrome has been amply described. People see through me now, or over me. They don't see me at all. Or they fix me with that plangent, aching stare: sympathy.

12   They offer too much assistance, scurrying to open doors, scrambling out of my way with unnecessary apologies, or they leave me no space at all, barking their shins on my foot pedals. My spirit rallies in the face of such humiliations; they have their comic aspect. What disturbs me most is not how others see me, but how I've lost my vision of myself.

13   Growing crippled is a bitch. First your body undergoes a strange enchantment. Circe's spell. Then your identity gives way. You become someone or something other, but for a long time you're not sure what that other is.

14   Along the way, I've had to give up activities and passions that define me, my safe position in society, my very sense of manhood. In our species, the pecking order is distinctly vertical. True for women. Doubly true for men. A man stands tall, stands firm, stands up for things. These are more than metaphors. The very act of sitting implies demotion. Anyone who's witnessed boardroom politics knows this much. Have a seat, barks the boss. It's not an invitation, it's an order.

15   Which brings me back to the gutter, where I lie listening to birdsong. Recognizing but not apologizing for the obstinacy that landed me here. For months my friends and family have watched my legs grow weaker. They've prodded me relentlessly to refit my van with a wheelchair lift in order to avoid just this disaster. But I've refused.

16   Twice a day at least, I've dragged my reluctant legs from beneath the steering column, hauled myself erect beside the driver's seat, inched my way down the roof rail to the rear stowage. And removed the chair by hand, standing.

17   Why have I clung to this ritual, knowing it's dangerous and futile? It's the only task I rise for anymore, in a sitting life. For a moment in the driver's doorway, I'm in control, unreliant on technology or assistance, upright. Or so I've told myself. But that moment is so fragile, the control so illusory.

18   When the time comes to change, I've said, I'll know.

19   Now I know.

20   I feel the lesson, sharp as the rap of a Zen master's stick. Lying in the hot gutter, I take a deep breath and my whole body relaxes. Tuning in to Rod Stewart's tiny wisdom from the window. Listening for a passing car or pedestrian.

21   Waiting.

Discussion Questions

1. Describe the tone of Soyster's essay. Identify specific lines that support your response. In what ways does the tone complement what Soyster is writing about?

2. Do you think Soyster wants his readers' pity? sympathy? compassion? What do you see as the purpose of his essay?

3. In paragraph 12, Soyster claims, "What disturbs me most is not how others see me, but how I've lost my vision of myself." Do you think Soyster *has* lost a vision of himself, or is he simply resistant to change? Explain your response.

4. Do you think Soyster's thinking is representative of most people when they become disabled? Why or why not?

5. Explain what you understand the last paragraph of Soyster's essay to mean. In what ways is it an apt conclusion?

At War with My Skin

John Updike

John Updike was born in 1932 and began his writing career as a staff writer for the New Yorker. *A prolific essayist, critic, poet, and novelist, Updike is most known for his series of* Rabbit *novels, beginning with* Rabbit, Run *(1960); and continuing with* Rabbit Redux *(1971),* Rabbit Is Rich *(1981),* Rabbit's Version *(1981); and ending with* Rabbit at Rest *(1990). His other novels include* The Poorhouse Fair *(1959),* The Centaur *(1963),* Of the Farm *(1965),* Couples *(1968),* A Month of Sundays *(1975),* Marry Me *(1976),* The Coup *(1978),* The Witches of Eastwick *(1984),* Roger's Version *(1986),* S. *(1988), and* Memories of the Ford Administration *(1992). Updike's essays and reviews appear in* Assorted Prose *(1965),* Picked-Up Pieces *(1985), and* Hugging the Shore *(1983). Updike's many honors include the National Book Award, the National Book Critics Circle Award, the Pulitzer Prize, the O. Henry Prize, the Rosenthal Award from the National Institute of Arts and Letters, the Macdowell Medal, and the American Book Award. Taken from his memoir,* Self-Consciousness *(1989),* "At War with My Skin" *is about psoriasis, a topic Updike has broached only twice before in his career as a writer.*

1   My mother tells me that up to the age of six I had no psoriasis; it came on strong after an attack of measles in February of 1938, when I was in kindergarten. The disease—"disease" seems strong, for a condition that is not contagious, painful, or debilitating; yet psoriasis has the volatility of a disease, the sense of another presence coöccupying your body and singling you out from the happy herds of healthy, normal mankind—first attached itself to my memory while I was lying on the upstairs side porch of the Shillington house, amid the sickly, oleaginous smell of Siroil, on fuzzy sun-warmed towels, with my mother, sunbathing. We are both, in my mental picture, not quite naked. She would have been still a youngish woman at the time, and I remember being embarrassed by something, but whether by our being together this way or simply by my skin is not clear in this mottled recollection. She, too, had psoriasis; I had inherited it from her. Siroil and sunshine and not eating chocolate were our only weapons in our war against the red spots, ripening into silvery scabs, that invaded our skins in the winter. Siroil was the foremost medication available in the thirties and forties: a bottled preparation the consistency of pus, tar its effective ingredient and its drippy texture and bilious color and insinuating odor deeply involved with my embarrassment. Yet, as with our own private odors, those of sweat and earwax and even of excrement, there was also something satisfying about this scent, an intimate rankness that told me who I was.

2   One dabbed Siroil on; it softened the silvery scales but otherwise did very little good. Nor did abstaining from chocolate and "greasy" foods like potato chips and french fries do much visible good, though as with many palliations there was no knowing how much worse things would be otherwise. Only the sun, that living god, had real power over psoriasis; a few weeks of summer erased the spots from all of my responsive young skin that could be exposed—chest, legs, and face. Inspecting the many photographs taken of me as a child, including a set of me cavorting in a bathing suit in the back yard, I can see no trace of psoriasis. And I remember, when it rained, going out in a bathing suit with friends to play in the downpour and its warm puddles. Yet I didn't learn to swim, because of my appearance; I stayed away from "the Porgy," the dammed pond beyond the poorhouse, and from the public pool in West Reading, and the indoor

pool at the Reading "Y," where my father in winter coached the high-school swimming team. To the travails of my freshman year at Harvard was added the humiliation of learning at last to swim, with my spots and my hydrophobia, in a class of quite naked boys. Recently the chunky, mild-spoken man who taught that class over thirty years ago came up to me at a party and pleasantly identified himself; I could scarcely manage politeness, his face so sharply brought back that old suppressed rich mix of chlorine and fear and brave gasping and naked, naked shame.

3   Psoriasis is a metabolic disorder that causes the epidermis, which normally replaces itself at a gradual, unnoticeable rate, to speed up the process markedly and to produce excess skin cells. The tiny mechanisms gone awry are beyond the precise reach of internally taken medicine; a derivative of vitamin A, etretinate, and an anticancer drug, methotrexate, are effective but at the price of potential side-effects to the kidneys and liver more serious than the disease, which is, after all, superficial—too much, simply, of a good thing (skin). In the 1970s, dermatologists at Massachusetts General Hospital developed PUVA, a controlled light treatment: fluorescent tubes radiate long-wave ultraviolet (UV-A) onto skin sensitized by an internal dose of methoxsalen, a psoralen (the "P" of the acronym) derived from a weed, *Ammi majus,* which grows along the river Nile and whose sun-sensitizing qualities were known to the ancient Egyptians. So a curious primitivity, a savor of folk-medicine, clings to this new cure, a refinement of the old sun-cure. It is pleasant, once or twice a week, to stand nearly naked in a kind of glowing telephone booth. It was pleasant to lie on the upstairs porch, hidden behind the jigsawed wooden balusters, and to feel the slanting sun warm the fuzzy towel while an occasional car or pack of children crackled by on Shilling Alley. One became conscious, lying there trying to read, of bird song, of distant shouts, of a whistle calling men back to work at the local textile factory, which was rather enchantingly called the Fairy Silk Mill.

4   My condition forged a hidden link with things elemental—with the seasons, with the sun, and with my mother. A tendency to psoriasis is inherited—only through the maternal line, it used to be thought. My mother's mother had had it, I was told, though I never noticed anything wrong with my grandmother's skin—just her false teeth, which slipped down while she was napping in her rocking chair. Far in the future, I would marry a young brunette with calm, smooth, deep-tanning skin and was to imagine that thus I had put an end to at least my particular avenue of genetic error. Alas, our fourth child inherited my complexion and, lightly, in her late teens, psoriasis. The disease favors the fair, the dry-skinned, the pallid progeny of cloud-swaddled Holland and Ireland and Germany. Though my father was not red-haired, his brother Arch was, and when I grew a beard, as my contribution to the revolutionary sixties, it came in reddish. And when I shaved it off, red spots had thrived underneath.

5   Psoriasis keeps you thinking. Strategies of concealment ramify, and self-examination is endless. You are forced to the mirror, again and again;

psoriasis compels narcissism, if we can suppose a Narcissus who did not like what he saw. In certain lights, your face looks passable; in slightly different other lights, not. Shaving mirrors and rearview mirrors in automobiles are merciless, whereas the smoky mirrors in airplane bathrooms are especially flattering and soothing: one's face looks as tawny as a movie star's. Flying back from the Caribbean, I used to admire my improved looks; years went by before I noticed that I looked equally good, in the lavatory glow, on the flight down. I cannot pass a reflecting surface on the street without glancing in, in hopes that I have somehow changed. Nature and the self, the great moieties of earthly existence, are each cloven in two by a fascinated ambivalence. One hates one's abnormal, erupting skin but is led into a brooding, solicitous attention toward it. One hates the Nature that has imposed this affliction, but only this same Nature can be appealed to for erasure, for cure. Only Nature can forgive psoriasis; the sufferer in his self-contempt does not grant to other people this power. Perhaps the unease of my first memory has to do with my mother's presence; I wished to be alone with the sun, the air, the distant noises, the possibility of my hideousness eventually going away.

6   I recall remarkably few occasions when I was challenged, in the brute world of childhood, about my skin. In the second grade, perhaps it was, the teacher, standing above our obedient rows, rummaged in my hair and said aloud, "Good heavens, child, what's this on your head?" I can hear these words breaking into the air above me and see my mother's face when, that afternoon, I recounted them to her, probably with tears; her eyes took on a fanatic glare and the next morning, like an arrow that had fixed her course, she went to the school to "have it out" with the teacher who had heightened her defective cub's embarrassment. Our doctor, Doc Rothermel in his big grit-and-stucco house, also, eerily, had psoriasis; far from offering a cure out of his magical expanding black bag, he offered us the melancholy confession that he had felt prevented, by his scaly wrists, from rolling back his sleeves and becoming—his true ambition—a surgeon. "'Physician, heal thyself,' they'd say to me," he said. I don't, really, know how bad I looked, or how many conferences among adults secured a tactful silence from above. My peers (again, as I remember, which is a choosing to remember) either didn't notice anything terrible about my skin or else neglected to comment upon it. Children are frank, as we know from the taunts and nicknames they fling at one another; but also they all feel imperfect and vulnerable, which works for mutual forbearance. In high school, my gym class knew how I looked in the locker room and shower. Once, a boy from a higher class came up to me with an exclamation of cheerful disgust, touched my arm, and asked if I had syphilis. But my classmates held their tongues, and expressed no fear of contagion.

7   I participated, in gym shorts and tank top, in the annual gym exhibitions. Indeed, as the tallest of the lighter boys, I stood shakily on top of "Fats" Sterner's shoulders to make the apex of our gymnastic pyramid. I

braved it through, inwardly cringing, prisoner and victim of my skin. It was not really *me,* was the explanation I could not shout out. Like an obese person (like good-natured Fats so sturdy under me, human rock, his hands gripping my ankles while I fought the sensation that I was about to lurch forward and fly out over the heads of our assembled audience of admiring parents), and unlike someone with a withered arm, say, or a port-wine stain splashed across his neck and cheek, I could change—every summer I *did* become normal and, as it were, beautiful. An overvaluation of the normal went with my ailment, a certain idealization of everyone who was not, as I felt myself to be, a monster.

8   Because it came and went, I never settled in with my psoriasis, never adopted it as, inevitably, part of myself. It was temporary and in a way illusionary, like my being poor, and obscure, and (once we moved to the farm) lonely—a spell that had been put upon me, a test, as in a fairy story or one of those divinely imposed ordeals in the Bible. "Where's my public?" I used to ask my mother, coming back from the empty mailbox, by this joke conjuring a public out of the future.

9   My last public demonstration of my monstrosity, in a formal social setting, occurred the day of my examination for the draft, in the summer of 1955. A year in England, with no sun, had left my skin in bad shape, and the examining doctor took one glance up from his plywood table and wrote on my form, "4-F: Psoriasis." At this point in my young life I had a job offer in New York, a wife, and an infant daughter, and was far from keen to devote two years to the national defense; I had never gone to summer camp, and pictured the Army as a big summer camp, with extra-rough bullies and extra-cold showers in the morning. My trepidation should be distinguished from political feelings; I had absolutely no doubts about my country's need, from time to time, to fight, and its right to call me to service. So suddenly and emphatically excused, I felt relieved, guilty, and above all ashamed at being singled out; the naked American men around me had looked at my skin with surprise and now were impressed by the exemption it had won me. I had not foreseen this result; psoriasis would handicap no killing skills and, had I reported in another season, might have been nearly invisible. My wife, when I got back to my parents' house with my news, was naturally delighted; but my mother, always independent in her moods, seemed saddened, as if she had laid an egg which, when candled by the government, had been pronounced rotten.

10   It pains me to write these pages. They are humiliating—"scab-picking," to use a term sometimes leveled at modern autobiographical writers. I have written about psoriasis only twice before: I gave it to Peter Caldwell in *The Centaur* and to an anonymous, bumptious ceramicist in the short story "From the Journal of a Leper." I expose it this third time only in order to proclaim the consoling possibility that whenever in my timid life I have shown some courage and originality it has been because of my skin. Because of my skin, I counted myself out of any of those jobs—salesman, teacher, financier, movie star—that demand being presentable. What did

that leave? Becoming a craftsman of some sort, closeted and unseen—perhaps a cartoonist or a writer, a worker in ink who can hide himself and send out a surrogate presence, a signature that multiplies even while it conceals. Why did I marry so young? Because, having once found a comely female who forgave me my skin, I dared not risk losing her and trying to find another. Why did I have children so young? Because I wanted to surround myself with people who did not have psoriasis. Why, in 1957, did I leave New York and my nice employment there? Because my skin was bad in the urban shadows, and nothing, not even screwing a sunlamp bulb into the socket above my bathroom mirror, helped. Why did I move, with my family, all the way to Ipswich, Massachusetts? Because this ancient Puritan town happened to have one of the great beaches of the Northeast, in whose dunes I could, like a sin-soaked anchorite of old repairing to the desert, bake and cure myself.

Discussion Questions

1. Do you think that Updike's seeming obsession with his skin is fairly typical of most people who have a noticeable flaw in their appearance? Why or why not?

2. What emotions do you think Updike wants his readers to feel after reading his essay? Support your answer by referring to specific lines in his essay that lead you to your response.

3. What sustains your interest in this essay as Updike describes his dermatological history?

4. How convincing is Updike when he claims in paragraph 10 that "whenever in my timid life I have shown some courage and originality it has been because of my skin"? Explain your response.

5. How would you describe Updike's attitude toward having psoriasis? What leads you to your answer?

Short Subject

Joseph Epstein

Born in 1937, Joseph Epstein is the editor of The American Scholar *and teaches writing and literature at Northwestern University. He is the author of such books as* Divorced in America: Marriage in an Age of Possibility *(1974),* Ambition: The Secret Passion *(1980),* Masters: Portraits of Great Teachers *(1981),* The Middle of My Tether *(1983),* Plausible Prejudices: Essays on American Writing

(1985), Partial Payment: Essays on Writers and their Lives *(1988),* The Goldin Boys' Stories *(1991), and* Pertinent Players: Essays on the Literary Life *(1993). In the following essay from* A Line Out for a Walk *(1991), Epstein provides a stunning list of short men as he examines his feelings surrounding his own height of 5 feet, 6 ½ inches.*

1   Should you urgently need to reach me, here, to save time, are a few places you are almost certain *not* to find me: browsing happily in the grain section of a health food store, sitting under a dryer reading *Popular Mechanics* during the final stages of a male permanent at Vidal Sassoon, pasting up Thank You for Not Smoking signs on firing-squad walls, shopping for a cabana suit at the M. Hyman and Son Big & Tall Men Store. Unless you happen to live in Chicago, there is every likelihood that you have never heard of M. Hyman and Son, where they claim to "suit the big guy at discount prices." I have no doubt that they do just that, but, reading the store's advertising copy, it occurred to me that no one has ever called me "big guy." Nor has anyone ever referred to me, as I seem to recall their female co-stars in the movies used regularly to refer to Clark Gable and John Wayne, as "you big galoot." Not even the very plainest woman, let alone Marlene Dietrich, has ever slung an arm around my neck, drawn me closer to her, and exclaimed, "Kiss me, big boy."

2   If you begin to gain the impression that I am not one of M. Hyman and Son's ideal customers, you are onto something. Although I have been called many things, I have never been in the least danger of being called Moose, Big Daddy, or Bubba. Quite the reverse; I have always considered myself fortunate to have evaded being called Pee-Wee, or Half-Pint, or Shorty. In a grammar school skit for an assembly on Lincoln's birthday, I, at age eleven or twelve, as the shortest boy in the class, played Stephen Douglas, the Little Giant, opposite the Abe Lincoln of Jack Sheasby, the tallest boy in the class, in a sensibly abridged version of the Lincoln-Douglas debates. This feels like the place in the paragraph where I should insert something like the following sentence: "However, in the summer between my junior and senior years of high school I grew eleven inches to my present height of 6'2"." That summer I may in fact have grown three-quarters of an inch. I kept waiting to "shoot up," in the phrase popular at the time, but never did. Today, in my early fifties, I am beginning to believe it may never happen.

3   Just how small is this guy anyhow? you may by now be asking. Have I all these years, you are perhaps wondering, been reading a dwarf? I shall set out some figures presently, but first I think it mildly interesting that most curiosity about male height seems to be not about how tall but about how short certain men are—and by certain men, I chiefly mean certain movie actors. When I was a boy there was much guessing about the exact height of Alan Ladd. Figures as low as 5'2" were bruited about. It was said that Ladd had to stand on a box to kiss his leading ladies. Edward G. Robinson, James Cagney, John Garfield, George Raft, Spencer Tracy

were scarcely suited to be power forwards in the National Basketball Association; Humphrey bloody Bogart is said to have been no more than 5'5½ " or 5'6", sweetheart.

4   Now it is the height of Robert Redford and Paul Newman that is in the flux of controversy. Evidently neither man will divulge his exact height. One would think that the science of investigative reporting could find a solution to this problem—have Bob Woodward or Carl Bernstein stand next to them and make some elementary deductions. Thus far neither Butch nor Sundance will apparently measure up. Estimates on their respective heights run from 5'5" to a respectable 5'10". Both actors are said to be rather touchy on the subject. Upon meeting either of them, it is probably wise not to begin your conversation by saying, "Loved your last flick, little guy."

5   I am nowhere near so touchy about my own height, though it, too, is in that same controversial flux. Nothing pleases a fat man more, said A. J. Liebling (himself a very fat man), than to be called muscular. What, similarly, pleases a short man is to be asked, "What're you, about 5'10"?" I was once asked, "What're you, about 5'9"?" and I glowed for a full week. I think of myself as 5'7", but I can't seem to get a clear consensus on it. I not long ago wrote an essay about living in Little Rock, Arkansas, where I have lived at two different times in my life, and in the course of the essay mentioned getting a letter from a Southern journalist who remarked that I was a small legend in Little Rock. In the essay, I noted this and my answer, which was to say that I didn't know about the legend but, being 5'7", I would accept the small part. The editor of the magazine in which the essay appeared, a friend of many years, changed my copy to read "but being *under* 5'7"" (italics mine, vicious tactlessness his), which is what I would call heavy editing.

6   Unfortunately, he turns out to have been factually correct. A few months later, I had a physical examination, during which I weighed in at 135 pounds and measured 66½ inches. When the physician wrote these figures down, he asked, rather perfunctorily, "What did I say, 67½ inches?" I nodded, lying, and added, "I believe so." I am now down in my own medical records at 5'7½ ". But what will happen when I next go in for a physical and it is discovered that I am in fact only 5'6½ "? Will my physician feel that I am too young to be losing height so rapidly? Will he order various CAT scans and other tests to be run in search of the cause of my lost inch? Will I be sent off to the Mayo Clinic? Or perhaps to Zurich, where there is doubtless a lost-height specialist, a man I imagine to be 4'11" with thick glasses and an impenetrable German accent? Complicated stuff, height, and not merely, as the sports announcers are wont to say about baseball, football, golf, and other sports, a game of inches.

7   Somerset Maugham, who was 5'7" and none too pleased about it, says somewhere that the world is an entirely different place to a man of 5'7" from what it is to a man of 6'2". Maugham's is a telling and true

point, so long as one does not push it over into the chief psychological cliché about shortness. I refer to the notion that short people, in particular short men, tend to overcompensate for their size through outsized aggression and ambition. In this reading, T. E. Lawrence, had he been five or six inches taller than his 5'4", could have devoted all his time to his wretched translation of Homer and let the Turks and the Arabs fight it out on their own. Ambition, ample and aggressive ambition, turns up in every shoe size. In literature, for example, Ivan Turgenev and George Orwell were nice-sized boys; so, in politics, were Franklin Delano Roosevelt and Charles de Gaulle. The theory of compensation, as an explanation for the behavior of small men, comes up way short. (Good old language, it never lets you down.) One of the nice things about having been Napoleon (at 5'2") is that at least no one could ever accuse you of having a Napoleonic complex.

8   Not that size doesn't have multitudinous influences on one's life. Although there have been witty big men—Oscar Wilde comes first to mind—wit and humor seem more in the province of the smaller man. Chaplin, Keaton, the Marx Brothers were all small men. We expect a comedian to be small. He may also be fat. W. C. Fields was fat; so was Oliver Hardy. Fat is funny, small is funny. Lou Costello, of Abbott & Costello, was small and fat—a winning comic combination. Tall isn't funny, perhaps owing to its being too imposing, even slightly menacing. Tall and handsome conjoined are, with rare exceptions, especially unfunny. One can always fall back on being the tall and silent type, of whom, in the movies, Gary Cooper was the apotheosis. But if one is small and silent, one is likely merely to be counted shy. Small men are under an obligation to do more talking; perhaps this is why so many among them are always joking.

9   We all have certain expectations about the physical size of the writers we read—expectations that are often wildly mistaken. One of the nicest compliments I ever received came from a man who, upon meeting me after having read my work for many years, remarked that he expected a fatter man. "You are too slender to be so funny," he said. So delighted was I by the remark that at my next meal I had two desserts. Along the same line, I always thought Chekhov short, possibly for so doltish a reason as his mastery of the short story. (He turns out to have been a bit taller than average and, when young, moviestar handsome.) Tolstoy, whom I should have thought tall, was smallish though sinewy; I have seen him described as a giant dwarf. William James had the elongated head of a tall man but was rather short; his body, after that fine head, rather disappoints. I tend on the other hand to think of Shakespeare, about whose height I know nothing, as having the large head of a short man. I recently read that Freud was 5'8", though he looks smaller, as do all his early followers. No one who has ever seen a photograph of Freud and his circle would mistake it for a photograph of the Los Angeles Lakers.

10   I should have guessed that Jane Austen was small, chiefly because of

the delicacy of her charmingly oblique observations. Wrong again. According to J. E. Austen-Leigh's memoir of his Aunt Jane, "in person she was very attractive; her figure was rather tall and slender, her step light and firm, and her whole appearance expressive of health and animation." In her novels Jane Austen frequently describes the figure and carriage of her characters, and it will scarcely come as a surprise that she held some extremely interesting views about size. Reading along in her novel *Perssuasion*, I discovered Miss Austen writing of a tertiary character that her amplitude made the expression of sorrow appear unseemly: "Mrs. Musgrove was of a comfortable substantial size, infinitely more fitted by nature to express good cheer and good humour, than tenderness and sentiment. . . ." Then, to reinforce her point, Miss Austen adds:

> Personal size and mental sorrow have certainly no necessary proportions. A large bulky figure has as good a right to be in deep affliction, as the most graceful set of limbs in the world. But, fair or not fair, there are unbecoming conjunctions, which reason will patronize in vain—which taste cannot tolerate—which ridicule will seize

The point is quite indefensible, even a little crazy, yet absolutely true: there is something slightly appalling about the spectacle of a large person expressing sorrow. When a small woman cries, she weeps; a large woman, doing the same thing, is more likely to be described as blubbering.

11   Dorothy Parker, herself a small woman, caught the same point in "Big Blonde," her best story. Her heroine, a former model named Hazel Morse, is a large sensual woman prevented by her nature from introspection and by her many men friends from giving vent to the sadness that so often swamps her. Big babes are not permitted to give way to depression, and Dorothy Parker emphasizes that women of Hazel's kind, who don't mind having a fellow who buys them clothes and maybe pays the rent, all tend to be large:

> They were all big women and stout, broad of shoulder and abundantly breasted, with faces thickly clothed in soft, high-colored flesh. They laughed loud and often, showing opaque and lustreless teeth like squares of crockery. There was about them the health of the big, yet a slight, unwholesome suggestion of stubborn preservation. They might have been thirty-six or forty-five or anywhere between.

The largeness of such women as Hazel Morse seems only to add to their vulnerability. When Hazel fails at an attempt at suicide through an overdose of Veronal tablets, a physician, looking down upon her large rumpled body, pronounces, "You couldn't kill her with an ax." There is a line whose jolt could drop a rhino.

12   If large men and women are nearly condemned to being robust, sporty, and full of high spirits, small men and women, however naturally full of bonhomie they may be, are often thought devious. In literature, treachery is frequently assigned to small people. Many of Robert Louis Stevenson's villainous characters turn out to be small; when Dr. Jekyll transmogrifies into Mr. Hyde, for example, he becomes shorter. I don't recall if Shakespeare ever refers to Iago's size, but no one, surely, would put him above 5'8". Cassius, of course, is "lean and hungry," but was he also short? An economist with whom I discussed this felt that Cassius is best thought of as having the head of John Kenneth Galbraith, though not quite his 6'8" frame.

13   "It's not what you have here," my father used to say, pointing to his flexed biceps, "it's what you have here," he added, pointing now to the right temple of his forehead. At 5'4" no Kareem Abdul-Jabbar himself, my father was fond of telling me the story of David and Goliath, with its salutary reminder of what a good little man can do. I have just reread the David and Goliath story, and, in retrospect, I'm not at all certain that it offers much in the way of consolation. To be sure, it took real courage to go up against this champion of Gath, "whose height was six cubits and a span"—by my reckoning 9'9", which makes him likely to have gone early in the NBA draft. David, a youngest son, is described as a "stripling"; he refuses armor, saying he hasn't earned the right to it. All very impressive. But the fact is that David got in the first and only shot—"And David put his hands in his bag, and took thence a stone, and slang *it,* and smote the Philistine in his forehead, that the stone sunk into his forehead; and he fell upon his face to the earth"—and scored something of a lucky punch; some might even compare it to a quick kick in the groin. I never raised this objection to my father. Nor, when he pointed to his biceps and then to his forehead, announcing that it was better to have it in the latter location than in the former, did I suggest, as it occurred to me often to do, that it might be best of all to have it in both places.

14   By the time I was seven or eight, I suspect I must have known that I was destined to be small and that, consequently, certain adjustments had to be made. Although I was a fairly good grammar school athlete, being small, I knew I was precluded from playing certain positions—first base in baseball, fullback in football—that called for being tall or powerful; I knew that it made no sense to swing for home runs or to attempt to knock the next guy off his feet through clean brutality. Violence as a mode of settling boyhood arguments was closed off to me, except with boys roughly my own size; in argument I would have to rely on cleverness and cunning. No point, either, in developing crushes on the taller girls in the class, no matter how pretty or sweet-natured they might be. By the time I was twelve, it was perfectly evident to me that central casting had not sent me to earth to be a tough guy, or the sort of boy girls would swoon over, or a hero generally. Central casting was a bit unclear about what role I was to play; I would have, over time, to develop my own.

15   I hope I have not given the impression that being smallish was painful. It wasn't. I had enough up here—see figure 1, not shown, short man pointing to right temple—to avoid ever being tormented or even teased about being small. Besides, I wasn't as small as all that; I was even rather tall for a short fellow. Yet, given a choice, I should much have preferred to have been the toughest kid in the class and the boy all the girls were daffy about. Being small did, however, teach early the lesson that life has its unalterable conditions and limitations. Size, or more precisely height, could not be changed through diet or calisthenics, pills or surgery, or psychological self-improvement programs. Your height is the one card you cannot toss in in exchange for another.

16   The genius of Sir Laurence Olivier, I have heard it said, included his ability to act much taller than he was, and to do so absolutely convincingly. I find this most impressive. I do not think myself an altogether unimaginative person; I can imagine myself a woman, a member of other races, all ethnic groups, tremendously rich, completely broke, a Medal of Honor winner, on the run from the police. But what I cannot successfully imagine myself is a foot taller than my actual height. On many occasions I have attempted to do so. The most recent of these was on a sunny afternoon while watching a baseball game at Wrigley Field in Chicago.

17   Four empty seats to my right sat a man, in his early forties I should guess, shirtless, in cut-off jeans, gym shoes, a dark beard, aviator sunglasses; well soaked with beer, he was regaling four youngish women, who looked to be office workers out for an afternoon in the sun, with loud accounts of his sexual daring and astonishing virility. Had I been a foot taller—6'7", let us say, if you will permit me to round off that odd half inch in my favor—I do believe I should have spoken to the fellow. Standing well above him, I might have said:

18   "Sir, I won't trouble you more than a moment. Your charm, I am sorry to report, has worn a little thin, and I must ask you to remain silent for the remainder of the game, with the exception of cheering for the team of your choice and singing "Take Me Out to the Ball Game" during the seventh-inning stretch. If these conditions seem to you too stringent, don't hesitate to say so, for I am sure another seat elsewhere in the ballpark can be found for you—and one I shall be delighted to carry you to, in a state of consciousness or unconsciousness, as you prefer. Do think about it."

19   A foot taller, might I not develop into a quiet, somewhat well-spoken, bully? Would I not suddenly find myself acting to rectify the many little rudenesses in life I find so wearying? I see myself, in a traffic jam, uncoiling my considerable length from behind the wheel of my car, stepping out into the street, my head high above the ruck, the calm enforcer, the man who straightens things out by speaking in the voice of true reason with just a hint in it of real menace. No, the more I think of it, the more I am inclined to believe my physique is nicely mated to my temperament, given my many passions, impatience, and strong opinions. It is probably best that I am not in a position to do much about these things except express them through talk and writing.

20   This same physique also neatly fits me for intellectual work. Not many university teachers, editorial workers, artists, my guess is, are on the select mailing list of M. Hyman and Son. Only among artists and journalists could Ernest Hemingway have got away with his bogus tough-guy act; the same act, attempted at the construction site or on the assembly line, would have had the old boy in the dentist's chair before lunch break. At most universities, however, it would have gone over beautifully. Outside the physical education department, faculties are not notable for their Olympic muscularity. If a university teacher is not short, there is every chance that he is underweight, overweight, has a slouch, is hiding a weak chin behind an unkempt beard, or is otherwise misfitted or mildly deformed. To walk around a university is to realize that natural selection never takes a day off.

21   Along with being a university teacher, an editorial worker, a bit of an artist—in sum, a member in good standing of the shorter classes—I am also Jewish. The notion of Jews as puny has been put to rout and final rest by the efficient ferocity of the Israeli army, or at least ought to have been. (Whenever he sees soldiers of the Israeli army on television, the comedian Jackie Mason reports, his first reaction is to think they are Puerto Ricans.) Yet I continue to think of Jews as characteristically short. Despite the notable Jewish boxers, power hitters, football and basketball players, I still think of a good-sized Jewish man as about 5'9". ("I'm a Jewish six-footer," someone once told me, "you know, about 5'10½".") A Jew much above six feet tall has always seemed to me overdoing it; he looks out of character, more than a touch odd, somehow slightly out of proper proportion. I think of such people falling into a category I call "Too Tall Jews," which has the same cheerful rhythm as the name of the 6'9" Dallas Cowboy defensive lineman Ed "Too Tall" Jones. If the late Harold Rosenberg, the art critic of *The New Yorker,* had not been 6'5" or so, would his criticism perhaps have seemed less cloudy? If Arthur Miller were not 6'2" or 6'3", would his plays have been more grounded in reality? Maybe so.

22   Forgive me for having dwelt so long on Jews and height, but being both Jewish and short I feel as if I belong to two ethnic groups simultaneously. When I learn, say, that Nijinsky was short, I feel an emotion akin to learning that Walter Lippmann was Jewish: "Ah," I say to myself in both cases, "one of our boys." Is there something similar to ethnic pride that might be called short pride? Not that I am about to begin wearing T-shirts that carry the message Short Is Beautiful, or When You're in Love, the Whole World's Smallish. Yet I am not, apparently, alone in feeling short pride. A friend, who is also short and a baseball fan, recently revealed to me that he has assembled an All-Time All-Star Short Players team, composed of players all of whom are under 5'8". Some of his selections are not surprising: "Wee Willie" Keeler at 5'4" was a cinch to make the team. But I didn't know that the great Cub slugger Hack Wilson was only 5'6". Sure'n' it's a great day for the Shortish.

23   The short have not exactly got long shrift in literature. There is the pathetic Tiny Tim, of course, and Walter de la Mare wrote a novel about a

young girl's growing up—or, more precisely, not having grown up—titled *Memoirs of a Midget*. But most writers do not bother to describe their characters' height, unless it is extraordinary. Nor do most autobiographers mention how tall they are. How tall was Rousseau? He tells us everything else about himself, but not, to the best of my memory, his height. I have always imagined Ben Franklin short and John Stuart Mill tall, but I don't think either refers to his height in his classic autobiography. Nor do I remember Henry Adams anywhere remarking that he is quite short—no more than 5'4" or 5'5", I'd say, judging from photographs. Would he have been less sour, I wonder, at 5'11"? Would the country have looked different to him at 6'1"?

24 Montaigne informs us that "I am a little below medium height" and that, frankly, it bugs him. It is not only a serious defect, he says, but a "disadvantage, especially for men in command or office; for the authority given by a fine presence and bodily majesty is lacking." He quotes Aristotle saying that little men may be pretty but not handsome. Warming to his subject, Montaigne adds:

> Where smallness dwells, neither breadth and roundness of forehead, nor clarity and softness of eyes, nor the moderate form of the nose, nor small size of ears and mouth, nor regularity and whiteness of teeth, nor the smooth thickness of a beard brown as the husk of a chestnut, nor curly hair [Montaigne was bald], nor proper roundness of head, nor freshness of color, nor a pleasant facial expression, nor an odorless body, nor just proportion of limbs, can make a handsome man.

It's almost enough to cause a man under six feet to send off for elevator shoes.

25 Henry James, whom no one is likely to have described as rangy, occasionally mentions the height of his characters, but chiefly, in my recollection, when they are especially small. A secondary character in *The Ambassadors* named John Little Bilham is referred to everywhere in the book as "little Bilham" because of his diminutive size. In *The Princess Casamassima,* the novel's tragic hero Hyacinth Robinson is time and again described as "little Hyacinth," even when he grows to adulthood. I once asked a class to whom I was teaching the novel why James seemed continually to emphasize Hyacinth's smallness. I was able to convince them, through the usual strong-arm tactics, that the answer might be because, given Hyacinth's relation to two women in the novel, James, by stressing his character's littleness, wished to take him out of sexual contention. One of the two women, the working-class Millicent Henning, for example, is always described as large and robust, and therefore any notion of Hyacinth being her lover is disqualified. "How small, exactly, do you think Hyacinth is?" I asked, hoping someone would answer five feet, perhaps 5'2" at the maximum. "Well, how small is he, Miss Palmer?" I asked,

when no one cared to hazard a guess. "I don't know," she said. "I suppose about your size." Ah, another magical moment in teaching.

26   "Stand tall, soldier," I can recall our elegant, whipper-lean 6'2" training sergeant Andrew Atherton bellowing, generally as a prelude to chewing out a recruit. Tall, for him as for most people, clearly was an approbative. In bygone movie days, tall was linked up with dark and handsome to describe, say, Cary Grant. Short, dark, and handsome somehow isn't the same. Splendid to be big-hearted, but you don't want to be thought small-minded. You want to be careful, too, about coming up short. *Petty* derives from *petite*, which is of course French for *small*. Small-fry, small change, small beer—all convey the notion of triviality. The word *little* has become an intensifier, applied to people who are not themselves necessarily small, chiefly to add a dollop of contempt or to suggest insignificance, as in "that little fool," or even "what a little monster he has turned out to be." In short (so to speak), the language is loaded against us.

27   Still, I can recall a time when being tall seemed to have its own drawbacks. A tall young girl was usually a shy young girl, and often today, most touchingly, still is. Tall boys came in two varieties: thin and gangly or thick and oafish. To have been more than, say, 6'3" in high school and even college was an almost certain guarantee of being ill-coordinated. With occasional exceptions, in sports the very tall seemed to convey an aura of hopelessness. (To be very tall and not compete in sports was, worse, to convey an aura of freakishness.) In basketball, where great height was an obvious advantage, the very tall were instructed to hang around near the baskets in the hope that the ball would fall into their hands, whereupon they could pass it along to someone shorter who would know what to do with it. At a side gym at the University of Illinois sometime in the middle 1950s, I recall watching no fewer than three coaches attempt to teach a 6'7", rather thickset freshman basketball player how to jump. I felt as if I were watching three trainers working with a bear.

28   As if to underscore the fundamental difference between the tall and the small, in the Chicago high school system of my boyhood two basketball divisions were created: junior basketball was for boys 5'8" and under; senior basketball for boys 5'8" and above. Connoisseurs tended to feel that junior basketball was superior; the players were better coordinated, size couldn't replace skill, the game was quicker and more sophisticatedly played. Junior basketball in Chicago may have been one of the few occasions in all Western history when a substantial number of young males lied about their height—lied, that is, downwardly. Each year there was an official measuring-in for junior basketball, and many boys who were 5'9" or 5'10", preferring to play junior ball, slumped and slouched up to the measuring standard, trying to lose an inch or two through poor posture. Many were the stories about boys staying up all through the night before in the hope that lack of sleep would diminish their already modest size. Of an older kid in our school named Harry Shadian, who was very kind to me when I was a freshman, it was said that, in the attempt to "measure in" for

juniors, he stayed up for two full nights drinking coffee and smoking cigarettes while carrying another boy named Dick Burkholder on his shoulders. The picture of the two of them continues to exert its fascination.
While Harry Shadian was smoking and drinking coffee, what, I have wondered, was Dick Burkholder, perched upon his shoulders, doing? Not, I
suspect, eating watercress sandwiches and reading La Bruyère.

29   Not only was junior basketball abolished in Chicago in my sophomore
year in high school—providing one of the few serious disappointments in
my otherwise agreeable youth—but then, ten or so years later, as if the
needle of evolution had jumped eight or ten grooves, suddenly large boys
and men became normally, in fact beautifully, coordinated. Earlier such
extraordinary professional basketball players as Bob Pettit and Dolph
Schayes, both well above 6'5", had moved with splendid fluidity, and one
was occasionally treated to the spectacle of a quick and graceful fatboy on
the football field, but all at once it seemed as if there were hundreds and
hundreds of such athletes. Now one regularly saw men of 6'6", 6'9", 7',
7'2", who with an antelope-like bound could spear a fly ball just as it was
about to leave a ballpark, or catch up with a man a foot or so shorter who
had a twenty-yard lead, or pop into the air with the clarity and tautness of
Massine, except that Massine, at the end of such an effort, never bothered
to finish off with a three-sixty, double-pump, in-your-face, slam diddle-do
dunk. Such men had names like Winfield, Bird, Strawberry, Magic, and
Julius Erving (a name at whose close I always await either the name
Horowitz or Shapiro, though it never arrives). These are men who regularly manage feats of coordination that men more than a foot shorter never
even thought to attempt. In sports, it has made the old concept of "the
good little man" rather obsolete. If one can't at least be more graceful
than larger people, what, one has to ask, is the point of being small?

30   Or, to put it even more blatantly, who needs small men? Certainly one
doesn't find much call for them in the classified section. When once briefly
unemployed and hence a powerfully close reader of all employment ads, I
do recall reading an ad asking specifically for small men—to clean out
heating ducts in large office buildings in Manhattan. I regret having failed
to apply; it could have been my one chance to have been turned away for
being too tall. To return to sports, horse racing requires that jockeys be
small, or at least light in weight, and diving, gymnastics, and figure skating
favor smaller competitors, who have less body to control in the difficult
physical configurations these sports all require. I tend to think of great
mathematicians—Einstein and Ramanujan are two examples—as smallish
men, and so, too, musicians: Beethoven, though stocky, cannot have been
tall; Toscanini was distinctly short, and the contemporary composer and
conductor Nicolas Slonimsky, in his recent autobiography, gives his height
as 5'5 3/4" (only a short man will take every quarter inch he can get).
Psychoanalysts I have met tend to be short, and so, too, violinists. The
shortest audiences I know are those that attend chamber-music concerts.
Pope, Keats, and Swinburne were all exceedingly short, and so was Dylan
Thomas, though, when fully sauced, his height was not the first thing

most folks generally noticed about him. Disraeli and Churchill, the greatest English politicians, of the nineteenth and twentieth centuries, were both fairly short. . . . But surely you can feel me struggling here, thrashing around, seeking a pattern.

31   Character, Heraclitus famously says, is fate, but how does one's size affect both character and fate? Had Pushkin been taller—and he was quite small—might he not more easily have walked away from the foolish duel over his honor as a husband that ended his life when he was only thirty-eight? Taller, would Evelyn Waugh still have been, as Cecil Beaton recalls him from school days, "a tiny but fierce ringleader of bullies"—for in some sense Waugh remained a small bully all his days. Not all the short tough guys were in the movies. Edmund Wilson, another short man on the stocky model, despite his deceptively friendly and furry nickname of Bunny, often played the intellectual bully. At 5'4" or so, Milton Friedman quickly makes it plain that he is not a man to be fooled with, at least in economic argument, where he could take your scalp off quicker than you can say Joan Robinson.

32   Height, if I may go off on a gender bender, is no very big deal for women. To be a woman above six feet carries, I am sure, its complications, but small women don't seem to operate under some of the same constraints, compulsions, pressures that small men sometimes do. The petite, moreover, is a category of feminine refinement. Women don't, when young, have to worry about being called Pip-Squeak, Twerp, or Half-Pint. ("Lay off the 'Shorty,'" says a petulant Spencer Tracy to Clark Gable at one point in the movie *Boom Town*.) Outside the duct-cleaning business, short men have never constituted an ideal type, but for a time in American life short women did. In the late 1940s and through the 1950s, the female type of the cheerleader—short, bosomy, full-calved, energetic—was much admired. Debbie Reynolds and, at a steamier level, Elizabeth Taylor represent the type in its Hollywood version. At my high school, they abounded; a few were named Mary Lou, but more than half seemed to be named Bobbie. "They may not be all that elegant," a wag with whom I went to school once remarked, "but they sure hold the road."

33   For a long while now the day of the Mary Lous and Bobbies has been over. Clothes have long since ceased to be designed with such women in mind, and they have no current representative in the movies. Tall and slender is nowadays the winning ticket, for both women and men. One sees this everywhere, and not least prominently in the elaborately mounted fantasies that are the magazine advertisements of the 5'6" clothing designer Ralph Lauren (né Lifschitz), which are populated exclusively with lithe and lanky WASPs lounging about in cowboy, tennis, or boating duds. Any man even roughly Ralph Lauren's own size showing up in any one of these fantastical ads is as unlikely as the appearance of the Modern Jazz Quartet at a Hasidic picnic.

34   Height may be one of the few departments in life where the best break comes with being average. Extremes to either side can be a serious nuisance: to be either 4'10" or 6'10" carries its own bedeviling inconve-

niences—from finding shoes small enough to finding beds big enough. What today is average height is not altogether clear. Like the poverty line, the average height line, one assumes, is going up all the time. When I was a kid, 5'8" or 5'9" seemed average height for a man; now 5'10" appears closer to the average. The higher the average rises, the lower I fall beneath it. It could get worse. As some people grow elderly, their faces become blurry, as if someone had fooled with their contrast button; while others, usually those who are small to begin with, tend to shrink in size. I believe I am going to be one of the shrinkers. I could one day look back at 5'6½" as my dinosaur age.

35   Although I have said that I cannot imagine myself truly tall, and although I have gone on about height at such (oops, sorry) length, neither do I tend to think of myself as small, at least not most of the time. Usually I think of myself as I appear to myself in my dreams: a man of average height, neutral looks, and medium build. And so in my workaday life do I think of myself until I stand next to someone quite large—as when I discovered myself, in the Los Angeles airport, standing alongside the 7'2" Wilt Chamberlain, into whose belt atop immense chocolate-colored velour trousers I found myself staring. At such moments I am brought up (sorry again) short. Yet otherwise I do not think overlong (*oy!*) about my physique and go about heightless and fancy-free.

36   Despite these disclaimers, I do feel there was something strongly formative about growing up on the short side. I cannot say why, exactly, but I sense that, had I been four or five inches taller, I should have been a radically different person than I am now. Discussing an acquaintance at lunch one day, a friend said to me, "He's the most underconfident tall man I know"—and then he paused, and added—"just as you are the most confident short man I know." That is an interesting distinction, and a compliment with lots of slack in it for interpretation. Does it mean that I am extraordinarily confident *for* a short man? Or does it mean that, given my shortness, it is remarkable that I am so confident. Life, like me, is too short to worry about such ambiguities—and besides, with my confidence, who cares? Yet I do have the distinct sense that my confidence and size, too, are somehow linked. As Emile Zola, Teddy Roosevelt, Lenin, Lord Beaverbrook, Fiorello La Guardia, Picasso, and a few other shortish fellows would be pleased to testify, there has never been a big demand for small underconfident men. Besides, as a man once told me, it isn't what you have here but what you have someplace else that counts. And that, Bubba, is about the size of it.

Discussion Questions

1. What, if anything, in Epstein's essay makes you care about his thoughts on being short?

2. Do you feel sympathy for Epstein? Do you feel scorn and embarrassment for him? Or is your reaction one of amusement? Explain your reaction.

3. Epstein waits until paragraph 7 to reveal his true height, teasing his readers with information on where they wouldn't find him, what derisive names he would never be called, etc. How effective is such a beginning? Is his waiting until the seventh paragraph to reveal his height a clue that he is troubled by being short? Explain your answer.

4. Throughout his essay, Epstein names dozens of actors, writers, athletes, and politicians in his discussion of height. What do these names add to his essay? Do you see them as name-dropping or as examples that prove there's nothing wrong with being short?

5. After having read his essay, do you think Epstein has reconciled himself to being 5 feet 6 1/2 inches tall? Explain in what ways Epstein's dealing with his height is similar to or different from John Updike's reconciliation to having psoriasis or Leonard Kriegel's to having polio.

Time in a Bottle

Linda Ellerbee

Linda Ellerbee was born in 1944 in Texas. A graduate of Vanderbilt University, Ellerbee is best known for her career as a television journalist and talk show host. She currently appears on Nickelodeon Nick/News W/5. *Ellerbee is the author of two books,* And So It Goes: Adventures in Television *(1986) and* Move On: Adventures in the Real World *(1991), in which the following essay appears. "Time in a Bottle" is a revealing look into Ellerbee's addiction to alcohol and her successful attempt to break the habit at The Betty Ford Clinic.*

The Daily Feelings Journal describes what you have experienced during the past 24 hours. By taking time to review your day and reflect on your behavior, you can become more aware of your feelings, actions and attitudes toward yourself and others. Generally one or two paragraphs will be enough. You may choose your own time to write in your journal so long as it does not interfere with other scheduled sessions. Each evening the journal is placed on the desk in the living room, where it is accessible to your counselor. The feelings journal is reviewed daily by your counselor. It is recommended you use at least four "feeling" words per day.

1   You want to know how I "feel"? I feel like Private fucking Benjamin, only not cute. I'm also not awake, I can't think of anything nice to say and I wish, *oh how I wish* I were home.

2   "Have you 'journaled' today?" they ask.

3   "There's a word for people who do that," I snap. "We call them journalists."

4   I am not doing well at The Betty Ford Center.

5   The question is, do I belong here? I never meant to be an alcoholic. All I did was decide to drink. They have asked me, for my assignment for tomorrow, to write down the consequences of my drinking. Let's see, there's been perhaps a bit of erosion in my health and some deterioration in my looks, maybe a little increasing sloppiness about my appearance, some puffiness around the eyes and okay, I'm overweight, but nothing I can't fix. It's true my social life's almost nonexistent; I work, I drink, I sleep. My dwindling interest in sex seems hardly worth mentioning. Sure, there's been some isolation from friends and alienation from my children because of certain inconsistent behavior on my part, and so what if I've been overbearing or stopped listening to any voice but my own—it's *my* life. Oh, I admit I've gotten pretty rotten at handling some of the details of my life, say, most of them—this constant forgetting and losing things— and yes, I am depressed most of the time now and cry for no reason or all of them and, yes, I did endanger my son's life that night I drove us to the country drunk in that mean storm. And, yes, I guess you could say that because of my behavior fluctuating so wildly behind my code of values, or what's left of it, that I've pretty much lost all self-esteem. Put another way, I guess you could say I hate myself. But I'm *not* angry. Last Thanksgiving a friend, watching while I sliced the goose in the kitchen, told me in the kindest way that Josh had said something to him about being worried about me, about my drinking, and I was calm, wasn't I, when I sliced my finger to the bone?

6   And, yes, my father was an alcoholic, goddammit.

7   I used to love to get up in time to watch the sun rise. I was moved by the wholeness of beauty, the fine way the parts were joined. Little by little, that beauty has broken into pieces for me. Pretty is all that's left. It's not enough.

8   Do I belong here?

9   I belong here.

10   It tells you something when you say to your family and very closest friends that you're going to The Betty Ford Center and no one asks why.

11   Oh, hell, if Murphy Brown can . . .

You will be assigned to one of four [4] living units. You are not to be involved in any way, or to enter, any other unit than your assigned unit. You are expected to be in your unit at 10 pm, and you must sign out and back in at the reception window in your unit.

12   My "unit" is North Hall. There are twenty of us, a mixture of men and women, but not in the bedrooms, which are all doubles except for one. A retired elementary school teacher from Des Moines who's been here a week but whose eyes are still blackened from being beaten up by her husband, also a drunk, told me this afternoon that "when Betty was admitted to the Long Beach Naval Hospital she insisted on a private room but they told her it didn't work that way and in time Betty decided they were right so when she started her own place, she said each unit should have rooms with two beds in them and one room with four beds in it for anybody who demands a private room."

13   Betty isn't here right now, she tells me. Except in spirit, she adds. Betty's in Colorado. I don't blame Betty one damn bit. The temperature today in Palm Springs is 122° and there are no celebrities here, none, but the retired elementary school teacher says she can show me just which unit and bed Elizabeth Taylor was in. Both times.

> You will not leave the campus at any time. You will become an important member of a new "family" of 20 peers as each day you form new and meaningful relationships.

14   One of the minor versions of hell: my roommate is thin, tanned, gorgeous and twenty-three. She listens to rap music on the portable tape player her boyfriend, the Hell's Angel, bought for her as a going-away-to-The-Betty-Ford-Center gift. Walkmans, she says (Walkmen?), are against the rules. Getting sober is going to be loud. Funny, the people here, the patients, don't look like drunks; they look like normal people, most of them, not counting the short fellow from Omaha with the twitch who says he designs security systems for missile bases.

15   Last night I went to my first AA meeting. They read from the Big Book. Every reference was to men. "If the alcoholic says to his boss . . . Some good news for the wife of an alcoholic is . . . "

16   My "peers" keep their distance. I've been to crime scenes that were friendlier. I am the new kid on their block. Also, some of them think I'm here to write an "exposé" of The Betty Ford Center. I tried to tell them I was here for the same reason they were, but there was trouble about my coffee cup. You're given a coffee cup for the duration. A punch-label with your name on it is glued to the cup. Mine says "Linda Smith." When I was registering, the lady at the desk said sometimes the press got a hold of the patient list and it wouldn't be good for me to be worrying about that while I was worrying about so many other things (she sounded as if there were a great many things about which I ought to be worrying and if I were not, certainly would be soon), so why didn't I pick another name. I said I didn't see how much could be accomplished if I had to lie to other people starting with basics like my name. She said it was only for the books, not

the people, and why didn't I just pick one, now. I said write down "Linda Smith."

17   "Surely you can be more creative than that."

18   "Maybe, but my parents couldn't."

> You are required to attend and participate in all aspects of the treatment program. You are asked to keep current by checking the bulletin board in your unit. You are responsible for your personal care, for keeping your room clean and for completing your daily therapeutic duty assignment. You are expected to launder your own clothes. No dry cleaning is available. Becoming responsible to self and others is an essential component of recovery.

19   They gave me a schedule and told me to thumbtack it on the bulletin board over the desk in my room. They gave me a thumbtack, too. Up at 5:30. "Meditation" walk, followed by breakfast, followed by my "therapeutic duty assignment." I am a busboy. After I clean tables, there is exercise, then a lecture, then an hour-and-a-half group therapy session and a community meeting. By now we have reached lunch, it says here. After lunch there's another lecture, another therapy session, more exercise, then study time, dinner, still another lecture or AA meeting, then return to my room to work on written assignments or my "journaling."

20   I've been examined physically and mentally for three days, the same questions over and over.

21   "How did you feel when you realized you had a blackout?"

22   "I didn't have blackouts." *Oh, maybe a few times I couldn't remember some things, but no blackouts.*

23   "When was the first time you got high?"

24   "When I was three years old and discovered how dizzy I could get rolling down a hill." *I liked that.*

25   "Did you use other drugs besides alcohol?"

26   "I don't recall, I was drunk at the time." *The drugs of my generation. I did the drugs of my generation.*

27   "What is your drug of choice?"

28   "Tequila." *Or vodka or rum or brandy or whatever you've got.*

29   "When did you take your first drink?"

30   "Sixteen. Cutty Sark on the rocks." *My father drank Cutty Sark.*

31   "Did you like drinking?"

32   "Loved it." *In the beginning, the high I got from drinking in some ways did resemble the rush you get falling in love, a sense of well-being, an optimistic view of tomorrow and a desire to see my "lover" again soon.*

33   "What did you love about it?"

34   "The taste."

35   "You loved the taste?"

36   "Yes." *I hated the taste.*

37   "Is that why you kept drinking?"

38   "I guess." *I also liked being one of the "guys." You know, after you get that story you all sit around the bar telling lies about how you got that story. And drinking.*

39   "Anything else?"

40   "No." *Yes. Drinking made it easier to talk to strangers. And friends. Drinking made me forget to think about what I never wanted to think about anyway. Drinking made me happy. Drinking made me stupid.*

41   "Are you an alcoholic?"

42   "Yes." *Am I really? I hate this.*

43   "When did you realize you were an alcoholic?"

44   "Gee, I can't remember." *What time is it?*

45   They have given me a printed sheet of "feeling words" for my journal in case I've forgotten what "apprehensive," "lonely" and "humiliated" mean.

> You may not use the phone for the first five days. After that you may use the phone during one, scheduled, 10-minute period each 24 hours. Mail is sorted at the reception desk. We have a need to inspect all deliveries, including packages sent or dropped off by family and friends.

46   Mail for me, a card from Lloyd Dobyns. On the outside of the card, one jellyfish says to another jellyfish (who's floating upside down with all its tendrils rising upright and stiff): "The first thing you've got to learn is to relax." Inside, he has hand-printed: "And the second thing you've got to learn is to answer the question, 'When the cocktail hour comes, what do I do with my hands?' One possible answer, Ellerbee, is to chew on them for a while. That way your mouth won't be busy either. Love, Lloyd." Telling him may have been something of a mistake.

> Once you are diagnosed as chemically dependent, it is your responsibility to do those things necessary to get well. You will learn about yourself and your disease. It is important to become involved during your first week and to increase that involvement daily.

47   "*Webster's*," says the lecturer, "defines disease as anything which interferes with the human organism's ability to function normally." Does this, I wonder, make a knife wound a disease?

48   My disease is defined as alcoholism, he says. My disease is chronic, progressive *(progressive as long as I drink)* and incurable *(it's impossible to take an alcoholic and make a controlled drinker out of him—her)*. My disease is characterized by a loss of control *(an alcoholic cannot predict how much she will drink or her behavior when she drinks)* over alcohol and other sedatives *(alcohol is merely one more sedative)*. My disease follows a natural course *(if untreated)*, has specific signs and clinical symptoms, a known

outcome *(I will drink until I die, drink until I'm insane or brain-damaged, or stop drinking)* and a very definite treatment.

49   Which starts with not drinking.

50   "The cause, like that of many cancers, diabetes and AIDS, is unknown," he tells us, "but it is not, as the post-Freudians thought, the symptom of some larger, underlying problem. There is no set personality structure."

51   I am not unique.

52   This right away is a problem. I have counted on my uniqueness for years, relied on it. Being told I'm one of 12 million makes me feel about as good as being told I'm doing the "in" thing by checking into a rehab center or that all the really interesting people these days are at AA meetings. I used to tell Betty Ford Center jokes. Now I am one.

53   At the lectures I take many and detailed notes, like a good student, or a good girl. I am eager to please, to do well. To *get* well?

54   "What is known," says the not-quite-retired surgeon with the strong face and no-bull bedside manner, also a recovering alcoholic (he looks like a well-aged Richard Widmark, but then so does Richard Widmark), "is that something happens when ethyl alcohol is taken into the body of an alcoholic drinker that does not happen when it's taken into the body of a non-alcoholic drinker; something happens in the brain that causes a small portion of the alcohol to be converted into a highly addictive substance referred to as THIQ (tetrahydronisoquinalone). This substance is not found in the brain of non-alcoholic drinkers and at this time, it cannot be detected nor removed. Except by autopsy. But testing has shown there exists in some people some sort of biochemical defect which causes the alcohol to be converted to THIQ, and that the defect is hereditary."

55   I know about my father. And me. But what will this mean to my children?

56   In bed tonight, I read more on the subject in one of the pamphlets I've been given. They're all I have to read, them and the AA Big Book. They took away the books I brought with me: a couple of serious novels I'd been meaning to get around to, another book about Washington politics and a handful of mysteries. "Here," they said, "read this, instead." And so I do. "The alcoholic," I read, "while not responsible for having the disease of alcoholism, is entirely responsible for his recovery."

57   A disease? I'm not so sure about this disease business. I was raised to believe we bring our troubles on ourselves and have done my part in this matter. The American Medical Association defined alcoholism as a disease in 1956; I still think of it as a moral failing. My drinking is not my disease. My drinking is my fault. And my addiction. Alcoholism is an addiction to alcohol. If I am an alcoholic, then I am an addict. Like a junkie. My "feeling word" for the day is "shitty."

You will become familiar with the twelve steps of the Alcoholics Anonymous program, which is the blueprint to your recovery.

58   Today a lecture about change happens. And I had thought I was the expert.

59   "It's really quite simple," says the psychologist. "First you identify the problem. The second step is to develop trust." I ask the psychologist what she means.

60   "Hope," she says. "You gotta hope."

61   The next step, she says, is the catharsis ("Ventilate. Ventilate.") followed by insight and then, finally, change. These, she points out, are also the first five steps of the AA twelve-step program, except for change. Change is all the steps after the first five.

62   Sure sounds simple. But then so does a sex-change operation and I wouldn't want to contemplate trying one of those in thirty days. Or a lifetime.

63   Tonight's AA meeting is better. Drunks are very funny when they're sober, I find out. The man who spoke to us tonight is not a patient—or "inmate," as I continue to call them. Us.

64   *Us.*

65   He's a retired carpenter and a drunk who's been sober fifty years now. I ask him how. He says there's nothing to it. All you do is don't drink and don't die.

> You will be assigned a counselor as your primary case manager. There are formal planning sessions for each patient; individual therapy sessions between counselor and patient and daily group therapy sessions. The daily group becomes the nucleus of your recovery program. Your participation is important.

66   I get it. The basic assumption of AA is that only another alcoholic can help an alcoholic. But I don't like this group therapy business. It's too personal. I don't know these ten people well enough to talk about, well, to talk about what I don't know these ten people well enough to talk about. Today I watched them doing it with one another and could not imagine my being able to be so candid with near strangers. I have used words to keep from saying much for such a long time now, and so deftly, I like to think.

67   And what of all this chumminess? What am I to make of grownups who hug people they aren't related to and chant: *North Hall had a ball, using drugs and alcohol! Now we're sober one and all! Rah!* This cheer or one like it is performed with the twenty of us standing in a circle, arms linked, five or six times a day. A required exercise. I'm sure it's a polite way to perform regular "bed checks," but I don't know; I feel so damned silly.

68   They keep telling us, "If you want what we have, do what we do." Do they mean I have to become a sheep? Shit. I tell my counselor when it comes to how things are run around here, I have feelings. I have feelings that are buried alive. She says feelings are always buried alive.

> Our feelings substantially color the way we see life and react to it. No longer are we persons who simply feel resentful; we are re-

sentful persons. We may discover we have become self-pitying persons. What was once a feeling has hardened into an attitudinal posture—a character defect. If we are to change this, we must first discover ourselves at the feeling level.

69   There's another good-bye party tonight. It's always someone's first day, someone else's last. We have fruit punch; you never saw so many people who know how to hold a glass.

70   Tomorrow's my turn to "share" my life story.

71   Is "wordy" a feeling?

72   Tonight I think about my life. My counselor tells me there is a Linda and a Linda Jane. Little Linda Jane. My counselor tells me I need to go back and find little Linda Jane, but I can't even remember where I left my shoes after lunch, or what I ate. They say it will take at least a year to get my short-term memory back, if it comes back. They do not coddle us about the facts; one of the first things they tell us is that more than half never make it.

73   Josh's high-school graduation. He was so fine. I was so drunk. And I told him what I thought of his class play, the one we'd all gone to see the night before graduation; I took it apart, front to back, gave it my *professional* best. Over and over, the way drunks do. My son directed that play. Neither of us will forget graduation day, I expect.

74   This road seems so long and hard and I am so tired and scared. Trying to see myself clearly these days is like trying to look backwards without turning around.

> Most of us think we know ourselves and are afraid of looking bad to others, so it's hard to take the risk of being revealing and genuine. But what have we got to lose? You're only as sick as your secrets.

75   "My, but you're touchy tonight."

76   Mike and I are walking back from dinner when he says this. It's not dark yet. We eat at 5 P.M., like convicts or nuns, or children. Mike and I have taken to one another, possibly because, except for a mild case of terminal smart mouth, we are unalike. Mike is from Chicago but lives in Florida now. He has no job; he used to sell shoes, and other things, he hints, but I don't know at what. Michael has pancreatitis. Unlike liver damage, it is irreversible. Sometimes he's in pain. When the pain gets really bad, they let him have an aspirin. Mike laughs about that. And at me. He says women are only good for one thing. He calls me one of "those feminists" and say it's my fault or the fault of women like me that the world's so screwed up because women are far superior to men and we blew it when we demanded equality. It was a step down, he says. Mike does not read enough and he thinks too much and it's nice to have a pal. But not tonight.

77   "I am not touchy. Please just shut up."

78   Today I gave my life story to the group. Gave. Now there's an interesting choice of words. I cried once in the telling when something reminded me of something else. When it was over, I felt drained and also part of this group of people for the first time. It was not a bad feeling. So why am I so touchy tonight?

79   "Alcoholics," says my counselor, "do everything the hard way."

80   Another card from Lloyd today. On the front, the famous Escher lithograph "Relativity," the one with the people climbing stairs that go every which way, no matter which way you look at it or turn the card. Inside, he's printed, "This is a test. If you're sober and half-psychotic, the drawing on the front is all fucked up. To me it's just a bunch of people wanting to go up or down stairs. Of course, I'm half-sober and completely psychotic. Love, Lloyd."

> Besides a physician, registered nurse, psychologist and chemical dependency counselors, our multi-disciplinary team includes clergy, family counselors, a registered dietitian and an exercise coordinator.

81   God, this is depressing. Not only am I a sick person, I'm a fat sick person. They gave me a questionnaire at lunch. At *lunch*. "Are you a Fitness Drop-out?" I got as far as the first five questions. "Do you remember the day you last exercised for at least 30 minutes without stopping? Do you hang your laundry on your exercise bicycle? Do your children roll their eyes when you say you're going to start exercising again? Do you know exactly where your walking shoes are?" And the worst: "Do you weigh at least 20% more than you did when you graduated high school?" Does it count that I know at least 20 percent more, too? No? I see.

82   I've lost six pounds. But who could tell?

83   The dietitian tells us there are 630 calories in a Whopper. This is information I've been living to hear.

84   There's a lot of joking goes on among the inmates about this place. It's a victim of its own success; we've all seen the before-and-after pictures of the famous who've been here and said so. We kid each other about when do we get our face-lifts? But there are no face-lifts here, no tucks, no facials, no body rubs, no masseuse at all. There is no fashion boutique, no tanning salon, no golden saving lotions: only the Exercycles, weights and the track. There is a swimming pool, but North Hall's time to use it (thrice weekly) is from four to five in the afternoon and by that time the sun has turned it into people soup. I seem to be waking earlier and earlier, 4:30 this morning, but the coffeepot in the kitchen is always on and I've come to enjoy walking alone at this time of day. Round and round the track, I watch the purple leave the mountains.

85   This religion thing: the trick, I've decided, is not to allow my lack of it

to get in the way of my getting sober. I am not going to be one of those people who runs around saying, "I found God at The Betty Ford Center." Father Joseph says I haven't lost my faith; he says it's just buried under a pile of shit. Do all Catholic priests talk like Father Joseph? Or is it only the Irish? Lapsed Methodists would like to know these secular secrets.

86   I woke up and heard someone crying in the night. Was it me?

> Those who do not recover are people who cannot or will not completely give themselves to this simple program, usually men and women who are constitutionally incapable of being honest with themselves. There are such unfortunates. They are not at fault; they seem to have been born that way. They are naturally incapable of grasping and developing a manner of living which demands rigorous honesty. Their chances are less than average.

87

Every day, more confusion in my head. I've become obsessed with the idea I'm one of the ones they're talking about, one of the "unfortunates" incapable of recovery. But how can you know for sure? I've lied to myself so often about drinking; am I lying to myself about wanting to stop drinking? About being able to? How well *does* a person know herself after the better part of a half a century? I look in my roommate's journal to see what she's written about me.

> Most events that occur during your stay fall under the heading of therapeutic. All aspects of this chronic disease must be treated. As you participate in the program you will experience many hills and valleys.

88   What a remarkable morning! I feel great for a change, woke feeling rested and yes, peaceful. The feeling lasted a whole day. (That's three "feeling words" in one paragraph, except all the "feeling words" are "feeling" words, which probably doesn't count.) Spent part of the morning in the Serenity Room. Can you believe they call it that? "If you're looking for Twyla Jean, she's meditating right over there in the Serenity Room, just past the nurses' station. Look out for the pillows on the floor. Have a nice day."

89   It *is* nice, though, this day, and this room: soft carpet, the pillows on the floor and a glass wall facing a small courtyard garden with a few desert blossoms and much sky. The first thing everybody says when they see the Serenity Room is, "Jesus, what a great place to get high." I try to meditate. I used to do that in the sixties or was it the seventies; naturally I can remember my mantra. Or can I? Surely a plain old ohhmmm will work.

90   Ohhmmmmmmmmm . . .

91   After a while, when nobody was around, I knelt and put my hands together, the way I did when I was a little girl and believed in Jesus, the tooth fairy and tomorrow. Part of me felt like a fool. Another part of me

asked the first part just which one was the fool here. When it started to go that way, I got up and left the Serenity Room before I lost the stupid feelings that took me there in the first place, but going out the door I turned back and without thinking said, "Thank you." To an empty room.

92   Yesterday's card from Lloyd was blue with a star of David and the words "On Your Bar Mitzvah" embossed on the front. His words inside: "What the hell, they don't make cards that say, 'On Your Sobriety.' Love, Lloyd."

93   They do make such cards, Lloyd. They sell them here at the book and sundry shop (we call it the mall), not too far from the Serenity Room, but I'd never tell you that. You would laugh and then I would laugh and we'd be making up badass cards and I'd forget the point of the whole exercise was to clean the swamp. Lloyd, you really are a shithead. Don't ask me to tell you about the Serenity Room.

94   This week I got my "Master Plan." There it is in writing: Patient does not understand disease concept as evidenced by her continuing guilt feelings over drinking. Patient exhibits low self-esteem by covering more sensitive parts of her personality with a tough facade. Patient exhibits extreme confusions and shame concerning what her drinking has done to her children.

95   What they don't know about English they apparently do know about me. The same day I got a letter from Allison. About children. They tell me there are no coincidences.

96   "Dear Linda: This is great. I can talk at you and you can't talk back! I've been on vacation this week but most of my time is spent worrying about the beastie boy [Tyler is three and wonderful] who has just started day camp. These folks take this whole school/day camp thing far too seriously. There are words like 'structured play' and 'unstructured play.' Before the group started, I went to a meeting and the group leader asked us what we looked for in a play group. Comments like 'meaningful interaction' and 'racial diversity' spewed forth from these suburban mouths. I said I first looked in the closets and if there were no kids bound and gagged, it was probably a swell program. Tyler's taken to going to the bathroom outside. He likes it best when a car is passing. I'm letting his father handle that situation. Linda, I'm bewildered by the one of him. When I think about having two so close in age, the way you did, and then trying to raise them alone, I think about slitting my throat. Don't know how you did it. Again, hope all is well, and Linda, *listen* to them."

97   I'm listening.

98   We talked about different levels of communication yesterday morning. This is all so terribly obvious. Or so obviously necessary.

99   The cliche: "My name is Bob and I'm an alcoholic."

100   The facts: "I'm from Ohio."

101   The opinion: "I believe alcoholism is a disease."

102   The feeling: "When I found out I was an alcoholic, I was devastated."

103   After lunch, pretending it wasn't a zillion degrees hot, a bunch of us

sat outside on the sidewalk and I got to thinking how much I liked these people and what an easy time I had talking to them. There wasn't a thing you could say you'd done that somebody else hadn't done worse. Black humor is made for them, for here; there's much laughter, almost as much laughter as there is sadness.

104   Yesterday afternoon we talked about co-dependence (basically, taking someone else's temperature to see how you feel) and when Sue said, "the co-dependent parent, the one who didn't drink, is the one children have the most issues with later in life," I was genuinely stunned, having assumed, without giving it much thought, that my anger at Mama, our constant fighting, had to do with my taste, politics, friends, men, choices, life or the fact we were a lot alike. It never occurred to me it had to do with her not being able to stop Daddy from drinking.

> Visiting hours are Sundays and holidays from 1:00 pm–5:00 pm. Visitors are to register at the reception desk and receive a visitor's badge that is to be worn during their visit. The badge is to be returned to the desk upon departure of the visitor.

105   Watching other people's families come to visit, I miss my own so much I'm determined to do what it takes to get back to them. Today my roommate talked about dropping out, leaving now. She's thinking of it. I was anxious for her but very nervous, because I have not thought about quitting, although I said, "Oh, sure I have," when she asked. "We all do," I said.

106   I'm too scared to quit. I don't want to go back to where I was. But I do want to get back to my family; and still it's pleasant tonight sitting in this room at this desk, alone. There's no light but that from my desk lamp, soft and yellow, no sound but the crickets and the sprinklers that keep the desert at bay (for considerable handfuls of money, I suspect). I do like moments like this; you feel most monk-like. It must be the cell-effect. There's a curious peace in distance. Once in a while I think I would like to spend long periods of time apart from the world. Can one meditate and write at the same time? Solitude will always be necessary, I think, but then solitude is not isolation, is it? How is it that so often here I get the feeling I've worked hard to learn something I already know, or knew, once. Is it their purpose to teach us what we know? Or to remind us where to look for it, touching the posts as we go, trying to find our way home in the dark?

107   The soft yellow light on my desk shines me to sleep.

> Confrontation is defined as "presenting a person with himself by describing how I see him." It takes courage to risk confronting. We are all dependent upon others for a completed picture of ourselves. Confrontation provides that.

108   Treatment, they tell you, works from the outside in. At some time everyone in the group is asked to evaluate your progress. Each person is

given a form and asked to check those statements most appropriate to you. There are two columns. In one column are the phrases that damn: Minimizes use. Doesn't ask for help. Too much outside focus. Seems arrogant and self-centered. In the other column: Realistic about self and problem. Is well focused on treatment. Takes responsibility for own behavior. Socializes well with peers. Both lists are long in case you want to really get down to it. When it was Tom's turn, he was excited because he thought he was doing so well; he could hardly wait to see what nice things were going to be said about him. Probably, he said, he'd be the first person to get no bad phrases at all. He was crushed after the papers were turned in and the counselor read the results. It seems everybody said terrible things about Tom. Acts immaturely. Glamorizes use. Over-intellectualizes.

109   "But didn't anybody have any nice things to say about you?" I ask him, feeling pretty awful for him myself.

110   "Only Miguelito."

111   Miguelito is a gardener from East Los Angeles. He's also a drug dealer who liked his wares and as a consequence has a little trouble now putting two sentences together without large gaps of time between the words. Verbs give him particular trouble.

112   "What did Miguelito say?"

113   "He said I 'seemed willing.' Tom seems willing, said Miguelito the drug dealer."

114   "It's not much, is it?"

115   On Saturdays, we have two-hour sessions, the four "units" together in the main hall where they can mess with all our minds at once. They are quite good at it. This Saturday was "Lifeboat Drill." They divided us into four groups of twenty each, told each group it was a lifeboat halfway between Europe and America, with food and water on board for only eighteen; therefore each group had to pick two people to throw overboard. And each group had to decide *how* it would pick the two people to throw overboard, with only two rules: no volunteers, none of this "Oh, I'm not worth a damn or I don't care, etc., so throw me over," and no lotteries.

116   Amazing the way we can become children, cruel children, with the least encouragement. In our group, we decided to go round the circle and have everybody say why it was they thought they deserved to be allowed to stay on board (to live), then we'd vote. People said the oddest things. "I'm a good fisherman or I could learn to be one fast." "I studied astronomy in high school. I could guide us." "I'm small; I don't eat much." "I'm a good person. I sing."

117   When everybody was done, the eight people who'd been tossed to the sharks had to get up on stage in front of the rest of us and say how they "felt" about it. One theoretically dead woman ran crying from the room. A yellow-haired man I'd seen throwing rocks at a duck one day, also theoretically dead, said he hated us all and we'd be sorry. Others were merely pissed. The woman my group voted to sink said she expected it; she was old and her arm was in a cast (which she'd said would be good for hitting fish on the

head when she was trying to think of a reason we shouldn't drown her). I was sad for her. Nobody felt sad for the other one we threw off our boat. He should have known better than to ask the tired, used people in that room (collectively among our group of twenty, we had 500 years of drinking) to spare him because he was only twenty-four and had his whole life in front of him; and still we might have, but he said he was going to be a lawyer.

118   Taking a closer look at the eight people on the stage, seven now, I notice we've thrown away the old, the injured, the weak, a homosexual, a black man and in the would-have-been-a-lawyer's case, the witless. I'm less sure what this says about us as a bunch of drunks than as a society, but we learned, each of us to some extent or another during "Lifeboat Drill," about how we regarded ourselves and how that affected the way the others saw us. I knew, going in, that if it were a game, I would be voted overboard. I also knew if it were for real, I would survive. I was not voted overboard. Not that day.

119   The retired schoolteacher from Des Moines said that "when Betty was in treatment they played this same game and Betty said, 'If you don't throw me overboard, you'll all have a better chance of living because they won't give up searching for an ex-president's wife so soon.'" Mrs. Ford was always practical.

120   Lloyd's card today is a detail from "Garden of Id," an original oil painting by Ilene Meyer of Seattle, Washington, it says on the back. A beautiful blonde woman in a white tunic stands in the middle of a forest, gazing into a crystal ball which she holds above her head. She is surrounded by three male elves and one female elf wearing a red dress. The elves are very ugly and they, too, are looking in the crystal ball. Inside the card, in Lloyd's script, it says, "I figure you've been there long enough I don't have to print anymore. The blonde in white sees a future without all these pointy-eared, little-dick men who can do nothing for her. She is, therefore, pleased. The blonde in red sees a future without the demanding giant bitch and with a different man for every night of the week. She is, therefore, pleased. It's all relative. Love, Lloyd." There's a man to have in a lifeboat.

> For the most part, defenses are unconscious and automatic shields against a real or imagined threat. By pointing out the defenses you are using, you have a better chance of letting down this wall that is locking others out and keeping you prisoner. Since defenses hide us from ourselves as well as others, it is important to identify them.

121   I hate this place. Today they made me be quiet for two hours. I wasn't allowed to say anything to anyone or explain why I could not, nor was I allowed to be by myself. I had to sit with people, go to lunch with people and the longer it went on the more awful it was. Being silent, I realized how much I talked in self-defense. Being silent, I felt naked. How dare they take away my clothes. I mean my voice. I was in a rage so black the

room went dark. No voice. No power. I would get even. I would show them who had the power. I would, I said to myself, drink. Drinking would give me a voice.

122   When you shut one eye you don't hear so good.

123   I hate this place. They're so . . . right.

124   Got to change my behavior, not my thinking. Check. Can't think my-self into better living; it was my best thinking got me here. Check. Maybe I can live myself into better thinking. Check. Why have I been sober for twenty-one days? Because I haven't had a drink in twenty-one days. Right. Fear comes out as anger. Anger suppressed comes out as guilt. Check. Remember, you were a codependent before you were an addict. And so what? You think you come from a dysfunctional family, Linda? Nobody named Beaver Cleaver can be healthy.

125   Right.

126   I wander around The Betty Ford Center early in the morning, noting the many places I have stopped to cry in three weeks' time.

127   Last night a splendid white-haired, tall woman spoke to us at the AA meeting. She lives in Palm Springs and also is the mother of a man I once saw a lot in, and of. Strange place to meet her. This lady opened with the traditional greeting only more so; instead of saying, "My name is Maureen and I'm an alcoholic," she said, "No matter what you've been told, this is a confidential society, not a secret one, so my name is Maureen *Jones* and I'm an alcoholic." She waits while we laugh. "And I was one before your mother was born. So don't try to con me."

128   Maureen Jones is not her real name, of course. None of the names I've mentioned are real, except for mine, but "Maureen Jones" *is* a real person and she's gotten me thinking about what it's going to be like when I leave here, which won't be long now. My struggle is no longer how to live drunk, but how to live sober.

129   "It's simple," says Maureen. "Go to meetings and don't drink."

130   It *is* simple. But who's good with simple? No, shut up. Do what you're told. For once.

> H: never get too hungry.
> A: never get too angry.
> L: never get too lonely.
> T: never get too tired.

131   *HALT,* they say to remember. If you don't want to relapse, *HALT.* More codes for kids. And go to meetings and don't drink; I know. I know. Or hope I know. Recovery is a process, not an event. I must think about that, think about who will expect me to come home "fixed," and what will I say to them.

132   Even this place is changed. Mike is gone. June is leaving tomorrow. She and I have become close, too, in the way women can in confined circum-stances, despite (or because of) these also being circumstances where you spend a good part of the day telling each other your faults. I look forward to

visiting her in Los Angeles. We will, I hope, stay friends. She is one of those women who moves things along. Herself. Me. The group. I envy that. June knows many things. She told me when she used to drink tequila and didn't want anyone to know, she'd eat an apple and it would take the smell away.

133   *Now you tell me?*

134   I will miss her.

135   Them.

136   They told us the real healing would go on in the halls, by the water fountain and across the breakfast table, but there are so many new people who've come in, so many old people gone. I'm by way of being senior around here now. There's a scary thought.

137   Here's another. I was walking across what I still cannot bring myself to call the "campus" tonight, walking back to my "unit," and it was so nice out, the air so heavy and hot, so filled with summer, that I stopped, took off my shoes and ran into the sprinkler, dancing a little, a step or two, singing some, until I was wet and cool. My feet squishing in the grass the rest of the way back, I could see the mountains, black holes against the starred night sky of the desert, and nothing happened, but I knew I wasn't alone and hadn't been for a long time, maybe ever.

138   And to think I could have missed it all . . .

> Women have traditionally been the hidden chemically dependent. It appears that in specialized treatment services for women there is less game-playing, less falling into traditional roles, and less tendency to sit back and let the focus be on others. Special emphasis is placed on helping each woman work on her anger, her guilt, her grief and on helping her begin to build a positive self-image.

139   My last assignment is to write a letter to Linda Jane, the girl I left behind me. A "hello" letter, says my counselor. My hand must be permanently bent, I think, from so much longhand writing. Not since high school have I been without a machine to make the words. But I have gotten used to what seem nonsensical assignments. I have even come to see their sense.

140   When quite young, I thought other little girls were not like me because I was aware, and aware that I was. I was a tree, a sun and a feather. I had leaves and was yellow warm and could float; and my leaves could turn brown and die, falling away; clouds could hide the world so I could not shine and somebody could pick at me until all the things that made me a feather were gone and I was a bone. Or maybe a balloon. I could tell you what it felt like to be red or big or salty. What it felt like to be born. To be hurt. I would touch the skin on my knee, feeling it smooth, then bleeding, scabrous, then smooth once more. I felt *everything*. I could do anything. The only thing I could not feel was nothing at all and the only thing I could not do was make time stand still or love last. Or make my daddy stop drinking. And I felt that most of all.

141   That little girl knew something I don't. I learned how to feel nothing at all—or how to drink until it seemed that way. But drinking never made time stop or love last, either. And my daddy died.

142   Am I ready to leave here? Yes. No.

143   What will I tell the people I don't know? Where will I say I've been? I can't tell them the truth, not the people with whom I'll be working. Networks don't like drunks, even sober. They don't like women drunks more, I'll bet. Redemption is not what they're into. I decide to practice my story. I call a network vice president, a man who signs an occasional paycheck of mine. "Hello," I say, all cheery. "How are you?"

144   "Fine," he says. "Where are you?"

145   "Oh," I say, ready to tell him I'm visiting friends in the desert, "I'm at The Betty Ford Center." *Jesus Christ*, Ellerbee, you just said you were *where? To a network executive? Have you lost it or what?* I start to sweat. There is a short pause while he takes in what I've said.

146   "My name is Dave and I'm an alcoholic."

147   Today I got my last card from Lloyd. He called to tell me so. He's leaving for Detroit, which, he says, still sucks. I ask him don't they have cards in Detroit? "No," he says, "they have cards. They have no stamps."

148   The last card features another detail from another original oil by Ms. Meyer of Seattle (I suspect a sale). This one is called "Sentinel." It shows three women more or less lying, sphinx-like, on a beach, a few steps shy of what appears to be primordial slime. The women have wings growing from their backs, the lower halves of their bodies are leopards and they have long dragon tails. Two men stand in the slime, looking bewildered and somewhat insignificant in the face of such improbable strength. It is the dawn of the world. "Dear Linda Jane," writes Lloyd, inside. "Since you share my fascination with the language, I believe that you will be as delighted as I was to see for yourself the etymology of that familiar phrase, 'a little piece of tail.' Love, Lloyd." I always will love him, you know.

> Hope is the thing with feathers
>> That purchase in the soul
>> That sings the song without the tune
>> And never stops at all.

149   My name is Linda and I'm an alcoholic.

150   In the summer of 1989, I turned to my son and said please hold my hand, I think I'm in terrible trouble. I'm going to telephone The Betty Ford Center. I don't know where else to call and if I take the time to find out, I'll chicken out.

151   In the summer of 1990, I celebrated my first year of sobriety.

152   "It's the thirteenth month that's the hardest," says a friend with ten years. "We get over the first year: we're successful and we alcoholics can't take that."

153   "But it's my fourteenth month and I'm still sober," I tell her. "And still here."

154   "And do you know why?"

155   "Yes. I didn't drink and I didn't die."

Discussion Questions

1. What in Ellerbee's essay lures you into her history as an alcoholic and the description of her stay at The Betty Ford Clinic?

2. Discuss how realistic and compelling you think Ellerbee is in recounting her stay at the clinic.

3. Throughout her essay, Ellerbee includes passages from the rules and regulations of the clinic. Explain why you think she includes them and whether she could have achieved the same effect without them.

4. Describe the tone of Ellerbee's essay. Is she angry? bitter? hateful? conciliatory? confused? Cite specific examples that influence your response. How does the tone complement the events she is describing?

5. Do you think Ellerbee will stay sober? Why or why not?

The Men We Carry in Our Minds
Scott Russell Sanders

Scott Russell Sanders was born in 1945 in Tennessee. He earned a B.A. degree from Brown University and a Ph.D. from Cambridge University in England. A professor of English at Indiana University, Sanders writes children's stories, essays, science fiction, folktales, and historical novels. Some of his publications include Wilderness Plots: Tales about the Settlement of the American Land *(1983),* Fetching the Dead: Stories *(1984),* Hear the Wind Blow: American Folksongs Retold *(1985),* Stone Country *(1985),* Bad Man Ballad *(1986) and* The Paradise of Bombs *(1987), in which the following essay appears. Sanders's writing has also been published in such journals as* North American Review, Georgia Review, Omni, Transatlantic Review, *and* New Dimensions. *He has written a column for the Chicago* Sun Times *and has been the recipient of a Woodrow Wilson Fellowship, a Marshall scholarship, and a Bennett Fellowship in creative writing. In the following essay, Sanders ruminates on what it means to be a man and how the models he witnessed as a boy are no longer helpful.*

1   "This must be a hard time for women," I say to my friend Anneke. "They have so many paths to choose from, and so many voices calling them."

2   "I think it's a lot harder for men," she replies.

3   "How do you figure that?"

4   "The women I know feel excited, innocent, like crusaders in a just cause. The men I know are eaten up with guilt."

5   We are sitting at the kitchen table drinking sassafras tea, our hands wrapped around the mugs because this April morning is cool and drizzly. "Like a Dutch morning," Anneke told me earlier. She is Dutch herself, a writer and midwife and peacemaker, with the round face and sad eyes of a woman in a Vermeer painting who might be waiting for the rain to stop, for a door to open. She leans over to sniff a sprig of lilac, pale lavender, that rises from a vase of cobalt blue.

6   "Women feel such pressure to be everything, do everything," I say. "Career, kids, art, politics. Have their babies and get back to the office a week later. It's as if they're trying to overcome a million years' worth of evolution in one lifetime."

7   "But we help one another. We don't try to lumber on alone, like so many wounded grizzly bears, the way men do." Anneke sips her tea. I gave her the mug with the owls on it, for wisdom. "And we have this deep-down sense that we're in the *right*—we've been held back, passed over, used—while men feel they're in the wrong. Men are the ones who've been discredited, who have to search their souls."

8   I search my soul. I discover guilty feelings aplenty—toward the poor, the Vietnamese, Native Americans, the whales, an endless list of debts—a guilt in each case that is as bright and unambiguous as a neon sign. But toward women I feel something more confused, a snarl of shame, envy, wary tenderness, and amazement. This muddle troubles me. To hide my unease I say, "You're right, it's tough being a man these days."

9   "Don't laugh." Anneke frowns at me, mournful-eyed, through the sassafras steam. "I wouldn't be a man for anything. It's much easier being the victim. All the victim has to do is break free. The persecutor has to live with his past."

10   How deep is that past? I find myself wondering after Anneke has left. How much of an inheritance do I have to throw off? Is it just the beliefs I breathed in as a child? Do I have to scour memory back through father and grandfather? Through St. Paul? Beyond Stonehenge and into the twilit caves? I'm convinced the past we must contend with is deeper even than speech. When I think back on my childhood, on how I learned to see men and women, I have a sense of ancient, dizzying depths. The back roads of Tennessee and Ohio where I grew up were probably closer, in their sexual patterns, to the campsites of Stone Age hunters than to the genderless cities of the future into which we are rushing.

11   The first men, besides my father, I remember seeing were black convicts and white guards, in the cottonfield across the road from our farm on the outskirts of Memphis. I must have been three or four. The prisoners wore dingy gray-and-black zebra suits, heavy as canvas, sodden with sweat. Hatless, stooped, they chopped weeds in the fierce heat, row after row, breathing the acrid dust of boll-weevil poison. The overseers wore dazzling white shirts and broad shadowy hats. The oiled barrels of their shotguns flashed in the sunlight. Their faces in memory are utterly blank. Of course those men, white and black, have become for me an emblem of racial hatred. But they have also come to stand for the twin poles of my early vision of manhood—the brute toiling animal and the boss.

12   When I was a boy, the men I knew labored with their bodies. They were marginal farmers, just scraping by, or welders, steelworkers, carpenters; they swept floors, dug ditches, mined coal, or drove trucks, their forearms ropy with muscle; they trained horses, stoked furnaces, built tires, stood on assembly lines wrestling parts onto cars and refrigerators. They got up before light, worked all day long whatever the weather, and when they came home at night they looked as though somebody had been whipping them. In the evenings and on weekends they worked on their own places, tilling gardens that were lumpy with clay, fixing broken-down cars, hammering on houses that were always too drafty, too leaky, too small.

13   The bodies of the men I knew were twisted and maimed in ways visible and invisible. The nails of their hands were black and split, the hands tattooed with scars. Some had lost fingers. Heavy lifting had given many of them finicky backs and guts weak from hernias. Racing against conveyor belts had given them ulcers. Their ankles and knees ached from years of standing on concrete. Anyone who had worked for long around machines was hard of hearing. They squinted, and the skin of their faces was creased like the leather of old work gloves. There were times, studying them, when I dreaded growing up. Most of them coughed, from dust or cigarettes, and most of them drank cheap wine or whiskey, so their eyes looked bloodshot and bruised. The fathers of my friends always seemed older than the mothers. Men wore out sooner. Only women lived into old age.

14   As a boy I also knew another sort of men, who did not sweat and break down like mules. They were soldiers, and so far as I could tell they scarcely worked at all. During my early school years we lived on a military base, an arsenal in Ohio, and every day I saw GIs in the guardshacks, on the stoops of barracks, at the wheels of olive drab Chevrolets. The chief fact of their lives was boredom. Long after I left the Arsenal I came to recognize the sour smell the soldiers gave off as that of souls in limbo. They were all waiting—for wars, for transfers, for leaves, for promotions, for the end of their hitch—like so many braves waiting for the hunt to begin. Unlike the warriors of older tribes, however, they would have no say about when the battle would start or how it would be waged. Their waiting was

broken only when they practiced for war. They fired guns at targets, drove tanks across the churned-up fields of the military reservation, set off bombs in the wrecks of old fighter planes. I knew this was all play. But I also felt certain that when the hour for killing arrived, they would kill. When the real shooting started, many of them would die. This was what soldiers were *for*, just as a hammer was for driving nails.

15   Warriors and toilers: those seemed, in my boyhood vision, to be the chief destinies for men. They weren't the only destinies, as I learned from having a few male teachers, from reading books, and from watching television. But the men on television—the politicians, the astronauts, the generals, the savvy lawyers, the philosophical doctors, the bosses who gave orders to both soldiers and laborers—seemed as remote and unreal to me as the figures in tapestries. I could no more imagine growing up to become one of these cool, potent creatures than I could imagine becoming a prince.

16   A nearer and more hopeful example was that of my father, who had escaped from a red-dirt farm to a tire factory, and from the assembly line to the front office. Eventually he dressed in a white shirt and tie. He carried himself as if he had been born to work with his mind. But his body, remembering the earlier years of slogging work, began to give out on him in his fifties, and it quit on him entirely before he turned sixty-five. Even such a partial escape from man's fate as he had accomplished did not seem possible for most of the boys I knew. They joined the army, stood in line for jobs in the smoky plants, helped build highways. They were bound to work as their fathers had worked, killing themselves or preparing to kill others.

17   A scholarship enabled me not only to attend college, a rare enough feat in my circle, but even to study in a university meant for the children of the rich. Here I met for the first time young men who had assumed from birth that they would lead lives of comfort and power. And for the first time I met women who told me that men were guilty of having kept all the joys and privileges of the earth for themselves. I was baffled. What privileges? What joys? I thought about the maimed, dismal lives of most of the men back home. What had they stolen from their wives and daughters? The right to go five days a week, twelve months a year, for thirty or forty years to a steel mill or a coal mine? The right to drop bombs and die in war? The right to feel every leak in the roof, every gap in the fence, every cough in the engine, as a wound they must mend? The right to feel, when the lay-off comes or the plant shuts down, not only afraid but ashamed?

18   I was slow to understand the deep grievances of women. This was because, as a boy, I had envied them. Before college, the only people I had ever known who were interested in art or music or literature, the only ones who read books, the only ones who ever seemed to enjoy a sense of ease and grace were the mothers and daughters. Like the menfolk, they fretted about money, they scrimped and made-do. But, when the pay stopped coming in, they were not the ones who had failed. Nor did they have to go to war, and that seemed to me a blessed fact. By comparison with the narrow, ironclad

days of fathers, there was an expansiveness, I thought, in the days of mothers. They went to see neighbors, to shop in town, to run errands at school, at the library, at church. No doubt, had I looked harder at their lives, I would have envied them less. It was not my fate to become a woman, so it was easier for me to see the graces. Few of them held jobs outside the home, and those who did filled thankless roles as clerks and waitresses. I didn't see, then, what a prison a house could be, since houses seemed to me brighter, handsomer places than any factory. I did not realize—because such things were never spoken of—how often women suffered from men's bullying. I did learn about the wretchedness of abandoned wives, single mothers, widows; but I also learned about the wretchedness of lone men. Even then I could see how exhausting it was for a mother to cater all day to the needs of young children. But if I had been asked, as a boy, to choose between tending a baby and tending a machine, I think I would have chosen the baby. (Having now tended both, I know I would choose the baby.)

19   So I was baffled when the women at college accused me and my sex of having cornered the world's pleasures. I think something like my bafflement has been felt by other boys (and by girls as well) who grew up in dirt-poor farm country, in mining country, in black ghettos, in Hispanic barrios, in the shadows of factories, in Third World nations—any place where the fate of men is as grim and bleak as the fate of women. Toilers and warriors. I realize now how ancient these identities are, how deep the tug they exert on men, the undertow of a thousand generations. The miseries I saw, as a boy, in the lives of nearly all men I continue to see in the lives of many—the body-breaking toil, the tedium, the call to be tough, the humiliating powerlessness, the battle for a living and for territory.

20   When the women I met at college thought about the joys and privileges of men, they did not carry in their minds the sort of men I had known in my childhood. They thought of their fathers, who were bankers, physicians, architects, stockbrokers, the big wheels of the big cities. These fathers rode the train to work or drove cars that cost more than any of my childhood houses. They were attended from morning to night by female helpers, wives, and nurses and secretaries. They were never laid off, never short of cash at month's end, never lined up for welfare. These fathers made decisions that mattered. They ran the world.

21   The daughters of such men wanted to share in this power, this glory. So did I. They yearned for a say over their future, for jobs worthy of their abilities, for the right to live at peace, unmolested, whole. Yes, I thought, yes yes. The difference between me and these daughters was that they saw me, because of my sex, as destined from birth to become like their fathers, and therefore as an enemy to their desires. But I knew better. I wasn't an enemy, in fact or in feeling. I was an ally. If I had known, then, how to tell them so, would they have believed me? Would they now?

Discussion Questions

1. Sanders provides a number of different models of men he encountered as a child. From your own experiences, can you identify with the types he describes? Why or why not?

2. Do you think women have the same problem with female models as Sanders had with males? Why or why not?

3. In paragraph 10, Sanders asks, "How deep is [the] past?" Based on your own observations and experiences, answer that question yourself.

4. In paragraph 18, Sanders explains why he was "slow to understand the deep grievances of women." Do you find his explanation believable? Why or why not?

5. What do you think Sanders learned from writing this essay? What did *you* learn?

Chapter 5 Writing Topics

1. Describe the "idealized" you, the person you dream of being. How did this image develop? How is that person different from the "real" you? What is preventing you from becoming that person?

2. Describe the ways in which you have seen yourself change as you have grown up—besides the obvious ones. Have you been pleased with the physical changes or disappointed with them? What do you suppose accounts for your reaction?

3. Write an essay in which you reflect on the following question: To what extent do you think your outward appearance reflects your inward being? Should it?

4. Many people have handicaps that are not readily apparent to others (e.g., learning disabilities, hearing or vision impairment). If you are one such person—or if you know someone who fits this description—write an essay in which you explore the ways you (or s/he) have been affected by the problem.

5. Imagine yourself at a different time in your life, say, middle or old age. Exactly how do you envision yourself? What does that image say about you as a person?

6. Choose a physical trait that you wish you didn't have and that is impossible to change (e.g., being tall, having freckles). Write an essay in which you describe the way you have come to terms with this trait.

7. Choose one of your physical characteristics and compare yourself with famous writers, athletes, actors or actresses, etc. who share the same feature. Have fun hobnobbing with the famous, much like Joseph Epstein did in "Short Subject."

8. Select a physical characteristic that some people might consider a liability. Show the ways in which it has been an asset. That is, shatter misconceptions that surround certain physical traits.

9. Select a painting, sculpture, or photograph that best represents either what you look like or what you would like to look like. Write an essay in which you investigate the likenesses you find between the image displayed in the piece of art and yourself. Be sure to address the reasons for your choosing that particular piece of art.

10. Can you recall a time when you did something unexpected or difficult in order to improve yourself (e.g., quit smoking, became a triathlete, drastically changed your appearance, etc.). How did your self-image change? How was your life affected? Were the effects long-lasting?

11. Write an essay in which you reflect on the importance that society and the media place on physical beauty. Given that there are very few truly beautiful people in this world and that most people would agree that "beauty is only skin deep," what do you think accounts for the obsession with appearance? Do you see it as something good or bad? Why?

12. Consider the female or male role models you had as a child. How did they help you to develop into the person you now are? Would you say that as an adult you emulate those models or act in defiance of them? Examine those questions in an essay that deals with what you think it means to be a woman or a man.

Chapter 6

Country and City Life

Every man, every woman, carries in heart and mind the image of the ideal place, the right place, the one true home, known or unknown, actual or visionary.

—Edward Abbey

Tell me the landscape in which you live, and I will tell you who you are.

—José Ortega y Gassett

Until I call attention to what passes before my eyes, I simply won't see it.

—Annie Dillard

True places are not found on maps.

—Herman Melville

The places we have known do not belong only to the world of space on which we map through our own convenience. None of them was ever more than a thin slice, held between the contiguous impressions that composed our life at that time; the memory of a particular image is but regret for a particular moment; and houses, roads, avenues are as fugitive, alas, as the years.

—Marcel Proust

O ften as important as the relationships we have with others is the relationship we have with our environment. Too many of us are unaware of the ways in which landscape helps to make us the individuals we are. Perhaps we take for granted where we live and our connection with that place. While we can relate a story or two about the place in which we live—the parched farmland from the drought of 1988 or the incapacitated cities from the blizzard of 1993—the tales usually focus on headline-type fare and not on the intricacies or subtleties that are peculiar to that special place and our attachment to it.

Not only can writing about our environment demonstrate the ways in which it affects us, such inquiry can illustrate the way we deal with nature, thus revealing much about us as people. Exploring the relationship between the two signifies the interconnectedness of humans and nature. The essays that follow attend to those very concerns.

Chapter 6 begins with Gretel Ehrlich's thorough and thoughtful description of Wyoming, a state she decided to call home after visiting there one summer. In "The Beautiful Places," Kathleen Norris reflects on the spiritual awakening she experienced while living in Lemmon, South Dakota. E. B. White returns to Walden Pond, the famed retreat of Henry David Thoreau, only to find that it hardly resembles the bucolic Walden of a hundred years ago. Then Edward Hoagland recalls his youth spent hunting turtles in the country and contrasts it with the painted turtles he finds for sale on the streets of New York City.

Pastoral settings are but one type of landscape, and the next three essays address the environment the authors found in urban settings. Elizabeth Hardwick discusses the "lost ideal" of Boston, and Anne Rivers Siddons reports on a disappointing visit to New York City. Then Phillip Lopate offers his initial impressions of Houston. Finally, William Zinsser describes Disneyland, the famous amusement park many people visit to escape the places they live—and, perhaps, the modern world.

All of the essays in this chapter present people confronting their natural—and unnatural—environments. Moving from rural to urban locales, they show people making sense of and coming to terms with the settings in which they find themselves. In all cases, the essays illustrate the following quote by Joseph Conrad: "My task . . . is, by the power of the written word, to make you hear, to make you feel—it is, before all, to make you see." As you read the selections, picture a place you have lived or visited that is significant to you. How you would characterize your relationship to it? What you have learned about the place—and about yourself—in the time you spent there?

The Solace of Open Spaces

Gretel Ehrlich

*B*orn in California in 1946, Gretel Ehrlich studied at Bennington
College in Vermont, the UCLA Film School, and the New School
for Social Research in New York. A poet, essayist, journalist, and film-
maker, Ehrlich is the author of two collections of essays: The Solace of
Open Spaces *(1985), in which the following essay appears, and* Islands, the Universe, Home *(1987). Ehrlich is also the author of a*
novel, Heart Mountain *(1988), and* A Match to the Heart *(1994),*
her account of being struck by lightning. She has lived in Wyoming
ever since she fell in love with the state while filming a documentary
on sheep herding for the American Public Broadcast system in 1976.
In the title essay from her 1985 book, Ehrlich describes the space, geog-
raphy, and people of Wyoming.

1   It's May and I've just awakened from a nap, curled against sagebrush
the way my dog taught me to sleep—sheltered from wind. A front is
pulling the huge sky over me, and from the dark a hailstone has hit me on
the head. I'm trailing a band of two thousand sheep across a stretch of
Wyoming badlands, a fifty-mile trip that takes five days because sheep
shade up in hot sun and won't budge until it's cool. Bunched together
now, and excited into a run by the storm, they drift across dry land, tumbling into draws like water and surge out again onto the rugged, choppy
plateaus that are the building blocks of this state.

2   The name Wyoming comes from an Indian word meaning "at the
great plains," but the plains are really valleys, great arid valleys, sixteen
hundred square miles, with the horizon bending up on all sides into
mountain ranges. This gives the vastness a sheltering look.

3   Winter lasts six months here. Prevailing winds spill snowdrifts to the
east, and new storms from the northwest replenish them. This white bulk
is sometimes dizzying, even nauseating, to look at. At twenty, thirty, and
forty degrees below zero, not only does your car not work, but neither do
your mind and body. The landscape hardens into a dungeon of space.
During the winter, while I was riding to find a new calf, my jeans froze to
the saddle, and in the silence that such cold creates I felt like the first person on earth, or the last.

4   Today the sun is out—only a few clouds billowing. In the east, where
the sheep have started off without me, the benchland tilts up in a series of
eroded red-earthed mesas, planed flat on top by a million years of water;
behind them, a bold line of muscular scarps rears up ten thousand feet to
become the Big Horn Mountains. A tidal pattern is engraved into the
ground, as if left by the sea that once covered this state. Canyons curve
down like galaxies to meet the oncoming rush of flat land.

5   To live and work in this kind of open country, with its hundred-mile

views, is to lose the distinction between background and foreground. When I asked an older ranch hand to describe Wyoming's openness, he said, "It's all a bunch of nothing—wind and rattlesnakes—and so much of it you can't tell where you're going or where you've been and it don't make much difference." John, a sheepman I know, is tall and handsome and has an explosive temperament. He has a perfect intuition about people and sheep. They call him "Highpockets," because he's so long-legged; his graceful stride matches the distances he has to cover. He says, "Open space hasn't affected me at all. It's all the people moving in on it." The huge ranch he was born on takes up much of one county and spreads into another state; to put 100,000 miles on his pickup in three years and never leave home is not unusual. A friend of mine has an aunt who ranched on Powder River and didn't go off her place for eleven years. When her husband died, she quickly moved to town, bought a car, and drove around the States to see what she'd been missing.

6   Most people tell me they've simply driven through Wyoming, as if there were nothing to stop for. Or else they've skied in Jackson Hole, a place Wyomingites acknowledge uncomfortably because its green beauty and chic affluence are mismatched with the rest of the state. Most of Wyoming has a "lean-to" look. Instead of big, roomy barns and Victorian houses, there are dugouts, low sheds, log cabins, sheep camps, and fence lines that look like driftwood blown haphazardly into place. People here still feel pride because they live in such a harsh place, part of the glamorous cowboy past, and they are determined not to be the victims of a mining-dominated future.

7   Most characteristic of the state's landscape is what a developer euphemistically describes as "indigenous growth right up to your front door"—a reference to waterless stands of salt sage, snakes, jack rabbits, deerflies, red dust, a brief respite of wildflowers, dry washes, and no trees. In the Great Plains the vistas look like music, like Kyries of grass, but Wyoming seems to be the doing of a mad architect—tumbled and twisted, ribboned with faded, deathbed colors, thrust up and pulled down as if the place had been startled out of a deep sleep and thrown into a pure light.

8   I came here four years ago. I had not planned to stay, but I couldn't make myself leave. John, the sheepman, put me to work immediately. It was spring, and shearing time. For fourteen days of fourteen hours each, we moved thousands of sheep through sorting corrals to be sheared, branded, and deloused. I suspect that my original motive for coming here was to "lose myself" in new and unpopulated territory. Instead of producing the numbness I thought I wanted, life on the sheep ranch woke me up. The vitality of the people I was working with flushed out what had become a hallucinatory rawness inside me. I threw away my clothes and bought new ones; I cut my hair. The arid country was a clean slate. Its absolute indifference steadied me.

9   Sagebrush covers 58,000 square miles of Wyoming. The biggest city has a population of fifty thousand, and there are only five settlements that could be called cities in the whole state. The rest are towns, scattered across the expanse with as much as sixty miles between them, their populations two thousand, fifty, or ten. They are fugitive-looking, perched on a barren, windblown bench, or tagged onto a river or a railroad, or laid out straight in a farming valley with implement stores and a block-long Mormon church. In the eastern part of the state, which slides down into the Great Plains, the new mining settlements are boomtowns, trailer cities, metal knots on flat land.

10   Despite the desolate look, there's a coziness to living in this state. There are so few people (only 470,000) that ranchers who buy and sell cattle know one another statewide; the kids who choose to go to college usually go to the state's one university, in Laramie; hired hands work their way around Wyoming in a lifetime of hirings and firings. And despite the physical separation, people stay in touch, often driving two or three hours to another ranch for dinner.

11   Seventy-five years ago, when travel was by buckboard or horseback, cowboys who were temporarily out of work rode the grub line—drifting from ranch to ranch, mending fences or milking cows, and receiving in exchange a bed and meals. Gossip and messages traveled this slow circuit with them, creating an intimacy between ranchers who were three and four weeks' ride apart. One old-time couple I know, whose turn-of-the-century homestead was used by an outlaw gang as a relay station for stolen horses, recall that if you were traveling, desperado or not, any lighted ranch house was a welcome sign. Even now, for someone who lives in a remote spot, arriving at a ranch or coming to town for supplies is cause for celebration. To emerge from isolation can be disorienting. Everything looks bright, new, vivid. After I had been herding sheep for only three days, the sound of the camp tender's pickup flustered me. Longing for human company, I felt a foolish grin take over my face; yet I had to resist an urgent temptation to run and hide.

12   Things happen suddenly in Wyoming, the change of seasons and weather; for people, the violent swings in and out of isolation. But good-naturedness is concomitant with severity. Friendliness is a tradition. Strangers passing on the road wave hello. A common sight is two pickups stopped side by side far out on a range, on a dirt track winding through the sage. The drivers will share a cigarette, uncap their thermos bottles, and pass a battered cup, steaming with coffee, between windows. These meetings summon up the details of several generations, because, in Wyoming, private histories are largely public knowledge.

13   Because ranch work is a physical and, these days, economic strain, being "at home on the range" is a matter of vigor, self-reliance, and common sense. A person's life is not a series of dramatic events for which he or she

is applauded or exiled but a slow accumulation of days, seasons, years, fleshed out by the generational weight of one's family and anchored by a land-bound sense of place.

14   In most parts of Wyoming, the human population is visibly outnumbered by the animal. Not far from my town of fifty, I rode into a narrow valley and startled a herd of two hundred elk. Eagles look like small people as they eat car-killed deer by the road. Antelope, moving in small, graceful bands, travel at sixty miles an hour, their mouths open as if drinking in the space.

15   The solitude in which westerners live makes them quiet. They telegraph thoughts and feelings by the way they tilt their heads and listen; pulling their Stetsons into a steep dive over their eyes, or pigeon-toeing one boot over the other, they lean against a fence with a fat wedge of Copenhagen beneath their lower lips and take in the whole scene. These detached looks of quiet amusement are sometimes cynical, but they can also come from a dry-eyed humility as lucid as the air is clear.

16   Conversation goes on in what sounds like a private code; a few phrases imply a complex of meanings. Asking directions, you get a curious list of details. While trailing sheep I was told to "ride up to that kinda upturned rock, follow the pink wash, turn left at the dump, and then you'll see the water hole." One friend told his wife on roundup to "turn at the salt lick and the dead cow," which turned out to be a scattering of bones and no salt lick at all.

17   Sentence structure is shortened to the skin and bones of a thought. Descriptive words are dropped, even verbs; a cowboy looking over a corral full of horses will say to a wrangler, "Which one needs rode?" People hold back their thoughts in what seems to be a dumbfounded silence, then erupt with an excoriating perceptive remark. Language, so compressed, becomes metaphorical. A rancher ended a relationship with one remark: "You're a bad check," meaning bouncing in and out was intolerable, and even coming back would be no good.

18   What's behind this laconic style is shyness. There is no vocabulary for the subject of feelings. It's not a hangdog shyness, or anything coy—always there's a robust spirit in evidence behind the restraint, as if the earth-dredging wind that pulls across Wyoming had carried its people's voices away but everything else in them had shouldered confidently into the breeze.

19   I've spent hours riding to sheep camp at dawn in a pickup when nothing was said; eaten meals in the cookhouse when the only words spoken were a mumbled "Thank you, ma'am" at the end of dinner. The silence is profound. Instead of talking, we seem to share one eye. Keenly observed, the world is transformed. The landscape is engorged with detail, every movement on it chillingly sharp. The air between people is charged. Days unfold, bathed in their own music. Nights become hallucinatory; dreams, prescient.

20   Spring weather is capricious and mean. It snows, then blisters with heat. There have been tornadoes. They lay their elephant trunks out in the sage until they find houses, then slurp everything up and leave. I've noticed that melting snowbanks hiss and rot, viperous, then drip into calm pools where ducklings hatch and livestock, being trailed to summer range, drink. With the ice cover gone, rivers churn a milkshake brown, taking culverts and small bridges with them. Water in such an arid place (the average annual rainfall where I live is less than eight inches) is like blood. It festoons drab land with green veins; a line of cottonwoods following a stream; a strip of alfalfa; and, on ditch banks, wild asparagus growing.

21   I've moved to a small cattle ranch owned by friends. It's at the foot of the Big Horn Mountains. A few weeks ago, I helped them deliver a calf who was stuck halfway out of his mother's body. By the time he was freed, we could see a heartbeat, but he was straining against a swollen tongue for air. Mary and I held him upside down by his back feet, while Stan, on his hands and knees in the blood, gave the calf mouth-to-mouth resuscitation. I have a vague memory of being pneumonia-choked as a child, my mother giving me her air, which may account for my romance with this windswept state.

22   If anything is endemic to Wyoming, it is wind. This big room of space is swept out daily, leaving a bone yard of fossils, agates, and carcasses in every stage of decay. Though it was water that initially shaped the state, wind is the meticulous gardener, raising dust and pruning the sage.

23   I try to imagine a world in which I could ride my horse across uncharted land. There is no wilderness left; wildness, yes, but true wilderness has been gone on this continent since the time of Lewis and Clark's overland journey.

24   Two hundred years ago, the Crow, Shoshone, Arapaho, Cheyenne, and Sioux roamed the intermountain West, orchestrating their movements according to hunger, season, and warfare. Once they acquired horses, they traversed the spines of all the big Wyoming ranges—the Absarokas, the Wind Rivers, the Tetons, the Big Horns—and wintered on the unprotected plains that fan out from them. Space was life. The world was their home.

25   What was life-giving to Native Americans was often nightmarish to sodbusters who had arrived encumbered with families and ethnic pasts to be transplanted in nearly uninhabitable land. The great distances, the shortage of water and trees, and the loneliness created unexpected hardships for them. In her book *O Pioneers!*, Willa Cather gives a settler's version of the bleak landscape:

> The little town behind them had vanished as if it had never been, had fallen behind the swell of the prairie, and the stern frozen country received them into its bosom. The homesteads were few and far apart; here and there a windmill gaunt against the sky, a sod house crouching in a hollow.

26   The emptiness of the West was for others a geography of possibility. Men and women who amassed great chunks of land and struggled to preserve unfenced empires were, despite their self-serving motives, unwitting geographers. They understood the lay of the land. But by the 1850s the Oregon and Mormon trails sported bumper-to-bumper traffic. Wealthy landowners, many of them aristocratic absentee landlords, known as remittance men because they were paid to come West and get out of their families' hair, overstocked the range with more than a million head of cattle. By 1885 the feed and water were desperately short, and the winter of 1886 laid out the gaunt bodies of dead animals so closely together that when the thaw came, one rancher from Kaycee claimed to have walked on cowhide all the way to Crazy Woman Creek, twenty miles away.

27   Territorial Wyoming was a boy's world. The land was generous with everything but water. At first there was room enough, food enough, for everyone. And, as with all beginnings, an expansive mood set in. The young cowboys, drifters, shopkeepers, schoolteachers, were heroic, lawless, generous, rowdy, and tenacious. The individualism and optimism generated during those times have endured.

28   John Tisdale rode north with the trail herds from Texas. He was a college-educated man with enough money to buy a small outfit near the Powder River. While driving home from the town of Buffalo with a buckboard full of Christmas toys for his family and a winter's supply of food, he was shot in the back by an agent of the cattle barons who resented the encroachment of small-time stockmen like him. The wealthy cattlemen tried to control all the public grazing land by restricting membership in the Wyoming Stock Growers Association, as if it were a country club. They ostracized from roundups and brandings cowboys and ranchers who were not members, then denounced them as rustlers. Tisdale's death, the second such cold-blooded murder, kicked off the Johnson County cattle war, which was no simple good-guy-bad-guy shoot-out but a complicated class struggle between landed gentry and less affluent settlers—a shocking reminder that the West was not an egalitarian sanctuary after all.

29   Fencing ultimately enforced boundaries, but barbed wire abrogated space. It was stretched across the beautiful valleys, into the mountains, over desert badlands, through buffalo grass. The "anything is possible" fever—the lure of any new place—was constricted. The integrity of the land as a geographical body, and the freedom to ride anywhere on it, were lost.

30   I punched cows with a young man named Martin, who is the great-grandson of John Tisdale. His inheritance is not the open land that Tisdale knew and prematurely lost but a rage against restraint.

31   Wyoming tips down as you head northeast; the highest ground—the Laramie Plains—is on the Colorado border. Up where I live, the Big Horn River leaks into difficult, arid terrain. In the basin where it's dammed, sand-

hill cranes gather and, with delicate legwork, slice through the stilled water. I was driving by with a rancher one morning when he commented that cranes are "old-fashioned." When I asked why, he said, "Because they mate for life." Then he looked at me with a twinkle in his eyes, as if to say he really did believe in such things but also understood why we break our own rules.

32   In all this open space, values crystalize quickly. People are strong on scruples but tenderhearted about quirky behavior. A friend and I found one ranch hand, who's "not quite right in the head," sitting in front of the badly decayed carcass of a cow, shaking his finger and saying, "Now, I don't want you to do this ever again!" When I asked what was wrong with him, I was told, "He's goofier than hell, just like the rest of us." Perhaps because the West is historically new, conventional morality is still felt to be less important than rock-bottom truths. Though there's always a lot of teasing and sparring, people are blunt with one another, sometimes even cruel, believing honesty is stronger medicine than sympathy, which may console but often conceals.

33   The formality that goes hand in hand with the rowdiness is known as the Western Code. It's a list of practical do's and don'ts, faithfully observed. A friend, Cliff, who runs a trapline in the winter, cut off half his foot while chopping a hole in the ice. Alone, he dragged himself to his pickup and headed for town, stopping to open the ranch gate as he left, and getting out to close it again, thus losing, in his observance of rules, precious time and blood. Later, he commented, "How would it look, them having to come to the hospital to tell me their cows had gotten out?"

34   Accustomed to emergencies, my friends doctor each other from the vet's bag with relish. When one old-timer suffered a heart attack in hunting camp, his partner quickly stirred up a brew of red horse liniment and hot water and made the half-conscious victim drink it, then tied him onto a horse and led him twenty miles to town. He regained consciousness and lived.

35   The roominess of the state has affected political attitudes as well. Ranchers keep up with world politics and the convulsions of the economy but are basically isolationists. Being used to running their own small empires of land and livestock, they're suspicious of big government. It's a "don't fence me in" holdover from a century ago. They still want the elbow room their grandfathers had, so they're strongly conservative, but with a populist twist.

36   Summer is the season when we get our "cowboy tans"—on the lower parts of our faces and on three fourths of our arms. Excessive heat, in the nineties and higher, sends us outside with the mosquitoes. In winter we're tucked inside our houses, and the white wasteland outside appears to be expanding, but in summer all the greenery abridges space. Summer is a go-ahead season. Every living thing is off the block and in the race: battalions of bugs in flight and biting; bats swinging around my log cabin as if the bases were loaded and someone had hit a home run. Some of summer's high-speed growth is ominous: larkspur, death camas, and green

greasewood can kill sheep—an ironic idea, dying in this desert from eating what is too verdant. With sixteen hours of daylight, farmers and ranchers irrigate feverishly. There are first, second, and third cuttings of hay, some crews averaging only four hours of sleep a night for weeks. And, like the cowboys who in summer ride the night rodeo circuit, nighthawks make daredevil dives at dusk with an eerie whirring sound like a plane going down on the shimmering horizon.

37　　In the town where I live, they've had to board up the dance-hall windows because there have been so many fights. There's so little to do except work that people wind up in a state of idle agitation that becomes fatalistic, as if there were nothing to be done about all this untapped energy. So the dark side to the grandeur of these spaces is the small-mindedness that seals people in. Men become hermits; women go mad. Cabin fever explodes into suicides, or into grudges and lifelong family feuds. Two sisters in my area inherited a ranch but found they couldn't get along. They fenced the place in half. When one's cows got out and mixed with the other's, the women went at each other with shovels. They ended up in the same hospital room but never spoke a word to each other for the rest of their lives.

38　　After the brief lushness of summer, the sun moves south. The range grass is brown. Livestock is trailed back down from the mountains. Water holes begin to frost over at night. Last fall Martin asked me to accompany him on a pack trip. With five horses, we followed a river into the mountains behind the tiny Wyoming town of Meeteetse. Groves of aspen, red and orange, gave off a light that made us look toasted. Our hunting camp was so high that clouds skidded across our foreheads, then slowed to sail out across the warm valleys. Except for a bull moose who wandered into our camp and mistook our black gelding for a rival, we shot at nothing.

39　　One of our evening entertainments was to watch the night sky. My dog, a dingo bred to herd sheep, also came on the trip. He is so used to the silence and empty skies that when an airplane flies over he always looks up and eyes the distant intruder quizzically. The sky, lately, seems to be much more crowded than it used to be. Satellites make their silent passes in the dark with great regularity. We counted eighteen in one hour's viewing. How odd to think that while they circumnavigated the planet, Martin and I had moved only six miles into our local wilderness and had seen no other human for the two weeks we stayed there.

40　　At night, by moonlight, the land is whittled to slivers—a ridge, a river, a strip of grassland stretching to the mountains, then the huge sky. One morning a full moon was setting in the west just as the sun was rising. I felt precariously balanced between the two as I loped across a meadow. For a moment, I could believe that the stars, which were still visible, work like cooper's bands, holding together everything above Wyoming.

41　　Space has a spiritual equivalent and can heal what is divided and burdensome in us. My grandchildren will probably use space shuttles for a honeymoon trip or to recover from heart attacks, but closer to home we might also learn how to carry space inside ourselves in the effortless way we carry our skins. Space represents sanity, not a life purified, dull, or "spaced out" but one that might accommodate intelligently any idea or situation.

42   From the clayey soil of northern Wyoming is mined bentonite, which is used as a filler in candy, gum, and lipstick. We Americans are great on fillers, as if what we have, what we are, is not enough. We have a cultural tendency toward denial, but, being affluent, we strangle ourselves with what we can buy. We have only to look at the houses we build to see how we build *against* space, the way we drink against pain and loneliness. We fill up space as if it were a pie shell, with things whose opacity further obstructs our ability to see what is already there.

Discussion Questions

1. What do you see as the purpose of Ehrlich's essay: to describe Wyoming? to justify her reasons for living there? to tell the story of how and why she decided to live there? to philosophize about Americans and their lifestyles? Explain your response.

2. Among the topics Ehrlich discusses in her essay are Wyoming's weather, landscape, ranch work, westerners, population, language, and history. Do you think there are too many areas covered? Why or why not?

3. Describe the way Ehrlich organizes her essay. To what extent do you think her choice of organization contributes to the essay's effectiveness?

4. What do you think Ehrlich means in the next-to-last paragraph when she states "Space represents sanity"? Explain your reasons for agreeing or disagreeing with that statement.

5. Do you agree with Ehrlich's observation in the last paragraph that "We [Americans] have a cultural tendency toward denial, but, being affluent, we strangle ourselves with what we can buy"? Why or why not? What in Ehrlich's essay supports this idea?

The Beautiful Places

Kathleen Norris

*K*athleen Norris *was born in Virginia and grew up in Illinois, Hawaii, Vermont, and New York City before moving to Lemmon, South Dakota, some twenty years ago. A poet and essayist, Norris has also worked as a bookkeeper and artist-in-residence in North and*

South Dakota schools. A freelance writer, Norris has been published in such journals as Beyond Borders, Gettysburg Review, Hungry Mind Review, Massachusetts Review, North Dakota Quarterly, *and* Northern Lights. *Norris is the author of* Dakota: A Spiritual Geography *(1993), in which the following essay appears. In this selection, Norris details not only South Dakota's landscape but the spiritual awakening she experienced when living there.*

> The Scarecrow sighed. "Of course I cannot understand it," he said. "If your heads were stuffed with straw like mine, you would probably all live in the beautiful places, and then Kansas would have no people at all. It is fortunate for Kansas that you have brains."
>
> —L. FRANK BAUM, THE WIZARD OF OZ

1   The high plains, the beginning of the desert West, often act as a crucible for those who inhabit them. Like Jacob's angel, the region requires that you wrestle with it before it bestows a blessing. This can mean driving through a snowstorm on icy roads, wondering whether you'll have to pull over and spend the night in your car, only to emerge under tag ends of clouds into a clear sky blazing with stars. Suddenly you know what you're seeing: the earth has turned to face the center of the galaxy, and many more stars are visible than the ones we usually see on our wing of the spiral.

2   Or a vivid double rainbow marches to the east, following the wild summer storm that nearly blew you off the road. The storm sky is gunmetal gray, but to the west the sky is peach streaked with crimson. The land and sky of the West often fill what Thoreau termed our "need to witness our limits transgressed." Nature, in Dakota, can indeed be an experience of the holy.

3   More Americans than ever, well over 70 percent, now live in urban areas and tend to see Plains land as empty. What they really mean is devoid of human presence. Most visitors to Dakota travel on interstate highways that will take them as quickly as possible through the region, past our larger cities to such attractions as the Badlands and the Black Hills. Looking at the expanse of land in between, they may wonder why a person would choose to live in such a barren place, let alone love it. But mostly they are bored: they turn up the car stereo, count the miles to civilization, and look away.

4   Dakota is a painful reminder of human limits, just as cities and shopping malls are attempts to deny them. This book is an invitation to a land of little rain and few trees, dry summer winds and harsh winters, a land rich in grass and sky and surprises. On a crowded planet, this is a place inhabited by few, and by the circumstance of inheritance, I am one of them. Nearly twenty years ago I returned to the holy ground of my childhood summers; I moved from New York City to the house my mother had grown up in, in

an isolated town on the border between North and South Dakota.

5   More than any other place I lived as a child or young adult—Virginia, Illinois, Hawaii, Vermont, New York—this is my spiritual geography, the place where I've wrestled my story out of the circumstances of landscape and inheritance. The word "geography" derives from the Greek words for earth and writing, and writing about Dakota has been my means of understanding that inheritance and reclaiming what is holy in it. Of course Dakota has always been such a matrix for its Native American inhabitants. But their tradition is not mine, and in returning to the Great Plains, where two generations of my family lived before me, I had to build on my own traditions, those of the Christian West.

6   When a friend referred to the western Dakotas as the Cappadocia of North America, I was handed an essential connection between the spirituality of the landscape I inhabit and that of the fourth-century monastics who set up shop in Cappadocia and the deserts of Egypt. Like those monks, I made a countercultural choice to live in what the rest of the world considers a barren waste. Like them, I had to stay in this place, like a scarecrow in a field, and hope for the brains to see its beauty. My idea of what makes a place beautiful had to change, and it has. The city no longer appeals to me for the cultural experiences and possessions I might acquire there, but because its population is less homogenous than Plains society. Its holiness is to be found in being open to humanity in all its diversity. And the western Plains now seem bountiful in their emptiness, offering solitude and room to grow.

7   I want to make it clear that my move did not take me "back to the land" in the conventional sense. I did not strike out on my own to make a go of it with "an acre and a cow," as a Hungarian friend naively imagined. As the homesteaders of the early twentieth century soon found out, it is not possible to survive on even 160 acres in western Dakota. My move was one that took me deep into the meaning of inheritance, as I had to try to fit myself into a complex network of long-established relationships.

8   My husband and I live in the small house in Lemmon, South Dakota, that my grandparents built in 1923. We moved there after they died because my mother, brother, and sisters, who live in Honolulu, did not want to hold an estate auction, the usual procedure when the beneficiaries of an inheritance on the Plains live far away. I offered to move there and manage the farm interests (land and a cattle herd) that my grandparents left us. David Dwyer, my husband, also a poet, is a New York City native who spent his childhood summers in the Adirondacks, and he had enough sense of adventure to agree to this. We expected to be in Dakota for just a few years.

9   It's hard to say why we stayed. A growing love of the prairie landscape and the quiet of a small town, inertia, and because as freelance writers, we found we had the survival skills suitable for a frontier. We put together a crazy quilt of jobs: I worked in the public library and as an artist-in-residence in schools in both Dakotas; I also did freelance writing and book-

keeping. David tended bar, wrote computer programs for a number of businesses in the region, and did freelance translation of French literature for several publishers. In 1979 we plunged into the cable television business with some friends, one of whom is an electronics expert. David learned how to climb poles and put up the hardware, and I kept the books. It was a good investment; after selling the company we found that we had bought ourselves a good three years to write. In addition, I still do bookkeeping for my family's farm business: the land is leased to people I've known all my life, people who have rented our land for two generations and also farm their own land and maintain their own cattle herds, an arrangement that is common in western Dakota.

10   In coming to terms with my inheritance, and pursuing my vocation as a writer, I have learned, as both farmers and writers have discovered before me, that it is not easy to remain on the Plains. Only one of North Dakota's best-known writers—Richard Critchfield, Louise Erdrich, Lois Hudson, and Larry Woiwode—currently lives in the state. And writing the truth about the Dakota experience can be a thankless task. I recently discovered that Lois Hudson's magnificent novel of the Dakota Dust Bowl, *The Bones of Plenty,* a book arguably better than *The Grapes of Wrath,* was unknown to teachers and librarians in a town not thirty miles from where the novel is set. The shame of it is that Hudson's book could have helped these people better understand their current situation, the economic crisis forcing many families off the land. Excerpts from *The Grapes of Wrath* were in a textbook used in the school, but students could keep them at a safe distance, part of that remote entity called "American literature" that has little relation to their lives.

11   The Plains are full of what a friend here calls "good telling stories," and while our sense of being forgotten by the rest of the world makes it all the more important that we preserve them and pass them on, instead we often neglect them. Perversely, we do not even claim those stories which have attracted national attention. Both John Neihardt and Frederick Manfred have written about Hugh Glass, a hunter and trapper mauled by a grizzly bear in 1823 at the confluence of the Little Moreau and Grand rivers just south of Lemmon. Left for dead by his companions, he crawled and limped some two hundred miles southeast, to the trading post at Fort Kiowa on the Missouri River. Yet when Manfred wanted to give a reading in Lemmon a few years ago, the publicist was dismissed by a high school principal who said, "Who's he? Why would our students be interested?" Manfred's audience of eighty—large for Lemmon—consisted mainly of the people who remembered him from visits he'd made in the early 1950s while researching his novel *Lord Grizzly.*

12   Thus are the young disenfranchised while their elders drown in details, "story" reduced to the social column of the weekly newspaper that reports on family reunions, card parties, even shopping excursions to a neighboring town. But real story is as hardy as grass, and it survives in Dakota in oral form. Good storytelling is one thing rural whites and Indians have in common. But Native Americans have learned through

harsh necessity that people who survive encroachment by another culture need story to survive. And a storytelling tradition is something Plains people share with both ancient and contemporary monks: we learn our ways of being and reinforce our values by telling tales about each other.

13   One of my favorite monastic stories concerns two fourth-century monks who "spent fifty years mocking their temptations by saying 'After this winter, we will leave here.' When the summer came, they said, 'After this summer, we will go away from here.' They passed all their lives in this way." These ancient monks sound remarkably like the farmers I know in Dakota who live in what they laconically refer to as "next-year country."

14   We hold on to hopes for next year every year in western Dakota: hoping that droughts will end; hoping that our crops won't be hailed out in the few rainstorms that come; hoping that it won't be too windy on the day we harvest, blowing away five bushels an acre; hoping (usually against hope) that if we get a fair crop, we'll be able to get a fair price for it. Sometimes survival is the only blessing that the terrifying angel of the Plains bestows. Still, there are those born and raised here who can't imagine living anywhere else. There are also those who are drawn here—teachers willing to take the lowest salaries in the nation; clergy with theological degrees from Princeton, Cambridge, and Zurich who want to serve small rural churches—who find that they cannot remain for long. Their professional mobility sets them apart and becomes a liability in an isolated Plains community where outsiders are treated with an uneasy mix of hospitality and rejection.

15   "Extremes," John R. Milton suggests in his history of South Dakota, is "perhaps the key word for Dakota . . . What happens to extremes is that they come together, and the result is a kind of tension." I make no attempt in this book to resolve the tensions and contradictions I find in the Dakotas between hospitality and insularity, change and inertia, stability and instability, possibility and limitation, between hope and despair, between open hearts and closed minds.

16   I suspect that these are the ordinary contradictions of human life, and that they are so visible in Dakota because we are so few people living in a stark landscape. We are at the point of transition between East and West in America, geographically and psychically isolated from either coast, and unlike either the Midwest or the desert West. South Dakota has been dubbed both the Sunshine State and the Blizzard State, and both designations have a basis in fact. Without a strong identity we become a mythic void; "the Great Desolation," as novelist Ole Rolvaag wrote early in this century, or "The American Outback," as *Newsweek* designated us a few years ago.

17   Geographical and cultural identity is confused even within the Dakotas. The eastern regions of both states have more in common with each other than with the area west of the Missouri, colloquially called the "West River." Although I commonly use the term "Dakota" to refer to both Dakotas, most of my experience is centered in this western region,

and it seems to me that especially in western Dakota we live in tension between myth and truth. Are we cowboys or farmers? Are we fiercely independent frontier types or community builders? One myth that haunts us is that the small town is a stable place. The land around us was divided neatly in 160-acre rectangular sections, following the Homestead Act of 1863 (creating many section-line roads with 90-degree turns). But our human geography has never been as orderly. The western Dakota communities settled by whites are, and always have been, remarkably unstable. The Dakotas have always been a place to be *from:* some 80 percent of homesteaders left within the first twenty years of settlement, and our boom-and-bust agricultural and oil industry economy has kept people moving in and out (mostly out) ever since. Many small-town schools and pulpits operate with revolving doors, adding to the instability.

18   When I look at the losses we've sustained in western Dakota since 1980 (about one fifth of the population in Perkins County, where I live, and a full third in neighboring Corson County) and at the human cost in terms of anger, distrust, and grief, it is the prairie descendants of the ancient desert monastics, the monks and nuns of Benedictine communities in the Dakotas, who inspire me to hope. One of the vows a Benedictine makes is *stability:* commitment to a particular community, a particular place. If this vow is countercultural by contemporary American standards, it is countercultural in the way that life on the Plains often calls us to be. Benedictines represent continuity in the boom-and-bust cycles of the Plains; they incarnate, and can articulate, the reasons people want to stay.

19   Terrence Kardong, a monk at an abbey in Dakota founded roughly a thousand years after their European motherhouse, has termed the Great Plains "a school for humility," humility being one goal of Benedictine life. He writes, "in this eccentric environment . . . certainly one is made aware that things are not entirely in control." In fact, he says, the Plains offer constant reminders that "we are quite powerless over circumstance." His abbey, like many Great Plains communities with an agricultural base, had a direct experience of powerlessness, going bankrupt in the 1920s. Then, and at several other times in the community's history, the monks were urged to move to a more urban environment.

20   Kardong writes, "We may be crazy, but we are not necessarily stupid . . . We built these buildings ourselves. We've cultivated these fields since the turn of the century. We watched from our dining room window the mirage of the Killdeer Mountains rise and fall on the horizon. We collected a library full of local history books and they belong here, not in Princeton. Fifty of our brothers lie down the hill in our cemetery. We have become as indigenous as the cottonwood trees . . . If you take us somewhere else, we lose our character, our history—maybe our soul."

21   A monk does not speak lightly of the soul, and Kardong finds in the Plains the stimulus to develop an inner geography. "A monk isn't supposed to need all kinds of flashy surroundings. We're supposed to have a beautiful inner landscape. Watching a storm pass from horizon to horizon

fills your soul with reverence. It makes your soul expand to fill the sky."

22   Monks are accustomed to taking the long view, another countercultural stance in our fast-paced, anything-for-a-buck society which has corrupted even the culture of farming into "agribusiness." Kardong and many other writers of the desert West, including myself, are really speaking of values when they find beauty in this land no one wants. He writes: "We who are permanently camped here see things you don't see at 55 m.p.h. . . . We see white-faced calves basking in the spring grass like the lilies of the field. We see a chinook wind in January make rivulets run. We see dust-devils and lots of little things. We are grateful."

23   The so-called emptiness of the Plains is full of such miraculous "little things." The way native grasses spring back from a drought, greening before your eyes; the way a snowy owl sits on a fencepost, or a golden eagle hunts, wings outstretched over grassland that seems to go on forever. Pelicans rise noisily from a lake; an antelope stands stock-still, its tattooed neck like a message in unbreakable code; columbines, their long stems beaten down by hail, bloom in the mud, their whimsical and delicate flowers intact. One might see a herd of white-tailed deer jumping a fence; fox cubs wrestling at the door of their lair; cock pheasants stepping out of a medieval tapestry into windrowed hay; cattle bunched in the southeast corner of a pasture, anticipating a storm in the approaching thunderheads. And above all, one notices the quiet, the near-absence of human noise.

24   My spiritual geography is a study in contrasts. The three places with which I have the deepest affinity are Hawaii, where I spent my adolescent years; New York City, where I worked after college; and western South Dakota. Like many Americans of their generation, my parents left their small-town roots in the 1930s and moved often. Except for the family home in Honolulu—its yard rich with fruits and flowers (pomegranate, tangerine, lime, mango, plumeria, hibiscus, lehua, ginger, and bird-of-paradise)—and my maternal grandparents' house in a remote village in western Dakota—its modest and hard-won garden offering columbine, daisies and mint—all my childhood places are gone.

25   When my husband and I moved nearly twenty years ago from New York to that house in South Dakota, only one wise friend in Manhattan understood the inner logic of the journey. Others, appalled, looked up Lemmon, South Dakota (named for George Lemmon, a cattleman and wheeler-dealer of the early 1900s, and home of the Petrified Wood Park— the world's largest—a gloriously eccentric example of American folk art) in their atlases and shook their heads. How could I leave the artists' and writers' community in which I worked, the diverse and stimulating environment of a great city, for such barrenness? Had I lost my mind? But I was young, still in my twenties, an apprentice poet certain of the rightness of returning to the place where I suspected I would find my stories. As it turns out, the Plains have been essential not only for my growth as a writer, they have formed me spiritually. I would even say they have made me a human being.

26   St. Hilary, a fourth-century bishop (and patron saint against snake bites) once wrote, "Everything that seems empty is full of the angels of God." The magnificent sky above the Plains sometimes seems to sing this truth; angels seem possible in the wind-filled expanse. A few years ago a small boy named Andy who had recently moved to the Plains from Pennsylvania told me he knew an angel named Andy Le Beau. He spelled out the name for me and I asked him if the angel had visited him here. "Don't you know?" he said in the incredulous tone children adopt when adults seem stupefyingly ignorant. "Don't you know?" he said, his voice rising, "*This* is where angels drown."

27   Andy no more knew that he was on a prehistoric sea bed than he knew what *le beau* means in French, but some ancient wisdom in him had sensed great danger here; a terrifying but beautiful landscape in which we are at the mercy of the unexpected, and even angels proceed at their own risk.

Discussion Questions

1. Do you think Norris's reasons for staying in South Dakota are convincing? What does her choice say about her as a person?

2. In paragraph 2, Norris states that "Nature, in Dakota, can indeed be an experience of the holy." Explain what you think she means by that statement and the ways in which she proves it.

3. Why do you think it is important for Norris to say in paragraph 7 that her move to South Dakota "did not take [her] 'back to the land' in the conventional sense"?

4. Explain what you understand Norris means when she invokes the idea of "inner geography" in paragraph 21 and "spiritual geography in paragraph 24.

5. Do you think there was anything about Norris's experiences that were peculiar to South Dakota, or could she have achieved a similar spiritual awakening in another locale—say, the Colorado Rockies or the Mississippi delta? Explain your response.

Walden

E. B. White

E (lwyn) B(rooks) White was born in 1899 and grew up in New York. He attended Cornell University, and his first job in journalism was working for The New Yorker. *In 1937, he began "One Man's Meat," a monthly column for* Harper's Magazine. *White was a prolific writer: his children's literature includes* Stuart Little *(1945),* Charlotte's Web *(1952), and* The Trumpet of the Swan *(1970); his collections of essays include* Every Day Is Saturday *(1934),* One Man's Meat *(1942),* The Second Tree from the Corner *(1954), and* The Points of My Compass *(1962). Many teachers and students know White from having read* The Elements of Style *(1959), a small book he edited for his professor from Cornell, William Strunk. White's many honors include the American Academy of Arts and Letters Gold Medal, a Presidential Medal of Freedom, and a National Medal for Literature. He died in 1985. White frames his essay as a letter to Henry David Thoreau and plays off Thoreau's famous essay that describes his home for two years,* Walden. *White's essay first appeared in his* Harper's *column in 1939.*

1   Miss Nims, take a letter to Henry David Thoreau. Dear Henry: I thought of you the other afternoon as I was approaching Concord doing fifty on Route 62. That is a high speed at which to hold a philosopher in one's mind, but in this century we are a nimble bunch.

2   On one of the lawns in the outskirts of the village a woman was cutting the grass with a motorized lawn mower. What made me think of you was that the machine had rather got away from her, although she was game enough, and in the brief glimpse I had of the scene it appeared to me that the lawn was mowing the lady. She kept a tight grip on the handles, which throbbed violently with every explosion of the one-cylinder motor, and as she sheered around bushes and lurched along at a reluctant trot behind her impetuous servant, she looked like a puppy who had grabbed something that was too much for him. Concord hasn't changed much, Henry; the farm implements and the animals still have the upper hand.

3   I may as well admit that I was journeying to Concord with the deliberate intention of visiting your woods; for although I have never knelt at the grave of a philosopher nor placed wreaths on moldy poets, and have often gone a mile out of my way to avoid some place of historical interest, I have always wanted to see Walden Pond. The account that you left of your sojourn there is, you will be amused to learn, a document of increasing pertinence; each year it seems to gain a little headway, as the world loses ground. We may all be transcendental yet, whether we like it or not. As our common complexities increase, any tale of individual simplicity (and yours is the best written and the cockiest) acquires a new fascination; as our goods accumulate, but not our well-being, your report of an existence without material adornment takes on a certain awkward credibility.

4   My purpose in going to Walden Pond, like yours, was not to live cheaply or to live dearly there, but to transact some private business with the fewest obstacles. Approaching Concord, doing forty, doing forty-five, doing fifty, the steering wheel held snug in my palms, the highway held grimly in my vision, the crown of the road now serving me (on the right-hand curves), now defeating me (on the lefthand curves), I began to rouse myself from the stupefaction that a day's motor journey induces. It was a

delicious evening, Henry, when the whole body is one sense, and imbibes delight through every pore, if I may coin a phrase. Fields were richly brown where the harrow, drawn by the stripped Ford, had lately sunk its teeth; pastures were green; and overhead the sky had that same everlasting great look which you will find on Page 144 of the Oxford pocket edition. I could feel the road entering me, through tire, wheel, spring, and cushion; shall I not have intelligence with earth too? Am I not partly leaves and vegetable mold myself?—a man of infinite horsepower, yet partly leaves.

5   Stay with me on 62 and it will take you into Concord. As I say, it was a delicious evening. The snake had come forth to die in a bloody S on the highway, the wheel upon its head, its bowels flat now and exposed. The turtle had come up too to cross the road and die in the attempt, its hard shell smashed under the rubber blow, its intestinal yearning (for the other side of the road) forever squashed. There was a sign by the wayside which announced that the road had a "cotton surface." You wouldn't know what that is, but neither, for that matter, did I. There is a cryptic ingredient in many of our modern improvements—we are awed and pleased without knowing quite what we are enjoying. It is something to be traveling on a road with a cotton surface.

6   The civilization round Concord today is an odd distillation of city, village, farm, and manor. The houses, yards, fields look not quite suburban, not quite rural. Under the bronze beech and the blue spruce of the departed baron grazes the milch goat of the heirs. Under the porte-cochère stands the reconditioned station wagon; under the grape arbor sit the puppies for sale. (But why do men degenerate ever? What makes families run out?)

7   It was June and everywhere June was publishing her immemorial stanza; in the lilacs, in the syringa, in the freshly edged paths and the sweetness of moist beloved gardens, and the little wire wickets that preserve the tulips' front. Farmers were already moving the fruits of their toil into their yards, arranging the rhubarb, the asparagus, the strictly fresh eggs on the painted stands under the little shed roofs with the patent shingles. And though it was almost a hundred years since you had taken your ax and started cutting out your home on Walden Pond, I was interested to observe that the philosophical spirit was still alive in Massachusetts: in the center of a vacant lot some boys were assembling the framework of the rude shelter, their whole mind and skill concentrated in the rather inauspicious helter-skeleton of studs and rafters. They too were escaping from town, to live naturally, in a rich blend of savagery and philosophy.

8   That evening, after supper at the inn, I strolled out into the twilight to dream my shapeless transcendental dreams and see that the car was locked up for the night (first open the right front door, then reach over, straining, and pull up the handles of the left rear and the left front till you hear the click, then the handle of the right rear, then shut the right front but open it again, remembering that the key is still in the ignition switch, remove the key, shut the right front again with a bang, push the tiny keyhole cover to one side, insert key, turn, and withdraw). It is what we all do, Henry. It

is called locking the car. It is said to confuse thieves and keep them from making off with the laprobe. Four doors to lock behind one robe. The driver himself never uses a laprobe, the free movement of his legs being vital to the operation of the vehicle; so that when he locks the car it is a pure and unselfish act. I have in my life gained very little essential heat from laprobes, yet I have ever been at pains to lock them up.

9   The evening was full of sounds, some of which would have stirred your memory. The robins still love the elms of New England villages at sundown. There is enough of the thrush in them to make song inevitable at the end of day, and enough of the tramp to make them hang round the dwellings of men. A robin, like many another American, dearly loves a white house with green blinds. Concord is still full of them.

10   Your fellow-townsmen were stirring abroad—not many afoot, most of them in their cars; and the sound that they made in Concord at evening was a rustling and a whispering. The sound lacks steadfastness and is wholly unlike that of a train. A train, as you know who lived so near the Fitchburg line, whistles once or twice sadly and is gone, trailing a memory in smoke, soothing to ear and mind. Automobiles, skirting a village green, are like flies that have gained the inner ear—they buzz, cease, pause, start, shift, stop, halt, brake, and the whole effect is a nervous polytone curiously disturbing.

11   As I wandered along, the toc toc of ping pong balls drifted from an attic window. In front of the Reuben Brown house a Buick was drawn up. At the wheel, motionless, his hat upon his head, a man sat, listening to Amos and Andy on the radio (it is a drama of many scenes and without an end). The deep voice of Andrew Brown, emerging from the car, although it originated more than two hundred miles away, was unstrained by distance. When you used to sit on the shore of your pond on Sunday morning, listening to the church bells of Acton and Concord, you were aware of the excellent filter of the intervening atmosphere. Science has attended to that, and sound now maintains its intensity without regard for distance. Properly sponsored, it goes on forever.

12   A fire engine, out for a trial spin, roared past Emerson's house, hot with readiness for public duty. Over the barn roofs the martins dipped and chittered. A swarthy daughter of an asparagus grower, in culottes, shirt, and bandanna, pedalled past on her bicycle. It was indeed a delicious evening, and I returned to the inn (I believe it was your house once) to rock with the old ladies on the concrete veranda.

13   Next morning early I started afoot for Walden, out Main Street and down Thoreau, past the depot and the Minuteman Chevrolet Company. The morning was fresh, and in a bean field along the way I flushed an agriculturalist, quietly studying his beans. Thoreau Street soon joined Number 126, an artery of the State. We number our highways nowadays, our speed being so great we can remember little of their quality or character and are lucky to remember their number. (Men have an indistinct notion that if they keep up this activity long enough all will at length ride somewhere, in next to no time.) Your pond is on 126.

14   I knew I must be nearing your woodland retreat when the Golden Pheasant lunchroom came into view—Sealtest ice cream, toasted sandwiches, hot frankfurters, waffles, tonics, and lunches. Were I the proprietor, I should add rice, Indian meal, and molasses—just for old time's sake. The Pheasant, incidentally, is for sale: a chance for some nature lover who wishes to set himself up beside a pond in the Concord atmosphere and live deliberately, fronting only the essential facts of life on Number 126. Beyond the Pheasant was a place called Walden Breezes, an oasis whose porch pillars were made of old green shutters sawed into lengths. On the porch was a distorting mirror, to give the traveler a comical image of himself, who had miraculously learned to gaze in an ordinary glass without smiling. Behind the Breezes, in a sun-parched clearing, dwelt your philosophical descendants in their trailers, each trailer the size of your hut, but all grouped together for the sake of congeniality. Trailer people leave the city, as you did, to discover solitude and in any weather, at any hour of the day or night, to improve the nick of time; but they soon collect in villages and get bogged deeper in the mud than ever. The camp behind Walden Breezes was just rousing itself to the morning. The ground was packed hard under the heel, and the sun came through the clearing to bake the soil and enlarge the wry smell of cramped housekeeping. Cushman's bakery truck had stopped to deliver an early basket of rolls. A camp dog, seeing me in the road, barked petulantly. A man emerged from one of the trailers and set forth with a bucket to draw water from some forest tap.

15   Leaving the highway I turned off into the woods toward the pond, which was apparent through the foliage. The floor of the forest was strewn with dried old oak leaves and *Transcripts*. From beneath the flattened popcorn wrapper (*granum explosum*) peeped the frail violet. I followed a footpath and descended to the water's edge. The pond lay clear and blue in the morning light, as you have seen it so many times. In the shallows a man's waterlogged shirt undulated gently. A few flies came out to greet me and convoy me to your cove, past the No Bathing signs on which the fellows and the girls had scrawled their names. I felt strangely excited suddenly to be snooping around your premises, tiptoing along watchfully, as though not to tread by mistake upon the intervening century. Before I got to the cove I heard something that seemed to me quite wonderful: I heard your frog, a full, clear *troonk*, guiding me, still hoarse and solemn, bridging the years as the robins had bridged them in the sweetness of the village evening. But he soon quit, and I came on a couple of young boys throwing stones at him.

16   Your front yard is marked by a bronze tablet set in a stone. Four small granite posts, a few feet away, show where the house was. On top of the tablet was a pair of faded blue bathing trunks with a white stripe. Back of it is a pile of stones, a sort of cairn, left by your visitors as a tribute I suppose. It is a rather ugly little heap of stones, Henry. In fact the hillside itself

seems faded, browbeaten; a few tall skinny pines, bare of lower limbs, a smattering of young maples in suitable green, some birches and oaks, and a number of trees felled by the last big wind. It was from the bole of one of these fallen pines, torn up by the roots, that I extracted the stone that I added to the cairn—a sentimental act in which I was interrupted by a small terrier from a nearby picnic group, who confronted me and wanted to know about the stone.

17   I sat down for a while on one of the posts of your house to listen to the bluebottles and the dragonflies. The invaded glade sprawled shabby and mean at my feet, but the flies were tuned to the old vibration. There were the remains of a fire in your ruins, but I doubt that it was yours; also two beer bottles trodden into the soil and become part of the earth. A young oak had taken root in your house, and two or three ferns, unrolling like the ticklers at a banquet. The only other furnishings were a DuBarry pattern sheet, a page torn from a picture magazine, and some crusts in wax paper.

18   Before I quit I walked clear round the pond and found the place where you used to sit on the northeast side to get the sun in the fall, and the beach where you got sand for scrubbing your floor. On the eastern side of the pond, where the highway borders it, the State has built dressing rooms for swimmers, a float with diving towers, drinking fountains of porcelain, and rowboats for hire. The pond is in fact a State Preserve, and carries a twenty-dollar fine for picking wild flowers, a decree signed in all solemnity by your fellow-citizens Walter C. Wardwell, Erson B. Barlow, and Nathaniel I. Bowditch. There was a smell of creosote where they had been building a wide wooden stairway to the road and the parking area. Swimmers and boaters were arriving; bodies plunged vigorously into the water and emerged wet and beautiful in the bright air. As I left, a boatload of town boys were splashing about in mid-pond, kidding and fooling, the young fellows singing at the tops of their lungs in a wild chorus:

> *Amer-ica, Amer-ica, God shed his grace on thee,*
>
> *And crown thy good with brotherhood—*
>
> *From sea to shi-ning sea!*

19   I walked back to town along the railroad, following your custom. The rails were expanding noisily in the hot sun, and on the slope of the roadbed the wild grape and the blackberry sent up their creepers to the track.

20   The expense of my brief sojourn in Concord was:

```
Canvas shoes . . . . . . . . . . . . . . .$1.95
Baseball bat . . . . . . . . . . . . . . . . . . .25 �️ gifts to take back
Left-handed fielder's glove . . . . . . .1.25 ⎦ to a boy
Hotel and meals . . . . . . . . . . . . . 4.25
                                        ─────
    In all . . . . . . . . . . . . . . .$7.70
```

As you see, this amount was almost what you spent for food for eight months. I cannot defend the shoes or the expenditure for shelter and food: they reveal a meanness and grossness in my nature which you would find contemptible. The baseball equipment, however, is the kind of impediment with which you were never on even terms. You must remember that the house where you practiced the sort of economy that I respect was haunted only by mice and squirrels. You never had to cope with a shortstop.

Discussion Questions

1. Have you ever been disappointed in or disillusioned by a place you have always wanted to see? Was your reaction as strong as White's was to Walden?

2. What is your reaction to White having framed his essay in the form of a letter? How would you have responded differently to it had it been written in the more conventional essay form?

3. At what point in the essay do you first detect White's cynicism? Could he have made his point as powerfully without using cynicism?

4. What do you think White's purpose was in mentioning automobiles and transportation throughout his essay when it was purportedly and principally about Walden?

5. Do you think White is justified in being disappointed by what he sees having overtaken Thoreau's once idyllic setting? Or are the changes simply the result of progress and modern technology?

The Courage of Turtles
Edward Hoagland

*B*orn in New York in 1932, Edward Hoagland received his education at Harvard University. His novels include Cat Man (1956) and Seven Rivers West (1986), and his travel books are Notes from the Century Before: A Journal from British Columbia (1969) and African Calliope: A Journey to the Sudan (1979). Hoagland also writes essays, which have been collected in Walking the Dead Diamond River (1973), Red Wolves and Black Bears (1976), The Tugman's Passage (1982), Heart's Desire (1988), The Courage of Turtles (1971), of which the following essay is the title piece, and Balancing Acts: Essays (1993). Hoagland has taught at Columbia University, Bennington College, and the University of Iowa. He divides his time between living in a New York City apartment and in a northeastern

Vermont cabin. "The Courage of Turtles" reflects those two markedly different worlds.

1   Turtles are a kind of bird with the governor turned low. With the same attitude of removal, they cock a glance at what is going on, as if they need only to fly away. Until recently they were also a case of virtue rewarded, at least in the town where I grew up, because, being humble creatures, there were plenty of them. Even when we still had a few bobcats in the woods the local snapping turtles, growing up to forty pounds, were the largest carnivores. You would see them through the amber water, as big as greeny wash basins at the bottom of the pond, until they faded into the inscrutable mud as if they hadn't existed at all.

2   When I was ten I went to Dr. Green's Pond, a two-acre pond across the road. When I was twelve I walked a mile or so to Taggart's Pond, which was lusher, had big water snakes and a waterfall; and shortly after that I was bicycling way up to the adventuresome vastness of Mud Pond, a lake-sized body of water in the reservoir system of a Connecticut city, possessed of cat-backed little islands and empty shacks and a forest of pines and hardwoods along the shore. Otters, foxes, and mink left their prints on the bank; there were pike and perch. As I got older, the estates and forgotten back lots in town were parceled out and sold for nice prices, yet, though the woods had shrunk, it seemed that fewer people walked in the woods. The new residents didn't know how to find them. Eventually, exploring, they did find them, and it required some ingenuity and doubling around on my part to go for eight miles without meeting someone. I was grown by now, I lived in New York, and that's what I wanted to do on the occasional weekends when I came out.

3   Since Mud Pond contained drinking water I had felt confident nothing untoward would happen there. For a long while the developers stayed away, until the drought of the mid-1960s. This event, squeezing the edges in, convinced the local water company that the pond really wasn't a necessity as a catch basin, however; so they bulldozed a hole in the earthen dam, bulldozed the banks to fill in the bottom, and landscaped the flow of water that remained to wind like an English brook and provide a domestic view for the houses which were planned. Most of the painted turtles of Mud Pond, who had been inaccessible as they sunned on their rocks, wound up in boxes in boys' closets within a matter of days. Their footsteps in the dry leaves gave them away as they wandered forlornly. The snappers and the little musk turtles, neither of whom leave the water except once a year to lay their eggs, dug into the drying mud for another siege of hot weather, which they were accustomed to doing whenever the pond got low. But this time it was low for good; the mud baked over them and slowly entombed them. As for the ducks, I couldn't stroll in the woods and not feel guilty, because they were crouched beside every stagnant pothole, or were slinking between the bushes with their heads tucked into their shoulders so that I wouldn't see them. If they decided I had, they beat their way up through the screen of trees, striking their wings danger-

ously, and wheeled about with that headlong, magnificent velocity to locate another poor puddle.

4   I used to catch possums and black snakes as well as turtles, and I kept dogs and goats. Some summers I worked in a menagerie with the big personalities of the animal kingdom, like elephants and rhinoceroses. I was twenty before these enthusiasms began to wane, and it was then that I picked turtles as the particular animal I wanted to keep in touch with. I was allergic to fur, for one thing, and turtles need minimal care and not much in the way of quarters. They're personable beasts. They see the same colors we do and they seem to see just as well, as one discovers in trying to sneak up on them. In the laboratory they unravel the twists of a maze with the hot-blooded rapidity of a mammal. Though they can't run as fast as a rat, they improve on their errors just as quickly, pausing at each crossroads to look left and right. And they rock rhythmically in place, as we often do, although they are hatched from eggs, not the womb. (A common explanation psychologists give for our pleasure in rocking quietly is that it recapitulates our mother's heartbeat *in utero*.)

5   Snakes, by contrast, are dryly silent and priapic. They are smooth movers, legalistic, unblinking, and they afford the humor which the humorless do. But they make challenging captives; sometimes they don't eat for months on a point of order—if the light isn't right, for instance. Alligators are sticklers too. They're like war-horses, or German shepherds, and with their bar-shaped, vertical pupils adding emphasis, they have the *idée fixe* of eating, eating, even when they choose to refuse all food and stubbornly die. They delight in tossing a salamander up towards the sky and grabbing him in their long mouths as he comes down. They're so eager that they get the jitters, and they're too much of a proposition for a casual aquarium like mine. Frogs are depressingly defenseless: that moist, extensive back, with the bones almost sticking through. Hold a frog and you're holding its skeleton. Frogs' tasty legs are the staff of life to many animals—herons, raccoons, ribbon snakes—though they themselves are hard to feed. It's not an enviable role to be the staff of life, and after frogs you descend down the evolutionary ladder a big step to fish.

6   Turtles cough, burp, whistle, grunt and hiss, and produce social judgments. They put their heads together amicably enough, but then one drives the other back with the suddenness of two dogs who have been conversing in tones too low for an onlooker to hear. They pee in fear when they're first caught, but exercise both pluck and optimism in trying to escape, walking for hundreds of yards within the confines of their pen, carrying the weight of that cumbersome box on legs which are cruelly positioned for walking. They don't feel that the contest is unfair; they keep plugging, rolling like sailorly souls—a bobbing, infirm gait, a brave, sealegged momentum—stopping occasionally to study the lay of the land. For me, anyway, they manage to contain the rest of the animal world. They can stretch out their necks like a giraffe, or loom underwater like an

apocryphal hippo. They browse on lettuce thrown on the water like a cow moose which is partly submerged. They have a penguin's alertness, combined with a build like a brontosaurus when they rise up on tiptoe. Then they hunch and ponderously lunge like a grizzly going forward.

7   Baby turtles in a turtle bowl are a puzzle in geometrics. They're as decorative as pansy petals, but they are also self-directed building blocks, propping themselves on one another in different arrangements, before upending the tower. The timid individuals turn fearless, or vice versa. If one gets a bit arrogant he will push the others off the rock and afterwards climb down into the water and cling to the back of one of those he has bullied, tickling him with his hind feet until he bucks like a bronco. On the other hand, when this same milder-mannered fellow isn't exerting himself, he will stare right into the face of the sun for hours. What could be more lionlike? And he's at home in or out of the water and does lots of metaphysical tilting. He sinks and rises, with an infinity of levels to choose from; or, elongating himself, he climbs out on the land again to perambulate, sits boxed in his box, and finally slides back in the water, submerging into dreams.

8   I have five of these babies in a kidney-shaped bowl. The hatchling, who is a painted turtle, is not as large as the top joint of my thumb. He eats chicken gladly. Other foods he will attempt to eat but not with sufficient perseverance to succeed because he's so little. The yellow-bellied terrapin is probably a yearling, and he eats salad voraciously, but no meat, fish, or fowl. The Cumberland terrapin won't touch salad or chicken but eats fish and all of the meats except for bacon. The little snapper, with a black crenellated shell, feasts on any kind of meat, but rejects greens and fish. The fifth of the turtles is African. I acquired him only recently and don't know him well. A mottled brown, he unnerves the greener turtles, dragging their food off to his lairs. He doesn't seem to want to be green— he bites the algae off his shell, hanging meanwhile at daring, steep, head-first angles.

9   The snapper was a Ferdinand until I provided him with deeper water. Now he snaps at my pencil with his downturned and fearsome mouth, his swollen face like a napalm victim's. The Cumberland has an elliptical red mark on the side of his green-and-yellow head. He is benign by nature and ought to be as elegant as his scientific name *(Pseudemys scripta elegans)*, except he has contracted a disease of the air bladder which has permanently inflated it; he floats high in the water at an undignified slant and can't go under. There may have been internal bleeding, too, because his carapace is stained along its ridge. Unfortunately, like flowers, baby turtles often die. Their mouths fill up with a white fungus and their lungs with pneumonia. Their organs clog up from the rust in the water, or diet troubles, and, like a dying man's, their eyes and heads become too prominent. Toward the end, the edge of the shell becomes flabby as felt and folds around them like a shroud.

10   While they live they're like puppies. Although they're vivacious, they

would be a bore to be with all the time, so I also have an adult wood turtle about six inches long. Her top shell is the equal of any seashell for sculpturing, even a Cellini shell; it's like an old, dusty, richly engraved medallion dug out of a hillside. Her legs are salmon-orange bordered with black and protected by canted, heroic scales. Her plastron—the bottom shell—is splotched like a margay cat's coat, with black ocelli on a yellow background. It is convex to make room for the female organs inside, whereas a male's would be concave to help him fit tightly on top of her. Altogether, she exhibits every camouflage color on her limbs and shells. She has a turtleneck neck, a tail like an elephant's, wise old pachydermous hind legs, and the face of a turkey—except that when I carry her she gazes at the passing ground with a hawk's eyes and mouth. Her feet fit to the fingers of my hand, one to each one, and she rides looking down. She can walk on the floor in perfect silence, but usually she lets her plastron knock portentously, like a footstep, so that she resembles some grand, concise, slow-moving id. But if an earthworm is presented, she jerks swiftly ahead, poises above it, and strikes like a mongoose, consuming it with wild vigor. Yet she will climb on my lap to eat bread or boiled eggs.

11   If put into a creek, she swims like a cutter, nosing forward to intercept a strange turtle and smell him. She drifts with the current to go downstream, maneuvering behind a rock when she wants to take stock, or sinking to the nether levels, while bubbles float up. Getting out, choosing her path, she will proceed a distance and dig into a pile of humus, thrusting herself to the coolest layer at the bottom. The hole closes over her until it's as small as a mouse's hole. She's not as aquatic as a musk turtle, not quite as terrestrial as the box turtles in the same woods, but because of her versatility she's marvelous, she's everywhere. And though she breathes the way we breathe, with scarcely perceptible movements of her chest, sometimes instead she pumps her throat ruminatively, like a pipe smoker sucking and puffing. She waits and blinks, pumping her throat, turning her head, then sets off like a loping tiger in slow motion, hurdling the jungly lumber, the pea vine and twigs. She estimates angles so well that when she rides over the rocks, sliding down a drop-off with her rugged front legs extended, she has the grace of a rodeo mare.

12   But she's well off to be with me rather than at Mud Pond. The other turtles have fled—those that aren't baked into the bottom. Creeping up the brooks to sad, constricted marshes, burdened as they are with that box on their backs, they're walking into a setup where all their enemies move thirty times faster than they. It's like the nightmare most of us have whimpered through, where we are weighted down disastrously while trying to flee; fleeing our home ground, we try to run.

13   I've seen turtles in still worse straits. On Broadway, in New York, there is a penny arcade which used to sell baby terrapins that were scrawled with bon mots in enamel paint, such as KISS ME BABY. The manager turned out to be a wholesaler as well, and once I asked him whether he had any larger turtles to sell. He took me upstairs to a loft room devoted to the

turtle business. There were desks for the paper work and a series of racks that held shallow tin bins atop one another, each with several hundred babies crawling around in it. He was a smudgy-complexioned, bespectacled, serious fellow and he did have a few adult terrapins, but I was going to school and wasn't actually planning to buy; I'd only wanted to see them. They were aquatic turtles, but here they went without water, presumably for weeks, lurching about in those dry bins like handicapped citizens, living on gumption. An easel where the artist worked stood in the middle of the floor. She had a palette and a clip attachment for fastening the babies in place. She wore a smock and a beret, and was homely, short, and eccentric-looking, with funny black hair, like some of the ladies who show their paintings in Washington Square in May. She had a cold, she was smoking, and her hand wasn't very steady, although she worked quickly enough. The smile that she produced for me would have looked giddy if she had been happier, or drunk. Of course the turtles' doom was sealed when she painted them, because their bodies inside would continue to grow but their shells would not. Gradually, invisibly, they would be crushed. Around us their bellies—two thousand belly shells—rubbed on the bins with a mournful, momentous hiss.

14   Somehow there were so many of them I didn't rescue one. Years later, however, I was walking on First Avenue when I noticed a basket of living turtles in front of a fish store. They were as dry as a heap of old bones in the sun; nevertheless, they were creeping over one another gimpily, doing their best to escape. I looked and was touched to discover that they appeared to be wood turtles, my favorites, so I bought one. In my apartment I looked closer and realized that in fact this was a diamondback terrapin, which was bad news. Diamondbacks are tidewater turtles from brackish estuaries, and I had no seawater to keep him in. He spent his days thumping interminably against the baseboards, pushing for an opening through the wall. He drank thirstily but would not eat and had none of the hearty, accepting qualities of wood turtles. He was morose, paler in color, sleeker and more Oriental in the carved ridges and rings that formed his shell. Though I felt sorry for him, finally I found his unrelenting presence exasperating. I carried him, struggling in a paper bag, across town to the Morton Street Pier on the Hudson River. It was August but gray and windy. He was very surprised when I tossed him in; for the first time in our association, I think, he was afraid. He looked afraid as he bobbed about on top of the water, looking up at me from ten feet below. Though we were both accustomed to his resistance and rigidity, seeing him still pitiful, I recognized that I must have done the wrong thing. At least the river was salty, but it was also bottomless; the waves were too rough for him, and the tide was coming in, bumping him against the pilings underneath the pier. Too late, I realized that he wouldn't be able to swim to a peaceful inlet in New Jersey, even if he could figure out which way to swim. But since, short of diving in after him, there was nothing I could do, I walked away.

Discussion Questions

1. To what extent is Hoagland's interest in turtles a natural child-hood instinct? Can you remember having a similar fascination with animals when you were a child?

2. Besides describing turtles in his essay, Hoagland introduces us to other animals. Explain what they add to the essay.

3. Throughout his essay, Hoagland provides detailed descriptions of turtles. What in these descriptions gives you a new under-standing of the animal?

4. How justified do you find Hoagland's tossing the wood turtle into the Hudson River in paragraph 14? What does his action say about Hoagland as a person? Would you have acted simi-larly? Why or why not?

5. Do you see any connection between the turtles Hoagland finds in New York and the Walden that E. B. White finds years after Thoreau lived there? Explain your answer.

Boston: The Lost Ideal

Elizabeth Hardwick

Elizabeth Hardwick was born in 1916 in New York. She received her B.A. and M.A. degrees from the University of Kentucky and pursued advanced study at Columbia University. She is the author of three novels, The Ghostly Lover *(1945),* The Simple Truth *(1955), and* Sleepless Nights *(1979) as well as three collections of essays,* A View of My Own *(1962),* Seduction and Betrayal *(1974), and* Batyleby in Manhattan *(1983). The recipient of the George Jean Nathan Award for dramatic criticism, a Guggenheim fellowship in fiction, and a National Book Critics Circle Award nomination, Hardwick is a professor at Barnard College and the founder and advisory editor of the* New York Times Review of Books. *In the following essay, Hardwick discusses the complex image of Boston and the ways in which that city's "grand old ideal" has changed.*

1   With Boston and its mysteriously enduring reputation, "the reverbera-tion is longer than the thunderclap," as Emerson observed about the tena-cious fame of certain artists. Boston—wrinkled, spindly-legged, depleted of nearly all her spiritual and cutaneous oils, provincial, self-esteeming—has gone on spending and spending her inflated bills of pure reputation decade

after decade. Now, one supposes it is all over at last. The old jokes embarrass, the anecdotes are so many thrice-squeezed lemons, and no new fruit hangs on the boughs.

2   All the American regions are breaking up, ground down to a standard American corn meal. And why not Boston, which would have been the most difficult to maintain? There has never been anything quite like Boston as a creation of the American imagination, or perhaps one should say as a creation of the American scene. Some of the legend was once real, surely. Our utilitarian, fluid landscape has produced a handful of regional conceptions, popular images, brief and naked; the conservative Vermonter, the boastful Texan, the honeyed Southerner. "Graciousness is ours," brays a coarsened South; and the sheiks of Texas cruise around in their desert.

3   The Boston image is more complex. The city is felt to have, in the end, a pure and special nature, absurd no doubt but somehow valuable. An author can hardly fail to turn a penny or two on this magical subject. Everyone will consent to be informed on it, to be slyly entertained by it. The image lends itself to exaggerations, to dreams of social and ethnic purity, to notions of grand old families still existing as grand old families are supposed to exist. *Actual* Boston, the living city, is governed largely by people of Irish descent and more and more, recently, by men of Italian descent. Not long ago, the old Yankee, Senator Saltonstall, remarked wistfully that there were still a good many Anglo-Saxons in Massachusetts, his own family among them. Extinction is foreshadowed in the defense.

4   Plainness and pretension restlessly feuding and combining; wealth and respectability and firmness of character ending in the production of a number of diverting individual tics or, at the best, instances of high culture. Something of that sort is the legendary Boston soul or so one supposes without full confidence because the old citizens of Boston vehemently hold to the notion that the city and their character are ineffable, unknowable. When asked for an opinion on the admirable novel, *Boston Adventure,* or even the light social history, *The Proper Bostonians,* the answer invariably comes, "Not Boston." The descriptive intelligence, the speculative mind, the fresh or even the merely open eye are felt to discover nothing but errors here, be they errors of praise or censure. Still, wrongheadedness flourishes, the subject fascinates, and the Athenaeum's list of written productions on this topic is nearly endless.

5   The best book on Boston is Henry James's novel, *The Bostonians.* By the bald and bold use of the place name, the unity of situation and person is dramatized. But poor James, of course, was roundly and importantly informed by everyone, including his brother William, that this too was "not Boston," and, stricken, he pushed aside a superb creation, and left the impregnable, unfathomable Boston to its mysteries. James's attitude toward the city's intellectual consequence and social charm is one of absolute impiety. A view of the Charles River reveals ". . . an horizon indented at empty intervals with wooden spires, the masts of lonely boats, the chim-

neys of dirty 'works,' over a brackish expanse of anomalous character, which is too big for a river and too small for a bay." A certain house has "a peculiar look of being both new and faded—a kind of modern fatigue—like certain articles of commerce which are sold at a reduction as shop-worn." However, there is little natural landscape in James's novel. The picture is, rather, of the psychological Boston of the 1870s, a confused scene, slightly mad with neurotic repressions, provincialism, and earnestness without intellectual seriousness.

6   James's view of Boston is not the usual one, although his irony and dissatisfaction are shared by Henry Adams, who says that "a simpler manner of life and thought could hardly exist, short of cave-dwelling," and by Santayana who spoke of Boston as a "moral and intellectual nursery, always busy applying first principles to trifles." The great majority of the writings on Boston are in another spirit altogether—frankly unctuous, for the town has always attracted men of quiet and timid and tasteful opinion, men interested in old families and things, in the charms of times recently past, collectors of anecdotes about those Boston worthies hardly anyone can still clearly identify, men who spoke and preached and whose style and fame deteriorated quickly. Rufus Choate, Dr. Channing, Edward Everett Hale, Phillips Brooks, and Theodore Parker: names that remain in one's mind, without producing an image or a fact, as the marks are left on the wall after the picture has been removed. William Dean Howells held a more usual view than Henry James or Adams or Santayana. Indeed Howells' original enthusiasm for garden and edifice, person and setting, is more than a little *exalté*. The first sight of the Chapel at Mount Auburn Cemetery moved him more than the "Acropolis, Westminster Abbey, and Santa Croce in one." The massive, gray stones of "the Public Library and the Athenaeum are hardly eclipsed by the Vatican and the Pitti." And so on.

7   The importance of Boston was intellectual and as its intellectual donations to the country have diminished, so it has declined from its lofty symbolic meaning, to become a more lowly image, a sort of farce of conservative exclusiveness and snobbish humor. Marquand's George Apley is a figure of the decline—fussy, sentimental, farcically mannered, archaic. He cannot be imagined as an Abolitionist, an author, a speaker; he is merely a "character," a very idiosyncratic and simple-minded one. The old Boston had something of the spirit of Bloomsbury: clannish, worldly, and intellectually serious. About the historian, Prescott, Van Wyck Brooks could say, ". . . for at least ten years, Prescott had been hard at work, harder, perhaps, than any Boston merchant."

8   History, indeed, with its long, leisurely, gentlemanly labors, the books arriving by post, the cards to be kept and filed, the sections to be copied, the documents to be checked, is the ideal pursuit for the New England mind. All the Adamses spent a good deal of their lives on one kind of history or another. The eccentricity, studiousness, and study-window slow pace of life of the historical gentleman lay everywhere about the Boston

scene. For money, society, fashion, extravagance, one went to New York. But now, the descendants of the old, intellectual aristocracy live in the respectable suburbs and lead the healthy, restless, outdoor life that atrophies the sedentary nerves of culture. The blue-stocking, the eccentric, the intransigent bring a blush of uncertainty and embarrassment to the healthy young couple's cheek.

9   Boston today can still provide a fairly stimulating atmosphere for the banker, the broker, for doctors and lawyers. "Open end" investments prosper, the fish come in at the dock, the wool market continues, and workers are employed in the shoe factories in the nearby towns. For the engineer, the physicist, the industrial designer, for all the highly trained specialists of the electronic age, Boston and its area are of seemingly unlimited promise. Sleek, well-designed factories and research centers pop up everywhere; the companies plead, in the Sunday papers, for more chemists, more engineers, and humbly relate the executive benefits of salary and pension and advancement they are prepared to offer.

10   But otherwise, for the artist, the architect, the composer, the writer, the philosopher, the historian, for those humane pursuits for which the town was once noted and even for the delights of entertainment, for dancing, acting, cooking, Boston is a bewildering place. There is, first of all, the question of Boston or New York. (The question is not new; indeed it was answered in the last decades of the last century in favor of New York as the cultural center of America.) It is, in our day, only a private and personal question: where or which of the two Eastern cities should one try to live and work in? It is a one-sided problem. For the New Yorker, San Francisco or Florida, perhaps—Boston, never. In Boston, New York tantalizes; one of the advantages of Boston is said, wistfully, to be its nearness to New York. It is a bad sign when a man who has come to Boston or Cambridge, Massachusetts, from another place begins to show an undivided acceptance of his new town. Smugness is the great vice of the two places. Between puffy self-satisfaction and the fatiguing wonder if one wouldn't be happier, more productive, more appreciated in New York a thoughtful man makes his choice.

11   Boston is not a small New York, as they say a child is not a small adult but is, rather, a specially organized small creature with its small-creature's temperature, balance, and distribution of fat. In Boston there is an utter absence of that wild electric beauty of New York, of the marvelous, excited rush of people in taxicabs at twilight, of the great Avenues and Streets, the restaurants, theatres, bars, hotels, delicatessens, shops. In Boston the night comes down with an incredibly heavy, small-town finality. The cows come home; the chickens go to roost; the meadow is dark. Nearly every Bostonian is in his own house or in someone else's house, dining at the home board, enjoying domestic and social privacy. The "nice little dinner party"—for this the Bostonian would sell his soul. In the evenings, the old "accommodators" dart about the city, carrying their black uniforms and white aprons in a paper bag. They are on call to go, anywhere, to cook and

serve dinners. Many of these women are former cooks and maids, now living on Social Security retirement pensions, supplemented by the fees for these evening "accommodations" to the community. Their style and the bland respectability of their cuisine keep up the social tone of the town. They are like those old slaves who stuck to their places and, even in the greatest deprivation, graciously went on toting things to the Massa.

12   There is a curious flimsiness and indifference in the commercial life of Boston. The restaurants are, charitably, to be called mediocre, the famous sea food is only palatable when raw. Otherwise it usually has to endure the deep-fry method that makes everything taste like those breaded pork chops of the Middle West, which in turn taste like the fried sole of Boston. Here, French restaurants quickly become tea-roomy, as if some sort of rapid naturalization had taken place. There is not a single attractive eating place on the water front. An old downtown restaurant of considerable celebrity, Locke-Ober's, has been expanded, let out, and "costumed" by one of the American restaurant decorators whose productions have a ready-made look, as if the designs had been chosen from a catalogue. But for the purest eccentricity, there is the "famous" restaurant, Durgin-Park, which is run like a boarding house in a mining town. And so it goes.

13   Downtown Boston at night is a dreary jungle of honky-tonks for sailors, dreary department-store windows, Loew's movie houses, hillbilly bands, strippers, parking lots, undistinguished new buildings. Midtown Boston—small, expensive shops, the inevitable Elizabeth Arden and Helena Rubinstein "salons," Brooks Brothers—is deserted at night, except for people going in and out of the Ritz Carlton Hotel, the only public place in Boston that could be called "smart." The merchandise in the Newbury Street shops is designed in a high fashion, elaborate, furred and sequined, but it is never seen anywhere. Perhaps it is for out-of-town use, like a traveling man's mistress.

14   Just as there is no smart life, so there is no Soho, no Greenwich Village. Recently a man was murdered in a parking lot in the Chinatown area. His address was given as the South End, a lower-class section, and he was said to be a free-spender, making enough money as a summer bartender on Cape Cod to lead a free-wheeling life the rest of the year. One paper referred to the unfortunate man as a "member of the Beacon Hill Bohemia set." This designation is of considerable interest because there is no "Bohemia" in Boston, neither upper nor lower; the detergent of bourgeois Boston cleans everything, effortlessly, completely. If there *were* a Bohemia, its members would indeed live on Beacon Hill, the most beautiful part of Boston and, like the older parts of most cities, fundamentally classless, providing space for the rich in the noble mansions and for the people with little money in the run-down alleys. For both of these groups the walled gardens of Beacon Hill, the mews, the coach houses, the river views, the cobblestone streets are a necessity and the yellow-brick, sensible structures of the Fenway—a plausible but unpoetical residential section

near the Art Museum—are poison. Espresso bars have sprung up, or rather dug down in basements, but no summer of wild Bohemia is ushered into town. This reluctance is due to the Boston legend and its endurance as a lost ideal, a romantic quest.

15   Something transcendental is always expected in Boston. There is, one imagines, behind the drapery on Mount Vernon Street a person of demo cratic curiosity and originality of expression, someone alas—and this is the tiresome Boston note—*well-born*. It is likely to be, even in imagination, a she, since women now and not the men provide the links with the old traditions. Of her, then, one expects a certain unprofessionalism, but it is not expected that she will be superficial; she is profoundly conventional in manner of life but capable of radical insights. To live in Boston means to seek some connection with this famous local excellence, the regional type and special creation of the city. An angry disappointment attends the romantic soul bent upon this quest. When the archaeological diggings do turn up an authentic specimen it will be someone old, nearly gone, "whom you should have known when she was young"—and still could hear.

16   The younger Bostonians seem in revolt against the old excellence, with its indulgent, unfettered development of the self. Revolt, however, is too active a word for a passive failure to perpetuate the ideal high-mindedness and intellectual effort. With the fashionable young women of Boston, one might just as well be on Long Island. Only in the nervous, shy, earnest women is there a lingering hint of the peculiar local development. Terrible *faux pas* are constantly being made by this reasonable, honorable person, followed by blushes and more false steps and explanations and the final blinking, retreating blush.

17   Among the men, the equivalent of the blushing, blurting, sensitive, and often "fine" woman, is a person who exists everywhere perhaps but nowhere else with such elaboration of type, such purity of example. This is the well-born failure, the amateur not by choice but from some fatal reticence of temperament. They are often descendants of intellectual Boston, odd-ball grandsons, charming and sensitive, puzzlingly complicated, living on a "small income." These unhappy men carry on their conscience the weight of unpublished novels, half-finished paintings, impossible historical projects, old-fashioned poems, unproduced plays. Their inevitable "small income" is a sort of dynastic flaw, like hemophilia. Much money seems often to impose obligations of energetic management; from great fortunes the living cells receive the hints of the possibilities of genuine power, enough to make some enormously rich Americans endure the humiliations and fatigues of political office. Only the most decadent and spoiled think of living in idleness on millions; but this notion does occur to the man afflicted with ten thousand a year. He will commit himself with a dreamy courage to whatever traces of talent he may have and live to see himself

punished by the New England conscience which demands accomplish-ments, duties performed, responsibilities noted, and energies sensibly used. The dying will accuses and the result is a queer kind of Boston inco-herence. It is literally impossible much of the time to tell what some of the most attractive men in Boston are talking about. Half-uttered witticisms, grave and fascinating obfuscations, points incredibly qualified, hesitations infinitely refined—one staggers about, charmed and confused, by the twi-light.

18   But this person, with his longings, connects with the old possibilities and, in spite of his practical failure, keeps alive the memory of the best days. He may have a brother who has retained the mercantile robustness of nature and easy capacity for action and yet has lost all belief in anything except money and class, who may practice private charities, but entertain profoundly trivial national and world views. A Roosevelt, Harriman, or Stevenson is impossible to imagine as a member of the Boston aristoc-racy; in Boston the vein of self-satisfaction and conservatism cuts too deeply. . . .

19   Harvard (across the river in Cambridge) and Boston are two ends of one mustache. Harvard is now so large and international it has altogether avoided the whimsical stagnation of Boston. But the two places need each other, as we knowingly say of a mismatched couple. Without the faculty, the visitors, the events that Harvard brings to the life here, Boston would be intolerable to anyone except genealogists, antique dealers, and those who find repletion in a closed local society. Unfortunately, Harvard, like Boston, has "tradition" and in America this always carries with it the risk of a special staleness of attitude, and of pride, incredibly and comically swollen like the traits of hypocrisy, selfishness, or lust in the old dramas. At Harvard some of the vices of "society" exist, of Boston society that is—ar-rogance and the blinding dazzle of being, *being at Harvard*.

20   The moral and social temptations of Harvard's unique position in American academic life are great and the pathos is seen in those young fac-ulty members who are presently at Harvard but whose appointments are not permanent and so they may be thrown down, banished from the be-atific condition. The young teacher in this position lives in a dazed state of love and hatred, pride and fear; their faces have a look of desperate yearn-ing, for they would rather serve in heaven than reign in hell. For those who are not banished, for the American at least, since the many distin-guished foreigners at Harvard need not endure these piercing and fascinat-ing complications, something of Boston seems to seep into their charac-ters. They may come from anywhere in America and yet to be at Harvard unites them with the transcendental, legendary Boston, with New England in flower. They begin to revere the old worthies, the houses, the paths trod by so many before, and they feel a throb of romantic sympathy for the directly-gazing portraits on the walls, for the old graves and old names in the Mount Auburn Cemetery. All of this has charm and may

even have a degree of social and intellectual value—and then again it may not. Devious parochialisms, irrelevant snobberies, a bemused exaggeration of one's own productions, pimple the soul of a man upholding tradition in a forest of relaxation, such as most of America is thought to be. Henry James's observation in his book on Hawthorne bears on this:

> . . . it is only in a country where newness and change and brevity of tenure are the common substance of life, that the fact of one's ancestors having lived for a hundred and seventy years in a single spot would become an element of one's morality. It is only an imaginative American that would feel urged to keep reverting to this circumstance, to keep analyzing and cunningly consider ing it.

21   If the old things of Boston are too heavy and plushy, the new either hasn't been born or is appallingly shabby and poor. As early as Thanksgiving, Christmas decorations unequaled for cheap ugliness go up in the Public Garden and on the Boston Common. Year after year, the city fathers bring out crèches and camels and Mother and Child so badly made and of such tasteless colors they verge on blasphemy, or would seem to do so if it were not for the equally dismal, although secular, little men blowing horns and the canes of peppermint hanging on the lamps. The shock of the first sight is the most interesting; later the critical senses are stilled as year after year the same bits are brought forth and gradually one realizes that the whole thing is a permanent exhibition.

22   Recently the dying downtown shopping section of Boston was to be graced with flowers, an idea perhaps in imitation of the charming potted geraniums and tulips along Fifth Avenue in New York. Commercial Boston produced a really amazing display: old, gray square bins, in which were stuck a few bits of yellowing, drying evergreen. It had the look of exhausted greenery thrown out in the garbage and soon the dust-bins were full of other bits of junk and discard—people had not realized or recognized the decorative hope and saw only the rubbishy result.

23   The municipal, civic backwardness of Boston does not seem to bother its more fortunate residents. For them and for the observer, Boston's beauty is serene and private, an enclosed, intense personal life, rich with domestic variation, interesting stuffs and things, showing the hearthside vitality of a Dutch genre painting. Of an evening the spirits quicken, not to public entertainment, but instead to the sights behind the draperies, the glimpses of drawing-rooms on Louisburg Square, paneled walls, and French chandeliers on Commonwealth Avenue, bookshelves and flower-filled bays on Beacon Street. Boston is a winter city. Every apartment has a fireplace. In the town houses, old persons climb steps without complaint, four or five floors of them, cope with the maintenance of roof and gutter, and survive the impractical kitchen and resign themselves to the useless parlors. This is life: the house, the dinner party, the charming gardens, one's high ceilings, fine windows, lacy grillings, magnolia trees, inside

shutters, glassed-in studios on the top of what were once stables, outlook on the "river side." Setting is serious.

24   When it is not serious, when a splendid old private house passes into less dedicated hands, an almost exuberant swiftness of deterioration can be noticed. A rooming house, although privately owned, is no longer in the purest sense a private house and soon it partakes of some of the reckless, ugly municipal neglect. The contrasts are startling. One of two houses of almost identical exterior design will have shining windows, a bright brass door-knocker, and its twin will show a "Rooms" sign peering out of dingy glass, curtained by those lengths of flowered plastic used in the shower bath. Garbage lies about in the alleys behind the rooming houses, discarded furniture blocks old garden gateways. The vulnerability of Boston's way of life, the meanness of most things that fall outside the needs of the upper classes are shown with a bleak and terrible fullness in the rooming houses on Beacon Street. And even some of the best houses show a spirit of mere "maintenance," which, while useful for the individual with money, leads to civic dullness, architectural torpor, and stagnation. In the Back Bay area, a voluntary, casual association of property owners exists for the purpose of trying to keep the alleys clean, the streets lighted beyond their present medieval darkness, and to pursue other worthy items of neighborhood value. And yet this same group will "protest" against the attractive Café Florian on Newbury Street (smell of coffee too strong!) and against the brilliantly exciting Boston Arts Festival held in the beautiful Public Garden for two weeks in June. The idea that Boston might be a vivacious, convenient place to live in is not uppermost in most residents' thoughts. Trying to buy groceries in the best sections of the Back Bay region is an interesting study in commercial apathy.

25   A great many of the young Bostonians leave town, often taking off with a sullen demand for a freer, more energetic air. And yet many of them return later, if not to the city itself, to the beautiful sea towns and old villages around it. For the city itself, who will live in it after the present human landmarks are gone? No doubt, some of the young people there at the moment will persevere, and as a reward for their fidelity and endurance will themselves later become monuments, old types interesting to students of what our colleges call American Civilization. Boston is defective, out-of-date, vain, and lazy, but if you're not in a hurry it has a deep, secret appeal. Or, more accurately, those who like it may make of its appeal a secret. The weight of the Boston legend, the tedium of its largely fraudulent posture of traditionalism, the disillusionment of the Boston present as a cultural force, make quick minds hesitate to embrace a region so deeply compromised. They are on their guard against falling for it, but meanwhile they can enjoy its very defects, its backwardness, its slowness, its position as one of the large, possible cities on the Eastern seacoast, its private, residential charm. They speak of going to New York and yet another season finds them holding back, positively enjoying the Boston life. . . .

26   . . . Outside it is winter, dark. The curtains are drawn, the wood is on the fire, the table has been checked, and in the stillness one waits for the guests who come stamping in out of the snow. There are lectures in Cambridge, excellent concerts in Symphony Hall, bad plays being tried out for the hungry sheep of Boston before going to the hungry sheep of New York. Arnold Toynbee or T. S. Eliot or Robert Frost or Robert Oppenheimer or Barbara Ward is in town again. The cars are double-parked so thickly along the narrow streets that a moving vehicle can scarcely maneuver; the pedestrians stumble over the cobbles; in the back alleys a cat cries and the rats, enormously fat, run in front of the car lights creeping into the parking spots. Inside it is cozy, Victorian, and gossipy. Someone else has *not* been kept on at Harvard. The old Irish "accommodator" puffs up stairs she had never seen before a few hours previously and announces that dinner is ready. A Swedish journalist is just getting off the train at the Back Bay Station. He has been exhausted by cocktails, reality, life, taxis, telephones, bad connections in New York and Chicago, pulverized by "a good time." Sighing, he alights, seeking old Boston, a culture that hasn't been alive for a long time . . . and rest.

Discussion Questions

1. Hardwick states in paragraph 2 that "all the American regions are breaking up." Can you think of cities other then Boston about which the same can be said?

2. Are Hardwick's reasons for Bostonians leaving their city valid? Why or why not? Do you find people in your own hometown leaving for similar or different reasons?

3. How much of the trouble Hardwick finds in Boston can be attributed to a legend that is impossible to live up to? Do you think that cities are obligated to live up to the legends with which they are associated? Explain your response.

4. Do you think Hardwick is justified in paragraph 25 when she states, "Boston is defective, out-of-date, vain, and lazy"? Why or why not?

5. Discuss the connections you see between E. B. White's description of Walden and Hardwick's description of Boston. How many of the changes the two authors find can be attributed to the nature of technology and growth?

I Don't Like New York in June

Anne Rivers Siddons

Anne Rivers Siddons was born in 1936. A graduate of Auburn University, she also attended the Atlanta School of Art. Before becoming a full-time writer in 1974, Siddons worked in advertising. A prolific writer, her novels include Heartbreak Hotel *(1976),* The House Next Door *(1978),* Fox's Earth *(1980),* Homeplace *(1987),* Peachtree Street *(1988),* King's Oak *(1990),* Outer Banks *(1991), and* Hill Towns*(1993), and* Downtown *(1994) . Her collection of essays, in which the following piece appears, is entitled* John Chancellor Makes Me Cry *(1975). In "I Don't Like New York in June," Siddons's description of a visit that she and her husband, Heyward, made to New York City provides ample evidence to support the title of her essay.*

1   On a day while we were in Princeton last June, before Reunion Week geared up, my husband and I went into New York for a flying visit. And wished we hadn't.

2   It had been precisely ten years since I had been to New York, but before that I'd visited often, staying with assorted city-struck friends in their impossibly cramped, cluttered, and overpriced cubbyholes in the East Eighties, sleeping on sofas and Hide-a-Beds and loving every hectic minute of it. It was the dream of all of us, stuck like yearning, iridescent flies in the amber of our Alabama college, to Go to New York when we graduated, but only a few of us did. In the late fifties, in the South, the distance to New York was measured in more than miles.

3   The New York to which we aspired never existed. It couldn't have. Nothing in it was real, and no subsequent visits ever breathed gritty, grimy life into it for those of us who didn't live there. It was a scale model built by Stanford White and Le Corbusier, threaded by shining streets from the MGM back lot. The people who lived in its Billy Baldwin-appointed apartments and worked in its Knoll-furnished offices (always advertising agencies and publishing houses) were Piper Laurie and Millie Perkins and Tony Franciosa and Cary Grant, if you needed an Older Man, or else Rona Jaffe had invented them. *The Best of Everything* was our field manual. Gordon Jenkins wrote the score.

4   I visited often enough then, in those pre-riot-and-rape days, to learn my way around the parts of New York that mattered to anyone I cared to know. The Eighties, where five underpaid sorority sisters who did not, after all, have Careers but only toiled as secretaries to underwriters, lived what had to be the Good Life in a one-bedroom apartment. There, in that badly painted, ostentatiously doormanned Xanadu, bullfight posters stood in for Billy Baldwin, but the address was good.

5   Central Park—the part with high curly bridges that was invariably photographed with Audrey Hepburn in blue jeans running through it.

Park-Fifth-Madison. The theater district, vaguely. The prescribed lap around the prescribed museums. One small area around Gramercy Park (I adored knowing you had to have a key to get into the park). I could eventually find my way to the Village, had been taken to Sutton Place, was fond of saying that Mary McCarthy made Tudor City fashionable with *The Group,* and was proud of myself for having ventured as far west as Columbus Circle to prowl through the Huntington Hartford.

6   It didn't occur to me that real people lived anywhere but my territorial Manhattan. I wouldn't have been interested in anybody who lived in the other four boroughs, didn't know about Long Island, sneered at the suburbs, and left midtown only once, when I took the wrong train and ended up somewhere near Carnarsie. To me, Brooklyn had a tree and a bridge.

7   But my ersatz Manhattan *was* a lovely place to visit, and so my memories of it were cherished, if celluloid: Watching the entire mounted patrol coming home two by two under the mist-haloed street lights one October evening. Flocks of birds—starling, I suppose—darting in luminous clouds around the top of the Empire State Building on a martini-enchanted June night. Standing in an April rain on the sidewalk outside McSorley's while my date had a beer inside, clutching his propitiary bunch of violets in white-gloved hands and finding nothing at all degrading about it. Talking to a man who turned out to be Robert Morse in P.J. Clarke's, drinking green beer in Costello's on St. Patrick's Day, having champagne with a peach in it at the Plaza (*Saratoga Trunk*-inspired champagne, canned peach). Dashing into Tiffany's as it closed in a new tweed suit from Bergdorf's to "pick up a little something for my hostess" (key ring). For years, I turned into Holly Golightly whenever my plane touched down at La Guardia.

8   Well knowing what usually happens to one's youthful Shangri-las when they are revisited, I should have been prepared. I should have suspected something when we learned that the ageless train that has always run from Princeton Junction to Penn Station—the one my husband remembers from his idyllic college years—didn't any more, with any regularity. Many people took the bus now, we were told, and it was only a nice, cool hour's ride straight into the New York Port Authority Terminal, where there was always a line of waiting cabs. So we dutifully bought our tickets on the nine-thirty bus to New York and went across the street to the bench in front of the main gate that is the bus stop to wait. It was nine-fifteen and we had a lunch date on Park. Plenty of time. No sweat.

9   Figuratively, anyway. At nine-fifteen in Princeton it was 92 degrees under a tree. I was dressed in what people who lunched on Park wore in my days there—little sleeveless linen dress, stockings, pumps. By the time the wayward bus coughed up to its stop at ten twenty-five, my pantyhose felt like a wet suit and my linen looked like used aluminum foil on a thawing chicken. We climbed aboard.

10   The bus windows were properly sealed to facilitate the air-conditioning that wasn't working. The driver was angry at having to stop for us and got angrier at each subsequent stop. They are legion between Princeton

and New York. All in towns that looked as though they had factories and mills that were at that moment violating the child labor laws. The towns of the Jersey flats are to me the saddest and seediest places I have ever seen, and the hottest. People who got on at the last stops along the route had to stand, and the lady who was standing next to my seat was sucking Certs, listening to a transistor playing "Honey," and poking my chin with a large, round plastic hatbox-thing that had a Caesar's Palace sticker on it. When I wriggled one foot out of its blue-and-white spectator pump, sweat had stained my foot blue. When I half rose to unwrinkle my linen behind, my sweat-slackened stocking foot slid around so that I had a blue ring around one entire ankle. It wasn't shaping up into any Gordon Jenkins day in New York.

11   Finally, we were disgorged into the maw of the Port Authority Terminal, which is as fearsome a place as I hope to encounter while living. A catacombs-like terminal area was spilling a lava of suburban types onto concrete aprons—nice little hatted ladies who'd brought their own E. J. Korvette shopping bags; vaguely middle-aged men in electric blue double-knits; young women in four-inch clogs and the varnished beehives and miniskirts of the late sixties; cool young black men in what I can only describe as pimp suits, with hard, measuring eyes; wiry young black women with the high, rolling gaits of Shetland ponies; one or two chic matrons with distaste ironed onto their faces; Heyward and me. The herd made for the terminal proper, where an arctic gust of public-smelling air-conditioning froze our steaming clothes to us in permanent ridges. Elbowed, jostled, and glared at in impersonal malice on all sides, I began to flinch.

12   This was no twilight-in-front-of-St.-Patrick's crowd. A young Puerto Rican was performing an eerie, slow-motion dance in a semicircle in front of a phone booth where no phone was, chanting to himself in high, sibilant island Spanish; his eyes were half-lidded and opaque, and he was smiling at his lost inner visions. An old man was slumped against a Keys-Made-While-U-Wait booth, asleep or drunk or ill or dead. He had soiled his pants. The key-maker was making keys and people were stepping over him and a cop down the arcade looked through him.

13   "Should we. . . ?"

14   "No."

15   Outside, where the taxi line waited, Port Authority veterans body-checked us away from cab after cab. In the last one, a driver with a tight, furious face fanned himself with a tabloid and listened to a talk show. Desperately knocking aside a small lady and her sullen teenaged daughter, we lunged at it, ripped open the door, scrambled in, and panted, "Park and Forty-seventh. Please."

16   "Whassamattercan'tyoureadthemuthuhfuckingoffdutysign?"

17   "It's not on," said Heyward, getting the flat, polite look on his face that means he's going to do battle even though he be slain for it.

18   I thought he probably was, and mewled smarmily, "Oh, that's all

right. We'll just wait for—"

19   "YOUR OFF-DUTY SIGN IS NOT ON AND WE WANT TO GO TO PARK AND FORTY-SEVENTH!" roared my husband.

20   "Muthuhfuckingsonofabitch," commented the driver, and clashed into gear and careened off across town.

21   It was after noon, and the traffic was hideous. The cab was plastered with stickers that read AMERICA—LOVE IT OR LEAVE IT and NIXON NOW, MORE THAN EVER. The plastic shield, designed, no doubt, to protect our driver's tender sensibilities from the dangerous, leftist likes of us, was opaque with grime, and the driver's neck had a carbuncle. He cursed monotonously and matter-of-factly and steadily, breaking his litany of choler only to shout perfunctory obscenities at other motorists, blow his horn, and thump on the side of his vehicle. I didn't really blame him. Every panel truck in Manhattan was double-parked along our route across town, effectively blocking any progress.

22   Approaching midtown, a shining cliff of a Lincoln just in front of us rammed the cab in front of it. Everything stopped. Horns started. The Lincoln's driver, a tanned, gray-frosted man in a silk suit got out and approached the other cab's driver, who was rolling down his window and turning a deep, dull red. The silk-suit man was an extra from *my* Manhattan; he looked like the Rector of Justin, and I was relieved to see that his type still existed. He looked into the cab's window and said in a satisfying bass Yale drawl, "I believe you were at fault."

23   "Go fuck yourself," said the cab's driver, uncoiling from his vehicle.

24   "Move that fucking thing!" roared our driver helpfully, leaning on his horn.

25   "I'll report you to the Hack Bureau," said the Rector of Justin, backing off slightly from his outraged adversary.

26   "I'll take you apart," said his driver, squaring off to do so.

27   "Go fuck yourself," the Rector of Justin said, and got back into his Lincoln and locked the door.

28   "Fuck you," said the cabbie, and got back into his cab and growled away.

29   "Fuck everybody!" shouted our driver creatively, and he blew his horn, and we were off again.

30   "If everybody in New York did that when somebody told them to, it would look like something Bosch painted," I told Heyward, reeling from the exchange. When we crawled out on our corner and Heyward tipped our driver, I think he advised us to perform the same anatomical impossibility upon ourselves.

31   We ran into Saks to pick up a gift for our hostess in Princeton. Saks is—or used to be—a great font of civility and comfort to me, and I approached the inevitable black-dressed, duchess-faced chatelaine of the department with relief and alacrity.

32   "I'm looking for something for a country patio—an Italian cachepot or a pottery box or something," I said, "for around fifteen dollars. I'd like

it in green and—"

33   "Pottery is in another department," snapped the Eighteenth Duchess of Saks. "All this is Limoges. I have to go to lunch now." And she did.

34   "Mmf-you," said my husband to her retreating ramrod back. And we left and walked across the street to keep our lunch date.

35   We were lunching with an old friend, a prep-school classmate of my husband's who is a long-time Manhattanite. He had visited us often in Atlanta, but we'd never called on him on his native turf. As he steered us out on Park into the lunchtime throng, he suffered a sea change into something rich and strange indeed. The amiable, graceful, urbane Charles I knew became a feral battering ram, cutting through the clotted crowd like a cruising shark. He towed me along behind him with a steel hand on my arm. "For Chrissake, how long has it been since you've been to New York?" he barked at me. "Only a damned fool would bring a handbag into the city. Every woman over twelve carries her money in her underwear, if she wears any. Give me that thing." And this shining six-foot son of St. Albans and Harvard went bruising down Forty-seventh Street clutching my dainty patent envelope to his chest and enjoining pedestrians he jostled to fuck themselves.

36   "New York is a summer festival," I quavered at him, hoping to inject a note of levity into the Bataan-like march to lunch.

37   "New York is a goddam muggers' convention and don't you forget it," he flared.

38   At lunch, the Charles I knew was back, lighting my cigarettes and nodding affably to his publishing peers and trading courtesies with the headwaiter, who fell on his neck the instant we entered and installed us at an impeccable banquette that did not, for the first time on one of my New York visits, back up to the kitchen. He crooned over us and suggested the ubiquitous striped sea bass that all of New York seems to lunch on. I had three Bloody Marys in rapid succession and felt better.

39   Lunch over, we trudged back to Charles's office on Park, dropped him off, and stood for a moment on a corner, sniffing the wind. Things were looking up. I had borrowed the key to the ladies' room from Charles's enameled secretary and washed my face and hands, scrubbed most of the manacle-like ring of blue shoe dye off my ankle, squirted on a reviving splash of Vent Vert, and combed my hair. At three o'clock, the shadows of encircling buildings had cooled Park a little, and the crowds had thinned down to good-looking women whisking out of stores and restaurants and good-looking men getting out of cabs with attaché cases. Only an occasional young, lounging, sleepy-faced felon had ventured, barracuda-like, out of his territory to stalk his prey. This was more like *my* Manhattan.

40   "Want to stay in town and see a show?" asked Heyward, basking in the sunlit edge of the jungle. And at that moment, we witnessed our first purse-snatching.

41   I'm sure it wasn't much of a purse-snatching, as such things go: a rapier-quick sortie by a blind-faced child—he couldn't have been more than twelve—at a woman coming out of Saks's revolving door across the street, up to her eyes in muted, tweed-patterned Saks boxes. He had her shoulder bag and was around the corner and gone before her boxes hit the sidewalk and her mouth opened. She never did scream. "Somebody just took my purse," she said to people passing on the sidewalk, in a funny, small Connecticut voice. "I just had my purse snatched." Nobody broke stride, but one man did turn to look at her. She picked up her boxes and went back into the cool, dark maw of Saks.

42   "Did you see that?" asked Heyward, mildly.

43   "Yes," I said. "I want to go back to Princeton." And we did.

44   Coming back on the plane to Atlanta after Reunion Week, I told my husband about my Manhattan, and the things I remembered, and how New York had gone unalterably and certainly to hell, and how I would probably never go back. "Atlanta has its problems," I said prissily, "but the whole *city* isn't a damned jungle. People don't curse you as a matter of course. People don't try to *kill* you at lunchtime."

45   We claimed our baggage, staggered with it out of the terminal, and lunged for the door of the last cab parked in the hack line under the canopy.

46   "Whassamatter," said the driver, "can'tyoureadthemuthuhfuckingoff-dutysign?"

Discussion Questions

1. Do you think that Siddons sets herself up for being disappointed; that is, was the root of her problem wanting and expecting the "dreams" she had of New York City instead of the reality of the place? Explain your response.

2. Throughout her essay, Siddons reels off names of specific places in New York (e.g., Sutton Place, McSorley's, the Plaza). Were you put off by this practice, or did it engage you in the essay? Discuss the effectiveness of this technique.

3. Describe what you learned about New York from Siddons's visit there. Do you think it accurately represents the city? Why or why not?

4. In what ways does humor balance the frustration Siddons experiences in New York? Why is this important?

5. What do you know about Siddons from reading her essay? How does she reveal her true self in the piece? Do you like the person you meet in the essay? Why or why not?

Houston Hide-and-Seek

Phillip Lopate

*B*orn *in 1943 in New York, Phillip Lopate earned his B.A. degree at Columbia University. He is the author of* Being with Children *(1975);* Confessions of Summer *(1979); and* Against Joie de Vivre *(1989), in which the following essay appears. The editor of the* Art of the Personal Essay *(1994), his work also has appeared in* Best American Essays, The Paris Review, Village Voice, Columbia Review, Yale Literary Review, *and the Pushcart Prize annuals. A recipient of Guggenheim and National Endowment for the Arts fellowships, Lopate is an associate professor at the University of Houston. He also teaches at Columbia University's graduate writing program. In the following essay, Lopate recalls his first impressions of living in Houston and the "bifocular vision" he developed living there.*

1   When I first moved to Texas in 1980 to teach at the University of Houston, I was struck by how many Houstonians asked me right away what I thought of the place; and then I would see their faces start to flinch in preparation for my not "getting it." Invariably I tried to frame a positive answer, to set them at ease, because I genuinely did like Houston, or the little I knew of it. I was, in fact, determined to like Houston. It seemed boorish to react like the all-too-typical New Yorker who keeps saying, "You call these bagels? You call this an Italian restaurant?" I knew I had not moved down to Houston in search of the perfect bagel. There would be enough local dishes and amenities to delight me, if I gave them the chance, and I quickly saw that when I expressed myself as even moderately well disposed toward their town, Houstonians would respond with a generosity, hospitality, and kindness I had not encountered anywhere else.

2   As I came to know Houston better, I began to get anxious watching visitors and new arrivals frame their own answers to the Houstonian's patient question, What do you think of our city? Often I was embarrassed to hear the newcomer's reply loaded with factual distortion, simplistic clichés, and superiority. But I was equally nonplussed at the Houstonian's grave, gentle nod of seeming agreement. The other side of the Texas-sized boast is a reserve, if not a kind of self-effacing modesty. One evening I asked a dear friend of mine—third-generation Houstonian, sixth-generation Texan—why she had not corrected the fatuous misstatements of several intellectual transients talking about her city at a dinner party we had both attended. Her reply was a weary, resigned "Why bother?" I wondered if this refusal to correct the newcomer's errors might be not just a case of good manners—native Houstonians have the finest manners—but something more aristocratically scornful as well. These people think we are fools, so let the truth be our secret and leave them to their own pitiful ignorance.

3   I have become enough of a Houstonian that now, when I go back to

New York for a season, I get enraged listening to the idiotic stereotypes that Manhattanites have of Houston. I never fail to defend its high level of civilization; then I return to the Magnolia City and have to do the reverse when Houstonians start in on their New York-hating routines. During the Mets-Astros baseball playoffs a few years ago, my divided loyalties made me feel like a counterspy wherever I turned. However, this very perspective (bifocular, émigré, divided) may allow me to shed some light on the mysteries of Houston, since the city now has many residents like myself in its midst, people who originated elsewhere and remain on the fence of geographical commitment.

4   My arrival in Houston, during the record heat of July 1980 (you may recall the thousands of chicks who died in their incubators), occurred in the midst of an economic boom. It was a giddy, heady, can-do atmosphere; funding seemed to exist for every new idea; skyscrapers were going up by the dozen; the art world was flourishing; and the residential real estate market was so lush that people claimed even a retarded Realtor could make a fortune here. Every time the price of oil went up a dime a new crop of millionaires was birthed. Having fled New York, which had just escaped a bankruptcy scare by laying off teachers and other municipal workers by the thousands, I could not help but be enticed by this atmosphere of easy money. Not that a writer ever hopes to cash in on such wealth, but one can at least enjoy the good life by subliminal proximity.

5   At the same time, I was a little put off by all the boosterish rhetoric I heard. Houston was billing itself as the City of the Future, the one that all others would have to emulate. These were the days when the words "world-class city" were flung around like rice at a wedding. Either Houston had just arrived on the international stage as a "world-class city," or it merely needed a (fill in the blanks: first-class opera house/mass transit system/new convention center/major Picasso from his cubist period) to become one. All this sounded, I'm sorry, rather dumb and yokel-like to me, because when a metropolis has achieved the status of a great world city—Paris, London, New York, Tokyo, Berlin, Beijing, Mexico City—everyone knows it and there is no need to keep acting as though one more item would push it over the top. Besides, this fuss to become a world-class city struck me as too outer-directed, too desperate to catch up, too futuristic without showing enough love for what Houston already had and was. (As it happens, Houston has since gotten its opera house, convention center, Picasso, and voter approval for a mass rail system—and the place still feels the same.)

6   Part of this hysteria to shed the city's more modest beginnings by trying to purchase "class" led to a kind of blue-chip approach in cultural decisions, a way of playing it safe that has, paradoxically, often resulted in Houston being taken for a ride. Again and again, the city has gone after the most established, distinguished names in the arts, with results that resemble every other provincial city on the make. Take, for example, Houston's public sculpture, entertaining in its way, but tame and pre-

dictable: one Henry Moore, one Dubuffet, one Miró, one Oldenburg, one Beverly Pepper, and so on down the line. Need a big, prestigious corporate architect? Hire I. M. Pei, of course. Hence the boringly correct Texas Commerce Center. A sculpture garden designer? Who else but Isamu Noguchi? The result is an uneasy cross between rock garden "retreat" and corporate plaza, which almost no one uses, set on a site crying for human movement. Maybe it would have been better to commission a provocative younger artist on the rise than to have approached a master in his doddering years, or one whose practice is so big he farms out most of it to underlings. When the Museum of Fine Arts needed a new wing they went after the best architect money could buy, Mies van der Rohe. The first austere glass wall Mies designed may have been top-notch, I wasn't around to see it; all I know is that in the museum's next expansion, which swallowed up the first, they have gone to the Miesian well once too often. The curved, band-shell facade we live with today is not thrilling design, Miesian or otherwise. The interior is a different story; yet one becomes adjusted even to the lunkish exterior after a while, and to cherish it for its very familiarity.

7   This is part of what I mean by the bifocular vision I've developed toward Houston. My aesthetic response seems to consist in tenderness for what's there, chagrin for what isn't. Sometimes one can come to find lovable in Houston what in another context might appear less so. Several years back I was showing an English literary critic around town, and I took him to the Shamrock Hotel for lunch, since I loved their cheeseburgers. As the Shamrock confronted us, this very cosmopolitan, well-traveled gentleman said, "My God, what an ugly building!" I was pained. He did not understand—how could he?—the significance of that very building on that particular site. Not that I'd forgotten that my own response on first seeing it had been somewhat similar. But over the years I had become so attached to that improbable step-backed cliff looming up and anchoring the neighborhood around the Medical Center; so fond of its goofy lemon-and-lime color and faded-fancy lobby shops and Olympic pool amid cabanas and palm trees; so aware of its historical meaning to Houstonians—the hotel's wildcatter builder, Glenn McCarthy; its spectacular opening in 1949, the bands that broadcast from the Shamrock nationwide when it was all the rage; the rites of passage round the pool for generations of Houston adolescents (the girls whose families could not get into the restricted country clubs would form desperate crushes on the lifeguards, and then meet their safer future husbands; here also, Air France, which used to lodge its stewardesses and pilots, providing an informal beauty pageant, fondly remembered by the locals, of the latest maillots and monokinis, and the first shocked glimpse of men's bikini briefs)—that I would almost have died at that moment rather than see it go. Little did I anticipate that I would soon be marching in a futile protest rally to save the Shamrock. That's when you know you love a town, when you start mourning the way it savages itself. . . .

8   I am, if not Houston proud, then Houston fond. Must our chests swell with pride in order for us to love a place? The affection I have for Houston collects around certain street corners, landscapes, cicada sounds, atmospheres, many of which have nothing to do with civic pride *per se*. If I tell you that I am moved by the chastened afternoon light in February, on a day of scattered clouds, as it bounces through the crape myrtle trees and onto the white clapboard houses with their subtropical peeling paint jobs, it's not something I expect to see in a Chamber of Commerce brochure. Equally unusable is the fact that I love to ride my bike through the Vietnamese neighborhood downtown, around Tuam and Main, past the Saigon Cafe with its beaded curtain and extra-strong coffee and tables occupied by serious young Asian men in white shirts, past the upstairs nightclubs with their melancholy Vietnamese pop chanteuses, the apothecary shops and groceries with their consonant-clotted signs, all that homesick re-creation of Indochina mushrooming for a few blocks and then disappearing into the weeds, as mysterious as the old dry-cleaning establishment nearby that, for some reason, is housed in what looks like a Greek temple.

9   There is something funky and moody about Houston's allure. It has to do with the way surprises crop up in the middle of nowhere: a beautifully tended front garden next door to a tumbledown shack; a house made of beer cans; a stunning Mexican-style apartment court like the Isabella on decaying lower Main Street; a glass-bricked, art deco printing plant near deserted warehouses and railroad tracks on the outskirts of town. (Sometimes it feels as though three fourths of this city lies at the edge of town.) It's an aesthetic of grace notes amidst emptiness; mirage and discontinuity. No matter how much they build up Houston, it will always resemble to me a warm smile with missing teeth. One reason is that it didn't grow up tightly and logically like other cities, which spread block by block in dense concentric rings, but kept jumping miles away from the center, establishing speculative outposts and overoptimistically expecting in-fill to come later. On the one hand, I regret Houston's refusal to play the game more like traditional European capitals, since there is a certain urbane synergism that can only be achieved when a metropolis is dependably dense, continuous, and citylike for miles and miles. On the other hand, as Kenneth Frampton has noted, "Given the distributive capacity of the freeway it is highly unlikely that we will ever return to the dense pattern of the traditional city." Besides, in an odd way I have come to enjoy the spaciness (in both senses) of this place. There is a weightless, eerie, floating quality about Houston, which comes partly from its decentralized clumps of skyscrapers rising with capricious verticality from the interminable flat horizon. Houston has the split personality of wanting to be both a big city and a small town, with backyard and lawn for every citizen; and the resulting schizoid contradictions of scale shouldn't, but do, form an oddly comforting meditational ground.

10   Driving along Kirby Avenue late at night—a nondescript nowhere

corridor with billboards and fast-food stands and darkness, a way to get from one place to another but without much profile in itself—you are sucked in, as with so much of Houston, invited farther and farther along with no real opposition, nothing to bounce off of, until you notice that the place you're sucked into is your own inner self. Somewhere, always just beyond reach, is the city, all that flat, exploding, diffuse, strip shopping center galaxy, outside, but never bigger than, one's car window. The automobile is a moving monk's cell, it forces you back on your thoughts, while only marginally attending the vaguely urban streets. "Perhaps only through a kind of inattention, the most benevolent form of betrayal, is one faithful to a place," writes architect Aldo Rossi. If so, Houston invites fidelity; it is a strangely nonimposing environment. . . .

11   Houston is perceived by the outside world as a thoroughly modern environment, a sterile mélange of concrete and glass, so that people who have never been here are surprised when you tell them that, first, it is an exorbitantly verdant place, and second, that it retains much that is old. For myself, who am by nature attached more to the past than the present, this evidence of the old is very healing. I keep trying to root out the vestiges of old Houston, to understand what it was like before I came. My archaeological itch has taken me to the various cemeteries around town, where I stare at headstones and fantasize about the days when people routinely picnicked among the graves if the weather was nice; it has taken me through the charming old residential neighborhoods like the Montrose, the Heights, the Binz, Southampton, MacGregor Drive—which comprise for me the true heart of Houston, with their wonderfully diverse stock of vernacular bungalows, split-level ranch houses, and Bauhaus-style cottages made elegant or cozy by their owners' loving touches; it has taken me into the old tumbledown wards and the new ethnic areas in search of a polyglot, international Houston; it has taken me into the orderly, regulated suburbs like Kingwood, where clotheslines are forbidden and where the American Dream has been achieved to a degree that scares the hell out of me; and into the abandoned suburbs far beyond Loop 610,[1] where the American Dream suddenly stopped in its tracks and ran out on its mortgage. In a vain effort to grasp firsthand the city's economy, I have ridden around the obscure area of the Ship Channel, whose construction sixty years ago catapulted Houston over Galveston into one of the major ports in North America (a fact one so often forgets, even living here); out by the oil fields where mechanical grasshoppers paw the ground; and through the

---

1   A belt highway, Loop 610 divides the older, inner city from the annexed suburbs. I am partial to life within the Loop, where the concentration of cultural institutions, downtown business district, and old neighborhoods connotes a life-style as well as an address—Manhattan might be a rough analogy—while what I would facetiously call Outer Loopovia refers to all that *terra incognita* (to me) of sprawling suburban subdivisions. Demographic figures show the population of Houston shifting more and more outside the Loop, which presents special problems for preserving and rejuvenating the old historical core of the city.

enormous Medical Center, a virtual walled empire of Disease (health care, not the oil business, is Houston's largest employer). But riding around and imagining can teach you only so much, and the history of Houston is not that easy to come by. This is not a city that wears its past on its sleeve. Quite the contrary, it is an amnesiac city, one that keeps forgetting its intriguing antecedents in a headlong rush to embrace the shock of the new (or the *schlock* of the new, like Jean-Michel Jarre's laser light show during Texas Sesquicentennial Year).

12   In the City of the Future, even native Houstonians fall into a state that has become predominantly urban but refuses to recognize the fact, has long been caught in the contradictions of that denial. The creation of public space is after all the most self-consciously urban act a municipality can undertake. It signifies a city's maturation, through the recognition of its responsibilities to the public to exist as a collectivity. Houston is often spoken of as an adolescent: the question is whether this immaturity is a phase (albeit a protracted one) or a permanent personality trait.

13   Some have argued that older cities had more of a need for good public space (as well as cafes, pubs, clubs, and community halls), because people's homes were generally less comfortable. In offering its citizens a much higher standard of domestic comfort, this argument goes, Houston represents a new type of suburbanized city where private convenience reduces the necessity, and the yearning, for public interaction. Perhaps, though I can't believe that the political vitality and conviviality of urban areas are not somehow diminished in the process. Still, most Houstonians do seem at peace with their city, find it reasonably easy to navigate, and don't seem to feel the same ache of placelessness that I, as a transplanted New Yorker, intermittently experience. For instance, I can't help noticing the oddity of two major thoroughfares crossing each other without anything more dramatic than a 7-Eleven convenience store and a gas station to mark the juncture. It seems to me that major intersections should be commemorated by an intensification of city life—a department store, a big movie theater, a dance hall, a public square or park, *something*—but Houstonians do not seem to share this uneasiness. Each Friday and Saturday night I look at the cars piling into the junction of Montrose and Westheimer streets, drawn by the magnetic attractions of these crossroads, and I think, Wouldn't it be better for these young people to have something to *do* once they got there, besides honk their horns and participate in gridlock? But no, they seem to like to sit bumper to bumper, perhaps entertaining the fantasy of picking up some cuties in the next car. Who knows?

14   The problem with looking at Houston from a strictly urbanistic perspective is that one inevitably falls into the trap of judging it by the cherished traditional values of urban form (real streets to walk in, real public spaces to be in). By these standards Houston must be seen as a failure, even while they ignore the degree to which it seems to work on its own terms. On the other hand, the proclamation of local champions to "Let

Houston be Houston" has a smug Panglossian ring and dodges responsibility for correcting the very real deficiencies of the place. If you ask me, Houston will never become a great, "world-class" city. But it's an intriguing, evocative, comfortable, one-of-a-kind place with plenty of surprises. So it seems that once again I'm parked at the intersection between Tenderness and Chagrin, where I'll leave it alone for the present.

Discussion Questions

1. Why do you think people resort to "idiotic stereotypes" of cities, especially when they resent others stereotyping their own places of residence?

2. In paragraph 7, Lopate uses the term "bifocular vision" to describe his view of Houston. Has there been a time when you had a bifocular vision of a place where you lived? Describe it so that others can see the dual vision.

3. Lopate describes Houston in paragraph 9 as "a warm smile with missing teeth." Given what Lopate has shared about the city, do you find that a fitting image? Explain your response.

4. In paragraph 11, Lopate states that the "evidence of the old is very healing" and explains that he keeps "trying to root out the vestiges of old Houston, to understand what it was like before I came." Do you think Lopate is typical of other residents in his wanting to know the history of a place? To what extent do *you* find comfort in knowing the background of the place where you live?

5. What exactly in Lopate's description of Houston allows you to see the city through his eyes? Did you have a similar reaction to it? If so, why? If not, why not?

Disneyland

William Zinsser

*B*orn in 1922, William Zinsser has worked as a columnist for Look *magazine,* Life *magazine, and* The New York Times. *He has also taught at Yale University. Zinsser's numerous publications include* Pop Goes America *(1963),* The Lunacy Boom *(1970),* Blair and Ketchum's Country Journal *(1979),* Writing with a Word Processor *(1983),* On Writing Well *(1991), and* American Places: A

Writer's Pilgrimage to 15 of This Country's Most Visited and Cherished Sites (1992), in which the following essay appears. Zinsser has also edited six books on the art and craft of writing biography, memoir, religious writing, political novels, writing for children, and travel writing. In "Disneyland," Zinsser examines the fascination Americans have with the landscape of fantasy.

1   When I first called Disneyland and was put on hold, the canned music I got was "When You Wish Upon a Star." It made my day, or at least that two minutes of it. Of all the affable songs that ran through the Walt Disney movies I grew up on, none conveyed with such assurance—not even "Some Day My Prince Will Come," from *Snow White and the Seven Dwarfs*—the Disney message of infinite possibility. When you wished upon a star, the song said, it didn't matter who you were; anything your heart desired would come true. Jiminy Cricket sang it in the opening scene of *Pinocchio,* 50 years ago, and in 1991 it was still on the job, epitomizing not only Disneyland but its surrounding homeland of southern California, world capital of make-believe.

2   It was to that far-off Eldorado that a young man named Cecil B. DeMille came from New York in 1913 on an exploring trip, dispatched by his partners—Jesse L. Lasky and Samuel Goldfish, who later changed his name to Goldwyn—in a newly formed film-producing company. Their first picture was *The Squaw Man,* and they needed a rural site that they could populate with cowboys and Indians. DeMille found an old barn with some fruit trees and chicken coops in a drowsy section of Los Angeles called Hollywood, and he proposed to Lasky that they rent the barn and an acre of land as their production center.

3   "O.K.," Lasky wired back, "but be careful."

4   That may have been the last time that restraint was urged on any of the moguls who founded "Hollywood," one of the most famous civilizations that man has built, a synonym in every corner of the world for glamour and wish fulfillment. Goldwyn would become the "G" of M-G-M, the mightiest dream factory of them all, and the second "M," Louis B. Mayer, would impose on the colony an almost religious belief in the happy ending and the punished sin. I was reared on the movies that were spun out of that factory, and when I grew up and toured the studios as a writer in the twilight of their golden age, in the 1950s, I saw the sets that had once transported me to distant lands and dynasties. I saw the Middle Kingdom pylons from *The Egyptian* and the medieval castle from *Prince Valiant* and the Siamese court from *The King and I.* I saw Caligula's Rome and Napoleon's Paris and Disraeli's London and Diamond Jim Brady's New York and Wyatt Earp's Dodge City. I saw the columns of Tara and the train that finished off Greta Garbo in *Anna Karenina.* I saw the Chinese village from *The Good Earth* and the picket-fenced street where Andy

Hardy lived. Huddled on the back lot, the ghostly sets waited to be reanimated by the rustle of costumed extras and the director's cry of "Action!"

5   Instead the sounds that were heard were the sounds of demolition. The founding moguls died, the back lots were sold off to developers, and a new breed of independent producers began to forge a new Hollywood, where agents would be quoted more often than stars, where studios would be bought and sold like junk bonds, and where the movies that did get produced were not made according to the gospel of Louis B. Mayer. Hollywood as the purveyor of happy dreams was shutting down. But 27 miles to the south, in Anaheim, on a rural acreage not unlike the one that DeMille and Lasky and Goldfish bought in 1913 to start it all, another dream merchant was about to take over the franchise.

6   Walt Disney first talked in the early 1940s about building a "magical little park" next to his movie studio in Burbank. It would cover eight acres and would feature pony rides, train rides, "singing waterfalls" and statues of Mickey Mouse, Donald Duck and other Disney cartoon figures with whom tourists could pose for pictures. He wanted to create something different in entertainment parks, having found as a father trying to entertain his young daughters that existing parks were "dirty, phony places, run by tough-looking people." His plans were halted by World War II, and when they were revived a decade later they had outgrown the small tract in Burbank, reaching a level of aspiration that was unheard of in America and unwelcomed by its banks. Bankers were not persuaded that a family park called Disneyland was what American families were waiting for.

7   "Dreams offer too little collateral," Walt later said, explaining the banks' aversion, and to raise the money he and his brother Roy did the traditional borrowing against their life insurance and selling of treasured assets that are the stuff of American capitalist legend. They bought 180 acres of orange groves in Anaheim, began "imagineering" the new kind of theme park they had in mind, cleared the land, built their Sleeping Beauty Castle and their Rocket to the Moon and their fantasy villages and rivers and rides, and opened on July 17, 1955. More than 300 million people have since paid their way in.

8   Thus Disney dreams were proved to be prime collateral after all, and in the 1970s they financed the orgy of land acquisition and construction in Florida that created Walt Disney World and Epcot Center. But Anaheim was where the brothers first tried out their idea on the American people and found that they had struck a deep psychic need. Disneyland, not Walt Disney World, was the true icon—carved, like Mount Rushmore, out of virgin America—and that's where I went next, flying to an airport so aptly named for Orange County, John Wayne Airport, that just landing there made me feel better. Walt and the Duke would watch over me and see that all my endings were happy.

9   The psychic need that Disneyland fills is the need to be whisked away to any time and place except present-day America. Being transported—on

mechanical rides or on the wings of imagination—is the essence of the park. Its central metaphor, anchoring all the other contraptions of escape, is the old-fashioned Main Street that constitutes its entrance. It looks the way we like to think America looked in its late-Victorian age of innocence, or at least the way Disney chose to reimagine his boyhood town of Marceline, Missouri, and as soon as I saw its genial facades and storefronts—mansard roofs with red-white-and-blue bunting, ice cream parlors and candy palaces and penny arcades—I gladly let myself sink into the warm bath of that turn-of-the-century world. Given a choice of turning centuries, there was no choice; Disney's late 1890s were a far nicer place than my 1990s, which I had left just outside the main gate—a vast tundra of asphalt, parked cars, tourist buses and sightseer hotels. Greater Anaheim was greater nowhere.

10   I began my visit by taking a ride on the old-fashioned steam train that leaves from an old-fashioned brick station at the head of Main Street. Hanging on the wall of the station was a French barometer in an ornate Victorian frame, and I wasn't surprised to see that its needle was at *très sec,* safely beyond *variable* and well past *grande pluie* and *tempête.* There is no *pluie* in Disneyland. Nor is there a speck of dirt, as I noticed when I got back to Main Street. The pavement is hospital clean, and even the horses that draw the horse-drawn trolleys leave no evidence behind. I stopped to look in the window of the clockmaker and the Blue Ribbon Bakery and the Silhouette Studio and the Market House ("Jellies and Jams") and then went up onto a turn-of-the-century front porch and sat on one of its turn-of-the-century chairs and watched the day's arriving crowds as they hurried by.

11   Actually they *strolled* by, their gait subliminally set by the music, all of which was in three-quarter time. One after another the gently lilting waltzes came and went—"East Side, West Side," "On a Bicycle Built for Two," "I'm in Love with the Man in the Moon"—and I realized that no other time signature in music is so suggestive of good old summer pleasures, of picnics in a grove and rowboats on a lake. Three-quarter time is an intravenous drip of yesteryear. Sometimes I heard competing music from the coin-operated nickelodeon in the Penny Arcade across the street, but it never violated the emotional codes—it was ragtime piano or steam calliope, ingenuous and jaunty, with no harsh edges, just as the colors of the buildings had no hard tones. They were pastel yellows and greens and gray-blues, or, at the loudest, the pink of a strawberry ice cream soda. The saleswomen in the shops wore peppermint-striped shirtwaists, high at the neck, and tied their hair up in ribbons—definitely not "tough-looking people." The men wore vests and suspenders and boaters, and occasionally four of them came gliding by on a bicycle built for four. It was an old Alice Faye Technicolor musical brought to life, and what it said as an architectural statement was that Main Street circa 1900 was America's lost paradise, recoverable only in facsimile.

12   I thought about that architecture, that Disney haute nostalgia. Hadn't I seen it somewhere else? I had. I had seen it replicated in upscale shopping malls in upscale towns across America—towns like Aspen, Colorado,

and Naples, Florida. I remembered from a visit to Naples that the twin ideas of "postmodern" (reinventing the past) and "retro" (re-creating the past) have merged there to form the collective taste. Though taste is seldom easy to define, Naples, it's safe to say, is united in the belief that yesterday was wonderful. Proof of that homage was a six-block complex of 110 stores, restaurants and art galleries that were as aggressively charming as the set of *Meet Me in St. Louis*. I also remembered a visit to the Georgetown section of Washington, D.C. Walking along its main street, admiring its authentic Federal facades, I turned through an archway and found myself in a vast turn-of-the-century world. It was a three-story mall called Georgetown Park, with every *faux* gaslight and lamppost and storefront in place—a pure appropriation, I realized, of Disneyland. I wondered whether this influence is taught in architecture schools. Just as America's postwar architects inflicted on our landscape the glass boxes of their revered Bauhaus modernism, their successors have taken their inspiration from Anaheim Victorian, building mini-Disneylands across the country to soothe our worries away. Thus Main Street America comes full circle. Though we have eagerly abandoned our actual Main Streets for the new mall out on the strip, we don't have to give up the *idea* of Main Street. Thanks to Disney, we can still make believe that the good old days never went away.

13   At the far end of Main Street, Disneyland fans out into other "lands," including Fantasyland, Frontierland, Adventureland, Tomorrowland and New Orleans Square—each of them, like Main Street, a perfect amalgam of preformed ideas and memories. Fantasyland, which I reached by crossing a moat perpetually washed by a dulcet rendition of "When You Wish Upon a Star," was "a timeless land of enchantment," as Walt Disney once called it, invoking two of the park's operative words. Many of its attractions have "enchanted" in their name, and what makes Fantasyland "timeless" is that it is a tapestry of images that go back to the fairy tales of our early childhood, which in turn go back to folk myth. Fantasyland could have been built by Bavarian elves, not Anaheim carpenters. The turreted Sleeping Beauty Castle was every castle from every illustrated storybook about princes, princesses, wicked stepsisters and enchanted toads, and the town that lies at its feet, with its half-timbered stucco houses and weathered beams, was every medieval European village from the tales of Grimm to the opera *Hansel and Gretel*.

14   No less familiar to me were the neighboring principalities of Adventureland and Frontierland, where I went next. Adventureland was all-purpose exotic: the South Seas of Maugham and Gauguin and Jack London, with an Amazon cruise and appropriate jungle drums thrown in. Every Pacific culture from Melanesia to Maui had been rifled for an identifying artifact—tribal masks and tiki statues, tapa cloth and thatched roofs, Hawaiian music and bamboo porch railings—and the resulting town was the generic "away" of every dreamer who dreams of getting away from it all, just as Frontierland was the generic Old West that Hollywood has

planted in our minds as the real Old West, instantly recognizable for its trading posts and cowboy outfitters and wooden sidewalks. The genius of Disneyland is that it has no shocks of nonrecognition; we are safely cushioned against change. Walt Disney wasn't Wilbur Wright, or Gutzon Borglum, or Thoreau; he was at the other end of the American rainbow from those peppery individualists. He was Mr. Mainstream, a boy who never entirely grew up and who intuitively knew that the rest of us haven't entirely grown up either.

15　　I spent my two days at Disneyland taking rides. I took a bobsled through the Matterhorn and a submarine under the Polar Ice Cap and a rocket jet to the Cosmic Vapor Curtain. I took Peter Pan's Flight, Mr. Toad's Wild Ride, Alice's Scary Adventures and Pinocchio's Daring Journey. I took a steamboat and a jungle boat. I took the Big Thunder Mountain railroad to coyote country and the Splash Mountain roller coaster to Critter Country. I took a "Pirates of the Caribbean" ride (black cats and buried treasure) and a "Haunted Mansion" ride (creaking hinges and ghostly laughter). I took monorails and Skyways and Autopias and PeopleMovers. More precisely, those rides took *me:* up and down and around sudden corners and through dark tunnels and over rooftops, and all I had to do was sit back and let whatever conveyance I was sitting in do the driving. I had no desire to be at the wheel myself. In Disneyland that primal American urge—the urge to drive—gets suspended, replaced by the still more primal urge to be eternally transported to timeless lands of enchantment.

16　　I didn't even mind waiting for the rides. The lines had been shrewdly configured in bends and loops to look shorter than they were, and the crowds moved along without impatience, the children cheerful and well behaved. Parents with very small children had dutifully left their strollers in one of the areas designated for "Stroller Parking": ultimate tidiness. The crowds were also very white. Although I noticed a number of Mexican-American and Asian tourists, I saw only one black family in two days. American blacks, I suspect, know that it will take more than wishing upon a star to make their hearts' desires come true.

17　　How the Disney people view their park—what dreams and needs they think their millions of visitors bring to Disneyland to be fulfilled—I never found out; they weren't allowed to talk to me. When I first called to introduce myself, I was told that if I were writing an article there would be no problem—I could interview anybody. But books were another matter: anything connected with a book had to be cleared by the Disney legal department.

18　　On one level that was good news. At a time when writing and reading are increasingly devalued, books were still important enough for lawyers to worry about. Books got into libraries. Magazines and newspapers were mere visitors in our midst, leaving no imprint on the culture; as a young reporter I was often told that the morning newspaper is what fish get wrapped in at night. But now, because I was working on a book, I would have to write Disneyland a formal letter of request. I did, and word came back that the legal department would process my letter soon. That "soon" never arrived. When I got to Disneyland the publicity staff refused to see me, or give me any publicity material, or even let me cross their doorstep. "Our hands are tied," they told me on the phone—the closest I came to meeting them—and no untying was ever done.

19   I couldn't help thinking about the American values I had seen certified and glorified on Disneyland's turn-of-the-century Main Street—such things as neighborliness and trust. At all my previous stops I had been replenished by hearing men and women talk about the place where they work and what it means to them. Their sense of work as useful and satisfying was an old-fashioned value that I found alive and well, especially in the National Park Service. In towns like Abilene, I was reminded that the people who traditionally lubricated small-town America in Disney's beloved yesteryear, helping people to get on with their lives, were the bankers and the doctors and the lawyers. None of them could have imagined that with the turn of another century Americans would be so protective of their image that they would cede to lawyers much of their freedom to act. Half the country, it often seemed, was waiting for legal clearance.

20   Because Disneyland is a collage of many cherished American myths, I found myself encountering in its synthetic "lands" many of the folk heroes I had met earlier on their authentic turf. The Mississippi steamboat I took in Frontierland was the *Mark Twain,* and the island it circumnavigated was Tom Sawyer Island. Davy Crockett, late of the Alamo, appeared to me three times. In Critter Country I rode in a Davy Crockett Explorer Canoe; in Frontierland I shopped in a store called Davy Crockett's Pioneer Mercantile; and at a nearby log stockade I saw a sign informing me that a string of such forts, like Fort Pitt and Fort Duquesne, once linked the American frontier. "Davy Crockett and other famous scouts," it said, "spent much time in and around such wilderness outposts acting as 'eyes and ears' of the woods."

21   Therefore I should have known that I hadn't seen the last of Abraham Lincoln. Earlier I had seen him in granite at Mount Rushmore and had felt his healing presence at Appomattox. Now, as I was about to leave, I noticed a building called the Disneyland Opera House. GREAT MOMENTS WITH MR. LINCOLN, its marquee said. That was for me—I'm always up for great moments with Mr. Lincoln. Inside, I watched a brief film in which Walt Disney explains his process of Audio-Animatronics, the technology that has become a trademark of his parks, enabling all manner of seemingly real people, animals, birds, fish and other critters to hail us as we come riding by. "Ever since I was a small boy I've had a great personal admiration for Abraham Lincoln," Disney says, recalling that he first Audio-Animated Mr. Lincoln for the New York World's Fair of 1964, using a life mask of the 16th President that was taken in 1860, before he grew a beard. "The final result is so lifelike you may find it hard to believe," the narrator of the film said, and we were duly ushered into a theater to try to believe it.

22   After a brief slide show recapitulating the Civil War, the curtain went up and I saw on the stage a tall man in a black suit who somewhat resembled Abraham Lincoln. He was sitting in a chair, with a diorama of the Capitol behind him, and something in me kept hoping he wouldn't try to get up. But he did, struggling arthritically to his feet and moving a few steps forward. He wanted to talk to us about liberty, he said, and he began to expatiate on respect for duty, the law, faith in divine Providence, and dangers facing the nation. They sounded like disconnected homilies, and as I later learned, they were: snippets plucked from five speeches delivered during the mainly beardless years of 1838 to 1864. This was not my writer's Lincoln. In fact, was it anybody's Lincoln? As the tall man rambled on, emphasizing his points with hand and arm gestures that were angular and spasmodic, his long legs just a little unsteady—would he *fall?*—I was reminded of another tall figure from the dim recesses of Hollywood make-believe who moved with the same mechanical vulnerability, the same endearing wish to be human. It was Boris Karloff in *Frankenstein.*

23   With mingled joy and regret, as they said in the old Hollywood travelogues, I bade farewell to Disneyland and stole out into the parking lot. There I caught a shuttle bus that took me to my modern hotel across a landscape that was not spotless and not beautiful; I didn't see a single orange tree. But it was real, and I was glad to get back to my America. Two days in Disneyland had been a welcome release from the stressful present into an America as long gone and as deeply longed for as the boyhood of Tom Sawyer. I could only tell myself that Walt Disney's turn-of-the-century Main Street and Mark Twain's mid-19th-century Hannibal—the handiwork of two masters of make-believe—were also not as ideal as they made themselves believe.

Discussion Questions

1. In paragraph 9, Zinsser states "The psychic need that Disneyland fills is the need to be whisked away to any time and place except present-day America." Do you agree with his explanation, or do see amusement parks filling other needs? Explain your response.

2. Why do you think it is important in paragraph 12 that "we can still make believe that the good old days never went away"? Do you agree with this observation? Why or why not?

3. Explain the importance of Zinsser naming all of the rides he went on at Disneyland and the significance of the names themselves.

4. In paragraph 20, Zinsser states that "Disneyland is a collage of many cherished American myths" and proceeds to identify some. Can you offer other myths that are found at amusement parks? Why are such myths important?

5. When Zinsser leaves Disneyland he claims to be "glad to get back to my America." Do you think other visitors share his reaction? Would you? Why?

Chapter 6 Writing Topics

1. Write an essay in which you describe what you appreciate about the place where you live. Make sure to describe it fully enough so that others can envision the place and what you value in it.

2. The inhabitants of a place sometimes reflect the "spirit" of their locale. Write an essay that describes the nature of the people who reside in and characterize a given place.

3. Has living in a particular place ever provided an occasion for you to learn something important about yourself that living in only that place could have elicited? Write an essay in which you examine such a place and time.

4. Sometimes places have unearned and unjust reputations. If you know of such a place, discuss the reputation it has, the reasons for that reputation, and what in your experience makes you think the reputation is unfair.

5. In an essay, trace your history of living in big cities, small towns, in the country, near mountains or water, etc. Examine the choice you made and what it says about you as a person.

6. Compare and contrast the native inhabitants of a place with their transplanted counterparts. What observations can you offer about the two sets of people?

7. Think of a place you have visited or lived that surprised you because it was unlike what you had expected. Write an essay in which you show the sharp contrast between your expectations and what you actually witnessed.

8. Choose a place you know very well that has changed considerably over the years. Describe the changes so that others can experience the differences you have noticed.

9. Using as many senses as possible, describe a place that means a lot to you (e.g., a city street, park, mountain hideaway, inlet, or room). Capture the essence of the place by using specific details to evoke what you find so alluring about it.

10. Write an essay in which you describe your "ideal place, the right place, the one true home" that Edward Abbey refers to in the epigraphs to Chapter 6. Make sure that you show why this place is perfect for you.

Chapter 7

Living in America

There may be said to be two classes of people in the world; those who constantly divide the people of the world into two classes and those who do not.

—Robert Benchley

From my point of view, no label, no slogan, no party, no skin color and indeed no religion, is more important than being human.

—James Baldwin

Society is like the air, necessary to breathe, but insufficient to live on.

—George Santayana

Society is always diseased, and the best is the most so.

—Henry David Thoreau

No one can make you feel inferior without your consent.

—Eleanor Roosevelt

From reading the essays in the previous six chapters of *The Voice of Reflection,* no doubt you have learned much about the authors from their accounts of their families, their educational experiences, their friends, their physical characteristics, and the geography that surrounds them. Other issues are of equal importance: people's experiences, observations, and reflections concerning race, ethnicity, and sexual orientation.

The stories and reflections of other cultures and races can provide not only an interesting and necessary education about other people and their heritages, they can open our eyes to our own beliefs, the cultural slant that informs our own thinking. *No one* is exempt from such a vantage point: everything we think and write is filtered through a societal background and belief system, whether we are consciously aware of it or not.

In Chapter 7, you will hear writers who voice their impressions of not only the society in which they live but the personal experiences that have informed their viewpoints. The chapter begins with three essays that deal with racial discrimination: Audre Lorde recalls the disappointing family vacation to Washington, D.C., where she was first confronted with discrimination. Then, Brent Staples reports on the way he was victimized because others thought he was an intruder and a threat. In the next essay, Mark Mathabane and Gail Mathabane, an interracial couple, describe the first time they appeared in public as a couple.

In "A Woman from He-Dog," Mary Crow Dog recounts her experiences as a Native American woman living in a white, male world. Arturo Madrid reflects on some experiences that precipitated his feeling of being "missing" in a white society, and Kesaya E. Noda examines the evolution of her identity as a Japanese-American woman. Finally, Louie Crew describes the ways in which, as a gay "outsider and an outcast," he is able to "thrive" in a heterosexual world.

Each of these writers has much to teach us about life experiences because their essays call into question the beliefs commonly held by people from societies and cultures different from their own. Most importantly, because of the writers' forthright reflections on their backgrounds and understandings of who they are as people, the essays encourage us to rethink our own beliefs and identities. That is, in coming to terms with themselves, the writers motivate us to do the same with ourselves.

The Fourth of July

Audre Lorde

Born in 1934 in New York City, Audre Lorde was educated at City University of New York, Hunter College, and Columbia University School of Library Science. She was an English professor at the City University of New York and Hunter College, and in 1981 co-founded Kitchen Table: Women of Color Press. Lorde is the author of thirteen books of poetry and essays, including Cables to Rage *(1970),* From a Land Where Other People Live *(1973), which was nominated for a National Book Award,* Coal *(1976),* Between Ourselves *(1976),* Sister Outsider: Essays and Speeches *(1984),* The Cancer Journals *(1980),* A Burst of Light *(1988), and her autobiography,* Zami: A New Spelling of My Name *(1982), in which the following essay appears. In 1991, Lorde was named poet laureate of New York State. "The Fourth of July" describes the graduation present her parents gave her, a family vacation in Washington, D.C., that unexpectedly turned out to be an encounter with racial discrimination. Lorde died of cancer in 1992.*

1   The first time I went to Washington, D.C., was on the edge of the summer when I was supposed to stop being a child. At least that's what they said to us all at graduation from the eighth grade. My sister Phyllis graduated at the same time from high school. I don't know what she was supposed to stop being. But as graduation presents for us both, the whole family took a Fourth of July trip to Washington, D.C., the fabled and famous capital of our country.

2   It was the first time I'd ever been on a railroad train during the day. When I was little, and we used to go to the Connecticut shore, we always went at night on the milk train, because it was cheaper.

3   Preparations were in the air around our house before school was even over. We packed for a week. There were two very large suitcases that my father carried, and a box filled with food. In fact, my first trip to Washington was a mobile feast; I started eating as soon as we were comfortably ensconced in our seats, and did not stop until somewhere after Philadelphia. I remember it was Philadelphia because I was disappointed not to have passed by the Liberty Bell.

4   My mother had roasted two chickens and cut them up into dainty bite-size pieces. She packed slices of brown bread and butter and green pepper and carrot sticks. There were little violently yellow iced cakes with scalloped edges called "marigolds," that came from Cushman's Bakery. There was a spice bun and rock-cakes from Newton's, the West Indian bakery across Lenox Avenue from St. Mark's School, and iced tea in a wrapped mayonnaise jar. There were sweet pickles for us and dill pickles

for my father, and peaches with the fuzz still on them, individually wrapped to keep them from bruising. And, for neatness, there were piles of napkins and a little tin box with a washcloth dampened with rosewater and glycerine for wiping sticky mouths.

5   I wanted to eat in the dining car because I had read all about them, but my mother reminded me for the umpteenth time that dining car food always cost too much money and besides, you never could tell whose hands had been playing all over that food, nor where those same hands had been just before. My mother never mentioned that Black people were not allowed into railroad dining cars headed south in 1947. As usual, whatever my mother did not like and could not change, she ignored. Perhaps it would go away, deprived of her attention.

6   I learned later that Phyllis's high school senior class trip had been to Washington, but the nuns had given her back her deposit in private, explaining to her that the class, all of whom were white, except Phyllis, would be staying in a hotel where Phyllis "would not be happy," meaning, Daddy explained to her, also in private, that they did not rent rooms to Negroes. "We will take among-you to Washington, ourselves," my father had avowed, "and not just for an overnight in some measly fleabag hotel."

7   American racism was a new and crushing reality that my parents had to deal with every day of their lives once they came to this country. They handled it as a private woe. My mother and father believed that they could best protect their children from the realities of race in America and the fact of American racism by never giving them name, much less discussing their nature. We were told we must never trust white people, but *why* was never explained, nor the nature of their ill will. Like so many other vital pieces of information in my childhood, I was supposed to know without being told. It always seemed like a very strange injunction coming from my mother, who looked so much like one of those people we were never supposed to trust. But something always warned me not to ask my mother why she wasn't white, and why Auntie Lillah and Auntie Etta weren't, even though they were all that same problematic color so different from my father and me, even from my sisters, who were somewhere in-between.

8   In Washington, D.C., we had one large room with two double beds and an extra cot for me. It was a back-street hotel that belonged to a friend of my father's who was in real estate, and I spent the whole next day after Mass squinting up at the Lincoln Memorial where Marian Anderson had sung after the D.A.R. refused to allow her to sing in their auditorium because she was Black. Or because she was "Colored," my father said as he told us the story. Except that what he probably said was "Negro," because for his times, my father was quite progressive.

9   I was squinting because I was in that silent agony that characterized all of my childhood summers, from the time school let out in June to the end of July, brought about by my dilated and vulnerable eyes exposed to the summer brightness.

10   I viewed Julys through an agonizing corolla of dazzling whiteness and

I always hated the Fourth of July, even before I came to realize the travesty such a celebration was for Black people in this country.

11   My parents did not approve of sunglasses, nor of their expense.

12   I spent the afternoon squinting up at monuments to freedom and past presidencies and democracy, and wondering why the light and heat were both so much stronger in Washington, D.C., than back home in New York City. Even the pavement on the streets was a shade lighter in color than back home.

13   Late that Washington afternoon my family and I walked back down Pennsylvania Avenue. We were a proper caravan, mother bright and father brown, the three of us girls step-standards in-between. Moved by our historical surroundings and the heat of the early evening, my father decreed yet another treat. He had a great sense of history, a flair for the quietly dramatic and the sense of specialness of an occasion and a trip.

14   "Shall we stop and have a little something to cool off, Lin?"

15   Two blocks away from our hotel, the family stopped for a dish of vanilla ice cream at a Breyer's ice cream and soda fountain. Indoors, the soda fountain was dim and fan-cooled, deliciously relieving to my scorched eyes.

16   Corded and crisp and pinafored, the five of us seated ourselves one by one at the counter. There was I between my mother and father, and my two sisters on the other side of my mother. We settled ourselves along the white mottled marble counter, and when the waitress spoke at first no one understood what she was saying, and so the five of us just sat there.

17   The waitress moved along the line of us closer to my father and spoke again. "I said I kin give you to take out, but you can't eat here. Sorry." Then she dropped her eyes looking very embarrassed, and suddenly we heard what it was she was saying all at the same time, loud and clear.

18   Straight-backed and indignant, one by one, my family and I got down from the counter stools and turned around and marched out of the store, quiet and outraged, as if we had never been Black before. No one would answer my emphatic questions with anything other than a guilty silence. "But we hadn't done anything!" This wasn't right or fair! Hadn't I written poems about Bataan and freedom and democracy for all?

19   My parents wouldn't speak of this injustice, not because they had contributed to it, but because they felt they should have anticipated it and avoided it. This made me even angrier. My fury was not going to be acknowledged by a like fury. Even my two sisters copied my parents' pretense that nothing unusual and anti-american had occurred. I was left to write my angry letter to the president of the united states all by myself, although my father did promise I could type it out on the office typewriter next week, after I showed it to him in my copybook diary.

20   The waitress was white, and the counter was white, and the ice cream I never ate in Washington, D.C., that summer I left childhood was white, and the white heat and the white pavement and the white stone monuments of my first Washington summer made me sick to my stomach for

the whole rest of that trip and it wasn't much of a graduation present after all.

Discussion Questions

1. Do you think Lorde's parents were right in "protecting" her the way they did or were they naive, unrealistic, and unfair? Explain your response.

2. Lorde comments in paragraph 7, "Like so many other vital pieces of information in my childhood, I was supposed to know without being told." Do you think this happens frequently in families? Can you offer some of your own examples that attest to Lorde's observation?

3. What do you see as the significance and underlying meaning of the statement in paragraph 11, "My parents did not approve of sunglasses, nor of their expense" having its own paragraph?

4. Why do you think Lorde chooses not to capitalize the word "America(n)"and United States in paragraphs 7 and 19?

5. Do you find the title of this essay fitting? Explain your answer.

Just Walk on By

Brent Staples

Born in 1951 in Pennsylvania, Brent Staples earned his B.A. degree from Widener University in 1973 and his Ph.D. degree from the University of Chicago in 1982. A reporter for the Chicago Sun-Times *and an editor of* The New York Times Book Review, *Staples has been the first assistant metropolitan editor of* The New York Times *since 1985. He is the author of* Parallel Time: A Memoir (1991). *The following essay, which describes his experiences with discrimination on evening walks in the city, first appeared in* Ms. *magazine in 1986.*

1   My first victim was a woman—white, well dressed, probably in her early twenties. I came upon her late one evening on a deserted street in Hyde Park, a relatively affluent neighborhood in an otherwise mean, impoverished section of Chicago. As I swung onto the avenue behind her, there seemed to be a discreet, uninflammatory distance between us. Not so. She cast back a worried glance. To her, the youngish black man—a

broad six feet two inches with a beard and billowing hair, both hands shoved into the pockets of a bulky military jacket—seemed menacingly close. After a few more quick glimpses, she picked up her pace and was soon running in earnest. Within seconds she disappeared into a cross street.

2   That was more than a decade ago. I was 22 years old, a graduate student newly arrived at the University of Chicago. It was in the echo of that terrified woman's footfalls that I first began to know the unwieldy inheritance I'd come into—the ability to alter public space in ugly ways. It was clear that she thought herself the quarry of a mugger, a rapist, or worse. Suffering a bout of insomnia, however, I was stalking sleep, not defenseless wayfarers. As a softy who is scarcely able to take a knife to a raw chicken—let alone hold it to a person's throat—I was surprised, embarrassed, and dismayed all at once. Her flight made me feel like an accomplice in tyranny. It also made it clear that I was indistinguishable from the muggers who occasionally seeped into the area from the surrounding ghetto. That first encounter, and those that followed, signified that a vast, unnerving gulf lay between nighttime pedestrians—particularly women—and me. And I soon gathered that being perceived as dangerous is a hazard in itself. I only needed to turn a corner into a dicey situation, or crowd some frightened, armed person in a foyer somewhere, or make an errant move after being pulled over by a policeman. Where fear and weapons meet—and they often do in urban America—there is always the possibility of death.

3   In that first year, my first away from my hometown, I was to become thoroughly familiar with the language of fear. At dark, shadowy intersections in Chicago, I could cross in front of a car stopped at a traffic light and elicit the *thunk, thunk, thunk, thunk* of the driver—black, white, male, or female—hammering down the door locks. On less traveled streets after dark, I grew accustomed to but never comfortable with people who crossed to the other side of the street rather than pass me. Then there were the standard unpleasantries with police, doormen, bouncers, cab drivers, and others whose business it is to screen out troublesome individuals *before* there is any nastiness.

4   I moved to New York nearly two years ago and I have remained an avid night walker. In central Manhattan, the near-constant crowd cover minimizes tense one-on-one street encounters. Elsewhere—visiting friends in SoHo, where sidewalks are narrow and tightly spaced buildings shut out the sky—things can get very taut indeed.

5   Black men have a firm place in New York mugging literature. Norman Podhoretz in his famed (or infamous) 1963 essay, "My Negro Problem—And Ours," recalls growing up in terror of black males; they "were tougher than we were, more ruthless," he writes—and as an adult on the Upper West Side of Manhattan, he continues, he cannot constrain his nervousness when he meets black men on certain streets. Similarly, a decade later, the essayist and novelist Edward Hoagland extols a New York where once "Negro bitterness bore down mainly on other Negroes." Where

some see mere panhandlers, Hoagland sees "a mugger who is clearly screwing up his nerve to do more than just *ask* for money." But Hoagland has "the New Yorker's quick-hunch posture for broken-field maneuvering," and the bad guy swerves away.

6   I often witness that "hunch posture," from women after dark on the warrenlike streets of Brooklyn where I live. They seem to set their faces on neutral and, with their purse straps strung across their chests bandolier style, they forge ahead as though bracing themselves against being tackled. I understand, of course, that the danger they perceive is not a hallucination. Women are particularly vulnerable to street violence, and young black males are drastically overrepresented among the perpetrators of that violence. Yet these truths are no solace against the kind of alienation that comes of being ever the suspect, against being set apart, a fearsome entity with whom pedestrians avoid making eye contact.

7   It is not altogether clear to me how I reached the ripe old age of 22 without being conscious of the lethality nighttime pedestrians attributed to me. Perhaps it was because in Chester, Pennsylvania, the small, angry industrial town where I came of age in the 1960s, I was scarcely noticeable against a backdrop of gang warfare, street knifings, and murders. I grew up one of the good boys, had perhaps a half-dozen fist fights. In retrospect, my shyness of combat has clear sources.

8   Many things go into the making of a young thug. One of those things is the consummation of the male romance with the power to intimidate. An infant discovers that random flailings send the baby bottle flying out of the crib and crashing to the floor. Delighted, the joyful babe repeats those motions again and again, seeking to duplicate the feat. Just so, I recall the points at which some of my boyhood friends were finally seduced by the perception of themselves as tough guys. When a mark cowered and surrendered his money without resistance, myth and reality merged—and paid off. It is, after all, only manly to embrace the power to frighten and intimidate. We, as men, are not supposed to give an inch of our lane on the highway; we are to seize the fighter's edge in work and in play and even in love; we are to be valiant in the face of hostile forces.

9   Unfortunately, poor and powerless young men seem to take all this nonsense literally. As a boy, I saw countless tough guys locked away; I have since buried several, too. They were babies, really—a teenage cousin, a brother of 22, a childhood friend in his mid-twenties—all gone down in episodes of bravado played out in the streets. I came to doubt the virtues of intimidation early on. I chose, perhaps even unconsciously, to remain a shadow—timid, but a survivor.

10   The fearsomeness mistakenly attributed to me in public places often has a perilous flavor. The most frightening of these confusions occurred in the late 1970s and early 1980s when I worked as a journalist in Chicago. One day, rushing into the office of a magazine I was writing for with a deadline story in hand, I was mistaken for a burglar. The office manager called security and, with an ad hoc posse, pursued me through the

labyrinthine halls, nearly to my editor's door. I had no way of proving who I was. I could only move briskly toward the company of someone who knew me.

11   Another time I was on assignment for a local paper and killing time before an interview. I entered a jewelry store on the city's affluent Near North Side. The proprietor excused herself and returned with an enormous red Doberman pinscher straining at the end of a leash. She stood, the dog extended toward me, silent to my questions, her eyes bulging nearly out of her head. I took a cursory look around, nodded, and bade her good night. Relatively speaking, however, I never fared as badly as another black male journalist. He went to nearby Waukegan, Illinois, a couple of summers ago to work on a story about a murderer who was born there. Mistaking the reporter for the killer, police hauled him from his car at gunpoint and but for his press credentials would probably have tried to book him. Such episodes are not uncommon. Black men trade tales like this all the time.

12   In "My Negro Problem—And Ours," Podhoretz writes that the hatred he feels for blacks makes itself known to him through a variety of avenues—one being his discomfort with that "special brand of paranoid touchiness" to which he says blacks are prone. No doubt he is speaking here of black men. In time, I learned to smother the rage I felt at so often being taken for a criminal. Not to do so would surely have led to madness—via that special "paranoid touchiness" that so annoyed Podhoretz at the time he wrote the essay.

13   I began to take precautions to make myself less threatening. I move about with care, particularly late in the evening. I give a wide berth to nervous people on subway platforms during the wee hours, particularly when I have exchanged business clothes for jeans. If I happen to be entering a building behind some people who appear skittish, I may walk by, letting them clear the lobby before I return, so as not to seem to be following them. I have been calm and extremely congenial on those rare occasions when I've been pulled over by the police.

14   And on late-evening constitutionals along streets less traveled by, I employ what has proved to be an excellent tension-reducing measure: I whistle melodies from Beethoven and Vivaldi and the more popular classical composers. Even steely New Yorkers hunching toward nighttime destinations seem to relax, and occasionally they even join in the tune. Virtually everybody seems to sense that a mugger wouldn't be warbling bright, sunny selections from Vivaldi's *Four Seasons*. It is my equivalent of the cowbell that hikers wear when they know they are in bear country.

Discussion Questions

1. Have you ever noticed people behaving the way Staples describes in his essay? What was your response?

2. What do you see as Staples's purpose in writing this essay? Do you think the essay accomplished its aims? Why or why not?

3. What do you think Staples means when he mentions "the language of fear" in paragraph 3?

4. In the last two paragraphs, Staples presents some precautions he has taken to make himself less threatening. Do you think he *should* take such measures? Why or why not?

5. How do you think the people who avoided Staples in the examples he presents would respond to his essay? Do you think their behavior would change after having read it? Why or why not?

Going Public

Mark Mathabane and Gail Mathabane

Mark Mathabane was born in 1960 in South Africa. An accomplished tennis player, Mathabane received an athletic scholarship to Limestone College in South Carolina after Stan Smith, the American tennis professional, recognized his talents and sponsored him. Mathabane is the author of two books that recount his experiences growing up under apartheid in South Africa: Kaffir Boy *(1986) and* Kaffir Boy in America *(1989). While a student at the Columbia University Graduate School of Journalism, Mathabane met Gail, a fellow graduate student, whom he would later marry. Together, they have written* Love in Black and White: The Triumph Of Love over Prejudice and Taboo *(1992), in which the following essay appears. He is also the author of* African Women *(1994). Since 1980, the number of interracial marriages has doubled; the Census Bureau reports that in 1992 there were 246,000 black-white couples, nearly four times the number twenty years ago. The Mathabanes' book chronicles their experiences as an African-American man and a Caucasian woman meeting, falling in love, marrying, and the way they have dealt with the prejudice against interracial marriages. "Going Public" describes the way each of them responded to appearing in public as a couple for the first time.*

Mark's View

1   Walking through Manhattan side by side, Gail and I blended into the diverse crowd of pedestrians, who ranged in color from as dark as I to as light and fair as Gail. Moving down the jammed sidewalks of Fifth Avenue at rush hour, we were inconspicuous in a throng that had to walk eight abreast to keep from tumbling off the curb and into the steady, noisy stream of traffic and honking yellow taxicabs. People bumped into each other in their mad dash for a vacant cab or a late appointment.

2   The smell of hot dogs and pretzels, blended with the malodorous steam rising from manholes, stung our noses; the blare of honking horns and corner evangelists shouting into loudspeakers deafened our ears. In such confusion and cacophony, it was easy to get lost in the anonymity of a crowd and still retain our individuality, without once letting go of each other's hand.

3   The subway was a different story. In a crowded train rumbling, rattling, and racing through the bowels of Manhattan, I would cling to the center pole and Gail would wrap her arms around my waist and hold on for dear life. She seemed oblivious to the fact that we stood out, and held onto me with unself-conscious ease. I, on the other hand, was hyperaware of people staring at us. Some would lift their weary eyes, ponder us for a moment, then resume reading the sports pages of the *New York Post, The New York Times,* or the *Daily News.* Older women would lean their faces together, gossiping in whispers, looking disdainfully at us from time to time. Others had seen it all before and were too jaded by New York even to cast a curious glance at us.

4   One evening as Gail and I hurried arm in arm from Fifth Avenue toward Port Authority, we passed two young black men.

5   "Hey, look at him," one young man shouted to his friend. "He got hisself a white girl. She be damn good lookin' too."

6   Such comments upset and saddened me. They reminded me of the pervasive stereotype that all black men are, at least subconsciously, out to "get a white girl." What did those two young men know about our relationship? Nothing. All they saw was black man, white woman.

7   Our first major evening out in public was to attend the 1985 Front Page Dinner Dance thrown by the Newswomen's Club of New York. Because she usually wore jeans and owned a scanty wardrobe of formal wear, Gail had to go out at the last minute and buy a new dress and shoes in which to receive her $2,500 Anne O'Hare McCormick scholarship. The dinner, an extravagant affair held in the Empire State Ballroom of the Grand Hyatt Hotel, was followed by an award ceremony for top journalists from *Newsday, The New York Times, The New Yorker,* ABC News "Nightline," and "20/20." I was the only black in the ballroom except for those stacking the dirty plates and clearing the clutter from the tables, which gave me a disquieting feeling of being back in South Africa, where blacks toiled as servants while whites were lavishly entertained. What was I doing in such a place?

8   But I quickly remembered my reason for being there when I watched

Gail ascend the steps onto the stage to receive her scholarship award. I felt proud: That was my "Sweets" up there. The president of the Newswomen's Club, Joan O'Sullivan of King Features, made a short speech about Gail's off-beat accomplishments: mastering Hungarian, German, and Russian; traveling alone to Budapest and talking her way into the university there; graduating from Brown; and writing for Minneapolis *City Pages.*

9   Few couples were dancing, but Gail, in her exuberant mood, dragged me onto the dance floor. We must have looked strange, a black man and a white woman, dancing together in the middle of a high-ceilinged ballroom while the white faces of the American media's movers and shakers looked on. I had been the only black in a room filled with whites many times, but never when I was dancing with a white woman. Some people gaped at us, a few with bemused indifference. I did my best to forget them and to focus on Gail, her happiness at receiving the award, and our joy at sharing a special moment.

10   Whenever I traveled to Long Island to lecture on South Africa and apartheid before various groups, Gail would accompany me. During these trips, we would never let on that we were anything more than friends. We wanted to keep our relationship private and, therefore, kept it a secret. It was easier to pretend to be platonic friends than to deal with people's prejudices. When we spent the night at a white minister's home, we requested separate rooms, despite his wife's attempt to coax us into revealing the true nature of our relationship.

11   "You *do* want to stay in the same room, don't you?" she said insinuatingly. "It would be fine with *us,* you know. *We* understand."

12   We insisted we were just friends and wanted separate rooms. In the morning at breakfast the minister spoke to me, in a confidential and fatherly tone, about the problems mixed couples confront and how difficult it is to stay married.

13   "I had a good friend once, a black man like yourself," the minister said. "He wanted to marry a white woman. Oh, I assure you I warned him against it. But no, he wouldn't listen to me. He went ahead and married her. And you know what happened? They're divorced now. I knew it would happen all along." He looked hard at me, then at Gail, then back to me, as if to say, "Don't make the same mistake."

14   Spring arrived and the weather grew warm. Gail and I went for regular runs along the Hudson River through Riverside Park, past rotting benches, screeching seagulls stained by the polluted air, and graffiti-covered stone walls. Whenever the exercise and warm weather made me sweat, I would peel off my shirt to cool down. People often stared at us, but we never heard a negative comment. Many were simply curious. Almost nothing can shock a New Yorker, not even people with pink hair, black lipstick, painted faces, or safety pins in their cheeks.

15   I felt completely natural around Gail when we were alone together, but as soon as we stepped out the door I became acutely sensitive to the way

people regarded us. It was difficult for me to regard our love as an aberration in social norms. Only when people stared did I remember how deeply race as an issue still permeated American society. At times it seemed that the only difference between white attitudes in South Africa and America was that white South Africans had made the mistake of institutionalizing their racism.

16   It seemed half the audience turned around whenever we sat down in a movie theater or concert hall. When we asked to be seated at an elegant restaurant on Fifty-second Street, the waiter led us to a bad table directly in front of the kitchen's swinging doors—there were a couple of empty tables in nicer locations—next to the only black couple in the restaurant. Gail was outraged and wanted to insist on better seating, but I was so accustomed to prejudice that I saw no point in arguing. We left without ordering.

17   "Racism makes me so mad," Gail said, still upset. "Why do people do this to each other?"

18   "I really don't know," I replied. "The best way to deal with racism is not to be obsessed by it. It can make you paranoid and even drive you mad. It gives racists satisfaction to know they're messing up your life. Life is simply too short to let bigots spoil its few moments of happiness with their venom."

19   "But shouldn't we fight to change people's attitudes?" she asked.

20   "Yes, we should," I said. "But let's be realistic. For some people racism is a way of life. It's deeply ingrained in their psyches. No amount of argument and reason will change attitudes based on ignorance and fear."

21   We fell silent for a while, and continued walking through the streets of Manhattan, looking for another place to dine. Suddenly Gail looked up and said, "Do you sometimes wish I were black?"

22   The question surprised me and made me somewhat defensive. "I fell in love with you as you are! Why in the world would I want you to be something you're not?"

23   "It would be easier for you, wouldn't it, if I were black?"

24   "Easier how?"

25   "I mean, we wouldn't be so odd and conspicuous as a couple. Therefore people wouldn't mind us."

26   "Why are you obsessed about what other people think?" I asked. "I thought you were the one who said nothing matters but the way we feel about one another."

27   "I did say that, and I meant it. But Mark, tell me the truth. Doesn't it bother you that I'm white?"

28   I denied that it did, but deep down I was troubled that people, especially blacks, misconstrued my reasons for dating a white. I knew that should I enter the limelight after the publication of *Kaffir Boy,* the issue would become magnified, especially as I might be regarded as some sort of spokesperson for the anti-apartheid struggle, a voice for the black community. What effect would my relationship with Gail have on my career as a writer? What sacrifices would it entail? Was I willing to make those sacrifices? Only time would tell.

29   The two friends I was eager for Gail to meet were Stew and Claudia, a mixed couple on Long Island with whom I lived for a summer. Stew, a black stockbroker for a major national firm, grew up in Winston-Salem, North Carolina. His wife, Claudia, an elementary school teacher from New England, was disowned by her parents for marrying Stew. They had two children whom I was sure Gail would adore.

30   I wanted the visit to be a surprise. As Gail and I rode the Long Island Railroad toward Bellport, she kept asking me questions about Stew and Claudia. I told her a little about each of them, but not enough to give away their races. I wanted her to meet my friends with fresh eyes and an open heart, and to assure her that we were not the only mixed couple on earth.

Gail's View

31 That weekend visit to Stew and Claudia's home on Long Island was both enlightening and troubling. First of all, it gave me a glimpse into suburban married life, which made me, a young graduate student with a fear of commitment, imagine that I would suffocate in such an environment. Like many women of my generation, I had not escaped the influence of radical feminism and was convinced that marriage and a house in the suburbs were nothing more than a paralyzing trap that transforms even the most talented and energetic women into unrespected housewives and overworked mothers.

32   Since the day I finished Betty Friedan's book *The Feminine Mystique* my sophomore year at Brown, I vowed I would never let myself become one of those complacent women with the frozen smiles in the laundry detergent commercials who derive their happiness from seeing dirty socks turn white. I swore I would never make the same mistakes as my mother, a brilliant woman who graduated from Mount Holyoke College at twenty; taught for a year; married a minister; then gave up her career ambitions under social pressure to devote herself to the church, her children, and her husband's career. She ended up feeling trapped and depressed for almost two decades.

33   Perhaps getting involved with a black man was my way of stating to the world that I would never succumb to the stereotype of the suburban housewife dressed in pink with the fake smile on her face hugging her three blond children. Falling in love with Mark, a nonconformist who throughout life had swum against the tide, gave me the feeling of being different.

34   But when I met Stew and Claudia, I realized that even mixed couples settle down at some point and have a fairly normal and routine life of grocery shopping, feeding the kids, washing the cars, and mowing the lawn. It upset me to learn that even mixed couples, those rebels against society,

cannot avoid the numbing effects of all-American family life, with its mortgage payments and church meetings and football games.

35   That weekend I turned twenty-three. I felt old all day long. I realized I had reached adulthood and that I should be very careful with my heart. I could not continue to fall in and out of love with men indefinitely. I felt I had to consider my relationship with Mark as potentially permanent or flee. I sensed Mark had partly taken me to Stew and Claudia's house to test me, to see how I would react to interracial marriage. If by the end of the weekend I felt life was too hard for mixed couples, I knew I would have to break up with Mark. It would not be fair to either of us to carry on a relationship that could not lead to marriage.

36   What disturbed me most about our visit was something Claudia said at dinner one night.

37   "A mixed couple is viewed as a black couple," she said.

38   I stared at her milky skin, thin nose, and almond-shaped eyes and wondered how on earth people could consider her black.

39   "What do you mean?" I asked.

40   "The white woman becomes black in the eyes of the community," she said, then went on to explain the trouble they had finding a real estate agent who would show them homes in white neighborhoods.

41   I stared at Stew and Claudia's children. Both the boy and girl, Sudi and Leta, had skin the color of café au lait, dark brown eyes, and curly black hair. To the outside world they were black; their mother's white skin would never change that. They would be as discriminated against and stereotyped as any black child in America.

42   The night was long and dark. I tossed and turned, deeply troubled. I struggled to understand how a white woman like Claudia could so willingly relinquish the love of her parents and give up her identity as a white person to become a black man's wife and the mother of two black children. Claudia had been cut off emotionally and financially from her parents when she married Stew, had sacrificed the approval of society to be with the man she loved. I admired her strength and hoped that someday I too could learn to love as deeply and selflessly as Claudia, but that night I knew I was wavering, tossed back and forth between my strong attachment to Mark and my ingrained desire to please my parents and do what was expected of me. My parents still did not know I was dating a black man.

43   As I lay awake watching Mark sleep, I realized, with a stab in my heart that took my breath away, that I wanted a baby with pink cheeks and blue eyes someday. I wanted what many of us want: a child that reminds us of ourselves as we once were. I always pictured my child having straight blond hair and big, bright eyes. I thought, *I want a baby who won't be labeled, categorized, or discriminated against. It would be selfish of me not to think of my child's future. Shouldn't I marry a white man for my baby's sake? It may be morally strengthening to battle societal stereotypes, but I want a baby with blue eyes.*

44   I fell asleep fantasizing about traveling through Finland and Russia,

meeting strong, blond men with blue eyes. In another dream I stood in a group of tall blond Russian intellectuals on the steps of the University of Moscow.

45   When I opened my eyes the next morning I saw Mark's dark handsome face kissing my lips and whispering, "Oh, Sweets, I love you." I threw my arms around him with more passion and vigor than ever and shut my eyes tight against his shoulder, trying desperately to force out all thoughts of race and society and blue eyes. I loved Mark, the human being, and that was all that mattered to me.

46   That afternoon Mark and I went for a walk on the beach, holding hands and feeling the warmth of the sun on our upturned faces. The waves rolled in rhythmically and crashed on the smooth, packed plane of sand. Ocean blended into sky and land like one immense orb. We were sitting on the sand, half-leaning against each other, when five-year-old Leta snuck up behind us and hummed the wedding march.

47   "I now pronounce you man and wife," she said in her girlish voice, grinning from ear to ear. "You may kiss the bride . . . on the lips!" Leta burst into giggles as Mark chased her around the beach trying to kiss her. "I'm not the bride!" she shrieked. "You're supposed to marry Gail! I wouldn't marry you for all the candy in the world!"

48   Mark caught Leta in a bear hug and gave her a kiss. She started screaming and crying so hard she hyperventilated, then sat up laughing with tear-filled eyes.

49   "She's pretty smart for a five-year-old," I said when Mark returned.

50   "That's nothing," Mark said. "When she first heard I had a girlfriend, she asked me, 'Does she have big boobs?'"

51   We burst out laughing. Leta came skipping gleefully down the beach to join us. Little did we know her playful marriage pronouncement would come true, and that two and a half years later she would be the flower girl at our wedding.

52   That evening Stew and Claudia threw a party for Mark and invited numerous friends: writers, peace activists, Unitarians, teachers. Mark sat on a sofa between me and best-selling mystery-suspense writer Phyllis Whitney, a small and sprightly woman in her eighties who gazed up at the young African with admiration. In the living room the five guests listened with rapt attention to Mark expounding his views on politics and life. I turned my attention to the eyes transfixed on him.

53   At such moments, I sensed that Mark was too overpowering for me, too much the focus of attention, too strong and talkative and persuasive. I wondered if my own identity, still developing and tentative, could flourish beside his. I sometimes felt a need to be away from him in order to grow.

54   After the crowd dispersed and we were alone together, I watched Mark read beside me, his head nodding sleepily and his short curly eyelashes shutting his tired eyes, and thought how much I loved him, though I loved in an envious, competitive, adoring, worshiping way, constantly wracked with doubts about our future as an interracial couple.

55   I did not understand the complexities of interracial love, because I was, for the most part, unaware of what it meant to be black in America. Like most whites, I rarely had to concern myself with race issues. My knowledge of civil rights and the 1960s had taught me that racial tensions could explode into riots and bloodshed, and talking to frustrated and embittered blacks in Harlem and black teenage mothers in the South Bronx had enlightened me further, but I still could not grasp what it truly meant to be discriminated against or oppressed simply because of one's skin color and the texture of one's hair.

56   In an attempt to think and feel, if only briefly, like a black person, I began reading the works of black writers: Alice Walker, Zora Neale Hurston, James Baldwin, Richard Wright, and Claude Brown. A certain line in Baldwin's *The Fire Next Time* struck me: "He was defeated long before he died because at the bottom of his heart, he really believed what white people said about him." It was then I realized that color consciousness is deeply rooted not only in whites, but in blacks as well. When you are treated all your life as an inferior being, it is easy to believe you are indeed inferior.

57   As I walked across the Columbia campus in the early spring of 1985 I began encountering groups of people gathered in tight circles, deeply involved in heated discussions, around card tables labeled Coalition for a Free South Africa. Their tables attracted considerable attention, and soon I saw a large number of students, both black and white, wearing the colors of the African National Congress and pins reading Free Mandela. I sensed they were up to something.

58   On April 3, 1985, on the seventeenth anniversary of the assassination of Martin Luther King, Jr., I saw a huge group of students gathering on the steps of Hamilton Hall, the main administration building. It was around eleven o'clock on a crisp, sunny spring morning. Out of curiosity I slipped through the crowd to see what was happening. Students had just finished wrapping a silver-link chain around the door handles. The building was barricaded for the first time since the student protests of 1968.

59   "What's this all about?" I asked a young man clad in faded jeans and wearing a huge Free South Africa button.

60   "We want Columbia to stop supporting apartheid," he said. "This university has thirty-three million dollars worth of stocks invested in companies that do business in South Africa. We're not unlocking this building until they dump those stocks. Some of the people here are on a hunger strike. They haven't eaten in two weeks. If you support us, boycott your classes. We're not leaving these steps until President Sovran listens to us."

61   For weeks they camped out on the steps, made tents to protect themselves from the rain, kept warm in cold weather by staying in their sleeping bags all day. The massive divestment protest lasted all month, received national media coverage, and sparked similar protests at universities across the country.

62   Our professors at the journalism school warned us from getting involved in the protest.

63   "A good journalist has to be objective," one of the deans said sententiously. We were assembled in the World Room for a special meeting, and he spoke from behind a podium. We could hear the protesters chanting at the rally below the window. "In a political controversy, you cannot advocate only one side," he said. "You must present a balanced view. You have to be professionals. You should weigh the statements made by the trustees against the slogans those students are shouting in that uproar out there."

64   Most of us were too curious and excited to heed the dean's warning, and knowing how Mark had suffered made me determined to do whatever I could to help stop apartheid. Whenever we J-school students could, we would cross the campus to Hamilton Hall and join in with the others as they chanted, "Apartheid kills, Columbia pays the bills" and "South Africa's stocks have got to go."

65   Six members of the Coalition for a Free South Africa were fasting to protest the university's investments. Two of them, both white, were in my Russian class. They stopped attending class, but I saw them every day on the steps of the administration building, growing thinner and more gaunt each day. Eventually they had to be hospitalized for dehydration.

66   Rumors spread that the administration threatened to deport any South African exchange students participating in the protest, so Mark kept a cautious distance from the rally. I attended for both of us. I was amazed by the large turnout of whites. Watching blacks and whites work together to fight injustice made me feel hopeful that racism might someday be defeated, not only in South Africa, but in this country as well.

67   By May graduation, the protest had lost its steam and still the university had not divested. Several months later, Columbia finally withdrew its holdings in companies that do business in South Africa, but the administration denied that its decision had anything to do with the student protests.

68   The protest made me think more deeply about the oppression of blacks, and in doing so, I thought about what it means to be a woman in America. Just as it bothers a black person to be seen only as a Negro rather than as a human being with dignity and pride, it bothered me when men saw me only as a female, as a sexual object for their fantasies. Knowing that many men read porno magazines, I often felt vulnerable when a strange man stared at me. But I never felt that way with Mark. I knew that he saw me as an individual first, not as a female or as a white woman.

69   In fact, Mark was repulsed and astounded by the emphasis Americans placed on sex. In his culture, lovemaking was natural and spontaneous, not associated with sin and scandal and fitness and baby oil and hot tubs and fraternities and Freud. It was part of love, but it was not a major component. It was a fact of life, but it was not an obsession. It had not been analyzed, studied, surveyed, written about, and mutilated into a mechanical act as it had been in America. It had not been advocated and promoted and overemphasized by a sexual liberation movement, therapists, sexologists, stimulating videos, and sexy television programs and ads or pulsating popular music with lewd lyrics. It was one of life's most precious mysteries—a mystery that was best left unexplained.

70   My strong desire to become a foreign correspondent led me to apply to Reuters News Service, based in London. Soon after I applied, a fellow journalism student from Texas congratulated me on getting the internship.

71   "What do you mean?" I said. "All I did was apply. There are thousands of applicants and they'll only select a few."

72   "I know," Jody replied. "But people are saying that if anyone at Columbia has one chance in hell to get into Reuters, it will be you."

73   All my hopes for the future were wrapped up in that one application to Reuters. When the letter from Reuters arrived, it was thin. They did not need me.

74   "Why are you so troubled?" Mark asked. "I don't know why you even applied to Reuters."

75   "I want to work abroad," I said. "I've studied German and Hungarian and Russian for so long. I want to use them!"

76   "But if you had joined Reuters, you would never have had time to write. You don't need a boss. All you have to do is choose a long-term goal and divert all your energy toward achieving it. One needs only two things: confidence and self-motivation. With those you can do anything you choose. You've already told me you want to become a writer. Why don't you focus on your writing?"

77   I smiled at his advice, not understanding how one could focus on writing without first having an income.

78   "Look at that!" Mark said, pointing to my two-foot stack of typed and bound journals I had kept since I was thirteen. "Look how much you've written already. All you have to do is harness that energy, discipline it."

79   His encouragement made me cry. None of my previous boyfriends had believed in me as much as Mark did.

80   "I care for you too deeply to see you this unhappy," Mark said, lightly rubbing my arms and looking at me with concerned, sad eyes. "I've never felt so precious to anyone besides you outside my immediate family. Of course, I'll miss you if you find a job abroad. But we could write to one another. If it's what you really want, I'd never stand in your way."

81   In early May 1985 I left New York for West Germany, where I was to be an intern at *Die Neue Presse* newspaper in Hannover. When I showed Mark my letter of acceptance, he was delighted that I had the opportunity to do what I wanted: travel to Europe, practice my foreign languages, and get journalism experience. It amazed me that his love was so unselfish that he was not afraid to let me go.

82   On the plane flying over the Atlantic Ocean, I gazed into the darkness, but saw only the image of my face reflected in the small window pane—a face expressing deep sadness. All I had to remind me of Mark was a black-and-white photograph I had developed and printed in the I-House darkroom. He was standing on the roof of the dorm on the first warm day of spring, bare chested, wearing a camouflage army hat. His longshot application for a green card as a writer was pending and I wondered if he would still be in the country when I returned.

83   Those first two weeks in Germany before I received a letter from him were filled with regret at having left New York. I missed my soul mate. During the first week the nine other American journalists and I were kept busy touring government buildings in Bonn, meeting reporters and editors, and reading German newspapers. The language around me had a new and exciting ring to it, the bakeries and shops were quaint and welcoming, and most of the Germans I met were well educated, philosophical, politically aware, and fond of conversation.

84   It was only at night, when I lay in the darkness thinking of Mark and feeling terribly alone in a foreign world, that I would ask myself if I had done the right thing, if I truly wanted to spend my life moving from place to place, clinging to nothing but my carer and leaping at every chance to advance it, breaking off relationships whenever they grew too constraining. Suddenly all the maxims I had learned while coming of age in America—Love them and leave them, Live life to the max, Indulge, Love the one you're with, Live for the moment, Be free and unfettered—grated on my ears like a pack of senseless formulas designed to produce the most intense feelings of misery and emptiness.

85   One morning when I passed a newstand in Hamburg, I spotted the cover of a *Spiegel* magazine that read, "*Rassen Krieg in Süd Afrika*—Race War in South Africa." I immediately bought a copy and learned what had happened: The South African government had declared martial law. The country was closed to foreign journalists. Children were being rounded up and detained without trial. I feared for the safety of Mark's family and wondered how Mark was taking the news. I wanted to be there for him. Was he still in America?

86   As soon as I had a chance I sat down and wrote him a long, heartfelt letter. I didn't care anymore that we were different colors. I loved him and wanted to commit myself to our relationship. I signed my letter *Na ku randa ngopfu,* his native language for "I love you very much."

87   Three weeks later I received the following reply, and felt excited and jittery as I withdrew it from its envelope.

    Gail, my dearest,

    I miss you terribly. Your trip to Germany has left my soul destitute of serenity and confidence. Never have I felt such a wretch emotionally. The first week without you was a nightmarish phantasmagoria. One moment—from reading, say, a good novel or poem, or listening to an uplifting classical music record—my heart and mind would be drunk with joy and hope and a sense of control and a love for life, all of which often lead young people to believe they can never die; the next—from thinking of you and longing to touch you and kiss you, to hear the wisdom of your mind and heart—I would be plunged into the deepest gloom and despair.

As the second week rolled around, reality still appeared discordant, like a punctured African drum, and meaningless, like the suffering of children. It was pure torture to contemplate the miles and miles of ocean and land, the hot months made of tedious days and minutes and seconds, that separate us.

One thing I did learn from those lonely days and nights of sunken spirits is that I'm madly in love with you. So much in love that it terrifies me. You possess me wholly, you know me deeper than I know myself, I hide nothing away from you. You know the taste of every drop of my bleeding heart—bleeding because of man's inhumanity to man. Think of me as I think of you, for inspiration against life's trials and tribulations.

P.S. My immigration situation looks promising.

88 We wrote to each other regularly: ten-page letters full of longing. The time apart strengthened our relationship. Through letters we could communicate on more profound levels, exploring our feelings and seeking to describe our thoughts on writing and literature with greater precision. We sent each other lengthy quotes from the books we had read, excerpts of poems, long descriptions of our thoughts and dreams. I carried the photograph of him with me everywhere. I did not feel complete without it. The aching hollowness in my chest did not go away no matter where I was or how many people were around me. Our correspondence inspired me so much I began writing short stories and, later, a novel. As I reflected on the months I had spent living in Budapest, in an old apartment overlooking the Danube, I came up with a plot for a novel about two Hungarian lovers fleeing the east bloc in search of artistic freedom.

87 When I was well into the first chapter, I wrote in a letter to Mark: "It seems the only way to escape the hectic rush and tense routine of life is to be creative. The only way to gain a feeling of control over the chaos of our lives is to express our inner selves."

90 Confident in our relationship, I threw myself into my work, submerged myself in German culture, read books in German, reported stories with seasoned journalists on the newspaper's staff, traveled to conferences with the other nine interns scattered all over Germany, and made trips to Stuttgart, Heidelberg, Berlin, and Vienna.

91 When I was not traveling, I lived with a German family in the farming village of Börssum, south of Hannover near Hildesheim. I did not hang my treasured photograph of Mark on the wall but kept it hidden. I did not think my host family would understand. They were conservatives who supported Chancellor Helmut Kohl's ruling party and believed that Turkish workers should be deported back to Turkey, in the same manner many whites in this country believed blacks should be sent back to Africa. The father had been a leader in the Hitler Youth when he was young. Like most Germans, they had lived in fear of Nazi informers and felt compelled to hang portraits of Hitler all over their house and greet neighbors with

"Heil, Hitler!" The grandmother, who lived on the second floor, had lost her husband when the American troops landed in Normandy and barely said a word to me the whole three months I was there.

92   When the last day of my internship came, I took the train to Frankfurt and excitedly boarded a plane for New York. Flying back across the Atlantic, I reread some of Mark's letters to me and wondered how we would combat the prejudices many people have toward interracial couples. Above all I wondered how my father would react if I ever mustered enough courage to tell him about Mark.

93   "How are things, darling?" Mark had written. "I got the letter in which you hinted that you might be willing to have us share an apartment in New York. I'm delighted."

94   At this I cringed, for I had changed my mind and decided to live with my brother Paul and sister-in-law, Debbie, on the Upper East Side. I was afraid of rushing things with Mark, and I wanted each of us to have enough space to maintain a healthy sense of independence. Most of all, my conscience had plagued me after I agreed to live with him. I could not fight the fact that I was a minister's daughter and that, deep down, I believed living together out of wedlock was somehow wrong. I continued reading: "I hope that your father (what a complex man!) will understand and give you his blessing."

95   I closed my eyes and imagined my father's probable reaction to the news that I was living with my boyfriend, who happened to be black. Would he rant, rave, question, pry, fume, apply pressure in all the right areas to make me leave Mark forever? I thought of my mother, who had once refused even to spend the night at a home in which the man and woman were not legally married.

96   I recalled my father's reaction when he met Carol's biracial boyfriend at a cocktail party during the weekend of Brown's 1984 graduation. He seemed to think interracial love should be addressed by textbooks on abnormal psychology. He was so absorbed in his career as a psychologist that his conversations were peppered with words like *schizophrenia, manic, incestuous tendencies, latent homosexuality, biofeedback, repressed anger,* and *psychotic behavior*. He and my brothers, who are also psychologists, seemed to speak a foreign language.

97   I gazed out the airplane window, picked up the letter from Mark, and read on.

98   "It is about time your father reconciled himself to the fact that he can never mold you after his own heart. You are a grown woman now, free to make your own decisions and choices and bear all responsibility. Though I have no doubt your father means well, he has his own life to live, and you have yours. I do not mind if your father chooses to hate me implacably; some day he will come to understand the depth of our feelings for each other, and understand too the spiritual, emotional and creative bond that has made our souls one, and made us such perfect complements of each other."

99   I smiled at Mark's optimism. I was not at all as confident that my father would accept my falling in love with an African. I was still not strong enough to follow my heart's desire, not courageous enough to live with Mark and risk the censure of my parents and relatives. Mark believed I was.

100   "One of the reasons I love you so much," he wrote, "is that you're a fighter for your rights as a woman, equal to, and as capable as, any man. Your attitude reminds me of my mother. That is why being with you has made me grow in so many ways. My mother was the first feminist to have a profound influence upon me. Your uncompromising defense of your womanhood is one reason I believe in you as a writer."

101   "Oh, Johannes, my love," I murmured as the plane touched down at Kennedy Airport, using Mark's middle name, the name he went by in his youth. "I've let you down. I wish I had your courage."

Discussion Questions

1. Mark Mathabane describes in some detail the first time he and Gail appeared together in public as a couple. How cognizant do you think most people are of interracial couples?

2. The Mathabanes believe they should "fight" to change people's attitudes. Do you think they should, or is their battle futile? Explain your response.

3. Do you think the Mathabanes' story would have been substantively different if he were Caucasian and she were an African-American? Why or why not?

4. In the first paragraphs of her view, Gail Mathabane contends that not "escap[ing] the influence of radical feminism" contributed to her desire "ever [to] succumb to the stereotype of the suburban housewife." In your own life, how have the sexual revolution and feminism affected the choices you make?

5. How realistic is Gail Mathabane when she dreams of a world in which people are not "labeled, categorized, or discriminated against"? What do you think it would take to end such labeling, categorization, and discrimination?

A Woman from He-Dog

Mary Crow Dog

Mary Crow Dog was born on a Sioux reservation in South Dakota in 1954. Forced to go to parochial school away from her home, she quit before graduating but was awarded a diploma anyway because of her tenacity. She later married Leonard Crow Dog, a famous medicine man and leader of the second Wounded Knee massacre. In Lakota Woman *(1990), written with Richard Erdoes, and from which the following essay is taken, Crow Dog describes how "just being Indian, trying to hang on to our way of life, language, and values while being surrounded by an alien, more powerful culture" made life so difficult. Crow Dog was given an American Book Award in 1991 for* Lakota Woman. *She has since changed her name to Mary Brave Bird and published* Ohitika Woman *(1993), a further examination of her life as a Native American.*

> A nation is not conquered until
> the hearts of its women
> are on the ground.
> Then it is done, no matter
> how brave its warriors
> nor how strong their weapons.
>
> —CHEYENNE PROVERB

1   I am Mary Brave Bird. After I had my baby during the siege of Wounded Knee they gave me a special name—Ohitika Win, Brave Woman, and fastened an eagle plume in my hair, singing brave-heart songs for me. I am a woman of the Red Nation, a Sioux woman. That is not easy.

2   I had my first baby during a firefight, with the bullets crashing through one wall and coming out through the other. When my newborn son was only a day old and the marshals really opened up upon us, I wrapped him in a blanket and ran for it. We had to hit the dirt a couple of times, I shielding the baby with my body, praying, "It's all right if I die, but please let him live."

3   When I came out of Wounded Knee I was not even healed up, but they put me in jail at Pine Ridge and took my baby away. I could not nurse. My breasts swelled up and grew hard as rocks, hurting badly. In 1975 the feds put the muzzles of their M-16s against my head, threatening to blow me away. It's hard being an Indian woman.

4   My best friend was Annie Mae Aquash, a young, strong-hearted woman from the Micmac Tribe with beautiful children. It is not always wise for an Indian woman to come on too strong. Annie Mae was found dead in

the snow at the bottom of a ravine on the Pine Ridge Reservation. The police said that she had died of exposure, but there was a .38-caliber slug in her head. The FBI cut off her hands and sent them to Washington for fingerprint identification, hands that had helped my baby come into the world.

5   My sister-in-law, Delphine, a good woman who had lived a hard life, was also found dead in the snow, the tears frozen on her face. A drunken man had beaten her, breaking one of her arms and legs, leaving her helpless in a blizzard to die.

6   My sister Barbara went to the government hospital in Rosebud to have her baby and when she came out of anesthesia found that she had been sterilized against her will. The baby lived only for two hours, and she had wanted so much to have children. No, it isn't easy.

7   When I was a small girl at the St. Francis Boarding School, the Catholic sisters would take a buggy whip to us for what they called "disobedience." At age ten I could drink and hold a pint of whiskey. At age twelve the nuns beat me for "being too free with my body." All I had been doing was holding hands with a boy. At age fifteen I was raped. If you plan to be born, make sure you are born white and male.

8   It is not the big, dramatic things so much that get us down, but just being Indian, trying to hang on to our way of life, language, and values while being surrounded by an alien, more powerful culture. It is being an iyeska, a half-blood, being looked down upon by whites and full-bloods alike. It is being a backwoods girl living in a city, having to rip off stores in order to survive. Most of all it is being a woman. Among Plains tribes, some men think that all a woman is good for is to crawl into the sack with them and mind the children. It compensates for what white society has done to them. They were famous warriors and hunters once, but the buffalo is gone and there is not much rep in putting a can of spam or an occasional rabbit on the table.

9   As for being warriors, the only way some men can count coup nowadays is knocking out another skin's teeth during a barroom fight. In the old days a man made a name for himself by being generous and wise, but now he has nothing to be generous with, no jobs, no money; and as far as our traditional wisdom is concerned, our men are being told by the white missionaries, teachers, and employers that it is merely savage superstition they should get rid of if they want to make it in this world. Men are forced to live away from their children, so that the family can get ADC—Aid to Dependent Children. So some warriors come home drunk and beat up their old ladies in order to work off their frustration. I know where they are coming from. I feel sorry for them, but I feel even sorrier for their women.

10   To start from the beginning, I am a Sioux from the Rosebud Reservation in South Dakota. I belong to the "Burned Thigh," the Brule Tribe, the Sicangu in our language. Long ago, so the legend goes, a small band of Sioux was surrounded by enemies who set fire to their tipis and the grass around them. They fought their way out of the trap but got their legs burned and in this way acquired their name. The Brules are part of the

Seven Sacred Campfires, the seven tribes of the Western Sioux known collectively as Lakota. The Eastern Sioux are called Dakota. The difference between them is their language. It is the same except that where we Lakota pronounce an *L,* the Dakota pronounce a *D.* They cannot pronounce an *L* at all. In our tribe we have this joke: "What is a flat tire in Dakota?" Answer: "A b*d*owout."

11 The Brule, like all Sioux, were a horse people, fierce riders and raiders, great warriors. Between 1870 and 1880 all Sioux were driven into reservations, fenced in and forced to give up everything that had given meaning to their life—their horses, their hunting, their arms, everything. But under the long snows of despair the little spark of our ancient beliefs and pride kept glowing, just barely sometimes, waiting for a warm wind to blow that spark into a flame again.

12 My family was settled on the reservation in a small place called He-Dog, after a famous chief. There are still some He-Dogs living. One, an old lady I knew, lived to be over a hundred years old. Nobody knew when she had been born. She herself had no idea, except that when she came into the world there was no census yet, and Indians had not yet been given Christian first names. Her name was just He-Dog, nothing else. She always told me, "You should have seen me eighty years ago when I was pretty." I have never forgotten her face—nothing but deep cracks and gullies, but beautiful in its own way. At any rate very impressive.

13 On the Indian side my family was related to the Brave Birds and Fool Bulls. Old Grandpa Fool Bull was the last man to make flutes and play them, the old-style flutes in the shape of a bird's head which had the elk power, the power to lure a young girl into a man's blanket. Fool Bull lived a whole long century, dying in 1976, whittling his flutes almost until his last day. He took me to my first peyote meeting while I was still a kid.

14 He still remembered the first Wounded Knee, the massacre. He was a young boy at that time, traveling with his father, a well-known medicine man. They had gone to a place near Wounded Knee to take part in a Ghost Dance. They had on their painted ghost shirts which were supposed to make them bulletproof. When they got near Pine Ridge they were stopped by white soldiers, some of them from the Seventh Cavalry, George Custer's old regiment, who were hoping to kill themselves some Indians. The Fool Bull band had to give up their few old muzzle-loaders, bows, arrows, and even knives. They had to put up their tipis in a tight circle, all bunched up, with the wagons on the outside and the soldiers surrounding their camp, watching them closely. It was cold, so cold that the trees were crackling with a loud noise as the frost was splitting their trunks. The people made a fire the following morning to warm themselves and make some coffee and then they noticed a sound beyond the crackling of the trees: rifle fire, salvos making a noise like the ripping apart of a giant blanket; the boom of cannon and the rattling of quick-firing Hotchkiss guns. Fool Bull remembered the grown-ups bursting into tears, the women keening: "They are killing our people, they are butchering them!"

It was only two miles or so from where Grandfather Fool Bull stood that almost three hundred Sioux men, women, and children were slaughtered. Later grandpa saw the bodies of the slain, all frozen in ghostly attitudes, thrown into a ditch like dogs. And he saw a tiny baby sucking at his dead mother's breast.

15   I wish I could tell about the big deeds of some ancestors of mine who fought at the Little Big Horn, or the Rosebud, counting coup during the Grattan or Fetterman battle, but little is known of my family's history before 1880. I hope some of my great-grandfathers counted coup on Custer's men, I like to imagine it, but I just do not know. Our Rosebud people did not play a big part in the battles against generals Crook or Custer. This was due to the policy of Spotted Tail, the all-powerful chief at the time. Spotted Tail had earned his eagle feathers as a warrior, but had been taken East as a prisoner and put in jail. Coming back years later, he said that he had seen the cities of the whites and that a single one of them contained more people than could be found in all the Plains tribes put together, and that every one of the wasičuns' factories could turn out more rifles and bullets in one day than were owned by all the Indians in the country. It was useless, he said, to try to resist the wasičuns. During the critical year of 1876 he had his Indian police keep most of the young men on the reservation, preventing them from joining Sitting Bull, Gall, and Crazy Horse. Some of the young bucks, a few Brave Birds among them, managed to sneak out trying to get to Montana, but nothing much is known. After having been forced into reservations, it was not thought wise to recall such things. It might mean no rations, or worse. For the same reason many in my family turned Christian, letting themselves be "white-manized." It took many years to reverse this process.

16   My sister Barbara, who is four years older than me, says she remembers the day when I was born. It was late at night and raining hard amid thunder and lightning. We had no electricity then, just the old-style kerosene lamps with the big reflectors. No bathroom, no tap water, no car. Only a few white teachers had cars. There was one phone in He-Dog, at the trading post. This was not so very long ago, come to think of it. Like most Sioux at that time my mother was supposed to give birth at home, I think, but something went wrong, I was pointing the wrong way, feet first or stuck sideways. My mother was in great pain, laboring for hours, until finally somebody ran to the trading post and called the ambulance. They took her—us—to Rosebud, but the hospital there was not yet equipped to handle a complicated birth, I don't think they had surgery then, so they had to drive mother all the way to Pine Ridge, some ninety miles distant, because there the tribal hospital was bigger. So it happened that I was born among Crazy Horse's people. After my sister Sandra was born the doctors there performed a hysterectomy on my mother, in fact sterilizing her without her permission, which was common at the time, and up to just a few years ago, so that it is hardly worth mentioning. In the opinion of some people, the fewer Indians there are, the better. As

Colonel Chivington said to his soldiers: "Kill 'em all, big and small, nits make lice!"

17   I don't know whether I am a louse under the white man's skin. I hope I am. At any rate I survived the long hours of my mother's labor, the stormy drive to Pine Ridge, and the neglect of the doctors. I am an iyeska, a breed, that's what the white kids used to call me. When I grew bigger they stopped calling me that, because it would get them a bloody nose. I am a small woman, not much over five feet tall, but I can hold my own in a fight, and in a free-for-all with honkies I can become rather ornery and do real damage. I have white blood in me. Often I have wished to be able to purge it out of me. As a young girl I used to look at myself in the mirror, trying to find a clue as to who and what I was. My face is very Indian, and so are my eyes and my hair, but my skin is very light. Always I waited for the summer, for the prairie sun, the badlands sun, to tan me and make me into a real skin.

18   The Crow Dogs, the members of my husband's family, have no such problems of identity. They don't need the sun to tan them, they are full-bloods—the Sioux of the Sioux. Some Crow Dog men have faces which make the portrait on the buffalo Indian nickel look like a washed-out white man. They have no shortage of legends. Every Crow Dog seems to be a legend in himself, including the women. They became outcasts in their stronghold at Grass Mountain rather than being whitemanized. They could not be tamed, made to wear a necktie or go to a Christian church. All during the long years when practicing Indian beliefs was forbidden and could be punished with jail, they went right on having their ceremonies, their sweat baths and sacred dances. Whenever a Crow Dog got together with some relatives, such as those equally untamed, unregenerate Iron Shells, Good Lances, Two Strikes, Picket Pins, or Hollow Horn Bears, then you could hear the sound of the can gleska, the drum, telling all the world that a Sioux ceremony was in the making. It took courage and suffering to keep the flame alive, the little spark under the snow.

19   The first Crow Dog was a well-known chief. On his shield was the design of two circles and two arrowheads for wounds received in battle—two white man's bullets and two Pawnee arrow points. When this first Crow Dog was lying wounded in the snow, a coyote came to warm him and a crow flew ahead of him to show him the way home. His name should be Crow Coyote, but the white interpreter misunderstood it and so they became Crow Dogs. This Crow Dog of old became famous for killing a rival chief, the result of a feud over tribal politics, then driving voluntarily over a hundred miles to get himself hanged at Deadwood, his wife sitting beside him in his buggy; famous also for finding on his arrival that the Supreme Court had ordered him to be freed because the federal government had no jurisdiction over Indian reservations and also because it was no crime for one Indian to kill another. Later, Crow Dog became a leader of the Ghost Dancers, holding out for months in the frozen caves and

ravines of the Badlands. So, if my own family lacks history, that of my husband more than makes up for it.

20   Our land itself is a legend, especially the area around Grass Mountain where I am living now. The fight for our land is at the core of our existence, as it has been for the last two hundred years. Once the land is gone, then we are gone too. The Sioux used to keep winter counts, picture writings on buffalo skin, which told our people's story from year to year. Well, the whole country is one vast winter count. You can't walk a mile without coming to some family's sacred vision hill, to an ancient Sun Dance circle, an old battleground, a place where something worth remembering happened. Mostly a death, a proud death or a drunken death. We are a great people for dying. "It's a good day to die!" that's our old battle cry. But the land with its tar paper shacks and outdoor privies, not one of them straight, but all leaning this way or that way, is also a land to live on, a land for good times and telling jokes and talking of great deeds done in the past. But you can't live forever off the deeds of Sitting Bull or Crazy Horse. You can't wear their eagle feathers, freeload off their legends. You have to make your own legends now. It isn't easy.

Discussion Questions

1. What do you think is the main purpose of this chapter from Crow Dog's book: to gain your sympathy? to describe the plight of Native Americans or of women? to decry whites' treatment of Native Americans? Explain your answer.

2. Crow Dog presents her stories matter-of-factly, without embellishments. Do you see this as an effective style? Why or why not?

3. When Crow Dog states in paragraph 4, "It is not always wise for an Indian woman to come on too strong," do you think Audre Lorde, Brent Staples, and Mark and Gail Mathabane would agree? Explain your reasons.

4. In paragraph 10, Crow Dog "start[s] from the beginning" and provides the history of her tribe. How necessary and helpful is that information? What does it add to the essay?

5. Explain your understanding of the last two sentences of Crow Dog's essay, "You have to make your own legends now. It isn't easy."

"Diversity and Its Discontents"
Arturo Madrid

*B*orn in 1939, Arturo Madrid was educated at the University of New Mexico and the University of California at Los Angeles where he received the Ph.D. degree in Spanish literature. He has taught at Dartmouth College, the University of California at San Diego, and the University of Minnesota, where he was also the Associate Dean of Humanities and Fine Arts. Currently, Madrid is president of the Tomas Rivera Center in Claremont, California, a research center he founded in 1985 to study educational, social, and economic issues that affect Hispanic-Americans. The original version of "Diversity and Its Discontents" was delivered at the 1988 meeting of the American Association for High Education; this current essay has been published in Academe. In it, Madrid reflects on the ways in which people of different races and ethnic backgrounds have been denied "voice or visibility or validity in American society and its institutions."

1   My name is Arturo Madrid. I am a citizen of the United States, as are my parents and as were my grandparents, and my great-grandparents. My ancestors' presence in what is now the United States antedates Plymouth Rock, even without taking into account any American Indian heritage I might have.

2   I do not, however, fit those mental sets that define America and Americans. My physical appearance, my speech patterns, my name, my profession (a professor of Spanish) create a text that confuses the reader. My normal experience is to be asked, "And where are *you* from?" My response depends on my mood. Passive-aggressive, I answer, "From here." Aggressive-passive, I ask, "Do you mean where am I originally from?" But ultimately my answer to those follow-up questions that ask about origins will be that we have always been from here.

3   Overcoming my resentment I will try to educate, knowing that nine times out of ten my words fall on inattentive ears. I have spent most of my adult life explaining who I am not. I am exotic, but—as Richard Rodriguez of *Hunger of Memory* fame so painfully found out—not exotic enough . . . not Peruvian, or Pakistani, or Persian, or whatever. I am, however, very clearly the *other*, if only your everyday, garden-variety, domestic *other*. I will share with you another phenomenon that I have been a part of, that of being a missing person, and how I came late to that awareness. But I've always known that I was the *other*, even before I knew the vocabulary or understood the significance of otherness.

4   I grew up in an isolated and historically marginal part of the United States, a small mountain village in the state of New Mexico, the eldest

child of parents native to that region and whose ancestors had always lived there. In those vast and empty spaces, people who look like me, speak as I do, and have names like mine predominate. But the *americanos* lived among us: the descendants of those nineteenth-century immigrants who dispossessed us of our lands; missionaries who came to convert us and stayed to live among us; artists who became enchanted with our land and humanscape and went native; refugees from unhealthy climes, crowded spaces, unpleasant circumstances; and, of course, the inhabitants of Los Alamos, whose socio-cultural distance from us was moreover accentuated by the fact that they occupied a space removed from and proscribed to us. More importantly, however, they—*los americanos*—were omnipresent (and almost exclusively so) in newspapers, newsmagazines, books, on radio, in movies and, ultimately, on television.

5   Despite the operating myth of the day, school did not erase my otherness. It did try to deny it, and in doing so only accentuated it. To this day, schooling is more socialization than education, but when I was in elementary school—and given where I was—socialization was everything. School was where one became an American. Because there was a pervasive and systematic denial by the society that surrounded us that we were Americans. That denial was both explicit and implicit. My earliest memory of the former was that there were two kinds of churches: theirs and ours. The more usual was the implicit denial, our absence from the larger cultural, economic, political and social spaces—the one that reminded us constantly that we were *the other*. And school was where we felt it most acutely.

6   Quite beyond saluting the flag and pledging allegiance to it (a very intense and meaningful action, given that the U.S. was involved in a war and our brothers, cousins, uncles, and fathers were on the front lines) becoming American was learning English and its corollary—not speaking Spanish. Until very recently ours was a proscribed language—either *de jure* (by rule, by policy, by law) or *de facto* (by practice, implicitly if not explicitly; through social and political and economic pressure). I do not argue that learning English was not appropriate. On the contrary. Like it or not, and we had no basis to make any judgments on that matter, we were Americans by virtue of having been born Americans, and English was the common language of Americans. And there was a myth, a pervasive myth, that said that if we only learned to speak English well—and particularly without an accent—we would be welcomed into the American fellowship.

7   Sam Hayakawa and the official English movement folks notwithstanding, the true text was not our speech, but rather our names and our appearance, for we would always have an accent, however perfect our pronunciation, however excellent our enunciation, however divine our diction. That accent would be heard in our pigmentation, our physiognomy, our names. We were, in short, the *other*.

8   Being the *other* involves a contradictory phenomenon. On the one hand being the *other* frequently means being invisible. Ralph Ellison wrote eloquently about that experience in his magisterial novel *The Invisible*

Man. On the other hand, being the *other* sometimes involves sticking out like a sore thumb. What is she/he doing here?

9   For some of us being the *other* is only annoying; for others it is debilitating; for still others it is damning. Many try to flee otherness by taking on protective colorations that provide invisibility, whether of dress or speech or manner or name. Only a fortunate few succeed. For the majority, otherness is permanently sealed by physical appearance. For the rest, otherness is betrayed by ways of being, speaking or of doing.

10   The first half of my life downplaying the significance and consequences of otherness. The second half has seen me wrestling to understand its complex and deeply ingrained realities; striving to fathom why otherness denies us a voice or visibility or validity in American society and its institutions; struggling to make otherness familiar, reasonable, even normal to my fellow Americans.

11   I spoke earlier of another phenomenon that I am a part of: that of being a missing person. Growing up in northern New Mexico I had only a slight sense of our being missing persons. *Hispanos,* as we called (and call) ourselves in New Mexico, were very much a part of the fabric of the society, and there were *hispano* professionals everywhere about me: doctors, lawyers, school teachers, and administrators. My people owned businesses, ran organizations and were both appointed and elected public officials.

12   My awareness of our absence from the larger institutional life of society became sharper when I went off to college, but even then it was attenuated by the circumstances of history and geography. The demography of Albuquerque still strongly reflected its historical and cultural origins, despite the influx of Midwesterners and Easterners. Moreover, many of my classmates at the University of New Mexico in Albuquerque were Hispanos, and even some of my professors were. I thought that would obtain at UCLA, where I began graduate studies in 1960. Los Angeles already had a very large Mexican population, and that population was visible even in and around Westwood and on the campus. Many of the grounds-keepers and food-service personnel at UCLA were Mexican. But Mexican-American students were few and mostly invisible, and I do not recall seeing or knowing a single Mexican-American (or, for that matter, black, Asian, or American Indian) professional on the staff or faculty of that institution during the five years I was there. Needless to say, persons like me were not present in any capacity at Dartmouth College the site of my first teaching appointment, and, of course were not even part of the institutional or individual mind-set. I knew then that we—a we that had come to encompass American Indians, Asian-Americans, black Americans, Puerto Ricans, and women—were truly missing persons in American institutional life.

13   Over the past three decades, the *de jure* and *de facto* types of segregation that have historically characterized American institutions have been under assault. As a consequence, minorities and women have become part

of American institutional life, and although there are still many areas where we are not to be found, the missing persons phenomenon is not as pervasive as it once was. However, the presence of the *other*, particularly minorities, in institutions and in institutional life, is, as we say in Spanish, a *flor de tierra* we are spare plants whose roots do not go deep, a surface phenomenon, vulnerable to inclemencies of an economic, political, or social nature.

14   Our entrance into and our status in institutional life is not unlike a scenario set forth by my grandmother's pastor when she informed him that she and her family were leaving their mountain village to relocate in the Rio Grande Valley. When he asked her to promise that she would remain true to the faith and continue to involve herself in the life of the church, she assured him that she would and asked him why he thought she would do otherwise. "Doña Trinidad," he told her, "in the Valley there is no Spanish church. There is only an American church." "But," she protested, "I read and speak English and would be able to worship there." The pastor responded, "It is possible that they will not admit you, and even if they do, they might not accept you. And that is why I want you to promise me that you are going to go to church. Because if they don't let you in through the front door, I want you to go in through the back door. And if you can't get in through the back door, go in the side door. And if you are unable to enter through the side door I want you to go in through the window. What is important is that you enter and that you stay."

15   Some of us entered institutional life through the front door; others through the back door; and still others through side doors. Many, if not most of us, came in through windows and continue to come in through windows. Of those who entered through the front door, some never made it past the lobby; others were ushered into corners and niches. Those who entered through back and side doors inevitably have remained in back and side rooms. And those who entered through windows found enclosures built around them. For, despite the lip service given to the goal of the integration of minorities into institutional life, what has frequently occurred instead is ghettoization, marginalization, isolation.

16   Not only have the entry points been limited, but in addition, the dynamics have been singularly conflictive. Gaining entry and its corollary, gaining space, have frequently come as a consequence of demands made on institutions and institutional officers. Rather than entering institutions more or less passively, minorities have of necessity entered them actively, even aggressively. Rather than waiting to receive, they have demanded. Institutional relations have thus been adversarial, infused with specific and generalized tensions.

17   The nature of the entrance and the nature of the space occupied have greatly influenced the view and attitudes of the majority population within those institutions. All of us are put into the same box; that is, no matter what the individual reality, the assessment of the individual is inevitably conditioned by a perception that is held of the class. Whatever our history, whatever our record, whatever our validations, whatever our accomplish-

ments, by and large we are perceived unidimensionally and dealt with accordingly. I remember an experience I had in this regard, atypical only in its explicitness. A few years ago I allowed myself to be persuaded to seek the presidency of a well-known state university. I was invited for an interview and presented myself before the selection committee, which included members of the board of trustees. The opening question of the brief but memorable interview was directed at me by a member of that august body. "Dr. Madrid," he asked, "why does a one-dimensional person like you think he can be the president of a multi-dimensional institution like ours?"

18   Over the past four decades America's demography has undergone significant changes. Since 1965 the principal demographic growth we have experienced in the United States has been of peoples whose national origins are non-European. This population growth has occurred both through birth and through immigration. A few years ago discussion of the national birthrate had a scare dimension: the high—"inordinately high"—birthrate of the Hispanic population. The popular discourse was informed by words such as "breeding." Several years later, as a consequence of careful tracking by government agencies, we now know that what has happened is that the birthrate of the majority population has decreased. When viewed historically and comparatively, the minority populations (for the most part) have also had a decline in birthrate, but not one as great as that of the majority.

19   There are additional demographic changes that should give us something to think about. African-Americans are now to be found in significant numbers in every major urban center in the nation. Hispanic-Americans now number over 15 million people, and although they are a regionally concentrated (and highly urbanized) population, there is a Hispanic community in almost every major urban center of the United States. American Indians, heretofore a small and rural population, are increasingly more numerous and urban. The Asian-American population, which has historically consisted of small and concentrated communities of Chinese-, Filipino-, and Japanese-Americans, has doubled over the past decade, its complexion changed by the addition of Cambodians, Koreans, Hmongs, Vietnamese, et al.

20   Prior to the Immigration Act of 1965, 69 percent of immigration was from Europe. By far the largest number of immigrants to the United States since 1965 have been from the Americas and from Asia: 34 percent are from Asia; another 34 percent are from Central and South America; 16 percent are from Europe; 10 percent are from the Caribbean; the remaining 6 percent are from other continents and Canada. As was the case with previous immigration waves, the current one consists principally of young people: 60 percent are between the ages of 16 and 44. Thus, for the next few decades, we will continue to see a growth in the percentage of non-European-origin Americans as compared to European-Americans.

21   To sum up, we now live in one of the most demographically diverse nations in the world, and one that is increasingly more so.

22   During the same period social and economic change seems to have ac-

celerated. Who would have imagined at mid-century that the prototypical middle-class family (working husband, wife as homemaker, two children) would for all intents and purposes disappear? Who could have anticipated the rise in teenage pregnancies, children in poverty, drug use? Who among us understood the implications of an aging population?

23   We live in an age of continuous and intense change, a world in which what held true yesterday does not today, and certainly will not tomorrow. What change does, moreover, is bring about even more change. The only constant we have at this point in our national development is change. And change is threatening. The older we get the more likely we are to be anxious about change, and the greater our desire to maintain the status quo.

24   Evident in our public life is a fear of change, whether economic or moral. Some who fear change are responsive to the call of economic protectionism, others to the message of moral protectionism. Parenthetically, I have referred to the movement to require more of students without in turn giving them more as academic protectionism. And the pronouncements of E. D. Hirsch and Allan Bloom are, I believe, informed by intellectual protectionism. Much more serious, however, is the dark side of the populism which underlies this evergoing protectionism—the resentment of the *other*. An excellent and fascinating example of that aspect of populism is the cry for linguistic protectionism—for making English the official language of the United States. And who among us is unaware of the tensions that underlie immigration reform, of the underside of demographic protectionism?

25   A matter of increasing concern is whether this new protectionism, and the mistrust of the *other* which accompanies it, is not making more significant inroads than we have supposed in higher education. Specifically, I wish to discuss the question of whether a goal (quality) and a reality (demographic diversity) have been erroneously placed in conflict, and, if so, what problems this perception of conflict might present.

26   As part of my scholarship I turn to dictionaries for both origins and meanings of words. Quality, according to the *Oxford English Dictionary,* has multiple meanings. One set defines quality as being an essential character, a distinctive and inherent feature. A second describes it as a degree of excellence, of conformity to standards, as superiority in kind. A third makes reference to social status, particularly to persons of high social status. A fourth talks about quality as being a special or distinguishing attribute, as being a desirable trait. Quality is highly desirable in both principle and practice. We all aspire to it in our own person, in our experiences, in our acquisitions and products, and of course we all want to be associated with people and operations of quality.

27   But let us move away from the various dictionary meanings of the word and to our own sense of what it represents and of how we feel about it. First of all we consider quality to be finite; that is, it is limited with respect to quantity; it has very few manifestations; it is not widely distributed. I have it and you have it, but they don't. We associate quality with

homogeneity, with uniformity, with standardization, with order, regularity, neatness. All too often we equate it with smoothness, glibness, slickness, elegance. Certainly it is always expensive. We tend to identify it with those who lead, with the rich and famous. And, when you come right down to it, it's inherent. Either you've got it or you ain't.

28   Diversity, from the Latin *divertere,* meaning to turn aside, to go different ways, to differ, is the condition of being different or having differences, is an instance of being different. Its companion word, diverse, means differing, unlike, distinct; having or capable or having various forms; composed of unlike or distinct elements. Diversity is lack of standardization, of regularity, of orderliness, homogeneity, conformity, uniformity. Diversity introduces complications, is difficult to organize, is troublesome to manage, is problematical. Diversity is irregular, disorderly, uneven, rough. The way we use the word diversity gives us away. Something is too diverse, is extremely diverse. We want a little diversity.

29   When we talk about diversity, we are talking about the *other,* whatever that other might be: someone of a different gender, race, class, national origin; somebody at a greater or lesser distance from the norm; someone outside the set; someone who possesses a different set of characteristics, features, or attributes; someone who does not fall within the taxonomies we use daily and with which we are comfortable; someone who does not fit into the mental configurations that give our lives order and meaning.

30   In short, diversity is desirable only in principle, not in practice. Long live diversity . . . as long as it conforms to my standards, my mind set, my view of life, my sense of order. We desire, we like, we admire diversity, not unlike the way the French (and others) appreciate women; that is, *Vive la difference!*—as long as it stays in its place.

31   What I find paradoxical about and lacking in this debate is that diversity is the natural order of things. Evolution produces diversity. Margaret Visser, writing about food in her latest book, *Much Depends on Dinner,* makes an eloquent statement in this regard:

> Machines like, demand, and produce uniformity. But nature loathes it: her strength lies in multiplicity and in differences. Sameness in biology means fewer possibilities and therefore weakness.

32   The United States, by its very nature, by its very development, is the essence of diversity. It is diverse in its geography, population, institutions, technology; its social, cultural, and intellectual modes. It is a society that at its best does not consider quality to be monolithic in form or finite in quantity, or to be inherent in class. Quality in our society proceeds in large measure out of the stimulus of diverse modes of thinking and acting; out of the creativity made possible by the different ways in which we approach things; out of diversion from paths or modes hallowed by tradition.

33   One of the principal strengths of our society is its ability to address, on a continuing and substantive basis, the real economic, political, and social problems that have faced and continue to face us. What makes the United States so attractive to immigrants is the protections and opportunities it offers; what keeps our society together is tolerance for cultural, religious, social, political, and even linguistic difference; what makes us a unique, dynamic, and extraordinary nation is the power and creativity of our diversity.

34   The true history of the United States is one of struggle against intolerance, against oppression, against xenophobia, against those forces that have prohibited persons from participating in the larger life of the society on the basis of their race, their gender, their religion, their national origin, their linguistic and cultural background. These phenomena are not consigned to the past. They remain with us and frequently take on virulent dimensions.

35   If you believe, as I do, that the well-being of a society is directly related to the degree and extent to which all of its citizens participate in its institutions, then you will have to agree that we have a challenge before us. In view of the extraordinary changes that are taking place in our society we need to take up the struggle again, irritating, grating, troublesome, unfashionable, unpleasant as it is. As educated and educator members of this society we have a special responsibility for ensuring that all American institutions, not just our elementary and secondary schools, our juvenile halls, or our jails, reflect the diversity of our society. Not to do so is to risk greater alienation on the part of a growing segment of our society; is to risk increased social tension in an already conflictive world; and, ultimately, is to risk the survival of a range of institutions that, for all their defects and deficiencies, provide us the opportunity and the freedom to improve our individual and collective lot.

36   Let me urge you to reflect on these two words—quality and diversity—and on the mental sets and behaviors that flow out of them. And let me urge you further to struggle against the notion that quality is finite in quantity, limited in its manifestations, or is restricted by considerations of class, gender, race, or national origin; or that quality manifests itself only in leaders and not in followers, in managers and not in workers, in breeders and not in drones; or that it has to be associated with verbal agility or elegance of personal style; or that it cannot be seeded, nurtured, or developed.

37   Because diversity—the *other*—is among us, will define and determine our lives in ways that we still do not fully appreciate, whether that other is women (no longer bound by tradition, house, and family); or Asians, African-Americans, Indians, and Hispanics (no longer invisible, regional, or marginal); or our newest immigrants (no longer distant, exotic, alien). Given the changing profile of America, will we come to terms with diversity in our personal and professional lives? Will we begin to recognize the diverse forms that quality can take? If so, we will thus initiate the process of making

quality limitless in its manifestations, infinite in quantity, unrestricted with respect to its origins, and more importantly, virulently contagious.

38   I hope we will. And that we will further join together to expand—not to close—the circle.

Discussion Questions

1. For which does Madrid make a stronger case: his being a "missing person" or an "other"? Do you think there are more "missing persons" than there are "others" in the United States? Explain your answer.

2. In paragraph 5, Madrid states that "what takes place in schools is more socialization than education." Based on your own experiences and observations, to what extent do you agree or disagree with him?

3. Madrid states in paragraph 13 that "minorities and women have become part of American institutional life. And although there are still many areas where we are not to be found, the missing persons phenomenon is not as pervasive as it once was." Provide specific examples that would prove Madrid's point.

4. What does the word "diversity" conjure up in your mind? Why? To what extent do you agree or disagree with Madrid's discussion of diversity? Explain your response.

5. How do you think Audre Lorde, Brent Staples, Mark and Gail Mathabane, and Mary Crow Dog would react to Madrid's essay? On what points would they agree and disagree?

Growing Up Asian in America
Kesaya E. Noda

Born in 1950 in California, Kesaya E. Noda was raised in New Hampshire. After graduating from high school, she spent eighteen months living and studying in Japan. Noda is the recipient of a master's degree from Harvard Divinity School and is studying for a doctorate in religious studies from Harvard University. She is the author of The Yamato Colony *(1981), a history of the California community where her parents grew up. The following essay, which discusses her growing sense of self-identity, first appeared in* Making Waves, *an anthology of Asian-American writing.*

1   Sometimes when I was growing up, my identity seemed to hurtle to-

ward me and paste itself right to my face. I felt that way, encountering the stereotypes of my race perpetuated by non-Japanese people (primarily white) who may or may not have had contact with other Japanese in America. "You don't like cheese, do you?" someone would ask. "I know your people don't like cheese." Sometimes questions came making allusions to history. That was another aspect of the identity. Events that had happened quite apart from the me who stood silent in that moment connected my face with an incomprehensible past. "Your parents were in California? Were they in those camps during the war?" And sometimes there were phrases or nicknames: "Lotus Blossom." I was sometimes addressed or referred to as racially Japanese, sometimes as Japanese-American, and sometimes as an Asian woman. Confusions and distortions abounded.

2   How is one to know and define oneself? From the inside—within a context that is self-defined, from a grounding in community and a connection with culture and history that are comfortably accepted? Or from the outside—in terms of messages received from the media and people who are often ignorant? Even as an adult I can still see two sides of my face and past. I can see from the inside out, in freedom. And I can see from the outside in, driven by the old voices of childhood and lost in anger and fear.

I Am Racially Japanese

3   A voice from my childhood says: "You are other. You are less than. You are unalterably alien." This voice has its own history. We have indeed been seen as other and alien since the early years of our arrival in the United States. The very first immigrants were welcomed and sought as laborers to replace the dwindling numbers of Chinese, whose influx had been cut off by the Chinese Exclusion Act of 1882. The Japanese fell natural heir to the same anti-Asian prejudice that had arisen against the Chinese. As soon as they began striking for better wages, they were no longer welcomed.

4   I can see myself today as a person historically defined by law and custom as being forever alien. Being neither "free white," nor "African," our people in California were deemed "aliens, ineligible for citizenship," no matter how long they intended to stay here. Aliens ineligible for citizenship were prohibited from owning, buying, or leasing land. They did not and could not belong here. The voice in me remembers that I am always a *Japanese*-American in the eyes of many. A third-generation German-American is an American. A third-generation Japanese-American is a Japanese-American. Being Japanese means being a danger to the country during the war and knowing how to use chopsticks. I wear this history on my face.

5   I move to the other side. I see a different light and claim a different context. My race is a line that stretches across ocean and time to link me to the shrine where my grandmother was raised. Two high, white banners lift in the wind at the top of the stone steps leading to the shrine. It is time for

the summer festival. Black characters are written against the sky as boldly as the clouds, as lightly as kites, as sharply as the big black crows I used to see above the fields in New Hampshire. At festival time there is liquor and food, ritual, discipline, and abandonment. There is music and drunkenness and invocation. There is hope. Another season has come. Another season has gone.

6   I am racially Japanese. I have a certain claim to this crazy place where the prayers intoned by a neighboring Shinto priest (standing in for my grandmother's nephew who is sick) are drowned out by the rehearsals for the pop singing contest in which most of the villagers will compete later that night. The village elders, the priest, and I stand respectfully upon the immaculate, shining wooden floor of the outer shrine, bowing our heads before the hidden powers. During the patchy intervals when I can hear him, I notice the priest has a stutter. His voice flutters up to my ears only occasionally because two men and a women are singing gustily into a microphone in the compound, testing the sound system. A prerecorded tape of guitars, samisens, and drums accompanies them. Rock music and Shinto prayers. That night, to loud applause and cheers, a young man is given the award for the most *netsuretsu*—passionate, burning—rendition of a song. We roar our approval of the reward. Never mind that his voice had wandered and slid, now slightly above, now slightly below the given line of the melody. Netsuretsu. Netsuretsu.

7   In the morning, my grandmother's sister kneels at the foot of the stone stairs to offer her morning prayers. She is too crippled to climb the stairs, so each morning she kneels here upon the path. She shuts her eyes for a few seconds, her motions as matter of fact as when she washes rice. I linger longer than she does, so reluctant to leave, savoring the connection I feel with my grandmother in America, the past, and the power that lives and shines in the morning sun.

8   Our family has served this shrine for generations. The family's need to protect this claim to identity and place outweighs any individual claim to any individual hope. I am Japanese.

I Am a Japanese-American

9   "Weak." I hear the voice from my childhood years. "Passive," I hear. Our parents and grandparents were the ones who were put into those camps. They went without resistance; they offered cooperation as proof of loyalty to America. "Victim," I hear. And, "Silent."

10   Our parents are painted as hard workers who were socially uncomfortable and had difficulty expressing even the smallest opinion. Clean, quiet, motivated, and determined to match the American way; that is us, and that is the story of our time here.

11   "Why did you go into those camps?" I raged at my parents, frightened by my own inner silence and timidity. "Why didn't you do anything to re-

sist? Why didn't you name it the injustice it was?" Couldn't our parents even think? Couldn't they? Why were we so passive?

12   I shift my vision and my stance. I am in California. My uncle is in the midst of the sweet potato harvest. He is pressed, trying to get the harvesting crews onto the field as quickly as possible, worried about the flow of equipment and people. His big pickup is pulled off to the side, motor running, door ajar. I see two tractors in the yard in front of an old shed; the flatbed harvesting platform on which the workers will stand has already been brought over from the other field. It's early morning. The workers stand loosely grouped and at ease, but my uncle looks as harried and tense as a police officer trying to unsnarl a New York City traffic jam. Driving toward the shed, I pull my car off the road to make way for an approaching tractor. The front wheels of the car sink luxuriously into the soft, white sand by the roadside and the car slides to a dreamy halt, tail still on the road. I try to move forward. I try to move back. The front bites contentedly into the sand, the back lifts itself at a jaunty angle. My uncle sees me and storms down the road, running. He is shouting before he is even near me.

13   "What's the matter with you?" he screams. "What the hell are you doing?" In his frenzy, he grabs his hat off his head and slashes it through the air across his knee. He is beside himself. "Don't you know how to drive in sand? What's the matter with you? You've blocked the whole roadway. How am I supposed to get my tractors out of here? Can't you use your head? You've cut off the whole roadway, and we've got to get out of here."

14   I stand on the road before him helplessly thinking, "No, I don't know how to drive in sand. I've never driven in sand."

15   "I'm sorry, uncle," I say, burying a smile beneath a look of sincere apology. I notice my deep amusement and my affection for him with great curiosity. I am usually devastated by anger. Not this time.

16   During the several years that follow I learn about the people and the place, and much more about what has happened in this California village where my parents grew up. The issei, our grandparents, made this settlement in the desert. Their first crops were eaten by rabbits and ravaged by insects. The land was so barren that men walking from house to house sometimes got lost. Women came here too. They bore children in 114-degree heat, then carried the babies with them into the fields to nurse when they reached the end of each row of grapes or other truck-farm crops.

17   I had had no idea what it meant to buy this kind of land and make it grow green. Or how, when the war came, there was no space at all for the subtlety of being who we were—Japanese-Americans. Either/or was the way. I hadn't understood that people were literally afraid for their lives then, that their money had been frozen in banks; that there was a five-mile travel limit; that when the early evening curfew came and they were inside their houses, some of them watched helplessly as people they knew went into their barns to steal their belongings. The police were patrolling the

road, interested only in violators of curfew. There was no help for them in the face of thievery. I had not been able to imagine before what it must have felt like to be an American—to know absolutely that one is an American—and yet to have almost everyone else deny it. Not only deny it, but challenge that identity with machine guns and troops of white American soldiers. In those circumstances it was difficult to say, "I'm a Japanese-American." "American" had to do.

18   But now I can say that I am a Japanese-American. It means I have a place here in this country, too. I have a place here on the East Coast, where our neighbor is so much a part of our family that my mother never passes her house at night without glancing at the lights to see if she is home and safe; where my parents have hauled hundreds of pounds of rocks from fields and arduously planted Christmas trees and blueberries, lilacs, asparagus, and crab apples; where my father still dreams of angling a stream to a new bed so that he can dig a pond in the field and fill it with water and fish. "The neighbors already came for their Christmas tree?" he asks in December. "Did they like it? Did they like it?"

19   I have a place on the West Coast where my relatives still farm, where I heard the stories of feuds and backbiting, and where I saw that people survived and flourished because fundamentally they trusted and relied upon one another. A death in the family is not just a death in a family; it is a death in the community. I saw people help each other with money, materials, labor, attention, and time. I saw men gather once a year, without fail, to clean the grounds of a ninety-year-old woman who had helped the community before, during, and after the war. I saw her remembering them with birthday cards sent to each of their children.

20   I come from a people with a long memory and a distinctive grace. We live our thanks. And we are Americans. Japanese-Americans.

I Am a Japanese-American Woman

21   Woman. The past piece of my identity. It has been easier by far for me to know myself in Japan and to see my place in America than it has been to accept my line of connection with my own mother. She was my dark self, a figure in whom I thought I saw all that I feared most in myself. Growing into womanhood and looking for some model of strength. I turned away from her. Of course, I could not find what I sought. I was looking for a black feminist or a white feminist. My mother is neither white nor black.

22   My mother is a woman who speaks with her life as much as with her tongue. I think of her with her own mother. Grandmother had Parkinson's disease and it had frozen her gait and set her fingers, tongue, and feet jerking and trembling in a terrible dance. My aunts and uncles wanted her to be able to live in her own home. They fed her, bathed her, dressed her, awoke at midnight to take her for one last trip to the bathroom. My aunts (her daughters-in-law) did most of the care, but my mother went

from New Hampshire to California each summer to spend a month living with Grandmother, because she wanted to and because she wanted to give my aunts at least a small rest. During those hot summer days, mother lay on the couch watching the television or reading, cooking foods that Grandmother liked, and speaking little. Grandmother thrived under her care.

23   The time finally came when it was too dangerous for Grandmother to live alone. My relatives kept finding her on the floor beside her bed when they went to wake her in the mornings. My mother flew to California to help clean the house and make arrangements for Grandmother to enter a local nursing home. On her last day at home, while Grandmother was sitting in her big, overstuffed armchair, hair combed and wearing a green summer dress, my mother went to her and knelt at her feet. "Here, Mamma," she said. "I've polished your shoes." She lifted Grandmother's legs and helped her into the shiny black shoes. My Grandmother looked down and smiled slightly. She left her house walking, supported by her children, carrying her pocket book, and wearing her polished black shoes. "Look, Mamma," my mom had said, kneeling. "I've polished your shoes."

24   Just the other day, my mother came to Boston to visit. She had recently lost a lot of weight and was pleased with her new shape and her feeling of good health. "Look at me, Kes," she exclaimed, turning toward me, front and back, as naked as the day she was born. I saw her small breasts and the wide, brown scar, belly button to pubic hair, that marked her because my brother and I were both born by Caesarean section. Her hips were small. I was not a large baby, but there was so little room for me in her that when she was carrying me she could not even begin to bend over toward the floor. She hated it, she said.

25   "Don't I look good? Don't you think I look good?"

26   I looked at my mother, smiling and as happy as she, thinking of all the times I have seen her naked. I have seen both my parents naked throughout my life, as they have seen me. From childhood through adulthood we've had our naked moments, sharing baths, idle conversations picked up as we moved between showers and closets, hurried moments at the beginning of days, quiet moments at the end of days.

27   I know this to be Japanese, this ease with the physical, and it makes me think of an old Japanese folk song. A young nursemaid, a fifteen-year-old girl, is singing a lullaby to a baby who is strapped to her back. The nursemaid has been sent as a servant to a place far from her own home. "We're the beggars," she says, "and they are the nice people. Nice people wear fine sashes. Nice clothes."

> *If I should drop dead,*
> *bury me by the roadside!*
> *I'll give a flower*
> *to everyone who passes.*

What kind of flower?

The cam-cam-camellia [tsun-tsun-tsubaki]

watered by Heaven:

alms water.

28   The nursemaid is the intersection of heaven and earth, the intersection of the human, the natural world, the body, and the soul. In this song, with clear eyes, she looks steadily at life, which is sometimes so very terrible and sad. I think of her while looking at my mother, who is standing on the red and purple carpet before me, laughing, without any clothes.

29   I am my mother's daughter. And I am myself.

30   I am a Japanese-American woman.

Epilogue

31   I recently heard a man from West Africa share some memories of his childhood. He was raised Muslim, but when he was a young man, he found himself deeply drawn to Christianity. He struggled against his inner impulse for years, trying to avoid the church yet feeling pushed to return to it again and again. "I would have done *anything* to avoid the change," he said. At last, he became Christian. Afterwards he was afraid to go home, fearing that he would not be accepted. The fear was groundless, he discovered, when at last he returned—he had separated himself, but his family and friends (all Muslim) had not separated themselves from him.

32   The man, who is now a professor of religion, said that in the Africa he knew as a child and a young man, pluralism was embraced rather than feared. There was "a kind of tolerance that did not deny your particularity," he said. He alluded to zestful, spontaneous debates that would sometimes loudly erupt between Muslims and Christians in the village's public spaces. His memories of an atheist who harangued the villagers when he came to visit them once a week moved me deeply. Perhaps the man was an agricultural advisor or inspector. He harrassed the women. He would say: "Don't go to the fields! Don't even bother to go to the fields. Let God take care of you. He'll send you the food. If you believe in God, why do you need to work? You don't need to work! Let God put the seeds in the ground. Stay home."

33   The professor said, "The women laughed, you know? They just laughed. Their attitude was, 'Here is a child of God. When will he come home?'"

34   The storyteller, the professor of religion, smiled a most fantastic tender smile as he told this story. "In my country, there is a deep affirmation of the oneness of God," he said. "The atheist and the women were having quite different experiences in their encounter, though the atheist did not know this. He saw himself as quite separate from the women. But the

women did not see themselves as being separate from him. 'Here is a child of God,' they said. 'When will he come home?'"

Discussion Questions

1. Noda asks in paragraph 2, "How is one to know and define one-self?" How would *you* answer that question?

2. Why do you think it is important for Noda to establish her self-identity? Why is it important for most people? Do you think at the end of the essay she succeeds? Why or why not?

3. Do you think that most people have difficulty establishing their sense of self-identity? Why do you think that is the case?

4. What does the Japanese folksong that Noda describes in paragraphs 27 and 28 add to her essay? How necessary is it?

5. What do you see as the purpose of Noda's epilogue? What does it add to the essay?

Thriving as an Outsider, Even as an Outcast, in Smalltown America

Louie Crew

Born in 1936, Louie Crew grew up in Alabama and earned his B.A. degree from Baylor University, his M.A. degree from Auburn University, and his Ph.D. degree from the University of Alabama. A gay activist and religious reformer, Crew is an essayist, poet, and a professor at Rutgers University. He also has taught in China. The founder of Integrity, a national organization for gay Episcopalians, Crew wrote the following essay as a response to the social problems he experienced while living in a small town in Georgia.

1   From 1973 to 1979, my spouse and I lived in Fort Valley, a town of 12,000 people, the seat of Peach County, sixty miles northeast of Plains, right in the geographic center of Georgia. I taught English at a local black college and my spouse was variously a nurse, hairdresser, choreographer for the college majorettes, caterer, and fashion designer.

2   The two of us have often been asked how we survived as a gay, racially integrated couple living openly in that small town. We are still perhaps too close to the Georgia experience and very much caught up in our similar struggles in central Wisconsin to offer a definite explanation, but our tentative conjectures should interest anyone who values the role of the dissi-

dent in our democracy.

3   Survive we did. We even throve before our departure. Professionally, my colleagues and the Regents of the University System of Georgia awarded me tenure, and the Chamber of Commerce awarded my spouse a career medal in cosmetology. Socially, we had friends from the full range of the economic classes in the community. We had attended six farewell parties in our honor before we called a halt to further fetes, especially several planned at too great a sacrifice by some of the poorest folks in the town. Furthermore, I had been away only four months when the college brought me back to address an assembly of Georgia judges, majors, police chiefs, and wardens. We are still called two to three times a week by scores of people seeking my spouse's advice on fashion, cooking, or the like.

4   It was not always so. In 1974 my spouse and I were denied housing which we had "secured" earlier before the realtor saw my spouse's color. HUD documented that the realtor thought that "the black man looked like a criminal." Once the town was up in arms when a bishop accused the two of us of causing a tornado which had hit the town early in 1975, an accusation which appeared on the front page of the newspaper. "This is the voice of God. The town of Fort Valley is harboring Sodomists. Would one expect God to keep silent when homosexuals are tolerated? We remember what He did to Sodom and Gomorrah" (*The Macon Herald*, March 20, 1975: 1). A year later my Episcopal vestry asked me to leave the parish, and my own bishop summoned me for discipline for releasing to the national press correspondence related to the vestry's backroom maneuvers. Prompted in part by such officials, the local citizens for years routinely heckled us in public, sometimes threw rocks at our apartment, trained their children to spit on us from their bicycles if we dared to jog, and badgered us with hate calls on an average of six to eight times a week.

5   One such episode offers a partial clue to the cause of our survival. It was late summer, 1975 or 1976. I was on my motorcycle to post mail at the street-side box just before the one daily pickup at 6:00 P.M. About fifty yards away, fully audible to about seventy pedestrians milling about the court house and other public buildings, a group of police officers, all men, began shouting at me from the steps of their headquarters: "Louise! Faggot! Queer!"

6   Anyone who has ever tried to ease a motorcycle from a still position without revving the engine knows that the feat is impossible: try as I did to avoid the suggestion, I sounded as if I were riding off in a huff. About half-way up the street, I thought to myself, "I'd rather rot in jail than feel the way I do now." I turned around, drove back—the policemen still shouting and laughing—and parked in the lot of the station. When I walked to the steps, only the lone black policeman remained.

7   "Did you speak to me?" I asked him.

8   "No, sir," he replied emphatically.

9   Inside I badgered the desk sergeant to tell her chief to call me as soon

as she could locate him, and I indicated that I would press charges if necessary to prevent a recurrence. I explained that the police misconduct was an open invitation to more violent hoodlums to act out the officers' fantasies with impunity in the dark. Later, I persuaded a black city commissioner and a white one, the latter our grocer and the former our mortician, to threaten the culprits with suspension if ever such misconduct occurred again.

10   Over a year later, late one Friday after his payday, a black friend of my spouse knocked at our door to offer a share of his Scotch to celebrate his raise—or so he said. Thus primed, he asked me, "You don't recognize me, do you?"

11   "No," I admitted.

12   "I'm the lone black policeman that day you were heckled. I came by really because I thought you two might want to know what happened inside when Louie stormed up to the sergeant."

13   "Yes," we said.

14   "Well, all the guys were crouching behind the partition to keep you from seeing that they were listening. Their eyes bulged when you threatened to bring in the F.B.I. and such. Then when you left, one spoke for all when he said, 'But sissies aren't supposed to do things like that!'"

15   Ironically, I believe that a major reason for our thriving on our own terms of candor about our relationship has been our commitment to resist the intimidation heaped upon us. For too long lesbians and gay males have unwillingly encouraged abuses against ourselves by serving advance notice to any bullies, be they the barnyard-playground variety, or the Bible-wielding pulpiteers, that we would whimper or run into hiding when confronted with even the threat of exposure. It is easy to confuse sensible nonviolence with cowardly nonresistance.

16   In my view, violent resistance would be counter-productive, especially for lesbians and gays who are outnumbered 10 to 1 by heterosexuals, according to Kinsey's statistics. Yet our personal experience suggests that special kinds of creative nonviolent resistance are a major source of hope if lesbians and gay males are going to reverse the physical and mental intimidation which is our daily portion in this culture.

17   Resistance to oppression can be random and spontaneous, as in part was my decision to return to confront the police hecklers, or organized and sustained, as more typically has been the resistance by which my spouse and I have survived. I believe that only organized and sustained resistance offers much hope for long-range change in any community. The random act is too soon forgotten or too easily romanticized.

18   Once we had committed ourselves to one another, my spouse and I never gave much thought for ourselves to the traditional device most gays have used for survival, the notorious "closet" in which one hides one's identity from all but a select group of friends. In the first place, a black man and a white man integrating a Georgia small town simply cannot be inconspicuous. More importantly, the joint checking account and other equitable economies fundamental to the quality of our marriage are pub-

lic, not private acts. Our denial of the obvious would have secured closet space only for our suffocation; we would have lied, "We are ashamed and live in secret."

19   All of our resistance stems from our sense of our own worth, our conviction that we and our kind do not deserve the suffering which heterosexuals continue to encourage or condone for sexual outcasts. Dr. Martin Luther King used to say, "Those who go to the back of the bus, deserve the back of the bus."

20   Our survival on our own terms has depended very much on our knowing and respecting many of the rules of the system which we resist. We are not simply dissenters, but conscientious ones.

21   For example, we are both very hard workers. As a controversial person, I know that my professionalism comes under far more scrutiny than that of others. I learned early in my career that I could secure space for my differences by handling routine matters carefully. If one stays on good terms with secretaries, meets all deadlines, and willingly does one's fair share of the busy work of institutions, one is usually already well on the way towards earning collegial space, if not collegial support. In Georgia, I routinely volunteered to be secretary for most committees on which I served, thereby having enormous influence in the final form of the groups' deliberations without monopolizing the forum as most other molders of policy do. My spouse's many talents and sensibilities made him an invaluable advisor and confidante to scores of people in the community. Of course, living as we did in a hairdresser's salon, we knew a great deal more about the rest of the public than that public knew about us.

22   My spouse and I are fortunate in the fact that we like the enormous amount of work which we do. We are not mere opportunists working hard only as a gimmick to exploit the public for lesbian and gay issues. Both of us worked intensely at our professional assignments long before we were acknowledged dissidents with new excessive pressures to excel. We feel that now we must, however unfairly, be twice as effective as our competitors just to remain employed at all.

23   Our survival has also depended very much on our thorough knowledge of the system, often knowledge more thorough than that of those who would use the system against us. For example, when my bishop summoned me for discipline, I was able to show him that his own canons give him no authority to discipline a lay person except by excommunication. In fact, so hierarchical have the canons of his diocese become, that the only laity who exist worthy of their mention are the few lay persons on vestries.

24   Especially helpful has been our knowledge of communication procedures. For example, when an area minister attacked lesbians and gays on a TV talk show, I requested equal time; so well received was my response that for two more years I was a regular panelist on the talk show, thereby reaching most residents of the entire middle Georgia area as a known gay person, yet one speaking not just to sexual issues, but to a full range of religious and social topics.

25   When I was occasionally denied access to media, as in the parish or diocese or as on campus when gossip flared, I knew the value of candid explanations thoughtfully prepared, xeroxed, and circulated to enough folks to assure that the gossips would have access to the truthful version. For example, the vestry, which acted in secret, was caught by surprise when I sent copies of their hateful letter to most other parishioners, together with a copy of a psalm which I wrote protesting their turning the House of Prayer into a Court House. I also was able to explain that I continued to attend, not in defiance of their withdrawn invitation, but in obedience to the much higher invitation issued to us all by the real head of the Church. In January, 1979, in the first open meeting of the parish since the vestry's letter of unwelcome three years earlier, the entire parish voted to censure the vestry for that action and to extend to me the full welcome which the vestry had tried to deny. Only three voted against censure, all three of them a minority of the vestry being censured.

26   My spouse and I have been very conscious of the risks of our convictions. We have viewed our credentials—my doctorate and his professional licenses—not as badges of comfortable respectability, but as assets to be invested in social change. Dr. King did not sit crying in the Albany jail, "Why don't these folk respect me? How did this happen? What am I doing here?" When my spouse and I have been denied jobs for which we were the most qualified applicants, we have not naively asked how such things could be, nor have we dwelt overly long on self-pity, for we have known in advance the prices we might have to pay, even if to lose our lives. Our realism about danger and risk has helped us to preserve our sanity when everyone about us has seemed insane. I remember the joy which my spouse shared with me over the fact that he had just been fired for his efforts to organize other black nurses to protest their being treated as orderlies by the white managers of a local hospital.

27   Never, however, have we affirmed the injustices. Finally, we simply cannot be surprised by any evil and are thus less likely to be intimidated by it. Hence, we find ourselves heirs to a special hybrid of courage, a form of courage too often ignored by the heterosexual majority, but widely manifest among sexual outcasts, not the courage of bravado on battlegrounds or sportsfields, but the delicate courage of the lone person who patiently waits out the stupidity of the herd, the cagey courage that has operated many an underground railway station.

28   Our survival in smalltown America has been helped least, I suspect, by our annoying insistence that potential friends receive us not only in our own right, but also as members of the larger lesbian/gay and black communities of which we are a part. Too many whites and heterosexuals are prepared to single us out as "good queers" or "good niggers," offering us thereby the "rewards" of their friendship only at too great a cost to our integrity. My priest did not whip up the vestry against me the first year we lived openly together. He was perfectly happy to have one of his "clever

queers" to dress his wife's hair and the other to help him write his annual report. We became scandalous only when the two of us began to organize the national group of lesbian and gay-male Episcopalians, known as IN-TEGRITY; then we were no longer just quaint. We threatened his image of himself as the arbiter of community morality, especially as he faced scores of queries from brother priests elsewhere.

29   Many lesbians and gay males are tamed by dependencies upon care-fully selected heterosexual friends with whom they have shared their se-cret, often never realizing that in themselves alone, they could provide far more affirmation and discover far more strength than is being cultivated by the terms of these "friendships." Lesbians and gay males have always been taught to survive on the heterosexuals' terms, rarely on one's own terms, and almost never on the terms of a community shared with other lesbians and gay males.

30   Heterosexuals are often thus the losers. The heterosexual acquain-tances close to us early on when we were less visible who dropped us later as our notoriety spread were in most cases folks of demonstrably much less character strength than those heterosexuals who remained our friends even as we asserted our difference with thoughtful independence.

31   My spouse and I have never been exclusive nor aspired to move to any ghetto. In December 1978, on the night the Macon rabbi and I had suc-cessfully organized the area's Jews and gays to protest a concert by Anita Bryant, I returned home to watch the videotape of the march on the late news in the company of eight house guests invited by my spouse for a sur-prise party, not one of them gay (for some strange reason nine out of ten folks are not), not one of them obligated to be at the earlier march, and not one of them uneasy, as most of our acquaintances would have been a few years earlier before we had undertaken this reeducation together.

32   Folks who work for social change need to be very careful to allow room for it to happen, not to allow realistic appraisals of risks to prevent their cultivation of the very change which they germinate.

33   Our survival has been helped in no small way by our candor and clarity in response to rumor and gossip, which are among our biggest enemies. On my campus in Georgia, I voluntarily spoke about sexual issues to an average of fifty classes per year outside my discipline. Initially, those en-counters sharpened my wits for tougher national forums, but long after I no longer needed these occasions personally for rehearsal, I continued to accept the invitations, thereby reaching a vast majority of the citizens of the small town where we continued to live. I used to enjoy the humor of sharing with such groups facts which would make my day-to-day life more pleasant. For example, I routinely noted that when a male student is shocked at my simple public, "Hello," he would look both ways to see who might have seen him being friendly with the gay professor. By doing this he is telling me and all other knowledgeable folks far more new infor-mation about his own body chemistry than he is finding out about mine. More informed male students would reply, "Hello" when greeted. With

this method I disarmed the hatefulness of one of their more debilitating weapons of ostracism.

34   All personal references in public discussions inevitably invade one's privacy, but I have usually found the invasion a small price to pay for the opportunity to educate the public to the fact that the issues which most concern sexual outcasts are not genital, as the casters-out have so lewdly imagined, but issues of justice and simple fairness.

35   Resistance is ultimately an art which no one masters to perfection. Early in my struggles, I said to a gay colleague living openly in rural Nebraska, "We must stamp on every snake." Wisely he counseled, "Only if you want to get foot poisoning." I often wish I had more of the wisdom mentioned in *Ecclesiastes,* the ability to judge accurately, "The time to speak and the time to refrain from speaking." Much of the time I think it wise to pass public hecklers without acknowledging their taunts, especially when they are cowardly hiding in a crowd. When I have faced bullies head-on, I have tried to do so patiently, disarming them by my own control of the situation. Of course, I am not guaranteed that their violence can thus be aborted every time.

36   Two major sources of our survival are essentially very private—one, the intense care and love my spouse and I share, and the other, our strong faith in God as Unbounding Love. To these we prefer to make our secular witness, more by what we do than by what we say.

37   I am not a masochist. I would never choose the hard lot of the sexual outcast in smalltown America. Had I the choice to change myself but not the world, I would return as a white male heterosexual city-slicker millionaire, not because whites, males, heterosexuals, city-slickers, and millionaires are better, but because they have it easier.

38   Yet everyone faces a different choice: Accept the world the way you find it, or change it. For year after year I dissented, right in my own neighborhood.

39   America preserves an ideal of freedom, although it denies freedom in scores of instances. My eighth-grade civics teacher in Alabama did not mention the price I would have to pay for the freedom of speech she taught me to value. I know now that the docile and ignorant dislike you fiercely when you speak truth they prefer not to hear. But I had a good civics class, one that showed me how to change our government rejoice.

40   Sometimes I think a society's critics must appreciate the society far more than others, for the critics typically take very seriously the society's idle promises and forgotten dreams. When I occasionally see them, I certainly don't find many of my heterosexual eighth-grade classmates probing much farther than the issues of our common Form 1040 headaches and the issues as delivered by the evening news. Their lives seem often far duller than ours and the main adventures in pioneering they experience come vicariously, through television, the movies, and for a few, through books. In defining me as a criminal, my society may well have hidden a major blessing in its curse by forcing me out of lethargy into an on-going,

rigorous questioning of the entire process. Not only do I teach *The Adventures of Huckleberry Finn,* my spouse and I have in an important sense had the chance to be Huck and Jim fleeing a different form of slavery and injustice in a very real present.

Discussion Questions

1. In paragraph 2, Crew states that his conjectures "should interest anyone who values the role of the dissident in our democracy." Even if you don't consider yourself "valu[ing] the role of the dissident in our democracy," what do you find interesting, informative, or important about his thinking?

2. Explain the difference Crew establishes in paragraph 15 between "sensible nonviolence" and "cowardly nonresistance." Can you offer some examples of each? Why might the former be considered preferable to the latter?

3. In the last paragraph, Crew claims that his former classmates' "main adventures . . . come vicariously, through television, the movies, and, for a few, through books." Do you see this as a fair and accurate assessment of most students? Why or why not?

4. What do you think "outsiders" can learn from Crew's essay? What did *you* learn? Be specific in your response.

5. Do you see this essay as optimistic or pessimistic? Explain your answer.

Chapter 7 Writing Topics

1. Recall a time when you experienced or witnessed an injustice taking place. What happened, and what was your role in the situation? What was the outcome? What did you learn about injustice from what transpired?

2. Write an essay in which you examine the term "victim." To what extent can *all* people be viewed as victims at some time in their lives? Draw on your own experiences and observations when answering this question.

3. Describe a situation in which you felt yourself threatened, whether the threat was real or imagined. Be sure to make the feelings you experienced at the time vivid and palpable.

4. Was there ever a time in your life when you resisted authority? What were the circumstances, and what was the outcome? If you had to do it again, would you act the same way or would you do things differently?

5. Think back to a time when you had power over other people (e.g., being an older sibling, a salesclerk in a crowded department store, a repair person, etc.). Describe the situation, the way you acted, and the behavior of those not in power. Discuss what you can surmise from the situation about the nature of power.

6. Reflect on a time when you met and "connected" with someone entirely different from you. Write an essay in which you relate the occasion for the meeting, what transpired, and your reflections on it.

7. Recall a time when you felt different from other people. Describe that feeling of "otherness" in such a way that others can understand and appreciate your feelings at the time.

8. Arturo Madrid writes about being a "missing" person. What in your experience and observations leads you to believe that there will always be a group of "missing persons" in the world, individuals who, for reasons beyond their control, are "on the fringes," outcasts from the mainstream? What does this situation say about society at large?

9. Look around your university campus and notice the ways in which people of different races, cultures, and sexual orientations are represented. What do your findings tell you about your school? Are you pleased with what you see, or do you find noticeable segments of the population missing? Where do *you* fit into the picture?

10. Write an essay in which you define who you are as a person, much like Kesaya Noda did in "Growing Up Asian in America." Be sure to show how you came to identify yourself in the way you do.

11. Recall an event in your life that markedly changed your self-perception or self-identity. Describe the circumstances of the event, and discuss the ways in which you were changed.

12. Consider the following questions: What is important for people to know about you? How much are you willing to reveal about yourself to friends and to strangers? How do you want others to view you? Write an essay in which your examination of these questions creates a thoughtful self-portrait.

13. Think about your family history and write an essay in which you account for the way in which history has affected you and your character.

14. Write an essay in which you imagine a world where people accept one another for who they are, where discrimination does not exist, where people live amicably. Why doesn't such a place exist? Can there ever be such a place? Why or why not? What do you envision as your role in such a utopia?

Chapter 8

....

The Circle Unbroken

In the midst of life we are in death.

—Book of Common Prayer

We shall not cease from/exploration/And the end to all our/exploring/Will be to arrive where we/started/And know the place for the first time.

—T.S. Eliot, "Little Gidding"

The whole life of the individual is nothing but the process of giving birth . . . indeed, we should be fully born when we die.

—Erich Fromm

All sorrows can be borne if you put them into a story or tell a story about them.

—Isak Dinesen

Death is the mother of beauty; hence from/her/Alone shall come fulfillment to our dreams.

—Wallace Stevens

One of the few things we can depend upon in life, ironically, is death. For as surely as we are born into this world, there comes a time for each of us to die. While this may sound unnecessarily morbid, it need not be viewed that way. Indeed, the essays in this chapter of *The Voice of Reflection* are moving tributes to the *lives* people have lived. They celebrate the majesty of life, the sacredness of the circle completed. The essays pay homage to life; they implore us to learn from others and rejoice in having known them. Oddly enough, to look at death then is also to look at life.

The essays in this chapter are also testimony to writing as a way of coming to terms with a topic you might prefer to avoid. At the very least, the writing helps us to sort out complex and thorny ideas and feelings; it provides a blueprint for the evolution of thought; it documents where we were at a certain moment in our process of understanding.

Chapter 8 begins with medical researcher Lewis Thomas reflecting on death as a "natural" process. In the next selection, Anatole Broyard describes his account of becoming ill and offers insights on the ways he came to view his malady. Then surgeon-turned-writer Richard Selzer provides the perspective of a physician whose patient dies on the operating table. Anne-Grace Scheinin, a woman who has attempted suicide, reflects on what she has learned from her mother's suicide.

The last three essays are written by surviving family members and friends: Wallace Stegner frames his essay in the form of a letter to his dead mother, telling her all she has meant to him. Then Andrew Holleran reflects on the ways in which AIDS-related deaths have affected his life. In the last essay, Barbara Lazear Ascher muses on the death of a beloved family member, her dog.

While it is natural to grieve the loss of life, these writers' perspectives transcend mourning to reach understanding, reconciliation, and learning. At some time in your life, you will be confronted with death (if you haven't been already). What in these essays can help you to better understand death? What can you offer from your own experiences and observations to help others make sense of the circle unbroken?

On Natural Death

Lewis Thomas

*ewis Thomas was born in 1913 in New York. The recipient of an
M.D. degree from Harvard University, he is the author of* The
Lives of a Cell: Notes of a Biology-Watcher *(1974),* The Nedusa and
the Snail: More Notes of a Biology Watcher *(1979), in which "On
Natural Death" appears,* The Youngest Science: Notes of a Medical-
Watcher *(1983),* Late Night Thoughts on Listening to Mahler's
Ninth Symphony *(1983), and* Et Cetera, Et Cetera: Notes of a
Word-Watcher *(1990). Many of his essays originally appeared in the*
New England Journal of Medicine. *An eminent physician and med-
ical researcher, Thomas has been the president of the Memorial Sloan-
Kettering Cancer Center in New York City and the recipient of the
National Book Award for nonfiction in 1974. Thomas died of cancer
in 1993. In the following essay, he posits the notions that death is quite a
natural occurrence and that we could learn from seeing the forms death
takes all around us.*

1   There are so many new books about dying that there are now special
shelves set aside for them in bookshops, along with the health-diet and
home-repair paperbacks and the sex manuals. Some of them are so packed
with detailed information and step-by-step instructions for performing the
function that you'd think this was a new sort of skill which all of us are now
required to learn. The strongest impression the casual reader gets, leafing
through, is that proper dying has become an extraordinary, even an exotic
experience, something only the specially trained get to do.

2   Also, you could be led to believe that we are the only creatures capable of the awareness of death, that when all the rest of nature is being cy-
cled through dying, one generation after another, it is a different kind of
process, done automatically and trivially, more "natural," as we say.

3   An elm in our backyard caught the blight this summer and dropped
stone dead, leafless, almost overnight. One weekend it was a normal-look-
ing elm, maybe a little bare in spots but nothing alarming, and the next
weekend it was gone, passed over, departed, taken. Taken is right, for the
tree surgeon came by yesterday with his crew of young helpers and their
cherry picker, and took it down branch by branch and carted it off in the
back of a red truck, everyone singing.

4   The dying of a field mouse, at the jaws of an amiable household cat, is
a spectacle I have beheld many times. It used to make me wince. Early in
life I gave up throwing sticks at the cat to make him drop the mouse, because the dropped mouse regularly went ahead and died anyway, but I always shouted unaffections at the cat to let him know the sort of animal he
had become. Nature, I thought, was an abomination.

5   Recently I've done some thinking about that mouse, and I wonder if

his dying is necessarily all that different from the passing of our elm. The main difference, if there is one, would be in the matter of pain. I do not believe that an elm tree has pain receptors, and even so, the blight seems to me a relatively painless way to go even if there were nerve endings in a tree, which there are not. But the mouse dangling tail-down from the teeth of a gray cat is something else again, with pain beyond bearing, you'd think, all over his small body.

6   There are now some plausible reasons for thinking it is not like that at all, and you can make up an entirely different story about the mouse and his dying if you like. At the instant of being trapped and penetrated by teeth, peptide hormones are released by cells in the hypothalamus and the pituitary gland; instantly these substances, called endorphins, are attached to the surface of other cells responsible for pain perception; the hormones have the pharmacologic properties of opium; there is no pain. Thus it is that the mouse seems always to dangle so languidly from the jaws, lies there so quietly when dropped, dies of his injuries without a struggle. If a mouse could shrug, he'd shrug.

7   I do not know if this is true or not, nor do I know how to prove it if it is true. Maybe if you could get in there quickly enough and administer naloxone, a specific morphine antagonist, you could turn off the endorphins and observe the restoration of pain, but this is not something I would care to do or see. I think I will leave it there, as a good guess about the dying of a cat-chewed mouse, perhaps about dying in general.

8   Montaigne had a hunch about dying, based on his own close call in a riding accident. He was so badly injured as to be believed dead by his companions, and was carried home with lamentations, "all bloody, stained all over with the blood I had thrown up." He remembers the entire episode, despite having been "dead, for two full hours," with wonderment:

> It seemed to me that my life was hanging only by the tip of my lips. I closed my eyes in order, it seemed to me, to help push it out, and took pleasure in growing languid and letting myself go. It was an idea that was only floating on the surface of my soul, as delicate and feeble as all the rest, but in truth not only free from distress but mingled with that sweet feeling that people have who have let themselves slide into sleep. I believe that this is the same state in which people find themselves whom we see fainting in the agony of death, and I maintain that we pity them without cause. . . . In order to get used to the idea of death. I find there is nothing like coming close to it.

Later, in another essay, Montaigne returns to it:

If you know not how to die, never trouble yourself; Nature will in a moment fully and sufficiently instruct you; she will exactly do that business for you; take you no care for it.

9   The worst accident I've ever seen was in Okinawa, in the early days of the invasion, when a jeep ran into a troop carrier and was crushed nearly flat. Inside were two young MPs, trapped in bent steel, both mortally hurt, with only their heads and shoulders visible. We had a conversation while people with the right tools were prying them free. Sorry about the accident, they said. No, they said, they felt fine. Is everyone else okay, one of them said. Well, the other one said, no hurry now. And then they died.

10   Pain is useful for avoidance, for getting away when there's time to get away, but when it is end game, and no way back, pain is likely to be turned off, and the mechanisms for this are wonderfully precise and quick. If I had to design an ecosystem in which creatures had to live off each other and in which dying was an indispensable part of living, I could not think of a better way to manage.

Discussion Questions

1. How do *you* account for the plethora of books on dying? Why do you think people are writing and reading them in growing numbers?

2. Do you agree with Thomas when he wonders in paragraph 5 whether the mouse's dying is different from the elm's? Explain your answer.

3. What point do you think Thomas makes by quoting Montaigne? How does this strengthen your understanding of death?

4. In paragraph 9 Thomas describes the worst accident he ever saw. What do you see as the purpose of this description? What can you learn from this incident?

5. In the last paragraph, Thomas states, "Pain is useful for avoidance, for getting away when there's time to get away, but when it is end game, and no way back, pain is likely to be turned off, and the mechanisms for this are wonderfully precise and quick." Do you agree with Thomas about pain being "useful for avoidance"? Does this statement explain why people, just before they die, are reported to experience peace and tranquility? Explain your response.

Intoxicated by My Illness

Anatole Broyard

*B*orn *in 1920 in Louisiana, Anatole Broyard received his educa-tion at Brooklyn College and the New School for Social Research. A lecturer in sociology and literature for some twenty years at the New School, Broyard worked as a book reviewer and feature writer for* The New York Times *after 1971. He is the author of* Aroused by Books *(1974) and* Men, Women, and Other Anticlimaxes *(1980), both col-lections of his* New York Times *reviews and essays, and* Kafka Was the Rage: A Greenwich Village Memoir *(1993). Before his death in 1990, Broyard also published* Intoxicated by My Illness *(1990). The following piece, from that book, was originally published in* The New York Times Magazine *in 1989. The essay describes Broyard's thoughts and feelings when he first learned he had prostate cancer.*

1   So much of a writer's life consists of assumed suffering, rhetorical suf-fering, that I felt something like relief, even elation, when the doctor told me that I had cancer of the prostate. Suddenly there was in the air a rich sense of crisis, real crisis, yet one that also contained echoes of ideas like the crisis of language, the crisis of literature, or of personality. It seemed to me that my existence, whatever I thought, felt or did, had taken on a kind of meter, as in poetry, or in taxis.

2   When you learn that your life is threatened, you can turn toward this knowledge or away from it. I turned toward it. It was not a choice, but an automatic shifting of gears, a tacit agreement between my body and my brain. I thought that time had tapped me on the shoulder, that I had been given a real deadline at last. It wasn't that I believed the cancer was going to kill me, even though it had spread beyond the prostate—it could proba-bly be controlled, either by radiation or hormonal manipulation. No, what struck me was the startled awareness that one day something, whatever it might be, was going to interrupt my leisurely progress. It sounds trite, yet I can only say that I realized for the first time that I don't have forever.

3   Time was no longer innocuous, nothing was casual any more. I un-derstood that living itself had a deadline. Like the book I had been work-ing on—how sheepish I would feel if I couldn't finish it. I had promised it to myself and to my friends. Though I wouldn't say this out loud, I had promised it to the world. All writers privately think this way.

4   When my friends heard I had cancer, they found me surprisingly cheerful and talked about my courage. But it has nothing to do with courage, at least not for me. As far as I can tell, it's a question of desire. I'm filled with desire—to live, to write, to do everything. Desire itself is a kind of immortality. While I've always had trouble concentrating, I now feel as concentrated as a diamond, or a microchip.

5   I remember a time in the 1950s when I tried to talk a friend of mine

named Jules out of committing suicide. He had already made one attempt and when I went to see him he said "Give me a good reason to go on living." He was 30 years old.

6   I saw what I had to do. I started to sell life to him, like a real estate agent. Just look at the world, I said. How can you not be curious about it? The streets, the houses, the trees, the shops, the people, the movement and the stillness. Look at the women, so appealing, each in her own way. Think of all the things you can do with them, the places you can go together. Think of books, paintings, music. Think of your friends.

7   While I was talking I wondered, am I telling Jules the truth? He didn't think so, because he put his head in the oven a week later. As for me, I don't know whether I believed what I said or not, because I just went on behaving like everybody else. But I believe it now. When my wife made me a hamburger the other day I thought it was the most fabulous hamburger in the history of the world.

8   With this illness one of my recurrent dreams has finally come true. Several times in the past I've dreamed that I had committed a crime—or perhaps I was only accused of a crime, it's not clear. When brought to trial I refused to have a lawyer—I got up instead and made an impassioned speech in my own defense. This speech was so moving that I could feel myself tingling with it. It was inconceivable that the jury would not acquit me—only each time I woke before the verdict. Now cancer is the crime I may or may not have committed and the eloquence of being alive, the fervor of the survivor, is my best defense.

9   The way my friends have rallied around me is wonderful. They remind me of a flock of birds rising from a body of water into the sunset. If that image seems a bit extravagant, or tinged with satire, it's because I can't help thinking there's something comical about my friends' behavior, all these witty men suddenly saying pious, inspirational things.

10   They are not intoxicated as I am by my illness, but sobered. Since I refused to, they've taken on the responsibility of being serious. They appear abashed, or chagrined, in their sobriety. Stripped of their playfulness these pals of mine seem plainer, homelier—even older. It's as if they had all gone bald overnight.

11   Yet one of the effects of their fussing over me is that I feel vivid, multicolored, sharply drawn. On the other hand—and this is ungrateful—I remain outside of their solicitude, their love and best wishes. I'm isolated from them by the grandiose conviction that I am the healthy person and they are the sick ones. Like an existential hero, I have been cured by the truth while they still suffer the nausea of the uninitiated.

12   I've had eight-inch needles thrust into my belly where I could feel them tickling my metaphysics. I've worn Pampers. I've been licked by the flames and my sense of self has been singed. Sartre was right: you have to live each moment as if you're prepared to die.

13   Now at last I understand the conditional nature of the human condition. Yet, unlike Kierkegaard and Sartre, I'm not interested in the irony of

my position. Cancer cures you of irony. Perhaps my irony was all in my prostate. A dangerous illness fills you with adrenaline and makes you feel very smart. I can afford now, I said to myself, to draw conclusions. All those grand generalizations toward which I have been building for so many years are finally taking shape. As I look back at how I used to be, it seems to me that an intellectual is a person who thinks that the classical clichés don't apply to him, that he is immune to homely truths. I know better now. I see everything with a summarizing eye. Nature is a terrific editor.

14   In the first stages of my illness, I couldn't sleep, urinate or defecate—the word ordeal comes to mind. Then when my doctor changed all this and everything worked again, what a voluptuous pleasure it was. With a cry of joy I realized how marvelous it is simply to function. My body, which in the last decade or two had become a familiar, no longer thrilling old flame, was reborn as a brand-new infatuation.

15   I realize of course that this elation I feel is just a phase, just a rush of consciousness, a splash of perspective, a hot flash of ontological alertness. But I'll take it, I'll use it. I'll use everything I can while I wait for the next phase. Illness is primarily a drama and it should be possible to enjoy it as well as to suffer it. I see now why the romantics were so fond of illness—the sick man sees everything as metaphor. In this phase I'm infatuated with my cancer. It stinks of revelation.

16   As I look ahead, I feel like a man who has awakened from a long afternoon nap to find the evening stretched out before me. I'm reminded of D'Annunzio, the Italian poet, who said to a duchess he had just met at a party in Paris, "Come, we will have a profound evening." Why not? I see the balance of my life—everything comes in images now—as a beautiful paisley shawl thrown over a grand piano.

17   Why a paisley shawl, precisely? Why a grand piano? I have no idea. That's the way the situation presents itself to me. I have to take my imagery along with my medicine.

Discussion Questions

1. Broyard begins his essay with what some may consider a surprising confession: he was relieved to hear he had cancer. How believable is such a response? Can you recall a time when you were relieved to hear a piece of bad news?

2. In paragraph 2, Broyard states that he "turned toward it [knowledge]." How common do you think his reaction was: do most people turn toward or away from life-changing news? How about you?

3. Broyard claims in paragraph 4 that "desire itself is a kind of immortality." Do you believe him, or do you see this kind of thinking a rationalization for being upbeat?

4. What do you think Broyard means when he states that in paragraph 13 "Cancer cures you of irony"?

5. To what extent does the essay convince you in paragraph 15 that "Illness is primarily a drama and it should be possible to enjoy it as well as to suffer it"?

Sarcophagus
Richard Selzer

Born in 1928, Richard Selzer earned his B.S. degree from Albany Medical College. Recently retired from his professorship in surgery at the Yale School of Medicine and his surgical practice in New Haven, Connecticut, Selzer now devotes his time exclusively to writing and lecturing at universities and medical schools around the world. He is the author of Rituals of Surgery *(1974),* Mortal Lessons: Notes on the Art of Surgery *(1976),* Letters to a Young Surgeon *(1982),* Taking the World in for Repairs *(1986),* Imagine a Woman and Other Tales *(1990),* Down from Troy: A Doctor Comes of Age *(1992),* Raising the Dead *(1994), and* Confessions of a Knife *(1979), in which the following essay appears. His work has also been published in such magazines as* Reader's Digest, Esquire, Vanity Fair, Harper's, The New York Times Magazine, *and* Literature & Medicine. *Selzer won the National Magazine Award in 1975 for his essays on medicine, an American Medical Writer's Award, and a Guggenheim. In "Sarcophagus," Selzer provides the surgeon's perspective on the death of a patient.*

1   We are six who labor here in the night. No . . . seven! For the man horizontal upon the table strives as well. But we do not acknowledge his struggle. It is our own that preoccupies us.

2   I am the surgeon.

3   David is the anesthesiologist. You will see how kind, how soft he is. Each patient is, for him, a preparation respectfully controlled. Blood pressure, pulse, heartbeat, flow of urine, loss of blood, temperature, whatever is measurable, David measures. And he is a titrator, adding a little gas, drug, oxygen, fluid, blood in order to maintain the dynamic equilibrium that is the only state compatible with life. He is in the very center of the

battle, yet he is one step removed; he has not known the patient before this time, nor will he deal with the next of kin. But for him, the occasion is no less momentous.

4   Heriberto Paz is an assistant resident in surgery. He is deft, tiny, mercurial. I have known him for three years. One day he will be the best surgeon in Mexico.

5   Evelyn, the scrub nurse, is a young Irish woman. For seven years we have worked together. Shortly after her immigration, she led her young husband into my office to show me a lump on his neck. One year ago he died of Hodgkin's disease. For the last two years of his life, he was paralyzed from the waist down. Evelyn has one child, a boy named Liam.

6   Brenda is a black woman of forty-five. She is the circulating nurse, who will conduct the affairs of this room, serving our table, adjusting the lights, counting the sponges, ministering to us from the unsterile world.

7   Roy is a medical student who is beginning his surgical clerkship. He has been assigned to me for the next six weeks. This is his first day, his first operation.

8   David is inducing anesthesia. In cases where the stomach is not empty through fasting, the tube is passed into the windpipe while the patient is awake. Such an "awake" intubation is called crashing. It is done to avoid vomiting and the aspiration of stomach contents into the lungs while the muscles that control coughing are paralyzed.

9   We stand around the table. To receive a tube in the windpipe while fully awake is a terrifying thing.

10   "Open your mouth wide," David says to the man. The man's mouth opens slowly to its fullest, as though to shriek. But instead, he yawns. We smile down at him behind our masks.

11   "OK. Open again. Real wide."

12   David sprays the throat of the man with a local anesthetic. He does this three times. Then, into the man's mouth, David inserts a metal tongue depressor which bears a light at the tip. It is called a laryngoscope. It is to light up the throat, reveal the glottic chink through which the tube must be shoved. All this while, the man holds his mouth agape, submitting to the hard pressure of the laryngoscope. But suddenly, he cannot submit. The man on the table gags, struggles to free himself, to spit out the instrument. In his frenzy his lip is pinched by the metal blade.

13   There is little blood.

14   "Suction," says David.

15   Secretions at the back of the throat obscure the view. David suctions them away with a plastic catheter.

16   "Open," commands David. More gagging. Another pass with the scope. Another thrust with the tube. Violent coughing informs us that the tube is in the right place. It has entered the windpipe. Quickly the balloon is inflated to snug it against the wall of the trachea. A bolus of Pentothal is injected into a vein in the man's arm. It takes fifteen seconds for the drug to travel from his arm to his heart, then on to his brain. I count them. In

fifteen seconds, the coughing stops, the man's body relaxes. He is asleep.

17   "All set?" I ask David.

18   "Go ahead," he nods.

19   A long incision. You do not know how much room you will need. This part of the operation is swift, tidy. Fat . . . muscle . . . fascia . . . the peritoneum is snapped open and a giant shining eggplant presents itself. It is the stomach, black from the blood it contains and that threatens to burst it. We must open that stomach, evacuate its contents, explore.

20   Silk sutures are placed in the wall of the stomach as guidelines between which the incision will be made. They are like the pitons of a mountaineer. I cut again. No sooner is the cavity of the stomach achieved, than a columnar geyser of blood stands from the small opening I have made. Quickly, I slice open the whole front of the stomach. We scoop out handfuls of clot, great black gelatinous masses that shimmy from the drapes to rest against our own bellies as though, having been evicted from one body, they must find another in which to dwell. Now and then we step back to let them slidder to the floor. They are under our feet. We slip in them. "Jesus," I say. "He is bleeding all over North America." Now my hand is inside the stomach, feeling, pressing. There! A tumor spreads across the back wall of this stomach. A great hard craterous plain, the dreaded linitis plastica (leather bottle) that is not content with seizing one area, but infiltrates between the layers until the entire organ is stiff with cancer. It is that, of course, which is bleeding. I stuff wads of gauze against the tumor. I press my fist against the mass of cloth. The blood slows. I press harder. The bleeding stops.

21   A quick glance at Roy. His gown and gloves, even his mask, are sprinkled with blood. Now is he dipped; and I, his baptist.

22   David has opened a second line into the man's veins. He is pumping blood into both tubings.

23   "Where do we stand?" I ask him.

24   "Still behind. Three units." He checks the blood pressure.

25   "Low, but coming up," he says.

26   "Shall I wait 'til you catch up?"

27   "No. Go ahead. I'll keep pumping."

28   I try to remove my fist from the stomach, but as soon as I do, there is a fresh river of blood.

29   "More light," I say. "I need more light."

30   Brenda stands on a platform behind me. She adjusts the lamps.

31   "More light," I say, like a man going blind.

32   "That's it," she says. "There is no more light."

33   "We'll go around from the outside," I say. Heriberto nods agreement. "Free up the greater curvature first, then the lesser, lift the stomach up and get some control from behind."

34   I must work with one hand. The other continues as the compressor. It is the tiredest hand of my life. One hand, then, inside the stomach, while

the other creeps behind. Between them . . . a ridge of tumor. The left hand fumbles, gropes toward its mate. They swim together. I lift the stomach forward to find that *nothing* separates my hands from each other. The wall of the stomach has been eaten through by the tumor. One finger enters a large tubular structure. It is the aorta. The incision in the stomach has released the tamponade of blood and brought us to this rocky place.

35   "Curved aortic clamp."

36   A blind grab with the clamp, high up at the diaphragm. The bleeding slackens, dwindles. I release the pressure warily. A moment later there is a great bang of blood. The clamp has bitten through the cancerous aorta.

37   "Zero silk on a big Mayo needle."

38   I throw the heavy sutures, one after the other, into the pool of blood, hoping to snag with my needle some bit of tissue to close over the rent in the aorta, to hold back the blood. There is no tissue. Each time, the needle pulls through the crumble of tumor. I stop. I repack the stomach. Now there is a buttress of packing both outside and inside the stomach. The bleeding is controlled. We wait. Slowly, something is gathering here, organizing. What had been vague and shapeless before is now declaring itself. All at once, I know what it is. There is nothing to do.

39   For what tool shall I ask? With what device fight off this bleeding? A knife? There is nothing here to cut. Clamps? Where place the jaws of a hemostat? A scissors? Forceps? Nothing. The instrument does not exist that knows such deep red jugglery. Not all my clever picks, my rasp . . . A miner's lamp, I think, to cast a brave glow.

40   David has been pumping blood steadily.

41   "He is stable at the moment," he says. "Where do we go from here?"

42   "No place. He's going to die. The minute I take away my pressure, he'll bleed to death."

43   I try to think of possibilities, alternatives. I cannot; there are none. Minutes pass. We listen to the cardiac monitor, the gassy piston of the anesthesia machine.

44   "More light!" I say. "Fix the light."

45   The light seems dim, aquarial, a dilute beam slanting through a green sea. At such a fathom the fingers are clumsy. There is pressure. It is cold.

46   "Dave," I say, "stop the transfusion." I hear my voice coming as from a great distance. "Stop it," I say again.

47   David and I look at each other, standing among the drenched rags, the smeared equipment.

48   "I can't," he says.

49   "Then I will," I say, and with my free hand I reach across the boundary that separates the sterile field from the outside world, and I close the clamp on the intravenous tubing. It is the act of an outlaw, someone who does not know right from wrong. But I know. I know that this is right to do.

50   "The oxygen," I say. "Turn it off."

51   "You want it turned off, you do it," he says.

52   "Hold this," I say to Heriberto, and I give over the packing to him. I step back from the table, and go to the gas tanks.

53   "This one?" I have to ask him.

54   "Yes," David nods.

55   I turn it off. We stand there, waiting, listening to the beeping of the electrocardiograph. It remains even, regular, relentless. Minutes go by, and the sound continues. The man will not die. At last, the intervals on the screen grow longer, the shape of the curve changes, the rhythm grows wild, furious. The line droops, flattens. The man is dead.

56   It is silent in the room. Now we are no longer a team, each with his circumscribed duties to perform. It is Evelyn who speaks first.

57   "It is a blessing," she says. I think of her husband's endless dying.

58   "No," says Brenda. "Better for the family if they have a few days . . . to get used to the idea of it."

59   "But, look at all the pain he's been spared."

60   "Still, for the ones that are left, it's better to have a little time."

61   I listen to the two women murmuring, debating without rancor, speaking in hushed tones of the newly dead as women have done for thousands of years.

62   "May I have the name of the operation?" It is Brenda, picking up her duties. She is ready with pen and paper.

63   "Exploratory laparotomy. Attempt to suture malignant aorto-gastric fistula."

64   "Is he pronounced?"

65   "What time is it?"

66   "Eleven-twenty."

67   "Shall I put that down?"

68   "Yes."

69   "Sew him up," I say to Heriberto. "I'll talk to the family."

70   To Roy I say, "You come with me."

71   Roy's face is speckled with blood. He seems to me a child with the measles. What, in God's name, is he doing here?

72   From the doorway, I hear the voices of the others, resuming.

73   "Stitch," says Heriberto.

74   Roy and I go to change our bloody scrub suits. We put on long white coats. In the elevator, we do not speak. For the duration of the ride to the floor where the family is waiting, I am reasonable. I understand that in its cellular wisdom, the body of this man had sought out the murderous function of my scalpel, and stretched itself upon the table to receive the final stabbing. For this little time, I know that it is not a murder committed but a mercy bestowed. Tonight's knife is no assassin, but the kind scythe of time.

75   We enter the solarium. The family rises in unison. There are so many! How ruthless the eyes of the next of kin.

76   "I am terribly sorry . . . ," I begin. Their faces tighten, take guard. "There was nothing we could do."

77   I tell them of the lesion, tell of how it began somewhere at the back of the stomach; how, long ago, no one knows why, a cell lost the rhythm of the body, fell out of step, sprang, furious, into rebellion. I tell of how the cell divided and begat two of its kind, which begat four more and so on, until there was a whole race of lunatic cells, which is called cancer.

78   I tell of how the cancer spread until it had replaced the whole back of the stomach, invading, chewing until it had broken into the main artery of the body. Then it was, I tell them, that the great artery poured its blood into the stomach. I tell of how I could not stop the bleeding, how my clamps bit through the crumbling tissue, how my stitches would not hold, how there was nothing to be done. All of this I tell.

79   A woman speaks. She has not heard my words, only caught the tone of my voice.

80   "Do you mean he is dead?"

81   Should I say "passed away" instead of "died"? No. I cannot.

82   "Yes," I tell her, "he is dead."

83   Her question and my answer unleash their anguish. Roy and I stand among the welter of bodies that tangle, grapple, rock, split apart to form new couplings. Their keening is exuberant, wild. It is more than I can stand. All at once, a young man slams his fist into the wall with great force.

84   "Son of a bitch!" he cries.

85   "Stop that!" I tell him sharply. Then, more softly, "Please try to control yourself."

86   The other men crowd about him, patting, puffing, grunting. They are all fat, with huge underslung bellies. Like their father's. A young woman in a nun's habit hugs each of the women in turn.

87   "Shit!" says one of the men.

88   The nun hears, turns away her face. Later, I see the man apologizing to her.

89   The women, too, are fat. One of them has a great pile of yellowish hair that has been sprayed and rendered motionless. All at once, she begins to whine. A single note, coming louder and louder. I ask a nurse to bring tranquilizer pills. She does, and I hand them out, one to each, as though they were the wafers of communion. They urge the pills upon each other.

90   "Go on, Theresa, take it. Make her take one."

91   Roy and I are busy with cups of water. Gradually it grows quiet. One of the men speaks.

92   "What's the next step?"

93   "Do you have an undertaker in mind?"

94   They look at each other, shrug. Someone mentions a name. The rest nod.

95   "Give the undertaker a call. Let him know. He'll take care of everything."

96   I turn to leave.

97   "Just a minute," one of the men calls. "Thanks, Doc. You did what you could."

98   "Yes," I say.

99   Once again in the operating room. Blood is everywhere. There is a wild smell, as though a fox had come and gone. The others, clotted about the table, work on. They are silent, ravaged.

100   "How did the family take it?"

101   "They were good, good."

102   Heriberto has finished reefing up the abdomen. The drapes are peeled back. The man on the table seems more than just dead. He seems to have gone beyond that, into a state where expression is possible—reproach and scorn. I study him. His baldness had advanced beyond the halfway mark. The remaining strands of hair had been gallantly dyed. They are, even now, neatly combed and crenellated. A stripe of black moustache rides his upper lip. Once, he had been spruce!

103   We all help lift the man from the table to the stretcher.

104   "On three," says David. "One . . . two . . . three."

105   And we heft him over, using the sheet as a sling. My hand brushes his shoulder. It is cool. I shudder as though he were infested with lice. He has become something that I do not want to touch.

106   More questions from the women.

107   "Is a priest coming?"

108   "Does the family want to view him?"

109   "Yes. No. Don't bother me with these things."

110   "Come on," I say to Roy. We go to the locker room and sit together on a bench. We light cigarettes.

111   "Well?" I ask him.

112   "When you were scooping out the clots, I thought I was going to swoon."

113   I pause over the word. It is too quaint, too genteel for this time. I feel, at that moment, a great affection for him.

114   "But you fought it."

115   "Yes. I forced it back down. But, almost . . . "

116   "Good," I say. Who knows what I mean by it? I want him to know that I count it for something.

117   "And you?" he asks me. The students are not shy these days.

118   "It was terrible, his refusal to die."

119   I want him to say that it was right to call it quits, that I did the best I could. But he says nothing. We take off our scrub suits and go to the shower. There are two stalls opposite each other. They are curtained. But we do not draw the curtains. We need to see each other's healthy bodies. I watch Roy turn his face directly upward into the blinding fall of water. His mouth is open to receive it. As though it were milk flowing from the breasts of God. For me, too, this water is like a well in a wilderness.

120   In the locker room, we dress in silence.

121   "Well, goodnight."

122   Awkwardly our words come out in unison.

123   "In the morning . . . "

124   "Yes, yes, later."

125   "Goodnight."

126   I watch him leave through the elevator door.

127   For the third time I go to that operating room. The others have long since finished and left. It is empty, dark. I turn on the great lamps above the table that stands in the center of the room. The pediments of the table and the floor have been scrubbed clean. There is no sign of the struggle. I close my eyes and see again the great pale body of the man, like a white bullock, bled. The line of stitches on his abdomen is a hieroglyph. Already, the events of this night are hidden from me by these strange untranslatable markings.

Discussion Questions

1. What do you make of Selzer in paragraph 1 almost forgetting that the patient is "struggling"? Would his momentary oversight increase or decrease your confidence in him as a physician?

2. Brenda states in paragraph 58 that it is "better for the family to have a few days . . . to get used to the idea of it [their family member dying]." Do you think it is preferable for people to have time to prepare for the death of a loved one or for the death to come swiftly and without notice? Why?

3. In paragraph 81, Selzer questions the terminology he should use in telling the family of the death. Why do you think he has trouble? What word(s) would you have preferred?

4. Discuss the use and effectiveness of one-sentence paragraphs and short, declarative statements throughout the essay.

5. What do you make of Selzer entering the operating room for the third time when the patient is dead and the surgical team has left? Why does Selzer describe the abdomen as a "hieroglyph" and the events as hidden by it?

The Burden of Suicide

Anne-Grace Scheinin

*A*nne-Grace Scheinin, a resident of Alameda, California, wrote *the following essay for the "My Turn" section of* Newsweek *magazine. First started on November 6, 1972, the column is, according to the magazine, "a personal page commentary to be written each week by a different guest columnist." In "The Burden of Suicide," Scheinin ruminates on suicide from an unusual perspective: that of someone who has attempted suicide herself and of the daughter of a suicide victim.*

1   My mother died seven years ago by her own hand. My father found her when he returned home from work that Friday, her body already cold where it lay huddled in the back of the little red Corvair Monza. A hose led from the exhaust pipe through the rear window of the car.

2   I can't imagine what he must have felt when he found her. I *can* imagine how my mother must have felt as she descended the stairs to the garage for the last time. There was a numbness, a sense of suspended disbelief; her body already seemed not to belong to her. In her anesthetized mind was a single spark of clarity, the knowledge, vivid and unfrightening, that the peace she had longed for was now, really and truly, to be hers. Maybe she left in anger, maybe that was why. But the only reality for her in those last moments was the desperate hunger for a final, eternal end to pain. She never fought against the blackness that swallowed her.

3   I know. I've been there. I tried suicide several times in my life when I was in my early 20s and was quite serious at least twice. I bitterly resented having my life saved. I despised and raged against the doctors and nurses who prevented my death, against the psychiatrists who locked me up until I was cajoled into wanting to live again, or was at least willing to give it a try. All I really wanted was the kind of peace of mind everyone in the whole world seemed blessed with except me. Was that asking too much?

4   **Nightmare:** Apparently so. A manic-depressive like my mother, I have a physiology that never seemed to give me an even break. Just when my internal seas began to calm and I began to think living might be palatable after all, minute chemicals in my brain would either recede or reassert themselves and I'd be off on another nightmare roller-coaster ride, out of control, a stranger to myself and to everyone who thought they knew me. Some manic-depressives are greatly helped by medication, notably lithium carbonate. Nothing seemed to help me. Suicide often seemed the most sane resolution to the insanity my body forced on me. Besides actually attempting suicide, I've wanted, wished and even prayed to die more times than I can count.

5   Well, I'm 32 now and I'm still alive. I'm even married and have moved from a secretarial position into entry-level management in a

Fortune 500 company. I keep house and look after my husband and our three cats, Lila, Blackberry and little Snailbait. I have bills to pay, a bus to catch every weekday morning, laundry that never seems quite white or bright enough, a body that refuses to conform to Cheryl Tiegs's configuration. I'm a lousy cook. But I'm alive because of my mother's death. She taught me that in spite of my illness I had to live. Suicide just isn't worth it.

6   I saw the torment my mother's death caused others: my father, my brother, her neighbors and friends. When I saw their overwhelming grief, I knew I could never do the same thing she had done—force other people to take on the burden of pain I'd leave behind if I died by my own hand.

7   Suicide is not a normal death. It is tragic beyond the most shattering experiences, and the ultimate form of abandonment. There is no fate on which to place the blame. It rests squarely on the shoulders of the victim and the people left behind, many of whom spend the rest of their lives wondering, never knowing, if there was anything they could have done to prevent such a tragedy.

8   There is something about suicide that, even when done as an escape from an agonizing terminal illness, signals complete and utter defeat. It is without any semblance of nobility or pride. Life can become too heavy a burden to bear, but the release that suicide offers is not a triumph of life, the ultimate mastery of self over fate, but a grim renunciation of hope and a failure of the human spirit. There may be legitimate rationalizations for committing suicide. But my experiences have taught me that suicide, by and large, is a decision made by a desolate soul. The many suicidal patients I met in my hospital stays had no philosophy of death; their desire to die was not a condemnation of current socioeconomic or political realities. They were in profound emotional pain, and all they wanted was an end to that suffering.

9   For years I was no different. My illness was a source of immeasurable pain to my family and friends, and seeing my irrationality and despair mirrored in their eyes was often unendurable. I still have seizures of profound depression, and I can still see that ugly self reflected in the faces of the people I love. Then, too, there is the stigma of being a mental patient, a victim of a major psychotic disorder, which is as humiliating as it has always been.

10   However, I will not, cannot, end my life as my mother did. Suicide no longer can offer me any peace.

11   **Wasteland:** She was 55 when she died. She looked behind her and saw a wasteland, never willing to accept that she was loved by many and had richly contributed to the lives of friends, family and strangers. She perished because she allowed herself to be deceived by her own mind into believing she was worthless. She refused professional help because, like many of her generation, she felt it was shameful to seek psychiatric aid. What would the neighbors and relatives think? She was consumed at the end by unbearable depression. The best thing she could do for those who cared about her was to remove herself from their presence—permanently. She could not have been more wrong.

12   She taught me the most valuable lesson of my life: no matter how bad the pain is, it's never so bad that suicide is the only answer. It's never so bad that the only escape is a false one. Suicide doesn't end pain. It only lays it on the broken shoulders of the survivors.

13   Ironically, my mother's final gift to me was not death, but life, a determination to live as she chose not to.

14   By the way: to all the doctors, nurses and psychiatrists who forced me to live when I didn't want to—thank you for keeping breath in my lungs and my heart beating and encouraging hope in me when I didn't have any hope.

15   I'm glad I'm alive to say that.

Discussion Questions

1. To what extent do you find Scheinin's essay more believable because she attempted suicide several times herself than if she had never attempted it at all?

2. Scheinin describes her rage and resentment at the medical team that saved her life. Do you think most other people who attempt suicide feel similarly, or do you think people who attempt suicide really wish to die? Explain your response.

3. In paragraph 5, Scheinin states that her mother taught her that "suicide just isn't worth it." Do you think it was her mother who taught her that, or do you see other factors influencing her? Explain your answer.

4. In paragraph 7, Scheinin states, "Suicide is not a normal death." How do you think Dr. Jack Kevorkian, the Michigan physician who assists terminally ill patients in their suicides, would respond to that statement?

5. To what extent do you think American society has a problem accepting suicide as a valid answer to an emotionally and/or physically painful existence? Explain your response.

Letter, Much Too Late

Wallace Stegner

Born in 1909 in Iowa, Wallace Stegner was a professor of English at the University of Wisconsin, Harvard University, and Stanford University, where he founded and directed the Stanford Writing Program until 1971. A prolific writer, Stegner's novels include The Big Rock Candy Mountain *(1943);* All the Little Live Things *(1967),* Angle of Repose *(1971), which won the Pulitzer Prize in fic-*

tion; The Spectator Bird *(1976), fiction winner of the National Book Award in 1977;* Recapitulation *(1979); and* Crossing to Safety *(1987). His nonfiction includes* Beyond the Hundredth Meridian *(1954),* Wolf Willow *(1963),* The Sound of Mountain Water *(1969),* The Uneasy Chair: A Biography of Bernard De Voto *(1974), and* Where the Bluebird Sings to the Lemonade Springs: Living and Writing in the West *(1993), which was nominated for a National Book Critics Circle Award. Stegner died in 1993 from injuries suffered in a traffic accident. The following essay first appeared in* Family Portraits: Remembrances by Twenty Distinguished Writers, *edited by Carolyn Anthony. In it, Stegner reminisces about the close relationship he had with his mother and the influence she still has on his life, despite her death thirty years earlier.*

1   Mom, listen.

2   In three months I will be eighty years old, thirty years older than you were when you died, twenty years older than my father was when he died, fifty-seven years older than my brother was when *he* died. I got the genes and the luck. The rest of you have been gone a long time.

3   Except when I have to tie my shoelaces, I don't feel eighty years old. I, the sickly child, have outlasted you all. But if I don't feel decrepit, neither do I feel wise or confident. Age and experience have not made me a Nestor qualified to tell others about how to live their lives. I feel more like Theodore Dreiser, who confessed that he would depart from life more bewildered than he had arrived in it. Instead of being embittered, or stoical, or calm, or resigned, or any of the standard things that a long life might have made me, I confess that I am often simply lost, as much in need of comfort, understanding, forgiveness, uncritical love—the things you used to give me—as I ever was at five, or ten, or fifteen.

4   Fifty-five years ago, sitting up with you after midnight while the nurse rested, I watched you take your last breath. A few minutes before you died you half raised your head and said, "Which . . . way?" I understood that: you were at a dark, unmarked crossing. Then a minute later you said, "You're a good . . . boy . . . Wallace," and died.

5   My name was the last word you spoke, your faith in me and love for me were your last thoughts. I could bear them no better than I could bear your death, and I went blindly out into the November dark and walked for hours with my mind clenched like a fist.

6   I knew how far from true your last words were. There had been plenty of times when I had not been a good boy, or a thoughtful one. I knew you could no longer see my face, that you spoke from a clouded, drugged dream, that I had already faded to a memory that you clung to even while you waned from life. I knew that it was love speaking, not you, that you had already gone, that your love lasted longer than you yourself did. And I had some dim awareness that as you went away you laid on me an im-

mense and unavoidable obligation. I would never get over trying, however badly or sadly or confusedly, to be what you thought I was.

7   Obviously you did not die. Death is a convention, a certification to the end of pain, something for the vital statistics book, not binding upon anyone but the keepers of graveyard records. For as I sit here at the desk, trying to tell you something fifty-five years too late, I have a clear mental image of your pursed lips and your crinkling eyes, and I know that nothing I can say will persuade you that I was ever less than you thought me. Your kind of love, once given, is never lost. You are alive and luminous in my head. Except when I fail to listen, you still speak through me when I face some crisis of feeling or sympathy or consideration for others. You are a curb on my natural impatience and competitiveness and arrogance. When I have been less than myself, you make me ashamed even as you forgive me. You're a good . . . boy . . . Wallace.

8   In the more than fifty years that I have been writing books and stories, I have tried several times to do you justice, and have never been satisfied with what I did. The character who represents you in *The Big Rock Candy Mountain* and *Recapitulation,* two novels of a semi-autobiographical kind, is a sort of passive victim. I am afraid I let your selfish and violent husband, my father, steal the scene from you and push you into the background in the novels as he did in life. Somehow I should have been able to say how strong and resilient you were, what a patient and abiding and bonding force, the softness that proved in the long run stronger than what it seemed to yield to.

9   But you must understand that you are the hardest sort of human character to make credible on paper. We are skeptical of kindness so unfailing, sympathy so instant and constant, trouble so patiently borne, forgiveness so wholehearted. Writing about you, I felt always on the edge of the unbelievable, as if I were writing a saint's life, or the legend of some Patient Griselda. I felt that I should warp you a little, give you some human failing or selfish motive; for saintly qualities, besides looking sentimental on the page, are a rebuke to those—and they are most of us—who have failed at them. What is more, saintly and long-suffering women tend to infuriate the current partisans of women's liberation, who look upon them as a masculine invention, the too submissive and too much praised victims of male dominance.

10   Well, you were seldom aggressive, not by the time I knew you, and you were an authentic victim. How truly submissive, that is another matter. Some, I suppose, are born unselfish, some achieve unselfishness, and some have unselfishness thrust upon them. You used to tell me that you were born with a redheaded temper, and had to learn to control it. I think you were also born with a normal complement of dreams and hopes and desires and a great capacity for intellectual and cultural growth, and had to learn to suppress them.

11   Your life gave you plenty of practice in both controlling and suppressing. You were robbed of your childhood, and as a young, inexperienced woman you made a fatal love choice. But you blamed no one but yourself.

You lay in the bed you had made, partly because as a woman, and without much education, you had few options, and partly because your morality counseled responsibility for what you did, but mostly because love told you your highest obligation was to look after your two boys and the feckless husband who needed you more even than they did. Your reward, all too often, was to be taken for granted.

12 Just now, thinking about you, I got out *The Big Rock Candy Mountain* and found the passage in which I wrote of your death. I couldn't bear to read it. It broke me down in tears to read the words that I wrote in tears nearly a half century ago. You are at once a lasting presence and an unhealed wound.

13 I was twenty-four, still a schoolboy, when you died, but I have lived with you more than three times twenty-four years. Self-obsessed, sports crazy or book crazy or girl crazy or otherwise preoccupied, I never got around to telling you during your lifetime how much you meant. Except in those moments when your life bore down on you with particular weight, as when my brother Cece died, and you turned to me because you had no one else, I don't suppose I realized how much you meant. Now I feel mainly regret, regret that I took you for granted as the others did, regret that you were dead by the time my life began to expand, so that I was unable to take you along and compensate you a little for your first fifty years. Cinderella should end happily, released from the dark unwholesome house of her servitude.

14 One of my friends in that later life that you did not live to share was the Irish writer Frank O'Connor, who was born Michael O'Donovan in a shabby cottage in Cork. His father was a drunk; his mother, he firmly believed, was a saint. He put her into many of his short stories, and he wrote her a book of tribute called *An Only Child*. Though he was not much of a Catholic, he expected to meet her in heaven, garbed in glory. From what he told me, she was much like you: she was incomparably herself, and yet she always thought of herself last. I can't believe that he is with her now in heaven, though I wish I could. I can't believe that eventually, pretty soon in fact, I will meet you there either. But what a reunion that would be! It would be worth conversation to assure it—the four of us enjoying whatever it is that immortals enjoy, and enjoying it together. I admired Frank O'Connor for his great gifts; but I loved Michael O'Donovan for the way he felt about his mother, and envied him for the chance he got, as a mature man, to show it. If the man-dominated world, with all its injustices, now and then produces women like his mother and mine, it can't be all bad.

15 I began this rumination in a dark mood, remembering the anniversary of your death. Already you have cheered me up. I have said that you didn't die, and you didn't. I can still hear you being cheerful on the slightest provocation, or no provocation at all, singing as you work and shedding your cheerfulness on others. So let us remember your life, such a life as many women of your generation shared to some extent, though not always with your special trials and rarely with your stoicism and grace.

16   I have heard enough about your childhood and youth to know how life went on that Iowa farm and in the town where everybody spoke Norwegian, read Norwegian, did business in Norwegian, heard Norwegian in church. The family Bible that somehow descended to me is in Norwegian, and in Gothic type at that. Next to it on my shelf is the preposterous five-pound book that they gave you on your fifth birthday: *Sandheden i Kristus,* Truths in Christ, a compendium of instructions and meditations geared to the religious year. You would have had to be as old as I am, and as rigid a Lutheran as your father, to tolerate five minutes of it.

17   Though your father was born in this country, you did not learn English until you started school. You learned it eagerly. Some of our mutual relatives, after five generations in the United States, still speak with an accent, but you never did. You loved reading, and you sang all the time: you knew the words to a thousand songs. When I was in college I was astonished to discover that some songs I had heard you sing as you worked around the house were lyrics from Tennyson's *The Princess.* Maybe you got the words from *McGuffey's Reader.* Where you got the tunes, God knows. You always made the most of what little was offered you, and you kept hold of it.

18   School was your happy time, with friends, games, parties, the delight of learning. You had it for only six years. When you were twelve, your mother died of tuberculosis and you became an instant adult: housekeeper to your father, mother to your two younger brothers and sister, farmhand when not otherwise employed. All through the years when you should have had the chance to be bright, girlish, even frivolous, you had responsibilities that would have broken down most adults.

19   Many farm wives had a "hired girl." You did not. You were It, you did it all. At twelve, thirteen, fourteen, you made beds, cleaned, cooked, sewed, mended, for a family of five. You baked the bread, biscuits, cakes, pies, in a cranky coal range. You made the *lefse* and *faiitgmand* and prepared the *lutefisk* without which a Norwegian Christmas is not Christmas. You washed all the clothes, and I don't mean you put lightly soiled clothes into a washing machine. I mean you boiled and scrubbed dirty farm clothes with only the copper boiler, tin tub, brass washboard, harsh soap, and hand wringer of the 1890s—one long backbreaking day every week.

20   At harvest time you often worked in the field most of the morning and then came in to cook dinner for the crew. You were over a hot stove in a suffocating kitchen for hours at a time, canning peas, beans, corn, tomatoes, making jams and jellies, putting up cucumber and watermelon pickles or piccalilli. When a hog was slaughtered, you swallowed your nausea and caught the blood for the blood pudding your father relished. You pickled pigs' feet and made headcheese. You fried and put down in crocks of their own lard the sausage patties that would last all winter. Morning and evening you helped with the milking. You skimmed the cream and churned the butter in the dasher churn, you hung cheesecloth bags of curd on the clothesline to drip and become cottage cheese. Maybe you got

a little help from your brothers and sister, especially as they got older; but they were in school all day, and whined about having homework at night.

21   I am sure there were times when you bitterly resented your bond-servant life, when you thumped your lazy and evasive brothers, or sent hot glances at your father where he sat reading *Scandinaven* in the parlor, totally unaware of you as you staggered in with a scuttle of coal and set it down loudly by the heater, and opened the heater door and lifted the scuttle and fed the fire and set the scuttle down again and slammed the heater door with a bang. Those were the years when you had unselfishness thrust upon you; you had not yet got through the difficult process of achieving it.

22   But however you might rebel, there was no shedding them. They were your responsibility and there was no one to relieve you of them. They called you Sis. All your life people called you Sis, because that was what you were, or what you became—big sister, helpful sister, the one upon whom everyone depended, the one they all came to for everything from help with homework to a sliver under the fingernail.

23   Six years of that, at the end of which your father announced that he was going to marry a school friend of yours, a girl barely older than yourself. I wonder if it was outrage that drove you from his house, or if your anger was not lightened by the perception that here at last was freedom and opportunity. You were eighteen, a tall, strong, direct-eyed girl with a pile of gorgeous red hair. In the tintypes of the time you look determined. You do not yet have the sad mouth your last photographs show. Maybe the world then seemed all before you, your imprisonment over.

24   But nobody had prepared you for opportunity and freedom. Nobody had taught you to dream big. You couldn't have imagined going to Chicago or New York and winning your way, you could never have dreamed of becoming an actress or the editor of a women's magazine. They had only taught you, and most of that you had learned on your own, to keep house and to look after others. You were very good at both. So when you were displaced as your father's housekeeper, you could think of nothing better to do with your freedom than to go to North Dakota and keep house for a bachelor uncle.

25   There you met something else they had not prepared you for, a man unlike any you had ever seen, a husky, laughing, reckless, irreverent, story-telling charmer, a ballplayer, a fancy skater, a trapshooting champion, a pursuer of the main chance, a true believer in the American dream of something for nothing, a rolling stone who confidently expected to be eventually covered with moss. He was marking time between get-rich-quick schemes by running a blind pig. He offended every piety your father stood for. Perhaps that was why you married him, against loud protests from home. Perhaps your father was as much to blame as anyone for the mistake you made.

26   You had a stillborn child. Later you had a living one, my brother Cecil. Later still, on a peacemaking visit back to Iowa, you had me. Then, as you told me once, you discovered how not to have any more, and didn't. You had enough to be responsible for with two.

27   To run through your life would be lugubrious if it were not you we were talking about. You made it something else by your total competence, your cheerfulness under most uncheerful conditions, your resilience after every defeat. "Better luck next time!" I have heard you say as we fled from some disaster, and after a minute, with your special mixture of endurance, hope, and irony, "Well, if it didn't kill us, I guess it must have been good for us."

28   Dakota I don't remember. My memories begin in the woods of Washington, where we lived in a tent and ran a lunchroom in the logging town of Redmond. By getting scarlet fever, I had balked my father's dream of going to Alaska and digging up baseball-sized nuggets. Then there was a bad time. You left my father, or he you; nobody ever told me. But Cece and I found ourselves in a Seattle orphans' home, stashed there while you worked at the Bon Marché. In 1913 you didn't have a chance as a husbandless woman with two children. When you found how miserable we were in that home, you took us out and brought us back to the only safety available, your father's house in Iowa.

29   I can imagine what that cost you in humiliation. I can imagine the letters that must have passed between you and my father. I can imagine his promises, your concessions. At any rate, in June 1914 we were on our way to join him in the valley of the Whitemud River in Saskatchewan. Perhaps it sounded romantic and adventurous to you, perhaps you let yourself listen to his come-all-ye enthusiasm, perhaps you thought that on a real frontier he might be happy and do well. Very probably you hoped that in a raw village five hundred miles from anywhere we could make a new start and be a family, something for which you had both a yearning and a gift. If you went in resignation, this time your resignation was not forced on you. It was a choice. By 1914, at the age of thirty-one, you had finally achieved unselfishness.

30   Saskatchewan is the richest page in my memory, for that was where I first began to understand some things, and that was where, for a half dozen years, we had what you had always wanted: a house of our own, a united family, and a living, however hard.

31   I remember good days for the shared pleasure we took in them—family expeditions to pick berries in the Cypress Hills, when we picnicked on the edge of Chimney Coulee and watched great fleets of clouds sail eastward over the prairie. Raising a sandwich to your mouth, you exclaimed, "Oh! Smell your hands!" and we did, inhaling the fragrance of the saskatoons, gooseberries, chokecherries, pin cherries, and highbush cranberries we had been working in. I remember that on our way home from one of those expeditions the democrat wagon tipped over on a steep hillside and spilled us and our overflowing pans and pails of berries out onto the grass. You took one quick look to see if anyone was hurt, and then began to laugh, pointing to the embarrassed and bewildered team standing among the twisted tugs. We sat in the sudden grass and laughed ourselves silly before we got up and scraped together the spilled berries and straightened

out the buggy and relieved the team and drove home. Singing, naturally. You never lost an opportunity to sing. You sang, too, among the rich smells in the kitchen as you made those wild berries into pies and jams and sauce and jellies and put a lot of them up in jars and glasses to be stored on the cellar shelves.

32   Do you remember a day on the homestead when Pa came back from Chinook with a big watermelon, and we cooled it as well as we could in the reservoir and then sat down in the shade of the shack and ate it all? How simple and memorable a good day can be when expectation is low! You made us save the rinds for pickles. Your training had been thorough, you never wasted anything. One of our neighbors, years later, wrote me about how amazed he was to see you, after you had peeled a lot of apples and made pies of them, boil up the peelings and turn them into jelly.

33   I think you loved that little burg in spite of its limitations. You loved having neighbors, visiting with neighbors, helping neighbors. When it was our turn to host the monthly Sunday-school party, you had more fun than the kids, playing crocinole or beanbag like the child you had never been allowed to be. You loved the times when the river froze without wind or snow, and the whole channel was clean, skatable ice, and the town gathered around big night fires, and skaters in red mackinaws and bright scarfs moved like Breughel figures across the light, and firelight glinted off eyeballs and teeth, and the breath of the community went up in white plumes.

34   You loved having your children in a steady school, and doing well in it. You read all the books you could lay hands on. When your North Dakota uncle died and left you a thousand dollars you didn't let my father take it, though I am sure he would have found a use for it. Instead, you bought a Sears, Roebuck piano and you set my brother and me to learn to play it under the instruction of the French doctor's wife. Alas, we disappointed you, resisted practice, dawdled and fooled around. Eventually you gave up. But you could no more let that piano sit there unused than you could throw perfectly good apple peelings out to the pig. You learned to play it yourself, painstakingly working things out chord by chord from the sheet music of popular songs. How hungry you were! How you would have responded to the opportunities ignored by so many who have them!

35   Many good days. Also, increasingly, bad ones. Hard times. While you lived your way deeper into the remote and limited place where my father's enthusiasms had brought you, he felt more and more trapped in what he called "this dirty little dung-heeled sagebrush town." On the homestead where we spent our summers, he had made one good and one average crop out of five. One summer he grew hundreds of bushels of potatoes on rented bottomland near town, and stored them in the basement of the hotel waiting for the right price, and the hotel burned down. That winter he supported us playing poker. By the summer of 1920 he was raging to get out, do something, find some way of making a real living.

36   Eventually he got his way, and we abandoned what little you had been able to get together as a life. During the next fourteen years you lived in

much greater comfort, and you saw a lot of the western United States. You continued to make a home for your boys and your husband, but it was a cheerless home for you. We lived in a dozen towns and cities, three dozen neighborhoods, half a hundred houses. My brother and I kept some continuity through school and the friends we made there, but your continuity was cut every few months, you lost friends and never saw them again, or got the chance to make new ones, or have a kitchen where women could drop in and have a cup of coffee and a chat. Too much of your time, in Great Falls, Salt Lake, Reno, Los Angeles, Long Beach, you were alone.

37   You believed in all the beauties and strengths and human associations of place; my father believed only in movement. You believed in a life of giving, he in a life of getting. When Cecil died at the age of twenty-three, you did not have a single woman friend to whom you could talk, not a single family of neighbors or friends to help you bear the loss of half your loving life.

38   You're a good . . . boy . . . Wallace. That shames me. You had little in your life to judge goodness by. I was not as dense or as selfish as my father, and I got more credit than I deserved. But I was not bright enough to comprehend the kind of example you had been setting me, until it was too late to do anything but hold your hand while you died. And here I am nearly eighty years old, too old to be capable of any significant improvement but not too old for regret.

39   "All you can do is try," you used to tell me when I was scared of undertaking something. You got me to undertake many things I would not have dared undertake without your encouragement. You also taught me how to take defeat when it came, and it was bound to now and then. You taught me that if it hadn't killed me it was probably good for me.

40   I can hear you laugh while you say it. Any minute now I will hear you singing.

Discussion Questions

1. What effect does Stegner create by framing his essay in the form of a letter? How does the letter format draw you into his writing?

2. In paragraph 3, Stegner confesses that even though he is almost eighty years old, he is "often simply lost, as much in need of comfort, understanding, forgiveness, uncritical love—the things you used to give me—as I ever was at five, or ten, or fifteen." Do you think most people feel similarly? Explain your response.

3. Stegner claims in paragraph 9 that his mother is "the hardest sort of human character to make credible on paper." Do you think some people are harder to "capture" in writing than others? Who are they, and why is that the case? Evaluate Stegner's success in describing his mother.

4. Explain what you understand Stegner to mean in paragraph 12 when he describes his mother as "a lasting presence and an unhealed wound." Have there been people in your own life about whom you could say the same thing? Why?

5. What do you see as Stegner's reason for describing his mother's background in an essay purportedly about his relationship with her?

Stars

Andrew Holleran

*A*ndrew *Holleran was born in 1943. His articles have appeared in such publications as* New York *magazine and* Christopher Street. *He is the author of* Dancer from the Dance *(1978) and* Nights in Aruba *(1983). The following essay appears in* Ground Zero *(1988), a collection of essays that examines pre- and post-AIDS gay life. In this selection, Holleran reflects on the ways in which his friends' and acquaintances' deaths from AIDS have affected his life.*

1   Walking is considered odd in this little town in the country—but since the laying of a sidewalk last summer, you can go all the way uptown now to the intersection where two highways crisscross each other beneath a traffic light, before the facade of a gas station, a fried-chicken franchise, and a stretch of railroad tracks. The intersection could be anywhere in the United States, anywhere at all, but on the way, you walk past particular things: the insurance agency, the nursery that failed last year in the freeze, the bank, the town hall, and the public park. In the park is a fountain that plashes in the still night for apparently nobody's benefit but my own; at night I am usually the only person out. Sometimes the lights are on above the tennis courts, and people are playing a game or are on the basketball court adjacent to the courts, shooting baskets. Sometimes I make out a solitary teenage boy dribbling a basketball in the dark (the lights now cost twenty-five cents every half hour; in the old days people walked away and left them burning) with the radio on in his car to keep him company. There is also a man who walks his poodle on a leash in his pajamas, and sometimes a policeman is sitting in his car by the public beach waiting for a crime to be committed. Twice I have been accused of a crime—most recently, a woman saw someone walk across her lawn, phoned the cops, and they stopped me and asked to see my footprints. (To take a walk in the United States is to be suspected either of poverty or criminal intent.) Sometimes it is overcast, and in the summer often too humid, but in winter it is mostly clear and dry, and when you finally go up the hill past the public beach and begin the last stretch along the dark, silent gardens of the houses on the lake, you are all alone beneath a cloudless sky. The stars in Florida in the

winter are mesmerizing—though it may be merely my imagination, they seem more thickly strewn across the sky than in the summer. Or perhaps the cool air merely leaves one free to look up at them undisturbed—no bugs to swat, no heat to make you want to get indoors to a ceiling fan or air conditioner. In winter, conditions for starwatching are perfect; the stars are plenteous and bright, and, if there isn't any moon, you stand there looking up with the distinct feeling that you are on the surface of a planet suspended in space shared by countless others that merely face you, like houses across the lake.

2   In a small town at night a walk clears the head, gets you out of the house, lets your mind wander, sets you free. I am upset when I meet someone else walking; I have grown accustomed to having the sidewalk to myself as I let unravel in the darkness whatever is on my mind, so that, returning an hour later, whatever facts, events, incidents have made that day good or bad seem to have played themselves out and become a little more ordered than they were on first receiving them. Sometimes I leave the house after a telephone call from New York. I digest the news—so dense with incident—in the silence exuded by the sleeping gardens. Sometimes the news is bad: a friend is sick, or dead. Tonight I'm told a man committed suicide rather than suffer any longer the deterioration caused by the virus. On the tennis courts I see two couples playing, and some kids on the basketball court beyond, borrowing their light, and the first thing I think about them is, *They do not have It. It has nothing to do with them.* The stars are very white above me when I put the tennis courts behind and go down the hill by the public beach, very thick and beautiful in the black sky—and I think, *R. belongs to that now, a part again of the universe, no longer in human form, a mix of elements, vaporized, cremated, gone, eternal, and dissembled: as unearthly as a star.* And he joins a constellation not marked in the maps of the heavens—of these friends and acquaintances who have now entered the past; I imagine them all out there, white pinpoints of light, stars.

3   Some of them were stars—to me, or the homosexual world of New York City, or the world in general. Some of them were men who were famous for designing clothes or buildings, or interpreting history, or composing music. Some of them were merely admired on Fire Island. Some were stars in pornographic films—like the man I saw in the slides flashed on the screen of a bar in Washington several years ago, one of the sexual icons of New York, who was in fact withering away even as the men around me paused in the conversation, their drinking, to admire his penis and his pectorals. And now this most recent, newest star: a man so good-looking everyone urged him to become a model, but who chose to remain in publishing, a copywriter, a man from California whose skin, hair, teeth, smile, and bright good looks were startling on the gray streets of Manhattan, whose grime and falling dust could not dim his blondness. He was so blond that is what I remember, and unlike everyone else I knew of that hue—whose appearance was affected by age, stress, fast living, the general

ash of the urban air—he looked as crisp and golden the last time I saw him as he did the day ten years before when we first met. His Western health was a kind of marvel. Why didn't the city get to him? He lived in a house with friends, and former lovers, in the city and commuted to Fire Island in the summers; he was a staple, an icon, of homosexual New York City— handsome but not vain, smart but not mean, blond but not wasted; so that when he got sick, we were all shocked as if it had never happened before, and when he killed himself, we felt a light had been extinguished— and a new star put up in the sky, beneath which I walk on these quiet nights with fear, dread, remorse, sadness, and disgust in the heart. Fear, of It. Dread: Who's next? Remorse: that we should have lived differently. Sadness: that friends suffered. Disgust: that something common as the flu, wretched as African pestilence, could destroy so much that was secure, beautiful, happy; that there should be such penalties for sex. I look at the public beach as I walk by—in a ravine, where a stream issues from another lake. I see a dark grove of live oaks draped with Spanish moss swaying in the breeze, a pale white dock and changing room whose white clapboard sides gleam in the streetlight refracted through the limbs of the trees—and want only one thing: to be alive, and able to swim when the weather gets warm this coming summer.

4   This ambition is somewhat scaled down from previous ones: I used to take this walk wondering if I should get in the car and drive to Jacksonville and visit the baths and bars. I felt on the loveliest nights—when the moon was new, and there was a soft, warm breeze, and the sensations that characterize a Southern Night were all in bloom—that such beauty, such a night, required a lover. Then I felt sorry for myself, annoyed that homosexual life was confined to cities, and in those cities to one-night stands. Now I have no such ambitions, do not demand a lover, merely want life. A decrease in expectations, the economists would call it; a rise in conservatism, the politicians; a return to morality, the priests. In fact it is fear and loathing; in reality it is the mind scrambling to accommodate itself to facts beyond its control. The town seems to me as exotic as a colony on the moon because it does not have it. The little old lady who sits alone in her tiny living room in the miniature house so near the sidewalk I can almost reach in through the window and touch her; the solitary adolescent dribbling his basketball on the cement court in the darkness, his bare chest flashing as he passes near the faint radiance of the streetlight; the children who have left their tricycles tilted in the sand of their driveway might as well be living on another planet—and as I walk past the bank whose sign flashes the time and temperature with a loud *clunk,* I feel I can deal with only two facts: *It is nine forty-three, it is sixty-three degrees.* That is all I want to know right now. I don't want any more phone calls, any more news—I have come to detest the sound of a ringing phone.

5   This shrinking—of the universe to a bank sign on this quiet night— while above me the eerie stars provoke dreary thoughts, this reduction of my dreams to the simple goal of being able to swim this summer, intensi-

fies as the roll call of expiring men expands. As every other day the television or newspaper carries some new fact—300,000 are exposed, Dr. Curran announces; 30,000 will get It in the next five years—one's desires, defiance, beliefs, wilt. One wonders if there isn't some way to fight back—besides celibacy, that is; a treatment of some kind that would allow one to go out and meet the barbarians rather than sit quietly in fear waiting for them to reach the gate. "It's so depressing," a friend says on the phone from New York, after telling me about his arrangements to increase his insurance and make out a will. "You mean all this grown-up stuff," I say. "No," he says, "I mean all this death stuff."

6   This death stuff is unnerving—one gets up each day, or walks through the quiet town at night, past the two-story houses with lights burning in cozy rooms, and dogs drooping on porches, and bicycles knocked over in the sand, and wonders just how many more facts one will have to absorb. When will it happen? Where do I want to be when it does? How will it happen? Friends say if you don't want to get it, you won't; but this seems to me silly; friends who did not want to die have. Your desire to live one, two, three, or four years is within your power, to a degree; but how much more? And you wonder as you walk through the sleeping town under a sky filled with crystalline stars how this happened, because on quiet nights in winter you have time to think over the past fifteen years and ask, *Could I have lived differently? Been a different kind of homosexual?*

7   Even as I do, a friend of mine ten years younger is living in the apartment above the first one I lived in, in New York, and writing me letters at three in the morning about the men he has just met, and in some cases slept with—and I thrill to this reenactment of the adventure I had when I moved to the city, and think happily, *It still goes on.* Yet I wonder if this vicarious pleasure is not foolish. In Florida as of February there are thirty-five new cases a month. Thirty thousand are predicted over the next five years in the nation. Promiscuity is, after all, like the engine of some giant ocean liner, which takes days to start once it is stopped. Promiscuity is so huge, so enormous, so habitual, so vital that it is brought to a halt very slowly, and only in the direst of circumstances: the equation of death with sex. There are homosexuals who say promiscuity is our right and cannot be taken away from us, but this sounds like the man on the bridge screaming he has a right to jump. Shut the whole vast machine down, with a shudder, and let us be quiet till this thing is trapped. Because each evening I take this walk, it is pure sentimentality to imagine friends who have disappeared as stars twinkling in the night sky above the earth—in fact they are just gone.

8   And the statue to be erected in Sheridan Square of two men on a bench seems oddly outdated now—perhaps a piece of marble with names engraved on it might make more sense. The town beneath these stars does not remember how blond, bright, witty, and well liked R. was; nor does the woman behind the counter of the Seven-Eleven store across the railroad tracks whose bright light brings me in out of the darkness. It is open

all night. Inside, the woman who works the register on the graveyard shift is talking to a customer buying Tootsie Rolls about a city they have both lived in: San Diego. I buy some cookies, and a wrestling magazine that features foldouts of ten wrestling stars who, both hairy and smooth-chested, wear elaborate belt buckles, tattoos, black bathing suits. It is the sort of magazine a ten-year-old boy might buy or a girl who follows the wrestlers on TV, I guess—neither of which I am, or both of which I am, as I walk home with the magazine folded in my pocket, feeling like a kid who hopes to grow up and have enormous muscles. I guess I still do. Walking home with my cookies, my wrestler magazine, the sound of my footsteps down the quiet street, I have regressed; I might as well be ten; my desires as chaste as stars. And soon I have left the light behind, and pass the boy still dribbling his basketball with an intensity that sounds odd in the deep darkness but comes no doubt from the fact that as he leaps up to make his shot, he too imagines he's a star. Down in the hollow, coming up from the beach, I think the real stars at this moment are the journalists, scientists, volunteers in New York and San Francisco, and wherever else, caring for the men determined to hang on to their human form. And the doctor who delivers us from this thing the brightest star of all. But enough of metaphors. Now the real stars make me stop on the sidewalk and look up: so cold and brilliant, so far away, so unlike anything we know. All that remains beneath them on this planet of hope and dread is the determination to remain terrestrial. All that beats in the stillness of the winter night is the basketball, and the horrified heart.

Discussion Questions

1. Describe the tone of Holleran's essay. Explain what leads you to your answer.

2. What do you see as the purpose of Holleran's essay? Explain your response.

3. Evaluate the effectiveness of Holleran's framing of his essay with his walks. Why do you think he chose to structure the essay that way?

4. After citing the "real" stars in paragraph 8, Holleran states, "But enough of metaphors." What do you think of his metaphors? Discuss what they add to the essay and evaluate their effectiveness.

5. Explain what you think the last two sentences of Holleran's essay mean.

The Death of a Dog

Barbara Lazear Ascher

*arbara Lazear Ascher was born in 1946 and practiced law before
becoming a full-time writer. Her essays have appeared in such
publications as the "Hers" column of* The New York Times, Saturday
Review, The Yale Review, *and* Vogue. *She is the author of two collections of essays,* Playing After Dark *(1987) and* The Habit of Loving
(1989), in which the following essay appears. She is also the author of
Landscape without Gravity: A Memoir of Grief *(1993). "The Death
of a Dog" recounts Ascher's thoughts upon the loss of an important
member of the family.*

1   In the days of the dog's dying a scent of decay suggested something
drastic beyond our vision and beyond our help.

2   We remembered recent hurricane victims, open-mouthed and incredulous as they stared into space once filled with the tops of trees. They
wanted to know, how could winds, weaker than predicted, fell a fifty-foot
oak? The answer was that the roots had rotted and could not brace a tree
against heavy weather. Rotted in the secret intimacy of deep soil while life
above went on as usual. Nests were built, tire swings hung, and picnic tables set in the shade of boughs. Weakened roots could support these fri
volities of spring and summer, but not the gales of autumn that hauled
them heavenward where branches used to be.

3   We, who have lost a dog, are as shocked as those who lost maples,
oaks, and pines. We shake our fists at fate and its stealth in snatching lives.
We stamp our feet and speak of fairness, as if life were a child's game
bound by rules determining wins, losses, and who gets to go first. As if
facts were marbles, smooth-surfaced aggies controlled by the swiftness of a
thumb. No fair! cry the cheated children. No fair that the dog grew old
and sick, that bones took dominion over spirit and flesh.

4   We knew the dog was leaving when he turned his back to our approach. We wondered, is it pride, or the deep privacy of death that turns
the dying from earthly love? But we weren't ready for abandonment and
stubbornly followed the path of his retreat.

5   I don't share prehistoric man's spiritual partnership with beasts. My
walls are not carved with images of horses and ibexes, and unlike tribal
hunters, I don't look to animals to learn how to live. And yet there is a
remnant of that ancient harmony as I face the death of a dog and find myself contemplating many deaths—real and imagined, past and anticipated.
What would my reactions have been had I been widowed instead? Would I
act as I do now, compulsively cleaning, determined to rout out death as if
it were a dust ball? As I throw out leash, collar, tick shampoo, and drinking
bowl I wonder, if my husband rather than the dog had died, and this bowl

were his shoes, would I drop them into a garbage bag along with all other possessions no longer possessed?

6   A parade of ghosts follows in the wake of my broom. Grandparents, old friends, the boy I loved at sixteen who died before we learned how to still our pounding hearts. I entertain a fantasy of heaven in which these ghosts would welcome the dog and take him running across that unbroken expanse of impersonal blue.

7   The mythologist Joseph Campbell has suggested that myth-making began with the first awareness of death, with the shock that a spirit could exist and then exist no more. I think that that shock gave birth to purpose, setting man forth on his eternal struggle to rationalize the irrational. Myths made it possible to deny finality by perceiving death as a journey and a transformation, the departing spirit moving on to take the form of constellations in the heavens, nymphs in wind and water, death-defying heroes in immortal tales.

8   Would we go mad without such thoughts of heaven? Without our ghosts and dreams of immortality? Who can accept that spirit can be snuffed out as finally as flame? That life is little more than a tease, dangling creatures before us to whom we will proclaim our love in song and sonnet before they are snatched back midsentence, leaving us to stare, open-mouthed into space?

9   Yet, trained in skepticism, I am awkward when asking the vet for a lock of fur before cremation. I am reminded of the discovery, not long ago, of Neanderthal men buried in Alpine caves with the bones of the bears they had hunted. It is unsettling to find myself seeking warmth by the fires of the ancients, sitting on my haunches and staring heavenward.

10   On the night of our dog's death, I bake an apple pie, open three dozen oysters and a fine, chilly wine, unaware that I am preparing a wake. There is an aspect of ritual that is unconscious and automatic.

11   The family gathers about the table and begins to reminisce. Smiles spread above chins shiny with brine as we recall when our daughter was five and announced that she wanted to marry the dog. My mother, who has the grace not to laugh at children unless they're asking for a laugh, fashioned a wedding gown of old lace curtains. The barefoot bride, fresh from the playground and smelling sweetly of child's sweat, rested her knuckles on the furry head as I performed the ceremony before our makeshift altar, the bathtub. I omitted, "till death do us part," considering that sounded too ominous for a child, and knowing that to own a dog is to deny that our life expectancy charts rarely merge. Unless you wait to become an owner when you are a 61.5-year-old male or 68.3-year-old female.

12   We recall when we first met the dog, opening our arms to capture the enthusiastic thrusts of sinew and bone, to hold him and make him ours. We conjure up that wild rush of life. It seems like yesterday, replacing yesterday in fact, a day of illness and worry. We have fulfilled the purpose of a wake.

13   In the days that follow, each of us feels the conflicting urge to tell the news and to hold grief unto ourselves. I want to tell strangers. I want to tell the man who sells me fish. As if saying the words will make it real. Just

as for children, learning to speak lifts life out of a dream state into the light of day. But for sudden, unexpected moments when there is the surprise of tears, the death of this dog does not seem real. The lock of golden fur still reflects light.

14   I have felt a kinship with those ancients who made their peace with life by denying the finality of its end. Although I may not share their firm belief in heavenly transport, I too am unable to accept the extinguished spirit. I see it in the unthinking acts—the moment when I start to save table scraps, or ask the butcher for a bone, or the times when I reach into the remaining box of Milk-Bone and pull out a biscuit.

15   My housekeeper, long-widowed, once saw me stare at the betraying hand and said: "You know, Mrs. Ascher, it's just like people. Sometimes, I set a place at the table for my husband."

16   I know the dog is dead. I have the bill from the vet and the cancelled check to prove it. Conversations about him are in the past tense. Yet we can't believe that he's gone—*really* gone. We trip over the space he's left behind.

Discussion Questions

1. How convincing is the analogy of the dog's death with the loss incurred by natural disaster in paragraph 2? Explain your response.

2. In what ways does the dog's death resemble that of a person's? What does this contribute to the essay?

3. Given the topic, Ascher's essay could have been maudlin and sentimental. How does she avoid falling into over-emotional and sappy writing?

4. To what extent do you agree with Ascher's observation in paragraph 7 about "Myths [making] it possible to deny finality by perceiving death as a journey and a transformation"? Explain your answer.

5. From Ascher's reflections, what have you learned about death and about Ascher as a person?

Chapter 8 Writing Topics

1. Think of a time when you (or someone you know) were seriously ill. Describe what happened to you (or the person). Pay special attention to your thoughts *and* feelings.

2. Given that most people have experienced or witnessed illness at some time in their lives, do you think they have truly learned something from their illness that they can carry with them when they are well? Write an essay in which you reflect on what you think illness can teach people.

3. What do you think of the language people often use for the word "death" (e.g., "passed away," "went to sleep," "went home," etc.)? Why do you think people use such euphemisms? What term do *you* use? Why?

4. Write an essay in the form of a letter, much as Wallace Stegner did, in which you address someone who has died. Explain to that person the ways she or he had an impact on your life.

5. Suicide attempts and fatalities are increasing these days, especially among teenagers. Why do you think that is the case? Write an essay in which you offer your own observations on this alarming fact.

6. In recent years, many people have had friends and acquaintances die from AIDS. Write an essay in which you explore the impact of this particular disease on the victim's surviving family and friends.

7. What do you make of the kinship some people have with their pets? Write an essay in which you examine such relationships.

8. If you have had a family pet die, describe the circumstances of his or her death. What impact did it have on you or on other members of the family?

9. Despite much that has been written about death, it is frequently considered a taboo subject. Why do you think this is the case? Do you think people are fearful of death—so much so that they prefer not to discuss it? Or is it ignorance or something dictated by their culture?

Acknowledgments and Credits

Index of Authors and Titles